EuroTragedy

A Drama in Nine Acts

ASHOKA MODY

OXFORD
UNIVERSITY PRESS

OXFORD
UNIVERSITY PRESS

Oxford University Press is a department of the University of Oxford. It furthers
the University's objective of excellence in research, scholarship, and education
by publishing worldwide. Oxford is a registered trade mark of Oxford University
Press in the UK and certain other countries.

Published in the United States of America by Oxford University Press
198 Madison Avenue, New York, NY 10016, United States of America.

Library of Congress Cataloging-in-Publication Data
Names: Mody, Ashoka, author.
Title: EuroTragedy : a drama in nine acts / Ashoka Mody.
Other titles: Euro Tragedy
Description: New York City : Oxford University Press, 2018.
Identifiers: LCCN 2017046690 | ISBN 9780199351381 (hardback) |
ISBN 9780199351398 (updf) | ISBN 9780199351404 (epub)
Subjects: LCSH: Europe—Economic integration—History. |
Europe—Economic conditions—1945– | BISAC: BUSINESS & ECONOMICS / International /
Economics. | BUSINESS & ECONOMICS / Economics / Macroeconomics.
Classification: LCC HC240.M694 2018 | DDC 337.1/4209—dc23
LC record available at https://lccn.loc.gov/2017046690

1 3 5 7 9 8 6 4 2

Printed and bound in Great Britain by Clays Ltd, Elcograf S.p.A.

To Shalini,
Who never asks for anything in return

CONTENTS

LIST OF FIGURES

ACKNOWLEDGMENTS

Willy Kiekens, formerly an IMF Executive Director, suggested in a phone conversation soon after I left the IMF that I write a book explaining the euro crisis. He set me off on an amazing journey.

My greatest debt is to George Akerlof. He understood what I wanted to write long before I did. Through many lunches over five years, he gave me an opportunity to talk about my findings and ideas. These ideas crystalized at a particularly long lunch in Georgetown in late 2016, when he prodded me on potential titles for the book and then came up with one himself: "EuroTragedy: A Drama in Nine Acts."

My other mentor during these past years was André Szász. My breath was taken away by his little but magnificent book, *The Road to European Monetary Union*. Following a long phone conversation with him, I visited him twice in Amsterdam. With a twinkle in his eye, he said to me that he would be my archive. Sure enough, over a period of three years, he wrote me beautifully composed emails, sometimes twice a week. His last email to me was on December 19, 2016. In place of his customary cheer, he wrote, "This makes it clear that when member states agreed to proceed toward a common currency, there was no consensus on important political implications, notably for national sovereignty. I think it is this fact that should be stressed." Two weeks later, through a common friend I heard, with great sorrow and dismay, that André had passed away.

Among other important influences, Liaquat Ahamed read several drafts and pointed me in the direction of writing a story instead of a conventional thematically organized economics book. He even drew me a flow diagram of how the story could evolve. Writing the book as a story has been so much fun—and it helped me recognize that often the story itself is the story.

In the honor list of those who read the entire manuscript are Madeleine Adams, Paulette Altmaier, Michael Bordo, Kevin Cardiff, James Conran, Barry Eichengreen, Henry Ergas, Edward Hadas, Juha Kähkönen, Elizabeth Litchfield, Mico Loretan, Thomas Mayer, Peter Smith, and Enzo Rossi. As the end approached, many of them became virtual coauthors in taking me to the finish line. I am grateful to them all. Their knowledge and their generosity was one of the many gifts of writing this book.

To my great delight, my 85-year old mother—a former school guidance counselor and someone who only skims the economics section of the *Times of India*—volunteered to read my final draft. By the time she completed reading the manuscript, she had strong views on needed changes; when she said the book was done, I was reassured that I was, in fact, done.

Several colleagues, friends, and family members kindly read chapters of the book. Among them were Suzanne Albers, Lee Buchheit, Ajai Chopra, Geoff Cooper, Michael Carlston, Stefania Fabrizio, Peter Hall, Rahul Jacob, Nigel Lawson, Michael Leigh, Paul Lever, Colleen McHugh, Graham McKee, Matina Meintani, Sophie Meunier, Kevin O'Rourke, Swaha Pattanaik, Morgan Steelman, Neil Unmack, and Emil Verner. David Wheeler, one of my PhD thesis advisors, played that role again with his matchless wisdom and humor. D. C. Rao, once a distinguished economist at the World Bank and ever since a spiritual teacher, acted as my guardrail. The mathematicians in the family, Krishnan and Andra, read parts of the manuscript with their customary attention to precision and logic, helping me think straight and thus greatly improving the exposition.

The Woodrow Wilson School at Princeton University was the perfect place to work on a book that aspired to blend economics, politics, and history. The school has it all: a vibrant academic community, bright and curious students, and extraordinary resources. Among colleagues, I was fortunate to learn from Yacine Ait-Sahalia, Markus Brunnermeier, Harold James, Robert Keohane, Andrew Moravcsik, and Sophie Meunier. Andy and Sophie also organized regular seminars on European economics and politics, to which they brought distinguished scholars and policymakers. Perhaps the most unexpected ideas for the book came from lively classes where my students challenged and probed. Teaching truly is an exciting way to learn. The librarians with their unflagging patience searched for the exact data and the perfect story. Elana Broch started me off, and Ashley Faulkner—for whom being a librarian is a calling—found me virtually anything I could dream of.

And Bobray Bordelon surely knows more about economic databases than any other human being.

I am grateful also to Jean Pisani-Ferry and, especially, to Guntram Wolff and Matt Dann for welcoming me over many summers to Bruegel and giving me access to their valuable platform to test some of my ideas. Jan Krahnen at Goethe University and the Centre for Financial Studies in Frankfurt also generously hosted me for a summer. Through these visits, I was able to meet and correspond with Otmar Issing, Horst Köhler, Romano Prodi, and Jean-Claude Trichet, to all of whom I am most grateful for their valuable time. Thomas Moser of the Swiss National Bank graciously gave me the opportunity to spend several weeks there.

On yet another roll of honor are my research assistants and students. With extraordinary diligence and pride in her work, Uuriintuya Batsaikhan did several iterations leading to the final production of the charts in the book. Several others helped me with the data analysis, proof reading, and editing: Nidhi Banavar, Rachel Lurie, Graham McKee, Giulio Mazzolini, Arvind Natarajan, Brandon Tan, Fabian Trottner, Aron Villarreal, Nancy Wu, and especially Junho Choi. Anton Pluschke was with me from the very start; with Daniela Gandorfer, at first, he translated German texts and gave comments on various aspects of the book. Hartley Miller and Andrew Atkins were my French consultants; and Maria Rusak worked on Italian translations. Quentin Becheau, Nick Ligthart, and Daniel Kang were students who gave me many specific data and written inputs; they also critically read large parts of the manuscript with the diligence and candor that makes students so special. Christine Östlund helped with many aspects of the book; perhaps most important, she pitilessly reminded me of opposing views and perspectives.

My editor, David McBride, gently pushed me to attempt greater clarity in my writing, all the while reassuring me that I was making progress. My previous editor, Scott Parris, was an especially important influence. He commissioned the book, commented on several drafts of chapters, and reread the final manuscript. From the very start, Scott gave me the opportunity to talk to him at great length about where I was going, and he expanded my horizons with several important suggestions. The ever-courteous Emily Mackenzie at Oxford University Press helped keep things moving. Deepti Agarwal shepherded the complex production process.

Through this all, Jyothsna, my wife for thirty-eight years, allowed the book to live with us for, oh, so many years. With her instinctive intelligence and empathy, she probably now knows more about Europe than I do. This is as much her book as it is mine.

LIST OF ABBREVIATIONS

ABCP	Asset-backed commercial paper
AfD	Alternative für Deutschland
AIB	Allied Irish Bank
AIG	American International Group
ARRA	American Recovery and Reinvestment Act
BBC	British Broadcasting Corporation
BDI	Bundesverband der Deutschen Industrie (Federation of German Industries)
BIS	Bank for International Settlements
BNP	BNP Paribas
BOE	Bank of England
BOJ	Bank of Japan
BRRD	Bank Recovery and Resolution Directive
CAP	Common Agricultural Policy
CDU	Christian Democratic Union
CSU	Christian Social Union
D-mark	Deutschmark
EBA	European Banking Authority
EC	European Community (see also EEC)
ECB	European Central Bank
ECJ	European Court of Justice
ECSC	European Coal and Steel Community
ECU	European Currency Unit
EDC	European Defense Community
EEC	European Economic Community

EFSF	European Financial Stability Facility
EFSM	European Financial Stability Mechanism
ELA	Emergency Liquidity Arrangement
EMS	European Monetary System
EMU	European Monetary Union
EONIA	Euro Overnight Index Average
ERM	Exchange Rate Mechanism
ESM	European Stability Mechanism
ESRI	Economic and Social Research Institute
EU	European Union
EURIBOR	European Interbank Offered Rate
FDIC	Federal Deposit Insurance Corporation
FDP	Free Democratic Party
FOMC	Federal Open Market Committee
GDP	Gross Domestic Product
GFSR	Global Financial Stability Report
IKB	IKB Deutsche Industriebank AG
IMF	International Monetary Fund
KfW	Kreditanstalt für Wiederaufbau
LIBOR	London Interbank Offered Rate
LREM	La République En Marche
LTCM	Long-Term Capital Management
LTROs	Longer-Term Refinancing Operations
MEP	Member of the European Parliament
MPS	Monte dei Paschi di Siena
NATO	North Atlantic Treaty Organization
NPL	Non-Performing Loan
OECD	Organisation for Economic Co-operation and Development
OIS	Overnight Index Swap
OMTs	Outright Monetary Transactions
PASOK	Panhellenic Socialist Movement
PISA	Programme for International Student Assessment
QE	Quantitative easing
R&D	Research and development
S&P	Standard and Poor's
SEA	Single European Act
SGP	Stability and Growth Pact
SMP	Securities Markets Programme
SPD	Social Democratic Party

SRB	Single Resolution Board
SRM	Single Resolution Mechanism
SSM	Single Supervisory Mechanism
TAF	Term Auction Facility
TARP	Troubled Asset Relief Program
UKIP	UK Independence Party
VIX	Measure of expected volatility in the US stock market
WAMU	Washington Mutual
WEO	"World Economic Outlook"

Introduction

Europe Ends Up Someplace Else

THE EURO—THE single currency shared by nineteen European nations—
is unique in human history. Never before has a group of countries created a brand-new currency that they would share with one another. Some idealists have seen this uniqueness as a virtue, as the harbinger of a better future world in which nations cooperate on a wider range of economic and political decisions. In due course, a political union might emerge; national parliaments would give increasing authority to a European parliament, which would make decisions for everyone. With this vision, almost half a century ago, European nations began exploring the idea of a single currency. Such a single currency, their leaders said, would bring greater prosperity and greater political unity.

At the time, Europe had a lot going for it. The wounds of World War II were receding into the past. Europeans had made another war unthinkable. They had learned to "fight across conference tables" rather than on battlefields.[1] They had opened their borders to allow greater trade with one another. None of this had been easy. They had wisely taken little leaps in the dark to slowly leave behind the shadows of two great wars fought earlier in the twentieth century, and they had learned to rely on one another's goodwill. They were rightfully proud of their success.

At that point, the essential historical purpose—to build the best human defense against another European war—was largely fulfilled. The question was how best to use the space opened up by this peace parenthesis. The task that lay ahead was to build on the liberal values that European citizens had come to cherish. To create an open society. To enable competition for ideas. To foster creativity and prosperity.

At The Hague in December 1969, European leaders, possibly unknowingly at first, took another leap in the dark: they set about creating a single currency. The thinking was that businesses and travelers would save the costs of exchanging currencies, and so they would trade more and travel more within Europe. Furthermore, with a European central bank, the eurozone would have a uniform monetary policy, which governments of member nations could not bend toward their purposes. Hence, to prevent domestic inflation and to promote domestic growth, the governments of all the countries would have to be fiscally responsible. Countries using the single currency would also need to coordinate their economic policies. And as they learned to cooperate, peace would be even more firmly established.

Despite the economic and political crisis of the eurozone over the past decade, some continue to believe in this vision.

In fact, as the history I document in this book shows, key decision makers came very quickly to understand the dangers of the leap they were taking. They understood that the benefits of easier transactions within Europe were small. What they possibly did not think clearly about is an economic proposition that comes as close to a theorem as economics can have. In a classic 1968 paper, Milton Friedman, one of the foremost economists of the twentieth century, explained that the main function of monetary policy is to help minimize a macroeconomic dislocation—to prevent an economic boom from getting too big and reduce the time that an economy spends in a recession.[2] Monetary policy, Friedman insisted, cannot help an economy *raise* its long-term growth prospects. And, here was the kicker: if monetary policy is badly implemented, it can cause lasting damage and can, hence, *reduce* long-term growth prospects. Like a "monkey wrench" thrown into a machine, ill-chosen and ill-timed monetary policy frustrates normal economic functioning.[3] By going down the route of monetary union, European leaders were making it more likely that European monetary policy would throw monkey wrenches into their economies.

European leaders may not have been aware of Friedman's near-theorem on the proper role and limits of monetary policy. They should have been aware that a single currency could not deliver economic prosperity. And they were surely aware that Italy and Greece had always bucked economic directives from European authorities, and thus these countries were unlikely to meet the standards of economic management needed to accompany a single currency, a single monetary policy.

European leaders also knew that the promised political gains were illusory. Although they often repeated the mantra of "political union," they knew they would not give up their own tax revenues to provide meaningful help to other nations in distress. They knew that the risk of economic conflicts of interest was real. And economic conflicts would create political conflicts. From the moment the single currency was proposed in 1969 to its introduction in 1999, validations of these forewarnings recurred. Again and again. But the risks were downplayed, and alternative viewpoints were deflected.

The essential flaw of the single currency was elementary. In giving up their national currencies, eurozone members lost important policy levers. If a member country went into recession, it would not have a currency it could devalue so that its businesses could sell abroad at lower US-dollar prices in order to boost exports and employment. The member country would also not have a central bank that could reduce *its* interest rates to encourage domestic spending and stimulate growth.

This basic flaw creates acute difficulties as soon as the economies of countries that share the currency diverge from one another. If the Italian economy is in trouble and the German economy is humming along, the common interest rate set by the European Central Bank (ECB) will be too high for Italy and too low for Germany. Thus, Italy's economic troubles will persist, and the German economy will get even more of a boost. It is in the nature of the single currency that once member economies begin to diverge from one another, the common interest rate will cause the divergence to increase.

These elementary problems considered, economists concluded by the late 1960s that if the single currency were to have a chance—any chance at all—there would need to be significant fiscal transfers from the humming countries to those that were in the dumps.[4] In a single-country, single-currency customs union such as the United States, states receive more funding from the federal budget; also, residents of states hit hard by recession pay reduced federal taxes relative to the residents of states that are less seriously affected. When such benefits are provided, no one fusses about them, because under the current political arrangement (the United States), they are legitimate. Indeed, some US states, such as Connecticut and Delaware, make large permanent transfers to states such as Mississippi and West Virginia. Economists thus concluded that for the euro leap into the dark, a common budget under a single fiscal authority would be needed.

If Europe wanted to go down this route, national parliaments would need to take back seats; they would mainly transfer resources to a common budget. A European finance minister reporting to a European parliament would use funds from a common European budget to stimulate the economy of the troubled country and thus shorten its recession. Fiscal transfers would not guarantee success, but without them, this was a dangerous venture.

From day one, however, it was clear that the Europeans would never be willing to agree on a common budget. The Germans were understandably worried that if they agreed to share their tax revenues, they would become the financier of all manner of problems in the rest of Europe. Thus, a common budget to smooth the path to the United States of Europe with the euro as its common currency was politically off the table.

Although they described the project in grand terms, Europeans set about creating an "incomplete monetary union," one that had a common monetary policy but lacked the fiscal safeguards to dampen booms and recessions. Within this incomplete structure, conflicts involving the conduct of monetary and fiscal policy were bound to arise.

To be clear, such conflicts arise even within nation-states. But within a nation, political procedures are typically in place to achieve some resolution. In the European single-currency project, there was no political contract for how the conflicts would be resolved. When financial crises occurred, there would be no mutually acceptable way to resolve them. Some countries would "lose," and others would "win"; the "winners" would become "more equal" than the others. Divergence among countries would increase, and the monetary union would become even more unmanageable. The incomplete monetary union contained the seeds of its own breakup.

To make matters worse, breakup of the incomplete monetary union would be extremely costly. If a country exited during a crisis, its domestic currency would depreciate rapidly, and the country's government, businesses, and households would need to pay their euro (or dollar) debts in their depreciated currency. Many would default. Especially if the country was large, the defaults could set off panic, leading to more exits from the euro and a widening circle of financial mayhem.

In this book, I ask a series of questions. Why did Europeans attempt such a venture that carried no obvious benefits but came with huge risks? How did they reconcile its obvious contradictions? How did these contradictions play out once the euro was launched? Where has Europe ended up?

There is an overarching answer to all these questions. European leaders had little idea why and where they were going. And as it has been said, if you don't know where you are going, you end up someplace else. This will be my story in the pages ahead: how, despite their idealistic vision, Europeans ended up someplace else. As could be expected, that someplace else has not been a good place. The euro has hobbled many of its member countries. It has created bitter division among Europeans. If Aristotle were alive today, he would see how "eminently good and just" men and women enacted the EuroTragedy, "not by vice or depravity," but by "error or frailty."

The rest of this introductory chapter narrates, in summary, the story I will tell. I have followed the discipline of never looking ahead to guess what people might have done with the benefit of hindsight. We will be witness to an economic and political drama played out over nearly half a century. The events will unfold, with the discussions, debates, and decisions reported as they happened.

Before the Euro: The Europeans Create a "Falling Forward" Narrative

In its origin, the single currency was a French initiative. French President Georges Pompidou called for a summit of European leaders at The Hague in December 1969. The process of opening borders, initiated by the Treaty of Rome in 1957, was well on its way. Stuck in an inertial mindset, Europeans were anxious to achieve more European integration. And, as if it were just a regulatory extension of Europe's expanding common market, Pompidou proposed a European monetary union. In fact, he said, monetary union must be made a priority.

France had suffered the humiliation of frequent devaluations of its currency, the franc. The country had lost the economic standing it had up to the mid-nineteenth century, and its political stature had declined through the course of the twentieth century. Pompidou established a French view that a European monetary union would gain France greater equality with an ascendant Germany.

The single currency was a bad idea at a bad time. Having given up their own currencies, countries that adopted a single currency would permanently fix their exchange rates with one another. Global productivity growth was slowing down, and the global economy had become more turbulent. The post-World War II Bretton Woods system of fixed-but-adjustable exchange rates was collapsing. Countries were required to keep their exchange rates fixed unless exceptional circumstances required adjustment. The exceptional circumstances were becoming more common and more disruptive. A consensus toward more flexibility, even floating, of exchange rates was emerging. The values of currencies would change continuously as national and global conditions changed.

German officials opposed a monetary union. Germans, traditionally more pro-market, were inclined toward floating exchange rates. But the French initiative to create a single European currency was pulling them in the opposite direction.

From the start, the political worry for Germans was that they would be sucked into paying for countries that had fallen into prolonged recessions and financial crises. Yet at The Hague, German Chancellor Willy Brandt did not disengage from the discussion. This moment of history is crucial. Brandt was keen to pursue *Ostpolitik*, bringing East and West Germany together. German leaders had personal memories of the war, and the French were never shy of reminding the Germans that they needed to be good Europeans.

Ironically, the one thing the French and the Germans agreed on was that there would be no common pool of funds to finance fiscal transfers. In 1954, the French National Assembly had rejected a proposal for a European army with its own budget. The French prized their sovereignty over tax revenues just as much as the Germans did. The French wanted a free lunch.

The December 1969 Hague summit appointed a committee led by Luxembourg Prime Minister Pierre Werner to lay out the plan for Europe's single currency. In October 1970, the Werner Committee completed its report.

In the pages of that report, a European narrative evolved. The report pledged that a single currency would *grow* into a more complete monetary union. This "falling forward" thesis became the European single currency's guiding philosophy. One thing would lead to another. Crises would make Europeans more determined to move forward. The contradictions of the single-currency project would not just be resolved, Europe would emerge stronger and more vibrant.

European leaders, introspectively, described this falling forward phenomenon as "pro-Europeanism." As custodians of pro-European philosophy, they believed that the great reconciliation after World War II, followed quickly by the opening of borders to trade, had established abundant goodwill, which would extend to new ventures.

But such extrapolation of postwar achievements to the creation and functioning of a monetary union was a mistake. The early successes had a sound foundation. Peace and open trade borders were clearly in the interests of all European nations. Importantly, neither of these goals required a surrender of core national sovereignty—the opening of borders to European trade required only minimal coordination. And the early postwar initiatives did not give any one nation intrinsically greater authority or influence over the conduct of European affairs. A monetary union would be in opposition to each one of the principles that had made the original successes possible. By the very nature of a single monetary policy, some nations would benefit more than others. Crucially, moreover, monetary union would require conceding a nation's core national sovereignty, the right to determine taxation policy and the distribution of a country's tax revenues, possibly to countries that its citizens might deem "unworthy" of such trust. And so it followed inevitably that monetary union would increase the political influence of some countries over others. Conceived originally as a community, even a brotherhood, Europe now would have a hegemonic governance structure.

Contemporaries warned that the contradictions would not be resolved; the single currency would not fall forward into a more robust monetary union. No European nation was willing to let go of its sovereign right to tax and spend, not even the French, despite their role as the prime movers toward monetary union. Countries would give up their currency and monetary policy, but no pan-European fiscal pool would be there to open its floodgates in a crisis. The problems would come, and it would be each ship on its own bottom.

But the small group of European leaders who mattered persuaded themselves that they could have their cake and eat it, too; essential national sovereignty over tax revenues could be preserved, and a monetary union could be made to work. No matter what, in order to erase the history of the wounds they had repeatedly inflicted on one another in the past, they would resolutely pursue a "pro-European" future.

I use the term *groupthink* to describe this unwavering collective belief.[5] European leaders fell into a groupthink that all would be well. The narrative of pro-Europeanism, of Europe as exceptional, would carry them forward. More Europe—an increased range of functions with an ever-expanding number of countries within its fold—was the common destiny. European leaders endlessly repeated this story. And a story told often enough is eventually embedded in people's psyches. Indeed, the story becomes the motivation to pursue an often-unrealizable agenda.[6]

The most prophetic critique of the proposed single currency—startling when read today—was by University of Cambridge economist Nicholas Kaldor.[7] In March 1971, just five months after the Werner Committee presented its single currency proposal, Kaldor wrote that European leaders were grossly underestimating the financial consequences of their plan. If they truly wanted a monetary union, a fiscal pool merely for crises would not be enough. Economically strong nations would need to finance some of the weaker nations on a more or less permanent basis. Could Kaldor have been thinking nearly four decades ahead of Greece in 2009? He warned that the single currency would divide Europeans, and, recalling the words used by Abraham Lincoln, Kaldor said that a house "divided against itself cannot stand." Rather than bringing Europeans together, a single currency would tear them apart.

They went ahead, nevertheless. Following the Werner Committee's recommendation, European nations took the first step toward monetary union by attempting to fix the exchange rates of their national currencies in an imaginatively named "snake-in-the-tunnel" system. The idea was to create a training ground for countries to learn to live with fixed exchange rates. It did not work. Exporters operating in countries experiencing high inflation rates lost competitiveness. National authorities were forced to devalue their currencies to help their exporters and boost domestic economic growth and employment. France dropped out of the snake arrangement, came back in, and dropped out again. The snake died, and countries floated their exchange rates.

In 1979, French President Valéry Giscard d'Estaing, still pursuing the goal of parity with Germany, pulled Europe back to the path set out in the Werner Committee report. German Chancellor Helmut Schmidt agreed, for his own mysterious reasons, to join the venture. Together, Giscard d'Estaing and Schmidt revived the snake. Only this time, they called it the European Monetary System (EMS). By now, the Bretton Woods system, the global arrangement of fixed-but-adjustable exchange rates, had irrevocably broken down, and the world was decisively moving toward more exchange-rate flexibility. Yet invocation of Europe's postwar achievements and exceptionalism continued. The myth of Europe began to form. I am reminded of an old Indian saying, "The bee came to suck the honey, but its feet got stuck in it."[8]

The EMS did not do any better than the snake. Many countries needed the option of devaluing their currencies. And no one took a deep breath to think ahead. Once these countries were in the eurozone, they would have no currency to depreciate. How would they manage then? The evidence made it clear that the warnings of contemporary economists against tightly fixed exchange rates within a monetary union were not just theoretical.

By now, the tradition and motivation were set. Following Pompidou and Giscard d'Estaing, a third French president, François Mitterrand, pushed for monetary union. In Germany, Helmut Kohl became chancellor. The year was 1982. He opposed the single currency. He rightly pointed out that a single currency, which would fix exchange rates, was ill suited for countries on divergent economic paths.

Kohl plays a central role in this drama. Although he was too young to have fought in World War II, he had seen the war's destruction and had suffered great personal loss. He described himself as the last pro-European chancellor and believed that as memories of the war faded, Germany's commitment to Europe would diminish. After the Berlin Wall fell on November 9, 1989, Kohl became the chancellor of German unity, bringing the East and West together. In German politics, he acquired exceptional autonomy and was able to make executive decisions in the manner of American presidents, relying on a small group of close advisers.

Riding on his extraordinary authority and invoking the themes of peace and friendship, Kohl came to believe it was his historical role to make a European single currency possible. His role is crucial, because the single-currency idea kept crashing into economic and political reality. Under ordinary circumstances and without a forceful champion, the idea would have gradually faded and disappeared. European "fixed" exchange rates remained fragile, causing crisis-like conditions and eventually requiring adjustment. The world continued to move toward floating rates.

Yet in December 1991, at Maastricht, Kohl, overriding the counsel of the Bundesbank (Germany's central bank) and the finance ministry, committed Germany to the single-currency project.

Even at this early stage, one country was deeply suspicious of the project. British Prime Minister Margaret Thatcher had been the single currency's fiercest opponent. Her opposition was based on exactly the right considerations: the lack of clear gains, the important risks, and the loss of national sovereignty. Thatcher's successor, John Major ensured that the United Kingdom had the right to opt out. Although the United Kingdom would continue in what would soon be called the European Union, it would be under no obligation to give up the pound and adopt the single currency.

Among those countries that did begin to move toward the single currency, a political rebellion began almost immediately. In a referendum held in June 1992, Danish voters said they wanted no part of the single currency. In September of that year, French voters almost walked away from the prized single currency that French presidents had dreamed of for so long. If another 1 percent of the French had voted no, there would have been no euro.

Amid this rebellion, the EMS, which had appeared for a short while to have stabilized, came under renewed fire. It was, in effect, dismantled and European currencies floated. While there was much hand-wringing about the breakdown of the EMS, few took heed of the troubling French referendum vote. French citizens who voted "no" to the single currency felt economically left behind and feared for their futures. European policies, many of them believed, were further restricting the limited opportunities of upward social mobility. They wanted France to disengage from European projects.

The French referendum was an early window into a widespread rift that was beginning to form between Europe's leaders and citizens. After the Maastricht Treaty was signed, public support for European institutions fell quite sharply in many prospective member states of the eurozone. Europe's leaders dismissed the warning. They continued to decide on European priorities and policies without public consultation. The leaders claimed that they had a "permissive consensus," the right to act on European matters without democratic authorization because the issues were too complex for most citizens.

But although the issues were complex, European decisions intruded ever more into daily lives, and people wanted more of a say. The problem was that they had no forum to express their concerns. Domestic issues dominated in national elections, giving little space for debate on European priorities. Only the rare referendum provided voters an opportunity to express their protest against the European project. The French referendum was such an expression. It was a pivotal moment in European history. Instead of heeding the voice of the people and healing the growing rift, European decision makers barreled on.

The rest of the 1990s belonged to Kohl. He gave the eurozone's group-think its roots. Kohl was a master of framing the political narrative. More than anyone else, he drilled into the European psyche the idea that the single European currency was an instrument for peace. The illogic of this proposition did not matter; a common currency has never been a deterrent to civil wars, and countries do not go to war with one another just because they have different currencies.

To deflect criticism and debate of the outlandish connection he made between the single currency and peace, Kohl continually repeated an aspiration for a European "political union." Of course, Kohl never literally intended that Germany would form a real political union with other European countries. In a real political union, German tax revenues could be spent on people in other countries. Thus, Kohl's genius was that he coded his logical contradictions in a suitably high-minded narrative. Within that narrative, everyone was free to believe that his or her cause was being served.

Kohl wanted the single currency to be his legacy as chancellor of European unity, but he understood that the German public fiercely opposed giving up the deutschmark. Hence, he endlessly reassured Germans that they would not pay to bail out other countries using the single currency. At the negotiating table, therefore, Germans insisted that the incomplete monetary union be governed by a fiscal rule, one that required member countries to keep their budget deficits below 3 percent of GDP.

They called this rule, in another masterly stroke of framing, a "convergence criterion." It created the illusion that the economies of countries that followed the rule would "converge" or align with the movements of other countries, making the single monetary policy more relevant to all. In June 1997, they made this rule the centerpiece of the Stability and Growth Pact (SGP). But of course, a budget rule, like a single currency, neither promotes convergence nor creates stability, as every economist recognized from the very start. To the contrary, a government forced by the rule to reduce its budget deficit during a recession will place its economy in a deeper recession. Divergent economies will not converge; they will diverge, and they will be more unstable.

Nevertheless, the budget rule got locked in, periodically tweaked through administrative changes, but shielded by a protective stability ideology. The view was that even a bad rule is better than no rule.

The ECB, set up to conduct the single monetary policy, reinforced the stability ideology through its commitment to price stability. Two Nobel Laureates in economics, Franco Modigliani and Robert Solow, warned that excessive commitment to price stability would restrain output growth and, hence, would raise the eurozone's unemployment rate. Moreover, like the budget rule, price stability when pursued unthinkingly, can—as it did during the eurozone's financial crisis—become a source of instability. But the ECB's stability ideology is even more insulated from criticism than the budget rule, because the ECB is accountable to no one. Germans insisted on this, believing that otherwise governments would try to bend ECB policy in their own favor. As a result, ECB mistakes can also remain unchecked, making a bad situation worse.

In addition to giving a boost to the groupthink within which the stability ideology gained adherents, the pro-European Kohl used his enormous authority to bring an obviously unprepared Italy into the inaugural group of eurozone member countries. This did neither Italy nor the rest of Europe any favors. Italy's politics were deeply corrupt, its governments were unstable, and by the 1980s, Italian businesses relied on a steady dose of industrial subsidies and repeated depreciations of the lira to sell their products in international markets. The all-would-be-well narrative said that the single currency would act as Italy's "external anchor." Without the crutch of a lira to depreciate, politicians and businesses would mend their ways.

Kohl had completed his historical role. He had navigated the single currency project through economic and political minefields. Without him, the project could easily have blown up. Kohl's euro gift package came with enticing visions of peace and political union, with a stability ideology that veiled the destabilizing nature of the eurozone, and with Italy among the inaugural members.

For three decades, French presidents had pushed for a euro, even though the French public cautioned against going ahead. Kohl made the euro possible, even though Germans would have much preferred to keep their deutschmark. The French had compromised by letting the Germans write the rules. It is not clear whether the protagonists had understood what they were really doing. They certainly seemed to believe their own rhetoric. On January 1, 1999, the single currency idea became a reality—a euro that French leaders had desperately wanted but that worked on German terms. That is the EuroTragedy.

After the Euro, Before the Crisis: In a Bubble

The new German chancellor, Gerhard Schröder, had no personal memories of the war. He was not shy to assert the German national interest. Economic unification of West and East Germany had not been the free lunch Kohl had promised. Higher inflation and higher taxes had put the economy in recession. Schröder, for good reasons, challenged the German-inspired stability ideology.

However, being the German chancellor, Schröder needed to keep up a façade of pro-Europeanism. He repeated the mantra that Europeans would eventually join in a "political union," although—as in Kohl's case—what Schröder meant by that remained fuzzy. In his signature pro-European gesture, Schröder waved Greece into the eurozone in 2001. As in Italy, Greek politics had been entangled in corrupt networks and governments had been dysfunctional. As in Italy, European rules had never reined in the Greeks. But Greece had a small economy. Schröder judged that there would be little trouble mopping up a Greek crisis.

Apart from those easy, feel-good measures for Europe, Schröder kept up a hard-nosed commitment to German interests. In European politics, he demanded greater German say. When European leaders met at a summit in Nice in December 2000, he fought for power and influence in running the European Union. He protected the German automaker Volkswagen by blocking a European Union corporate takeover code, which would have made hostile takeovers easier. The euro was in its early years. Predictions of falling forward into greater political unity were already crumbling.

Serious economic handicaps, hitherto largely ignored, now came into focus. For the previous three decades, productivity growth had been slowing in all advanced economies, but now eurozone productivity growth was particularly anemic. Loss of productivity momentum is never welcome but it was an especially serious problem for eurozone countries. Having given up national monetary policy and lacking a national currency that they could depreciate to boost exports and employment, member countries of the eurozone needed the benefit of strong productivity growth to pull themselves out of recessions. Yet another serious problem was that European nations had inherited bloated banking sectors, which their governments had promoted and coddled for years in the hope that domestic banks would act as agents of economic growth. Europe was "overbanked," the banks earned low returns on their assets, and they were looking for easy ways to make money.

These liabilities—no independent currency and monetary policy, low productivity growth, and large banking sectors—fashioned the next phase of the eurozone's evolution.

Between 2004 and 2007, amid a global financial euphoria, the eurozone had its own bubble. The financial bubble was sustained by a cognitive bubble, a widespread belief among European policymakers that the euro was proving to be a great success. Riding on the global wave, economic growth in the eurozone picked up. But even in those hospitable years, there was no evidence that the sudden turn in fortunes was due to the euro's promised economic dividends. A prominent econometric study had claimed that the euro would boost trade among European nations. However, the study proved to be flawed, and the original author later retracted his claim. The fact is that the share of trade among eurozone nations was steadily falling. As another achievement, European officials pointed to lower inflation rates, which they said were a direct benefit of the ECB's wise monetary policy. But average inflation rates in the eurozone declined exactly in step with global trends. European countries that had not adopted the euro did just as well in maintaining moderate and stable inflation.

While there were no evident benefits from the euro, predictions that a single monetary policy would increase divergence among countries did come to pass. The "periphery" countries—Greece, Ireland, Italy, Portugal, and Spain—experienced higher-than-average inflation rates, their products became more expensive for foreigners, and their exporters lost competitiveness to Chinese and Eastern European producers. Nevertheless, banks from the "core" countries—especially German and French banks—were keen to lend to borrowers in the periphery. Higher inflation gave the periphery borrowers more euros to repay debts. Core banks lent them more money, which pushed inflation rates further up, which attracted more lending from core banks. Economic divergence—in this case, inflation divergence—was actively at work.

Along with the divergence came financial bubbles in the periphery countries. With their especially low productivity growth rates, they were inflating their economies and, hence, losing international competitiveness; all the while, they were gorging on debt. Ireland and Spain, moreover, had particularly outsized property price bubbles, which fostered a frenzy of construction activity. After initial worries that this could all go wrong, concerns abated. Instead, a euphoria settled in, drawing attention away from the fundamental problem of weak productivity growth in the periphery. Italian and Portuguese GDPs barely grew even in these bubble years. European policymakers believed all was going well. The narrative was that the euro made their economies more stable. They could handle a financial bust should one occur.

It is remarkable that despite the elites' sense of well-being, political discontent was brewing among European citizens. The concern was that European institutions and policies were acquiring too much influence in people's lives. In 2005, Dutch and French citizens decisively rejected a largely symbolic European constitution. As in the French vote on the Maastricht Treaty, low-income, poorly educated citizens voted against the European initiative. Many believed that European decisions, handed down without a democratic vetting process, were making already onerous social inequalities worse. By now, the votes showed, the young were also growing disenchanted with Europe.

Ignoring these concerns and irritants, with eurozone banks enmeshed in the burgeoning global financial crisis, European leaders celebrated the first decade of the single currency in 2008. They took particular delight in ridiculing critics who had predicted that the euro would fail. Those celebrations proved premature.

Eurozone's Rolling Crisis: Policymakers Respond with Half-Measures

Already by mid-2007, the gathering financial crisis in the United States had trapped several eurozone banks seduced by apparently easy pickings in the subprime market. By mid-2008, at home in the eurozone, banks began to totter as property prices collapsed and economies fell into recession.

As eurozone economic activity fell, the ECB, keeping faith with its stability ideology, focused on the threat of inflation and raised its interest rate.

Rhetorically, the Europeans denied that they had a crisis on their hands; they insisted that the crisis was mainly an American problem, which the Americans deserved for having lived well beyond their means. Thus, while the eurozone and US GDPs fell at around the same pace, only the US Federal Reserve (Fed) eased monetary policy.

Acting on the time-honored risk management principle that a stitch in time saves nine, the Fed started lowering its interest rate in September 2007. The goal was to put more money in people's pockets so that they would spend more and help revive economic activity. By December 2008, having concluded that reducing its own interest rate was not enough to stimulate the economy, the Fed established quantitative easing (QE), a bond-buying program to speed up the decline in long-term interest rates, such as mortgage rates. These Fed actions eased fears of a severe economic crunch and slowly helped revive spending.

The ECB, in contrast, remained unwilling to back off from its stability focus and waited. Only after the near global meltdown following the Lehman Brothers bankruptcy in mid-September 2008 did the ECB lower its interest rate for the first time. Its subsequent rate reductions were always too little, too late. Not surprisingly, in late 2009 and early 2010, the eurozone recovered at a slower pace than the United States. The ECB, which had forecast a quicker return to better times, lost credibility that it could assess risks appropriately and act in time to ward off a gathering crisis. Milton Friedman's ghost was at work: monetary policy badly implemented was causing long-term harm.

The eurozone's home-grown crisis started in October 2009 when the Greek government revealed that its budget deficit for the year was much larger than anticipated. European authorities could now no longer blame the Americans. The crisis was squarely in their backyard, and European leaders had two choices. They could let the Greek government default on its creditors, which many rightly argued was the proper course to take. Or they could stick to the doctrine espoused by both ECB President Jean-Claude Trichet and US Treasury Secretary Timothy Geithner that a Greek default would cause contagious financial panic and inflict incalculable damage. Eurozone policymakers chose to drum up anxiety about contagious panic. There was little basis for such fearmongering. Greek banks and borrowers had limited interconnections in the global financial system. If a panic did occur and depositors and creditors did begin to pull funds out of financially sound banks, the ECB could have provided those banks with cheap funds.

By preventing the Greek government from defaulting on its debt, European authorities made their own task more difficult. They did not have a fiscal transfer system to give Greece financial assistance. Thus, European leaders waited in the hope that the Greek problem would go away. They relied on "cheap talk"—optimistic rhetoric—in the hope that their upbeat words would entice investors into lending to the Greek government at lower interest rates and would thus help tide the government over a rough patch. But the Greek government was not merely going through a rough patch. It was in severe financial distress, and investors remained wary. The Greek government needed its debts restructured quickly, official financial assistance, and a program of moderate fiscal austerity. The delay in mounting an early response only deepened the Greek distress.

The flaws of Europe's incomplete monetary union were now starkly evident. In the United States, states in financial crisis automatically received large financial transfers, which aided their recovery. These US financial transfers were part of the political contract. No one questioned why Nevada was a net recipient of funds from the federal government, some part of which was coming from taxes collected in Connecticut. The eurozone did not have such a system of transfers, as Kohl had repeatedly emphasized in order to reassure German voters.

Finally, when no good options were left, European governments and the International Monetary Fund (IMF) loaned the Greek government a large sum of money to repay its private creditors. Greece still had the same amount of debt to repay. But now the government had to repay mainly its official creditors and the remaining private creditors. For this privilege of keeping its unpayable debt burden unchanged, Greece agreed to extraordinary fiscal austerity, which soon crushed the Greek economy.

Through the evolution of the Greek crisis in 2010, German Chancellor Angela Merkel became the de facto European chancellor. No decision was possible without German backing; hence, Merkel acquired veto power. But she was a reluctant European. Born in 1954, she had no direct connection to the war. The daughter of a pastor, she had grown up in East Germany. Until the Greek crisis started, Merkel showed little inclination for pro-European causes or rhetoric. Protecting Germany's interests was her primary goal, and she was cautious by nature. She delayed the loans to Greece until it became clear to her that any further delay could cause a financial meltdown with widespread consequences. In a pattern that would recur, she made her decisions at the last moment and then only to extend bare-minimum support to defuse the ongoing crisis rather than to solve the problem decisively.

The inequality in power relationships, always inherent in the incomplete monetary union, now became manifest. Germany became "more equal than others." This was the European quandary. Without Merkel in a coordinating role, the European response might well have been chaotic, since national interests would have been difficult, if not impossible, to align. But with Merkel steadily increasing her reach, resentment of German dominance and euro skepticism grew.

The euro crisis entered its darkest phase in the first half of 2011, when the entire eurozone adhered to the norms of fiscal austerity and price stability. These German norms became, as it were, defining features of the European identity. Instead of a European Germany, as Kohl had promised, a German Europe was now in place.

On top of severe fiscal austerity adopted across the eurozone, the ECB raised interest rates in April and July 2011 to fight a phantom inflation scare. The July 2011 interest-rate hike was surely the most egregious policy error of the crisis. The ECB had received repeated warnings from investors and analysts that especially the July rate hike would do incalculable damage. The unaccountable ECB stuck in its isolation to a misguided assessment of the eurozone's economic condition. It thus generated intolerable financial stress and pushed the eurozone economy into a new crisis. Now Milton Friedman's ghost was really at work.

Italy's Mario Draghi became ECB president in November that year, and while he reversed the egregious rate hikes from earlier in the year and while he spoke of more forceful monetary stimulus, the actual stimulus the ECB delivered remained meager as the German members of its governing council continued to hold back ambitious measures. Under the double squeeze of fiscal austerity and tight monetary policy, euro-area economies struggled in what seemed like perpetual economic recession.

Investors lost confidence in the ability of the Italian and Spanish governments to repay their debts, and in mid-2012, a debt default seemed imminent. In July 2012, Draghi famously announced that the ECB would do "whatever it takes" to save the eurozone. For political support, Draghi needed Merkel's tacit approval to follow through on his announcement. Merkel had no wish to lay out German money to save Italy and Spain, but she was not ready to see the eurozone melt down. The ECB's promise of "unlimited" financial help relieved pressure on Italian and Spanish bonds. Thus, Merkel held political control of Europe, but at this critical moment, she needed the ECB's deep pockets to achieve her objectives. The power in the eurozone was now definitively concentrated in a few hands.

Throughout these years, resentment against Merkel increased. Especially governments and citizens of the periphery countries viewed the policy of all pain and no gain as a German imposition. Merkel's association with the departure of the Greek and Italian prime ministers in November 2011 heightened the perception of German imperialism; that perception intensified when pro-European technocrats took over as prime ministers in Greece and Italy in a bid to cut through political gridlock and implement stricter austerity. In Greece, anti-German sentiment fueled the rise of the radical Syriza party. In Italy, popular support for the anti-euro Five Star Movement soared. In Germany, many citizens had the opposite anxiety that Merkel was being soft on undisciplined countries. In September 2012, rebels within the Christian Democratic Union (CDU) began an anti-euro movement, which then emerged as the Alternative für Deutschland (AfD) in February 2013. Thus, political fissures among eurozone member countries widened.

The Italian Fault Line

For the period 2014 to 2017, I focus on how the ECB made an already bad Italian situation worse. All the pathologies of the eurozone—low productivity, high government debt, chaotic banks, short-lived governments, receding opportunities for upward social mobility, and euro skepticism—come together in Italy. And Italy is several times larger than Greece. Italy, I believe, is the eurozone's fault line.

In early 2014, the ECB's monetary policy was still too tight. With Italy in near-perennial recession since 2011, its economy had so weakened that a price-deflationary tendency had begun to set in. While too high inflation causes loss of international competitiveness, too low inflation creates its own ills. Once they experience an extended period of low inflation, businesses and consumers begin to postpone purchases, believing that the inflation rate could decline further, and prices might actually fall. The slow pace of spending, in fact, keeps inflation low. And low inflation and low growth make existing debt burdens more onerous, which further restrains spending and growth. As growth suffers, financial vulnerabilities increase.

To gain perspective on Italy's economic problems, a comparison with Japan's lost decade of the 1990s is helpful. Because of delayed and timid monetary policy responses to the property and stock market crash that began in 1990, the Japanese economy slid into almost perpetual "lowflation," long periods of very low inflation interspersed with brief periods of declining prices. The lesson from Japan is that once it sets in, such a lowflation tendency is very difficult to reverse. Inflation does rise for short periods but tends to come down quickly. Essentially, as Japan's experience shows, the central bank loses the credibility that it has the competence and patience to bring inflation back up to normal rates.

In January 2015, Draghi and his ECB colleagues belatedly began purchasing eurozone government bonds to bring long-term interest rates down. Yes, for those keeping track, this was just more than six years after the Fed had begun similar action in December 2008. The eurozone's "core" inflation rate—the inflation rate stripped of volatile food and energy prices—barely budged. While the average core inflation rate stayed around a low of about 1 percent, even lower inflation rates appeared to have set in to large parts of the eurozone, adding to their many vulnerabilities.

Throughout these years, eurozone authorities touted one solution to get them out of their morass: structural reforms. Structural reforms were a code phrase for making it easier to fire workers. Sure enough, in 2015, Italian Prime Minister Matteo Renzi's Jobs Act, following the playbook, made it easier to fire workers. Judging by a vast amount of past evidence, the measures will do little to help economic growth. To the extent that they make jobs more precarious, they will reduce the incentives to invest in raising worker productivity. Thus, if anything, measures taken under the Jobs Act will hurt long-term growth prospects and increase financial vulnerabilities. Moreover, these "labor market reforms" will increase social inequalities as some workers are trapped in temporary and insecure jobs.

Italy's true problems lie elsewhere. With low levels of research and development (R&D), lagging educational standards, and many college-educated Italians migrating, Italian productivity growth seems likely to remain low. Without inflation and growth, government debt will tend to stay at high levels, and while banks are beginning to get over their worst phase, their journey out of trouble is a long one. An economic or financial tremor in Italy or in the global economy could open up Italy's cracks, which could radiate earthquakes and cause damage along other vulnerable fault lines.

Amid Renewed Optimism, the Reality of a Divided Europe

Starting in mid-2017, optimism spread through much of the world economy. The optimism raised world trade growth and, thus, brought economic and financial cheer also to the eurozone. But this short-term relief rally faced the force of long-term trends that pointed to a more worrying future. Productivity growth rates had declined during the crisis years from already low levels; meanwhile, populations were barely growing and could start declining in some countries within the next generation.

Thus, once the current global sweet spot receded, economic growth rates in the eurozone countries seemed set to fall back down to their low potential. Eurozone economies remained well behind the United States in R&D intensity, and they were falling behind the most dynamic Asian economies not only in R&D but also in the international league tables of university rankings. A severe long-term growth and competitiveness challenge lay ahead for the countries in the eurozone.

Moreover, within the eurozone, after nearly ten years in and out of crisis, the economic divide across member countries had widened—and, hence, political divisions had also sharpened and become more entrenched. Nicholas Kaldor's predictions from 1971 were proving eerily correct. In the successful "northern" eurozone group, led by Germany, citizens had reason to be optimistic over the long term. Their economies were productive by European standards, their government debt burdens were back to or below pre-crisis levels, and their young could find jobs. These countries were relatively insulated from the eurozone in the sense that they were not severely hurt by the orthodoxies and errors in eurozone policies.

However, even in these relatively successful countries, nationalism and euro skepticism had steadily increased. Northern governments were ever more fearful of footing the bill for southern countries. A large number of citizens in the northern countries had not experienced material gains for nearly a generation. Such left-behind citizens were stuck on the lower rungs of the economic ladder. Their fears that their economic security was slipping away fed the fear of refugees and migrants. Thus, as the populations of the northern nations turned their gazes inward, their governments were increasingly constrained in their ability to make pro-European gestures.

On the other side of this divide, the southern countries had low productivity growth rates, high government debt burdens, bleak work opportunities for their young population, and schooling systems that did a poor job of lifting children above the economic and social status into which they were born. All these problems were rooted in weak governance and institutional structures, which weakened growth prospects by creating incentives for corruption, raising costs of doing business, inducing people to work in the so-called "shadow" economy, and lowering the quality of education that schools and universities delivered—to different degrees in different countries. Moreover, the eurozone's ideologically driven policies inflicted the most harm to growth potential in the south. Because the southern countries had remained in recession-like conditions for long periods, businesses had cut back on long-term investments and R&D, and unemployed workers had lost skills or otherwise become unemployable. Of the southern countries, Italy, as

I have pointed out, had the most grievous long-term problems and posed the greatest risk to the eurozone's integrity. But France, too, I believe, was now squarely in the southern part of the eurozone.

Looking ahead, I am afraid the groupthink will continue. Dismissing the evidence of the past several years, eurozone leaders continued to assert that the euro delivered "huge, often invisible benefits."[9] As past generations of leaders spoke of "political union," the new leadership talked of "governing together," "shared sovereignty," "pooling of sovereignty," and "European sovereignty," they spoke of a "eurozone finance minister" and a "European budget."[10] As in years past, the different actors used the same sets of words and phrases to represent their very different interests and preferences.

And they repeated the mantra of "democratic accountability," knowing that real European accountability could be achieved only if national parliaments were subordinated to the European Parliament. Even if such a far-reaching outcome was ultimately desirable—and it is debatable whether it was—no one believed that Europeans would ever be ready for such a big leap. Thus, responsibility and accountability in the governance of the eurozone remained hard to pin down. Who was responsible for fiscal and labor market policy, the national government or European authorities? Who was to blame when policies implemented had counterproductive consequences? If they were upset, whom should citizens vote out of office? As economic historian Alan Milward wrote in 2005, European democracy was slipping "between the interstices of the nation states and the supranation."[11] Which only added to economic and political anxiety.

Rather than evolving into a politically legitimate governing system, the eurozone is set to continue on an inward-looking involutionary path of newly invented administrative measures. Groupthink will continue to lull European leaders into a false sense of confidence that another clever measure will strengthen the eurozone. However, history keeps reminding us that the fundamental national unwillingness to share tax revenues will severely limit what can be achieved.

Unfortunately, few European leaders recall and learn from that history. Thomas Schelling, Nobel laureate in economics, wrote in a 1988 essay, it is in the nature of us human beings to forget that we keep forgetting.[12] In the eurozone, repeated efforts, unburdened by the memory of past failures, return to circle around the same themes; each time, with the same words and the same arguments, the hope is that the latest effort will finally pay off. Instead of falling forward, instead of an evolution, "involution" continues.[13]

The next financial crisis will start from a point of greater economic and financial vulnerability than the last one did. Meanwhile, as the economic divide between member states stays wide—and possibly widens—the sense of nationalism and euro skepticism in the north and south will grow steadily more acute. The next crisis could tear Europe's delicate fabric apart.

A New Pro-Europeanism

In these introductory pages, I have given the reader the essence of a nearly seventy-year history of postwar Europe. One message comes across through these long years. The sovereignty barrier remains alive. Why is that? True falling forward required the euro project to deliver tangible benefits to spark increased popular willingness to share sovereignty. That would have led to greater willingness to share tax revenues and agree to democratically legitimate European governance mechanisms. That has not happened because the euro has predictably not generated any noticeable economic benefits, and the costs imposed by the euro in people's lives have often been stark. Without real evidence that the euro improves the economic welfare of a substantial number of European citizens—and basic economic principles tell us that the prospects of that happening are not good—administrative efforts to pool sovereignty will not mobilize the needed political legitimacy and the euro scaffolding will, therefore, remain fragile under conditions of stress.

Those who are already persuaded by my interpretation of the history and the conclusions that they lead to will, I hope, read on to relive in greater detail the economic and political drama as it unfolded. You will hear the principal actors as they framed the European narrative and worked with—and continue to work with—its contradictions.

For those who are skeptical, I hope you, especially, will read on. I say—with no attempt at irony—that I have written this book as a pro-European. I do not believe in more Europe or even a cleverly reengineered Europe. The lack of political legitimacy will continue to undermine the credibility of European institutions that step into domains reserved for national sovereigns. Instead, I believe it is time to change the narrative of what truly is pro-Europeanism. True pro-European values can flourish only when the bonds that tie Europe so tightly today are loosened. As a first step toward that goal, I offer some technical suggestions on necessary policy steps.

But more important, I believe, is that it is time to recommit Europe to its principles of an open society, with its emphasis on democracy, social protection, freedom of travel, and cultural diversity. Europe had embarked on exactly this path in the early postwar decades before the euro project led it astray. To achieve an open society, Europe must go back to the model within which the Enlightenment flourished between the sixteenth and eighteenth centuries. In that model, nation-states competed in the marketplace of ideas. Such a new European Republic of Letters will erase the harm done by the euro and will make Europe a stronger contender in the global economic race. It will shrink social inequalities, and will strengthen the European identity.

CHAPTER I

Three Leaps in the Dark, 1950–1982

I T WAS A little after six p.m. in Paris on May 9, 1950. At a hurriedly arranged press briefing, French Foreign Minister Robert Schuman announced that France and Germany had agreed to operate their coal and steel industries under unified supervision.[1] Such "solidarity in production," Schuman said, would make war between France and Germany "not merely unthinkable, but materially impossible."[2] Schuman also invited other European nations to join the Franco-German venture. Together, he promised, they would all take "a first step in the federation of Europe."

Although World War II had ended five years earlier, its long shadows still fell across the European continent. It was time, Schuman said in his bold declaration that evening, to lay "common foundations for economic development" to strengthen European solidarity and preserve peace.

That soaring vision and rhetoric meant little to the gathered journalists. They wanted to know how the extraordinary transnational plan would work, and Schuman seemed unwilling, or unable, to give details. A frustrated newspaperman finally asked him, "In other words, it's a leap in the dark?" Surprised by the question—and mindful that he needed to rush to catch his train to London—Schuman instinctively replied, "Yes, that's what it is, a leap in the dark."

The previous evening, Schuman had sent his proposal to German Chancellor Konrad Adenauer. The Federal Republic of Germany ("West Germany") had been constituted only the year before, in 1949. Adenauer had swiftly replied that he accepted the proposal with "all his heart."[3] To his aides, the elated Adenauer exclaimed, "'Das ist unser Durchbruch'— this is our breakthrough."[4] Sharing German sovereignty over coal and steel production was a small price to pay for reintegration into Europe and the international community.

The Schuman Plan created advantages for France as well. Germany's economy, having long since surpassed that of France (figure 1.1), was now poised to surge even further ahead based on its strengths in machine, automobile, and pharmaceutical production. France, in danger of losing European and global influence, feared that it would be left merely with the thankless task of monitoring a politically quarantined but economically dominant Germany.[5] By making Germany more of a political partner, the Schuman Plan would open an opportunity for France to shape Europe's future.

The newly formed "High Authority," a central feature of the plan, would supervise the transnational coal and steel production facilities. In this authority lay the seed of a visionary post-nineteenth-century state within which sovereign nations would work together—perhaps in an increasingly federal structure—toward a "pro-European" future.

While the goal was political reconciliation and eventually a European federation, the methods were economic. Under the proposed arrangement, rearmament efforts, which required ramped-up coal, iron, and steel production, would be easy to detect. But Schuman also emphasized that pooling of coal and steel production was the first step in laying "common foundations

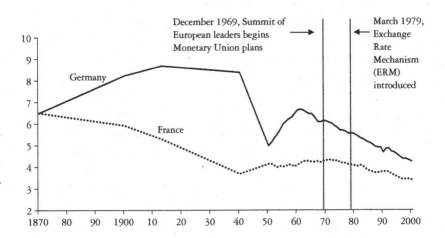

FIGURE I.I. France falls behind Germany starting around 1870.

(Each country's share of world GDP, percent)

Sources: Angus Maddison. "Historical Statistics of the World Economy: 1–2008 AD." University of Groningen, available from: http://www.ggdc.net/maddison/oriindex.htm, series "GDP." The values for 2009 and 2010 are from the Conference Board (GDP adjusted for purchasing power parity, series "GK GDP"), available from https://www.conference-board.org/data/economydatabase/index.cfm?id=27762.

for economic development." Working together to raise standards of living would be the glue of a politically united, postwar Europe.

In his instantly historic declaration, Schuman had outlined the basic contours of postwar European integration: centralized governance and the promise of economic prosperity. The details were to be decided once European nations were airborne on their first leap into the dark.

Paris 1951: The First Leap

Jean Monnet followed Schuman to London. Born in November 1888, Monnet had left school at the age of sixteen, set up a canned-food business, sold cognac for his family's company, been a merchant banker, and become an "entrepreneur in the public interest."[6] In May 1950, as head of the French Planning Commission, Monnet was also the author of the Schuman Plan.

Monnet was keen for the British to sign on to the Schuman Plan and give the fledgling initiative gravitas and momentum. But the skeptical British saw the French initiative as an effort to create an unaccountable European bureaucracy, which could override the decisions of the British government and parliament. As Monnet himself later reported in his memoirs, a section of the British press "recoiled at the word 'federation'" and expressed alarm that the plan would "be the end of British independence."[7]

British officials were polite but firm. The plan, they said, was too vague and open-ended. In particular, they questioned the need for a "High Authority," which they feared would acquire great powers and undermine British sovereignty. But to Schuman and Monnet, a "High Authority" was crucial and, hence, nonnegotiable. Monnet's final meeting on that London trip was with Sir Stafford Cripps, Chancellor of the Exchequer, Britain's finance minister. When Cripps refused to budge, Monnet darkly warned him that the British would regret their stubbornness and eventually "adjust to the facts" after seeing Europe "succeed."[8]

Four other countries—Italy, Belgium, Luxembourg, and the Netherlands—responded to Schuman's call. Country representatives soon met to discuss and negotiate the way forward. Those were heady days for Europe. François Duchêne, an Anglo-Swiss public intellectual and longtime aide to Monnet, would write that the officials who negotiated the Schuman Plan "thought of themselves as laboring together for a common good." Their shared sense of history and purpose "created a brotherhood of politicians and high officials."[9]

When national leaders gathered on April 18, 1951, to sign the Treaty of Paris and formally create the Coal and Steel Community, a number of matters remained unresolved; indeed, there was no real treaty to sign. Luuk van Middelaar, a European scholar and former senior Eurocrat, writes that the ministers (including Adenauer for Germany and Schuman for France) "signed a blank sheet of paper." Such was the sense of goodwill: "Europe began on an unwritten page."[10] Monnet was appointed the first president of the High Authority of the European Coal and Steel Community, and the first European institution was in place.

The main goals of Schuman's leap-in-the dark strategy—political reconciliation and European security—were achieved. Germany was brought back into the fold. The Coal and Steel Community created forums for economic and political coordination, and European leaders learned to speak to and work with one another.

But could Europe develop further, as Schuman had visualized, into a "federation"? The signs were not promising. Even with the goodwill at the time, the Treaty of Paris had dropped any reference to a European "federation." Instead, the German negotiators had proposed the word *Gemeinschaft*, translated into English as "community." Van Middelaar explains that *Gemeinschaft* signifies a stable and durable association, and the principle was that member states, working together in a "community spirit," were to be "all equal under law."[11] Thus, rather than rushing into hierarchical relationships within the rigid structure of a federation, the consensus was to gain strength from durable ties among equals.

Nevertheless, the idea of a European federation remained alive. In the summer of 1950, soon after Schuman's historic declaration but before the Treaty of Paris was signed, new tensions prompted another initiative. The Americans began insisting that Germany needed to rearm itself as part of a broader European defense against the Soviet threat. "Once again," Monnet wrote, "there was talk of an arms race, and above all of returning to the former aggressor the weapons he had seemed glad to lay down."[12] The French were aghast at the thought of a German army. French leaders and citizens alike asked, "Are we going to have to go through it all over again?"[13] The Americans, however, remained insistent.

The French were in a dilemma. Although they abhorred the idea of a rearmed Germany, the risk was that Americans might give Germany the legitimacy and latitude to form its own army. If that happened, Germans could decide to walk away from Schuman's proposed Coal and Steel Community.[14] Monnet was also concerned that Germans were becoming more "nationalistic."[15] In a bid to prevent the Americans and the Germans from getting too far ahead, French Prime Minister René Pleven reluctantly proposed the creation of a European army under the supervision of a European Defense Community (EDC).[16] The goal was to embed German forces within a newly assembled European army operating under the control of a European minister of defense, with the policies and strategic objectives set by a Council of Ministers from member states. Although it was a response to American pressure, the ambition of the latest plan was breathtaking. With its European governance structure and its own budget, the EDC remains to this day Europe's most far-reaching initiative to achieve political union.

The EDC Treaty, signed on May 27, 1952, was ill fated. The Germans bristled at the "blatantly inferior" ranks at which their soldiers were to be included in the European army.[17] Despite such reservations, the German parliament, the Bundestag, did ratify the treaty in March 1953. Adenauer supported the EDC because Germany was still an "occupied territory" and "a mere object in diplomatic contests"; the EDC offered Germany another opportunity to become a "co-actor" in European and global affairs.[18] The French, however, having initiated the project reluctantly, had second thoughts. They were not ready for a rearmed Germany, and they were unwilling to see their own army disappear into a "stateless hotch-potch."[19] Moreover, with France experiencing "defeat and humiliation in Vietnam," the new prime minister, Pierre Mendès France, decided that his tenuous coalition government could crack if he insisted on a vote in favor of the EDC Treaty.[20] With no advocate, the French National Assembly unceremoniously rejected the treaty on August 30, 1954.

The words *federal* and *supranational* became tainted, and "the idea of a Europe in some sense above nations" was discredited.[21] Although memories of World War II were still fresh and the ground for political unity was more fertile than it had ever been, the French refused to cross a threshold that compromised core fiscal and political sovereignty. The EDC, despite its original impetus from the Americans, was a real effort toward a United States of Europe. But the ambition overreached. As Mendès France bluntly said, "In the EDC there was too much integration."[22]

Soon even the Coal and Steel Community came to be viewed as intrusive and irrelevant. Ostensibly, there were technical difficulties with the coordination of production. The real problem, however, was that Monnet began stepping on the toes of national politicians. He tried to shape the High Authority as a European administration run by a technocratic elite based in Brussels. He asserted the right to levy taxes, with only the obligation to consult the Council of Ministers.[23] The High Authority quickly became the largest foreign issuer of bonds on the New York market in its effort to be "the hub of Community investment."[24] Asserting that he was Europe's representative, Monnet established direct relations with foreign governments. Put simply, Monnet was performing tasks reserved for national governments elected through a democratic process. The smaller member states felt particularly threatened by him.[25]

European leaders aspired to do more but they were uncertain about what should come next. In his biography of Monnet, Duchêne has sympathetically described that moment of contemplation. Contemporaries recognized that Europe could not be built through either "security or political means."[26] Instead, they concluded that "approaches henceforth would have to take more oblique—meaning, in practice, *economic*—avenues." This renewed emphasis on the economic interests of European nations was a return to Schuman's message that peace and European integration required long-term commitment to deliver material progress. While Schuman had focused on immediate postwar priorities, he had said that Europe could be successful only if it raised people's standards of living. It is to the credit of European leaders that they recognized that efforts to forge ahead with political structures would only lead to more dead ends, and thus that it was time to change course. Thus, the first leap ended with an institutional framework to discuss matters of common European interest. More important, it made clear the limits of how deeply Europeans were willing to integrate with one another and imparted the momentum to begin a second leap to the Treaty of Rome.

Rome 1957: The Second Leap

Belgian Foreign Minister Paul-Henri Spaak led the effort and drew on the Dutch for support. These two smaller European nations had been minor bystanders in the "first" Europe; they now pushed to promote their interest, which lay in greater commercial integration. Being small countries, they relied heavily on international trade and stood to benefit considerably from reduced barriers to trade. The Spaak Committee's report, published in April 1956, emphasized that all European nations would gain from expanded opportunities for trade with one another.[27] Indeed, Europe had no choice, the report warned. Failure to generate more prosperity through trade would cause Europe to fall farther behind the United States.

The political logic behind this new initiative was also sound. More trade reduces the risk of war by creating mutual economic interests and personal empathy among businesses transacting across borders.[28] Importantly, this gain is achieved without sacrificing national sovereignty. Instruments to foster trade require minimal international supervision and allow nations to retain their core sovereign authority based on national democratic processes.

Germany and France, for their different reasons, resisted this new effort at first. Ludwig Erhard, Germany's economics minister (1957–1963) and later chancellor (1963–1966), wanted borders opened to all countries, not only to European nations; the French did not want borders opened, not even to European nations.[29]

The French exacted a price for moving forward. To protect their inefficient farmers, French authorities persuaded other European nations to join in subsidizing all European farmers. Thus was born the Common Agricultural Policy (CAP), which created egregiously large and long-lasting costs for Europe and for the world. Indeed, the CAP was postwar Europe's most disgraceful economic policy. It led to wasted food, lower prices for developing country farmers, and a heavy drain on the meager European budget (see Appendix at the end of this chapter).

. The rest was smooth sailing. Global economic forces were favorably powerful. World trade was growing rapidly, and the Europeans stood to gain from joining rather than opposing this opportunity.[30] On March 25, 1957, the "original six," those that had formed the Coal and Steel Community, signed the Treaty of Rome. They now joined to form the European Economic Community (EEC), which started functioning on January 1, 1958.

The Treaty of Rome responded to the clear message from member nations that they would push back against efforts to encroach on their sovereignty. As Duchêne sums it up: "The governments rejected anything or anyone that threatened, like Monnet, openly to compete with their monopoly."[31] Hence, the European Commission, which replaced the unpopular High Authority, was given reduced powers so that another president of Monnet's standing could not expand the range of actions taken at the European level. The new commission's tasks were limited to drafting proposals for European laws and conducting the "day-to-day business" of implementing policies and spending European funds.[32] Even Charles de Gaulle, who had opposed the treaty before he became France's president in 1958, ultimately reconciled himself to it.[33] The Treaty of Rome, de Gaulle wrote in his memoirs, was "an improved treaty of commerce that does not alter the sovereignty of the Six [members], notably in political matters."[34]

The engagement of the smaller countries in forging and implementing the treaty allowed a clearer expression of "community spirit." The community functioned to strengthen economic links but did not relegate the smaller member states to a second-tier status from where they would have to work harder to preserve their sovereign status. As historian Alan Milward would write in 1992, the European community, with its shared institutional structure, "rescued" the nation-state. Member nations, differing in their economic capabilities and social priorities, could work within a system that extended their ability to bring opportunities to their citizens but, at the same time, treated all nations in a fair manner and as equals.

As a trade agreement, the Treaty of Rome set out with modest ambitions. Tony Judt, historian and author of the classic *Postwar*, reminds us that the treaty was "for the most part a declaration of future good intentions."[35] It outlined a process rather than specific goals and measures. The Treaty of Rome nevertheless succeeded so spectacularly because it was ideally suited to the times. Benefiting from the momentum of postwar recovery, GDP growth rates were still high. World trade was expanding rapidly, and the need to reduce the barriers to trade—even if not recognized at first by all participants—soon became self-evident. France was the last nation to board the Treaty of Rome bandwagon. All member states of the European Economic Community (EEC) found it in their interest to reduce tariffs, lowering them faster than proposed in the treaty.[36] Quantitative restrictions on trade virtually disappeared by 1961. In pushing ahead with freer trade in its self-interest, Europe also led the global effort to bring trade barriers tumbling down.

This happy coincidence of trade integration, economic progress, and European "self-confidence" continued during these years despite de Gaulle's efforts to disrupt the European sense of collegiality and community. De Gaulle believed that the community's institutions, unless checked, would override national authority and undermine French priorities. For de Gaulle, European institutions were of value only if they promoted French interests, if they were, in his words, "the means for France to recover what she ceased to be after Waterloo: first in the world."[37]

In 1960, de Gaulle began an effort to coordinate European defense and foreign policy under French leadership.[38] De Gaulle had an ally in Adenauer, who, having gained legitimacy for Germany, was willing to bypass EEC institutions in favor of an intergovernmental approach. Adenauer's support for de Gaulle was sometimes grudging, not least because de Gaulle made no effort to hide his contempt for "les petits gens de Bonn" (the little people of Bonn).[39] Adenauer, however, played along because he shared de Gaulle's instincts to curtail European authority; Adenauer was a "Gaullist" on matters related to Europe.[40]

Dutch Foreign Minister Joseph Luns led the fight against de Gaulle's effort to take charge of Europe. De Gaulle's project, Luns said, would "serve as the infrastructure of the greater French international power position" and do nothing "to strengthen European unity and integration."[41] Fierce Dutch and Belgian resistance ensured that de Gaulle's first attempt to hijack Europe went nowhere.

De Gaulle created the next governance crisis between March 1965 and January 1966. He was responding, in part, to a European Commission effort to gain taxation authority. If that proposal went into effect, the eminent Eurocrat Robert Marjolin noted, "the Commission would [have] become, in budget matters, a kind of government of the Community."[42] All member states had reacted angrily to the commission's encroachment on sovereign rights. But de Gaulle went a step further. He tried to undo the Treaty of Rome's provision for decisions by majority vote and sought, instead, a right for member states to veto European proposals. Eventually, under the so-called Luxembourg Compromise of January 1966, European leaders agreed that they could veto decisions on matters they considered to be of very high national interest. With that, as Marjolin summed up: "The Community was stripped of the few supranational elements that had been written into the Treaty of Rome."[43] De Gaulle instigated this outcome, but the others, especially the Germans, found the arrangement entirely congenial.

Yet through these power struggles during the first half of the 1960s, the Treaty of Rome continued to function smoothly. The treaty was a magnificent achievement precisely because it did not depend on elaborate coordination among nation-states or on supranational regulation. As commerce among the EEC members expanded, so did public support for Europe. Reflecting back on those years, with some pride in the role he played, Marjolin later described the decade after the signing of the Treaty of Rome—the years from 1958 to 1967—as the "springtime of Europe." A widespread "spirit of self-confidence" accompanied the "feeling that great things were happening."[44]

By the mid-1960s, it was possible to look back with a sense of accomplishment and pride. The first two leaps in the dark, despite their despondent moments, had proven to be historically courageous and wise. For political idealists, there was much to celebrate. As Oxford University's Timothy Garton Ash has written, although Europe was an "externally ill-defined, internally diverse, and historically disorderly" continent, Europeans had developed mechanisms for institutional cooperation.[45] Europe had made big strides toward a "liberal order"; the people of Europe could pursue "different ends," and although these ends could not all be "reconciled," they could "coexist peacefully."[46] For economic idealists, Europe's nation-states had adapted to the needs of an interconnected global economy, and commercial relationships within the community had increased the sense of European identity and deepened the foundations of peace. The essential purpose of postwar Europe was complete.

Europe at a Critical Juncture

The contrast with what came next is stark. The postwar boom began to fade by the late 1960s. Amid growing worries about Europe's economic future, European leaders sought to push European integration but without a sense of where they were going or, indeed, why more integration was needed. "The world had changed," writes Duchêne.[47] Germany did not need Europe for political recognition, and de Gaulle had made it legitimate for European nations to reject anything perceived as "outside interference." In addition, whereas in the previous two decades the world economy had been generally buoyant, now the postwar economic miracle years were ending. Perhaps most important, differences in national economic performance had thus far not been especially relevant for the construction of Europe. But now, as Europe took its next steps, widening inflation differentials across countries were signs that European nations were moving on different economic paths.

A notable troubled spot was France. Although buoyed by the postwar momentum and expanding world trade, the French economy had "aged," wrote economic historian Charles Kindleberger. The loss of vitality had steadily strengthened "vested interests" and created a sense of being entitled to a higher standard of living.[48] Businesses had reaped easy gains from the favorable economic environment but had not adapted to the needs of a competitive global economy. French government policies propped up consumption and reduced incentives for risk-taking. The result was frequent bouts of inflation, and "when all groups demand 110 percent of the national income, and government is unable to resist them, 10 percent inflation is inevitable."[49]

This tendency to experience bouts of domestic inflation caused a recurring headache for France with its international finances. At the heart of the international problem was the exchange rate, the price at which one currency buys another. Under the postwar Bretton Woods international monetary system, countries were required to keep their exchange rates "fixed"—the price of the currency was to remain within a narrow band around an agreed parity. This system did not suit France. With the French franc's exchange rate fixed, French exporters struggled. If, as their domestic costs went up, they kept US dollar or German deutschmark (D-mark) prices for their international buyers unchanged, their profits would be squeezed; if they raised their international prices to compensate for rising domestic costs, they would sell less abroad. Also, a fixed exchange rate induced French consumers and businesses facing high inflation at home to buy the now less expensive goods from abroad. Thus, France developed a tendency to sell less abroad than it imported; this shortfall of exports over imports, the "current account deficit," had to be financed by borrowing from lenders abroad. It was neither prudent nor possible to keep running deficits, because the country would become overly indebted to the rest of the world.

About every ten years, the pressure became unbearable, and French authorities were forced to devalue the franc to make imports more expensive and exports cheaper.[50] In principle, devaluation (formally, "downward adjustment of the parity") required the permission of the International Monetary Fund (IMF)—guardian of the global monetary system under the Bretton Woods Agreement. French authorities tried to bypass the humiliation of seeking the IMF's nod. But with or without the IMF's concurrence, devaluation was seen as an admission that the country's authorities had mismanaged their economy.

Repeated devaluations were truly embarrassing. Following a devaluation of the franc in 1948, the reprieve quickly wore off, and it was devalued by more than 30 percent during 1957-1958. French inflation, however, remained too high, and pressure for another devaluation kept building.[51] In its annual review of the French economy in 1968, the IMF said that France had not kept pace with international competition at least since 1960.[52] The French executive director of the IMF objected to this characterization, but other directors endorsed the bleak assessment of French competitiveness.

The underlying structural problem was that French businesses were unable to raise their productivity rapidly enough to compete in the global marketplace and France, as a nation, was, therefore, unable to live within its means. Exchange-rate devaluations were not a solution to France's long-term problems. Devaluations can help only temporarily to revive economic activity, and each devaluation makes the country poorer, since more domestic goods have to be sold abroad to buy the same quantity of imports. Rather than continuing to rely on frequent devaluations, the French economy needed fundamental changes. Businesses needed to become more innovative, and workers needed to moderate their wage demands. Progress on both those fronts would have dampened domestic inflationary pressures, made the French economy more competitive, and made French citizens more prosperous.

The contrast with German economic performance was striking. German companies held a dominant position in the global exports of sophisticated industrial products. Moreover, with German citizens still haunted by the memories of interwar hyperinflation and the accompanying political calamity, the Deutsche Bundesbank, Germany's central bank, had kept a determined lid on inflation. The combination of high productivity growth and low inflation led to large excesses of exports over imports and, hence, to chronic current account surpluses.[53] Because German products were in such great demand, international buyers perpetually scrambled for German D-marks, and German authorities were always under pressure to revalue the D-mark (to make it more expensive) and thus dampen the incentive of foreign buyers to purchase German goods.

For France, the strong D-mark and the weak franc became depressing symbols of German ascendancy and French decline. Things came to a head with the French student uprising in May 1968 and the workers' strikes in June. The government's efforts to pacify students and workers "satisfied no one."[54] The huge increase in workers' wages increased demand for domestic goods and services, fueling a new bout of inflation.[55] French investors lost confidence in their own government's ability to stabilize the economy and so rushed to convert their francs into safer D-marks, which were expected to rise in value. To meet this panicky demand for D-marks, French authorities drew down their reserves of gold and US dollars, according to one estimate, from nearly $6 billion in April 1968 to $3 billion by November 22 that year; of that total, $1 billion was drawn down after November 14 as investors fled with their money.[56]

On November 22, finance ministers of leading industrial nations met in Bonn. It was widely anticipated that the French would announce devaluation of the franc, which would make D-marks more expensive for French residents and, hence, slow the outflow of funds from France.[57] In France, the prospect of devaluation was read (correctly) as a sign of national decline, and it caused widespread dismay. The Germans intensified the hurt. The most mild-mannered jibe came from the usually strident German tabloid *Bild-Zeitung*, which carried the headline "Germany is number one again."[58] German Finance Minister Franz Josef Strauss dealt French prestige a blow by preemptively announcing that the franc would be devalued.[59] And the French felt the greatest sense of shame when the newspaper *Le Monde* reported that German journalists had "passed the hat for France" at a news conference.[60] These German assaults registered deep in the French psyche. Michel Debré, de Gaulle's foreign minister, looking back at this event in his memoirs, wrote: "I know the Germans sufficiently to be aware that they abuse their power as soon as they are in a position to do so."[61]

We can only speculate how de Gaulle felt about France's shame on November 22. The next day, he called a cabinet meeting at three thirty in the afternoon and kept the meeting running for hours as reporters and investors waited for his decision. Late in the evening, a brief statement from the Presidential Palace read: "The present parity of the French franc is maintained."[62] The franc would not be devalued after all. De Gaulle went on to impose austerity measures to reduce imports; in addition,

France borrowed from abroad (including from Germany) to finance its current account deficit.[63]

De Gaulle briefly regained the adulation of the French people, who were elated by his willingness to "fight" the foreigners in a "financial war."[64] The drama of de Gaulle's defiance was exhilarating, but France's economic and social problems had not gone away. French exporters needed a weaker franc to be competitive in international markets, and a misguided attachment to the strength of the currency only prolonged the anguish and made matters worse. By thumbing his nose at the Germans, de Gaulle had, one last time, given French citizens something to cheer about. But he could offer no longer-term vision consistent with the aspirations of the people. On April 27, 1969, French citizens voted against de Gaulle's proposals for changes to the French constitution. De Gaulle had lost the confidence of French citizens and he resigned on April 28. He died in November 1970, having completed only the first volume of his *Memoirs of Hope*.

History's currents were meeting. Georges Pompidou, who had served under de Gaulle as prime minister between 1962 and 1968, was about to take over as president. The French economy was falling behind the German economy and needed a boost from the devaluation that de Gaulle had valiantly withheld. Pompidou did not share de Gaulle's disdain for Europe. And so Pompidou wondered if "more Europe" could solve France's problems and help it catch up. True, the European integration process had reached a successful end. But the narrative of more integration as a solution for European problems was still alive. Psychologists Amos Tversky and Daniel Kahneman coined the phrase "availability heuristic" to explain that human beings instinctively believe the world will continue to work in the future as it has in the recent past.[65] Europe's infrastructure seemed "available" to take another leap.

The Hague 1969: The Third Leap

Georges Pompidou was elected president of France in June 1969. The franc came under pressure again, and the new president waited until August 8 to announce another devaluation.[66] In the meantime, he had called for European leaders to meet at The Hague later that year.[67] One of the topics of discussion at the leaders' summit was European monetary union. It was thus that France led Europe to take its third leap in the dark.

Although a Gaullist and therefore protective of symbols of French sovereignty, Pompidou decided it was time to give up de Gaulle's allegiance to the cherished French franc.[68] The franc, in his view, had become a perpetual headache. Pompidou persuaded himself that the way forward lay in monetary union, in which France and Germany would use the same currency. Once the franc disappeared into the miasma of a single currency, the need for humiliating devaluations would disappear. Thus, the French would not have to suffer continuous reminders of German economic superiority.

Pompidou was willing to give up de Gaulle's assertive nationalism, but he retained the Gaullist instinct that Europe must serve France's purpose. For him, "containing Germany" was the principal objective.[69] As would become clearer over time, "containing Germany" was mainly a code phrase indicating the goal of gaining economic parity with Germany. Parity, however, could be achieved only in the superficial sense. A single currency would eliminate the glaring difference between the strength of the D-mark and the French franc. But, to gain real parity, French leaders needed to build a more dynamic economy.

"Monetary union must be our priority," Pompidou declared. "This is where concrete results can be achieved."[70] Hubert Védrine, who later served as one of the closest advisers to French President François Mitterrand, later wrote that from Pompidou onward, monetary union became "a principal goal of French diplomacy."[71]

Pushing Back the Tide of History

A single currency within a monetary union would fix the exchange rates among France, Germany, and other member states that joined the monetary union. Member countries sharing the currency would also share a central bank that set a single monetary policy for all of them. French authorities would no longer have a currency that they could devalue if businesses in France lost competitiveness, nor would they be able to reduce domestic interest rates to pull the French economy out of a recession. Instead, France would depend on a European central bank that set the common interest rate and thus steered the exchange rate for the entire single-currency area. That common interest rate and exchange rate would depend, importantly, on the German economy, which could well be performing strongly and running current account surpluses at the same time. A European central bank could not respond to France's domestic economic needs.

It is helpful here to step back in time to fully recognize the folly of Pompidou's monetary union proposal. That proposal attempted to push back against the rushing tide of international monetary history. The experience of the past nearly one hundred years had plenty of cautionary warnings to offer about the risks of fixing exchange rates and giving up national monetary policy. The one apparent exception was the period between 1880 and 1913 when fixed exchange rates had, indeed, served the international community well. During those years, the world's major economies exchanged their currencies for a fixed amount of gold, giving rise to that system's name as the "gold standard." The world enjoyed rapid economic growth and, for the most part, achieved financial stability.[72] Because the gold standard and global prosperity coexisted, many observers inferred that the prosperity was the result, at least in part, of the gold standard and, therefore, fixed exchange rates were the only proper way to organize the international monetary system.

In truth, however, fixed exchange rates are helpful only during periods of economic calm. Economic historians Barry Eichengreen and Peter Temin have explained that "in good times," the ability to conduct international transactions at unchanging exchange rates creates an additional sense of stability. But "when times are bad," fixed exchange rates "intensify problems."[73] After 1913, governments of high-inflation countries often urgently needed to devalue their currencies to prevent excessively large current account deficits. Because such governments were held back from devaluing, they imposed harsh domestic austerity to restrict imports. That led to high unemployment. The problem became especially acute during the Great Depression in the 1930s, and according to Eichengreen's influential analysis, the gold standard had greatly added to the misery of the Great Depression.[74]

Thus, the interwar period—and, especially, the experience during the Great Depression—undermined the rationale for fixed exchange rates.[75] However, the world's policymakers had not fully absorbed the lessons from the Great Depression when they met at Bretton Woods, New Hampshire, in July 1944 to decide on a new international monetary system. They did recognize that requiring rigidly fixed exchange rates would be foolish. And so, in a modest concession to that reality, they had allowed for "adjustment" of exchange rates under international supervision. That, then, was the origin of the postwar "fixed-but-adjustable" exchange rates.

The new system had serious problems, as became quickly evident to University of Chicago economics professor and later Nobel laureate Milton Friedman. First in 1950 and again in 1953, Friedman explained that when exchange rates are fixed, warnings of trouble are initially not striking enough. Governments, therefore, delay their response, hoping that matters will be set right. But the "disequilibrium" in the current account grows (the current account deficit increases) to "crisis dimensions, requiring drastic action at home, international consultation, and help from abroad."[76]

Almost as if he could foresee the recurring need to devalue the French franc and the tendency for French authorities to cling to the fixed rate and delay that decision until a financial crisis loomed, Friedman called for abandoning the Bretton Woods system.[77] It was time, he insisted, for currencies to float freely: the exchange rate—the currency's price—should not be decided once every several years by the government or the IMF but should be determined continuously by market forces of supply and demand. Under floating or "flexible" exchange rates, the value of the currency would, he said, respond to rising inflation and widening current account deficits well before crisis-like conditions set in. The exchange rate, a "sensitive" price, would act like a shock absorber.

Over the two decades that followed, Friedman was proven right in his diagnosis of the shortcomings of fixed exchange rates. The Bretton Woods system was poorly equipped to deal with persistent differentials in inflation rates across countries. All politicians—not just those in France—preferred to delay devaluations because reducing the value of the home currency was associated with public loss of face and prestige; and the international community discouraged devaluations because one currency's devaluation could set off cascading "competitive devaluations" by others seeking to regain export advantage. The delays encouraged speculators to test if governments would keep their commitment to the fixed rate. Policymakers fought back with a mélange of responses, including controls on imports and capital movements.[78]

But growing numbers of international investors were willing to speculate on impending devaluations by selling the currency whose value they expected would fall. To maintain their commitment to the fixed rate, governments had to use their foreign-exchange reserves to buy their own currency, and when the reserves began to fall too low, governments that refused to devalue had to either hike interest rates or impose fiscal austerity to restrain imports and, hence, contain the current account deficit. However, higher interest rates and austerity caused domestic economic activity to slow down and threatened to raise unemployment to politically intolerable levels. Speculators understood that governments would not be able to withstand the political pressure arising from a slowing economy and widespread unemployment and hence that the governments would eventually capitulate and let the currency depreciate.

As French authorities surely understood, for countries that were losing international competitiveness, it was not possible in a world of active financial speculators to maintain a fixed exchange rate and simultaneously conduct domestic macroeconomic policy to meet the country's growth and employment objectives. France's problem was not Germany. France, quite simply, had been unable to get its own house in order.

By the late 1960s, many countries found it impossible to live within the constraints of fixed exchange rates and the postwar Bretton Woods system of fixed-but-adjustable exchange rates was slowly breaking down. The United States, the linchpin of the system, struck the final blow. Running high inflation rates, it could not sustain its commitment to pay $35 for an ounce of gold. On March 15, 1968, a "two-tier" system was introduced under which central banks would continue to transact with one another at the $35 price but would not interfere in the setting of gold's market price. At that point, monetary historian Michael Bordo says, the Bretton Woods system effectively ended, although an attempt to stay within a fixed exchange rate regime continued for some years.[79]

In March 1969, another towering economist, Harry Gordon Johnson, repeated Friedman's call for flexible exchange rates. Such was Johnson's intellectual heft that Yale University economist James Tobin (and future Nobel laureate) later wrote of him: "For the economics profession throughout the world, the third quarter of this [the twentieth] century was the 'Age of Johnson.' [He] bestrode our discipline like a colossus."[80] Johnson pointed to an embarrassing void in the economics profession: "little reasoned defense of the fixed exchange rate system has been produced beyond the fact that it exists and functions after a fashion, and the contention that any change would be for the worse."[81] In contrast, he said, the case for flexible exchange rates was undeniable. Friedman, Johnson said, was right. Greater exchange-rate flexibility would give countries greater insulation from macroeconomic shocks and would allow national authorities more freedom in the pursuit of domestic policy objectives.

Thus, while in 1957 the Treaty of Rome had been in the vanguard of international trade liberalization, in late 1969, Pompidou's call for permanently fixed exchange rates embedded in a European monetary union was not just an eccentric priority for France, it was mystifyingly opposed to the global trend toward a system of flexible exchange rates. In seeking what appeared to him an easy fix, Pompidou was shirking his true obligation to seek real solutions to France's long-term competitiveness problems. He was, moreover, pulling other European nations into a gamble whose historical context and risks he evidently did not understand and whose complexities he had no idea how to manage. Pompidou was doing everyone a disservice.

Of course, Pompidou's proposal could have simply died at the meeting in The Hague. There was, after all, the matter of Germany. Germans shared with many in the English-speaking world, the "Anglo-Saxons," a respect for the market economy. In the 1950s, Ludwig Erhard, seeking to foster truly competitive markets in Europe, had wanted Europe's trade borders to be opened to all countries—and not just to other European nations. Similarly, to German officials, it now made sense that the price of the currency was best set by market forces.

Indeed, although the US-based Friedman had given impetus to the concept, German scholars were the real aficionados of flexible exchange rates ("flexible Wechselkurs" or "schwankender Wechselkurs") (see figure 1.2). They had run with this theme faster than the Anglo-Saxons had. And, in this respect, German scholars were a world removed from their French counterparts. In France, academics, bureaucrats, and politicians remained steeped in a dirigiste mindset: the idea that governments could (and should) manage virtually all aspects of the economy. Not surprisingly, the French showed little interest in exchange-rate flexibility ("taux de change flexible" or "taux de change flottant"). To them, it seemed unimaginable that anyone other than the government would set the price of a country's currency.

On September 29, 1969, two months before the summit at The Hague, Germany let the D-mark's exchange rate float against the dollar. Soon after, the German authorities did peg the D-mark again. However, German officials had shown a willingness to move toward a floating-rate regime. As

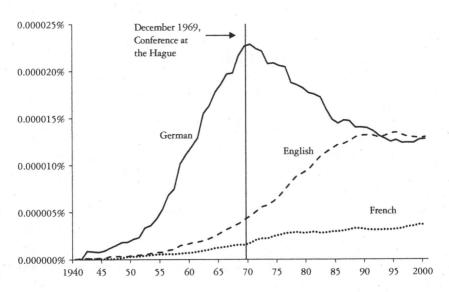

FIGURE 1.2. Germans led the intellectual inquiry into "flexible exchange rates." (Frequency of reference to "flexible exchange rate" in books digitized by Google)
Note: The graph was created using the Google Books Ngram Viewer (https://books.google.com/ngrams/info). It reports the frequency with which the phrase "flexible exchange rate" is mentioned in the books scanned by Google. The term "flexible Wechselkurs" was used for German books, and "taux de change flexible" was used for French books. The English variation "floating exchange rate," the German variation "schwankender Wechselkurs," and the French variation "taux de change flottant" yielded similar trends.

Robert Hetzel, economist at the Federal Reserve Bank of Richmond, would later explain: "Germany's commitment to a free market economy pushed it to reject fixed exchange rates and adopt floating exchange rates."[82]

Thus, in proposing a monetary union, Pompidou was defying not only the global experience that was causing fixed-exchange-rate systems to break down, but he was also ignoring the clash between the French dirigiste temperament and the German market-oriented economic ideology. Pompidou nevertheless pushed ahead, because a quarter century after World War II had ended, he believed that France still had leverage as "moral guarantor for the Federal Republic [of Germany]."[83]

As the Hague summit approached, Pompidou pushed harder. Two days before the summit, on Saturday, November 29, the *New York Times* reported that Pompidou would "press for closer monetary links within the European Economic Community" at the summit.[84] Pompidou's finance minister, Valéry Giscard d'Estaing, added that the summit would chart a path toward a common European monetary policy.

The Germans could have said no and walked away. Germany was an economically powerful nation. It preferred floating exchange rates. The idea of a European monetary union would have been shelved in the archives.

The Shadow of the War Continues to Fall on Germany

Germany's politics and leadership were also changing. The Christian Democratic Union (CDU) had finally lost its postwar grip on power, and Willy Brandt of the Social Democratic Party (SPD) had just become chancellor. Brandt had left Germany in 1933 soon after Hitler came to power.[85] When he returned to Germany in 1947, some Germans considered him a traitor for living abroad while they had endured unspeakable tyranny at home. However, on his return, he wrote and spoke eloquently about German responsibility. He came "to symbolize a Germany of peace, tolerance and a measure of modesty."[86] Brandt became mayor of West Berlin in 1957 and West German chancellor in 1969.

Above all, Brandt wanted to atone for German brutality and crimes. In December 1970, a little more than a year after he became chancellor, Brandt traveled to Warsaw to lay a wreath at the Monument to the Ghetto Heroes. There, in an unplanned and unexpected gesture of penance, he bowed and went down on his knees. Amid the stunned silence, clicking cameras captured images of that remarkable "Warsaw Genuflection."[87] Years later, Brandt wrote: "From the abyss of German history, under the burden of millions of victims of murder, I did what human beings do when speech fails them."[88] He was awarded the Nobel Peace Prize in 1971 for his "attempt to bury hatred" and his courage in promoting peace and detente.[89]

Although he set high value on establishing international harmony, Brandt had a skeptical view of the European project. He wrote in his memoirs that "emotional" calls for European integration were common, but "national prejudice and recalcitrance" shaped real decisions. European politicians, he went on, found it "easy to soar above national egocentricities on the wings of rhetoric, but this achieved little more than a Europe of declamations."[90] Brandt's "financial experts" warned him that the French proposal for European monetary union was not in Germany's best interests. The experts asked him "to exercise the utmost caution."[91] Brandt himself was clear that "structural disparities between member countries and divergences in economic aims and practices were real problems" in moving toward monetary union.[92] Thus, neither a greater European cause nor a specific idea of European monetary union enthused Brandt.

Brandt's overriding priority was *Ostpolitik*, reconciliation between West and East Germany. "We must prevent a further drifting apart of the German nation," he said, and begin working "with each other."[93] This was a historic task, to which there was great resistance. Within West Germany, Brandt faced opposition from the Christian Democrats.[94] Abroad, reconciliation and eventual German reunification aroused fear of renewed German nationalism. Thus, although the war had ended more than a quarter century earlier, it continued to cast its shadow on Europe. *Ostpolitik* was still too radical, and Brandt needed allies to make progress.

In a bid to gain French support for *Ostpolitik*, Brandt showed willingness to discuss Pompidou's monetary union idea. Since his experts were trying to dissuade him from going down this path, Brandt consulted Jean Monnet. For Monnet, "more Europe" was always the right way forward. He never quite grasped the strength of the European nation-state.[95] Monnet "encouraged" Brandt to consider establishing a European Reserve Fund, a concept long advocated by Robert Triffin, the Belgian-born Yale economist and avid proponent of monetary unions.[96] The Reserve Fund would pool contributions from member states to lend to countries running current account deficits and even to promote growth.[97]

Karl Schiller, German minister of economic affairs, strongly opposed the Reserve Fund.[98] Schiller's position and that of other German "experts" was that Germany would discuss a common fund only after other European economies had "converged"—in other words, had achieved economic performance standards acceptable to Germans. Otherwise, Germans could end up financing those running persistent fiscal and current account deficits. Nevertheless, at the Hague summit, Brandt, who knew nothing of these matters and had barely given them any thought, agreed to further consider a European Reserve Fund.[99]

After the summit, the European public was excited by the possibility that Britain would finally become a member of the EEC. Having rejected Monnet's overtures to join the Coal and Steel Community in 1950 and having also chosen to stay out of the EEC created by the Treaty of Rome in 1957, Britain fell into a despondent mood of national "declinism."[100] British leaders had begun knocking on Europe's doors, believing that joining the EEC would "remedy" Britain's economic failures and increase its international political influence.[101] Twice, in 1963 and 1967, de Gaulle vetoed British entry. De Gaulle was convinced that Britain's true allegiance was with the United States and that as a proud, seafaring nation, Britain would disrupt a truly "European Europe."[102] However, de Gaulle was now gone, and Pompidou believed that Britain would help counter Germany's growing influence in European matters. Brandt, for his part, understood that Britain would not be an "easy partner." But, he believed, "Britain's steadfast resistance in World War II, her sacrifices and sufferings, should not be consigned to oblivion. Hadn't they already demonstrated their membership in Europe's darkest hour?"[103]

In public appearances after the summit, French and German leaders declared that their friendship was again driving European progress by enlarging membership in the EEC. Among other countries expected to join at that time were Denmark, Ireland, and Norway (Norway ultimately stayed out).

Tensions continued to bubble behind the public face of Franco-German amity. Brandt's preliminary agreement to the European Reserve Fund meant little because he himself was worried about divergent countries living within a monetary union; for which reason, both he and his officials were worried that Germany may be called to finance deficits in other countries. And, despite Pompidou's claim, France could no longer exercise any leverage as Germany's "moral guarantor." German newspapers reporting on the Hague summit emphasized that Germany was not only a superior economic power but had "emerged as at least equal to France in political weight."[104] Germany's economic ideology and national interest did not favor a monetary union, and Brandt attached no special value to European integration. A Franco-German tug of war was about to begin over what was as yet a hazy monetary union.[105]

1970: *Werner Committee Proposes an Incomplete Monetary Union*

At their summit in The Hague, European leaders set up a committee to chart a path toward monetary union.[106] Led by Luxembourg Prime Minister Pierre Werner, the committee immediately confronted the fundamental problem of monetary unions. When national authorities give up the ability to conduct monetary policy tailored to their domestic needs, they lose an essential macroeconomic management tool. Domestic monetary policy is typically in the front line of efforts to deflate excessive economic exuberance and help pull the economy out of recessions and crises. Within a monetary union, however, a common monetary policy applies to all members. If the common monetary policy is set to meet the needs of the "average" nation, inflation will rise faster in rapidly growing, high-inflation countries; countries struggling with a weak economy and low inflation will be further handicapped by what, for them, would be a too-tight monetary policy. Bringing countries into a monetary union was, therefore, a bad idea when countries were diverse and their performances were on divergent trajectories.

In an article published in September 1961, Robert Mundell, then an economist at the IMF and later a Nobel laureate, explained that a monetary union could succeed if workers were willing to migrate from struggling to booming economies.[107] However, the likelihood that European workers would migrate in sufficient numbers from one member country to another in response to shifting economic fortunes seemed unrealistic. Compared with US workers, who moved in significant numbers across states, European workers were much less mobile across national boundaries or even within their own countries.[108] In 1969, economist Peter Kenen, then a professor at Columbia University, argued that even if workers were mobile, a stable monetary union also required a substantial pool of centralized funds: a smoothly functioning monetary union needed a "fiscal union."[109] Such central funding, delivered through the federal government, was available in the United States.[110] The US government provided temporary relief to states facing short-term distress and gave long-term support to chronically underperforming states. No such funding was available, or seemed possible, in Europe.

The US government also facilitated private "risk sharing," which further evened out economic conditions across its various states.[111] Uniform regulations, federally backed deposit insurance for banks, and social security transfers from the federal government created an integrated national economy. A business could operate nationally rather than primarily within a single state, a bank could borrow and lend throughout the country, and households were willing to own stocks and bonds that financed companies with offices and production facilities nationwide. Thus, financial risks were diversified across states, and such diversification—like the flow of migrants—helped absorb the shock of economic contraction in a particular state.

The Werner Report, published in October 1970, recognized Europe's evident handicaps in creating a successful monetary union. In the report's words, European workers did not circulate across borders "in an entirely satisfactory way," and the "community budget" that was needed to support a fiscal union would always be "insufficient."[112] The report stated plainly that European nations needed to form a political union—a unified, democratically legitimate, political entity—to achieve sizable pooling of tax resources and thus operate a budget appropriate to the needs of a monetary union. The report's conclusion was straightforward: monetary union would be "unable to do without" political union.[113] Without political union, the necessary fiscal safeguard could not be established, and without that safeguard, the monetary union would remain fragile and would not survive.

Based on its analysis, the Werner Committee could easily have said that a European monetary union was a bad idea and needed to be stopped in its tracks. Europe could not mobilize sufficient political unity to achieve a safely functioning monetary union. Even in the shadow of World War II, when goodwill for other European nations and the sense of "brotherhood" was greatest, willingness to compromise on core sovereign rights had been absent. Taxation was a core sovereign right. No European nation was willing to hand over sufficient tax revenues to a European authority to make a monetary union work. Everyone on the Werner Committee understood that.

However, instead of counseling European leaders to abandon the venture, the Werner Committee discovered reasons to move ahead. The committee's report predicted that the inevitable tensions and pressures within the incomplete monetary union would force member nations toward "progressive development of political cooperation." Thus, the incompleteness of the monetary union was actually a virtue: it would be the "leaven," the yeast, that would cause Europe to ferment and transform into "political union."[114] The Werner Committee was expressing the French "monetarist" position: monetary union was the path to political union. Faith in such transformation lay in Jean Monnet's proposition that when Europe stumbled and fell, it got up to move forward. Monnet expressed this falling-forward idea in throwaway, but memorable words: "I have always believed that Europe would be built through crises, and that it would be the sum of their solutions."[115]

The Werner Committee members did understand that even if this benign progression unfolded, its end-point—a political union—could take decades to reach. But the Committee did not draw the obvious conclusion. As long as the "community budget" remained "insufficient," costly financial crises could occur. Was that good reason to put monetary union on hold?

The committee was under pressure to deliver something. Drawing on extensive correspondence during that time, David Marsh, author of *The Euro: The Battle for the New Global Currency*, writes that French leaders continued to push for monetary union. They were concerned that Germany was speaking in "a loud voice" because the D-mark was so strong. The risk, as the French saw it, was that Germany would be "master of Europe" for a long time.[116] The Germans were worried that the French were trying to put "shackles" on what they regarded as Bundesbank's "sinister" monetary policy, which kept interest rates too high for the comfort of other nations.[117] Hence, German leaders, unwilling to be "shackled," continued to resist monetary union.

The Werner Committee said to the French, "there is, in fact, a way forward," and to the Germans the committee said the way forward "is on your terms." The German terms were simple. All countries should manage their economic policy just as the Germans did.

Translating the German terms into a concrete proposal, the Werner Committee's report asserted that an incomplete monetary union could work if all member states agreed to "norms" of fiscal prudence, around which they would "harmonize" their policies.[118] The norms would include the "size" and "variation" of public budgets; and they would "be made *increasingly restrictive*."[119] To ensure compliance with the norms, a central authority would "*control*"—indeed, exercise a "*decisive*" influence" over—the budgetary and economic policy of member states.[120] Eventually, responsibility for all policy decisions would transfer from the national to Community authorities.[121] These steps to support a single currency, the Werner Report concluded, would "ensure growth and stability within the Community," and "make it a pillar of stability," in the world economy.[122]

Thus, a European "stability ideology" was born. The Werner Committee report did not even try to present an economic logic to justify its strange proposal, which had no historical precedent or analytical basis. The committee did not explain why "harmonization" around unenforceable "norms" would help ensure a workable monetary union. Nor did it explain why national parliaments would agree to steadily give up their budgetary authority to Community institutions.

But with its sights set on an illusory—certainly distant—political union, the Werner Committee declared that Europe was ready to begin its uncharted journey to an incomplete monetary union. In such a monetary union, member states would no longer be able to use domestic monetary policy and exchange rate changes to deal with their economic booms and busts. Neither would they have access to alternative support mechanisms to dampen the inevitable economic fluctuations. Countries would be especially vulnerable during recessions and financial crises. Europe could reach such an incomplete monetary union within a decade, the Werner Committee said. [123] The committee thus delivered on the political objective that Pompidou had set.

It is unclear if the economic absurdity of their proposal was evident at the time to the members of the Werner Committee. Certainly, some who were closely involved in the committee's deliberations looked back in horror. Hans Tietmeyer, member of the German delegation to the Werner Committee and President of the Bundesbank between 1993 and 1999, later wrote that the Werner Committee had tried to reconcile the irreconcilable.[124] Another contemporary observer, André Szász—a former Dutch central bank official and author of perhaps the most insightful and engaging history of Europe's single currency odyssey—had more biting criticism. The Werner Committee's report, Szász said, was not a compromise in the conventionally understood sense. European governments did not resolve their differences by meeting each other "on intermediate positions." Rather, "they agreed on documents that left them free to push for their own preference."[125] They agreed to use suitably nebulous words, such as "harmonization," "coordination," and "union," which later left them free to interpret the documents in a manner that most suited their ideologies and interests.

Such were the cynical beginnings of the European monetary union.

The Stability Ideology Takes Center Stage

A month after the report's publication, Samuel Brittan, economics commentator at the *Financial Times*, said the EEC was heading into "the worst of all worlds." Countries would no longer be able to change their exchange rates, but the new machinery put in place would not be sufficient "to make such changes unnecessary." Monetary union, Brittan said, would not work without "a common budget, political union, and some form of European Government." The only explanation for the initiative, he concluded, was that the heads of government had little idea what they were doing but believed they could score an "impressive" public relations triumph without too much effort.[126]

Four months later, in March 1971, Nicholas Kaldor, the University of Cambridge economist, wrote an extended critique of the Werner Committee's report. Kaldor was one of the most distinguished economic theorists of his generation. More than half a century after he proposed them, the "six Kaldor facts on economic growth" are still a subject of live academic discourse. On the policy front, Kaldor was a public finance expert; his ideas on expenditure taxes remain influential.

In his critique of the Werner Committee's report, Kaldor focused his fire on the Werner Committee's reliance on fiscal harmonization to make the monetary union work. Harmonization would actually make matters worse, Kaldor wrote. Insisting on rigid fiscal benchmarks during periods of distress would prolong the distress. Even in the long term, Kaldor argued, harmonization could constrain and set back the less prosperous and slower-growing countries. It would be essential, he emphasized, for a central authority to move fiscal resources from the stronger to the weaker countries.[127] And because such movement of resources required a democratically legitimate political contract, "The objective of full monetary and economic union," Kaldor repeated, would be "unattainable without a political union."[128]

But, perhaps, Kaldor's most scathing and prescient comment was on the Werner Committee's promise that Europe would stumble into a political union. An incomplete monetary union, he said, would "prevent the development of a political union, not promote it."[129] National conflicts within the incomplete monetary union would fester, which would undermine European unity. Kaldor grimly concluded that a European monetary union would be like the house which "divided against itself cannot stand."

Kaldor's instinctive political analysis received ample support years later from US political scientists. Researchers did acknowledge that policies introduced without public consultation and support could sometimes gain citizens' backing and political momentum over time. The iconic example of such a success was the social security program in the United States. Introduced in 1935 by President Franklin D. Roosevelt, the reliable social security checks created a large constituency of political supporters, especially low-income senior citizens. Such beneficiaries have ever since actively defended their benefits from repeated efforts to roll back the program.[130]

But when a policy that is parachuted into people's lives delivers small or "capricious and arbitrary" benefits, the public quickly views the policy and, indeed, the government itself "with mistrust and skepticism."[131] Public opposition to the policy steadily increases and undermines it. The problem is even more acute when a policy creates conflicts, as Stanford University economist Avner Greif and political scientist David Laitin explain. Those who lose because of the policy try to gut it. The conflicts intensify, and the policy eventually collapses.[132]

The benefits of the European monetary union were, at best, "capricious and arbitrary." And conflicts were inbuilt: an easy monetary policy for some is too tight for others. Governments resist the prospect of paying to rescue other governments. Nothing in the economics of the single currency or in the recent political history of European integration gave reason to believe that these limitations and tensions would go away on their own.

France itself stood in the way of a true monetary union. After the Schuman Declaration's brief glorious moment in 1950, France had rejected the European Defense Community and had acted as a petulant laggard in the Treaty of Rome negotiations. In the 1960s, de Gaulle had disrupted Europe's institutions and even tried to reverse their course. Now Pompidou had made it clear that he would reject any attempt to fold France into a European political union. He had instructed the French representatives on the Werner Committee to scrub out "rhetorical references" to political union from the committee's documents.[133] And when the committee's report nevertheless appeared with unacceptable phrases such as "progressive development of political cooperation" and "leaven for political union," an angry Pompidou reprimanded the chief French negotiator on the Werner Committee, Bernard Clappier, for signing the report.[134] All Pompidou really wanted was "an improved support mechanism for the franc."[135] He and other Gaullists were not prepared to surrender their fiscal sovereignty and French state authority.[136] The more traditional Gaullists, such as Michel Debré, were even more upset. They opposed the very concept of a single currency. To them, it was unacceptable that Pompidou was proposing to give up the franc, the emblem of the French government's sovereignty.[137]

There seemed no meeting point. The possibility that Europe would fall forward into political union was unthinkable. And without such a prospect, any move toward monetary union was foolhardy, as Kaldor had warned. By now, Brandt's brief flirtation with the monetary union was also over. In the days after the summit, Brandt took the lead in opposing France's monetary union idea.[138] It soon proved hard even to find a point of congruence in the Werner Committee's proposal of fiscal norms enforced by a central authority. German officials demanded more surrender of French economic sovereignty and "greater supranational control of its economy than the French were willing to concede."[139] Brandt refused to agree to a "firm timetable for monetary union," and Pompidou's goal—echoed by the Werner Report—of a monetary union in ten years faded away.

Nevertheless, the Werner Report did have the last laugh. It had sown the seed from which slowly emerged a widely accepted European economic and political ideology. As sociologist and philosopher Max Weber has explained, ideologies change at critical junctures in history.[140] At such junctures, when alternative paths are possible, new ideologies can form to justify choices made. At this critical juncture in European history, with a nebulous sense that European integration needed to be deepened, the dirigiste French and the more market-oriented German ideologies were hard to reconcile.

In that vacuum, "stability" was a congenial idea to everyone. It was in accord with the German preference for low inflation and fiscal prudence. Stability also meant discipline, a powerful consideration for the smaller countries, which had always sought a degree of predictability. For example, the Netherlands, Austria, Belgium, and Luxembourg had, for long, tied their exchange rates to the D-mark. For France, the discipline demanded by the single currency created the possibility of an "external anchor," a way to tame the internal politics of incessant claims on the budget. The Italians, who at this time still felt the lingering glow of their nation's postwar economic miracle, thought of themselves as on the same side as the Germans but perceived value in Europe's "external anchor" role. Creating ties that bound nations tightly seemed an attractive idea.

Thus, the notion of "stability" became a "pro-European" virtue. The view took hold that commitment to monetary stability would guide Europe in a falling forward process to a political union in the indefinite future. The monetary union project—although delayed into an indefinite future—remained alive. The committees and institutional infrastructure established kept the project going. Europe extended its reach into the nation-state.

The vision was far-fetched. It was also economically and politically risky. And so it necessarily came about that a small group of European political leaders and senior bureaucrats rhetorically reinforced one another's belief in the virtues of a stability-based pro-Europeanism. Psychologist Irving Janis coined the word *groupthink* to describe a group's uncritical commitment to an ideology or course of action.[141] Once the group commits to that idea, its members tend to dismiss the fallacies and risks, and they rule out alternative options.[142] Indeed, when the evidence contradicts the groupthink, rather than stepping back, the likely response is an escalating commitment. Economist Robert Akerlof says that even when they see the dangers of their views and actions, group members suppress their misgivings because they value the approval and respect of the other group members and fear exclusion from the social circle of prestige.[143] Stories become important. In 1995, explaining the collective disregard of warnings before Mexico's financial crisis, Paul Krugman, then an economics professor at Stanford University, wrote:

> People believe certain stories because everyone important tells them, and people tell those stories because everyone important believes them. Indeed, when a conventional wisdom is at its fullest strength, one's agreement with that conventional wisdom becomes almost a litmus test of one's suitability to be taken seriously.[144]

Thus the story, the groupthink, continued. The experience with fixed exchange rates had highlighted that the illusion of stability could persist for long periods even as increasingly worrisome macroeconomic imbalances accumulated. The spell eventually broke in a furious burst of instability. National conflicts were deep-rooted and unlikely to disappear. Yet the Werner Report had proposed an ideology that Europeans found plausible. The question was whether this incipient groupthink would take hold and lead Europe to a safe and workable monetary union, or whether it would merely hide serious underlying differences in French and German ideologies and interests. And if it only served to hide the differences, would the groupthink encourage easy but dangerous decisions?

1971: On an Uncharted Journey

For now, the German-French differences threatened to derail the project. In May 1971, the Germans floated the D-mark, this time for a more extended period than in September 1969. At the Franco-German consultations in July 1971, the Germans reported on "the advantages it had already brought."[145] In October 1971, at the annual meetings of the World Bank and the IMF, German Economics Minister Karl Schiller said: "the mechanism of exchange rate adjustment has been far too rigid . . . it is important that unrealistic parities [exchange rates] should be adjusted promptly and sufficiently. We ought to look at parity changes not as matters of political prestige and of victory and defeat but from a sober economic point of view."[146] This was the first cautious official call for a global shift to exchange rate flexibility based on economic considerations rather than political drama.[147]

Schiller was a Social Democrat, not a liberal free-market economist like his famous predecessor Ludwig Erhard, the Christian Democrat. Schiller was more receptive than Erhard to the government's role in boosting demand for recovery from economic slumps. But Schiller and Erhard shared a common German acknowledgment of the proper role of market forces. Exchange rates could never be completely depoliticized, but once the currency was floated, political interference in setting its value became much more difficult.

Pompidou might have believed that France was Germany's "moral guarantor" and could therefore exercise leverage over German policies. But he was misreading history. As Marjolin pointed out, even Adenauer had been unwilling to accept French demands when they encroached on "fundamental German interests."[148] Thus, in late 1971 and early 1972, when Pompidou and Brandt met several times, the sticking point was always the same. Pompidou pressed the Germans for greater "community monetary effort"; Brandt and Schiller predictably asked who would pay if the weaker member states, including France, needed to be bailed out.[149] The Germans did not want to be called on "to support poorer or less productive partners."[150]

The French said that monetary union would lead to political union. The official German position was that monetary union could not start without political union. But the Germans were playing with the phrase "political union." They were unwilling to share their valuable tax revenues in the cause of the monetary union, and "political union" without shared tax revenues was an oxymoron. Germans, in their public position, conveniently hid behind the facade of a mythical political union, which they knew Pompidou would not accept. French and German ideologies and national interests were still far apart.

However, Germans also wanted to be perceived as good European citizens. They did not want to be seen as setting back European integration. In the struggle to resolve this tension, they gradually moved toward the French ideological position on exchange rates. Although German scholars remained much more interested in floating rates than their French counterparts, references to floating exchange rates in German writings began to fall (see figure 1.2).

Protected by the stability ideology, a process of seemingly easy compromises began. In April 1972, German authorities returned to the European fixed-exchange-rate fold. The first step in the Werner Committee's recommendations was the "snake-in-the-tunnel" arrangement. The "snake" required European currencies to stay within narrow bands of agreed parities with one another, and the "tunnel" allowed European currencies to fluctuate in a wide range around their respective parities with the US dollar.[151] The Germans joined that initiative. The experiment would include the entire EEC, which was to increase in size to nine members once Britain, Denmark, and Ireland joined on January 1, 1973. Britain, in fact, joined the snake in May 1972, in anticipation of its EEC membership.

Could fixed exchange rates work this time? It should have been no surprise that some members of the snake arrangement, including France, could not uphold their commitment to the narrow exchange-rate bands. Germany, as the "safe haven," received large flows of capital from the other countries. The D-mark perpetually tended to strengthen, while the other currencies tended to weaken below the agreed benchmark. The French wanted the Germans to help the weaker currencies, to display "solidarity," by reducing D-mark denominated interest rates.[152] The Germans refused, saying that all countries needed to keep their own houses in order. The obvious disagreements led speculators to bet that participants in the snake would not be able to maintain their commitment to exchange-rate parities. As Milton Friedman had predicted nearly two decades earlier, the threat of unbearable speculative pressure and exchange-rate crises grew. Britain left the snake in June 1972, a month after it had joined.

In September, the Germans acted to discourage the flood of capital inflow, but Bundesbank President Karl Klasen was pessimistic. "We are still struggling," he said, "to keep alive the snake in the tunnel."[153] Klasen added that the plan to introduce a single European currency by the end of the decade was completely unreasonable. Klasen's prediction gained credibility as Italy's miraculous postwar economic recovery came to an abrupt end. The Italian economy seemed unable to make the transition from the easier task of postwar rebuilding to a more demanding, productivity-driven growth model. In February 1973, the Italian lira left the snake, and Italian authorities let the lira float. A parallel effort to revive the Bretton Woods system failed, and in March, the D-mark was floated again.[154] Less than a year later, on January 19, 1974, France floated the franc.

The key player in this next round was Valéry Giscard d'Estaing. Upon Pompidou's sudden death in April 1974, Giscard d'Estaing defeated François Mitterrand in a closely fought election to become France's president on May 19, 1974. Born in February 1926, he was forty-eight years old and was often compared with former US President John F. Kennedy.[155] At the age of sixteen, Giscard d'Estaing had joined the French resistance, and after World War II ended, he completed military duties in North Africa. He studied in France's elite schools and received their highest academic honors.

Giscard d'Estaing, like his former boss, Pompidou, was convinced that the growing German economic lead over France was intolerable. Both men believed that the best way to close that gap was by creating a European monetary union. However, rather than unthinkingly continue down that path, Giscard d'Estaing had good reason to rethink his way forward. With France's inflation virus persisting, the franc had crashed out of the narrow exchange-rate bands allowed by the snake. And a few weeks before he became president, a frustrated Giscard d'Estaing had said that the snake was "an animal from European monetary prehistory."[156] Even so, he decided that the discipline required to keep the franc within the snake would help him enforce greater austerity at home, which he believed would spur renewed French economic dynamism.

He made it a priority to bring the exchange rate value of the franc back to within the bounds set under the initial snake arrangement. He achieved that goal in July 1975. However, nothing else had changed, and the French economy again struggled within the restraints of exchange-rate bands. As before, French inflation remained high, the current account deficit remained large, and the franc was perennially under stress. The high unemployment rate created pressure to devalue the franc. In March 1976, nine months after reentering, France withdrew from the snake a second time. Over the next four months, the franc depreciated by over 10 percent. The strong German D-mark remained a depressing reminder of the gap that France had not been able to bridge.

Insiders Try to Stop the Monetary Union

While Europe was failing in its effort to live within the bounds permitted by the snake, the European Commission set up a "study group," chaired by Robert Marjolin, to examine what had gone wrong and assess the prospects of launching the European monetary union.

By any metric, Marjolin was pro-European, and as a longtime senior Eurocrat, he understood the mechanics by which Europe moved forward. Marjolin had played a key role in the negotiation and implementation of the Treaty of Rome. He had worked particularly hard to persuade his fellow French leaders and citizens to give up their protectionist instincts and sign on to opening France's borders to trade.[157]

However, the Marjolin Committee was not helpful to the cause of European monetary union. Extrapolating from the need for—and success of—open trade borders to monetary union was "naive," the committee said. Its report, submitted in March 1975, pointed out that under the "customs union" established by the Treaty of Rome, member nations had given up limited national authority. They had surrendered "the instruments of commercial policy, notably customs duties and quantitative restrictions," but had retained "all other instruments of economic and monetary policy." In contrast, monetary union required governments to transfer critical elements of national political authority to "Community institutions," which could then impose their decisions on member states.[158]

The committee's conclusion was simple. Since the political willingness to subordinate national interests to "Community institutions" was clearly absent, no plan for a monetary union could be credible. Marjolin vigorously stood by these views, first in lectures he gave in 1980 (where he reproduced some of the words cited in the preceding paragraph) and then again in his 1986 memoirs.[159]

In his memoirs, Marjolin would also reject the "falling forward" thesis, the idea that monetary union would force agreement to political union. European leaders, he said, were "obviously not ready" to give up their core sovereign functions; the change required was simply too "profound."[160] He saw no reason to expect that the passage of time—or the hard knocks of experience—would alter the resolve to retain national fiscal and, hence, political sovereignty. It would be a "fundamental error," he said, to expect that a government would "relinquish sovereignty simply because an 'inner logic'—the reality of which is moreover debatable—left it no alternative."[161]

Two years later, another committee, this one under Donald MacDougall, a British civil servant with long tenure in economic policymaking, insisted that a US-style federal taxation structure was essential to operate a monetary union. The MacDougall Committee recognized that Europe could not match the scale of federal taxation possible in the United States. The committee concluded that a monetary union required the support of a central budget that was at least 5 to 7 percent of aggregate GDP of the member states.[162] Reaching that level would take a huge effort since the Community's budget at that time was just 0.7 percent of member states' GDP. But only with the much larger budget envelope could the Community provide meaningful help, including grants and social insurance, to member states facing financial distress. Anything less could not sustain a monetary union.[163]

Europe was at a crossroads. The snake, which had tried to restrict exchange-rate movements, was dying. Two committees appointed by the European Commission had said, "don't do it." It would be unwise for Europe to embark on the monetary union journey. The global Bretton Woods system had broken down, and advanced economies outside Europe were "learning to float" their exchange rates.[164] Here was another opportunity for Europe to abandon its monetary union venture.

Europe's urgent priorities were to revive economic growth and renew a sense of optimism. The impressive recovery from the Great Depression of the 1930s and the wreckage of World War II was over.[165] Productivity growth was slowing down; a European economic "sclerosis" seemed to be setting in.[166] European governments found it increasingly hard to deliver on the public's expectations.[167] The oil-price hike in 1973 had stoked higher inflation; a "kind of civil war between the various social groups, . . . each wanting to get as large a share of the cake as possible," was adding to inflationary pressures.[168] The optimism of the postwar years was turning into a "deep pessimism."[169]

Europe had serious economic problems for which monetary and exchange-rate arrangements could do little. In another iconic paper, with echoes in German intellectual and policy discourse, Milton Friedman had written: "We are in danger of assigning to monetary policy a larger role than it can perform, in danger of asking it to accomplish tasks that it cannot achieve."[170] Friedman had noted in particular that monetary policy could not create a sustained increase in employment opportunities. The implications for European policymakers were clear. They needed to focus on initiatives to jump start productivity growth and expand employment opportunities. Yet, they continued to place their faith in monetary union, a fixed-exchange-rate system under a common monetary policy, which they believed would help achieve macroeconomic policy discipline and would thus solve Europe's most pressing problems.

1978: Giscard d'Estaing Tries Again

Giscard d'Estaing pushed to fix exchange rates within a newly fashioned European Monetary System (EMS).[171] His goal was "to make France the equal of Germany."[172] Germany, Giscard d'Estaing said, had reached the "forefront of the industrialized nations," and it was not good for "only one" European economy to be at that advanced level. It was therefore "important for France to be influential in Europe . . . of the same order as West Germany."[173] Such equality between France and Germany, Giscard d'Estaing insisted, would be "in the best interest of all European countries."[174]

For Giscard d'Estaing, the "currency link" was the best way to achieve parity with Germany.[175] He gave respectability to the idea that the requirement to maintain the value of the franc against the D-mark would establish for France an "external anchor." French policymakers would be forced to maintain a disciplined macroeconomic policy, from which other good things would follow, especially equality with Germany's economic prowess. Giscard d'Estaing should have known better. France had been unable to live within exchange-rate bands for the past three decades. If French authorities now kept their interest rates high and practiced fiscal austerity to keep the franc within a designated band, at least at first, unemployment would rise and there could be no presumption that productivity growth would follow. But the legend stuck. And with Italy now going through a phase of high inflation and large current account deficit, Italian bureaucrats and some politicians were also attracted to European monetary arrangements to anchor their unruly political system.[176]

In May 1974, a few weeks before Giscard d'Estaing was elected French president, Helmut Schmidt had unexpectedly become German chancellor after Willy Brandt's resignation upon discovery of an East German spy in his entourage. Schmidt, like most German leaders and officials, was against the idea of fixing exchange rates. "You cannot," he had said some years earlier, "link currencies closely if you are going to permit the economies to veer apart."[177] This also remained the strongly held view in the German Ministry of Finance and in the Bundesbank. However, seeing that Giscard d'Estaing was so keen on fixed exchange rates, Schmidt softened his own views "out of deference to his French partner's views."[178]

Schmidt found his own reasons for supporting Giscard d'Estaing. He persuaded himself that a European monetary system would help protect Germany from the weakness of the US dollar. How he arrived at this conclusion remains a mystery. Even Robert Solomon, a monetary historian and director of the US Federal Reserve Board's Division of International Finance in the mid-1970s, was unable to fathom Schmidt's convoluted reasoning. Solomon wryly wrote: "What matters is Chancellor Schmidt's perceptions, not analytical niceties."[179] Perhaps Schmidt's opportunistic support for monetary union was motivated by his interest in a common European defense policy, made necessary, he insisted, by US President Jimmy Carter's "unpredictable security policy."[180] The EMS, Giscard d'Estaing made sure to claim, "was mainly my idea"; a defense policy for Europe was Schmidt's.[181] Thus, in his bid to achieve European cooperation in defense, which he must have or should have known was a nonstarter, Schmidt became an advocate of the EMS.

Once again, a coincidental historical event, the coming together of Giscard d'Estaing and Schmidt, each with his own narrow objective, was shaping European history. It is a measure of the idiosyncrasy of their initiative—and of their insecurity in the merits of their own venture—that Giscard d'Estaing and Schmidt worked with only their closest advisers so that their plans would receive no public scrutiny and they could present the project as a fait accompli.[182] They did not even inform the heads of other European governments.

Schmidt, especially, had reason to keep things hush-hush; he knew that the Bundesbank and his Finance Ministry would oppose the idea. In particular, he knew that they would oppose his promise to Giscard d'Estaing that, unlike with the snake, Germany would share the adjustment burden within the EMS; by revaluing the D-mark or with other measures, Germany would support weaker currencies under devaluation pressure.[183] Schmidt's agreement to "symmetrical" adjustment was a victory for Giscard d'Estaing, who claimed it as such when the plans went public in November 1978.[184]

Schmidt could not deliver. He should have known that. German officials stepped in and rebuffed Schmidt's promises. Giscard d'Estaing, meanwhile, had raised expectations and could not now walk away without losing face. Therefore, he agreed to resuscitate the snake. On March 13, 1979, the snake was renamed the EMS, with the Exchange Rate Mechanism (ERM) as its centerpiece. Under the ERM, countries would keep their bilateral exchange rates within narrowly defined bands. Not for the first—or, indeed, for the last—time, little thought was given to how the system would work. With his always-acute analysis, André Szász wrote: "Participants entered into the European Monetary System in 1979 without having either a common strategy or common tactics. . . . They did not even try to reach prior agreement on these issues. Had they tried, they would have failed. The EMS would not have started."[185]

With that background, this time could not be any different. The same pressures and tensions that had bedeviled the Bretton Woods and snake arrangements rapidly surfaced. The passage of time had done nothing to dull Friedman's warning. Fixed exchange rates did not allow prompt corrective response. Inflation differentials across the EMS countries increased. Indeed, as economists Barry Eichengreen and Charles Wyplosz have documented, the differentials within the group of EMS countries grew larger than across European countries that "did not participate in the system."[186]

Soon EMS countries with high inflation began to lose competitiveness to the low inflation member countries, and their "fixed" exchange rates needed to be regularly "realigned," the official term for devaluation. Italy's postwar miracle had by now truly faded, and spells of high inflation were followed by five devaluations between March 1981 and July 1985, accumulating to a nearly 25 percent depreciation against those currencies whose rates were not realigned.[187] Giscard d'Estaing's boast that France had brought inflation under control proved premature.[188] Still unable to deal with the rigors of fixed exchange rates, French authorities devalued the franc by around 15 percent between October 1981 and April 1986. As Britain's prime minister, Margaret Thatcher, wrote in her autobiography, in those turbulent times, an exchange rate that was "right" today could be "wrong" tomorrow, and vice versa.[189] Hence, every country that wished to realign was ultimately able to do so. The system became dysfunctional and pointless.

One Leap Too Many

As this thirty-five-year period—from the Schuman Declaration in 1950 to the mid-1980s—came to an end, the good news was that Europe's first two leaps had succeeded. The first visionary leap in 1950 brought European nations together in a spirit of reconciliation and laid the basis for the postwar European institutional framework. In 1957, the second leap with the Treaty of Rome enabled the flowering of Europe as an economic community. By the mid-1960s, with the European structure in place, it was time for nation-states to play their distinctive roles, which was to equip their citizens with the ability to participate in an increasingly competitive global economy.

Instead, Europe began a third leap in 1969, as if extending the reach of Europe deeper into the nation-state was a self-evidently desirable goal. External critics and sympathetic insiders made it clear—and German chancellors seemed to understand—that economic disparities among the member states would undermine the monetary union project. The predictable failures of repeated efforts to fix exchange rates were further warnings that pursuit of monetary union, which would more firmly fix the exchange rates, created great risks and did little for Europe's real economic problem of generating long-term growth and reducing unemployment. Put simply, Europe's leaders were trying to find a solution to symptoms—inflation and currency crises—rather than to the under-lying causes of these symptoms, the lack of dynamism in their economies.

A pro-European rhetoric that monetary union would deliver financial sta-bility and ultimately political unity kept this process going. But although dressed in that rhetoric of solidarity, adversarial relationships among member nations of the EEC persisted, and national stereotyping was creeping back into European discourse.

Despite the often-heard claim that France and Germany were united in pursuit of a more perfect Europe, the reality was quite different. The relation-ship between the two countries had always been lopsided. Through the early postwar years, the Germans were desperate to emerge from political purga-tory and had no choice but to follow the French lead. But by the mid-1960s, Germany had reestablished its economic primacy in Europe, and it was an increasingly self-confident political power. Tensions in the Franco-German relationship grew as a result. German leaders and media were all too ready to proclaim Germany's ascendancy, but they rejected any suggestion that Germany had any obligation to support other European nations financially. This combination of German economic and political clout with unwilling-ness to aid others had created resentment since the early 1970s; conflicts could only increase within a monetary union.

Europe was moving in a direction profoundly opposed to its original postwar purpose. Europe's finest achievement, the Treaty of Rome, had worked because it preserved the sovereign rights of the nation-state while creating a European space and identity.[190] The Treaty of Rome had largely eliminated trade barriers within Europe and thereby established a Europe-wide level playing field on which businesses could pursue their material interests with minimal interference from European bureaucracy. Moreover, as commercial relationships deepened across Europe, they created an economic basis for peaceful coexistence among citizens of European nations.

Monetary union could do little to level or extend the playing field. Worse, pursuit of the monetary union institutionalized Germany's economic dominance in Europe. Monetary arrangements, as Szász highlighted, are built on power relationships.[191] A single monetary policy could not be right for different countries, and the risk was ever present that one country would end up paying the bills for others. Since that country was most likely to be Germany, Germans increasingly got to exercise veto over key decisions.

A successful monetary union required Europeans to go where they had refused to go. To arbitrate the differences in national interests, democratically legitimate and accountable European governance was needed. Simply put, monetary union required political union, as the Werner Report itself had made clear. But while Europe's political leaders endlessly repeated that political union was their goal, this was never a real possibility. From virtually the moment of the Schuman Declaration in 1950, European nations had made it clear that they would not cede core sovereign rights to a supranational authority. Since it was virtually impossible to break the sovereignty barrier, instead of bringing them together, the monetary union ambition was driving European nations further apart from each other. Therein lay the tragedy.

With Europe still airborne on its third leap, the risk of a hard fall was increasing. Europe's leaders could yet, if they wished, land safely and walk away from their monetary union project.

Appendix: Possible Motivations for European Monetary Union

In this chapter, I have described the evolution of Europe's monetary union as a French initiative motivated by the goal of achieving monetary and, hence, economic parity with Germany. In Pompidou's biographies or contemporary reporting, I find no evidence of other considerations that may have set Europe off on this journey. But it is helpful to review other possibilities that have since been put forward.

An early speculation—one that lingers to this day—was that France was trying to protect the retrograde common agricultural policy it had foisted on Europe. Some have argued that fixed exchange rates were needed to prevent large currency fluctuations and thus preserve the finely negotiated balance in agricultural prices. However, no documentary evidence exists to support the idea that this consideration was ever a serious basis for such a far-reaching change as monetary union. Former Dutch central banker André Szász reviewed the argument. He noted that there were well-understood and straightforward ways of adjusting agricultural prices in response to exchange-rate movements.[192] Real progress, though, required the French to give up their insistence on subsidies to large European farmers. The subsidies, which in many years soaked up 70 percent of Europe's meager budget, worked "chiefly to the advantage of big grain and dairy producers," offering "much less to the growers and sellers of olives, vegetables, fruit, and wine."[193] The subsidies induced European farmers to produce large grain surpluses, which brought world grain prices down and hurt farmers in poor countries.

Another concern at the time was that in the absence of an internationally accepted system of fixed exchange rates, countries would regularly devalue their currencies to help their exporters gain an edge over foreign competitors. In a 1998 interview, Giscard d'Estaing said that it was the fear of such competitive devaluations that caused European leaders to pursue monetary union:

> We could see the coming end of the Bretton Woods system, the grid of fixed exchange rates that had protected free trade since World War II. . . . We realized that the Common Market, with no trade barriers, would not last long with fluctuating currencies. That would have left the door open to competitive devaluations. Countries could resort to lowering their currencies' value in order to make their goods cheaper and increase exports through this artificial competitiveness. A commercial war of that sort would destroy the Common Market because countries would take protectionist measures in self-defense and re-erect the trade barriers we were trying to do away with.[194]

Giscard d'Estaing's retrospective rationale is not evident in official documents or newspaper reporting. Neither the communiqué from the Hague summit nor the Werner Report refer to this concern. I also could not find any earlier statement on this matter by Giscard d'Estaing himself. In any event, the worry about competitive devaluations faded by the mid-1970s, because it was in no one's interest to indulge in such a practice. Currency devaluation does temporarily boost exports, but it also makes imports more expensive. Therefore, countries that devalue repeatedly become "poorer," because they need to export more to buy the same goods and services from abroad. Also, by raising the prices of imports, devaluation stokes domestic inflation. With inflation stubbornly high, especially after the first oil shock in 1973, currency devaluation was not welcome, even from a domestic perspective. Thus, as the Fed official and monetary historian Robert Solomon has written, competitive devaluation ceased to be "a live issue."[195] Advanced economies outside Europe gradually "learned to float" without disrupting the global trading system.[196]

Much later, a new—and longer-lasting—economic argument emerged in the European discourse to justify a monetary union. Since within a monetary union it would no longer be necessary to convert from one currency to another, costs of international transactions would be lowered, and the uncertainty arising from exchange-rate fluctuations would be eliminated. The proposition was that lower transaction costs and reduced uncertainty about future exchange rates would promote trade among members of the monetary union, which, in turn, would increase economic prosperity. Because this reasoning for monetary union appeared only later, it is discussed in the next chapter.

The final economic argument, which also appeared only much later, was based on the briefly popular "two poles" view.[197] By then, floating exchange rates had become the global norm. But Stanley Fischer, then the IMF's first deputy managing director, also proposed that truly fixed exchange rates (as within a monetary union) were also a reasonable choice. The real problem, he said, was with "intermediate" exchange-rate regimes, which were neither floating nor fixed. In intermediate regimes, the government's commitment to its promise was unclear and was likely to be tested by financial markets. But as Robert Mundell and Peter Kenen had made clear a long time ago, fixed exchange rates gave up monetary authority and, without appropriate safeguards, created the potential for more severe economic and financial instability.

Was the monetary union intended to preserve European peace? If such a connection had been on the minds of French and other European leaders, it would have been on display at the Hague summit. But while the communiqué after the summit reaffirmed European resolve to protect peace, it made no attempt to link monetary union to peace. Only later, when Germany proved a reluctant partner in this venture, a frustrated Pompidou asserted, "To France it is important that Germany understands that [the single currency] is not about a simple economic objective but is rather about Community morality."[198] But the refrain that peace in Europe required monetary union picked up only later, when German Chancellor Helmut Kohl made it his mantra.

| Kohl's Euro, 1982–1998

THROUGHOUT 1981 AND 1982, the ERM—the set of fixed-exchange-rate agreements within the broader EMS—kept unraveling. Italy had fallen from the highs of its postwar economic miracle, and the government's large budget deficits were fueling inflation. Although Italian authorities protested that devaluation of the lira was unthinkable, in March 1981, they finally broke their commitment to the fixed exchange rate and devalued the lira by 6 percent relative to a central reference point. In October, the Italians and the French together devalued their currencies by 3 percent, and together they devalued again in June 1982.[1] Meanwhile, Germany significantly revalued the deutschmark relative to the same reference point. Thus, in little more than a year, relative to the D-mark, the lira was devalued by almost 25 percent, and the franc was devalued by around 20 percent. Italy and France did not belong in the same economic club as Germany.

Although the German economy was performing better than other European economies, it had its own problem of rising unemployment. Indeed, all of Europe and also the United States were making a difficult economic transition. The postwar economic boom was long since over, productivity growth was declining globally, and the two most recent hikes in global oil prices in 1979 and 1981 had pushed up headline inflation rates. Stagflation—low growth and high inflation—seemed to have settled in. Amid high inflation and fast-moving international capital, fixing a currency's exchange rate was economically unwise and financially risky. Therefore, countries were gradually shifting to more flexible exchange rate arrangements.

On October 1, 1982, Helmut Kohl became German chancellor. When he was the opposition leader, he had opposed Europe's perennially troubled system of fixed exchange rates.[2] Kohl was moved principally by his sense of Germany's political history. He was born in 1930, and by "the grace of a late birth," as he himself said, he did not go to the battlefront in World War II. He did, however, experience the war's traumas. Kohl often told the story of his father's return from the war in Poland. "When we have to pay for what we have caused there," he quoted his father saying, "we will never again have anything to laugh about."[3] Kohl lost his uncle to the war. The death of his brother Walter, killed at the age of nineteen during an air raid in November 1944, was a profound shock.[4] To the editor-in-chief of *Le Monde*, Kohl said, "I want the unification of Europe because I promised it to my mother."[5] Scholar of German history Clay Clemens says that "gaining political consciousness amid the ruins of war gave [Kohl] an unshakeable belief in a need to contain nationalism within an over-arching sense of common European values."[6]

On October 4, 1982, three days after he became chancellor, Kohl traveled to Paris to meet French President François Mitterrand. By way of introduction, Kohl narrated to Mitterrand the loss of his uncle and brother in World War II. "You should have no illusion," Kohl said to Mitterrand, "I am the last pro-European chancellor. . . . far-reaching decisions will take place in the coming years, decisions on foreign policy, on security policy."[7]

The historian in Kohl—he had earned a doctorate in history with a Ph.D. dissertation on West Germany's political parties since 1945—looked all the way back to the 1870s, when a newly unified Germany under his predecessor Otto von Bismarck had destroyed Europe's post-Napoleon political equilibrium, triggering decades of conflict and devastation. In concluding his conversation with Mitterrand, Kohl recognized that Germany would remain a colossus in the center of the continent and thus a potential menace. He told Mitterrand that he would make every effort to prevent a Bismarckian German state from reappearing.[8]

On September 22, 1984, recorded in memorable photographs, Kohl and Mitterrand silently held hands for several minutes at the War Memorial at Verdun, the site of a climactic, months-long and bloody French-German battle during World War I.

Kohl had made clear his intention to keep nationalistic tendencies in check and work toward a pro-European future, but what that meant in practical terms was unclear. It was hard being pro-European in the early 1980s. Postwar Europe, with its institutions for European dialogue and open trade borders, was largely in place by the mid-1960s. Within that structure, member nations could generally assume that no single member would dominate

Europe and that each would have equal opportunity for progress. Thus, as I argued in chapter 1, the central objective of postwar Europe had already been achieved. The imperative to establish peace had passed, said Robert Marjolin, a prime mover during the Treaty of Rome negotiations in 1955 and later a senior European Commission official.

Marjolin went on to say that the effort to press for more integration could backfire. Nation-states were reasserting themselves. Too many European leaders "underestimated the strength and vitality of the nation-state."[9] The effort to smother national sovereignty with a more onerous European super-structure could revive the very nationalism it was supposed to contain.

The movement toward monetary integration had stalled. The EMS was barely holding up. In every initiative to forge stronger monetary ties, con-flicts among member nations quickly became apparent. In any case, Kohl appeared to be no fan of monetary integration.

Four years after Kohl became chancellor, the only pro-European advance was the 1986 Single European Act (SEA).[10] But even the SEA was hemmed in by protectionist barriers. In principle, the SEA was mainly an extension of the 1957 Treaty of Rome, which had so successfully opened European borders to traded goods during the 1960s. The SEA's emphasis on easier international flow of services, however, met with greater national resistance. Service providers from low-wage countries often stationed their workers— for example, construction crews—in higher-wage countries. The presence of low-wage foreigners caused resentment among domestic providers of similar services because they paid much higher wages to their employees and, hence, felt competitively disadvantaged. Nevertheless, British Prime Minister Margaret Thatcher worked energetically to negotiate and implement feasible compromises. As she wrote in her autobiography, "I had one overriding goal. This was to create a single Common Market."[11] Princeton political scientist Andrew Moravcsik says Thatcher played "a skeptical but ultimately con-structive role."[12] In contrast, Kohl, despite his pro-Europeanism, supported the SEA only passively.[13]

In the listless years after Kohl became chancellor, prospects of monetary unity receded further. By April 1986, the lira and the franc had devalued against the D-mark by close to 35 percent each.

In France, Mitterrand had become president in May 1981, defeating his long-time rival Valéry Giscard d'Estaing. As president, Mitterrand had inherited a "poorly performing economy."[14] At first, his socialist instincts led him to pump the economy with increased government spending. The stepped-up spending increased budget deficits and raised the inflation rate. A familiar French pattern followed.[15] Financial speculators repeatedly bet against the franc, knowing that French authorities would eventually devalue it. On each occasion, as capital fled France in anticipation of the devaluation, French authorities, at first, tried unsuccessfully to defend the value of the franc by selling their precious foreign-exchange reserves. But the reserves were limited.

Starting around 1983, the Banque de France tightened monetary policy, and the Mitterrand government, with Finance Minister Jacques Delors in charge, began efforts to rein in the budget deficit.[16] As a result, the inflation rate came down. But by curbing demand to reduce inflation, monetary and fiscal austerity caused an alarming increase in unemployment. This outcome—a mere shift from inflation to an unemployment problem—was more proof of Milton Friedman's 1968 theorem that macroeconomic policy, especially monetary policy, cannot solve a country's fundamental economic ills.[17] French leaders needed to raise long-term growth and productivity; they needed to create more opportunities for all so that proliferating interest groups would reduce their claims on the French budget. Monetary and fiscal austerity could not resolve France's deep-rooted challenges. French leaders were still looking at the symptoms rather than the causes of their ills.

That they needed to look elsewhere was, in fact, clear to some French policymakers. They had argued since the early 1980s that it was well past time to abandon the pursuit of fixed exchange rates and European monetary unity; they understood that they needed to explore more promising avenues to make real progress.[18] But alternative ideas did not take root. Those, such as Delors, who believed that fixed exchange rates were the only means for French authorities to maintain macroeconomic discipline, won the day. The fact that repeated experiments with fixed exchange rates had not solved France's problems did not get in the way.

Thus, at a meeting with Kohl in August 1986—even more aggressively than his predecessors Georges Pompidou and Giscard d'Estaing had done with their German counterparts—Mitterrand renewed France's demand that Europe move beyond mere fixed exchange rates to a single currency. As before, a French president began pursuing an elusive economic cure for his country, and by seeking to eliminate franc devaluations, he again hoped to create greater perception of equality with Germany. Mitterrand made clear that the "currency" was his priority rather than other plans for extending Europe's reach, including common European defense and foreign policy.

As Mitterrand continued to press his case for a single European currency, Kohl pushed back. The idea, he dismissively said, had "problems." It was, he explained, like a "grand speech made on a Sunday," and the "rest of the week we deal with reality, which is a bit awkward."[19] Kohl's reasons for holding back were sensible. Disparate nations would strain the ties of a single currency. Kohl also distrusted his foreign minister, Hans-Dietrich Genscher, who was eager to see the formation of a European monetary union. Kenneth Dyson and Kevin Featherstone, European scholars and authors of a comprehensive history of the EMU, say that the "result was a degree of uncertainty and unpredictability about whether, when, and how far Kohl might lead on EMU."[20]

Through 1987 and the first half of 1988, Mitterrand began doubting Kohl's claim to pro-Europeanism. The main reason was that Kohl remained "sceptical about monetary union."[21] At the Hanover summit in June 1988, Kohl did agree to the setting up of another committee to explore the monetary union idea. But Kohl's priority was free movement of capital, which worried the French because the franc would become subject to more intense speculative attacks; in contrast, the French wanted tax harmonization and a rapid move to single currency.[22] The Hanover summit appointed Delors, now president of the European Commission, as chair of this latest committee to design a European monetary union.

May 1989: *Kohl Pulls Back from Monetary Union, for Good Reasons*

Bundesbank President Karl Otto Pöhl was the most important member of the Delors Committee. Like every Bundesbank president before and after him, Pöhl expressed loyalty to the greater goal of European integration, but also like them all, he believed that European monetary union could work only under tightly specified conditions. The two Bundesbank conditions were sound public finances and an independent ECB that ensured price stability in all member countries. Pöhl convinced himself that if dauntingly high technical standards were set on achieving these budget-discipline and price-stability conditions, several countries would be intimidated, and the ill-considered project would fade away. He appears to have persuaded other skeptics—chief among them Bank of England (BOE) Governor Robin Leigh-Pemberton—that, rather than spending their energies in actively opposing monetary union, they should insist on hard-to-achieve technical requirements to undermine the project.

The Delors Committee could not disregard Pöhl and accepted the requirements he had set out. Pöhl had scored his technical victory, and his political analysis seemed sensible. Leigh-Pemberton later told European scholar

Alasdair Blair, "most of us, when we signed the [Delors Committee] Report in May 1989 thought that we would not hear much about it."[23]

But the Delors Committee's report had more life than Pöhl or Leigh-Pemberton had imagined. Although mainly a rewarmed version of the Werner Committee's report, the Delors Report staked out a new economic claim. A single currency, it asserted, would bolster commerce within Europe, because it would "remove intra-Community exchange rate uncertainties and reduce transactions costs."[24] Speaking to European parliamentarians in Strasbourg a few days before the release of the report, Delors said that the "inter-dependence" of European economies and the development of a single market made a single currency "indispensable."[25] A French official commented that although not quite "indispensable," a single currency would improve the "efficiency" of the single market.[26] Some voices did protest. For instance, the *Financial Times* wrote that the benefits were "unlikely to be very large."[27] But the myth began to take root. (See box 2.1.)

In Germany, the domestic politics was unfavorable to the idea of a monetary union. German businesses were keen to block the initiatives likely to emerge from the soon-to-be completed Delors Committee report. On June 3, 1989, three weeks before European leaders gathered in Madrid to consider the recommendations of the Delors Report, Germany's apex business association highlighted the risks. Siegfried Mann, director general (chief executive) of the Bundesverband der Deutschen Industrie (BDI, Federation of German Industries), representing nearly all industrial associations, wrote:

> Prematurely abandoning the possibility of responding to divergent economic developments and structural changes by means of exchange rate arrangements might confront the European Community with considerable strains. Europe's economically and structurally weaker regions would thus be deprived of an important instrument, the option of exchange rate adjustment. Locational disadvantages would be preserved or even exacerbated. This would result in appeals for new financial adjustment mechanisms or structural funds to ensure the necessary balance. High expectations pinned on wage and price flexibility then required in the EC countries would tend to be dashed.[28]

That statement distilled the essence of the argument against a single currency. As discussed in chapter 1, the University of Cambridge economist Nicholas Kaldor had reached an identical conclusion in his March 1971 critique of the Werner Report. Like Kaldor then, the BDI director general was warning that the weaker countries of the union could fall farther behind in a monetary union, in which case they would require long-term financial assistance from

BOX 2.1. The Foundational Economic Myth

The claim was that by freezing their exchange rates vis-à-vis one another, members of the monetary union would benefit from lower costs and reduced uncertainty in international transactions. Monetary union, the argument went, would boost commerce and make its member countries more prosperous.

Otmar Emminger, president of the Deutsche Bundesbank from 1977 to 1979, had tried to counter such claims in a 1982 monograph: "Financial institutions, exporters and importers have learnt to cope with such short-term [exchange-rate] fluctuations, and to cover themselves against such risks" (Emminger 1982, 15). The government, he insisted, should not be an insurance agency for exporters.

The earliest—and, for long, the most influential—econometric analysis cited in support of fixing exchange rates to stimulate trade is a 1989 study by two Italian economists Francesco Giavazzi and Alberto Giovannini. In fact, the authors found that the exchange rate regime—fixed or flexible—made no difference to the volume of international trade" (Giavazzi and Giovannini 1989, 4). Giavazzi and Giovannini nevertheless justified their support for fixed exchange rates by appealing to European exceptionalism.

A year after the Delors Report was published, a European Commission study, "One Market, One Money," made the most aggressive economic case for a single currency in support of a single market. The study recognized that there was no evidence that fixed exchange rates would increase European trade (European Commission 1990, 21). It nevertheless speculated that significant "dynamic" gains would be unleashed. Economic uncertainty would decline, businesses would ramp up investment, and unemployment would decrease (9–10). As evidence for dynamic gains, a claim that had no basis in the economics literature, the Commission reported that company managers surveyed to assess the gains were "very positive" about prospects within a monetary union. Such was the cavalier evidence for a momentous economic and political decision.

In 1993, Barry Eichengreen—economics professor at the University of California, Berkeley, and perhaps the most important chronicler of the EMU—brusquely said, "I dispute the belief that a single currency is a technically necessary concomitant of a single market in capital, labor, and goods." Eichengreen explained that the decline in transactions costs achieved through a single currency would be trivial and the dividends from reduced exchange rate uncertainty would be "quite small" (Eichengreen 1993, 1322). Just as Emminger had pointed out a decade earlier, Eichengreen said that "the existence of forward markets in foreign exchange permits traders to hedge currency risk at low cost" (1327). Subsequent studies have confirmed that when exchange rates are flexible, businesses buy insurance to protect themselves from currency movements (Patnaik and Shah 2010; Kamil 2012).

In contrast to the dubious claims that a single currency would increase European prosperity, it was evident that without their own exchange rates and monetary policies, many European nations would be handicapped because they would lack crucial economic and financial shock absorbers. The evidence for this handicap stared people in the face: fixed exchange rates led to accumulation of inflation differentials, which caused speculative attacks and required costly and damaging responses.

Germany. The remarkable fact is that German business opposed the single currency even though the single currency would likely be weaker than the D-mark and give German exports a boost. But such export gains were uncertain. In particular, the single currency would likely be too strong for several European countries, which would cause their economies to slow down, and, hence, their citizens would be less able to afford German products.

The political process kept moving. On June 26–27, 1989, European leaders "adopted" the Delors Report at their summit in Madrid. The "adoption," however, meant little, as Mitterrand recognized. There was no agreement on a timetable of implementation. Moreover, "The minute the Madrid summit ended, key participants started disputing the implications of their possibly historic agreement."[29] While the British objections were well known, Kohl also rejected the "ill-considered rush."[30] He recognized the resistance of German business interests. In addition, many of the (economic) liberals in his party opposed the move to a single currency.[31]

Hubert Védrine, a close Mitterrand adviser and later a foreign minister, described the frustration in the French camp after the summit. Védrine recalled the following conversation between Mitterrand and Kohl:

MITTERRAND: It's necessary for you to commit to the monetary union. . . .
KOHL: Abandoning the Mark is a great sacrifice for the Germans. Public opinion is not yet ready for it.
MITTERRAND: I know it, but do it! European public opinion awaits it. You are moving towards German reunification. You must show that you continue to believe in Europe.[32]

Not for the first (and not for the last) time, a French president was lecturing a German chancellor on the pulse of European opinion and asking that he act in the European interest. Much of the French negotiating strategy in this period was to remind the Germans that they needed to be good Europeans. Kohl responded by stalling. His tactic was to prolong the process. Authorization of the use of a single currency required changes to the Treaty of Rome, which governed the EC. Changes made to an existing treaty or a new treaty required first an intergovernmental conference to negotiate and draft the terms acceptable to member states. Kohl insisted that a date for such a conference could not be set without "complete and adequate preparation."[33] Thus, to Mitterrand's great annoyance, Kohl created an open-ended delay.

From then through the rest of the year, Bundesbank President Pöhl became an outspoken critic of the single currency. In an interview with the *Financial Times* on July 1, he said that British Prime Minister Thatcher, the single currency's fiercest political opponent, better recognized the pitfalls of the project than his own chancellor did. Thatcher's overriding concern was that a monetary union, however cleverly designed, would always infringe on a country's ability to set its tax policy. This was unacceptable to her, because, she said, "The ability to set one's own level of taxation is a crucial element of national sovereignty."[34] Pöhl wondered if this basic issue "has been understood by Chancellor Helmut Kohl."[35] Britain's Thatcher, the London *Economist* noted, had an "unlikely ally" in Germany's Pöhl.[36]

Thatcher, in fact, had a more important German ally. In October 1989, when Mitterrand continued to berate the chancellor, Kohl responded angrily: "It [the single currency] poses a heap of problems for me, my majority is reluctant, the business community doesn't want it, the time is not right."[37]

Berlin Wall Falls; Kohl Increases Resistance to Monetary Union

The Berlin Wall, which had separated East and West Germany since 1961, fell unexpectedly on November 9, 1989. A miscommunication that day by an official of East Germany's ruling party led East Berliners to believe they could start traveling to the West immediately. Thousands gathered at the checkpoints in the Berlin Wall, and the guards had no alternative but to let people cross into West Germany. The "heavily armed border" opened "literally overnight."[38] Reunification of the two Germanys had seemed a distant goal. Now that goal was within reach.

With Kohl preoccupied, Pöhl had space to maintain his offensive against monetary union. Once a journalist himself, Pöhl returned to make his case in the media. In a remarkable interview on BBC Television on November 19, Pöhl called for a slowdown in the pace of monetary unification. He reiterated his opposition to the "French-backed" rush to an intergovernmental conference. The only reason for the rush, Pöhl said, was that France and Italy "wished to topple the D-Mark from its pre-eminent position." Pöhl questioned if European leaders understood what they were getting into, and he called for a two-year waiting period to determine "whether a consensus really existed for further integration."[39]

Pöhl had good reason to call for a delay, at least a pause. "The economies of the member states were too divergent," he said in the BBC interview. Kohl had long agreed with that central concern and repeated it himself on November 27, when he wrote to Mitterrand, "I am especially worried about the fact that even though our countries have undertaken major steps in order to reach convergence, severe intra-community divergences regarding the development of stability continue to exist."[40] Kohl sternly added, "They [the divergences] might even get worse."

Then the action speeded up. On November 28, Kohl announced a ten-point plan to unify the two Germanys. He had forewarned no one. Neither his foreign minister, Genscher, nor any of the European allies had any idea that such an announcement was coming.

American President George H. W. Bush was the first international leader to receive word, but even Bush heard of the plan only after Kohl began presenting it to the Bundestag.[41] Bush and his national security team were annoyed. Kohl, however, compensated by making very clear that he was committed to the North Atlantic Treaty Organization (NATO). Kohl understood that the Americans were mainly interested in preserving NATO's integrity.[42]

Mitterrand was outraged that he had been kept out of the loop. When Genscher arrived in Paris to pacify him, Mitterrand shouted, "You don't have to be a psychologist to recognize that Germany is currently dragging its heels on economic and monetary union."[43] He added ominously that it was essential for Germany to commit itself to the European monetary union, or else "We will return to the world of 1913."[44]

Mitterrand, however, knew that the unification ship was sailing. The East German economy was "on the verge of collapse."[45] East Germans had risen in peaceful protest against an oppressive regime and were pouring out of the openings created in the Berlin Wall. Any attempt to slow down the pace of unification would have implied blocking the East German exodus, and doing that could have rapidly transformed the peaceful transition into a violent confrontation.

Thus, with the East Germans making reunification a near inevitability, Mitterrand was losing any veto authority over that decision. If ever he intended to use it that way, he was losing the reunification bargaining chip. In his public appearances, Mitterrand asserted that he was not afraid of reunification.[46] And now trying a different approach to reach his goal, Mitterrand offered Kohl a tempting carrot in exchange for monetary union. The carrot came in the form of a promise of "political union."

Mitterrand understood that this ill-defined and inflated concept was dear to Kohl's heart. What exactly was political union? In 1957, the Treaty of Rome had called for "an ever closer union." This noble, but deliberately vague sentiment framed Europe as greater than the sum of its member nations. Around the same time, the term "political union" appeared in the scholarly European literature, in French as "union politique," in German as

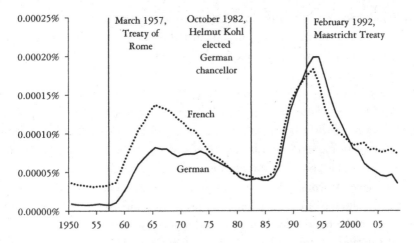

FIGURE 2.1. The beat of Europe's "political union" mantra.
(Frequency of reference to "political union" in French and German books digitized by Google)
Source: Google Books NGram Viewer. Notes: In French, the curve is the sum of references to "Union politique," "Union Politique," and "union politique"; there were no search results for "union Politique." In German, the curve is the sum of references to "politische Union" and "Politische Union"; there were no search results for "politische union" and "Politische union."

"politische Union" (figure 2.1). Like "ever closer union," political union was a feel-good concept that had no practical implication, and so, along with the prospects of European integration, it faded in the 1970s and reached a low ebb by the mid-1980s. However, Kohl had revived the narrative of political union. Mitterrand was playing on that weakness of Kohl's.

While Kohl often invoked the term and rarely said what it meant to him, on one rare occasion, he did say that a "political union" would include a common European foreign and security policy, which, he added, needed to be "worthy of their names."[47] Kohl also wanted increased powers for the European Parliament and more European decisions based on agreement among a majority of the countries rather than on unanimity. Despite these bold ideas, Kohl's vision never included ceding German fiscal sovereignty. Thus, however noble his intentions, if Kohl was unwilling to contribute German tax revenues to a central European budget, which would assist countries in economic distress, his talk of political union had little bearing on the construction of a monetary union.

The French conception of political union was even fuzzier. For a long time, France's leaders had resisted common European policies or stronger European institutions. In 1954, they had rejected the European Defense Community, intended to create a European army, because there was "too much integration" in it.[48] The idea of a European "federation" was particularly abhorrent in France. Some years later, in a January 1995 essay for the newspaper *Le Figaro*, former French President Giscard d'Estaing would airily describe political union ("union politique") as a "shared political vision backed by a common European will."[49]

Thus, with his monetary union project stuck, for Mitterrand it made sense to set up a false bargain. In a letter to Kohl on December 1, 1989, a week before the Strasbourg summit, Mitterrand first insisted on an expeditious move to monetary union. He then vaguely deferred to Kohl's equally vague demand for political integration, and—grudgingly—accepted a parallel intergovernmental conference on political union. He wrote that he saw "no disadvantage" in such a conference, but it could come "only *after* concluding on the treaties for economic and monetary union."[50]

Mitterrand's letter did not fool the Germans. They knew Mitterrand had little interest in anything other than the monetary union. In memos to Kohl on December 2 and 3, Kohl's adviser Joachim Bitterlich emphasized that Mitterrand's paramount aim was the economic and monetary union; the other "cluster of questions," Bitterlich wrote, had "a minor importance for him." Bitterlich added that Mitterrand and his circle of advisers viewed Kohl's demand for more far-reaching political integration as a "diversionary tactic from the monetary union."[51]

On December 3, Kohl had dinner with US President George H. W. Bush in Laeken, just outside Brussels. Historian Mary Elise Sarotte reminds us that this could have been a tense and confrontational meeting.[52] Kohl had blindsided Bush with his surprise ten-point plan for German unification, and the two were meeting "face to face" for the first time since the Berlin Wall had come down. "Bush would have been well within his rights to be displeased with Kohl," Sarotte writes. Instead, the Laeken dinner became, "in [National Security Adviser] Brent Scowcroft's terms, a major 'turning point.'" At Laeken, "Bush decided to give the strongest possible support to the chancellor's plans." Bush was "deeply impressed by Kohl and his plans and "made remarks along the line of, I'm with you, go for it." Bush later said that he believed Kohl would "not lead the Germans down a special, separate path" that downplayed the importance of NATO.[53]

East Germans were rushing to the west, and Kohl had just obtained Bush's backing for German unification. With that, on December 5, just days before the Strasbourg summit, Kohl wrote to Mitterrand, saying there did not even exist a "basis" to establish a monetary union.[54] Kohl said that, first, a new expert group should determine if there was even any point in moving ahead with an intergovernmental conference.[55] He restated that his primary goal was a European political union, of which the monetary union would be only a part.

On December 6, the *Frankfurter Allgemeine Zeitung* reported that Kohl had met with a wide cross section of Germans in the preceding weeks.[56] In those conversations, he referred to the imminent start of the uncontroversial first stage of the monetary union—the liberalization of capital flows—as "forward movement." Under the SEA, EC members had agreed to allow free flow of capital, a commitment that even Britain supported. Knowing that Mitterrand was pressing for a much bigger prize, Kohl resolutely refused to go any further. Britain's Thatcher had reason to think that she had Bundesbank's Pöhl and Chancellor Kohl as allies in opposition to monetary union.

On December 6, Mitterrand traveled to Kiev hoping that Mikhail Gorbachev, president of the Soviet Union, would use his influence to slow the pace of German unification. But Mitterrand came away from the meeting empty-handed. Overwhelmed by the "flood of events in Eastern Europe," Gorbachev was in no position to hold back history, and he had little to offer.[57] Mitterrand's frustration showed when, speaking to reporters after meeting the Soviet leader, he "warned West Germany not to push for reunification with East Germany, saying it could upset the delicate balance in Europe and slow integration of the European Community."[58]

The French persisted. On the morning of December 8 (the day the Strasbourg summit started), a French official made a not-so-veiled and over-the-top threat: "We're going to have to see how the Germans behave. But if they don't push ahead, there will be a terrible backlash in Europe."[59]

December 1989: Does Kohl Give the Green Light at Strasbourg?

Kohl was riding the historical tide of German unification. He understood that a monetary union of divergent economies was not viable. The economic divergences, in his own words, could "even get worse." Yet when European heads of state met at Strasbourg, Kohl, to the surprise of German officials present, abandoned his call for "complete and adequate preparation." He agreed to the start of an intergovernmental conference on the monetary union before the Italian presidency of the EC ended in December 1990.

However, since Kohl had surprised everyone, no one was clear what came next. As the Dutch central banker André Szász emphasized, observers at that time scratched their heads. Much work lay ahead, and member states had opposing views on many sensitive matters.[60] After all, the Strasbourg summit also had supportive words for a parallel conference on a political union, an idea that predictably went nowhere.

Kohl's green light at Strasbourg for discussions on monetary union to begin has led many to conclude that he "conceded" the euro then, because, otherwise, he feared the French would block German unification. But that story, although often told, is not correct. The single currency was not a quid pro quo for German unification. First, Kohl had all the cards on his side. Unification was already happening, and any attempt to stop it could have caused a human catastrophe. Kohl had received Bush's personal assurance of support on December 3, five days before Strasbourg. The Americans saw German unification as in their strategic interest. Sarotte points out that "the cold war order in Europe had collapsed."[61] To fill the vacuum left behind, the Americans wanted to establish a "new order" built around a unified Germany. Bush had good reasons to say he trusted Kohl. Kohl's generation of Germans had deep democratic roots and a commitment to preserve peace in Europe. Bush followed up on his end of the bargain, and by early 1990, "cooperation between Washington and Bonn switched into high gear."[62]

While the bargain with Soviet leader Mikhail Gorbachev was not complete before the Strasbourg summit, the path ahead on that matter was clear. The Soviet Union was weak and in desperate need of financial help. In a series of phone calls that began on September 7, 1990, Kohl quite simply bought Gorbachev's agreement to reunification. After much haggling, Kohl agreed to give the Soviet Union a large financial gift, 12 billion D-marks without any strings and a 3-billion-D-mark interest-free loan. Gorbachev signed off, and Germany was formally unified on October 3, 1990.[63] Joyous Germans, chanting "Helmut, Helmut," celebrated at the Brandenburg Gate, which had stood cordoned off on the east side of the Berlin Wall all these years. The truth is, Kohl would have given 100 billion D-marks if Gorbachev had bargained better. Thus, Kohl knew that German unification would happen. He did not need Mitterrand's concurrence.

Moreover, in the language of economists, any promise at Strasbourg was "time inconsistent." It would have been perfectly normal for Kohl to go back on a promise he made under duress. German Chancellor Konrad Adenauer had reneged on a promise to French President Charles de Gaulle. In 1963, the German Bundestag had diluted the Élysée Treaty of Franco-German friendship by strengthening the German tie with the United States. Adenauer had thus undercut de Gaulle's principal purpose for the treaty, to reduce America's geopolitical reach. There was not much de Gaulle could do, and so he had remarked, "Treaties, you see, are like girls and roses. They last while they last."[64] Kohl himself had earlier refused to honor his agreement to a French plan for tax harmonization.[65] Kohl's finance minister, Theo Waigel, had objected to the proposal, and Kohl announced his reversal to the Bundestag without warning Paris.[66]

At Strasbourg, Kohl merely agreed to an intergovernmental conference for drafting a treaty; he had made no further commitment. Mitterrand had agreed to a similar conference on "political union" to appease Kohl briefly. Mitterrand knew that Kohl understood that Mitterrand would gut the political-union project at the earliest opportunity. Why Kohl agreed to play that kabuki game is a mystery. Surely Kohl understood that just as Mitterrand could walk away from his promise, so could he.

One person who would know what transpired between Mitterrand and Kohl was Mitterrand's adviser Elisabeth Guigou. In a conversation with historian Tilo Schabert, Guigou said quite definitively that there was no bargain: "In 1989, I was present at all the meetings that François Mitterrand had with Helmut Kohl on Germany and Europe. There was never any bargaining: approval of reunification, in exchange for progress in the European sphere."[67]

Guigou speculated that a link between reunification and the single currency might well have existed in Kohl's own mind. Kohl had acted on his own at Strasbourg, and only he and his nearest advisers could reveal what he was thinking. Perhaps Kohl's personal memories of the war weighed on him at that defining moment. Perhaps at Strasbourg, Kohl saw and heard the anxiety of the other heads of state who feared a suddenly expanded Germany in the middle of Europe. Right after the Strasbourg summit, Kohl explained to US Secretary of State James Baker that the Bundesbank firmly opposed the single currency plan and that he himself agreed it was "against German interests."[68] He had chosen nevertheless to move ahead because it was "politically important" to do so. Germany, he said, "needs friends."

These were still early days. How Kohl would trade off friendship and national interests was still unclear.

1990–1991: Kohl Gains Political Autonomy

Kohl had declared his independence from conventional political and bureaucratic restraints on November 28, 1989, when he announced the ten-point German unification plan. From that point on, historian Sarotte emphasizes, on matters related to unification, Kohl and his closest aides were "distinct from the government of West Germany."[69] The historian Schabert says that the ten-point plan was "born in a network of small informal circles that intersected around the chancellor."[70] Similarly, on European matters, Kohl had begun to adopt his "imperial chancellorship" style: at Strasbourg, overriding official advice, he had given the go ahead on the long-debated intergovernmental conference on monetary union.

Kohl continued to broaden his authority as "party, parliament, and even the cabinet were largely excluded" from key decisions.[71] In early 1990, he applied that imperial approach to the monetary unification of the two Germanys. The two questions were how soon should that unification occur and at what rate should the East German Ostmark convert to the West German D-mark? Bundesbank President Pöhl and his East German counterpart, Horst Kaminsky, both opposed hasty monetary unification. On February 6, 1990, on the steps of the Staatsbank (the East German central bank), the two presidents told reporters that it was "premature" even to consider "such a far-reaching step." On the same day—indeed, almost at the same moment—Kohl announced an end-of-June target for German monetary unification.[72] David Marsh, journalist and Bundesbank historian, writes, "Pöhl had good reason for feeling slighted. Kohl could easily have warned him, but chose not to."[73]

With monetary unification a fait accompli, the Bundesbank, as well as the finance and economic ministries, strenuously opposed a one-for-one conversion of Ostmark to D-mark. In early 1990, currency traders demanded seven Ostmarks for one D-mark. Pöhl and Finance Minister Waigel proposed what for East Germans would be a very generous conversion rate of two Ostmarks for a D-mark.[74] In early April, Kohl appeared to support the Pöhl-Waigel position. However, in late April, he peremptorily announced a one-for-one conversion, evidently hoping to gain favor in the East German elections scheduled for May.[75] As a commentator later remarked, "Chancellor Kohl barreled over all objections on the ground that the political reality of German unification would allow nothing less."[76]

Kohl's autonomy had worked out well when on November 28, 1989, correctly sensing the political mood, he announced the ten-point unification plan. But Kohl also chose to scorn economics. Ostmarks were converted to D-marks at midnight on June 30, 1990, and, as a meticulously documented and damning scholarly indictment in early 1991 concluded, "One of the worst and sharpest depressions in European history had begun."[77] Two of the authors of that analysis were George Akerlof (who later received the Nobel Prize for Economics) and Janet Yellen (who became chairman of the Fed). They explained the unfolding disaster. At the unreasonably generous conversion rate, East German wages had become far higher than justified by labor productivity (which was around 30 percent that of West German workers). Thus, saddled with extraordinarily high production costs and inferior product quality, East German enterprises struggled to operate profitably. Moreover, because the unions did not allow the wages to fall to match lower East German labor productivity, unemployment rose quickly, driving workers to seek jobs elsewhere. Akerlof, Yellen, and their coauthors predicted that the distress would deepen, a prediction that would prove only too true.[78]

But those problems would be faced in the future. For the moment, Kohl had gained the political momentum he wanted. Turning his attention to the first post-unification election, he promised riches to the East at no cost to the West. But these promises were not credible. As East Germans grew increasingly anxious about their futures and West Germans recognized the inevitability of higher tax burdens, Kohl's electoral prospects wavered. He then changed his approach and tapped into the emotional elation of unification. He turned the campaign away from the "complex and uncertain problems" Germany faced and converted it into "a simple celebration of unity, an expression of nationalist joy."[79] Kohl's "brilliant election tactic," wrote journalist Tony Allen-Mills, drove "his opponents to despair."[80]

Now, at the height of his personal popularity, Kohl brought together the themes of German and European integration. "German unity and building the united states of Europe," he exhorted, "that is the reality of tomorrow!"[81] A grander future waited, Kohl said, and Europe could no longer be merely "a glorified free-trade zone."[82] As he continued his campaign for reelection, he heard the siren call of history. His goal, Kohl said, was to build "a shining tower of achievements that may endure for the next 1,000 years."[83] Somewhere along the way, the distinction between Kohl's personal ambition and German and European progress blurred. As Dyson and Featherstone observed, "the Chancellor was not immune to the seductions of writing himself into the history books of the future." Kohl, they wrote, "was intent on making the two issues of German unification and European unification his own."[84]

Despite his extraordinary popularity and approaching moment of triumph, Kohl did not think it right to seek the German public's mandate for giving up the D-mark and adopting a European currency. He knew that, by a consistently large margin, the German public opposed the single currency, and he feared that if he became widely seen as the man causing Germans to give up their prized D-mark, his electoral prospects would suffer.

Kohl was also a master at manipulating allegiances within his party, the CDU. Reelected in December 1990 as chancellor—with almost two-thirds of the Bundestag seats for his CDU and its coalition partners—Kohl squashed democracy within the party and "ran roughshod" over potential rivals for the chancellorship.[85] A bitter rival said of Kohl that he believed "he can increase his own stature by cutting other people down."[86] During his long tenure as German chancellor and party leader, Kohl used "familiar, personalized methods" to secure loyalties to his personal agendas.[87] Kohl ensured that "every single CDU Bundestag deputy and party member owed him something," and, hence, large numbers of party members "depended exclusively on him for advancement" and were "unlikely to question what he did."[88]

While Kohl was a master of German politics, his true political genius lay in the way he framed his message. Journalist Jens Peter Paul says that Kohl countered critics of the single currency by portraying them as "nationalistic, chauvinistic, and anti-European."[89] Similarly, Dyson and Featherstone write that Kohl equated opposition to the monetary union with "discredited nationalist politics."[90] This framing, Dyson and Featherstone astutely note, allowed Kohl to "transform the debate and escape from some of the restrictions he faced." Linguist George Lakoff, longtime professor of cognitive science at the University of California at Berkeley, has highlighted the decisive political advantage gained from political framing and messaging. A politician who aggressively describes opponents in offensive language wins the debate; indeed, if opponents fight back by denying the accusations, they keep alive the words and thus reinforce the suspicion of truth in the original charges. Lakoff's most recent example is US President Donald Trump's characterization of the media as the "enemy."[91] Those who protested that the media was "not the enemy" fell into the framing trap: by repeating the phrase, they gave plausibility to the idea that, in fact, the media could be the enemy. Similarly, those accused by Kohl of being nationalistic or anti-European had no easy defense. If they had responded that they were "not chauvinistic" or "not anti-European," they would—by reusing Kohl's language—have helped his case. Kohl had other metaphors to put his opponents on the defensive. As the date of the Maastricht summit approached, he drummed up the narrative of war and peace to deter any last-minute opposition to his monetary union plans.[92]

One irksome critic threatened to overpower Kohl's monumental political advantages. In March 1991, Bundesbank President Pöhl said at an event in Brussels that the "disastrous" monetary union of East and West Germany should be a warning against rushing to a European monetary union.[93] Pöhl said that the conversion of one Ostmark to one D-mark had been a disaster because it had occurred "almost without preparation and without any possibility for adjustment and at the wrong exchange rate." A similar disaster awaited the EMU, he predicted, unless there was "a very high degree of economic convergence" among European nations.[94] Pöhl's critical remarks came in the midst of the intergovernmental conference in the Dutch city of Maastricht, where country negotiators were trying to find common ground on how the monetary union would operate. Pöhl's comments implied that European nations were not ready for monetary union and that the ongoing preparatory process was definitely premature.

By insisting on greater convergence as a precondition for the success of the EMU, Pöhl was merely repeating the position that Kohl himself had taken with Mitterrand eighteen months earlier. But Kohl had since then undergone a conversion; he was now impatient and unwilling to wait in the hope that European economies would converge closer to one another. Pöhl's comments were unwelcome because they threatened to disrupt Kohl's plans to move rapidly forward. Kohl made matters worse for himself by reprimanding Pöhl, who, as a result, gained public stature for his principled position.[95] Karl Schiller, the former German economics minister, who had called for more flexible exchange-rate arrangements when Bretton Woods was breaking down, said, "Pöhl is doing the right thing."[96] Pöhl, however, got tired of the fight and resigned later that year.

The new Bundesbank president, Helmut Schlesinger, and his vice president, Hans Tietmeyer (who, in October 1993, would succeed Schlesinger as the bank's president), continued to speak out against rapid introduction of the single currency.[97] In testimony to the Bundestag's finance committee in September 1991, with the intergovernmental conference still in progress, Tietmeyer spelled out "uncompromising preconditions" for establishing European monetary union.[98] Monetary union could not start, he said, without ensuring rigorous budget discipline, backed by rules and sanctions. Tietmeyer and Schlesinger repeated similar remarks, but they did not predict a "disaster" or a "collapse" of the monetary union project. They said their pieces but stayed within the bounds acceptable to Kohl.

With a sense of pride, Kohl later told journalist Paul, "in the case of the euro, I was like a dictator."[99] Members of the Bundestag were afraid to voice opposition to his legislative initiatives, and Kohl was not embarrassed to confirm, "We never had a formal party agreement on whether the euro should be adopted. We just announced it."[100]

Because he had so much autonomy, it is unlikely that there will ever be a definitive understanding of why Kohl, who started as a critic, turned so passionate about favoring the single currency. US presidents, who enjoyed similar autonomy in their pursuit of the Vietnam War, left a sparse document trail, and the documents themselves give few clues about their motives.[101] That is also true in Kohl's case. He might have believed that the single currency guaranteed peace, or he could have been wishing to write himself into the history books, or some combination of both. He clearly came to believe that he was indispensable to Europe's future.

Over the next seven years, Kohl would use his autonomy at several crucial junctures to push the single currency toward the finish line. To that last phase, we must now turn.

1991: At Maastricht, Germans Demand Commitment to Stability

Starting in early 1991 and through the end of the year, negotiators from member countries of the EC worked in Maastricht to determine the rules under which the single currency would operate. Although, in principle, all member countries participated, the French and the Germans made all the key decisions. Jean-Claude Trichet, director of the French treasury, led the French team, and Horst Köhler, state secretary in the German finance ministry, headed the German team. A British team was also involved. However, the British role was limited. Although John Major, the new prime minister since November 1990, was not as outspoken as Thatcher had been, Britain was clearly going to stay out of the single-currency business.[102]

An intellectual consensus existed that Europe's monetary union needed a supporting fiscal union. In such a union, all member countries would pool some part of their tax revenues into a European budget, and that budget would assist countries when they fell into temporary distress. This was not a controversial "Anglo-Saxon" view. Senior European officials understood that without a fiscal union, countries within a monetary union could fall into spells of prolonged economic and political pain, which would make the union itself unstable. As I described in chapter 1, the Werner Report in 1970 had said so, and, more forcefully, the MacDougall Report in 1977 had emphasized the need for a sizable central budget, perhaps on the order of 5–7 percent of GDP. Even the Delors Report, although only in a little-noticed appendix, had conceded that monetary unions in federal states "possess a large central budget relative to GDP."[103] That rarely read appendix in the Delors Report was written by Alexandre Lamfalussy, who, as the first president of the European Monetary Institute from 1994–1997, laid the groundwork for the ECB.

Several years later, Lamfalussy repeated that it had been a mistake to launch the euro without a larger central budget.[104]

Yet it was clear that a fiscal union was impossible, because European nations were unwilling to surrender a significant share of their tax revenues to a European authority. Each nation wanted to retain its sovereign right to tax its citizens and spend the revenues in line with national aspirations and priorities. This was the position in 1970, when a monetary union was first considered as a serious possibility, and it remained the position throughout 1991, as officials worked at the intergovernmental conference in Maastricht to hammer out the details of the proposed monetary union.

At Maastricht, Delors and other officials knew that if they pushed for a central budget, the Germans would walk away. Kohl disdainfully accused others of "nationalism, chauvinism, and anti-Europeanism," and he spoke with great passion about "political union." But he was always clear that his government's tax revenues were only for the benefit of German citizens. The German public and government feared that a European fiscal union could open them to the risk of perpetually paying the bills of other European nations. Protection from such a risk was vital, because the French did not exactly hide their intention of using the monetary union to "pursue relatively expansionist policies."[105] The Dutch were the Germans' allies on such matters. Marius Holtrop, president of the Dutch central bank from 1946 to 1967, characterized Germany as "the prudent ant" and France as the irresponsible cricket. Could the ant, he asked, "be expected to put its stored resources at the disposal of the cricket?"[106] Similarly, in 1965, Johan Witteveen, then Dutch finance minister and later managing director of the IMF, explained in comments to the Dutch Parliament that a single currency gave rise to the risk that member states would present blank checks to one another.[107]

Without a political union to encompass a democratically legitimate fiscal union, there was only one way forward. For nearly one hundred years, from the 1840s to the Great Depression, the US monetary union had worked on the principle that if state and local governments borrowed too much and could not repay their debts in full, private creditors would bear the losses.[108] Operating within this system, creditors were cautious in their lending, and borrowers made greater effort to live within their means. If a state nevertheless did fall into financial distress, it defaulted on its creditors and did not require help from other states.

But European officials did not trust the disciplining powers of financial markets. They chose to believe that financial markets may either be too soft on governments or act in "sudden and disruptive" ways.[109] Hence, they were unwilling to seriously consider the possibility that financially distressed member nations might usefully reduce their debt obligations by defaulting on private creditors.

A muddled agreement emerged. The draft Maastricht Treaty prepared during the course of 1991 did say that one member state would not repay another member state's debts. The implication, therefore, was that if a member nation could not repay its debts, its private creditors would bear losses. In principle, then, the Maastricht Treaty had a "no bailout rule": European governments would not bail out either a member country or its private creditors. But the policy emphasis on the capriciousness of financial markets raised a question mark about whether the "no bailout" clause would be enforced if a sufficiently large crisis occurred.

With fiscal union ruled out and ambiguity about the possibility that fiscally stressed member nations could gain breathing room by delaying or reducing repayments to their private creditors, the right conclusion should have been that a European monetary union was not possible. However, the commitment to monetary union at all costs remained. Thus, monetary and fiscal rules came to occupy center stage.

The virtually exclusive reliance on rules in the Maastricht contract was a triumph of hope over good sense. To be legitimate and enforceable, rules for a monetary union also required a political union. Who would decide whether a rule was being applied fairly? Rigid enforcement of rules could create an unacceptable level of administrative intrusiveness in national authority. Moreover, as Kaldor had explained two decades earlier, uniform rules applied to divergent countries could increase the divergence, making management of the monetary union even harder.[110]

The muddle was made worse by the strange rule at the heart of the surveillance system. The idea, which originated in the Delors Report, was to place binding upper limits on the budget deficits and debts of member countries.[111] Delors himself was unhappy with such numerical limits. He tried, in fact, to water down the idea just after European leaders endorsed his report at Madrid in June 1989. He mumbled to reporters that, in practice, the rules "could be less binding than the report suggested."[112] But in 1991, as the negotiations on monetary union unfolded, Delors recognized that without such binding limits enshrined in the treaty, the Germans would reject the monetary union, but continued to hope that they would be satisfied with lip service to the rules.

Delors guessed correctly on one of the two rules; on the other, he went horribly wrong. The negotiators at Maastricht at first agreed that each member country would be required to keep its debt-to-GDP (its debt ratio) below 60 percent of GDP. But this limit quickly became irrelevant. Many countries had significantly higher debt ratios and could not realistically bring them below 60 percent of GDP within a short time period. If the debt ratio rule had been enforced, there would have been no eurozone. The negotiators, therefore, agreed that it was sufficient if the debt ratio was clearly coming down toward 60 percent of GDP. This was a vague and, therefore, meaningless rule.

The real drama centered on the rule for budget deficits. In their proposal, submitted on February 25, the Germans proposed the "golden rule": a government should run a deficit only to invest in long-term assets such as infrastructure.[113] The golden rule has a certain logic, and governments often use it to guide budgetary policy. But such a rule is not easy to implement, because the boundary of what constitutes long-term investments is fuzzy. For the EMU, it was unworkable. Member countries could easily disguise their regular expenditures as investments in infrastructure and run up large deficits.

Eventually, the French proposed, as an alternative to the golden rule, a simpler budget deficit limit, one that had a quixotic origin in the early 1980s. Facing soaring fiscal deficits, Mitterrand had asked the budget department in the French finance ministry to propose a rule that would help rein in public spending. Two young civil servants pointed out that a limit of 2 percent of GDP would be too hard to achieve consistently, whereas 4 percent of GDP would give too much latitude. So they proposed a limit of 3 percent of GDP, which the Mitterrand administration then began using for its internal guidance. The French now suggested that the same limit should apply to all members of the monetary union.[114] Journalists Eric Aeschimann and Pascal Riché report that in place of the complicated golden rule, "Paris proposed a less subtle barrier: limiting public deficits to 3% of GDP."[115] Why 3 percent? "François Mitterrand decided that the French deficits would never again reach the 3% level."[116] The 3 percent limit, Mitterrand believed, would satisfy German insistence on a rule, and France would be safe in a comfortable zone where the rule was not binding.

The political attraction of a fixed number was clear. No judgment or analysis would be required, and the expectation, therefore, was that the possibility of fudging and haggling would be reduced. The Germans quickly agreed and made it their guiding mantra. Although the rule was economic nonsense (see box 2.2), it would come to exercise a powerful hold on the European psyche.

The Germans also insisted on a procedure to correct "excessive" fiscal deficits. It seemed natural to them that deficits above 3 percent of GDP be considered "excessive." In the litany of bad ideas, the most bizarre was the German demand that sanctions, including fines, be imposed on countries whose deficits were deemed excessive. Such penalties made even less sense than the rule itself. Penalties would only inflict more pain on the distressed country's finances.[117] Moreover, the "threat" of penalties could only be an empty one, because peers would be reluctant to impose more pain on those whose goodwill they might one day need if they themselves were in violation of the rule in the future.[118]

Delors tried again to put a stop to this. In the final phase of the inter-governmental conference, he briefly joined forces with an odd ally, British Chancellor of the Exchequer Norman Lamont, who opposed the very idea of a single currency so dear to Delors. Delors disapproved of sanctions because, he said, they would unreasonably infringe national sovereignty; Lamont argued that sanctions were not required because "markets would discipline profligate governments by demanding higher rates of interest."[119]

The effort went nowhere. In October 1991, two months before national leaders were to gather at Maastricht to sign the treaty, Lamont and Delors "conceded defeat."[120] Lamont had no stake in the outcome, since Britain had decided to "opt out" of the monetary union. Lamont later wrote that most finance ministers opposed the fiscal rules (and not just the sanctions), "but the Germans were adamant and in the end got their way."[121]

Unlike Lamont, who could and did walk away, Delors had a long-standing stake in this enterprise. He had come so close to the monetary union he so desperately wanted. In the end, he was willing to make an essential compromise. In his 2004 memoirs, Delors also blamed the Germans. He wrote that he had protested against the German obsession with fiscal "stability," but his pushback "was not well-received by the super-orthodox Germans and Dutch."[122]

The Germans also insisted that the new central bank be independent, a demand consistent with German tradition and the global trend at the time. The laudable goal was to minimize political interference in the central bank's operations. But at Maastricht, in a significant departure from international practices, Europe's proposed central bank was set up to be super-independent. Elsewhere, even "independent" central banks are accountable to elected representatives. In the United States, the General Accounting Office has "wide latitude to review Fed operations," and the US Congress exercises oversight of the Fed's operations to ensure that monetary policy is conducted "reasonably and in the national interest."[123] In principle, Congress can also change the Fed's mandate. Such oversight of central banks is not controversial. However, the European monetary union's proposed central bank would have no formal accountability to member-state governments, and changing its mandate would be virtually impossible.

BOX 2.2. In Never-Never Land: The 3 Percent Rule

The 3 percent rule surprised everyone. There had been no public discussion or debate about the rule. Indeed, when the French negotiator Jean-Claude Trichet and the German negotiator Horst Köhler shook hands to make it official, few even at Maastricht understood its implications.

After the Maastricht Treaty was signed in February 1992, a flurry of studies appeared, all of them critical. They highlighted the same economic principle, that a fixed budget limit delays recovery from an economic crisis. When an economy falls into a downturn, its budget deficit rises (since revenues decline and expenditures for social support increase). Fiscal austerity to keep the budget deficit within a pre-set limit becomes self-defeating. Austerity—through reduced spending or higher taxes—causes economic growth to slow down further. The government's budget deficit and debt rise, rather than fall. (This logic was forcefully demonstrated, especially between 2011 and 2013; as countries undertook severe austerity, they helplessly watched their debt burdens grow. See chapter 7.) For this reason, considerable fiscal latitude is needed during recessions and crises. To be sure, such latitude must be exercised with judgement and wisdom; however, rigid rules hurt, and when uncritically applied, do long-term damage.

In September 1992, a little over six months after the Maastricht Treaty was signed, researchers at the Federal Reserve Bank of San Francisco reported that monetary unions often did not have fiscal rules; members of the union used the flexibility allowed to counter economic recessions. Even by the standards of monetary unions that did have fiscal rules, the Maastricht criteria were "excessively rigid" (Glick and Hutchison 1992).

In November, Charles Bean, London School of Economics professor and later deputy governor of the Bank of England, bluntly concluded: "if the price of monetary union is the adoption of inappropriate fiscal policies, then it is probably a price that is not worth paying." The fiscal rules proposed at Maastricht, he said, were "not just irrelevant, but may be positively harmful because of the limits they place on the scope for national fiscal policies." To emphasize his concern, Bean added, "Active national fiscal policies will be needed more than ever after monetary union, and imposing unnecessary constraints is a major error, especially in the absence of a Community-wide fiscal system" (Bean 1992, 48, 51).

And in 1993, a galaxy of international economists—including Economics Nobel laureate Robert Solow, Columbia University economics professor and future Economics Nobel laureate Edmund Phelps, and Olivier Blanchard, economics professor at MIT and future chief economist of the IMF—warned against the proposed fiscal rule. "It would be untenable," they wrote, "to expect governments faced with poor conditions to remain passive, or even to have to act in a way that is likely to deepen a domestic recession." After reviewing the experience in the United States where every state chooses its own fiscal disciplining method, they concluded that instead of requiring all countries to follow a common rule, each European government should "enjoy fiscal policy independence" (Fitoussi et al. 1993, 14–15).

Thus, in the year after Maastricht, there was only one intellectually respectable view. The Maastricht budget-deficit rule had no redeeming feature. Again, this was not just an "Anglo-Saxon" view. European scholars, policymakers, and leaders knew what they were getting into. The Lamfalussy appendix to the Delors Report had laid out the problems and the implications of the system being set up (Lamfalussy 1989).

Only an outsider could question such sweeping independence for the ECB. In 1997, Paul Volcker, the legendary former chairman of the Fed and himself an uncompromising advocate of central-bank independence, emphasized that central banks needed nevertheless to be politically accountable. A central bank, he said, "must be able to justify its policies to the general public and to political leaders."[124] Volcker was, therefore, sympathetic to the French demand for regular communication between the ECB and an intergovernmental council; in such a forum, governments would convey their economic and political priorities to the ECB.

But there was no easy way to hold the ECB politically accountable. Even in a national context, the line between communication of governmental priorities and political interference is a thin one. In an international context, where the countries adopting the single currency did not trust one another, the prime objective was to ensure that a member state could not hijack the central bank. On this matter, the Germans were unwilling to make concessions, especially as the French had made it clear that they would attempt to influence European monetary policy if they could. The German position won the day because there appeared to be no other legitimate option.

The proposed central bank's independence necessarily came with a simple rule to determine the conduct of monetary policy. Achieving price stability would be the only goal of the ECB. Unlike the Fed, which famously had a "dual mandate" of fostering both price stability and "maximum sustainable employment," the ECB would not act specifically to improve employment prospects. The ECB's focus on price stability was less controversial than the simple fiscal rules were. Some prominent voices, however, did object. Franco Modigliani, an MIT economics professor and Nobel laureate, along with his colleague and fellow Nobel laureate Robert Solow, warned that the ECB's mandate would make it focus obsessively on keeping inflation low. Interest rates, therefore, would be too high. This, they said, was a problem because European unemployment rates were worryingly high, and a monetary policy that overemphasized price stability would make the unemployment problem worse. They recommended that the ECB follow the Fed and adopt a "dual" mandate so that monetary policy not only would reflect inflation concerns but would also proactively ("on an equal footing" with the price-stability goal) work to increase employment opportunities. They said they were "confident" that the ECB could do more to alleviate Europe's employment problem "without renouncing or sacrificing its commitment against inflation."[125]

Modigliani also criticized the budget-deficit rule, because by restricting the deficit in recessionary periods, that too would tend to raise long-term unemployment.[126] Thus, as a piece of European economic history trivia, two MIT-based Nobel laureates, Franco Modigliani and Robert Solow, spoke out loudly against the two central pillars of the European single currency: the budget-deficit rule and the ECB's mandate to maintain price stability.

The Germans had achieved what they wanted: a fiscal rule that they believed in and an independent central bank devoted to price stability. It is important that they had elevated stability as a core economic ideology in European discourse. The Werner Report in 1970 had initiated the creation of this ideology.[127] Just more than two decades later, in 1991, that ideology was about to be enshrined in the Maastricht Treaty. As it met its economic and political contradictions, a European groupthink would protect it and carry it forward.

What about the forward movement to political union that Kohl spoke of so ardently? That idea had reached a dead end in September 1991. Fearful that his legacy might slip away, Kohl instructed his negotiators that progress on political union was no longer a priority.[128] Thus, Kohl gave up the long-held German view that monetary union must come only after political union; instead, he adopted the French "monetarist" position: it was necessary to push ahead with monetary union, for only such a push could create the momentum for European political unity.

In early December 1991, the Maastricht contract was in place. By then, the world had long-since moved away from a hard commitment to fixed exchange rates (figure 2.2). In contrast, European leaders had agreed that they would adopt a single currency and, thus, would fix their exchange rates with one another in a manner that would be extraordinarily costly to reverse. Whatever the illusory gains from the single currency, the costs associated with it were well understood. Countries in the single currency club would no longer be able to lower their interest rates, they would have little or no room for fiscal stimulus if their economies fell into a slump, and they would be unable to depreciate their exchange rates to regain lost competitiveness.

This was not a monetary union, even though Europeans called it so. A fiscal union, an essential safety net to complete the monetary union, was politically impossible. Hence, the fiscal rule—to keep the government's budget

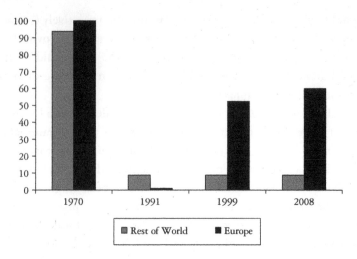

FIGURE 2.2. Europe's monetary union goes against the global tide.
(Share of countries on "hard-pegged" exchange-rate regimes, percent.)
Source: IMF Annual Report on Exchange Rates Regimes and Monetary Restrictions, 1971, 1992, 2000, and 2009. These reports distinguish among three groups of arrangements: hard pegs (arrangements with fixed exchange rates that are difficult to modify, such as currency boards), soft pegs (arrangements with exchange rates based around a central rate or bandwidth that may be adjusted, such as conventional fixed pegs and crawling pegs), and floating arrangements (arrangements without exchange-rate anchors, such as managed floating and independently floating). The ERM is classified as an intermediate regime in 1991. The IMF has deferred to the European authorities and defines the euro as floating (because it floats vis-à-vis the rest of the world); but it is shown here as a hard peg from 1999 onward. The sample of countries on which this is based are "developed countries," as listed on the MSCI Developed Markets Index, and "developing and emerging market nations," as listed on the MSCI Emerging Market and/ or EMBI+ indices. The figure is based on twenty-one European countries and thirty-four countries that represent the "rest of the world." In the rest of the world, Canada and South Korea were categorized as "floating" regimes in 1970, and Ecuador, Hong Kong, and Panama had "hard pegs" in 2008.

deficit below 3 percent of GDP—was invented as a substitute. The rule, however, was not a substitute for a fiscal union. To the contrary, instead of helping as a safety net during an economic downturn, it would, all economists agreed, force unwarranted austerity during a slump and make it worse.

When it came down to it, a small group of European leaders had decided that Europe should proceed with such an "incomplete monetary union." No leader had encouraged domestic debate to obtain a national consensus for such a major decision. Once the single currency was in place, neither the ECB nor those administering the fiscal rule would be accountable to European citizens for their actions.

The Maastricht contract essentially said that if a member country had a heart attack, it would receive no emergency care; it would need to rely for recovery on the equivalent of a regimen of diet and exercise. The supposed stability of the entire structure rested on this one threat that a country would receive no or only token assistance if it got itself into trouble. This threat was expected to induce good behavior and thus prevent the heart attack from occurring in the first place. But even with the best of intentions, human beings do have heart attacks, and countries do fall on bad times. The Maastricht plan, in its zealous emphasis on nipping in the bud all behavior tainted by moral hazard, defied economics, politics, and history.

Lamont wrote that during the Maastricht negotiations, he alerted those who would listen to him that Europe was setting itself up for trouble. Many privately agreed with the concerns he raised. Among them, former French President Giscard d'Estaing, ardent champion of European monetary unity, responded, "The points you make [against the intended construction] are good, but it's going to happen."[129]

December 1991: Kohl Keeps Monetary Union Alive

Giscard d'Estaing believed "it's going to happen," but although all their conditions had been met, the Germans were not ready to sign on. Kohl still had no domestic mandate for a single currency. The German public did not support it, and neither did the German business community. On September 8, 1991, three months before European heads of government were to meet in Maastricht to seal the deal, Ludolf von Wartenberg, previously a minister in the Kohl administration and at that time BDI's director general, explained the business perspective to the Bundestag's finance committee:

> It is senseless to believe that because of its export relationships in the European Community, German industry automatically values a single European currency. That view does not represent entrepreneurial reality. The benefits from easier trade transactions made possible by a single currency are immeasurably small. A political union must be interwoven with the monetary union, the rules for entry must be strict, and the central bank must be committed to stability. On these essential principles, there can be no compromises.[130]

Thus, through the yearlong negotiations, lacking a domestic consensus, the Germans had refused to commit to a launch date. "The only thing that was accepted," Védrine reported, "was a 'date to rendezvous'—December 30, 1996," when it would be decided what came next.[131] To move forward at that time would require that enough countries met macroeconomic checks of good health. The risk was that without a precise launch date, the momentum would fade and the project would run adrift.

At dinner on December 8, Mitterrand and Italian Prime Minister Giulio Andreotti fretted that the uncertainty about the precise date was proving intolerable.[132] Mitterrand was impatient with the "hesitations" and "time-wasting maneuvers" of finance ministers and their advisers on an "opening date."[133] He and Andreotti agreed that they would push for a firm date of January 1, 1999, no matter how many countries met the entry criteria.

At breakfast the next morning, the discussions began with the twelve heads of governments, their foreign ministers, and select aides. Mitterrand quickly insisted that it was "necessary to fix a date" for the introduction of the single currency and that unless, in the meantime, an earlier date could be justified, "the date of January 1, 1999, should fall like a guillotine blade."[134]

Mitterrand's adviser Guigou wrote that she was surprised that Mitterrand was so aggressive. She thought he had abandoned the idea of including a starting date in the text of the treaty. The French had repeatedly tested the idea, and the Germans had repeatedly rebuffed them.[135] Mitterrand was aggressive that morning, Guigou thought, because he anticipated that Kohl would make a binding decision then and present it as a done deal to his cabinet, the Bundesbank, and the Bundestag.[136]

Kohl's agreement to a definite date for the introduction of the euro was the biggest surprise of Maastricht. Once again, Kohl blindsided senior German officials. When word of his decision filtered out, the three top German officials present at Maastricht—Finance Minister Waigel, Bundesbank's Tietmeyer, and Köhler—all reacted with "horror."[137]

Védrine, however, was pleased. He described Kohl's decision to keep the process moving as the quintessence of "French-German harmony."[138] Mitterrand had an even grander view: the Maastricht Treaty, he said, had "made war impossible between the enemies of yesterday."[139] The political reflexes in these statements are revealing. They lay bare the self-congratulation, the invocation of peace as an objective of monetary union, and the reinforcement of the mythology of Franco-German friendship.

To symbolize the expectations of greater material prosperity and political unity, the European Community was renamed the European Union (EU). This enticing term had first surfaced in the early 1970s. When at the time French Foreign Minister Michel Jobert asked his cabinet colleague Édouard Balladur (a future French prime minister) what it meant, Balladur reportedly replied, "Nothing. But then that is the beauty of it."[140]

For Kohl, Maastricht had set Europe on the path to an idealistic post-nineteenth-century state. Upon his return from Maastricht, he explained in a speech to the Bundestag that he had achieved only some of what he wanted but that the force of history would now take over. He emphasized that sovereign nations had agreed on the absolute need for fiscal discipline and, hence, had committed to keeping budget deficits below 3 percent of GDP.[141] And although the movement toward political union had stalled, the movement toward monetary union, Kohl said, was now unstoppable. The union with a common currency would unleash a "dynamic process," which would sweep away narrow nationalism, and Europe would emerge in a political form not seen before.[142] This dynamic union would soon extend from "Copenhagen to Madrid, from The Hague to Rome."[143]

On February 7, 1992, European leaders signed the Maastricht Treaty, formally the Treaty on the European Union.

1992: Europe's Citizens Rebel, and the Monetary System Cracks

Instead of creating forward political momentum for European solidarity, Maastricht, as if on cue, opened the floodgates of public anxiety. When European citizens woke up to the reality of a single currency, they suddenly realized that the pain of monetary and fiscal austerity evidently lay ahead, but the single currency offered few solutions for the real problems they faced.

Maastricht offered little help for the most pressing problems of the day: growing unemployment and the dependence of ever-larger groups of people on the social protections made available by European governments. Europe's postwar momentum had long since vanished. Unemployment was on the rise (figure 2.3). In 1969, when the journey to monetary union began, Germany's unemployment rate was 0.6 percent. Yes, it was less than 1 percent. At Maastricht, the German unemployment rate was 5 percent and rising. In France, where it had risen to 8 percent, and more so in Italy, where it had reached 10 percent, unemployment was rooting itself more deeply.

Meanwhile, government expenditure had increased rapidly (figure 2.4). The expansion occurred especially in the provision of health services and social security.[144] The rapid rise in public expenditure alongside weak economic growth caused the governments' debt burden (the debt-to-GDP ratio) to increase, gradually in France and Germany but explosively in Italy. The Italian debt-to-GDP ratio reached 120 percent of GDP in the mid-1990s.

Although this debt-based expansion of public services was not sustainable, a generation had grown up believing that the government's safety net

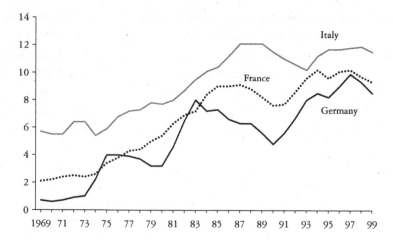

FIGURE 2.3. The rise of unemployment.
(Unemployment rates, percent)
Source: OECD, ALFS Summary Tables, Series: "Rate of Unemployment as a % of Civilian Labour Force."

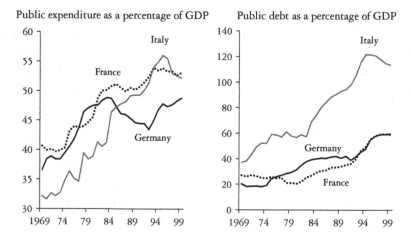

FIGURE 2.4. The rise of public expenditure and debt, from the Hague to the euro.
Source: Carlo Cottarelli and Andrea Schaechter. 2010. "Long-Term Trends in Public Finances in the G-7 Economies." International Monetary Fund Staff Position Note 2010/13. https://www.imf.org/external/pubs/ft/spn/2010/spn1013.pdf.

would always protect them. Many European nations had lived beyond their means, and something, indeed, needed to be done. But decisions were being handed down from Bonn and Brussels without domestic political debate and engagement. The concerns and resentments were felt most acutely among those who saw their pensions and health security to be at risk. These were the

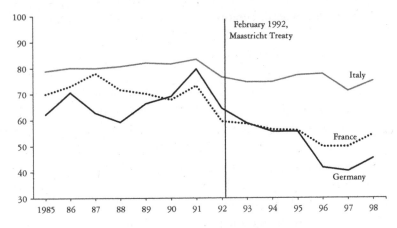

FIGURE 2.5. German and French support for Europe collapses around Maastricht.
(Percent of respondents who said EC or EU is a "good thing")
Source: Eurobarometer (http://ec.europa.eu/public_opinion/archives/eb_arch_en.htm); Leibniz Institute for the Social Sciences (http://zacat.gesis.org/webview/).
Note: Support for Europe is measured as the percentage of respondents who said their country's membership in the EC (before 1994) or the EU (on and after 1994) was a "good thing."

same people who could expect few direct economic benefits from the single currency.

Support for Europe among European citizens dropped dramatically (figure 2.5).[145] The most dramatic decline in support occurred in the two protagonist countries, France and Germany. German opinion polls showed that an overwhelming majority (80 percent of the respondents in a respected poll) opposed the single currency. Speaking on television, Foreign Minister Klaus Kinkel grumbled that the benefits of a "united Europe" were hard to explain but that people would soon recognize its value in their lives.[146] In Italy, support for Europe held up better, because Italian citizens still hoped that European strictures would discipline their wayward politicians. But even the Italians began to turn away from Europe. On the eve of Maastricht, citizens' support for Europe had stood at the highest recorded level. That peak was never regained—in any member country.

The "permissive consensus" on Europe was breaking down. That consensus had allowed a small group of European leaders to make consequential decisions without consulting European citizens. Jean Monnet, often regarded as the intellectual father of European integration, had legitimized such disregard: the peoples of Europe, he had said, had no experience of the complexities of Europe's policies and institutions.[147] Mitterrand's adviser Védrine was more daring: "Let us not be afraid to say it: . . . all the major decisions to move towards European integration . . . were the pure product of a modern form of enlightened despotism."[148] Critics of this "enlightened despotism" approach were dismissed with the assertion, "Europe is good for you."[149] At a working lunch during the intergovernmental negotiations at Maastricht, Dutch Finance Minister (and later Prime Minister) Wim Kok had rejected the idea that the single currency should be subject to the rigors of a democratic debate. If people were to vote against it, Kok said, "Europe will never find its destiny."[150]

Well, now some people did get a chance to vote, and a new citizens' activism revealed that people did want to determine their own destiny. In a public referendum held on June 2, 1992, the Danes rejected the Maastricht Treaty. Although the polls had indicated that such an outcome was possible, Danish authorities and the entire European establishment were shocked. They had believed that the higher purpose and calling of Europe would prevail. But European elites had lost touch with the popular mood. The Danish public, traditionally wary of Europe, had rebelled against more intrusion by the Brussels bureaucracy in their workplaces and homes. Indeed, the symbolism of renaming the EC as the EU had proven so offensive to the Danish public that the "pro-Europe" Danish prime minister had thought it wise to stop using the word *union* in the final days before the vote.[151]

The Danes believed, as the British did, in free trade within Europe. In the October 1972 referendum, they had voted enthusiastically to join the EC, and they had voted again in February 1986 to endorse the SEA. But they saw no value in the further march to union.

In France, Mitterrand took a political gamble and announced a referendum on June 3, 1992. Claiming the high ground a few days later, he told political science students, "A decision which might commit France forever could not be taken as though in hiding, with the people absent."[152] In truth, Mitterrand hoped to gain a tactical political victory. He expected that the vote would divide the opposition, while an easy public approval of the single currency would bolster his sagging political fortunes.[153]

But Mitterrand misjudged. "The high-tide of Europeanism," one writer vividly said, "may now be ebbing away."[154] There was no assurance anymore that the Maastricht Treaty would reach "safe harbor." Suddenly, the single currency began to look like a distant goal. Thus, a shadow fell over the ERM, the centerpiece of the EMS.

Exchange-rate parities within the ERM had remained unchanged for the past five years. Many had come to believe that this stability was the dividend of painful but necessary macroeconomic discipline, and they had hailed the advent of a "new" ERM.

The system, however, was fragile. In a 1986 essay, Alan Walters, a British economist and adviser to Prime Minister Thatcher, had pointed to a particularly perverse consequence of fixed exchange rates.[155] Under fixed exchange rates—and, hence, under a single currency—credit booms grow bigger, making the bust deeper and more chaotic. The basic problem stems from the fact that high inflation in Italy makes Italian borrowers more creditworthy from the perspective of German lenders! The reason for this curious outcome is that with a fixed exchange rate, Italian consumers with rapidly rising wages and businesses that are hiking their prices have steadily more inflated liras to repay loans in German D-marks. German investors—either directly, but more often through Italian banks—are, therefore, happy, even keen, to lend to Italians. To protect themselves, German lenders make loans only of short maturity so that they can pull out quickly if a lira depreciation become imminent. But, meanwhile, as lenders roll over old short-maturity loans and extend new ones, the lending spree fuels even higher Italian inflation, causing Italian exporters to lose international competitiveness. The perversity arises because even as Italy loses competitiveness and, hence, the country's GDP growth slows and the unemployment rate rises, Italians become more indebted. Walters' analysis explained precisely the reason for the repeated failure of European fixed exchange rate systems in the 1970s and 1980s. His analysis predicted the difficulties encountered under the ERM in the early 1990s. High inflation countries—Italy and the United Kingdom—experienced large capital inflows, which fed domestic credit booms. Lars Svensson, the international macroeconomist and later deputy governor of the Swedish Riksbank, added that the promise to maintain fixed exchange rates had kept the capital inflows charged until the very end: foreign creditors who were lending to the weakening economies sought to earn the last extra buck, making the judgment that they would exit before the system collapsed.[156]

Now, suddenly in early September 1992, it did seem that the system could collapse. Under the phased timetable for monetary union, the uncontroversial step of eliminating capital controls was largely complete.[157] Investors began moving their funds from the vulnerable countries, Italy and the United Kingdom, and sought refuge in German bonds. The pressure to revalue the D-mark increased, as did the need to devalue the lira and the British pound.

On September 3, Mitterrand faced the charismatic opposition spokesman Philippe Séguin in a televised debate at the Sorbonne. Séguin made the case that the single currency would undermine French national sovereignty and its democracy.[158] Mitterrand, in an effort to grab the French public's attention, asserted that the French and other governments would direct the ECB's actions. "I hear it said everywhere," he exclaimed, "that this ECB will be master of its decisions! That is not true!"[159] The European Council (European heads of state), Mitterrand said, would determine monetary policy; the ECB would only implement that policy.

To the Germans, the prospect of any French influence on ECB policy was abhorrent, which is why the Maastricht Treaty had ruled out such interference. Kohl, who was present during the television debate on a live link, could have objected to Mitterrand's bizarre claim. He chose to stay silent, presumably for fear that Mitterrand's credibility and, with it, the referendum would be lost. A little more than two decades later, recalling Mitterrand's stunning rejection of a core Maastricht principle and the outrage that followed in the German press, Szász wrote: "The German press gave the statement much publicity, suggesting that this did not bode well for the monetary union. Bundesbank president Helmut Schlesinger told me that German journalists had asked for his comment on Mitterrand's pronouncement, but he had declined with the excuse that his French was not good enough to understand it!"[160]

To investors, the signs were worrying. The European public was anxious, unemployment was running high, the state of government finances was alarming, and Mitterrand had added another element of uncertainty into an already volatile situation. The tipping point had come. By September 11, investors were fleeing from the lira. It was time for the Germans to help the Italians, to display "solidarity." The understanding was that in such situations, the Bundesbank would lower its interest rate to slow down the flight of capital into Germany. The Bundesbank, however, refused to budge, keeping its interest rate at an "excessively high" level and thus reinforcing the flight away from the beleaguered Italian lira.[161]

The Italians should have known that the Germans would help only up to a point. For a long time, German leaders and policymakers had made it clear that they did not believe in "symmetrical adjustment." Stated simply, the Germans did not believe that they had an obligation to help relieve the distress of weaker members of the union. Indeed, unknown to most, the Bundesbank had specifically acquired the authority to act primarily in what it judged was the German interest. That authority was recorded in a

November 1978 letter written by then Bundesbank President Emminger and approved by German Chancellor Schmidt.[162]

The Emminger letter was now in operation. The Bundesbank, by holding its interest rate firm despite the pressure on the lira, conveyed to investors that rescuing other European nations was in conflict with the German interest. Financial-market panic spread. On September 16, which instantly became known as Black Wednesday, the British pound was forced to leave the ERM. The lira left the next day.

Once again, it was time to ask questions about the future of Europe. Did fixed exchange rates make any sense in a modern globalized economy? In Europe, with differential inflation rates in countries on divergent economic paths, could a monetary union work?

1992: The French Citizens' Cry Goes Unheeded

When Mitterrand had announced the referendum in June, it appeared, as the Americans might have said, to be a slam dunk. Polls gave a yes vote for the Maastricht Treaty a big lead. Mitterrand had reason to think he could raise his stature as a statesman and strengthen his hold over French politics.

Although opposed by Philippe Séguin, Mitterrand had the backing of two powerful political foes. Paris mayor Jacques Chirac represented the nationalist, "Gaullist" perspective, but persuaded himself that supporting the single currency would enhance his European credentials and strengthen his presidential bid. Former president Valéry Giscard d'Estaing had a long-standing political rivalry with Mitterrand. Giscard d'Estaing had defeated Mitterrand in the presidential race in 1974 and had lost to him in 1981. Many of Giscard d'Estaing's followers sympathized with Séguin. Yet, Giscard d'Estaing—who had put France through the failed "snake-in-the-tunnel" and ERM arrangements—still believed that fixing exchange rates with a single currency was essential for France.

France's top leaders came together, but the polls showed a narrowing gap between yes and no vote supporters. On the day before the referendum, yes and no were in a statistical dead heat. On September 20, the yes side squeaked through with a 51-49 percent victory. Mitterrand's traditional followers among France's working class said no to his single-currency project; Giscard d'Estaing's backing made possible the narrow victory.

Exit polls after the referendum gave a rare and prescient insight into not just French but Western democracy. Those who voted against the treaty were

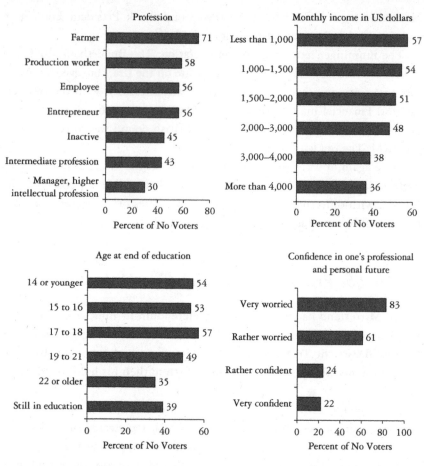

FIGURE 2.6. Who voted "no" to Maastricht in the French referendum?
Source: Christian de Boissieu and Jean Pisani-Ferry. 1995. "The Political Economy of French Economic Policy and the Transition to EMU." CEPII. http://www.cepii.fr/PDF_PUB/wp/1995/wp1995-09.pdf.

less educated and either unemployed or in low-income jobs (figure 2.6). A large number of no voters had given up on the mainstream French political parties and had wandered to either the extreme right or the extreme left, or they simply said they did not support any party. The no voters were united by one overriding concern, that they would remain trapped in their grim lives because their leaders could not—or would not—act to create a better future for them.[163]

Commenting on the referendum results, a writer for *Le Monde* observed, "France, which rejected the Maastricht Treaty, is above all the one suffering because she is the principal victim of unemployment, exclusion, and poverty, she feels abandoned, and she is fearful of the future."[164] Other *Le*

Monde commentators wrote similar accounts. The no voters lived in towns "where the factories had closed their doors leaving behind only wasteland."[165] They lived in places such as Calais, Boulogne sur Mer, Pas de Calais, Amiens, Somme, and Saint Quentin, where whole sections of the population lived in poverty and misery. The yes vote prevailed in the large metropolitan areas, in the "chic neighborhoods" of Paris and the residential suburbs of Lyon.[166] Here lived the educated, professional, and high-income French. The Maastricht vote had revealed a France split not just by economic success but also by geography, foreshadowing today's politics in virtually all Western democracies.

Some French leaders did hear the message correctly. Prime Minister Pierre Bérégovoy recognized that "the French most exposed to the harshness of existence" had voted against the Maastricht Treaty. The vote had revealed, Bérégovoy said, "a rupture between the people and their representatives."[167]

France, in its bid to keep the franc within the ERM, had tightened monetary policy. The government had also raised taxes to contain the fiscal deficit. Some of these taxes, such as employer social security contributions, discouraged hiring of workers.[168] This "franc fort" policy, which had started after the franc devaluations between 1981 and 1983, had continued ever since and had managed to squeeze French inflation down to German—and, by now, even lower—levels. But higher interest rates and austerity had also squeezed consumption and investment and had pushed French unemployment steadily to a record level of more than 10 percent.[169]

The premise of the franc fort strategy was that it would, over time, help improve the competitiveness of the French economy, and the unemployment problem would diminish and disappear. But these policies mainly created an economy that favored the well educated and those networked into French and European commerce and finance. The economy was leaving behind a large number of French citizens. France was dividing into two economic groups. Each group had its politics.

Dealing with this economic and political divide was France's major challenge, Séguin argued in early 1993. France's social contract needed to change to create a fresh sense of optimism for all. Such fundamental transformation, Séguin said, could not occur with the gun of German-inspired austerity held to French heads. France needed time, and it was therefore best to let the French franc float. A weaker franc would stimulate exports and employment, which would allow more modestly paced austerity while French leaders launched a parallel effort to create a more prosperous and equitable nation. France, Séguin said, should shape its own future rather than trying to fit itself into a German mold.[170]

In a curious parallel, also in the first half of 1993, Rudi Dornbusch, an MIT economics professor and perhaps the most influential international macroeconomist of his generation, had reached the same conclusion as Séguin. Commenting in 1996 on the paper by Barry Eichengreen and Charles Wyplosz about the breakdown of the EMS in 1992, Dornbusch said, "In France, the one sound strategy would be to let the currency float." French policymakers refused to take that obvious step, Dornbusch said, because they were "fixated by" and under the "magic spell" of the D-mark. And the fixation remained because France suffered from a "lack of confidence in its policies."[171]

The French referendum had raised serious questions about the economic and political future of France and Europe. Indeed, by highlighting the drift away from mainstream political parties to purveyors of extremism or into political alienation, the French vote had raised deep questions about the future of Western democracy.

Even on a more mundane and pragmatic level, the French public was trying to disabuse its leaders of their notion—carried from Pompidou to Giscard and now to Mitterrand—that the single currency would help France achieve greater economic parity with Germany. Two-fifths of French citizens who voted against the single currency in the referendum said they did so because they anticipated that under a single currency, Germany would exercise a dominating influence on European macroeconomic policy.[172]

But for Mitterrand, this was no time to pause and reflect. Paying little attention to the vote's message of economic and political anxiety, a tiring Mitterrand, recently diagnosed with prostate cancer, celebrated the "Community's joy" at being able to continue the European journey.[173]

Investors, however, were not yet done. They sensed that France was politically fragile and its economy was vulnerable. They began dumping the franc, preferring instead to hold the safer D-marks. The franc came under a full-scale attack just like the ones that had only recently knocked the Italian lira and the British pound out of the ERM. The French central bank, the Banque de France, was unequal to the task. Raising interest rates to bring investors back, and thus preserve the value of the franc, would only make the unemployment problem worse. Instead, the Banque de France began using its precious foreign-exchange reserves to prevent a steeper decline in value.

The future of Europe was again in question. If the franc fell out of the ERM, the idea of monetary union would likely die. The political fissures were already out in the open; although the yes vote had squeaked through, French voters were not so sure that they wanted a more integrated Europe. Germans also began to question whether more European integration made sense.[174] Public opinion had turned against, even become hostile to, a single currency. Germans remained strongly opposed to giving up the D-mark.[175]

But the Bundesbank, which had let the lira and the pound slide out of the ERM, used its vast resources to stabilize the franc. Either under pressure from Kohl or in the belief that it was in Germany's interest, for six consecutive days, the Bundesbank fought back against currency speculators who had been dumping the franc and buying D-marks.[176] The speculators eventually tired and went away. It was September 25, just five days since the French referendum. It had seemed a lifetime. The Bundesbank had calmed currency markets.

What came next for Europe? European leaders had an opportunity in September 1992 to reconsider their future course of action. The breakdown of the fixed-exchange-rate system under the ERM was a warning that inflation rate differentials would persist and financial disruptions would recur within the context of a single currency. Recent history had insistently conveyed that lesson. For nearly half a century, starting with the Bretton Woods system, then within the European snake in the tunnel, and now under the ERM, fixed rates had generated crises without providing any benefits. Moreover, the worry that floating-exchange-rate systems would be prone to "competitive devaluations," with countries matching the devaluations undertaken by competitor countries, had definitely faded. Was it time, maybe, to give up the frustrating search for European monetary unity?

1992–1993: *When Kohl Refused to Take No for an Answer*

On September 25, 1992, while the Bundesbank was shooing the last speculators away, Kohl tried to renew faith in Europe. Speaking to the Bundestag, he said that a united Europe must urgently work to serve the cause of world peace. Just as it was self-evident that the moment to unify Germany was at hand when the Berlin Wall fell in November 1989, "so too we must now have the courage to move ahead rapidly." If Europe failed to move forward, Kohl said, it would fall behind and "be rolled over by the events of history." Therefore, he concluded, "my government and I will work with all our energy to implement the Maastricht Treaty as planned." The turmoil in the summer of 1992 had not changed Kohl's mind. In trademark fashion, he ended, "Germany is our fatherland, Europe is our future."[177]

Kohl was using his inimitable rhetorical skills to sweep aside the economic problems that made monetary unity so difficult. Although he acknowledged that currency gyrations were the "necessary outcome of economic imbalances," he offered no ideas on how to prevent recurrence of those imbalances once the single currency was in place.[178]

It was a bad moment to downplay European economic problems. Italy had perennial macroeconomic imbalances: high inflation and unemployment. The three most recent entrants to the EEC—Greece, Spain, and Portugal—had the same inflationary tendencies that Italy did. Greece, which had joined the EEC in 1981, suffered from chronic high inflation and therefore was considered unprepared for the ERM. Spain and Portugal had joined the EEC in 1986, and although they did enter the ERM, their bouts of inflation created a struggle to keep exchange rates fixed, which is why they were allowed to maintain some controls on speculative capital flows.[179] Unemployment, a worry everywhere, was becoming more acute.

On the larger question of Europe's obligations to its citizens, Kohl had nothing to say. He did not even bother to address the anxieties of those, throughout Europe, who were worried about their futures and who believed that European institutions were not serving their interests. At home, German citizens wanted a scaling down of the monetary union ambition. In Denmark and Britain, citizens were tiring of the European project and saw the rush to monetary union as intolerable European overreach.[180] As British Chancellor of the Exchequer Norman Lamont said, "You can't get too far ahead of public opinion or you will be in trouble."[181]

In the summer of 1993, renewed speculation threatened to push the French franc out of the ERM. The French economy was in recession, weighed down by a weak global economy and domestic (monetary and fiscal) austerity induced by the franc fort policy. Jobless figures were increasingly gloomy. France desperately needed lower interest rates to revive growth and employment. However, lower interest rates could cause investors to dump the French franc and seek safe returns in D-mark assets. The French therefore faced a choice: abandon the high-interest-rate franc fort policy and accept another devaluation of the franc, or face rising unemployment.

Once the speculation started, French authorities again needed lower German interest rates to slow down investor flight from the franc. But unlike in September 1992, the Bundesbank refused to support the French cause. The German inflation rate was worryingly high, having jumped because of extensive public spending to rebuild East Germany. Bundesbank President Schlesinger later described how he saw things at the time: "Domestically, there was no clear indication to support another reduction in interest rates."[182] As always, the Germans were clear that their domestic interest came ahead of a European neighbor's needs. The embarrassment was acute, because European

Commission President Delors had recently praised the smooth functioning of the ERM. "The system," he had prematurely declared, "is not dominated by one single country or currency."[183]

On August 1 and 2, 1993, EC finance ministers and central bank governors met to consider the alternatives. When some of them called for a "fast-track move" to a monetary union, the Germans rejected the idea "as a joke."[184] Instead, the German finance ministry and the Bundesbank said, perhaps it was time to float all European currencies. That radical proposal was an ideological nonstarter. With red lines thus drawn, European leaders once again chose to fudge. They retained the fiction of the ERM, but the bands within which currencies could fluctuate were made so wide (15 percent on either side of the central parity) that European currencies were, in effect, in a floating regime. Some countries in the years ahead did try to keep the movements of their currencies within a smaller range, but crucially, they no longer had a commitment to do so. Hence, if economic pressures had increased, the option existed to let the currency drift down without fear of destabilizing market speculation.

Left there, Europe might well have adapted and—like the rest of the world—gradually learned to float. The German public, after all, was overwhelmingly against giving up the D-mark. According to the polls, Germans clamored to vote in a referendum and promised to reject the Maastricht Treaty decisively.[185] Schlesinger highlighted that German business continued to have "reservations about a common currency."[186] Horst Köhler recalled to me, in Berlin in the summer of 2014, that in 1993, as he was leaving his position in the Ministry of Finance, Kohl was worried about the aversion of German business to the prospect of a single currency. One of Kohl's last requests to Köhler was for him to help persuade German bankers and manufacturers that the single currency would be good for them and for Germany.

On October 12, 1993, the German constitutional court, after a seemingly interminable delay, confirmed that the Bundestag had the authority to ratify the Maastricht Treaty. The Bundestag, the court said, needed first to certify that a European monetary union was in Germany's interest. Then it needed to remain vigilant, for ratification now did not imply that Germany was agreeing "to an uncontrollable, unforeseeable process which will lead inexorably toward monetary union." The Bundestag's final decision to join the monetary union required proof of "permanent stability of the budgetary and financial policy of the participating Member States." The court's conclusion was simple: "The future European currency must be and remain as stable as the Deutsche Mark."[187]

Kohl now had a choice. The Constitutional Court had given him the green light. The court's stern message of stability, dear to his own heart, was firmly enshrined in the Maastricht Treaty. However, since the agreement at Maastricht in December 1991, economic and political developments were a warning of the perils that lay ahead. These developments called for a pause, even a long pause, while European countries resolved their domestic troubles. If he paused, the risk was that even a short delay could easily extend into an uncertain future, and there might never be a European monetary union.

Roger Boyes of the London *Times* wrote at the time that for Kohl, the monetary union had "become a deeply personal matter." He had become convinced that he was "the last chancellor capable of pushing through the Maastricht agenda."[188] Kohl was almost surely right that no future chancellor could summon his level of energy and political command to push the euro into reality. The question was whether Kohl, rather than focusing on the economic and political merits of a single currency, was acting to fulfill his personal aspirations. Was he imposing an unwarranted burden on future generations of Europeans? No one really was thinking of that legacy.

Kathryn Dominguez, professor at the University of Michigan, has written: "In a display of amazing (or some might say reckless) resolve, after surviving the currency turbulence in 1992 and 1993, European leaders stayed the course toward monetary union."[189]

1994–1998: Against All Opposition, Kohl Steers toward the Finish Line

On September 1, 1994, two leaders of Germany's CDU, Wolfgang Schäuble and Karl Lamers, warned that Europe was drifting apart and that it faced "existential internal problems."[190] Schäuble was the CDU's chairman and head of the party's legislators in the Bundestag; Lamers was the party's foreign policy spokesman. Europe, Schäuble and Lamers said, was too unwieldy to move forward together. It was best, they said, that France and Germany lead a "hard core" of European countries—a "Kerneuropa"—toward deeper economic and political integration. Their proposed core included the Netherlands, Belgium, and Luxembourg; they pointedly excluded Italy, one of the original six members of the Coal and Steel Community in 1950.[191] Excluding Italy was offensive but not surprising, since virtually everyone agreed that Italy was not ready to join a monetary union.

Beginning small was a sensible way to test the monetary union. German business was more comfortable with such a two-speed approach, with only the strongest allowed membership and the others asked to wait until they were ready.[192] Kohl was briefly tempted. Although he insisted that the Schäuble-Lamers proposal was merely an idea for discussion and not his government's policy, he agreed that laggards should not hold back the progress of the union.[193] And this idea of a two-speed Europe had its echoes in France. Prime Minister Balladur had made a similar proposal.[194] Perhaps the most famous voice in favor of such an idea was that of former French President Giscard d'Estaing.[195] For him, countries of Europe's "hard center" ("noyau dur") would align their domestic policies to support monetary union; others would wait in the European "space" until they were ready.

Tempting though these proposals were, they were never realistic. Schäuble and Lamers had proposed that the European Commission would function with the "features of a European government," with the authority to take important and binding policy decisions. No country would be able to veto efforts to "intensify cooperation and deepen integration."[196] Thus, the European Commission could override national parliamentary decisions. Such far-reaching authority was, of course, unacceptable to the Germans themselves, as Lamers soon conceded. Lamers clarified that countries could veto European decisions made on "the most important financial matters."[197] Lamers was inevitably echoing Kohl, who had repeatedly assured the Bundestag that Europe would have no claims over German tax revenues. In an interview with several European newspapers, Kohl said, "For a long period there must be a right to veto on certain issues."[198]

Kohl needed to be particularly careful, because he was in a tight race for reelection in October. His popularity had declined rapidly. He had told the West Germans that they would not have to pay for unification; now it seemed certain that subsidies from the West to the East would be required for many years. East Germans were struggling. By 1993, one out of six East German manufacturing jobs had disappeared.[199] The IMF said that the "open" unemployment rate in East Germany at 15 percent was misleadingly small, since many East Germans had given up and vanished from the roster of potential workers.[200] There seemed no end to their economic distress. The glow of reunification had waned quickly.

For Kohl, European unity was now his greater ambition. In an interview with European newspapers, he said, "we—in other words, governments—should avoid giving the impression that European unity is about technical issues. It must always be clear that it is also a matter for the heart."[201] Some days later, at a press conference, Kohl said that he had two challenges in his next term as chancellor: "One is German unity. The other—and please don't misunderstand me—is more important for me at the moment. We have to make another decisive step forward in building the European House." Ever conscious of his own historical role, he added, "If you ask my colleagues in any capital of the European Union, they'll tell you 'we want Helmut Kohl to be there because we need another push and the Germans have a special role here.'"[202]

Thus, Kohl squashed rumors that he would, if elected, hand over the chancellorship to the younger Wolfgang Schäuble. Only Kohl could see the single-currency project through to its end. As he later said, his presence remained necessary, because "who else could have ensured the euro?" Kohl was all too aware that Germans had deep misgivings about giving up the D-mark, and he was therefore worried that Schäuble would not be able to muster enough support for a single European currency, and without that keystone, "Europe would have collapsed."[203] He reiterated in late 1996, "I could retire tomorrow. Everybody expects me to retire. I'm staying on because I want to make sure the single currency goes ahead."[204] Whenever Kohl spoke of constructing the "European House," he meant establishing a single currency, which he saw as his crowning achievement.

In October 1994, Kohl's CDU-led coalition squeaked through to victory. But because three of the coalition parliamentarians voted against him in a secret ballot, Kohl returned as chancellor with a margin of one vote. Asked if his thin majority in the Bundestag would slow down his plans for Europe, he insisted, "If Germans don't understand that the historical gift of unity will be wasted if European unity doesn't proceed in parallel, then everything is lost."[205] The idea of "hard-core" Europe disappeared. Even Schäuble conceded that the term *hard core* was "clumsy."[206] The real intent of his proposal, Schäuble said, was to create a "magnetic core," which would attract all European nations to march forward together.

The single-currency offensive was now on. In an interview with the *Financial Times* in March 1995, Schäuble made a reckless claim. A single currency, he said, would give Europe an additional weapon in the fight to lower unemployment and improve competitiveness.[207] In January 1996, Giscard d'Estaing asserted that economic gains from a single currency should be self-evident. He said that once people became accustomed to the convenience of a single currency, they would look back and "recall that we were using 14 different currencies in the European Union, it will seem like a joke." Giscard d'Estaing said some Europeans lacked faith, and to educate such skeptics, he called on the European Commission to conduct an "objective" study to spell out the benefits of more "stable" exchange rates.[208]

Some months after Giscard d'Estaing's claim that the economic benefits of a single currency were self-evident, MIT's Dornbusch wrote an essay, as if in response to Schäuble and Giscard. With its provocative title, "Euro Fantasies," the essay argued that a single currency was, at best, irrelevant to Europe's serious economic challenges. "Experimenting with a new money is a bad idea," Dornbusch said, because "new money creates insignificant benefits." It would be of no help, he emphasized, in dealing with Europe's most urgent priorities, which were to "reintegrate millions of unemployed into a normal working life, deregulate statist-corporatist economies, and cultivate the supply side of its economy." Although Europe needed fiscal austerity, Dornbusch warned that the pace at which it was being enforced would "stunt growth and raise unemployment." He concluded, "The costs of getting there [to a functioning single currency] are large, the economic benefits minimal, and the prospects for disappointment major." To make his prediction vivid, he added, Italy was the country most likely to be disappointed.[209]

This sense of unease had spread to European leaders. Belgian Prime Minister Jean-Luc Dehaene said that "nobody has anything to gain by monetary overkill; competitive disinflation would be as disruptive as competitive devaluation."[210] Giscard d'Estaing, echoing a widely held French sentiment, called for a more flexible interpretation of the fiscal austerity demanded by the Maastricht Treaty. Because France was in a recession, he said, tax revenues had fallen and the deficit had increased. This temporary "recession effect," Giscard d'Estaing said, would go away when the economy recovered. Imposing austerity on a weak economy only inflicted unnecessary pain.[211] For once, Giscard d'Estaing was right.

Some European leaders suggested that it was best to delay the single currency's introduction. Among them, Spanish Foreign Minister Carlos Westendorp said it would be best to "stop the clock" on the single-currency timetable.[212] German Finance Minister Theo Waigel was sympathetic to the idea: rushing to the euro, he felt, was less important than meeting the criteria to be part of the single-currency area.[213]

It was time for rallying cries. Mitterrand had recently died, so the task fell to Delors and Kohl. To a Brussels audience, Delors said that "the political end of European construction is forgotten . . . the single currency must be based on the 'will to live together,' on motivations of peace, solidarity and democracy."[214] Some days later, Kohl added that "the policy of European integration is a matter of war and peace in the 21st century." He understood, he said, that a European monetary union posed for many a huge psychological challenge. But, he asked, "Have Europeans once again become weary of European integration?"[215]

Economic realities kept intruding. French truckers went on strike in November. Even though the strike created huge disruption, the truckers enjoyed public sympathy. French unemployment had crossed the 12 percent mark, and the prospect of further budget cuts implied greater hardship. The government seemed helpless.[216] German authorities were also struggling. The unemployment rate was now more than 10 percent, and it was proving ever harder to rein in the budget deficit. In December, Edward Mortimer of the *Financial Times* wrote, "France and Germany, the two locomotives of European integration, are now grinding and sputtering up the last steep slope leading to European monetary union."[217]

That slope got steeper in 1997. On June 1, France's new prime minister, socialist leader Lionel Jospin, promised to halt austerity and announced that his government would disregard the 3 percent of GDP limit on the budget deficit. His spokesman, future French President François Hollande, said, "We are for Europe, but we want the passage to a single currency to respond to certain demands."[218] Those demands included more attention to reducing unemployment, a weaker exchange rate, and greater political control of the proposed monetary union. Meanwhile, in Germany, Waigel was having his own problems in bringing the German budget deficit below 3 percent of GDP. With Kohl's tacit support, Waigel tried to revalue gold held by the Bundesbank so that the additional value could bring the year's deficit below the 3 percent limit.[219] The ruse, however, did not work, because the Bundesbank insisted that the revaluation would not count for 1997, the assessment year for entry to the eurozone.[220]

Kohl's response to the criticism of the gold revaluation fiasco was typical, an escape into soaring rhetoric. He said to the Bundestag, "We need the joint European currency. It is the basic precondition for peace and freedom and for building the European House."[221] But Kohl's rhetoric was becoming anachronistic. In a *New York Times* op-ed piece on June 5, Tony Judt wrote:

> An ever-closer union, of the kind that seemed so admirable and necessary in 1957 when the Treaty of Rome was drawn up, may no longer be the best way to insure peace and stability in Europe. Melding the economies of countries as different as Austria and Britain, France and Portugal, Sweden and Greece (not to mention Poland or Hungary) is both impossible and unwise: Contrasting social and economic practices are born of longstanding political and cultural differences that cannot be obliterated with the wave of a magic monetary wand.[222]

The economic straitjackets to qualify for the euro club, Judt said, encouraged "budgetary sleight of hand," fostering a culture of "political dishonesty and bad faith." His conclusion was simple: "the move to a closer monetary union is actually driving Europeans further apart." Judt, a historian who described himself as "a public intellectual voice within the American Left," had arrived at the same criticism of the single-currency project as mainstream American economists.[223]

On June 16 and 17, 1997, European leaders met in Amsterdam. If the French were allowed to increase public spending to reduce unemployment, Waigel feared that Germany would end up having to pay even more for Europe's upkeep.[224] Hence, at Amsterdam, rather than give in to French calls for flexibility in the budget-deficit rule, the Germans insisted on renewed commitment to that rule. The French could have walked away at Amsterdam. Under a floating exchange rate, they would have had more time to bring their deficit under control. But it was too late. The French had come too far. They had pushed the single currency for more than a quarter century, since 1969. They could not now blow up the idea. Perhaps the French did not trust themselves to use fiscal policy wisely. They gave in, the Germans got their way, and together they found a compromise in words. The Germans readily agreed to the French request for a "face-saving device": instead of calling the budget rule and its procedures for enforcement the Stability Pact, the Germans agreed that, in recognition of the French demand for more emphasis on promoting economic growth, the governing rulebook would be called the Stability and Growth Pact (SGP).[225] Not one thing had changed to justify the change in name. Philip Stephens of the *Financial Times* aptly commented: "We are accustomed to Eurofudge, but rarely has it been so richly sweetened with cynicism."[226]

On his return home from Amsterdam, Kohl said in the Bundestag that a retreat now from monetary union would set back German exports, investment, and jobs, and it would hurt Europe's integration. "We would all," he asserted, "pay dearly for the failure of the euro." Kohl was "uncharacteristically defensive" as he tried to persuade skeptical members of the Bundestag that the Amsterdam leaders' summit had advanced European integration on many fronts. "The euro is coming," he said four times.[227]

Kohl had some unfinished tasks. German opinion polls showed a sharp fall in the number of those who saw the euro as "a good thing."[228] Most Germans preferred a delay in introducing the euro. But Kohl steadfastly refused to open up a public discussion, because, he explained, emotional attachment to the D-mark made a "rational discussion" impossible. Instead, he hoped that optimistic rhetoric would persuade the skeptics. The single currency, he emphasized, would move European integration forward and thus prepare Europe for "peace and freedom in the 21st century." He repeated this, by now, standard theme: "We have to take advantage of the historical chance we have with the introduction of the euro."[229]

There was, of course, one last hurdle. The French had agreed in Amsterdam to the rigors of the SGP; now they needed to meet the budget-deficit target. German conservatives insisted that there be no special treatment for France. Bavarian Prime Minister Edmund Stoiber, who, in principle, was Kohl's ally, led that charge.[230] Stoiber emphasized that the deficit limit was "3.0" percent of GDP, highlighting the zero after the decimal point to argue that France must be denied entry even if its deficit exceeded the limit by a narrow margin.[231]

Despite its quirky history and lack of economic logic, the deficit limit became the symbol of a "stable euro." Kohl rejected Stoiber's call for "controlled delay" in launching the euro and impatiently retorted, "The chemistry-scale weighting has gone too far."[232] In any event, France met the "3.0" percent criterion. A payment from French Telecom to the government helped bring down the deficit for that year, although in return, the government took on the company's pension obligations due in later years.[233] Similarly, the Germans sold shares of Deutsche Telecom and other assets. Such sales helped the budget only in the year of sale and did not close the budget hole more durably.

European leaders, having fallen into their own rhetorical trap on the single currency and, in a bid to rush to that goal, were now engaged in exactly the kind of fiscal fudges that the IMF normally frowns on. The IMF could—and should—have protested more insistently that Europe was embarking on an unwise venture. The IMF was the guardian of international exchange-rate systems and global financial stability. Yet, it failed in its task of counseling Europeans to step back from their single-currency venture (box 2.3).

With the IMF's stamp of approval, a new European "economic regime" was in place: fixed exchange rates, price stability, and fiscal austerity. There was no evidence that this combination could deliver on the promise of economic prosperity. The combination, however, did conform to the German, and now European, stability ideology.

To make matters more ominous, Germans would have a huge say in how the eurozone operated. German officials had invented the system and Germany's large economic size gave it disproportionate political influence. This was exactly the type of centralized and hegemonic regime that political scientist Robert Keohane had explained would not work.[234] Keohane had said that international agreements worked only when based on "reciprocal

BOX 2.3. The IMF Waves the Euro On

Having witnessed and overseen the dismantling of the Bretton Woods system in 1971, the IMF understood the fragilities of rigid exchange-rate arrangements. But in the three decades from the Hague Summit in December 1969 to the euro's launch in January 1999, the IMF chose to remain a conspicuous bystander.

Even at crucial junctures, the IMF was disengaged. In September 1992, as the ERM imploded, many European officials were in Washington for the annual World Bank-IMF meetings. James Boughton, the longtime IMF resident historian, reports that the Europeans kept the IMF's staff out of their deliberations, reflecting their "long-standing reluctance to seek the Fund's advice" (Boughton 2012, 121). In any case, Boughton points out that the IMF lacked a clearly articulated position on European monetary affairs.

On the euro, IMF staff was divided, but management insisted on supporting the European decisions. Successive European managing directors—who as ministers and civil servants had played an active role in the single-currency debates—steered the IMF clear of what they deemed an internal European matter. In March 1996, the IMF's executive board—representing the IMF's member governments—met to discuss the impending monetary union, and some directors did express doubts about its viability. Egypt's Shakour Shaalan asked if the single currency was "in Europe's best interests," and others, prominent among them Daniel Kaeser, the Swiss executive director, suggested that the start date be delayed.

Even directors from EU member countries were worried that the intense fiscal austerity to shrink budget deficits before the euro's target launch date of January 1, 1999, was pushing unemployment too high. However, the Americans did not object to European initiatives, and even the reluctant among the EU members were not going to air their differences at the IMF. Thus, the IMF's board placed its faith in the astonishing powers of the single currency and said that "no matter how difficult the process turned out to be, its successful conclusion was critically important for Europe, and for the rest of the world" (Boughton 2012, 122).

In March 1997, the IMF's managing director, Michel Camdessus, formerly governor of the Banque de France, said the euro would deliver a great economic bounty: "Certainly, Europe will reap a number of economic benefits from the introduction of a sound common currency. A common currency will lower transaction costs, reduce exchange risk, stimulate competition, and facilitate the broadening and deepening of European financial markets." There was little, if any, evidence to support such claims of euro-induced benefits. IMF scholars surely knew the contrary views of such scholars as Barry Eichengreen. Camdessus went on to say, "EMU is the crowning achievement of four decades of European economic integration." It was, he said, "above all, an essential building block in Europe's growing political unity" (International Monetary Fund 1997a, 102). The words were always the same: "essential," "crowning achievement." With those cheery words, and the Executive Board already having given the green signal, the IMF's management punted on the world's most consequential international monetary policy decision taken since the Bretton Woods conference in July 1944.

trust." In contrast, centralized rules backed by hegemony created distrust and resentment. Thus a politically corrosive system that created incentives for member states to cheat came into place.

Some Europeans continued to argue that Maastricht was an intermediate step, which would lead to greater political unity. In an early 1997 essay titled "The Case for EMU: More Than Money," Peter Sutherland, former European commissioner and director general of the World Trade Organization, spoke for many Europeans when he said that "the ultimate rationale of monetary union lies in its contribution to the larger political strategy of European integration. This is a profoundly political act."[235] Even more so to non-Europeans, who emphasized the economic flaws of the single currency, the project only made sense if it fulfilled a political ambition. Thus, in November 1997, with the single-currency project nearing its finish line, Harvard University's Martin Feldstein explained the euro as motivated by "deeply held political views about the appropriate future of Europe."[236]

Dogged external critics, however, refused to accept even the logic of political unity through the single currency. Among them, British economist Nicholas Kaldor had warned as early as March 1971 that the fiscal governance system would deepen political divisions.[237] In November 1997, Milton Friedman predicted that the euro's flawed economics would "exacerbate political tensions by converting divergent shocks that could have been readily accommodated by exchange rate changes into divisive political issues." The Europeans had it backward, Friedman concluded: "Political unity can pave the way for monetary unity. Monetary unity imposed under unfavorable circumstances will prove a barrier to the achievement of political unity."[238]

Kohl: "Not Without Italy, Please"

As one of the original six nations that had formed the European Coal and Steel Community in 1950, Italy was a founding member of postwar Europe. Italy at the time was experiencing an "economic miracle." As Europe evolved—through the Treaty of Rome—into the EEC, the Italian economic miracle continued to deliver its bounty. Italy's automobile and machinery industry gained global recognition, and Italians aspired to achieve economic parity with Germans. Italy seemed insulated from the plague of perennial inflation and loss of competitiveness, which was chewing away at France's national reputation and psyche.

However, even in those apparently successful years, a deeply dysfunctional system was taking root, as Guido Carli narrates in a vivid and unsparing chronicle. Carli was governor of the Italian central bank, Banca d'Italia, between 1960 and 1975, and as finance minister between 1989 and 1992, he was responsible for the Italian negotiating position at Maastricht. Italy's "tumultuous" growth in the 1950s and 1960s, Carli says, occurred within an increasingly corrupt political framework where legal norms were "violated with impunity."[239] Opportunities and temptation for corruption grew as the government, which had inherited extensive state-owned production activities from the earlier fascist regime, expanded its ownership and control of Italian infrastructure, industry, and banks. The virus spread wider as political leaders and bureaucrats installed an enervating system of "internal protection"—through financial aid, tax credits, and subsidies—to shield Italy's privately owned businesses from foreign competition.[240] As Carli put it, the "shell" of the capitalist system was maintained, but the "pillars of the market economy were hollowed."[241]

Italy's public corruption flourished under a special postwar political arrangement. By a domestic and international consensus, the Communists, who formed the main political opposition, could not be in a government. Thus, the Christian Democratic Party held a virtual monopoly on power, which it reinforced by sharing the dividends with the political opposition.[242] As historian Tony Judt has written, "In time, the clientelistic system of patronage and favors put in place by the Christian Democrats came to characterize national Italian politics as a whole."[243] Everyone in the country's small governing elite had an incentive to be corrupt, and no one was accountable. In a cynical twist, corruption and accompanying "internal protectionism" were given respectability by appeals to "catholic solidarity" and the Marxist ideology of egalitarianism.[244]

The Italian government was unable to mount an effective and sustained response to the challenges it faced in the late 1960s. The momentum of postwar reconstruction ran out. Italy's economic future suddenly looked bleaker, and labor unrest, terrorism, and the vast criminal economy created unbearable social tensions. The government chose the easy option and rapidly increased expenditures to appease warring constituencies. Part of this expansion was intended to increase economic opportunities and strengthen the public safety net in the lagging south (the *Mezzogiorno*); however, a much broader set of social transfers and a particularly generous pension system were put in place and soon became embedded in the country's fabric.[245]

The unbridled public expenditure led to higher inflation, which raised the costs of domestic production and compromised the ability of Italian businesses to compete internationally. Unable to deal with the country's fundamental problems, Italian authorities had no choice but to devalue the lira. Italy crashed out of the snake-in-the-tunnel fixed-exchange-rate system in February 1973, and Italian authorities let the lira float. As Italian inflation gathered pace, the value of the lira steadily depreciated, helping businesses claw back some of their lost competitiveness. However, in March 1979, Italian authorities chose to join the latest fixed-exchange-rate system, the ERM. But chronic inflation had taken root in Italy, and by the early 1980s, just when Kohl became German chancellor, repeated lira devaluations became the norm. In September 1992, Kohl and the Bundesbank watched the show as speculators forced Italy out of the ERM.

Italy clearly could not live with a fixed exchange rate. Through nearly three decades, from the early 1970s to the approaching launch of the euro in 1998, lira devaluation had been an essential crutch for Italy. In 1970, one D-mark bought 170 liras; in 1998, a D-mark could buy nearly 1,000 liras (figure 2.7).

Meanwhile, the nexus of political corruption and corporate subsidies became entrenched. Italian businesses seemed unable to wean themselves off subsidies. A 1990 study by the Paris-based Organisation for Economic Co-operation and Development (OECD) reported that the Italian government's industrial subsidy bill was 16 percent of manufacturing value-added, the highest among OECD economies, matched only by similarly generous Greek subsidies.[246] Corruption did decline somewhat in the 1990s, as popular demand for greater government accountability and judicial prosecution of corrupt politicians weakened the Christian Democratic Party's grip on power.

However, as economists Andrei Shleifer and Robert Vishny explain, once corruption is widespread, it is hard to roll back.[247] In Italy, political scientist

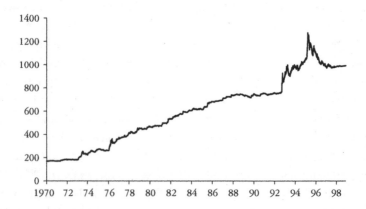

FIGURE 2.7. The depreciating lira.
(Number of liras for one D-mark)
Source: Banca d'Italia. https://tassidicambio.bancaditalia.it/timeSeries.

Sergio Fabbrini says, "the institutional structure shaped by half a century of cartel politics" proved "sticky."[248] There was little incentive to shine "light in dark corners," and the networks of political corruption kept reproducing and evolving.[249] Similarly, Judt writes, "In the 1950s, large-scale corruption was a near-monopoly of Christian Democrats; in later decades the Socialists who governed the great cities of the North emulated them with considerable success."[250] Through the 1990s, the international watchdog Transparency International ranked Italy the most corrupt Western market economy.[251]

Italians remained unable to establish a consensus for investing in their country's future. The different interest groups refused to concede their entitlements, hard decisions proved impossible, and the economic and political malaise continued. Italian educational achievements fell behind those of global competitors, research and development lagged, and productivity growth slumped. Italy's economic system was not sustainable in an increasingly competitive world. Thus, when ferocious Asian "tigers" burst onto global markets in the 1980s and Eastern European production sites opened up in the 1990s, Italian industry was completely unprepared and began to lose ground rapidly.

Through the past four decades, the expectation had been that the European Community would act as an external anchor, a constraint that would enforce discipline on its member nations. However, domestic Italian politics overwhelmed any external restraining influence. As Carli bluntly put it, in Italy, European strictures and appeals counted for virtually nothing.[252]

Yet despite the repeated failure of European institutions to instill discipline, many—including Carli—believed that the single currency and the broader legal framework of the Maastricht Treaty would finally restrain Italian authorities and thus create lasting economic benefit for Italian citizens. The premise was that since the Italians would no longer have the option of devaluing the lira, they would collectively act to modernize their economy.

At Maastricht, governments had promised to keep their debt and deficits within prescribed limits. The government's debt limit for prospective eurozone member states was set at 60 percent of GDP. However, since that limit would have kept too many countries out of the eurozone, the entry requirement was softened to allow those with declining debt-to-GDP ratios to also qualify.[253] Even so, it appeared unlikely that Italy would qualify. The Italian government's debt-to-GDP ratio was 120 percent; with productivity growth rate so low, the debt ratio would come down only slowly.

The bleak assessment of Italy's eurozone prospects changed suddenly and dramatically. In January 1998, James Blitz, writing for the *Financial Times*, captured the widely shared incredulity: "Pinch yourself. It now looks a pretty safe bet that Italy will be a founder member of Europe's economic and monetary union at the start of next year."[254]

The Italians had pressed their case. Prime Minister Romano Prodi emphasized the "extraordinary" progress achieved. In a frantic bid to adopt the euro, the government seemed to have brought its budget under better control. Italian authorities promised to continue the pace of deficit reduction and bring the debt-to-GDP ratio from 120 percent to the required 60 percent threshold by 2009. These promises renewed hopes among investors that Italy was turning the corner, and the lira strengthened.

Skeptics, however, questioned the government's numbers and the realism of the sudden "renaissance." One writer mockingly described the reported progress and promised pace of debt reduction as never seen before in the "history of global finance."[255] Critics projected that the debt ratio would remain above the Maastricht threshold until 2030.[256] In retrospect, the critics might have given the Italians too much credit; in 2017, the Italian debt ratio was more than 130 percent, with little likelihood that it would fall to 60 percent anytime soon.

Dutch authorities opposed Italian entry until the very end. Because of his strident tone, Italians accused Dutch Finance Minister Gerrit Zalm of "spaghettiphobia."[257] Prime Minister Wim Kok had to deny that the Dutch had threatened to stay out of the eurozone if Italy was granted entry.[258]

The most strenuous opposition to Italian entry came from Kohl's senior officials and well-wishers. Dispatches from the German embassy in Rome and assessments in Berlin all reached the same conclusion. It seemed as if every German other than Kohl wanted to keep Italy out. No German official took seriously the Italian authorities' claim that they had begun correcting their ways. Italy had gone down the wrong path for half a century; nobody believed that the history could be reversed by a few years of budget tightening. In mid-March, Horst Köhler wrote an unsolicited letter to Chancellor Kohl, warning him that Italy posed "a special risk" to the euro.

Disregarding all advice, Kohl pleaded the Italian case; he insisted that Italians would continue "structural reforms," enabling them to overcome their handicaps "in the coming years." Ultimately, his was not an economic but a political decision. Kohl felt the "weight of history," his adviser Joachim Bitterlich has recorded. "Not without the Italians, please. That was the political motto."[259] Kohl made that decision, virtually single-handedly, on behalf of all Europeans.

Kohl had one last task to complete. On April 23, 1998, the Bundestag ratified Germany's adoption of the single currency. In his speech that day, Kohl assured parliamentarians that the European leaders had continued to reinforce the fiscal rules first agreed to at Maastricht. They had promised to honor these rules to ensure the "stability" of the monetary union. Since those "stability" rules were firmly in place, Kohl said he could pledge that monetary union would create no added financial burden on Germans. "Ladies and Gentlemen," Kohl solemnly said, "according to the treaty rules, the community shall not be liable for the commitments of the member states and there are no additional financial transfers." For emphasis, he repeated those words, "According to the treaty rules, the community shall not be liable for the commitments of the member states and there are no additional financial transfers."[260] One more time, Kohl reminded them that they were voting for peace.[261]

On May 2, at a meeting in Brussels, European leaders waived Italy in, and the eurozone had its first eleven members: Austria, Belgium, Finland, France, Germany, Ireland, Italy, Luxembourg, the Netherlands, Portugal, and Spain.

An Era Ends, but a Legacy Lives On

At Brussels that day, the real drama came after the quick decisions on membership of the first euro club. For the next twelve hours, the leaders fought bitterly over who would be the ECB's president. Wim Duisenberg, the governor of the Dutch Central Bank, was widely presumed to have that job. But Jacques Chirac, Mitterrand's successor as French president since May 1995, had other ideas. In November 1997, Chirac announced that he wanted Jean-Claude Trichet, by now governor of the Banque de France, to be the ECB's first president.[262] Despite outrage expressed by Dutch Prime Minister Kok and unencumbered by a personal relationship with Kohl, Chirac continued to press his claim.

Kohl was livid. The Brussels summit was to be his crowning party. But Chirac was blocking his nominee for the position of ECB president. The loss of face in the German public's eyes could prove costly in the elections due in September. Former Swedish Prime Minister Göran Persson later recalled Kohl was so upset that he referred to himself as a monkey, the butt of everyone's ridicule.[263] In his rage, he ate a dozen cubes of butter—and when a new bunch arrived, he ate those too before he started to calm down.

Ultimately, British Prime Minister Tony Blair, whose country was not even going to be in the euro area, brokered the agreement on the leadership of the ECB because Britain held the Presidency of the EU for that six-month period and, as a result, he was chairing the meeting. The compromise was that

Duisenberg would be the first president but would "voluntarily" relinquish his position before his term was complete. Kohl's historical role was over. He stayed on the sidelines, calling for a "wise compromise." As Lionel Barber of the *Financial Times* concluded, "Chirac had pressed the French cause with scant attention to the re-election interests of a hard-pressed Helmut Kohl, nominally his closest ally and the man who has made a career of subjugating German national interests in the name of Europe."[264]

Marginalized on the European scene, Kohl was defeated in the 1998 German elections. He had been chancellor for sixteen years. His popularity, which had been falling since the highs reached in 1990, had plummeted in recent years. As he exited, he risked being "booed off stage."[265] He later wrote in his memoirs that backing the euro cost him his chancellorship; the German public felt let down by his decision to give up the D-mark.[266]

In November 1999, allegations surfaced that Kohl's CDU had received covert cash payments for years, including allegedly from Mitterrand's slush funds.[267] Kohl acknowledged that between 1993 and 1998, he received around 2 million D-marks in contributions for his party, but he refused to reveal the source of the funds.[268] Thus, during the very years when Kohl had most intensely promoted the single currency on the wings of high-minded rhetoric of European peace, it now appeared that he had indulged in petty illegal activity.

On December 21, 1999, a relatively unknown CDU functionary named Angela Merkel—until recently a minister in Kohl's cabinet and a protégé of his—wrote an op-ed for the *Frankfurter Allgemeine Zeitung*. She stated that Kohl had "damaged the party."[269] With clinical words, she brought the Kohl era to an end: "The Party must learn to walk now and dare to engage in future battles with its political opponents without its old warhorse, as Kohl has often enjoyed calling himself. We, who now have responsibility for the Party, and not so much Helmut Kohl, will decide how to approach the new era."[270]

Kohl might not be guilty in eyes of the law, Merkel said, but he had no place in the CDU community. "The party has a soul," she emphatically concluded. Referring to Merkel's rebellion, the cover story of the *Frankfurter Allgemeine Zeitung* that day carried the title "The Days of Helmut Kohl Are Irretrievably Over."

Kohl had been booted off the European stage, and the party he had led for sixteen years had ostracized him. The Kohl era surely was over.

But his legacy lived on. Kohl had taken Europe to a point of no return. As poet Robert Frost wrote, "Yet knowing how way leads on to way, I doubted if I should ever come back." Just as surely as Merkel had dismantled the Kohl era, she would inherit his legacy and grapple with it for years.

We have Kohl's word that he was pro-European, and we have his gift: the euro. Kohl might well have believed that a single currency used by all Europeans was essential to securing peace. However, in pursuing that vision, he—hesitantly at the start but decisively in the end—overrode economic and political good sense. He refused to hear his critics, whether they were senior German officials or respected international economists. He rejected the wisdom of public opinion. Kohl created the stability ideology that masked the destabilizing nature of the eurozone's policies and institutional structure. He gave the eurozone Italy. Perhaps, above all, he legitimized the use of rhetoric and groupthink as a substitute for real economic and political analysis. Even if grudgingly or unwittingly at first, a generation of European "elites" joined and then carried on Kohl's chorus of unthinking idealism, while all-too-real tensions tugged at Europe's delicate fabric.

| Schröder Asserts the German
National Interest, 1999–2003

E VEN AS EUROPEAN nations moved to launch the euro, Gerhard Schröder, leader of Germany's Social Democratic Party, proposed that they pause. In March 1998, campaigning to replace Helmut Kohl as chancellor, Schröder rightly observed that some countries would struggle to survive the rigors of the monetary union.[1] It would be better, he said, to delay the euro's birth rather than start with members that had not achieved the required fiscal discipline. The single currency, Schröder said, would be a "sickly premature baby."[2]

Europe's peace parenthesis had closed. Now more than half a century after the war, Germans were ready to put the terrible memories behind them. Schröder, who had no personal experience of the war, represented the inevitable generational change. When he was born in April 1944, his father, Fritz Schröder, a 32-year-old Wehrmacht lance corporal, was on the Balkan battlefront. Upon learning of his son's birth, the young father wrote to his wife, Erika, saying he would visit them soon. Fritz Schröder never did come home. He died six months later, in October 1944, as the Soviet army overwhelmed German soldiers in Romania's Transylvania region. The son, Gerhard, kept on his desk a black-and-white photograph of his father wearing a military uniform and Wehrmacht helmet. Thus, while the photograph was a daily reminder of the father he had never known, Gerhard Schröder was connected to recent German history by a weaker link than the firsthand experiences and extensive ties that weighed on his postwar predecessors.

Indeed, not just the generation but also the political mood in Germany was changing. As Roger Cohen of the *New York Times* wrote in the final phase of the election campaign, "Now, whether under Mr. Schröder, or under Mr.

Kohl, or, indeed, some other chancellor, the country clearly feels it has the right and might to make its voice heard, and to do so without any complexes."[3] Even Kohl, the self-proclaimed pro-European, had understood the limits of Germany's appetite for Europe. In his campaign for an unprecedented fifth term as chancellor, he had dialed down his customary European rhetoric. He had shifted his emphasis: "We do not want a European superstate. We want a strong Germany in Europe."[4]

Schröder was elected chancellor in October 1998. His hands were tied. Earlier in the year, in April, the Bundestag had authorized Germany's shift from the D-mark to the euro. Germany had made commitments to its European partners, and preparation for launch of the euro was in full swing. The German public—overwhelmingly opposed to the euro until 1997—was also ready to move on. In opinion polls, the euro ranked eighteenth on the list of people's fears; Germans had turned their worries to the destruction of Amazonian rainforests and the loss of jobs to Eastern Europeans.[5] Even if Schröder had really believed that it was right to delay the euro, he was now no longer in a position to stop the process. Investment plans and financial contracts anticipating the euro were in place. Exchange rates among currencies of prospective eurozone members were to disappear into a single currency on January 1, 1999. Any hint of delay would have raised the possibility that this might never happen. Exchange rates would have gyrated wildly, causing incalculable financial disruption. His bravado fizzled, and Schröder stoically declared, "We must make the euro a success."[6]

A British cynic, concerned that his government may soon adopt the euro, did wonder if trouble lay ahead. He predicted that European authority would reach much deeper into member nations, but it would do little to relieve Europe's real problem: unemployment:

The euro will soon be deployed,
A madness we just can't avoid.
It's part of our fate:
Join a great Federal state
And the ranks of the mass unemployed.[7]

But for most Europeans, the inevitability of the euro had sunk in. The political fever had ebbed. The French, having almost voted to stay out of the single currency, displayed little sentiment at the loss of their franc.[8] In Ireland, there was no "late outbreak of nostalgia for the Irish punt."[9] In Portugal, a representative of a consumers association said: "We Portuguese are an easy-going nation, and we will get used to the euro like we get used to everything else."[10]

The euro was born uneventfully on January 1, 1999.[11] The technical anxiety continued for a few more days. But bank balances and securities portfolios had been converted from national currencies to the euro, and the market and settlement infrastructure was in place.[12] The euro traded for the first time on Australian financial platforms. On Monday, January 4, at 5:00 a.m. Sydney time, the euro was valued at US$1.175.[13] Later that day, when the markets opened in Europe, the euro had become pricier and bought $1.1855.[14] And when the German stock exchange rang its opening bell that morning, the screens displayed share prices in euros.[15] It was a flawless debut.

Euro-area leaders celebrated and promised a brighter future. French Finance Minister Dominique Strauss-Kahn declared that euro-area member states were ready to work together to spur growth and reduce unemployment. "When everybody pushes in the same direction," he said, "everybody goes quicker."[16] Schröder chimed in: "I know the importance of this currency. I know that it will make Europe move forward."[17]

Schröder kept up the narrative of Europe's eventual political awakening. In January 1999, soon after he became chancellor, he even called for greater European "political union." He was following in Kohl's steps, who had given this phrase a European gravitas.[18] Kohl had used "political union" mainly as a slogan, while always undermining that lofty goal by insisting that the German government's tax receipts would not, in any significant way, be shared with other European nations. Schröder continued to pitch this much-abused phrase. In his usage, "political union" was a fuzzy label for his vague proposal to harmonize indirect taxes and coordinate direct taxes.[19] Like Kohl, he cynically exploited the latitude in the European discourse to claim pro-European credentials without needing to take any meaningful steps.

Alongside the obligatory European rhetoric, Schröder had to deal with domestic economic problems that were set to clash with the eurozone's recently enshrined operational principles and rules. Germany was still dealing with the aftermath of its historic unification in 1990. The government-financed construction boom in East Germany in 1991 and 1992 had caused the budget deficit to rise to about 3 percent of GDP and had pushed inflation briefly above an annual rate of 4 percent. These numbers were worrisome, but German authorities overreacted. With greater zeal than necessary, the government raised taxes to reduce the deficit. The Bundesbank raised its interest rate. Even the IMF criticized the Bundesbank for keeping monetary policy tight for too long. High taxes and interest rates did bring down the budget deficit and inflation, but, predictably, German economic growth also slowed.

The Eurozone Confronts an Economic Growth Problem

Slow growth was a more widespread eurozone problem, as became quickly evident in the value of the euro. When financial markets believe that a country is likely to grow slowly, they also expect that the monetary authorities of that country will keep interest rates low to stimulate domestic consumption and investment. The lower interest rates make it less attractive for foreigners to make financial investments in that country, and the value of its currency declines. The eurozone was not one country, but it had one monetary policy. Slow eurozone growth created expectations of lower financial returns and a weaker euro.

The exchange value of the euro started falling quickly after its dream opening. By early March 1999, a euro bought only $1.09, down from the $1.18 at the opening. Foreign exchange traders sold the euro expecting that the European Central Bank (ECB) would reduce interest rates to match the eurozone's weaker growth prospects. In addition, European companies made the judgment that buying American companies and thus buying into the exciting American story was a better value than investing at home.[20] Capital flowed from Europe to America, in the process causing the euro to depreciate vis-à-vis the dollar.

The United States was experiencing an economic renaissance. Central to this renaissance was a sustained rise in productivity growth since around 1995. Productivity—output per worker or the more inclusive "total factor productivity," which measures output produced by a bundle of capital and labor inputs—was rising quickly. High-tech sectors—computer hardware and software, pharmaceuticals, and biotech—were booming, and the stock market was buoyant. In contrast, European productivity was growing slowly, well below the pace in the United States.[21]

This US-Europe productivity growth difference reflected the fact that although both had been in the economic doldrums for much of the 1970s and 1980s, the American economy had reinvented itself and the European economy had not. The new "American dominance," Northwestern University economist Robert Gordon wrote, arose in large part from "the fruitful collaboration of government research funding, world-leading private universities, innovative private firms, and a dynamic capital market."[22] Europe had nothing comparable to offer.

The new European Central Bank, in its inaugural *Monthly Bulletin* in January 1999, highlighted serious impediments to growth in the eurozone and began what would be a ritualistic call on national governments to undertake "necessary structural reforms to increase the flexibility and efficiency of markets."[23]

In March 1999, the IMF completed the first of its planned twice-a-year assessments of the eurozone economy. It began with the mandatory official applause: the launch of the euro was "a defining event in the history of modern Europe" and "an unparalleled example of economic and political cooperation."[24] However, the IMF emphasized that the lack of an internal growth dynamic in the eurozone was "likely to impede the effective operation of the monetary union."[25] The eurozone's economic performance had been "lackluster" because of "deep structural rigidities" in public finances and labor markets. Because of these rigidities, economies of the member nations would not easily respond to monetary policy measures. In carefully crafted bureaucratic language, the report said that "early fulfillment" of the eurozone's promise of "greater economic stability and enhanced economic performance" was "uncertain."

Besides their general lack of growth momentum, all eurozone member economies—all heavily dependent for their economic good health on international trade—faced an immediate problem. In 1998, world trade suddenly slowed to 4.5 percent, abruptly down from an average of 9 percent a year in the previous four years. The slowdown was triggered by financial crises in a number of emerging markets. Starting in Thailand in mid-1997, the crises spread and engulfed, among other countries, South Korea and Indonesia. The Japanese economy, highly interdependent with the emerging Asian economies, went into recession. These Asian economies had, in recent years, become the most dynamic nodes of world trade, importing substantial amounts of inputs from the rest of the world, processing these inputs, and exporting products such as engineering goods, consumer and industrial electronics products, and clothing into the world economy. With the emerging Asian economies in crisis and Japan in a recession, crucial nodes in world trade were malfunctioning.

Slower world trade had a limited impact on the US economy, which marches to its own rhythm and is generally able to withstand economic weakness elsewhere in the world. But the force of the world trade slowdown was felt in Europe, especially in Germany. The German economy is geared to respond quickly to world demand for its superbly engineered and high-quality products. As the global demand for those goods fell, German exports stuttered in late 1998, German GDP contracted in the final quarter of 1998, and "economic activity remained sluggish in the first half of 1999."[26] GDP growth fell also in other countries of the euro area as their exports also suffered. And a weaker German economy added to European woes, since German imports from the rest of Europe stalled.[27]

The Schröder government responded to the fall in German GDP by mounting a concerted attack on the ECB. The attack began in late 1998, when the ECB was not even in full command of monetary policy. Schröder and his finance minister, Oskar Lafontaine, began "badgering it almost daily to open up the monetary spigots and generate more jobs." Schröder described German growth as too "damn little" to mount "a big offensive" on Germany's high unemployment level. The ECB, he said, had responsibility not just "for monetary stability but also for economic growth in a sensible way." German officials also complained about the ECB's secretive decision-making process, which they said was "pre-democratic."[28] This full-scale assault on the central bank was not very German. Schröder was contesting a principle that Kohl had fought for: an ECB that was focused on maintaining price stability and doing so without any political interference.

Germany's struggles were only just beginning. On March 11, Lafontaine resigned. Because he had tried to browbeat the ECB into lowering its policy interest rate, the press described him as the "first big political victim of the single currency."[29] Lafontaine's exit, however, had more to do with domestic politics. His effort to raise corporate taxes had caused him to fall afoul of struggling German business. His successor, Hans Eichel, was expected to be more conservative in his views and realistic in his goals.

Economic prospects briefly improved. The global economy and world trade strengthened, because the emerging market crises eased more quickly than expected and the US economy continued to power along.[30] And the euro's depreciation made euro-area exports cheaper for foreigners.[31] However, not impressed by this recovery, the IMF insisted in its August 1999 review that the euro area's medium-term growth potential remained "sluggish" and that "structural reform efforts fell far short of what was needed to lay the foundation for a vigorous sustained economic expansion."[32]

European leaders needed to create and sustain domestically generated growth momentum that would be commensurate with the aspirations of their people. The ECB believed that the euro area's large economic size would allow the creation of a vibrant domestic economy that did not just bob up and down with world trade.[33] At least for now, though, the euro area remained very much at the mercy of the global economy's fortunes.

On August 23, the German chancellor's official residence returned to Berlin from Bonn.[34] This was perhaps the last symbol of the German unification process, which had begun almost a decade earlier. There was also better short-term economic news toward the end of the year. But German and eurozone prospects remained worrying, and pessimistic traders continued to push the euro lower. By the end of December, the euro bought around one US dollar, nearly a 15 percent decline in value since its launch in January.

The euro had grown from a premature baby to a year-old infant. A moderate storm had buffeted the eurozone economy. Amid that economic storm, the Germans had quickly asserted their national interest by seeking aggressively to steer ECB policy in a direction favorable to Germany. Although the ECB remained unmoved, the message was clear. When euro-area rules and priorities conflicted with the German interest, European institutions could expect a fight.

A new European stage was set. On it were national actors with different economic and political strengths and moving to different rhythms. The euro, which tied them together, created economic conflicts and political tensions. These conflicts and tensions—foretold by critics and by Europe's experiments with monetary unity in the past decades—had surfaced quickly after the euro's introduction. The question was whether European leaders would have the wisdom—and the stature—to counteract these divisive tendencies.

Greece Is Invited

Adding to this fractious mix, Greece was on the verge of entering the eurozone. Greece's journey to Euroland was an improbable one. It began in July 1974, when the military junta collapsed after a brief but disastrous war with Turkey over control of the island nation of Cyprus. As prime minister of a new regime seeking to reestablish democracy, Konstantinos Karamanlis urgently renewed a long-standing Greek effort to join the EEC. Karamanlis held the view, shared by many, that Greeks were not fully ready to govern themselves in a prudent manner. He and others believed that European rules would act as "an external anchor," which would ensure Greece's economic stability and protect its democracy.[35]

On June 12, 1975, Greece applied to join the EEC. Seven months later, on January 29, 1976, the European Commission sent a memorandum to the European Council expressing several concerns. In particular, Greek industry was weak and would not be able to withstand the competition when Greece, in accordance with European rules, dismantled its system of subsidies and opened its borders to allow more trade.[36] Greece was welcome, the commission said, but needed "a considerable amount of joint preparatory work."[37] Since the commission was unwilling even to set a timetable for entry, some commentators inferred that Greece could join no earlier than 1984.[38] The Karamanlis government, however, reacted angrily and lobbied hard.

On February 9, 1976, less than two weeks after receiving the European Commission's memorandum, which had advised against rushing Greek EEC membership, European heads of state snubbed the commission and called for negotiations to "take place as soon as possible in a positive spirit."[39] French President Giscard d'Estaing personally intervened to keep the process on track.[40] Some speculate that Giscard d'Estaing and other European leaders wanted to protect the fledgling Greek democracy.[41] But that could not be the whole story. France, in particular, would later "put up strong opposition" to entry by two other new democracies, Portugal and Spain.[42] In those instances, French authorities gave lower priority to nurturing democracy than to protecting French farmers from highly competitive Portuguese and Spanish farm products. Greece, however, was a small and poor country, and its farmers were no threat. Thus, Greece sailed in, at least in part, because Greek entry into the EEC was an easy victory for European enlargement.

On May 29, 1979, Greece signed the Treaty of Accession with the EEC at a ceremony held "in the marble Zappeion hall in the shadow of the 2,500-year-old Acropolis." Karamanlis told the European dignitaries present, "She [Greece] joins you in the struggle for the creation of a new Europe which will change the destiny of our continent and, perhaps, of the world." Those words would acquire tragic meaning, which Karamanlis could not possibly foresee. Giscard d'Estaing, who signed the treaty on behalf of the EEC, also failed to recognize how much was about to change. Opposition leader Andreas Papandreou and other members of his party, the Panhellenic Socialist Movement (PASOK), boycotted the accession ceremony. They said that Greece would be "subjugating itself to monopolies and cartels" in other EEC countries.[43]

On January 1, 1981, Greece was ushered into the EEC, and in October, Papandreou, who had led the opposition, became Greek prime minister. Public finances deteriorated quickly, as did external finances.[44] As the commission had anticipated, the Greek economy handled external pressure poorly. The IMF reported that as customs duties were lowered, imports increased "substantially."[45] Many businesses proved unequal to meet the increasing global competition and moved into the "informal" sector, where they could avoid paying their taxes.[46]

In eight years, from 1981 to 1989, Papandreou—and a compliant Europe—oversaw the evolution of deep-seated political and economic pathologies in Greece. Even as the government's revenue base declined, the Papandreou administration went on a spending spree, establishing a vast network of entitlements, including generous pensions. But perhaps the most corrosive legacy of the period was the unbounded expansion of employment in the government and in enterprises run by the public sector. Altogether, government expenditures rose, the quality of public employees fell, and patronage and corruption became endemic.[47] Between 1980 and 1990, the Greek government's expenditures increased from 21 to 40 percent of GDP, and its debt grew from 25 to 70 percent of GDP.[48]

Instead of acting as an anchor, Europe, in effect, licensed irresponsible behavior. Ongoing European financial assistance to Greece, which amounted to between 3 and 5 percent of Greek GDP in the 1980s, abetted unbridled growth of the Greek public sector. Such was Greece's appetite for funds that in December 1985, Greece also borrowed 1.75 billion European currency units (ECUs) (around $1.5 billion, 5 percent of GDP) from the EEC. The government disregarded the conditions for reform that accompanied the loan. European authorities just made it easier for the Greek government to go on a spending splurge, which fed Greece's corruption machine.

In June 1989, Papandreou's PASOK lost its majority in the parliament. After repeated elections, a government finally formed in April 1990 under the center-right New Democracy Party leader Konstantinos Mitsotakis. The challenge for the incoming government was daunting. In its annual survey of the Greek economy that year, the IMF dryly stated: "Greece's economic performance in the 1980s compared unfavorably with that of its EC partners and with its own earlier experience." Output growth was low, inflation was high, and current account deficits had widened. Overall government debt and debt owed to foreigners had risen to levels that created "a serious burden on the economy."[49]

However, breaking with the past proved impossible. Papandreou-style populism inevitably carried on; the networks of entitlement were so entrenched that it was easier for the New Democracy government to align itself with and participate in those networks rather than try to buck them.[50] Greece was in a high-corruption, low-productivity trap. Economists Kevin Murphy, Andrei Shleifer, and Robert Vishny explain that once the extent of corruption exceeds a threshold, the incentives and institutions to counteract corruption weaken.[51] While corruption offers easy rewards, the expected returns from risky long-term investments stay low because corrupt officials might expropriate hard-earned gains. Productive activity suffers, incentives for corruption remain high, and collective action for the greater good of all seems a quaint and idealistic notion.

By early 1991, the Mitsotakis government was discussing another loan from the EEC. On this occasion, the European authorities made a fuss. In March 1991, they did extend a loan of 2.2 billion ECU (just less than $3 billion), but they threatened dire consequences if Greek authorities failed to behave. Once again, however, Greece did not live up to the terms of its loans. Although Mitsotakis had promised a "meritocratic" system to appoint senior public officials, he was soon under pressure from party members to "share in the spoils," and the plum jobs went to "the party faithful."[52] In a blunt statement, the governor of the Greek Central Bank, Demetrios Chalikias, said, "I am pessimistic about the Greek economy. . . . Nothing works correctly in the state mechanism."[53] European creditors disbursed only the first tranche of the loan.[54] The economic imbalances continued to mount.

In 1996, Konstantinos Simitis of PASOK became prime minister. His government incongruously began an effort to adopt the prospective single European currency. The effort led to some improvement in macroeconomic indicators, but in May 1998, European leaders sensibly excluded Greece from the first batch of euro entrants.

However, European leaders' realism on Greece lasted all too briefly. By early 1999, the word was that Greece's fiscal deficit was "under control," and although the debt-to-GDP ratio was at a high 90 percent of GDP, the defense offered was that it was falling and was less than that of Italy and Belgium.[55] One last technical hurdle remained. Greece's inflation rate was too high to justify entry into the eurozone. But Dutch Finance Minister Gerrit Zalm, who had heroically—even if briefly—stood in the way of Italy's eurozone membership, assured his Greek counterpart that the inflation criterion for entry "could be interpreted in some circumstances."[56] Technical rules could always be "interpreted," if politicians were willing to do so.

In October 1999, Schröder visited Athens to discuss Turkey's accession to the EU. He used that occasion to express his "huge respect" for the Greek government's achievements and especially noted the "progress" in fulfilling the criteria for admission to the euro area. The German daily *Frankfurter Allgemeine Zeitung* reported that Schröder "promised Germany's absolute support for Greece's entry to the eurozone."[57] In November, Greece was taken off the list of "excessive deficit" offenders, and Zalm commented: "Their progress has been fantastic over the last few years. I give them my compliments."[58] In December, when ECB President Duisenberg was asked if Greece would soon be a euro-area member, he replied, "That could be. Greece has made remarkable progress over the past three or four years towards meeting the convergence criteria [for joining monetary union]."[59] In mid-January 2000, a spokesman for the German Ministry of Finance said Greece should join the euro "as soon as possible."[60] Greece had not even formally applied to join the eurozone, but all the heavy hitters had spoken. The deal was done.

Just as Giscard d'Estaing had helped usher Greece into the EEC, Schröder had now given the green light for Greece to join the eurozone. For Schröder, the decision seemed economically and financially inconsequential. After all, Greece would form only 2 percent of the euro-area economy; its ups and downs would be barely noticeable in euro-area averages; Greece would have no bearing on euro-zone institutions and policies. Giscard d'Estaing in 1976 and Schröder in 1999 both acted to strengthen their European standing. An expanding Europe was an essential feature of pro-Europeanism.

On March 9, 2000, Greece applied for eurozone membership. This time, the European Commission did not make a fuss. In early May, the commission said Greece was ready. The commission's economics and monetary affairs chief, Pedro Solbes, reported that Greece had achieved a "high degree of sustainable convergence."[61] In early June, the eurozone's finance ministers gave Greece the green light.[62] On June 19–20, the European Council of national leaders completed the formality at their summit at Santa Maria da Feira, Portugal. The statement read: "The European Council congratulates Greece on the convergence achieved over recent years, based on sound economic and financial policies, and welcomes the decision that Greece will join the Euro area on 1 January 2001 which constitutes an additional positive step in the monetary integration of the Union."[63] As the day approached, Duisenberg celebrated Greece's entry into the eurozone: "It is indeed an historic and a very satisfying and gratifying moment. It shows the extent to which entry into monetary union can act as catalyst for more sound public finances, low inflation and appropriate monetary policies."[64]

To be sure, there were dissenting voices along the way. Duisenberg's deputy, ECB Vice President Christian Noyer, had expressed concern that Greece's low reported inflation rate was deceptive; the reduction in value-added tax rates had temporarily brought inflation down. Moreover, as Greek interest rates fell closer to euro-area rates, inflation would rise.[65] In Germany, an influential critic was Bavaria's Prime Minister Edmund Stoiber, who later led the conservative challenge against Chancellor Schröder in the 2002 elections.[66] Citing Noyer's misgivings, Stoiber insisted that Greek accession to the euro would send "the wrong signal."[67] Hans-Olaf Henkel, president of the BDI, said what was on many minds: although Greece had made a big effort, it would be a "herculean task" to sustain that discipline.[68]

Sustaining Greek performance was also a worry within Greece. Finance Minister Yannos Papantoniou acknowledged, "Greece has a strong tradition of protecting different sectors of the economy against new entrants. . . . Vested interests are skilled at putting obstacles in the path of outside investors." Any change, he said, would be slow.[69] As the date of Greek euro entry approached, the Association of Greek Industries and a Greek think tank warned that the government's privatization program had stalled, the reform momentum was fizzling, and business conditions were deteriorating.[70] None of this was a surprise to European and Greek scholar Kevin Featherstone, who described Greece as a "foot-dragger" on structural reforms.[71]

The dissenting voices were marginal and easily dismissed; in contrast, the pressure to join the eurozone groupthink was great. Inclusion of Greece in the euro area was part of the onward march of Europe; opposing it carried the risk of being labeled euro-skeptic. In Germany, the two top leaders of the Christian Democrats did not object. Angela Merkel, recently appointed chairman of the party, maintained a studied silence on Greece. Even Wolfgang Schäuble, who had advocated in 1994 that only an inner core of member states should move ahead toward monetary union, stayed quiet.

A December 2004 audit of Greek fiscal accounts revealed that Greece's fiscal deficit around the time of the euro entry decision was, in fact, significantly higher than reported and, as such, was well above the limit to qualify for entry. Günther Hanreich, head of Eurostat, the European statistical agency, wrote in the *Financial Times*: "there was a clear under-reporting by the Greek authorities of military expenditure irrespective of the accounting method used, an over-reporting of revenues from social security and an incorrect treatment of a significant amount of capitalised interest on government bonds." Moreover, "in spite of the repeated concerns publicly expressed by Eurostat, the information provided by the Greek authorities did not allow Eurostat to arrive at correct deficit figures for Greece."[72]

Put simply, Greece had never met the entry criteria. Joaquín Almunia, the European economic and monetary affairs commissioner, said that Greece's euro entry decision relied on the "best available evidence" at the time.[73] But he acknowledged: "We had a very sad experience in the case of Greece."[74]

Denmark Stays Out, and All Nations Assert Their Sovereignty

In a June 1992 referendum, Danish citizens had refused to ratify the Maastricht Treaty and so had voted to stay out of the euro area.[75] That vote had surprised European authorities, and its symbolism had caused anxiety in financial markets. That anxiety contributed to the breakdown of the ERM, the arrangement under which several European economies fixed their exchange rates with one another. Denmark received assurances that it would have no legal obligation to join the eurozone. On that basis, Danes voted again and ratified their diluted participation in the EU.[76]

In March 2000, Danish Prime Minister Poul Nyrup Rasmussen pressed the country's citizens for their authorization to join the eurozone. The political establishment, business interests, and the media actively supported Rasmussen.[77] The supporters promised a yes vote would deliver a bounty of riches. On September 28, the Danish public voted no again, this time with a bigger margin than in 1992. Rasmussen, who had worked tirelessly to make his case, was in tears as he conceded "defeat."[78]

The euro-area finance ministers—recently come together as the Eurogroup—expressed their regret in an unusual midnight communiqué. They declared that, with or without Denmark, the monetary union was a "great project for European integration which will ensure sound and job-intensive growth."[79] When the Eurogroup assembled the next day, ECB President Duisenberg, who also attended those meetings, took a shot at the Danes. "The Danish people," Duisenberg said, "have chosen to deprive themselves of benefits in the form of an increase in the rate of growth and the welfare of the economy that would have otherwise taken place and that is already taking place within the euro area."[80] Charitably, Duisenberg's claim was unproven. In fact, it was a false assertion. Duisenberg showed utter contempt for both economics and the democratic process. In his world, the Greeks were smart, the Danes were fools.

The Danish vote against the euro came despite the knowledge that the central bank would continue to tie the Danish krone to the euro, just as it had historically tied the krone to the D-mark.[81] From an economic standpoint, Denmark would be in the eurozone. Their vote against the euro was a political statement. The Danish people were unwilling to accept an intrusive European "super state" in their lives. Echoing a widely held interpretation of the result, Geoff Winestock and Marc Champion of the *Wall Street Journal* wrote that the "referendum reflected voters' deep distrust of efforts to transfer more power from national capitals to the EU headquarters in Brussels."[82]

The division between euro ins and outs, which had been quietly brewing, now became more evident. The Danish vote made it less likely that either Sweden or the United Kingdom would join the eurozone. In Sweden, the opinion polls had been drifting toward a no vote in an anticipated Swedish referendum.[83] The Danish vote strengthened that trend.[84] In the United Kingdom, Prime Minister Tony Blair insisted that nothing had changed, but his plan of holding a referendum was now even less credible, since the sentiment toward the euro in Britain was much more negative than that in either Denmark or Sweden. As one commentator remarked, "Denmark on paper does not matter, but psychologically it matters a lot."[85] The nation-state was asserting itself.

Against this background, European leaders met at Nice between December 7 and 10, 2000, to take stock of the challenges of governing an expanding Europe. It was yet another moment of high political rhetoric. German Foreign Minister Joschka Fischer recognized that the Danish referendum highlighted the political rather than economic weakness of the eurozone. His solution: the EU must "act and reform itself."[86] Fischer had recently proposed a plan for a "federal" Europe. Another idea was French President Chirac's proposal for "enhanced cooperation" among some European countries to show the way ahead to a deeper union. There had been many such proposals over the years. In 1994, Wolfgang Schäuble and Karl Lamers, both leaders of Germany's Christian Democratic Union, had proposed a "hard core" Europe (see chapter 2). The ideas kept repeating themselves in new words.

Behind these perennial feel-good plans for federation and cooperation lay a more hardnosed reality. Each member state wanted to have a greater say in the functioning of the EU. At the Nice summit, leaders focused their attention on power-sharing arrangements in Europe, a matter that had acquired greater urgency with a number of Eastern European countries expected to join the EU over the coming years. The summit predictably turned into a contentious fight for influence in running the EU. As Lionel Barber of the *Financial Times* wrote: "Nice is about the distribution of power in an enlarged Union. No one wants to lose ground before the entry of poorer newcomers over the next five to 10 years." The debates centered around the number of members who would represent a country in the European Parliament and the number of commissioners from each country in the European Commission.

But the most important source of contention was the distribution of voting rights in the council of ministers, where the key decisions were made. Voting rights, Barber wrote, "go to the heart of national sovereignty."[87] France fought back Germany's claim to a larger vote share, which more adequately reflected its larger population and economic size. The open friction between Chirac and Schröder chipped away at any sense of partnership.[88] The French held on to the notion that a Franco-German partnership of equals was an essential anchor for postwar Europe. But the always lop-sided Franco-German "friendship" had decisively shifted in favor of Germany, which had naturally emerged as "more equal than others."[89] German leaders did not have formal veto power over many decisions but they could guide Europe's destiny even as they pursued their national interest. In 1953, novelist Thomas Mann had called on the rising generation to reject a "German Europe" and embrace a "European Germany." Chancellor Kohl had often repeated the call but had all along protected the German interest. A "German Europe" was inevitable in a monetary union. Now it came into clearer focus.

The ECB Falls Behind the Curve

Eurozone authorities were preoccupied with internal matters—ushering Greece in, reacting petulantly to the Danish rejection, and establishing national interests at the summit in Nice. The eurozone economy continued to experience convulsions and the value of the euro continued to fall.

In March 2000, the US "dot-com" bubble burst. The tech-heavy NASDAQ index, which had risen from 400 in March 1990 to cross the 5,000 mark on March 9, 2000, fell by 30 percent in six weeks, down to below 3,500 on April 20. For now, the tech frenzy was over. The American consumption boom of the past decade began to fizzle, stock markets around the world swooned, and world trade stopped increasing. Despite the cheaper euro, weaker foreign demand for imports caused much of the eurozone economy to slow down. The German economy rapidly decelerated in the second half of 2000. Strong global forces were still whipping the eurozone economy around.

By September 5, 2000, one euro bought around 90 US cents. By now, currency traders were selling the euro simply because they anticipated that it would depreciate further, which ensured that the slide continued. The next "wave of selling" occurred when "it became clear that the currency was moving decisively below 89 cents."[90] Although German authorities generally denounced such financial speculation, Schröder welcomed the decline in the euro's value. A weak euro, he said, "should be more a reason for satisfaction than for concern."[91] That statement predictably caused the euro to fall further.

With the euro down to around 85 US cents in mid-September 2000, the consensus was that speculative forces had pushed the euro well below its fair value. On September 19, the IMF's chief economist, Michael Mussa, said that the euro had fallen too much and needed official support.[92] A day later, his new boss, IMF Managing Director Horst Köhler (previously Germany's chief negotiator at Maastricht) bluntly repeated that message.[93] And on September 22, coordinated purchases of the euro by the ECB and the central banks of the United States, Japan, the United Kingdom, and Canada helped it steady.[94] The

ECB reported that it had intervened again on November 3, this time acting on its own.[95] The euro finally stopped falling.

But the important task was not yet done. The ECB still refused to reduce its interest rate to help revive the eurozone economy. Duisenberg said that the eurozone's economy did not need help: it had sufficient internal strength to withstand adverse global developments. In December 2000, the ECB's Governing Council—its rate-setting body—decided to hold the policy interest rate unchanged at 4.75 percent (figure 3.1). Duisenberg said that America's troubles would prove to be a "weak wind," the eurozone's "underlying growth dynamism" would prevail.[96] In February 2001, Duisenberg repeated that "the impact of events outside the euro area is of a rather limited significance to the euro area." [97] Euro-area GDP, he predicted, would grow by 3 percent in 2001 and in 2002.

In contrast to the ECB's holding pattern, the Fed moved quickly. On January 3, 2001, Chairman Alan Greenspan initiated a conference call with his colleagues on the Federal Open Market Committee (FOMC)—the Fed's rate-setting body. Although the data was not yet alarming, Greenspan was worried about disturbing signs of economic deceleration. The American economy, he said, was "in the position of the person falling off the 30-story building and still experiencing a state of tranquility at 10 floors above the street."[98] The FOMC decided it was time to

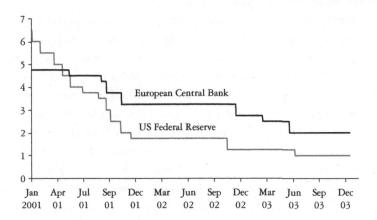

FIGURE 3.1. The US Federal Reserve leads, the European Central Bank follows.
(Policy interest rates, percent)
Sources: Federal Reserve Bank of New York. "Federal Funds Data Historical Search." https://apps. newyorkfed.org/markets/autorates/fed-funds-search-page. European Central Bank Main Refinancing Operations," variable rate tenders, https://www.ecb.europa.eu/stats/policy_and_exchange_rates/key_ ecb_interest_rates/html/index.en.html.

act and cut the Federal funds rate, the Fed's main policy interest rate by 50 basis points (100 basis points equal 1-percentage point). Among themselves, FOMC members agreed that they would follow up soon with more rate cuts. Greenspan expressed the hope that financial markets would read the bold measure that day as a signal that the Fed was beginning a series of rate cuts to stabilize growth preemptively well before the economy was at risk of crash landing.

While the Fed followed up quickly on its implied promise to reduce interest rates, the ECB held still. On April 11, the ECB refused again to reduce its interest rate.[99] Duisenberg acknowledged that GDP growth would be lower than he had forecast in February, but growth would still be robust, he insisted. By now, Duisenberg's statements had a theme: eurozone member countries needed to set their own houses in order. Crucially, they needed to consolidate their budget deficits. Member countries, he said, had taken a "solemn oath" to abide by the SGP and keep budget deficits definitely below 3 percent of GDP; preferably, governments would maintain a budget surplus.[100] In his other refrain, Duisenberg advised national governments to implement "comprehensive structural reform policies aimed at an increased labour market participation rate and improved investment incentives."[101] Through these repeated pronouncements, the ECB became the locus of the eurozone's "stability ideology." While committing itself to maintaining "price stability," the ECB exhorted member governments to be fiscally prudent and implement structural reforms.

A central bank needed to stay focused on price stability, Duisenberg said, because it could do little to "lift the euro area's growth potential."[102] In a narrow sense, this was, of course, a correct statement. The University of Chicago's Nobel laureate Milton Friedman, in his classic 1968 paper, had made it perfectly clear that monetary policy could not raise an economy's long-term or potential growth rate.[103] But Friedman had also warned that if a central bank failed to counteract recessionary conditions quickly and forcefully, growth potential would fall because long-term investment would decline and some of the unemployed resources would become obsolete![104] Bad monetary policy, he had said, was like a "monkey wrench," which jams up the economy. The ECB was placing a monkey wrench in the eurozone economy by failing to reduce interest rates so that investment and employment would return quickly to normal levels. The longer low investment and high unemployment persisted, the greater would be the damage to long-term growth prospects.

Ben Bernanke, at the time a professor of economics at Princeton University, had recently criticized the Bank of Japan (BOJ) for "exceptionally poor monetary policy-making" in the 1990s precisely because it did not expeditiously extend sufficient monetary stimulus to pull the Japanese economy out of the slump that began when Japanese stock and property prices crashed in late 1990.[105] That hesitant response prolonged Japan's recession, Bernanke said, and the stress of low growth made it politically difficult to undertake the structural reforms that the BOJ was advocating. The failure to act in time had consequences.

Duisenberg and his colleagues seemed uninterested in learning from the Japanese experience or, for that matter, from the Fed's ambitious ongoing monetary policy. When asked by a reporter if the ECB had heard the insistent calls to lower the policy rate, Duisenberg famously responded, "You might say I hear but I do not listen."[106]

On April 26, the IMF's Mussa took Duisenberg to task. Not the typical international civil servant, Mussa's words were hard-hitting: "the euro area as the second largest economic area in the world, needs to become part of the solution rather than part of the problem of slowing global growth." In response to a journalist's question, he said there was little risk of inflation but strong evidence of a slowdown in growth. Hence, a reduction in interest rates was the right policy. By failing to act, Mussa said, the ECB was hurting not only the eurozone but also the world economy. He then repeated: "In a slowdown such as we're now experiencing, every little bit helps, and it is desirable that the central bank of the second largest monetary area in the world be part of the solution rather than part of the problem going forward."[107]

In May, the IMF said, "prospects for global growth have weakened significantly."[108] With economic activity slowing down, inflationary pressures were easing.[109] The euro area's GDP was increasing at an annual pace of less than 1 percent rather than the 3 percent that Duisenberg had forecast in February. And, as elsewhere in the world, inflation was moderating.

At its meeting in May, the ECB did lower its rate, at which point the Fed and the ECB briefly had the same policy rate of 4.5 percent. In June, however, the ECB chose to keep its interest rate unchanged at 4.5 percent. The Fed was by then down to 3.75 percent. Duisenberg's and the ECB's analysis remained very different from Greenspan's or Mussa's. While Duisenberg recognized that a temporary increase in energy prices had boosted the headline inflation rate, he was concerned that the demand for higher wages would keep inflation higher than the ECB's comfort zone allowed. He repeated the phrase "price stability" eleven times at his June press conference. In contrast to his inflation fears, Duisenberg reiterated that economic growth was not a worry. He again called on member states to accelerate "structural reforms" to achieve "flexible functioning of the economy."[110]

This perennial mantra of structural reforms was the ECB's shield for its ideology of price stability.

Thus, continuing to keep its eye on a receding inflation, the ECB remained stubbornly unwilling to provide needed monetary stimulus to the eurozone economy.

Someone was bound to be unhappy. The ECB's first extended conflict, oddly enough, was with the German government. It turned out that Germans had less of a commitment to the "stability" ideology than may have been presumed from their earlier aggressive insistence on establishing the eurozone's rules embodying that ideology. Anxious to pull the German economy out of its recessionary conditions, Schröder was ready to set the price and fiscal stability rules aside. He called, instead, for greater priority to stimulating growth. By shifting the emphasis away from stability to growth, Schröder fell in step with French presidents and turned his back on traditional German positions, especially those of his predecessor Helmut Kohl.

Since the very start of his chancellorship in late 1998, Schröder had pushed the ECB for an easier monetary policy. Now that the ECB had dug in to an overly conservative stance, he had more reason to be upset. A few days after the ECB's June 2001 meeting, Schröder said that the global economic downturn was causing great pain in Germany and that his government had few domestic options to revive growth. Unlike the French, who were publicly contemplating the use of fiscal stimulus, Schröder said that Germany would not want to transgress European fiscal norms. Instead, he was asking the ECB to help Germany, although he coyly added that he did not doubt the ECB's independence.[111]

The ECB held firm until August, when it lowered its policy rates by 25 basis points. The global panic that followed the September 11 terrorist attacks on the United States prompted the ECB and the Fed, as well as several other central banks, to cut their interest rates by 50 basis points on Monday, September 17. However, with the ECB's policy interest rate still too high at 3.75 percent, Schröder's patience was running out. The ECB held steady in October. The Fed's policy rate was down to 2.5 percent, and the US government, in response to the terrorist attacks, began adding significant fiscal stimulus.[112]

Schröder was not alone in his impatience; other euro-area leaders were just as concerned. With world trade contracting rapidly, the entire euro-area economy was reeling, and every new forecast painted a grimmer picture of what lay ahead. The French economy had decelerated sharply since early 2001.[113] On October 16, Belgian Finance Minister and chair of the Eurogroup Didier Reynders spoke plainly to reporters in Luxembourg: "There is more room for maneuver on the monetary side than on the budgetary side."[114] Schröder decided to go a step further. In Frankfurt some hours later, he impatiently asked if ECB officials lacked common sense.[115]

The ECB's pushback against Schröder came the next day from Otmar Issing, a former high-ranking Bundesbank official who had become the ECB's chief economist in January 1999. Issing said that the ECB's commitment to price stability was particularly relevant amid the prevailing uncertainty in financial markets. The commitment was essential to restore and maintain "trust and confidence."[116] Issing's claim was that high interest rates kept prices "stable," and stability generated confidence in the future, which encouraged long-term investment and spurred growth. This plausibly stated sentiment was a dodge. The eurozone was not at risk of instability caused by runaway inflation. The need of the moment was to jump-start the economy. And with the ECB unwilling to provide more stimulus, GDP growth kept slipping. From 3.8 percent in 2000, GDP growth fell not to the 3 percent that Duisenberg had promised but to 2.2 percent in 2001 and to less than 1 percent in 2002.

Not only had the ECB failed in its first test to provide needed stimulus, it had also lost credibility. Ultimately, the ECB, having run out of excuses for inaction, did lower interest rates. But because the rate cuts were always late and reactive, their stimulus value was greatly diluted. The ECB had refused to listen to Nobel laureates Franco Modigliani and Robert Solow, who in 1998 had warned that obsessive focus on price stability would cause the ECB to keep interest rates too high, which would then reduce the pace of GDP growth and hence, would raise unemployment (see chapter 2). That is precisely what happened.

Price stability at all costs had the further implication that the interest rate would be particularly high for some countries. It is a historical irony that Germans, who had insisted on the goal of price stability, were the first victims of the structural problem that monetary policy will inevitably be too tight for some members of the single currency area. Even the IMF sympathized with Schröder's predicament. In September 2001, as the German economy headed into a recession, an IMF report said, "From a purely German perspective lower interest rates would be welcome."[117] In October 2002, with Germany now in an entrenched recession, the IMF repeated that the long period of high interest rates—initiated by the Bundesbank and continued by the ECB—had taken a toll on the German economy.[118]

With virtually no help from monetary stimulus, could member state governments use fiscal measures—lower taxes and increased expenditures—to revive their economies? The eurozone's rules placed severe limits on efforts to inject fiscal stimulus. A clash was thus set up between member states and the rules.

The "Stupid" SGP

The rules—enshrined in the SGP—were another product of German ideology. They required eurozone governments to strive for balanced budgets, and they carried the threat of penalties if the budget deficit exceeded 3 percent of GDP. This requirement allowed little latitude for fiscal stimulus to pull the economy out of the recession (see chapter 2). In late June 2001, Pedro Solbes, European Commissioner for Economic and Monetary Affairs, blacklisted France, Germany, Italy, and Portugal as budgetary offenders. Instead of maintaining balanced budgets or, better still, budgets in surplus, the governments of these countries were allowing their deficits to rise dangerously.[119] Issing was again the ECB's ideologue. In October 2001, with the world economy reeling, he said that the euro area needed fiscal discipline; "I might even say [it needs] a jacket." With customary central bank obscurity, he added, "but it's not a straitjacket."[120]

Ever since the agreement on monetary union at Maastricht in 1991, European officials had dismissed the basic economic principle that fiscal austerity prolongs economic distress (see chapter 2). Charles Wyplosz, the seasoned European scholar and commentator, reminded European policymakers of that principle. "The very rigorous interpretation" of the euro area's rules, he said, "is a problem."[121] Echoing Chancellor Schröder's words of criticism for the ECB, Wyplosz said of the fiscal rules: "Europe needs to respond in a way that makes sense." The IMF—normally an ardent advocate of fiscal austerity—advised the German government, "Don't do it." In a September 2001 report, IMF analysts "questioned the appropriateness" of sticking to the deficit reduction goals for 2001 and 2002.[122] The "untimely expenditure squeeze" was "unwarranted in the present setting"—it would make the recession worse.

There was something odd about European authorities pushing the German government to reduce its budget deficit. From large deficits that had followed unification in 1990—reaching 9 percent of GDP in 1995—the government had steadily moved its budget into a surplus by 2000. The spike in deficit in 2001 to just over 3 percent of GDP was due to the sudden stop in world trade, which had caused the German export engine to sputter. Especially in the absence of adequate monetary stimulus from the ECB, Germany needed fiscal stimulus, not austerity. But despite the illogic of more austerity, German officials—feeling duty-bound to honor the SGP—continued to make an effort to consolidate the government's budget.[123] That effort only induced a further slowdown in German GDP growth, which reduced tax receipts and increased the government's social support expenditures, making the task of consolidating the budget deficit harder.

By early 2002, the lower-than-anticipated tax revenues and rising payments to the unemployed pushed up the German budget deficit to about 3.5 percent of GDP. To keep the deficit below 3 percent of GDP would have required once again some combination of raising taxes and reducing spending, which would create a further drag on German growth. Frustrated by unending European Commission criticism of Germany's increasing budget deficit, Finance Minister Eichel shockingly called for reconsideration of the SGP rules.[124] Eichel's comments made a great deal of economic sense but they were politically highly inappropriate, especially from a senior German policymaker. Eichel quickly retracted his statement, but the battle lines were drawn.

The SGP procedures required the European Commission to warn a country whose budget deficit was approaching 3 percent of GDP. The commission could have reasonably concluded that it was neither practical nor sensible for the German government to stop the slide into a deeper deficit. Instead, the commission prepared a draft of a warning letter.[125] The next step was for the Council of European Finance Ministers to make the warning official by delivering the letter to Eichel. But a group of peers naturally hesitates to reprimand one of its own for fear of being at the receiving end of such a reprimand some time in the future. Portugal was facing the same censure as Germany. The United Kingdom was similarly at risk of triggering an unwelcome warning from the commission. As always, France was flirting with deficit limits and, in fact, had announced fiscal stimulus measures (income support for low-wage earners and corporate investment incentives).[126] By February 2002, when the finance ministers met, Germany had predictably gathered political support, and presumably, the draft warning letters were shredded.[127] ECB President Duisenberg and Bundesbank President Ernst Welteke had "lined up aggressively" behind the commission, but the disciplinary mechanism proved to be unworkable.[128]

At their Barcelona summit in March, European leaders again pledged allegiance to the SGP, promising to balance their budgets by 2004. It was an empty pledge, and Chirac, who was fending off an electoral challenge, quickly announced a plan for tax cuts and increased spending.[129] European leaders were outraged that Chirac, while paying lip service to the rules, was openly disregarding them. An angry Eichel said, "I don't understand how

Chirac can agree [on the budget target] at the Barcelona summit, and how a few weeks later this counts for nothing."[130] But Eichel, more so than anybody else, should have understood that the slowing economy was pushing budget deficits up everywhere. By May 2002, most observers agreed that Germany would not balance its budget even by 2004.[131]

In September 2002, the IMF reported that the global recovery would be slower than anticipated in April. The euro-area economy, the IMF said, was particularly weak, lagging behind the United States and emerging Asia.[132] The Fed had reduced its policy rate from 3.5 percent in September 2001 to 1.75 percent, and the government had injected substantial fiscal stimulus. A US economic recovery was taking shape. In contrast, the ECB had gingerly lowered its rate by a whisker from 3.75 to 3.25 percent. And the European Commission was bearing down on the weak economies to reduce their fiscal deficits. For Germany, the IMF recognized that trying to balance the budget by 2004 would place "excessive strain on the economy;" but reversing its sensible position from a year ago that austerity was being overdone, the IMF joined forces with the European Commission and said it was essential for Germany to undertake "credible" fiscal consolidation.[133] The French were much clearer on this matter. In early October, French Finance Minister Francis Mer gave up the pretense. Balancing the budget, he said, was not a high priority for France.[134]

European Commission President Romano Prodi, a former economics professor and Italian premier between 1996 and 1998, was unhappy with the task that awaited him. It would soon be time to prosecute France and Germany for exceeding the budget-deficit limit of 3 percent of GDP. The Maastricht Treaty and the SGP required that a serial budget-deficit offender be shamed publicly and possibly even fined.[135]

The whole idea of punishing a country in distress was absurd, and in an interview with French newspaper *Le Monde* on October 18, Prodi stated the obvious: "I know very well that the Stability Pact is stupid, as are all rigid decisions."[136] Prodi added that the SGP needed to be intelligent and flexible. At the European Parliament a few days later, Prodi stood by his words and insisted: "It is time to say the same things in public that we say to each other in private."[137] Others shared Prodi's assessment. Pascal Lamy, a Eurocrat of great distinction, had earlier described the SGP as a "medieval" construct that needed to go.[138] More graphically, French Finance Minister Mer compared the SGP to a "procrustean bed," which was "too small for some, too large for others, and a torture for all."[139]

However, the establishment forces quickly rallied. The ECB and the IMF vigorously defended the rules. In a press release on October 25, the ECB said that the SGP was indispensable: it had promoted sound public finances and was in the interests of member states. "Problems have arisen," the ECB insisted, "not because the rules are inflexible, but as a result of some countries' unwillingness to honour their commitment to respect the rules."[140] The ECB, with its unfailing insistence on honoring the SGP rules, extended its claim to be the intellectual heavyweight of the eurozone's stability ideology. The evidence calling for a reassessment did not matter.

At the IMF, Michael Deppler, the director of the European Department, echoed the ECB. Although the IMF had recognized that the fiscal rules were placing "excessive strain" on the German economy, Deppler returned to the IMF's conventional position. He said that the SGP was "fundamentally sound" and had the IMF's "strong support." And even as he announced that the euro-area growth rate was continuing its fall, he added: "The core of the problem is the fact that the three largest countries [Germany, France, and Italy] basically have not lived up to the rules." These countries, Deppler said, needed "to make a credible, responsive effort to fall into line with the SGP."[141]

Did this advice make any sense? How much more fiscal consolidation did Germany need to do? The official view was that monetary and fiscal stimulus would do the German economy little good since it was not in a short-term slump. Instead, the economy had deep-rooted problems, which required the German government to tighten its budget and simultaneously undertake structural reforms to stimulate growth. This view that Germany needed serious long-term medicine was made popular by the *Economist* in June 1999, when it described Germany as "the sick man of Europe."[142] The phrase caught on, and some wondered if Germany was "too sick to be cured."[143]

True, German authorities had their homework to do. The East German economy had long-term problems. Despite improvement in productivity, the high initial wages set by the 1:1 conversion of the Ostmark to the D-mark continued to undermine the competitiveness of East German firms, exactly as Professors George Akerlof and Janet Yellen had predicted (see chapter 2). Hans-Werner Sinn, President of the Munich-based Ifo Institute for Economic Research and a prominent voice in public debate, wrote that unemployment and business insolvencies in eastern Germany were still rising, and that the "flourishing landscapes," which Chancellor Helmut Kohl had breezily promised, were nowhere to be seen.[144] The east remained dependent on "costly subsidies," requiring a transfer each year of between 4 and 5 percent of West German GDP to the east.[145] The overall tax burden had increased to finance the subsidies to eastern Germany.

West German companies, however, were in relatively good shape. Although hampered by high taxes and tight monetary policy, many of these companies were investing in manufacturing innovation, redefining employer-employee relationships and work practices, and expanding operations to low-cost locations in eastern European economies.[146] A fruitful transition to a more competitive economy was ongoing.

To speed up that transition, Germany needed a modest fiscal stimulus. Especially since world trade had decelerated, good sense required that the economy receive monetary and fiscal help to tide over the difficult period. That is precisely the point of fiscal and monetary policy: to shorten the periods of economic dislocation.

The ECB had refused to budge. The prospects of realism in fiscal policy were also fading.

Despite his moment of intellectual clarity, Prodi fell back in with the European bias for rules and discipline. In the end, he was less interested in sensible economic policy than he was in asserting the authority of the European Commission. Prodi favored flexibility in the interpretation of the SGP but only as long as he got to decide how much flexibility and for whom.

Although eurozone leaders said that they also believed in flexibility, they were unwilling to give Prodi and the commission the power to determine national budget deficits. If the commission were to be in charge, as Prodi demanded, member states would suffer an unacceptable loss of sovereignty. Moreover, there would always remain the worry of unequal treatment; the commission might deal with some countries harshly but let others off the hook. Every member state would always perceive unfairness in the commission's actions.

Member states could have recognized that they needed no rules; each country could adopt its own fiscal disciplinary procedure as in other monetary unions.[147] And if a country lived beyond its means, it would need to face the wrath of private creditors. For, if there was to be a rule, only a rigid one—which allowed little latitude in interpretation—could be acceptable to all. And any rigid rule was bound to be economically indefensible, as countless economists had pointed out (see chapter 2).[148] European authorities had heard those criticisms, but, as Duisenberg might have said, they had chosen not to listen. Even having experienced its arbitrariness and dysfunctionality, they continued to persuade themselves that the hallowed 3 percent benchmark was better than no rule at all. It now fell on Prodi to enforce that "stupid" rule.

A French Chancellor in Berlin

Schröder and Chirac set up a common front against Prodi and, indeed, against the ECB. It was an alliance of convenience. Until then, the two leaders had fought each other on all crucial matters, including at Nice on the issue of voting rights in European decisions. By early 2002, relations had deteriorated to a low point. One commentator remarked that Schröder had "allowed the anemic Franco-German partnership to become the axis of indifference."[149]

But in late 2002, German and French national interests were suddenly aligned. The alignment was manifest in the transformed personal relationship between Schröder and Chirac. Their "awkward, even tense" personal interactions were gone, and they started greeting each other with "bear hugs."[150]

German GDP had fallen through the first half of 2002 and, after brief relief, was again contracting in the final months of the year. Monetary conditions were tight. The ECB's policy rate had been higher than that of the Fed since September 2001. With the ECB's rate now expected to remain above the Fed's rate, euro-denominated assets had become more attractive, and the euro had slowly strengthened. By May, the euro's value had returned to close to where it had started in January 1999, with one euro buying $1.14.

On November 19, 2002, with the German economy stuck in recessionary conditions, Prodi astonishingly recommended to the Council of Finance Ministers the start of a sanctions procedure against Germany.[151] Fiscal consolidation of the size recommended by the European Commission would have throttled the German economy. On January 21, 2003, the council concluded that Germany had breached the "excessive deficit" threshold and needed to demonstrate sufficient austerity measures ("rigorous budget execution") to achieve deficit reduction of 1 percent of GDP by May.[152]

Eichel gave up the pretense. In May 2003, he announced that not only would the deficit for 2003 exceed the 3 percent threshold, but it "would take a miracle" to achieve a balanced budget by 2006.[153] Schröder went on the offensive. He repeatedly complained that the strength of the euro was holding back German exports.[154] On July 11, after the ECB held its policy rate at 2 percent, and Duisenberg rebuked German authorities for mismanaging their public finances, Schröder said that the ECB's leadership surely had "intelligent people," but he wondered if they asked themselves every day "whether they have done enough in the context of the dollar/euro exchange rate to maintain the competitiveness of exports from Europe."[155]

Schröder then announced a fiscal stimulus package of tax cuts and stepped-up government spending. He abandoned even polite deference to the SGP and insisted that it be interpreted flexibly, emphasizing growth and not just fiscal discipline.[156] His new approach melded perfectly with that of the French, who received their "excessive deficit" warning in June 2003.[157]

Together, France and Germany joined in open violation of the SGP. It was a rare moment of Franco-German friendship. Such was the meeting of minds that in October 2003, French President Chirac represented Germany's 80 million citizens at the leaders' summit in Brussels because Schröder needed to be in Berlin for a crucial parliamentary vote.[158] A German official remarked, "Gerhard trusts Jacques."[159] Germany and France were ready to mount a political offensive against the eurozone's fiscal rules.

On November 17, Eichel made one final plea for economic good sense. A senior European leader has never since made a clearer and more cogent public statement on the fundamental problem with the SGP. In an opinion piece for the *Financial Times*, Eichel explained that the German authorities had made every effort to rein in their fiscal deficit. Despite those efforts, the deficit had continued to widen because the economy was stuck in extended recessionary conditions. Eichel rightly insisted that more austerity would be counterproductive.

He went on to say, "A policy geared solely to attaining quantitative consolidation targets in the short term runs the risk not only of curbing growth but also of increasing debt." This was the key sentence of Eichel's op-ed: austerity can actually increase the debt burden because it causes GDP to decline and hence the debt-to-GDP ratio to rise. Eichel concluded that European authorities should use the SGP not as a "code of sanctions" but rather as an "adaptable" framework that took into consideration each country's specific circumstances.[160]

No one disputed the German finance ministry's assertion that it had implemented deficit reduction measures agreed with the European Commission "to the letter."[161] To ask for more amid the "sluggish economy"—the "weakest in a decade"—was perverse, ministry officials correctly argued.

On November 25, when the Council of Finance Ministers met, Eichel's economics carried little weight. Importantly, however, Germany and France had gathered sufficient political support for their cause. In its decision, the council, in effect, said it loved the SGP and promised to implement it fairly but not for Germany and France at this time. The press release, without any apparent sense of irony, first stated, "The Council reaffirms the determination to implement the provisions of the Stability and Growth Pact by ensuring equality of treatment across Member States"; the menacing implication was that Germany and France would pay for their transgressions. But the statement sheepishly concluded that the excessive-deficit procedure against Germany and France would be held "in abeyance."[162]

Schröder hailed the waiver of sanctions as "a wise decision."[163] Italian Finance Minister Giulio Tremonti, who chaired the meeting of the ministers, more somberly said to reporters: "At the end of the day, this was the only solution possible and therefore it is the best solution."[164]

There were howls of protest. The European commissioner for economic and monetary affairs, Pedro Solbes, who, along with Prodi, had brought the action against Germany and France, complained that European ministers had together brazenly violated the letter and spirit of the SGP.[165] Dutch Finance Minister Zalm also protested.[166] But the loudest wails came, once again, from the ECB. In a quickly released press statement, the ECB said: "The Governing Council deeply regrets these developments, [which] carry serious dangers. The failure to go along with the rules and procedures foreseen in the Stability and Growth Pact risks undermining the credibility of the institutional framework and the confidence in sound public finances of Member States across the euro area."[167]

Prodi and the commission's staff continued to fret that Germany was violating the rules. But Eichel—by now clearly with the upper hand—advised the commission to "come out of its corner and stop sulking."[168] Prodi responded in January 2004 by escalating the fight. He appealed to the European Court of Justice (ECJ) to overturn the council decision. He had a weak case: the treaty gave the council of ministers the authority to decide if a breach of the SGP had occurred. On July 17, the ECJ confirmed that the council had acted within its rights.[169] The ECJ did say that the commission could make its case again; an excessive deficit could not continue indefinitely. However, Prodi acknowledged the political reality and gave up.

Thus, in these early euro years, monetary and fiscal policy had been put through a stress test. Eurozone authorities had refused to adapt and evolve. Instead, they had withdrawn into an involutionary preoccupation with price and fiscal stability rules, which caused them to lose perspective on the economic consequences of their decisions. Meanwhile, the United States benefited from its more active monetary and fiscal stimulus. By late 2001, US GDP began to grow faster than that of the eurozone; stock markets waited somewhat, but by late 2002, US stocks also pulled ahead (figure 3.2).

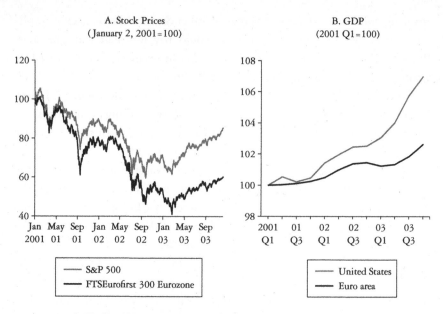

| A. Stock Prices | B. GDP |
| (January 2, 2001 = 100) | (2001 Q1 = 100) |

Legend A:
— S&P 500
— FTSEurofirst 300 Eurozone

Legend B:
— United States
— Euro area

FIGURE 3.2. Earlier US recovery in stock prices and GDP.
Sources: FTSEurofirst 300 Eurozone (FTEUEBL(PI)) from Datastream; S&P 500 (^GSPC), online at https://finance.yahoo.com/q/hp?s=^GSPC&a=00&b=1&c=1999&d=11&e=31&f=2003&g=d. For GDP, OECD Statistics "B1_GE: Gross domestic product—expenditure approach; LNBQRSA: Millions of national currency, chained volume estimates, national reference year, quarterly levels, seasonally adjusted," available from stats.oecd.org.

From the Euro's First Five Years: Echoes into the Future

No lessons were learned. Economist Adam Posen wrote in 2005 that only when "seen through some European eyes" could Germany's refusal in 2003 to undertake more fiscal consolidation be seen as improper or a "threat to the viability of the eurozone." Germany, he wrote was responding in a "rational, if not optimal" manner to the economic realities it faced.[170]

To most European officials, however, the brief German rebellion was—and remains—an instance of blatant and willful abuse of the rules. Indeed, in 2011, in the frenzied phase of the eurozone's sovereign debt and banking crisis, Schröder himself did an about-face on this matter. Although he continued to mumble that Germany deserved special treatment in 2002 and 2003, he expressed regret at having shown disrespect for the SGP.[171]

Meanwhile, the ECB quickly established itself as a practitioner of monetary policy dominantly focused on controlling inflation. To be sure, the ECB did lower its interest rates when economic weakness persisted. But unlike the Fed, which acted preemptively to prevent a crash landing, the ECB was always behind the curve. For that reason, investors remained uncertain about the ECB's intent, and the monetary stimulus was less effective in promoting economic recovery. Financial markets quickly recognized that the ECB had no intention of changing course and would keep its interest rates relatively high, even though the eurozone's economic recovery was weaker and growth prospects poorer compared with the United States. The resulting expectation of continued high interest rates caused the euro to strengthen; by early 2004, one euro could buy more than $1.20. The tendency for the euro to remain strong—and hence dampen exports from several eurozone countries—would persist.

Thus, an opportunity had arisen to change the fundamental economic framework of the eurozone. If one person could have promoted such change, it was Schröder. He certainly understood the problems that the prevailing ideology created. However, he was either too preoccupied with German problems, or he foresaw that Germany would one day want to impose on other countries the very rules against which he had rebelled.

In politics, cynicism and divisions came to the fore. Schröder encouraged the admission of Greece into the euro area in a vain gesture, which he thought would be costless to Germany and would gain him European brownie points. Thus, one more country, which would obviously not be able to take care of its own affairs, entered the eurozone's fold in the belief that the single currency would induce its policymakers to finally undertake the needed societal transformation. Greece was now in the company of France, Italy, Portugal, and Spain, all hoping that the eurozone would act as an "external anchor." In contrast, citizens in more self-confident nations—Denmark, Sweden, and the United Kingdom—protested against further European encroachment into their lives and thus ensured that their governments would not join the eurozone. The Danes in September 2000 and the Swedes three years later voted to keep their own currencies. In the United Kingdom, Prime Ministers Tony Blair and Gordon Brown recognized that a referendum defeat on the euro could cripple them politically, and so they stuck with the pound.

Political divisions in Europe became steadily more acute.[172] The larger member states threatened to reduce their contributions to the EU budget. Although there was reason to celebrate the accession of ten new member states from Eastern Europe—nations that had lived under communism and Soviet domination for nearly half a century—the enlargement of the EU already created new fault lines. Some of the new member states supported the United States in its pursuit of the Iraq War and thus invited the ire of French President Chirac. The contentious tussle for voting rights, which had overwhelmed the summit at Nice in December 2000, continued in December 2003. When European leaders met in Brussels on December 12 and 13, Spain and Portugal fought to preserve their vote shares while France and Germany demanded more for themselves. The differences proved insurmountable. As Prodi reported: "Today it was not possible to reach an agreement. Any deal would have been below expectations and no one wanted that."[173] Pro-Europeanism was mainly a rhetorical veneer that attempted without success to hide powerful national interests.

Little came of the Werner Report's promise in 1970 that the single currency would act as "a leaven for the development of political union."[174] In October 2003, delivering the Pierre Werner Lecture in Luxembourg, former Bundesbank President Hans Tietmeyer had a judicious assessment. "Up to now," he said, "the euro has played only to a very limited extent, the role that many people expected of it, as a catalyst of more political common ground in EMU. I am convinced that Pierre Werner would assess the situation in a similar way."[175]

The absence of political progress created a governance vacuum that coincided with Germany's readiness to leave behind postwar hesitations in pursuing its national interests. In 1998, Roger Cohen of the *New York Times* had written that Schröder represented "a more self-confident Germany, unburdened by its past." And he had presciently added: "[The] truth is that . . . Germany is likely to flex its muscle more in the coming years."[176]

Schröder had little patience for grand European designs. In February 2002, when asked if he believed in the "United States of Europe," he had impatiently replied, "What a child wants to call it is not as important as the substance." While he lamely added, "we need much more—let's call it coordination and cooperation," Schröder acted almost always to undermine European coordination and cooperation.[177] For good reason, he battled the ECB and the European Commission to gain respite for the German economy. But he refused to take leadership in overhauling the system, even though Germany was steadily becoming Europe's economic and political hegemonic power. Rather than assume the responsibilities of a hegemon, Schröder obsessively pursued German national interest, even when that pursuit clearly damaged European integration. In an episode with echoes in the present, Schröder acted to protect automaker Volkswagen, on whose supervisory board he had sat as governor of the state of Lower Saxony; he blocked an EU-wide corporate takeover code that would have made hostile takeovers easier.[178] By shielding one of Germany's largest companies, Schröder legitimized the idea that countries would protect their "national champions" from the discipline of financial markets.

On December 18, 2003, George Parker of the *Financial Times* wrote, "The last year has been an unmitigated disaster for supporters of the cause of greater European integration, as national self-interest reasserts itself across the continent." The mood at the Brussels headquarters of the EU, he said, was dark. As the "Brussels elite" climbed into BMWs for their Christmas breaks, the fear was that after the "dismal year" just past, "things could be even worse" when they returned.[179]

For the eurozone, it was an eventful first five years. Little had gone right. But sadly, European leaders made no attempt at economic or political course correction. More such years—and a more severe crisis—would further weaken the eurozone economy and pull harder at its political fabric. There was, however, a glimmer of hope. The world economy was beginning to grow, and if it continued to do so, perhaps, the rising tide would lift all boats.

CHAPTER 4 | Irrational Exuberance, 2004–2007

A T THE START of 2004, the eurozone's economy was still weak. The unemployment rate had climbed to 9 percent, and forecasters projected it would remain stuck there for the next few years. In contrast, the US economy, recharged with monetary and fiscal stimulus, was roaring ahead. Moreover, the US technology boom and productivity growth continued to provide long-term growth impetus. The US unemployment rate was at 6 percent and rapidly falling.

However, by mid-year, a strong global economic recovery was underway and lightened Europe's economic gloom. Buoyant US stock markets had already spread their cheer to European markets. More importantly, world trade growth accelerated to historically high rates, a special boon to European nations, which all rely heavily for their economic well-being on international trade. The US consumer's apparently limitless appetite for foreign goods fueled the acceleration in world trade. And as the Chinese manufacturing machine geared up to feed that voracious US demand, China itself emerged as a global locomotive. Chinese production sites rapidly became the world's hub for trade in manufactured goods, exporting vast quantities of products and importing raw materials, semi-finished goods, and machines to feed the exponentially multiplying factories. Affluent Chinese citizens rushed to buy global luxury goods. As the IMF wrote, between mid-2003 and mid-2004, China powered an "exceptionally rapid expansion" of the world economy.[1]

The IMF projected that the pace of world trade growth would jump from 5 percent in 2003 to 9 percent in 2004 (and when the numbers were later tallied, world trade in 2004 actually grew at more than 11 percent.).[2] That buoyancy was set to continue over the next few years. The times suddenly had turned visibly good. The dangers lay hidden.

With improved trade opportunities, even the struggling German economy began to show signs of life. Even as domestic demand in Germany remained "dormant," the growth of exports picked up, and the IMF projected that the German economy, which had contracted in 2003, would grow by 2 percent in 2004.[3] In Ireland, the property price boom continued unabated, and while Irish manufacturing jobs did begin moving to lower-wage Eastern European countries, US multinationals—with their long-standing presence in Ireland—egged on the Celtic tiger. Only Italy seemed stuck in its economic and psychological rut.

Suddenly, it seemed as if a new window was opening up for the eurozone to finally demonstrate its potential and deliver on its promises of economic prosperity, stability, and European harmony. In the eurozone's first five years, poor economic performance and national anxieties had given rise to assertive nationalism. A return to steady economic growth would dampen financial anxieties, which would, perhaps, kindle greater empathy for other Europeans and stir greater willingness to practice solidarity.

There were, however, worrying signs. While the United States was experiencing real economic progress, it was also in a phase of "irrational exuberance."[4] Alan Greenspan, legendary chairman of the Fed, cautioned as early as December 1996 that prices of US assets, such as stocks and homes, were reaching "unduly" high levels.[5] Yet, with a brief interruption after the bursting of the dot-com bubble in 2000 and the September 11 attacks, the exuberance continued almost unabated. Soon, in the same way as the United States was transmitting its domestic consumer-led economic growth to the rest of the world, the United States sparked global financial exuberance. Banks and investors worldwide wanted their share of the growing financial bounty in the United States, or else they sought easy riches nearer home. The risk was real that US and global asset prices would keep rising and then quickly and sharply reverse, as they had in Japan in 1990.

The person who sounded the loudest warning was Yale University economist Robert Shiller. He emphasized that bouts of irrational exuberance had recurred throughout history. Each bout arose from the same fundamental "human vulnerability to error" and did not just cause gyrations in financial markets but created pervasive instability in the "capitalist system."[6]

Many European policymakers believed that Europe was less susceptible to irrational exuberance and to the instability it could spawn than the United States was. Europeans saved more than Americans did. The United States had a large current account deficit (its imports greatly exceeded its exports), which required significant borrowing from abroad; the eurozone had a nearly balanced current account since it was formed and, in fact, had a surplus since 2001. The eurozone's financial system depended heavily on banks, which the eurozone authorities believed were safer than the allegedly fickle equity and bond markets that played a much more important role in the United States. Moreover, the eurozone's leaders actively espoused an ideology of stability, with its emphasis on fiscal austerity and price stability. Thus, while there were pockets of rapid property price increases, as in Ireland and Spain, altogether it seemed possible that the eurozone could benefit from rising global trade but remain insulated from irrational exuberance and instability.

The eurozone, however, had its own sources of economic and financial vulnerabilities. One source of instability was inherent in monetary unity, an instability that was vividly manifest during the crisis of the European ERM in the early 1990s.[7] British economist Alan Walters had explained that under a unified monetary policy, interest rates paid in the member countries would converge close to one another. The interest rate, therefore, would be too low for some countries, and such countries would experience rapid, possibly exuberant, credit-fueled growth along with high inflation and loss of international competitiveness. The credit boom could then unwind quickly and precipitate a financial crisis (see chapter 2).

A longer-term problem was the stability of banks in the eurozone. While eurozone authorities believed that banks acted prudently and were therefore a source of financial and economic stability, a worrying macroeconomic problem in fact was brewing. Banks had grown at an unusually rapid pace in the previous half century, but the banks' borrowers had struggled to raise their productivity (figure 4.1). The impending arrival of the eurozone had accelerated this problem in the 1990s; banks had expanded even while productivity growth had continued to slow down. This inverse relationship between ever larger banking systems and declining productivity growth was ultimately not sustainable. Economists Gary Gorton and Guillermo Ordoñez have documented that when productivity growth is low or falling, credit expansions typically end in default and tears.[8]

This, then, was the situation on both sides of the Atlantic in mid-2004. Growth prospects had brightened in the United States. The US economy had experienced a productivity renaissance in the previous decade and rising stock and property prices had sent the US consumer on a spending binge. "Now, tell me again, why exactly I should save for the future" was a common sentiment. US consumption growth gave a huge fillip to Chinese growth, and the global trade upsurge that followed gave European nations a renewed

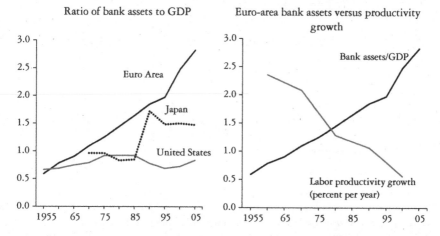

FIGURE 4.1. Euro area: Bank assets race ahead as productivity falls.

Note: Euro-area countries include Belgium, Germany, Italy, Spain, and the Netherlands (due to availability of reliable longtime series data). Labor productivity growth is the average annual increase in GDP/hour from the previous decade.

Source: Bank assets are from Sam Langfield. "Bank Bias in Europe: Effects of Systemic Risk and Growth." Available at http://www.samlangfield.com/research.html. Labor productivity growth is from "The Conference Board Total Economy Database," May 2015, http://www.conference-board.org/data/economydatabase/.

sense of economic confidence. And while vulnerabilities were accumulating in US financial markets in a manner that, at least initially, had some policymakers worried, the eurozone seemed largely immune to financial risks. The eurozone's increasing vulnerabilities lay hidden under a less well-understood combination of convergence of interest rates, an overgrown banking system, and declining productivity growth.

As the good times continued, policymakers and investors on both sides of the Atlantic concluded that they could ignore the financial risks. In 2004, concern about "irrational exuberance" peaked, and the "great moderation" narrative gained strength (figure 4.2). The "great moderation" narrative relied on studies which showed that, in the previous two decades, most advanced economies had experienced infrequent and shallow recessions.[9] The inference that an increasing number of observers drew was that this benign economic state would continue. The further inference was that economic expansions mainly reflected a welcome upsurge in productivity and that there was little reason to worry about financial excesses and crises. In fact, although Greenspan had made the phrase "irrational exuberance" popular, he believed that much of the ongoing exuberance was a rational response to new productive opportunities.[10] He believed, moreover, that advances in information and communication technologies would prevent financial risks from becoming dangerously

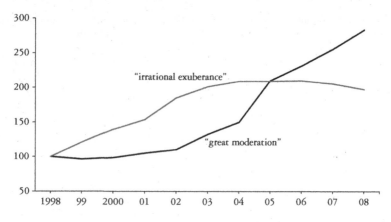

FIGURE 4.2. "Great moderation" overcomes "irrational exuberance."
(Indices of usage of phrases "great moderation" and "irrational exuberance" in books digitized by Google)
Source: Google Books Ngram Viewer.

concentrated in a few hidden pockets and that over time, financial markets would better serve the common good. As if to validate the great moderation narrative, during the course of 2004, the global "fear" index—the VIX, a measure of future volatility of the US stock market—fell steadily toward 15, well below its historical average of 20.

Crucial to the benign "great moderation" view was the growing presence of "independent" central banks. Many economists and policymakers believed that central banks, now impressively insulated from self-serving and short-sighted politicians, had the right incentives and tools to dampen harmful economic booms and prevent—or at least moderate—the busts. Central banks could keep the economy in a Goldilocks world, not too hot and not too cold.

For this reason, eurozone authorities could feel especially confident that they had the tools to tame financial risks. The ECB was hyper-independent: as a central bank without a nation-state, it operated with virtually no political oversight.[11] Hyper-independence was not necessarily a good thing, as Paul Volcker, former chairman of the Fed, had pointed out. The ECB's lack of political accountability could lead to errors and instability. However, European policymakers regarded the ECB's independence as an unmixed virtue. In February 2004, Tommaso Padoa-Schioppa, a leading European economist and among the first members of the ECB's executive board, lauded the "macroeconomic stability" that the ECB had established in the euro area. He added that by keeping its own house in order, the ECB had also "contributed to global stability in a significant way."[12]

A concern did arise in the early years of the eurozone that banks, lulled by the perception of diminished risk, might expand recklessly. But when asked whether the euro area needed a centralized bank supervisor to establish rigorous, common standards of safety and oversee national banking systems, Padoa-Schioppa said: "The system that exists today is a system that has no loopholes, no areas that are covered by uncertainty."[13]

Other observers joined in by applauding financial developments in the euro area. Economists Giancarlo Corsetti and Paolo Pesenti said: "In terms of its impact on financial market integration, the European Monetary Union is performing well above expectations." Corsetti and Pesenti predicted that the deeper-than-before equity and bond markets would intensify "competition among sovereign issuers, providing strong incentives for them to reform markets and pursue greater efficiency and transparency."[14]

Thus, the story of the next three years—from mid-2004 to mid-2007—revolves around a contest between the forces of great moderation and irrational exuberance. In the eurozone, as member states benefited from an improving global economy, a belief in the ECB's distinctive ability to maintain stability reinforced the narrative of great moderation. With the ECB in charge, the perception of risk-free lending took root, and euro-area banks expanded at home and abroad with abandon and with little financial cushion to protect themselves against adverse shocks.

The eurozone was being tested again, not for the performance of its stability ideology as in the first five years but for a more fundamental reason: could diverse countries fit into a single-currency area? Moreover, was there a risk that European banks, in a bid to boost their meager profits, would prey on, and hence magnify, this diversity to an extent that rendered policy actions toothless?

Europe's Fascination with Banks

Banks had seemed an irrelevant consideration in the decision to give up national currencies and adopt a single European currency. But banks were a historically powerful economic and political force in Europe. For nearly one hundred and fifty years, governments of the countries now in the eurozone had actively used banks to spur economic growth. In 1864, Emperor Napoleon III of France had authorized the establishment of Société Générale "to promote trade and industry in France."[15] From that early start, as University of California, Berkeley, political scientist John Zysman has written, banks steadily became the French government's "principal mechanism of policy."[16] Directing banks to serve public policy blended well with the French dirigiste philosophy, the view that governments should intervene in and override market forces to promote social objectives.

Other countries followed. Although German governments interfered much less in the working of the market economy than French governments did, banks became an important instrument of public policy even in Germany. In the late nineteenth century, as Harvard economic historian Alexander Gerschenkron first highlighted, the German government promoted domestic banks to help close the industrialization gap with Britain.[17] Thus emerged the *Kreditbanken* ("universal" banks, in modern terminology), which combined investment and commercial banking. These banks financed the ramping up of capital-intensive industries such as steel and machinery production. Also in the second half of the nineteenth century, state and local governments established and encouraged "savings" banks, the *Sparkassen*, to finance small and medium-sized enterprises.

Other European banking systems combined German and French features. In Italy, for example, large German-style "universal" banks became an important source of industrial finance in the nineteenth century.[18] Italy has also had its version of small community banks. Following a financial crisis in the early 1930s, the Italian government became a more active participant in banking, either as an owner or as an intrusive regulator.

European banks played their most valuable role after World War II. Economic output per capita had collapsed to around one-third the level of that in the United States (figure 4.3). The task, then, as economist Barry Eichengreen has written, was to finance "extensive growth"; the financing needs were obvious, the technology was familiar, and the risks were small. Banks financed the building of new factories that operated "along the lines of existing factories" and put people to work on "familiar tasks."[19] In the "golden decades" of the 1950s and 1960s, banks performed their task admirably: they channeled credit to where the needs and growth opportunities were greatest.[20] Banks "followed enterprise," as the great Cambridge University economist Joan Robinson might have said.[21]

By the early 1970s, average incomes in euro-area countries had climbed back to around 70 percent of the US level, about where they were at the onset of the Great Depression.[22] Banks assets (loans and other investments) had reached around 100 percent of GDP, which made the European banking system somewhat bigger than those in Japan and the United States. Postwar

FIGURE 4.3. Europe's impressive postwar economic recovery.
(Euro-area GDP per capita as percent of US GDP per capita, three-year moving averages)
Note: This chart plots the weighted average per capita GDP (in purchasing power parity terms) of euro-area countries as a ratio of US per capita GDP. Nine of the first twelve members represent the euro area in this chart. Greece, Ireland, and Luxembourg were not included, because data on these countries were not available for the entire period. Given the relatively small size of the omitted countries, the picture looks much the same if they are included for the years for which their data are available.
Sources: Angus Maddison. "Historical Statistics of the World Economy 1-2008 AD." series "GDP" and "Population" http://www.ggdc.net/maddison/oriindex.htm.

reconstruction was over, and the fruitful relationship between banks and economic growth was ending.

This was a moment for European policymakers to put the brakes on the growth of banks and, instead, begin promoting more nimble financial markets, which would bet on creative entrepreneurs. To further catch up with the United States, it was no longer sufficient to build more factories. Growth now required much greater reliance on "innovation."[23]

That shift did not occur. Many governments still either owned or controlled large parts of the banking sector. They pushed bank lending in the belief that providing more credit would help raise standards of living. This continued tendency to use banks as an instrument of public policy was prevalent in many parts of what is now the eurozone, but it was especially strong in the French civil law countries (France, Belgium, Italy, Portugal, and Spain), where governments were either the principal owners of banks or had a heavy hand in directing the flow of credit.[24] However, unlike in the "golden years," the latest round of credit expansion often favored specific regions or special interests; credit flows were misdirected and fostered public corruption.[25]

In France, for example, President Giscard d'Estaing began this latest phase of bank expansion in 1974, and President Mitterrand continued the process in May 1981, soon after taking office, when he nationalized thirty-six banks, placing around 60 percent of bank deposits in the hands of the state.[26] Harvard University political scientist Peter Hall has concluded that these efforts did more harm than good; the government used its "considerable control over the flow of finance" to channel funds "towards declining sectors."[27] In Italy, government-owned banks pushed subsidized credit to the politically well connected.[28] Although the Italian government claimed it was promoting "industrial restructuring and growth," as in France, Italian banks were significant funders of declining sectors and low-productivity projects.[29]

Even when the lending was well intentioned, European businesses, instead of investing in creative effort or in stepped-up worker training, focused mainly on replacing workers with more machines. This strategy could generate only limited productivity gains. With the aid of more machines, workers did produce more output per hour, but the gains steadily diminished. Growth in the all-important "total factor productivity," which accounts for both labor and capital inputs, decelerated quickly.[30]

Oddly, slower productivity growth made it easier for banks to expand. When growth slows, households do not typically reduce the share of their incomes that they save. The savings add to household wealth, and, hence, the wealth-to-income ratio increases. The slower the rate of economic growth, the faster the increase in the wealth-to-income ratio. Economists Thomas Piketty and Gabriel Zucman find that starting precisely in the early 1970s, wealth-to-income ratios increased through much of the industrialized world but especially rapidly in Europe, where growth had slowed the most.[31] Households parked more of their wealth as deposits and other financial investments in banks. With added funds, banks stepped up their lending, but running out of profitable opportunities in their traditional lending to businesses, they expanded into new and riskier areas of home financing and consumer credit.[32]

During the 1970s and 1980s, bank assets doubled in size relative to the economy, reaching 200 percent of GDP in 1990. All the while, productivity growth fell sharply. Through these years, banks also became powerful domestic political players.[33] They nurtured long-term lending relationships with their often equally influential borrowers.

Banks Merge and Expand As Euro Approaches

This European banking legacy soon met and interacted powerfully with the other great historical force: the drive toward a single currency. In the early 1990s, capital controls were dismantled, as a first step on the way to the single currency. Suddenly, banks faced the threat that a "giant" German bank would compete with them in their hitherto protected domestic markets. Bankers and policymakers drew the inference that "only the giants" would survive.[34] Thus, in anticipation of the euro's introduction, European banks frantically sought merger partners with whom they hoped to stake out positions of greater strength. The vast majority of mergers were domestic, as governments encouraged their banks to merge and create "national champions," which could then "compete in the European or global marketplace."[35] Only the Belgian government was not especially concerned about "national champions," and among the few cross-country mergers, three—ING, Fortis, and Dexia—had a Belgian partner.

This, then, is the history that the euro area inherited. From its very start, the euro area was "overbanked." Bank assets equaled 250 percent of GDP, far higher than in the United States or even in Japan. The density of bank branches in the largest euro-area economies—Germany, France, Italy, and Spain—was also much higher than in the United States or Japan.[36] And the overbanked euro area faced slowing productivity growth, which could deliver only meager returns on traditional lending activities.

Moreover, the rush to merge had made some banks too big to fail.[37] As early as 2001, the IMF cautioned that systemic financial risks were brewing in the euro-area member states. If a large bank became insolvent and was unable therefore to repay its creditors, cascading effects through the financial system would inflict significant costs on the government and eventually on the entire economy.[38] The IMF grimly warned that some banks were so large that rescue efforts would strain the financial resources of the government.[39]

To make matters worse, since the mergers had not made the banks more efficient, these outsize banks began taking greater risks in the hope of making easy money.[40] Instead of relying mainly on their depositors for a stable source of funding, banks increasingly raised funds in temperamental "wholesale" money markets. These markets are run by money managers who, in turn, are funded by large investors such as insurance companies and pension funds. The money managers lend for short durations and so can refuse to roll over their loans to banks. When financial stress looms, money managers can declare a strike and freeze funding, placing the ability of troubled banks to continue their operations in jeopardy. But with the then-plentiful supply of short-term money market funds, banks financed activities such as mergers and acquisitions of European corporations. They sought new profit-making opportunities, including stepped up trading of financial assets and packaging of loans to create new securities.[41] "On balance," the IMF paper ended, "these trends raise serious issues regarding key aspects of financial oversight."[42] Translated from IMF language, the regulators were asleep at the wheel.

Regulators Allow Banks to Take On More Risk

Ironically, because banks had grown so large, national regulators throughout the euro area had developed a commitment to helping banks find ways of bolstering the returns that the banks paid to their investors. A particularly crucial regulatory decision was on how much capital banks needed to hold to cover potential losses on their increasingly risky operations. Regulators allowed the banks to hold only modest amounts of "high-quality" capital— cash and equity rather than bonds of various kinds that required repayment to creditors.[43] Thus, banks could invest in government bonds without setting aside any capital; regulators assumed that governments would not default on their bonds. In addition, riding on Basel I, a 1988 international agreement on minimum capital requirements, regulators allowed banks to classify home mortgages as relatively low-risk assets, which, therefore, required limited capital backing. Then after 2004, the "light-touch" regulation philosophy in an updated international accord, Basel II, gave "sophisticated" banks great latitude in reaching their own judgments on how risky their assets were and, therefore, on how much capital they needed to set aside for potential losses. Banks had more scope to under-report and even hide their risks.

European regulators made one especially important concession to their banks. Unlike their US counterparts, European regulators did not require banks to hold minimum amounts of "equity" capital as a reliable cushion to absorb losses on risky assets.[44] In the United States, if a bank's assets increased disproportionately relative to its equity (in the language of regulators and financial markets, if its leverage ratio rose above a threshold), the bank needed to take "prompt corrective action" to reduce its assets or increase its equity. Equity capital is so crucial because it is the investment made by the bank's owners, and so it is their skin in the game. Equity takes the first hit when a bank is in trouble.[45] When owners have more skin in the game, the bank has greater ability to repay its depositors and creditors even in adverse conditions; this equity "buffer" makes it less likely that the bank will need official financial assistance if it runs into trouble.

European regulators allowed assets of banks to grow much faster than their equity: eurozone banks were becoming more leveraged (figure 4.4). Moreover, banks increased their leverage at the same time as they increased their reliance on "wholesale" money market funds to increase their lending. Thus,

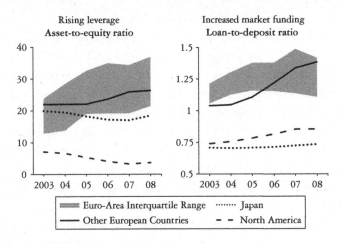

Rising leverage
Asset-to-equity ratio

Increased market funding
Loan-to-deposit ratio

Euro-Area Interquartile Range ········ Japan
—— Other European Countries – – North America

FIGURE 4.4. Euro-area bank funding becomes riskier.
Source: Bankscope.

euro-area banks were boosting their lending with unreliable funds and weak capital shock absorbers. European banks were becoming steadily riskier, but their regulators were not concerned.

To be sure, some large US banks developed the same fragilities as European banks. After all, Fed Chairman Greenspan was the philosopher who promoted "light-touch" regulation and its transformation into Basel II.[46] The cap on leverage for US investment banks was lifted in 2004 by their regulator, the US Securities and Exchange Commission (SEC). Investment banks promptly ratcheted up their leverage and used the borrowed funds to invest furiously in mortgage-backed securities.[47] The US Financial Crisis Inquiry Commission would later conclude: "The Securities and Exchange Commission's poor oversight of the five largest investment banks failed to restrict their risky activities and did not require them to hold adequate capital and liquidity for their activities."[48]

But Basel II had its true home in Europe, where regulators applied it indiscriminately across the continent's vast banking system. Sheila Bair, chairman of the US Federal Deposit Insurance Corporation and therefore a regular participant in international discussions on the amount of capital banks needed to hold, says European regulators took "industry self-regulation to new extremes, . . . articulating high-level standards but then leaving it to the banks themselves to interpret and enforce those standards."[49] At an October 2006 meeting of the Basel Committee, European members fiercely opposed the idea of an internationally agreed cap on the leverage ratio, "out of concern that its level would force some European banks to reduce assets or increase capital."[50] But that is precisely the purpose of a leverage cap: to force banks to reduce assets and increase capital. Williams College economics professor and former World Bank expert on bank regulation Gerard Caprio has also emphasized that "regulatory laxity was . . . a clear concern in continental Europe, where a devotion to Basel was perhaps most intense."[51] European banks became adept at exploiting the regulatory framework.[52]

Especially worrisome was the further fact that the limited equity holding by European banks was earning meager returns. It should have been the opposite. In principle, when only a limited amount of equity euros backs up a bank's business, equity investors should earn higher returns. If, for example, €100 of bank assets generate a return of €1, then a bank with €10 of equity earns a 10 percent return for its equity investors, but a bank with only €5 of equity earns a 20 percent return. Euro-area banks not only had less equity relative to their assets, but until 2005, most euro-area banks also earned lower returns on equity than did US banks or banks elsewhere in Europe (figure 4.5).[53] The reason for the low returns was simple: assets of banks in the euro area were not sufficiently productive. Simply put, the euro area was "overbanked" and had low productivity growth; there were too many banks, and the businesses to which they lent were not growing quickly enough. Hence, banks in the euro area needed to rely on the risky strategy of increasing their leverage to generate high equity returns. Only

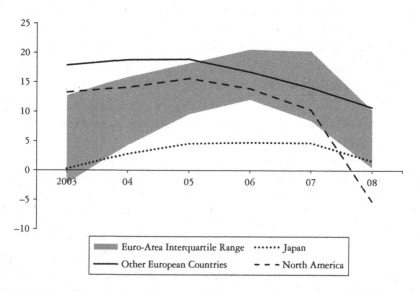

FIGURE 4.5. Euro-area banks use greater leverage to earn higher return on equity.
(Return on equity, percent)
Source: Bankscope.

briefly, in 2006 and 2007, when the leverage ratio of eurozone banks reached dangerous heights, did investors in eurozone banks earn high equity returns.

With Productivity Growth Stalled, Impatient Banks Take New Risks

The problem was that while the euro gave new impetus to the eurozone's banks, it did little to boost productivity growth, which remained weak. As Northwestern University's Robert Gordon noted, Europe was "left at the station when America's productivity locomotive departed."[54] Between 1995 and the early 2000s, US companies employed more workers and used technical advances to make them more productive.[55] But European businesses missed that window.[56] Even German and French productivity had failed to keep pace with US progress; Italy and Spain performed even worse (figure 4.6).

European authorities had recognized that the slow pace of productivity growth was a problem soon after the euro was introduced. At the summit in Lisbon on March 23–24, 2000, Eurozone leaders had ostentatiously pledged to "enhance" innovation and "modernize" education and thus make Europe's

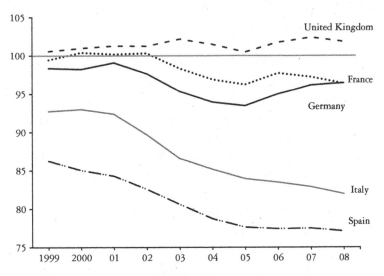

FIGURE 4.6. Euro-area productivity growth falls behind.
(Total factor productivity relative to the United States, US = 100.)
Source: Antonin Bergeaud, Gilbert Cette, and Remy Lecat. 2016. "Productivity Trends in Advanced Countries between 1890 and 2012." *Review of Income and Wealth* 62, no. 3: 420–444. Data available at www.longtermproductivity.com.

economy "the most competitive and dynamic knowledge-based economy in the world."[57] They had listed 102 specific targets for national authorities to achieve by 2010, with the goal of raising GDP growth by one percentage point a year.

A flurry of activity followed. Soon there were "Competitiveness Councils, Directorates for Enterprise and Information Society, Innovation Platforms, Growth Plans and High-Level Working Groups."[58] These ceremonial committees and processes became ends in themselves. As anthropologist Clifford Geertz might have said, European authorities had taken another "involutionary" turn.[59] Economists Guido Tabellini and Charles Wyplosz criticized the Soviet-style quantitative targets set under the Lisbon Agenda. They ruefully remarked, "Governments want to show that they have done something, and yet nothing of substance is affected. It seems a joke, but it is not."[60] MIT's Olivier Blanchard described the Lisbon boast—to make the EU the world's most dynamic and competitive economy—as "largely empty and pathetic."[61]

There was one other possibility. Perhaps, as the promoters of the euro had promised, use of the single currency would set off business decisions that would deliver a big productivity prize. Economist Andrew Rose of the University of California, Berkeley, believed such gains were likely. He predicted that "one money" would induce more trade within the euro area, which, he said, would increase competition and force businesses to sharpen their performances. Using modern econometric techniques, he asked how countries in prior currency unions had fared. Extrapolating from that earlier experience, Rose estimated that the euro could double, even triple the trade among member states.[62] Rose was not quite sure why a single currency would increase trade by such large amounts. He acknowledged that reduced transaction costs and lower exchange-rate volatility could not deliver such large dividends.[63] With little else to go on, he said, "It is wisest to conclude that we simply do not know why a common currency seems to facilitate trade so much."[64] Nevertheless, the euro, Rose twice insisted—at the start of his article and again at the end—would deliver "undisputed benefit."[65]

Rose had everyone's attention. In reports for the British and Swedish governments, he repeated the claim that by adopting the single currency, their countries also could double or even triple trade with euro-area countries.[66] Rose was telling the two European nations held back by domestic politics that they were missing large economic gains by not joining the euro area.[67]

Ben Bernanke, a Princeton University economics professor until 2002, when he was appointed a governor of the Federal Reserve Board, was skeptical of Rose's claims. In February 2004, Bernanke pointed out that several countries, including Germany, were reducing—not increasing—their share of trade with other euro-area members. The share of trade within the euro area, he said, had fallen "noticeably below" the peak reached in the early 1990s.[68] Italy's share of trade had declined the most, but the Germans and the French were also exporting less to the euro area (figure 4.7). Growing opportunities for increased trade lay outside Europe, especially with the dynamic United States and emerging market economies. Therefore, the most reasonable conclusion was that the euro had no effect on trade patterns. The most careful econometric study came only much later. That study said that the countries that had joined the euro area had long had strong trade ties with one another; once these old ties were accounted for, the influence of the euro was essentially zero; and even later, Rose, with coauthor Reuven Glick of the Federal Reserve Bank of San Franciso, offered a "mea culpa," pleading it was wrong to have extrapolated from data on other currency unions and claims of trade benefits from a single currency did not apply to the eurozone.[69]

There were no magical solutions for Europe's productivity problem. Gordon recommended an overhaul of educational and R&D systems and efforts to attract skilled foreigners, develop equity finance, and promote venture capital.[70] A report written by leading European economists had reached the same conclusion: to close the gap with the United States, the priorities had to be "more retraining, greater reliance on market financing, and higher investment in both R&D and higher education."[71] These were important and urgent tasks. The frontiers of research and educational skills were expanding

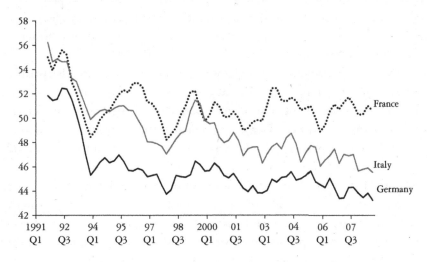

FIGURE 4.7. Trade shares of principal euro-area countries with their euro-area partners fall or stay flat.
(Percent, three-quarter moving average)
Source: IMF Direction of Trade Statistics.

rapidly.[72] The until-recently low-wage Asian nations were investing vast resources in education, and their businesses were making big strides in developing their technological capacities. In Europe, EU institutions and coordination had little to offer. Each member nation had to urgently do its own homework and embark on what was bound to be a long-haul journey.

Thus, with no immediate prospect that eurozone productivity growth would accelerate, banks began tiring of the limited profit potential at home and they sought new opportunities abroad. German and French banks, in particular, joined the irrational exuberance in the United States. They borrowed US dollars from US money markets and invested them in dodgy securities, including "subprime mortgages."[73] Working through the "shadow banking" system, they added significantly to financial excesses in the United States.[74]

German and French banks also led a homegrown irrational exuberance. They rapidly increased their lending to the eurozone's so-called periphery countries: Greece, Ireland, Portugal, and Spain. The periphery countries now suddenly looked "risk-free." Before the euro's introduction, these countries could, and did, devalue their national currencies. After the devaluation, domestic borrowers found it harder to repay international debts denominated in US dollars or German marks. Hence, anticipating possible devaluation, foreign lenders charged high interest rates as compensation for the risk they were taking. Now, with the single currency, the devaluation risk had disappeared, which made these countries appear safer. Reflecting that perception of greater safety, foreign lenders lowered the interest rates they charged to periphery borrowers (figure 4.8). Lenders were happy with the new business, and periphery borrowers quickly became more indebted.

What was remarkable, though, was that interest rates to the periphery had not just come down, but also virtually equalized across eurozone member countries. Thus, Greek borrowers paid nearly the same interest rate as German borrowers. German and French lenders were assuming that Greeks and other periphery borrowers would not default on their debts and that if they came close to doing so, European authorities would bail them out. Maurice Obstfeld, then a professor of economics at the University of California, Berkeley, emphasized that by treating government bonds held by banks as risk-free, European authorities had signaled that they would very likely find ways of repaying creditors who had lent to governments on the verge of defaulting; similarly, when the ECB lent to banks, it regarded government bonds of all member nations as having equal security value. Thus, Obstfeld said, the eurozone's financial framework encouraged investors to lend cheaply to governments with shaky public finances.[75]

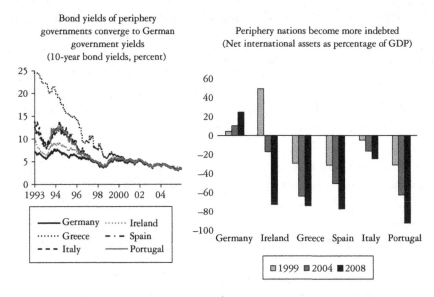

FIGURE 4.8. As interest rates fall, countries in the euro-area periphery become more indebted.

Note: Negative values of net assets indicate that the country is a net debtor.

Sources: Eurostat, "EMU Convergence Criterion Series—Monthly Data" (irt_lt_mcby_m); Eurostat, Data Series, "International Investment Position—Annual Data" (bop_ext_intpos); "GDP and Main Components (Output, Expenditure and Income) (name_10_gdp)."

In fact, the forces driving the credit flows to the periphery were even more powerful than Obstfeld had portrayed them. The triumph of politics over economics had brought the euro to life, but Alan Walters's ghost was lurking, and economics was about to take its revenge. Economics almost always exacts its revenge.

Walters's Ghost Takes Banks on a Lending Spree

Padoa-Schioppa was particularly proud that the ECB had successfully kept "inflation and inflation expectations stable and anchored to its very demanding definition of price stability."[76] Similarly, Jean-Claude Trichet, who had succeeded Wim Duisenberg as ECB president on November 1, 2003, said that with its "steady posture" and "alertness," the ECB had conveyed a message of calm and had thus achieved low and stable inflation with minimal activism.[77]

This self-congratulation missed the point. Sweden and the United Kingdom, having consciously stayed out of the eurozone, had also achieved low inflation rates. Even Poland, much poorer than euro-area countries and hence more likely to experience bursts of inflation, had contained its inflation to near the euro-area average. Indeed, inflation had rapidly come down throughout the world. As Kenneth Rogoff, then the IMF's chief economist and director of its research department, explained, competition from Chinese and other Asian exporters had "put downward pressure" on prices.[78] Inflation had come down everywhere, in large part because cheap Chinese manufactured goods were keeping a lid on prices.

In fact, the euro area had a serious inflation problem. The average inflation rate, around 2 percent, hid a large and worrying divergence in inflation rates. As Hans-Werner Sinn, president of the Munich-based Ifo Institute, had noted in 2003, and Bernanke reiterated in early 2004, Germany's inflation rate was "perhaps, uncomfortably low," while the Irish inflation rate was consistently too high.[79] This inflation differential was a problem because it created potent incentives for a credit boom.

Alan Walters, nearly two decades earlier, had explained how the link between inflation differentials and credit booms worked.[80] The observed interest rates, which had converged to near equality across the eurozone, were "nominal rates," the rates consumers and businesses paid on their borrowings. Economic decisions, however, are based on the "real interest rate," the difference between the nominal interest rate and the inflation rate. Debts are easier to repay when nominal interest rates are low and when inflation rates are high. High inflation creates a temptation to borrow today, because a business can expect to charge higher prices and consumers can expect rising salaries and wages to help repay the debt. For many periphery borrowers, real interest rates were low or even negative; inflation eroded the value of debt faster than interest payments grew. Moreover, Walters pointed out that lenders also find inflation attractive, an observation that recent research has confirmed.[81] For German and French lenders, rising prices and wages in the periphery ensured that the borrowers there would have plentiful euros to repay their debts. The strange consequence of eliminating currency devaluation was that higher inflation made periphery borrowers less competitive but, at least temporarily, more creditworthy.

Thus, in an almost perfect replication of Walters's prediction, foreign capital flowed to countries with high inflation rates; the inflow of capital raised the inflation rates further, which, in turn, caused more capital to flow in (figure 4.9). With a single monetary policy, the ECB had no way to stop this self-reinforcing process. Meanwhile, German and even French inflation remained relatively low, because their banks were pushing funds toward the periphery. The ECB was essentially powerless to deal with the inflation

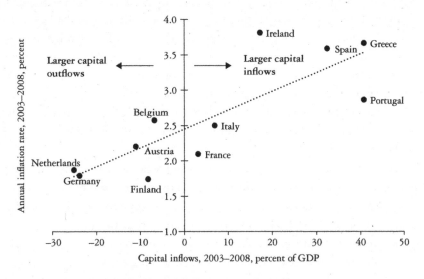

FIGURE 4.9. Gush of foreign capital inflows raises inflation rates, 2003–2008.
Note: Foreign capital inflows are the cumulative financial account. The larger the positive number, the greater the capital inflows; the larger the negative number, the greater the capital outflows.
Source: World Bank, World Development Indicators.

divergence across the eurozone's member states. If it wished to dampen the frenzy in the periphery, the ECB would have had to raise interest rates so high that the Germans and the French would have squealed, which they had not been shy to do between 2001 and 2003.[82] Philip Lane, then an economics professor at Trinity College, Dublin, dryly noted in 2006, "Common monetary policy has not suited all member countries at all times."[83] Unlike in the United States, where differences in inflation rates across states and regions were quickly reversed by labor mobility and fiscal transfers, the euro area's inflation divergence persisted because labor mobility was low, fiscal transfers were virtually nonexistent, and, above all, euro-area policymakers seemed oblivious to the ongoing credit expansion-inflation cycle.[84]

To make matters worse, while money was pouring into the periphery, borrowers were becoming less able to repay their debts. Rising inflation had led to higher costs of production, and signs of declining international competitiveness were already evident. Exporters from the periphery countries were being "displaced from their foreign markets" by competitors from China and Eastern Europe.[85] The growth rates of exports from the periphery countries were falling, their imports were growing rapidly, and, hence, their current account deficits were steadily widening. Declining international competitiveness because of continued high inflation was bound eventually to shrink the profits of domestic firms and raise their risk of default.

The risk was particularly acute because productivity growth had come to a virtual standstill in the euro area's periphery economies. Even by the low standards of the eurozone when compared with the United States, productivity growth in the eurozone's periphery was abysmal. Especially in the boom years between 2003 and 2008, as capital gushed into the periphery, productivity growth in these countries was close to zero. In fact, for short periods, productivity actually fell: the economies became less efficient in using capital and labor to produce output.

Low productivity growth in the periphery was neither accidental nor a temporary aberration. These countries lacked the foundations needed to compete in a more knowledge-intensive international economy. Standards of education and especially of R&D had fallen behind even by the modest standards of the eurozone (figure 4.10). There was no reason to expect a productivity resurgence. The euro-area periphery was experiencing the archetype of a "bad credit boom," which too frequently ends badly, as economists Gorton and Ordoñez have documented. Credit was fueling domestic demand, but loss of competitiveness and low productivity growth made the eventual task of repaying the debt increasingly difficult.

Europe had seen this movie before. In 1992–93, the ERM system, through which European nations fixed their exchange rates vis-à-vis one another, had broken down following precisely the logic spelled out by Walters.[86] High-inflation countries had attracted foreign capital for a while,

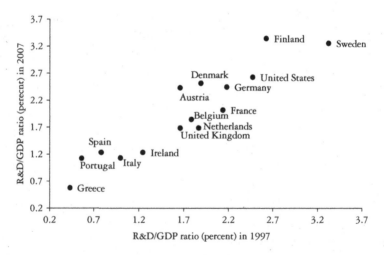

FIGURE 4.10. R&D rates were low in the euro-area periphery in 1997 and stayed low in 2007.
(R&D as a percentage of GDP, 2007 versus 1997)
Source: OECD Statistical Database.

but their competitiveness had continued to decline; eventually, lenders had decided it was time to take their profits and run. Now, in the rerun of the ERM movie, the problem was even more serious. European banks had become larger, the perception that lending to the periphery was risk-free was more deep-seated, and the rate of productivity growth in the countries receiving foreign capital had declined since the ERM crisis.

Financial and Cognitive Bubbles in the Eurozone's Periphery

Although the Walters mechanism operated in the same way throughout the periphery, each country had a different story. Italy did not have a credit boom; it just did not grow. In Ireland and Spain, the credit flows fed into spectacular property price and construction frenzies. Greece and Portugal suffered principally from deep loss in international competitiveness.

ITALY

Italy received only modest foreign capital, and its inflation rate remained relatively low. Thus, Italy did not have a financial bubble. Italy had long-term problems, which would become clearer a few years further down the road: the Italian economy simply seemed unable to grow and the Italian banking system was too large.

IRELAND

Ireland had the biggest bubble, which had a dramatic history in the making. In the 1970s and into the 1980s, Ireland was, like Greece, Portugal, and Spain, a relatively poor and mismanaged European economy. Plagued by high unemployment and high inflation, Irish authorities frequently needed to devalue their currency, the pound, to compensate for the country's high inflation. In January 1988, the London *Economist*'s special survey on Ireland showed a young woman clothed in rags and holding a little girl in her arms; on the pavement in front of her, she had placed a begging bowl. The not-so-subtle theme was that "poor Ireland" perpetually lived beyond its means.[87]

However, starting in the late 1980s and into the early 1990s, several favorable factors turned the Irish economy around. American multinational companies in the expanding information-technology industry and established pharmaceutical producers decided to take advantage of Ireland's low-tax regime. They set up manufacturing facilities in Ireland, which brought jobs and created spillover benefits for Irish suppliers. Dublin's international financial center attracted global financial firms. Educational standards rose, and generous aid from the EU financed much-needed infrastructure. In less than a decade, Ireland's per capita income had skyrocketed to one of the highest in the world. The *Economist*'s May 1997 cover proclaimed Ireland as "Europe's Shining Light."

Critics complained that Ireland's progress was vastly overstated. One journalist wrote that Ireland had become "a laundering operation for multinational industry in order to avoid tax."[88] Indeed, foreign companies used various accounting tricks to record their global profits in Ireland. These vast profits, seemingly generated in Ireland with very few workers, gave the statistical illusion of soaring Irish productivity growth. However, Ireland had more going for it than mere statistical jugglery by multinational corporations. Economists Patrick Honohan and Brendan Walsh established that after stripping out the illusion created by the tax-avoidance shenanigans, Irish progress, although not "miraculous," was "solid."[89]

Thus, unlike their counterparts in the other periphery countries, Irish authorities and citizens did not see the European single currency as an "external anchor," a mechanism to instill domestic policy discipline. Moreover, by joining the single-currency area, Ireland stood to make virtually no economic gain. For Ireland, even the transactional convenience was limited since its principal trade and investment connections were with the United Kingdom and the United States. In October 1996, a report by the Economic and Social Research Institute (ESRI), a Dublin-based think tank, recognized that a common European monetary policy would not serve Irish needs.[90] Honohan, one of the principal authors of the ESRI report and later governor of Ireland's central bank, conceded that the economic argument for joining the euro was "not particularly decisive."[91] But the ESRI report did lean in favor of Ireland joining the single-currency area. Their reason for doing so was odd: interest rates would decline and create jobs in the building sector.[92]

Because the Irish economy's "solid" progress was recent, the legacy of its less-developed past remained. Even in the 1990s, the Irish had not fully transitioned from agricultural to urban activities. And conversion of agricultural land to allow residential and commercial property construction was creating the potential for huge financial gains. County councilors, who held the authority to rezone land, leveraged that authority for financial gain and political power. The government was priming the pump with incentives such as grants for first-time home buyers, mortgage-interest deduction, and tax breaks on urban-renewal schemes and capital gains.[93] In 1996, the IMF had noted the disturbingly rapid increase in property prices and had warned against policy measures to stimulate construction.[94] However, an insidious nexus of relationships was forming among politicians, property developers, and banks. Rising property prices increased the incentives and potential for corruption.

A series of judicial investigations, which began in November 1997, eventually led to jail sentences for Liam Lawlor and Ray Burke, senior members of the ruling Fianna Fáil party.[95] The investigations tainted successive Fianna Fáil prime ministers Charles Haughey, Albert Reynolds, and Bertie Ahern.[96] The network of corruption extended throughout the party. A key figure in its fundraising operation during those years reportedly said: "Fianna Fáil was good for builders and builders were good for Fianna Fáil, and there was nothing wrong with that."[97]

There were probably several reasons for Ireland to join the eurozone, including a (misguided) sense fostered by officials that otherwise the government would lose access to EC funds, a legacy of its "poor" past. The Irish also wanted to create greater political distance from the United Kingdom.[98] But the ruling Fianna Fáil party maintained resolute commitment to the European single currency also because it attached great importance to low interest rates, which would keep up the momentum of construction activity spurred by rising property prices.

Once Ireland joined the eurozone, interest rates did plummet, and since inflation shot up, "real interest rates" turned negative.[99] Irish property developers and their banks were delighted. Cheap and plentiful credit fed property price gains of between 10 and 15 percent every year between 2001 and 2003.

Amid this craziness, it was the IMF's job to worry about financial risks, and indeed, in August 2003, the IMF's annual consultation report warned that Ireland's spectacular credit and property price "boom" was probably a "bubble."[100] There was "substantial risk," the IMF said, that houses prices were "significantly overvalued."[101] The Irish authorities pushed back. Household indebtedness, they countered, was not especially high, and a young population with a bright future would be well able to repay its debts.[102] The IMF withdrew its warning and concluded that the likelihood of defaults was low and risks to the financial sector were "manageable."[103]

After a brief pause in 2003, "real" property prices (house prices adjusted for inflation in the consumption price index) rose by between 15 and 20 percent a year from 2004 to 2007 (figure 4.11). Even more so than in Spain, Ireland's property bubble had crossed the line into a "mania." Financial historians Charles Kindleberger and Robert Aliber have written that a bubble forms when people buy assets with the expectation that they can still sell

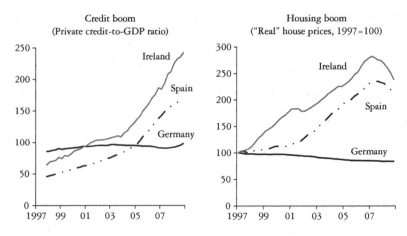

FIGURE 4.11. Ireland and Spain: credit and house prices boom.
Note: Credit is measured as stock of loans to other residents (loans to borrowers other than monetary and financial institutions and the government) granted by monetary and financial institutions (other than the European System of Central Banks) as a percentage of GDP (chain-linked volume), quarterly frequency.
Sources: ECB, Statistical Data Warehouse, sdw.ecb.europa.eu; OECD Statistical Database for "real" house prices.

them at a higher price to a "bigger fool."[104] A mania, in contrast, is pure frenzy.

Irish banks drove this mania. Setting the pace in Ireland was Anglo Irish, a bank that grew as if on steroids. With little shareholder equity that had its own skin in the game, Anglo Irish's management lent furiously to the Irish property market. Because customer deposits were flowing in too slowly, Anglo relied ever more on short-term, wholesale, money market funds. This was great business: borrowing short-term funds at low interest rates and lending to the property sector at premium rates.

With Anglo setting the new norms, all banks—including the two major banks, Allied Irish Bank (AIB) and Bank of Ireland—felt compelled to join the gold rush.[105] The pressure to follow Anglo Irish increased as its growth drew rave reviews from highly regarded international analysts. In December 2006, an assessment by Goldman Sachs "was positively effusive on Anglo's prospects."[106] New York-based financial consultancy Oliver Wyman was an even bigger fan, describing Anglo Irish as a "supermodel" and ranking it as the world's best-performing bank in 2007.[107]

These were intoxicating years. In a 2011 retrospective commissioned by the Irish parliament, Peter Nyberg, a former Finnish regulator, reported that the Irish Financial Services Regulatory Authority was "clearly aware of many of the problems" brewing in Ireland's banks.[108] But "light-touch," "principles-based" regulation was in fashion, and banks were allowed considerable freedom to manage their own risks. And banks brazenly abused that autonomy.[109] Auditors and the regulatory authority had independently observed that Anglo and other Irish banks had "materially deviated" from required procedures.[110] But hey, everyone loves success, and no one was willing to spoil the party.

Even the IMF changed its tune. In 2006, by which time the bubble was surely a mania, the words "boom" and "bubble" found no place in the IMF's annual review.[111] To the contrary, the IMF's special assessment of the Irish financial sector delivered a glowing report. Yes, some tweaking was necessary, but it was all good, the IMF concluded.[112] Nyberg wrote that the IMF's endorsement reinforced confidence in the "soundness" of the banking system and in the system's guardians, the central bank and the financial regulator.[113]

Yale University's Robert Shiller says that in all episodes of irrational exuberance, initial concerns give way to the belief that this time is different. Some of those who see the craziness and hold back are sucked in to the euphoria eventually. "People who thought there was a bubble, and that prices were too high, find themselves questioning their own earlier judgments, and start to wonder whether fundamentals are indeed driving the price increase." They come to believe that "the fundamentals will go on forever."[114]

SPAIN

The Spanish property-credit boom gained momentum in late 2003, around a decade after it started in Ireland. In Ireland, the single currency amplified an ongoing boom; in Spain, the recently introduced single currency triggered the boom. As in Ireland, observers expressed early concerns when the risks were beginning to build. Worried by the gathering pace of property prices, IMF staff advised the Spanish government in late 2003 to phase out "generous incentives" for home ownership.[115] But, as in Ireland, Spanish authorities responded that the demands of a growing population rather than financial speculation were causing property prices to increase, a position which the IMF accepted.[116]

However, many in Spain remained alarmed. Among them was Miguel Ángel Fernández Ordóñez, who had held a number of official positions in the 1990s, including secretary of state for the economy. In late 2003, and not a government official at the time, Fernández Ordóñez repeatedly cautioned that Spain was living on borrowed money and time. He was worried that the substantial amount of foreign capital that was pouring in would need to be repaid by increasing exports and curbing imports, a task that would become harder as Spain lost competitiveness. "The future may be long in coming," Fernández Ordóñez grimly warned, "but it will come."[117]

The Bank of Spain was also worried. The bank's April 2005 *Economic Bulletin* concluded that property prices had "departed from their fundamentals" and had disconnected from reality. To buy increasingly expensive homes, Spanish households were rapidly becoming more indebted. A pause in the good times would make debt harder to repay, increasing the likelihood of distress and default.[118]

Kindleberger and Aliber tell us, "Fraudulent behavior increases in economic booms. . . . individuals become greedy for a share of the increase in wealth and swindlers come forward to exploit that greed."[119] Spain, just as Ireland had some years earlier, fell prey to the menace of corruption. But in Spain, a darker stream of transactions also emerged. In March 2005, a police investigation, "Operation White Whale," established that international criminals and mafias were using their undeclared cash to buy Spanish property.[120] An investigation in March 2006 led to the arrest of several municipal officials in the coastal town of Marbella, where two earlier mayors had been charged for fraudulent practices and links with Italian and Russian mafias.[121] While regional authorities and the central government in Madrid moaned about the damage being done to Spain's reputation, they did little to rein in municipal bosses; instead, they "looked the other way—with or without open palms extended backwards."[122]

As in Ireland, regional and municipal governments authorized land development; but in Spain, they also controlled large numbers of savings banks, the *cajas*.[123] Although *cajas* were technically private institutions, politicians were on their governing boards, and "many were run at some point or another by prominent local politicians or even national ones."[124] By leading the rush to provide property credit, the *cajas* played the same role in Spain as Anglo Irish did in Ireland. Just as AIB and the Bank of Ireland had felt compelled to follow Anglo, other Spanish banks competed to keep pace with the *cajas*. In the process, Spanish *cajas* and banks became highly leveraged and increasingly reliant on "wholesale funding."[125]

In mid-2006, the narratives began to diverge. The official view remained upbeat. The IMF in its mid-2006 review said that Spain's financial sector was "highly dynamic and competitive," and its safety was ensured by "strong prudential supervision and regulation."[126]

But worrying messages continued. In April 2007, financial and property stocks fell when a prominent property developer was found to have "inflated profits."[127] The most serious warning came in May from the Bank of Spain's bank inspectors, who rebelled against the official effort to downplay the risks. In an extraordinary letter to Deputy Prime Minister Pedro Solbes, the inspectors insisted that their boss, Bank of Spain Governor Jaime Caruana, was misleading the Spanish public and investors. He was minimizing "the latent risk in the Spanish financial system" and ignoring the "predictable consequences" of a sudden adverse change in the Spanish and global economies. "Based on our experience and knowledge of the complex financial supervisory tasks," the inspectors wrote, "the risks are not under control as the Governor asserts, nor is it probable that the consequences will be as limited as he suggests."[128] The inspectors went a step further. They asserted that Caruana was deliberating downplaying the dangers that lay ahead because he had allowed reckless lending practices to spread and was now unwilling to acknowledge the risks that the country's economy and financial system were facing.

In July 2006, Caruana's term as the governor ended, and he moved to a senior position at the IMF. His successor was the same Miguel Ángel Fernández Ordóñez who had warned of a coming financial crisis in late 2003. Now in a different role, he adopted a more soothing tone. In April 2007, as the subprime crisis heated up in the United States and questions about property valuations in Spain and elsewhere grew more insistent, Fernández Ordóñez maintained that property prices and the economy would glide down from their giddy heights to a "soft landing." Banks, he said, had the financial cushions to absorb losses.[129] In June, as further signs of distress in US mortgage markets emerged, he said that demand for homes would hold up in Spain, and extensive defaults on mortgages were unlikely.[130] And in September, by which time financial markets were truly nervous, Fernández Ordóñez said: "Spanish lenders face this period of turbulence from a position of strength."[131] The banks, he again asserted, had built up large buffers during the good times precisely to help tide them over in such periods of stress. The IMF reinforced the optimism: the economy would slow down only gradually, and the future looked "bright."[132]

GREECE AND PORTUGAL

In Greece and Portugal, property price bubbles played a less prominent role than in Ireland and Spain. However, as in Ireland and Spain, the high rate of domestic price inflation caused Greece and Portugal to lose international competitiveness. Hence, in all four countries, imports increased at a faster pace than exports, which meant that their current account deficits with the rest of the world widened. International investors financed those deficits, and so the periphery countries became more indebted to foreigners.

In an elegant research paper presented in late 2002, MIT's Olivier Blanchard and Bocconi University's Francesco Giavazzi celebrated the rise in Greek and Portuguese external debts, giving credit to the euro for making this desirable outcome possible.[133] Blanchard and Giavazzi made a logically appealing case. Greece and Portugal, they explained, were the "poorest" of eurozone countries. Because they were "poor," they almost certainly had vast untapped investment opportunities. Foreign capital flowing into these two countries, they said, would help step up productive investment, which would raise Greek and Portuguese growth rates. And while foreign funds worked to raise domestic growth, Greek and Portuguese citizens could afford to export less than they imported—and save less than they invested—because greater prosperity would soon help them repay their foreign debts.[134] Moreover, foreigners themselves would earn higher rates of return by investing in Greece and Portugal than they could by investing at home. Everyone stood to gain. Blanchard and Giavazzi concluded that governments would do well to step aside and let the process unfold. A policy of "benign neglect," they counseled, "appears to be a reasonable course of action."[135]

Blanchard and Giavazzi presented their paper to a gathering of leading economists at the Washington-based Brookings Institution's Panel on Economic Activity. In a prepared response, Princeton economist Pierre-Olivier Gourinchas questioned the realism of the Blanchard-Giavazzi logic.

In past episodes of rapid inflows of foreign capital, Gourinchas said, foreign investors had only infrequently invested in productive enterprise and had done little to spur significant domestic productive investment. As in those earlier instances, he said, Greek and Portuguese debts would keep piling up, but the ability to repay would not improve.[136] The "specter of default" would surely rise. It was not too early, Gourinchas advised, for the Greek and Portuguese governments to tighten their fiscal belts and start saving up for the day when the bills would surely come due.

Another Princeton economist, Christopher Sims, spoke next, and he had the same message: "Opening up capital markets in poor countries has often led initially to large inflows and later to financial problems."[137] Sims also warned of the risk of sovereign defaults.

In August 2003, economists Carmen Reinhart and Kenneth Rogoff noted that Greece and Portugal belonged to the small club of "serial defaulters."[138] Both had defaulted on external creditors multiple times in the nineteenth century. Rogoff was still the IMF's chief economist and Reinhart was one of his deputies. Together with their colleague, Miguel Savastano, they reported that serial defaulters had "weak fiscal structures and weak financial systems," which persisted for years. Political systems in such countries remained unable to overcome their failings. Reinhart, Rogoff, and Savastano predicted that countries with a history of past defaults would continue to default. It was "sheer folly," they said, to assume that the history of serial default could be erased by new monetary and financial arrangements.[139]

The IMF's operational staff members were also worried. They knew, first-hand, that Greece had weak fiscal and financial systems. Successive cohorts of staff had maintained a record of Greece as a country that had lurched from crisis to crisis since joining the EEC in 1981.[140] Repeated Greek failures reflected deep pathologies. The economy had failed to diversify; much of the economic activity was conducted in the "black market," beyond the tax net; and corruption was deeply rooted in the political culture.

In June 2003, the IMF's annual review noted that the profitability of Greek banks had fallen, and their capital buffers were eroding; hence, they would face considerable stress in an economic downturn.[141] The IMF report politely called for "added supervisory vigilance" and "a strengthening of banks' capital."[142] The IMF had other concerns. The government's expenditures on pensions and healthcare were rising quickly and were set to explode as the country's population aged.[143]

An abiding reason for the fragility of Greek public finances was endemic tax evasion. In a fascinating study, economists Nikolaos Artavanis, Adair Morse, and Margarita Tsoutsoura reported that banks considered individuals who were adept at tax evading as more creditworthy.[144] The tax offenders were typically professionals. They described themselves as self-employed in medicine, law, engineering, education, and the media. Artavanis, Morse, and Tsoutsoura estimated that in the second half of the 2000s, such tax evaders cost the Greek government revenues of between 5 billion and 10 billion euros annually, which was 50 to 100 percent of the government's budget deficits in those years.[145]

Between 2004 and 2008, the IMF warned repeatedly that Greece's economic growth was unsustainable and was bound to falter.[146] But the IMF's Cassandra-like warnings about unsustainable growth and the dangers of rising debt were beginning to appear overdone. The Greek economy had grown at an average rate of 4 percent a year, a pace higher than that achieved by most other eurozone member states. The bubble had defeated the IMF's forecasts. Perhaps the Greek economy would grow out of its debt. The IMF relented. On March 20, 2008, just days after US authorities bailed out investment bank Bear Stearns and as the world economy was sliding toward a precipice, IMF staff wrote an upbeat assessment of Greek economic prospects. The staff's report to the Board of Executive Directors had the customary caveats, but the bolded headlines read: "The Greek economy has been buoyant for several years and growth is expected to remain robust for some time. The Greek banking sector appears to be sound and has thus far remained largely unaffected by the financial market turmoil."[147]

Like Greece, Portugal had a budget-deficit problem. The more serious Portuguese problem was its current account deficit, which was *the* largest among industrialized countries.[148] When foreign banks financed this external deficit, the funds flowed into Portuguese banks, which, in turn, lent them to Portuguese borrowers. But unlike in Greece, where foreign funds kept the economy bubbling, Portuguese economic growth was slowing. Hence, debt burdens were growing rapidly. As early as 2002, the IMF noted that household and business indebtedness was "rising at an unsustainable rate."[149]

In 2006, Blanchard returned to his study of the Portuguese economy. He was dismayed. He began his report dramatically: "The Portuguese economy is in serious trouble." The catalog of ills was short but devastating. "Productivity growth is anemic. Growth is very low. The budget deficit is large. The current account deficit is very large."[150]

Portuguese wages had risen briskly. The exchange value of the euro against the dollar and other international currencies—after a sharp initial fall starting in 1999 and continuing into early 2002—had risen considerably. With the twin handicaps of rising domestic costs and a stronger euro, Portuguese exporters found it ever harder to sell their goods into world markets at competitive prices. They steadily lost ground to Chinese and other low-wage Asian producers. Investment shifted away from manufactured exports to sectors such as wholesale and retail trade, education and health services, and social work, where foreign competition could not intrude.[151] Portuguese businesses lacked both the capacity and the incentives to substantially raise product quality or establish sophisticated, skill-intensive production processes. Educational standards continued to lag, and the government made no effort to encourage R&D. Politically favored firms were given preferential access to capital and so had little reason to try harder.[152] Unable to generate economic growth, Portugal was drifting into a debt crisis.

By late 2007 and into early 2008, the financial bubbles in the eurozone's periphery had persisted for at least five years. These periphery countries possibly would have run into economic and financial problems even if they had their own currencies and monetary policies. But certainly, the common monetary policy—powerless to deal with their relatively high inflation rates—had made it financially attractive for eurozone banks to behave irresponsibly; and the financial fragilities had persisted so long because the supporting cognitive bubble, which accompanies every financial bubble, was reinforced by the perception that the euro had eliminated risk. The eurozone's fiscal rules, under the SGP, had proven unequal to the task of enforcing discipline. By now, a widespread practice of fudging fiscal numbers was in place.[153] Instead of providing an anchor in a safe harbor, the euro had steered the periphery countries into dangerous waters, where rapid credit expansion continued alongside no productivity growth.

The Political Promise Also Fades

The euro's further promise was that it would hasten Europe's political progress. The mere existence of a single currency, the so-called "monetarists" had predicted, would create the impetus for countries to come together in closer political embrace.[154] As I described in chapter 3, that political progression had not occurred during the euro's first five years. To the contrary, with the eurozone economies under pressure, national interests had quickly taken center stage with little willingness to compromise.[155] But since mid-2004, the growth outlook had improved, and financial excesses in the periphery were still regarded as a sign of euro-zone success. Could it be that seeing potential benefits from the euro, citizens across member nations were ready to create stronger political ties with one another?

A real-life test of this "falling forward" thesis came in the context of an initiative for a European constitution. Former French President Giscard d'Estaing, now an elder European statesman, was the "moving force" behind the constitution project. He had travelled through Europe for two years, selling its message of freedom and democracy.[156]

In October 2004, Europe's leaders signed a treaty to create a "constitution" for the "citizens and States of Europe."[157] Its goals, somewhat removed from its lofty words, were, for example, to consolidate past treaties into a single EU treaty and give greater weight to larger countries in European decision-making.[158] The proposed changes were desirable, but they certainly did not add up to a new "constitution." In a scathing critique, Princeton political scientist Andrew Moravcsik commented that with the powers they already had, European authorities could have made the changes sought. The constitution, in Moravcsik's view, was mainly a public relations effort "to reverse the sagging popularity of the organization."[159] Even viewed more generously, it was at best a flamboyant gesture, intended to promote a greater sense of European community and identity. Real political progress was not possible. Symbols had to play a big role.

French and Dutch citizens objected even to that symbolism. Despite Giscard d'Estaing's warning that failure to ratify the Constitutional Treaty would create chaos in Europe, on May 29, 2005, the French public voted in a referendum to reject the constitution by a decisive 55–45 percent margin.[160]

France's leaders had not been listening to their own people. Back in September 1992, French citizens had nearly rejected the Maastricht Treaty, the European contract to form a single-currency area. The no vote had come mainly from the most economically vulnerable citizens, who had blamed their economic distress on the austerity pursued to achieve European monetary-policy objectives.[161] The Maastricht no votes were important because they had revealed that French society was fracturing into "winners" and "losers." Economic winners believed in and supported more integration; the losers feared that Europe was working against them.

In 2005, the social fractures had not healed. At the time of the referendum on the Constitutional Treaty, the unacceptably high unemployment rate— recorded at more than 10 percent in early May—had become the "prime voting motivation."[162] As was true for the Maastricht referendum, those who voted against the constitution typically lacked college degrees; many were unemployed or worked in precarious, low-paid jobs.[163] The message this time was louder. Some who believed in 1992 that they would eventually join the winners had by now given up hope. Jean-Marie Colombani, editor of the French daily *Le Monde*, said that France as a nation had "lost confidence," and increasing numbers among the French public feared the future.[164]

The young, who had held faith with Europe in the vote on the Maastricht Treaty, now felt especially betrayed by French and European leaders. Among those younger than twenty-four, the unemployment rate had remained stuck near 20 percent since 1991.[165] Such persistently high unemployment among the young was acting "as a cancer on France's social structure."[166] However, France's leaders seemed unable to recognize and respond to the corrosive disease. President Chirac helplessly said, "This fear of young people I don't understand."[167] Whether because they were afraid or were angry, one-third of the eligible voters between the ages of eighteen and twenty-four did not vote in the Constitutional Treaty referendum, and of those who did vote, nearly 59 percent rejected the constitution.[168] The next-higher age group, between twenty-five and thirty-nine, responded with the same anger.

The geographical divide, starkly manifest in the vote on the Maastricht Treaty in 1992, appeared once again in sharp relief. Outside of the metropolitan areas, the mood was grim in all age groups. The unemployment rate was 20 percent, twice the national average, in Mantes-la-Jolie, "a poverty-stricken small town to the west of Paris." The town's voters turned out in large numbers to register "a protest vote against the government."[169] In Courcelles-les-Lens, a small mining town in the north of France, the unemployment rate was also 20 percent. "Like so many other grimy, weed-choked towns in the Pas de Calais region," Courcelles-les-Lens was "a hotbed of want and despair," suffering from an epidemic of alcoholism, domestic violence, and suicide. Four out of five voters in the town rejected the European constitution.[170]

It was easy and perhaps unfair for voters to place the entire blame for their economic woes on Europe. France had its own long-standing economic and social problems. Productivity growth was weak. The French public felt entitled to generous welfare payments, which the government could not afford. Quite independent of European constraints, French leaders had run out of ideas on how to reinvigorate France's economy and society.

But voters who rejected the Constitutional Treaty were persuaded that leaders were under the spell of a European ideology that favored a form of "raw Anglo-American style capitalism" predisposed to "squeeze the wage earners."[171] Voters' fear of "ultra-liberal," open-door policies was reinforced by the inflow of low-paid workers from the new member states of Eastern Europe and by the growing tendency of domestic companies to move their operations to low-wage locations.[172] And the emphasis in European rules on fiscal austerity cast a continuous threat on social protection, which added to people's anxieties.

On June 1, three days after the French vote, the Dutch rejected the Constitutional Treaty by an even bigger 62–38 percent margin.[173] In the closing days before the referendum, Prime Minister Jan Peter Balkenende pleaded with his nation to vote yes, or else he would "look like a fool."[174] The prospect of making their prime minister look like a fool only added to the passion with which such a large majority of the Dutch voted no.

The economic pattern of the Dutch no vote was virtually identical to that in the French votes on the Maastricht Treaty and the Constitutional Treaty. Indeed, the economic anxiety expressed in the Dutch vote was even greater than in France. In the French vote a few days earlier, just more than 50 percent of those without college degrees had voted no; in the Netherlands, two-thirds of such voters said no.[175] In France, two-thirds of "manual workers" rejected the treaty; in the Netherlands, more than three-quarters rejected it.

And more starkly than in France, young Dutch voters rebelled against Europe. Around half of those younger than forty did not show up to vote, and among those who did vote, more than two out of three rejected the constitution. Put differently, only one out of six Dutch voters younger than forty actively backed the treaty.

In surveys, 40 percent of the Dutch public said that Europe was "moving too fast."[176] As the largest contributors to the European budget in per capita terms, the Dutch were frustrated by what they perceived as a wasteful use of those funds; particularly egregious to them was the French insistence on subsidies to farmers. The euro, the Dutch fretted, diluted national policy authority. The new Eastern European member states created a politically charged concern that the Netherlands would need to host more migrants.

In downplaying the role of the nation-state, European leaders had unwittingly but inescapably embraced the principles of free movement of capital and labor. While European leaders were publicly contemptuous of the heartless Anglo-Saxon model of unbridled competition, they had—in their bid to build a supranational state—created a system that featured all of the downsides of "ultra-liberal" capitalism. For European citizens, more European integration had understandably become associated with "hyper-globalization," with all its ills. And despite Europe's promise to honor its "social model" and provide greater social protection, its institutions and policies offered little hope for those who were being left behind by the competitive forces unleashed. Voters in France and the Netherlands had reason to believe that Europe was working against the interests of those whose jobs were in jeopardy. And because the most anxious voters saw their own leaders as captured by European political and economic ideologies, they were turning to nationalistic forces within the country.[177]

Even though they were not directly related to the euro, the referendums did not augur well for the single currency and its governance. Italian ministers mumbled about leaving the eurozone.[178] Belgian economist Paul de Grauwe was rightly concerned that political integration needed for successful working of the euro would become much harder.[179]

The vehemence of the French and Dutch votes surprised European leaders. After all, the matter at hand was only the innocuous Constitutional Treaty. However, few European leaders understood that voters did not care what precisely the vote was about. In a way that national elections could not, the referendum gave French and Dutch citizens a rare opportunity to express unmistakable opposition to the way Europe was working and where it was heading. Given that opportunity, they had let their frustrations out, not against the constitution *per se* but against the European agenda.

Irish political scientist Peter Mair concluded that the French and the Dutch had rejected the Constitutional Treaty because there was no regular "political arena" in which to "mobilize opposition in Europe" and "hold European governance accountable."[180] National elections dealt with multiple domestic matters, and European considerations did not get priority. The referendums allowed focus on the principles and consequences of Europe.[181] You cannot keep building the architecture of Europe without talking to us, the voters had just said.

The political basis of Europe was changing. Since its inception, the European construction had relied on a doctrine attributed to Jean Monnet. Europe's leaders, Monnet believed, had the "permissive consensus" of European citizens to put in place policies that were too complex for democratic debate but were nevertheless a force for good. European matters could not be subject to democratic accountability. That "permissive consensus" had begun to erode with France's Maastricht referendum in 1992 and had now broken down.

Mair's interpretation of the referendum results and his critique of European democracy drew on the trailblazing analysis of Yale University's political theorist Robert Dahl. In a 1965 essay, Dahl had observed that governments in all Western democracies had become centralized and bureaucratic "Leviathans," run by "professional and quasi-professional leaders." This small group of "highly organized elites," Dahl wrote, worked within a narrow range of policy options and effectively shut out alternative views.[182] European governance mechanisms, Mair concluded, had greatly amplified this historic tendency to disenfranchise the public.

Few European insiders understood the force of Mair's analysis. Hubert Védrine was one of them. He had been one of Mitterrand's closest advisors and later served as French foreign minister from 1997 to 2002. In a comment after the Dutch no vote, Védrine said that Europe had walked into a crisis because its "integrationist elite" believed that a "forced march" to closer union was "necessary whatever the criticism from the people."[183] Védrine, once an ardent advocate of the Maastricht Treaty, had had a recent conversion. He now said that the French public's fierce opposition to the Maastricht Treaty had been "an early-warning signal." Instead of heeding that signal, the "elites" had "marched on," blaming those who opposed the onward march as nationalists. But citizens' views could not be continually dismissed. Their desire to regain national sovereignty, Védrine said, was understandable and legitimate.

The dominant European view, however, did not change. To the contrary, leaders reinforced their own caricatures as antidemocratic and unwilling to listen to citizens' concerns. Luxembourg Prime Minister Jean-Claude Juncker crankily insisted that the French would need to repeat their referendum, and keep repeating it, until they got the vote "right."[184]

The Euro's First Ten Years: Taking Stock

The euro's first decade fell into two halves. During the first five years, amid a slow-growing world economy, the eurozone's policymakers tightly enforced their stability ideology, which prolonged recessionary conditions and delayed economic recovery. In the next five years, riding now on the back of a buoyant world economy, the eurozone seemed to its policymakers to be in robust health, poised for stable growth. However, along with growth came financial exuberance. The ECB's single monetary policy could do little to prevent frothy property prices and high inflation in the eurozone's periphery economies. The financial exuberance and inflation together created a tantalizing opportunity for the eurozone's vast inherited banking sector, which suffered from chronic low profitability. Searching for easy and seductively safe gains, the banks dangerously aggravated financial imbalances in the periphery.

Taking stock, then, of the euro's first ten years, the headline messages were simple. The eurozone's operating ideology had made the recession in the first five years worse than it would otherwise have been; and the inability to tailor monetary policy to diverse countries had caused the bubbles in the next five years to grow to sizes that few could have imagined. In compensation, the eurozone delivered no evident gain. Most worryingly, productivity growth remained low.

On the politics, in the first five years, European leaders had repeatedly clashed in pursuit of their national interests. In the next five-year period, significant majorities in the French and Dutch referendums on the Constitutional Treaty placed a renewed spotlight on the social fracture between those who were afraid of the future and others who were more self-confident. The vulnerable French and Dutch—who now included a large number of young citizens—protested against "more Europe" run by faceless elites; they protested against the uncritical adoption by their national leaders of Europe's "ultraliberal" policies that caused hardship but offered little hope. European leaders no longer had a blank check to drive the European agenda.

In July 2007, the global financial crisis had begun to rumble more ominously, and euro-area banks that had indulged in the US subprime folly were in the thick of a gathering storm; indeed, a small German bank, IKB, was about to blow up a crucial source of global dollar funds, the asset-backed commercial paper market.

The IMF was upbeat about the eurozone. Just back from consultations with the euro-area authorities, IMF staff wrote: "The outlook is the best in years. A benign external environment, favorable financing conditions and generally sound policies have set the stage for a sustained economic expansion."[185] Labor-market reforms, the IMF continued, had "clearly paid off, leading to a significant strengthening of employment growth."[186] Even the moribund "Lisbon Agenda," intended to raise European productivity but written off as a bad joke, appeared set for renewal.[187] As the

IMF graciously noted, it was fifty years since the signing of the Treaty of Rome. The praise was effusive: "The achievements are major and justify optimism."[188]

At first, the ECB's words lacked the IMF's flair. The July 2007 Monthly Bulletin of the ECB was content to say, "The medium-term outlook for economic activity remains favorable. The conditions are in place for the euro-area economy to continue to grow at a sustained rate."[189] In September, Trichet highlighted the euro area's low and stable inflation as the ECB's signature achievement.[190]

But in June 2008, on the verge of being sucked into a fearsome financial crisis, Trichet decided it was time to stop this dull recitation of the eurozone's many achievements. It was time to celebrate. "This relatively short period of time," he said, "has been rich in successes." He repeated those words to dramatize his message: "The euro has been a remarkable success." Then, trying hard to contain his elation, Trichet said he did not want to "name and shame" those who had predicted that the euro would fail. Instead, overcome by the exhilaration of the moment and at a loss for words, he breathlessly concluded by once again saying, "A success indeed."[191]

As George Orwell might have written, Trichet was narrating history "not as it happened, but as it ought to have happened."[192]

Outside that cognitive bubble, the facts told a more troubling story. Despite several years of a relatively "benign" global environment, too many European citizens remained unemployed or worked in precarious jobs. Economic historians Michael Bordo and Harold James were worried that with the recent buoyant world growth subsiding, GDP growth rates in Europe would fall back to their low potential and conflicts among member states on appropriate monetary policy would reemerge.[193] But a more immediate threat loomed. With its severe financial vulnerabilities, the euro area stood delicately poised at the edge of a growing crisis.

CHAPTER 5 | After the Bust, the Denial,
2007–2009

IN THE UNITED STATES, the financial rumbles heard since early 2007 grew louder in June. Two hedge funds operated by the investment bank Bear Stearns suffered large losses on their subprime assets, the securities backed by pools of risky home loans. But such losses were seen as isolated events, which inflicted deserved pain mainly on investors who had taken excessive risks. It was tempting to deny that a crisis was looming. On July 26, US Treasury Secretary Henry Paulson said, "I don't think [the subprime mess] poses any threat to the overall economy."[1]

A eurozone bank triggered the first widespread disruption in US financial markets. On July 30, IKB Deutsche Industriebank AG (IKB), a small German bank, announced that it expected to suffer large losses on its subprime investments.[2] The Düsseldorf-based IKB was a strange presence in the US subprime business. Owned principally by the government's development bank, Kreditanstalt für Wiederaufbau (KfW), IKB was set up to lend to Germany's small and medium-sized companies, the fabled *Mittelstand*. But intense competition from other German banks had curtailed profitable lending opportunities at home, and the US subprime market was irresistible.[3]

To make its subprime investments, IKB had borrowed from the so-called asset-backed commercial paper (ABCP) market. In the ABCP market, "conduits" run by asset managers connected borrowers such as IKB to major "real money" investors, including insurance companies and pension funds.[4] When IKB announced its large losses, the real money investors became worried that other borrowers might harbor similar problems.[5] The investors instructed the conduits to pull back, and the $1.2 trillion ABCP market began to collapse (figure 5.1).[6] The consequences were far-reaching. European banks that

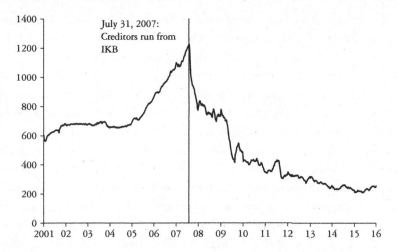

FIGURE 5.1. Germany's IKB sparks the collapse of the ABCP market.
(Size of ABCP market, US dollars, billion)
Source: Federal Reserve Bank of St. Louis, code ABCOMP. https://research.stlouisfed.org/fred2/series/ABCOMP#

had invested in subprime assets relied heavily on continuously rolling over their dollar funding obtained in the ABCP market. If the ABCP asset managers refused to roll over maturing loans, the banks would need to conduct a "fire sale" of their assets to repay their debts. Meanwhile, panic in the ABCP market spread fear to all short-term funding markets, "even those that were not exposed to risky mortgages."[7] The largely unknown IKB thus became the symbol of a major fault line in the global financial system.

Other German banks—including Commerzbank, Germany's second-largest bank—acknowledged that they had also incurred losses on their US subprime assets.[8] Jochen Sanio, president of the German financial supervisory authority, dramatically declared that Germany faced its "worst banking crisis since 1931."[9]

On Thursday, August 9, BNP Paribas, the largest French bank, notified investors that they could not withdraw their money from three of their funds that had purchased US subprime mortgages.[10] The market value of the mortgages was declining, and BNP did not want to be left holding worthless assets while investors took their money and walked away. The BNP announcement was like a "match [that] had been lit in a dry forest."[11] Ben Bernanke, chairman of the Board of Governors of the Federal Reserve System since February 2006, later wrote that what had thus far been a "correction" in the subprime market was now a "crisis."[12]

The interbank market, the nervous system of international banking and finance, threatened to shut down. In the interbank market, banks lend their excess cash to other banks that are temporarily short of cash. The interest rate on overnight interbank loans is usually close to the policy interest rate set by the central banks. Over longer maturities of one and three months, however, adverse unforeseen developments become a greater risk. Especially in periods of financial stress, the probability of default on the loans rises; hence, the interest rate for such loans includes a small "default" or "term" premium (also referred to as "term spread"). On August 8, the day before the BNP announcement, the premium on a three-month loan in the US dollar market was 13 basis points (0.13 percent), only slightly higher than the 5–10 basis points it had been in the past year (figure 5.2).[13] Thus, default risk was still considered very low. However, after the BNP shock on August 9, default risk increased and the term premium jumped to 40 basis points. This was a frightening new development; only the world's best-known banks participate in the interbank market. The fear that even such banks might not be able to repay their loans made banks wary of lending to each other.

Within hours of the BNP announcement, the ECB made unlimited funds available to banks.[14] By the end of the day, forty-nine banks had borrowed

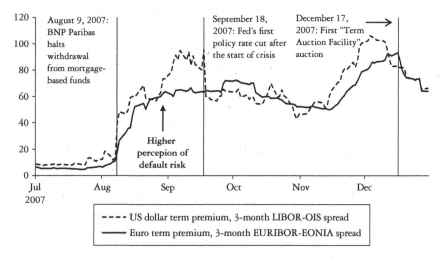

FIGURE 5.2. BNP Paribas causes a jump in interbank stress.
(Term premium on three-month interbank lending)
Notes: One hundred basis points equal 1 percentage point. A higher premium indicates a perception of higher default risk. The term premium for US dollars is the difference between the three-month London Interbank Offered Rate (LIBOR) and the Overnight Indexed Swap (OIS). The difference between the three-month Euro Interbank Offered Rate (EURIBOR) and the Euro Overnight Index Average (EONIA) measures the term premium when borrowing in euros.
Source: Bloomberg

€94.8 billion, on average, almost €2 billion each.[15] Banks needed cash to repay their lenders who were unwilling to roll over their loans. Banks also started hoarding cash for turbulent times ahead. The next day, August 10, the Fed followed the ECB and authorized increased liquidity to banks operating in the United States.[16]

At the Fed, the members of its decision-making body, the Federal Open Market Committee (FOMC), were especially worried that many European banks were running short of dollar funds. Without the supply of ABCP and interbank dollars, European banks might begin dumping their assets at fire-sale prices, which would greatly increase stress in the global financial system. Timothy Geithner, president of the Federal Reserve Bank of New York and vice chairman of the FOMC, anticipated that financial distress in Europe would intensify. Bernanke noted that the Fed would need to make special arrangements to supply dollar liquidity to euro-area banks.[17]

Despite stepped-up ECB and Fed liquidity to dampen the scare in the interbank market, the term premium kept rising. By the end of August, the premium was 73 basis points in US dollars and 64 basis points in euros. The premium was somewhat higher in dollar markets because European banks were bidding up demand for the dollars they urgently needed to fund their dollar-denominated investments.[18]

The pressures on euro-area banks were building from all sides. They had relied heavily on the supply of dollars from the ABCP market, which was rapidly drying up. As described in chapter 4, compared with US banks, euro-area banks had smaller capital buffers to guard against adversity.[19] A matter of great concern was that euro-area banks were deeply interconnected with one another; they traditionally lent and borrowed more from one another than US banks did. These interconnections implied that distress in a few banks could spill over into other banks quickly, creating the risk that the entire system would crash.[20]

At the end of August 2007, the question facing policymakers on both sides of the Atlantic was a difficult one. Was what they had witnessed over the previous weeks merely a temporary scare? Would it be enough if they continued to provide banks with more liquidity until the scare died down and banks began to trust one another again? Or was it prudent, in the words of Princeton economics professor Alan Blinder, to take the "dark" view that a giant financial bust had begun, which could tip the economy and financial system into free fall?[21]

The ECB took the view that the financial turbulence would soon pass. The Fed acted on the darker view that it would not.

Fed Injects Stimulus, the ECB Waits: September 2007–February 2008

Thus far, the Fed had provided liquidity to calm the panicked scramble for funds and to increase the financial system's capacity to lend. But enhanced lending capacity does not create demand for credit. The primary need was to increase demand through an interest-rate cut. As Robert Hetzel, economist at the Federal Reserve Bank of Richmond, explains, lower interest rates "put money into the people's pockets," which encourages households and businesses to spend.[22] And the ability to increase spending, along with the observation that others have stepped up their spending, improves the economic sentiment.[23]

On Tuesday, September 18, 2007, financial markets were expecting the Fed to lower the federal funds rate, its policy interest rate, by 25 basis points (a quarter of a percentage point). Instead, FOMC members quickly agreed to a 50-basis-point cut, bringing the federal funds rate down from 5.25 to 4.75 percent (figure 5.3). Blinder was appalled that the Fed had waited so long, "a full forty days after Paribas day."[24] But late though it was, the Fed's move that day proved to be the start of a new and fruitful strategy. The transcripts of the closed-door FOMC discussions, which have since been made public, reveal the philosophy that guided the members. Janet Yellen, then president of the Federal Reserve Bank of San Francisco

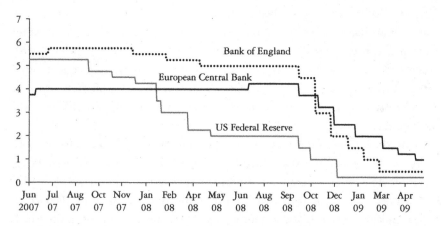

FIGURE 5.3. Interest-rate cuts: Federal Reserve leads, BOE follows, European Central Bank lags.

(Policy interest rates, percent)

Sources: Federal Reserve Bank of New York, "Federal Funds Data Historical Search,"; ECB, "Main Refinancing Operations" fixed rate tenders; BOE, http://www.bankofengland.co.uk/boeapps/iadb/Repo.asp.

and an FOMC member, said, "I honestly don't know what the risks are." But financial disruptions, she said, could generate "negative, non-linear dynamics."[25] Translation: things could get ugly quickly. Members of the FOMC agreed that it was necessary to act before things got ugly. The press release accompanying the rate-cut announcement said, "Today's action is intended to help forestall some of the adverse effects on the broader economy that might otherwise arise from the disruptions in financial markets." The key word was "forestall." It emphasized the FOMC's "risk-management" perspective, "insurance" against a "downward spiral that is hard to control."[26] In more familiar terms, it was the "stitch-in-time-saves-nine" strategy. There was also promise of more rate cuts to come. The press release's reassuring words said that the committee would continue to assess the effects of the financial stress on economic prospects and "will act as needed."[27]

Investors were impressed by the size of the rate cut and by the promise of more. Stock markets reacted enthusiastically.[28] Over the next two years, such market surges in response to policy actions proved a good leading indicator of stronger economic activity.[29] The term premium on interbank borrowing declined somewhat, indicating reduced banking stress.

Over the next few months, the Fed continued to cut its policy rate to raise confidence and sustain economic activity. The ECB kept its interest rate unchanged at 4 percent, on vigil against the threat of inflation and ready to raise interest rates. The Fed and the ECB were going in opposite directions.

Why did the two central banks respond so differently to the financial crisis? The two central banks were reading virtually the same data. The inflation rates on both sides of the Atlantic were almost identical (figure 5.4a) Growth in industrial production was slowing down at the same pace; indeed, starting in the second half of 2008, euro-area production actually began to fall faster (figure 5.4b).

Was the divergence the result of differences in the mandates—the objectives—that the two central banks were set up to fulfill? The Fed had a dual mandate: to support employment and to maintain price stability.[30] In contrast, the ECB's only objective was to maintain price stability. However, these mandate differences do not explain why the Fed and the ECB went in opposite directions.[31] The ECB was required to achieve price stability over the "medium term," over a two-year period during which slowing activity was likely to lower the inflation rate. Trying to bring inflation down instantly could only choke the economy and cause an unnecessarily painful economic downturn. In practice, therefore, central banks with a price stability objective act to counter recessions in the same way as the dual mandate Fed does. Even if inflation does rise temporarily in the effort to revive the

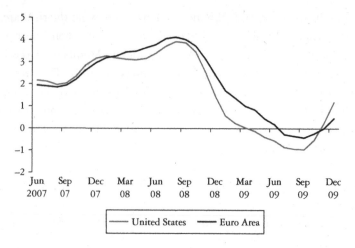

FIGURE 5.4a. Little difference between US and euro-area headline inflation rates.
(Annual inflation rates, percent; three-quarter moving averages)
Note: Headline inflation is computed as the three-month average of inflation over the same three months in the previous year.
Source: US: https://fred.stlouisfed.org/series/PCEPI; euro area: http://ec.europa.eu/eurostat/data/database?node_code=prc_hicp_midx.

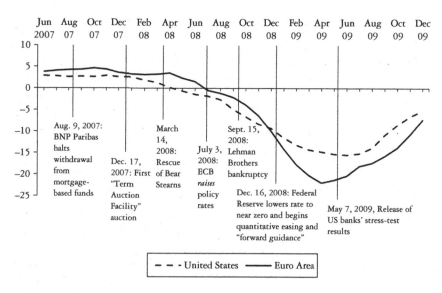

FIGURE 5.4b. Euro-area industrial production growth falls behind.
(Annual growth rates, percent; three-quarter moving averages)
Note: The three-month average of growth over the same three months in the previous year.
Source: World Trade Monitor, https://www.cpb.nl/en/data.

economy, there is time within the 2-year horizon to bring inflation down once the economy is in a more stable condition.[32]

But even from a purely price stability perspective, the ECB's stance was mystifying. Preoccupation with inflation was utterly misplaced. It is true that the inflation rate in mid-2007 was more than 2 percent a year and likely to rise. But the inflation rate was responding to global commodity and agricultural price increases. The last phase of the boom in emerging markets had not yet died down. Prices of food, metals, commodities, and crude oil were inertially rising at a fast pace. But commodity prices are known to reverse quickly, and as the financial crisis grew in strength, a possibly precipitous decline in output and inflation was likely. Thus, the Fed disregarded the current inflation rate and focused instead on preventing a dangerous crisis.

The difference between the Fed and the ECB reflected a different perception of the ongoing crisis and a different attitude toward the likely damage the crisis could inflict. In the Fed's dark view, the financial crisis could cause a huge loss of wealth, which could tip the economy and the financial system into a free fall.[33] This was the essence of Yellen's "non-linear" perspective. Hence, the Fed acted on two fronts. Like the ECB, it provided liquidity to banks and financial markets to calm the panicked search for immediate funding. But the Fed did more. Unlike the ECB, it brought down its interest rate rapidly to increase spending power and economic activity, believing that such activity could act to counter the economic disruption arising from the crisis.[34]

The ECB followed its diagnosis that the financial tensions were due to a temporary scare that had caused banks to hoard cash and thus restrict lending to other banks. The ECB, therefore, concluded that its main task was to provide more liquidity until markets resumed normal functioning. And the ECB leaned toward unchanged—or even higher—interest rates because it refused to recognize that the ongoing price inflation would naturally subside with the weakening economy. Instead, ECB President Jean-Claude Trichet built a narrative that rising commodity prices would feed into higher wages and cause an upward spiral of wages and prices. He reinforced his case for stable or rising interest rates by adding an optimistic spin to the economic and financial outlook. For instance, in November 2007, when the ABCP market was still collapsing and the term premium on interbank lending was rising, Trichet hopefully said that the ECB had "observed a progressive appeasement of tensions in the money market."[35]

The exact same difference between the Fed and ECB philosophy and response had appeared between 2001 and 2003. In January 2001, Fed Chairman Alan Greenspan had also deployed a risk management strategy. He had described the American economy as "in the position of the person falling off the 30-story building and still experiencing a state of tranquility at 10 floors above the street."[36] In the spirit of spreading a safety net before the falling person crash-landed, the FOMC had initiated a series of rate cuts. In contrast, the ECB between 2001 and 2003 had remained rooted in its stability ideology, reluctant to reduce interest rates, claiming that doing so would cause inflation to flare up. Without the necessary help from the ECB, the euro area's recessionary conditions had lasted longer, and its recovery had been slower.[37]

Nothing had changed. The Fed was again in the lead. The ECB's stability ideology remained intact, and the euro area was in danger of falling back again.

The Fed was reinforcing its position as the world's central bank. With its proactive approach, it was setting the benchmarks and the pace of global monetary policy. The Fed held special clout also because it managed the world's most-used currency. With the euro area so dependent on scarce dollars, the Fed was doing more to help the eurozone than the ECB itself was doing. On December 11, 2007, the FOMC authorized two new liquidity facilities, the Term Auction Facility (TAF) and dollar swap lines for foreign central banks. Both initiatives would ease the world-wide shortage of dollars. Oddly, Trichet delayed the announcement of these facilities by a day. As Bernanke later explained, Trichet wanted the announcements timed so that they would be seen as "a solution to a U.S. problem, rather than an instance of the Fed helping out Europe. His goal was to avoid highlighting the dollar funding difficulties faced by European banks."[38] But in trying to divert attention from the euro area's fragilities, Trichet only increased the panic.

As soon as the TAF became operational on December 17, euro-area banks, desperate for dollars, grabbed a large chunk of the funds. Of the initial allocation of $20 billion from the TAF, American banks used just $1 billion, while euro-area banks borrowed $16 billion. For euro-area banks, this was the first moment of relief since August 9, when BNP Paribas had triggered tensions in the interbank market. The term premium in euro interbank markets finally fell noticeably, two weeks after a similar fall had begun in dollar markets. When the Fed doubled the availability of dollars in early January, euro-area banks, still hungry for dollars, nearly doubled their borrowing to $30 billion. Among the earliest borrowers were many troubled euro-area banks, including DEPFA, Dexia, Fortis, and some German *Landesbanken*.[39]

The Fed also made dollars available directly to the ECB and the Swiss National Bank through the "swap facilities"; the two central banks then distributed the available funds to banks in their jurisdictions. By early January, euro-area banks received another $20 billion from the swap facilities. Over the next several months, as the Fed expanded its international dollar provision, euro-area banks were major beneficiaries. Trichet might have wished to convey the impression that the subprime crisis and its aftershocks were a US problem. But euro-area banks were still desperately scrambling.

Meanwhile, although economic and financial conditions had continued to worsen, the ECB maintained its passive policy of liquidity provision and refused to actively stimulate the economy by lowering interest rates to "put money in people's pockets."

The Fed had brought the policy rate down by 100 basis points to 4.25 percent by the end of 2007. On Monday, January 21, 2008, US financial markets were closed for Martin Luther King Jr. Day, but Asian and European markets were sinking. In a hastily arranged conference call with FOMC members, Bernanke insisted on a 75-basis-point cut in the policy rate. William Poole, president of the Federal Reserve Bank of St. Louis, objected that by acting between scheduled meetings, the Fed would set a bad precedent. Markets would come to expect a Fed response between meetings whenever stock prices fell steeply or economic data were especially gloomy.[40] The opposing argument was that the psychology of fear needed to be broken before it "spiraled" to cause widespread damage.[41] Here is the remarkable thing. In January 2008, US industrial production was still growing at an annual rate of 2.5 percent. Yet, echoing most on the FOMC, Bernanke warned, "We are facing, potentially, a broad crisis. We can no longer temporize. We have to address this crisis. We have to try to get it under control. If we can't do that, then we are just going to lose control of the whole situation."[42]

Again, note the sentiment: the fear of "losing control" and, hence, the need to stay ahead of the game before events, rather than policy actions, dictated the future. Bernanke got his way.[43] Early the following morning, before US financial markets opened, the FOMC announced a 75-basis-point cut, the largest cut in twenty-five years.[44] The press release announcing the reduction in the interest rate carried the customary promise to monitor inflation but emphasized that the economy faced "appreciable risks" and that the FOMC would "act in a timely way to address these risks." In other words, more rate cuts were coming. Sure enough, less than ten days later, at the conclusion of the regularly scheduled January 29–30 meeting, the Fed lowered the rate by another 50 basis points, down to 3 percent. The message was unmistakable: more monetary stimulus was on the way. While some market participants did worry that the Fed was going overboard, most saw the Fed as "ahead of the curve."[45] And investor sentiment lifted stock markets.

We are not privy to discussions in the ECB's Governing Council, because transcripts—or even minutes—of the meetings are not available.[46] But at his press conference on January 10, Trichet stayed on script, denying that there was a problem and keeping up the optimistic tone. The indicators, he emphasized, "generally remain at levels that continue to point to ongoing growth." Reiterating that the ECB's greater concern was a further rise in inflation, Trichet said that the Governing Council had held off from raising rates, but it maintained a "tightening bias."[47]

By the time of the ECB's February 7 rate-setting meeting, the Fed had reduced its rate by 125 basis points in a little more than two weeks. At the press conference after the meeting, a reporter asked Trichet if the Fed's actions were "an effort to stop an economic contraction that is already underway or highly proactive risk management."[48] The question was a relevant one. The Fed was slashing its policy rate even though the IMF's growth projections for the United States and the euro area were very similar.[49] While Bernanke and his FOMC colleagues were making the judgment that the economic outlook was rapidly worsening, Trichet's response to the reporter was that things were still OK. He emphasized that corporate profitability had been "sustained" and that unemployment rates had "fallen to levels not seen for 25 years." Looking ahead, he did concede that the economy would slow down; he maintained, however, that domestic and foreign demand would "support ongoing growth."[50] Trichet repeated his standard mantra: the Governing Council remained concerned that inflation would flare up.

The ECB's technical reasons for staying its course remain a puzzle. The strategy had not worked between 2001 and 2003; the high and persisting costs of delays in needed monetary policy stimulus were evident in Japan. And the Fed was taking aggressive action based on a clear and widely shared diagnosis of the challenge the world confronted. The ECB itself has never offered a reasoned defense of its strategy; minutes—much less transcripts— of the Governing Council's deliberations have not been made public. The ECB's first president, Wim Duisenberg had said, "I hear, but I don't listen." Trichet was continuing that honored tradition.

The ECB was not accountable. Wrong-headed decisions continued because the ECB did not have to defend its position to anyone. Its mandate could not be changed without a wrenching treaty renegotiation. And, therein, lay the failure of the democratic process. The presumption in giving a small, unaccountable group of European officials the independence to make consequential decisions was that they knew what they were doing, that they worked in the best interests of the eurozone's citizens. But the officials remained wrapped up in an ideology of stability, protected by a defensive groupthink that extended beyond ECB officials to the narrow "elite" group of European

Commission officials and national leaders. Together, they legitimized the ECB's insistence on stability as justified by European virtues of prudence.

This was not Europe's crisis, they said. The United States was in a crisis because of its incurable tendency to live beyond its means and because of its complex financial structures. With great self-confidence and, indeed, disdain, the European elite sneered at reckless Americans. Joaquín Almunia, European commissioner for monetary and economic affairs, said in January 2008, "big imbalances have built up over the years in the US economy—a big current account deficit, a big fiscal deficit and a lack of savings." Almunia gratuitously added that he was "not engaged in any criticism but these [US] imbalances are the root cause of the current turbulence." In contrast, he said, because of the eurozone's positive current account, sound fiscal position, and plentiful savings, "we are well prepared to weather this situation." In even more abrasive remarks, Jean-Claude Juncker, head of the Eurogroup (the group of eurozone finance ministers), said, "We have to be concerned, but a lot less than the Americans, on whom the deficiencies against which we have warned repeatedly are taking bitter revenge."[51]

The crisis was about to take the darker turn that Fed officials had worried about. Any claim that this was a liquidity crisis, a temporary scare that would go away, would now lose all credibility. Any claim that this was only an American crisis, which the euro area could ride out, would only delay essential change in the ECB's policy position—and it would delay the repair of the euro area's banks.

Bear Stearns Triggers "Nonlinear" Dynamics: March–April 2008

As the smallest of Wall Street's five top-tier investment banks, Bear Stearns had been in trouble since June 14–15, 2007, when two of its hedge funds imploded. Its stock price had closed at $150 per share at the end of that episode.[52] Over the next six months, the stock steadily lost value, reaching $70 in early January 2008. In pretrading at eight a.m. on Friday, March 14, the stock price was $57. Then, a little before the opening bell, Bear's management announced that they were running out of cash.[53] Creditors were refusing to renew their lending. The stock started tumbling, and for a short while after ten a.m., the price fell by a dollar every second.[54] The closing stock price that evening was $30.

Over the weekend, Geithner, as president of the New York Federal Reserve, hammered out a deal under which JPMorgan Chase agreed to buy Bear Stearns at a price of $10 per share. If, however, JPMorgan discovered larger than anticipated losses, it could bill the Fed up to $29 billion. All of Bear Stearns's creditors were to be paid in full.

Bear Stearns was an accident waiting to happen. The investment bank had borrowed $35 for every dollar of capital it held.[55] It had borrowed funds to invest in highly risky mortgage-related securities. Bear Stearns's creditors knew these facts. The creditors included some of the world's most sophisticated investors, and they knew exactly the risk they were taking. Yet US authorities had chosen to bail them out, sending the clear signal that creditors would not take losses. As if to reinforce the message, on Sunday, March 16, the Fed announced the creation of the Primary Dealers Credit Facility, which, for the first time, allowed investment banks to borrow from the Fed.[56] This lifeline further signaled the intention to protect creditors of investment banks.

Financial markets understood that stockholders would take losses, but creditors would go scot-free. On Monday, March 17, stock prices of investment banks fell. Among those who took an especially hard knock were shareholders of Lehman Brothers, the investment bank whose practices most resembled those of Bear Stearns.[57] But because Bear Stearns's creditors had been protected, financial indicators for creditors improved. The stress level in the interbank market—the term premium—fell for US banks but remained about the same for European banks. In the United States, there was also a small decline in the premium to insure against the risk that a bank would default on its debts.[58]

Author and journalist David Wessel later wrote, "there will always be Before Bear Stearns and After Bear Stearns."[59] In his memoirs, Bernanke described the Bear Stearns episode as "the end of the beginning."[60] The crisis was evidently no longer about a temporary shortage of liquidity. Some banks were insolvent; they had made bad bets. The froth of the pre-crisis bubble had hidden the weaknesses of specific banks and had blurred the shaky state of the banking system. Now the hidden and blurry images were coming into sharper focus.

The Bear Stearns episode will forever be at the center of the policy debate on "moral hazard." Were the officials right in using public funds to bail out creditors? Among those who forcefully said yes was Timothy Geithner. There was no alternative, Geithner later wrote. If creditors had not been paid in full, he argued, they would have defaulted on their own creditors, causing "cascading defaults" and greatly "amplifying" the damage.[61]

Patting himself on the back, Geithner said, "I thought we were pretty creative."[62] And he recalled with some delight that ECB President Trichet congratulated him for doing a "masterful job."[63] On the need to bail out creditors, US and euro-area authorities were of like mind.

Geithner acknowledged the opposing view, only to dismiss it. "We did create some moral hazard by protecting creditors and counterparties from the consequences of a Bear default," he said. Creditors quickly recognized that government, having bailed them out this time, would be under pressure to do so again. Thus, with a government safety net extended, creditors could afford to take unwarranted risks in the hope of making big gains. But such moral hazard, Geithner wrote, "was unavoidable."[64] He said that the desire to punish errant creditors only made crises worse.

Geithner's professed concern that if creditors bore losses, "cascading defaults" would follow had no evident factual basis. He said that such defaults had occurred in emerging markets in the 1990s. But the only major default then was by the Russian Federation in August 1998. The panic that followed was hard to isolate from the disruption caused by the collapse of the hedge fund Long-Term Capital Management (LTCM), which had made unwise bets on emerging markets. More important, the panic had been quickly contained. The New York Federal Reserve had persuaded a consortium of financial institutions that it was in their interest not to let LTCM collapse entirely and, instead, to provide emergency funds to allow for an orderly unwinding; simultaneously, the FOMC aggressively eased its policy to support the macroeconomy. Those who had invested foolishly had lost money, and the turbulence was brief.[65] This combination of creditors bearing losses and the central bank easing policy was a well-understood practice for limiting moral hazard and preventing cascading defaults.

An immediate, prominent critic of the Fed-subsidized Bear Stearns rescue was former Fed Chairman Paul Volcker. The Fed's action, he said, had gone "to the very edge of its lawful and implied powers, transcending certain long embedded central banking principles and practices." Volcker went on to say that actions taken in the Bear Stearns operation "will surely be interpreted as an implied promise of similar action in times of future turmoil."[66] In other words, investors would have reason to gamble, knowing that they would keep the winnings and the taxpayer would bear the losses. Another stinging critique came from Vincent Reinhart, until recently the director of the Fed's division of monetary affairs and secretary of the FOMC. On April 29, at a seminar at the Washington-based think tank, the American Enterprise Institute, Reinhart described the decision to bail out Bear Stearns as the Fed's "worst policy mistake in a generation." It "eliminated forever," he said, "the possibility that the Federal Reserve could serve as an honest broker." Reinhart later wrote at greater length on this theme.[67]

Bear Stearns was only the first in a sequence of events confirming that the crisis was not a temporary scare, which would go away on its own. Many bets made during the exuberant years had gone bad. Many of those bad bets were made by financial institutions in the euro area. On Monday, March 17, as the fallout of the weekend operation on Bear Stearns was felt in US and world markets, most Irish stock traders were taking the day off. It was St. Patrick's Day. But in what was quickly dubbed the St. Patrick's Day massacre, global investors dumped shares of the rogue bank Anglo Irish. Problems at Anglo Irish had been brewing since the start of the year. Although the financial consultancy firm Oliver Wyman had described Anglo Irish as a "supermodel" and the world's best-performing bank in 2007, the bank's stock price had been trending down since the start of 2008, and fearful depositors were withdrawing their money. On St. Patrick's Day, journalist Simon Carswell wrote, stock traders in Dublin watched their computer terminals in horror as Anglo's share graph descended "almost vertically."[68] Irish authorities dismissed the decline in Anglo's share price as due to "false and misleading rumors" about the bank's financial health.[69] John Hurley, governor of the Central Bank of Ireland, asserted: "The Irish banking sector remains robust." Anglo's stock price regained some lost ground.[70]

Banks in the eurozone's core, particularly German and French banks, facing their own mounting problems because of their US subprime misadventures, defensively began a retreat from the periphery soon after the Bear Stearns episode (figure 5.5). They refused to roll over their loans. Periphery banks now had the additional burden of repaying the retreating banks.

Irish and Spanish banks were now acutely short of funds. Spanish banks fared better initially. They had been required to set aside extra capital for such a moment; they managed to attract deposits through their "extensive branch networks."[71] But the stressed Irish banks needed to repay creditors who wanted their money back. The ECB began replacing the fleeing funds. But the necessary temporary prop was not accompanied by an effort to anticipate and address the imminent insolvency of some Irish banks. Thus, the likelihood increased that the Irish government would use taxpayer funds to place its banks on financial life support and, as a consequence, would take on a fiscal burden that would be much greater than the one that the Fed had assumed in support of Bear Stearns. The Irish government's finances were already strained, because financial sector and construction activity—the growth drivers of recent years—were now collapsing, and tax revenues were therefore evaporating. The possibility that banks might need

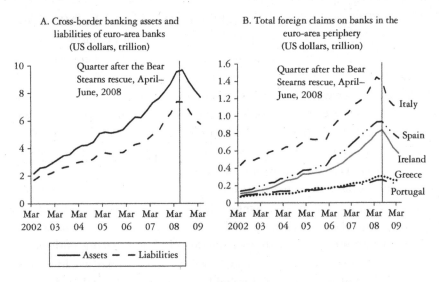

FIGURE 5.5. European international banking flows reverse after Bear Stearns.
Source: Bank for International Settlements. Panel A: Locational banking statistics, table 5A, http://stats.
bis.org/statx/srs/table/A5?c=5C&p=20151&i=3.6. Panel B: Consolidated banking statistics, table B4,
http://stats.bis.org/statx/srs/table/b4.

support made the government's finances more suspect. For the greater risk
they were bearing, bondholders demanded higher interest rates on the Irish
government's bonds. On March 17, 2008, the interest rate on a ten-year Irish
bond was just more than 4 percent; by early June, that interest rate had risen
to nearly 5 percent. Reflecting Ireland's greater risk, the difference between
the rates the Irish and German governments paid also rose, although only
modestly at this stage.

What began as a subprime "correction" in the United States had, by now,
disabled large parts of the global financial system. The sense of an economic
slowdown was palpable. In the United States, the FOMC met on March 18,
the day after bank stocks had fallen sharply. Setting the tone, Yellen said
that "every single data point was dismal."[72] She predicted that the United
States would go into a possibly prolonged recession starting immediately.
Elaborating on her theme of "negative, non-linear dynamics," about which
she had spoken at the September 2007 FOMC meeting, she said that the US
economy was in an "adverse feedback loop."[73] The idea once again was that
lots of bad things were happening at the same time, and each one made the
others worse. Yellen recommended an interest cut of 75 basis points, and
although a few FOMC members hesitated, the Fed later that day announced
exactly such a cut from 3 percent to 2.25 percent.

A global economic slowdown had begun. On April 3, the IMF's twice-a-year "World Economic Outlook" noted, "The global expansion is losing speed in the face of a financial crisis." The IMF said that there was now a 25 percent risk of a global recession, which it defined as world GDP growth of less than 3 percent.[74] In Yellen's terminology, the world—and not just the United States—was in "an adverse feedback loop." With international trade rapidly decelerating, the global trading system, which had been the source of great bounty in recent years, was now spreading economic malaise. As each country's economic growth slowed, it imported less from trading partners, which caused them to export less, and so the circle of distress widened. Even Germany, which had no domestic housing or credit boom and bust, felt the impact as the apparently insatiable appetite for its cars and machinery began to diminish. For the euro area, the IMF said, the economic outlook was turning "increasingly negative," and, hence, the inflation rate would steadily decline to the ECB's 2 percent threshold.[75] It was time, the IMF said, for the ECB to ease its monetary policy.

If the ECB's Governing Council heard the IMF's call, it did not listen. Meeting on April 10, for the first time after the Bear Stearns collapse almost a month earlier, the Governing Council kept the ECB's interest rate unchanged. At the press conference that followed, Trichet insisted that the euro-area economy was growing at a moderate but steady pace, it had "sound fundamentals," and it suffered from no "major imbalances." He said he "was no more and no less worried" about the global financial turbulence than he had been since the start.[76] The ECB was doing its bit by supplying plentiful liquidity to banks. Trichet, however, feared that inflation was likely to rise, and it was necessary, therefore, for the ECB to keep its interest rate on hold at 4 percent. The Fed, at its April 29–30 meeting, brought its interest rate down by another 25 basis points to 2 percent.

ECB Tightens Monetary Policy amid Collapsing Economy: July 2008

After its late-April rate cut, the Fed, for the first time since the start of the crisis, became concerned about inflation.[77] The reason for this changed emphasis is unclear. The financial system remained fragile, and the economy showed more signs of weakness. Consumer confidence, unemployment claims, retail sales, and industrial production all pointed to a worsening economic outlook. Indeed, US industrial production had steadily declined since

April. Even the IMF, an institution generally inclined to worry about inflation, projected lower inflation because of the expected "sharp" weakening of the global economy in the second half of 2008.[78] For this reason, many analysts have criticized the Fed's pause in interest rate cuts.[79] In his memoirs, Bernanke's explanation is that an "unreasonable" rise in "hawkishness on the Committee [FOMC]" held him back.[80]

Although the Fed had slowed its pace of rate cuts, the stunning contrast with the ECB continued. Whereas earlier the Fed was lowering rates and the ECB was holding steady, now the Fed paused and the ECB prepared the ground for raising its policy rate. The ECB did acknowledge that "the level of uncertainty resulting from the turmoil in financial markets remains unusually high and tensions may last longer than initially expected."[81] But this recognition, quite evidently, had little influence on its assessment of the economic outlook and inflation. The ECB's management continued to worry that inflation would rise. In an April speech in Brussels, ECB Governing Council member and chief economist Jürgen Stark insisted that the ECB must stick to "a policy uncompromisingly geared to pursuing price stability."[82] Central bankers know that there is no such thing as "uncompromising" pursuit of price stability. Stark was not speaking about the ECB's mandate for price stability, which, properly interpreted, required only that the ECB's 2 percent or less inflation target be achieved "over the medium-term." In the meantime, the ECB's task was to support economic activity so that the inflation rate did not fall too low and create new pathologies. Stark's "uncompromising" voice was that of an unaccountable ideologue who refused to heed the gush of evidence and the counsel of outsiders who suggested a change of course. To "outside observers" who called for monetary stimulus, Stark repeated a worn and misdirecting refrain, used earlier in the decade by his predecessor Otmar Issing. Any deviation from the ECB's established policy stance "would only exacerbate uncertainty without helping to resolve the causes of the turbulences, which are outside the realm of monetary policy."

In May, Trichet said that the Governing Council was unanimous in not easing monetary policy, and in June, he reported that the Governing Council had discussed the possibility of *raising* the interest rate before deciding to leave it unchanged. Although the global economic outlook had rapidly worsened, commodity prices had continued their rise. The price of Brent crude oil had risen from $55 per barrel in January 2007 to $95 per barrel in December 2007 and then further up to $130 per barrel by June 2008. The risk, the ECB said, was that inflation would become "entrenched." In other words, as commodity prices rose, people would expect prices to rise further, which would increase the demand for higher wages. Expectation of higher inflation would become self-fulfilling.[83] But such fears had no basis.

Rather, rapid deterioration in economic conditions was apparent. In late June, French President Nicolas Sarkozy warned that an ECB hike in the interest rate could choke the economy.[84] Spanish prime minister José Luis Rodríguez Zapatero made similar remarks. In discussions just before the ECB's July rate decision, the IMF also made clear its views: "staff does not see a compelling case for tightening."[85] In the polite world of international bureaucratic communication, this was the equivalent of saying "Don't do anything stupid."

Only the Basel-based Bank for International Settlements (BIS) stayed in the ECB's corner. The BIS, a forum for central bankers to exchange views, said that inflation was "actually rising," while significantly slower growth was "only a possibility."[86] Central banks must raise interest rates, the BIS said.

The ECB raised its interest rate by 25 basis points on July 3. At the press conference, Trichet said the measure would diminish price and wage pressures.[87] It is possible that the ECB's staff did not yet know that the euro area's industrial production in the three months from May to July was below the level in the same three months the previous year. The ECB had chosen to hike its interest rate at the very moment when the euro area was entering a prolonged recession. The ECB refused to listen to critics who warned that the higher interest rate on top of the economic drag from rising commodity prices would further hurt growth prospects. Stock prices in the euro area had fallen in anticipation of the decision, reflecting the market's view that an increase in interest rates was unwelcome.[88]

After the Lehman Moment, a Rush to Bailout: September 2008

In June 2008, Lehman had reported its first loss since 1994, and its stock had continued to slump through the summer.[89] Yet Lehman's management had continued with brash business decisions, presumably in the hope of striking gold and thus overcoming accumulated financial liabilities. Lehman's creditors did not seem to care. After the Bear Stearns rescue in March, virtually everyone was convinced that the Fed and the US government would protect the creditors. In July, the *Washington Post* summarized the widely held view: "We're not predicting that Lehman will fail—it won't, because of the

Federal Reserve, which has let it be known that it will lend Lehman (and any other investment bank it deems worthy) enough money to avoid collapsing."[90] Paul Volcker had said that the Bear Stearn bailout would "surely be interpreted as an implied promise of similar action in times of future turmoil." As if to validate Volcker, on September 7 the government took over the day-to-day operations of mortgage giants Fannie Mae and Freddie Mac and, hence, became responsible for repaying their debts.

Then, in a development that few observers anticipated, the US political establishment suddenly lost "the stomach for another bailout."[91] The US Congress was outraged about taxpayer-subsidized bailouts of financial firms. The two presidential candidates, Senators Barack Obama and John McCain, opposed pampering rich financiers. Many mocked Treasury Secretary Paulson as "Mr. Bailout." And so, "Mr. Bailout" Paulson, feeling political heat, decided that this was the time to stand firm against rescuing Lehman.[92] Without Bear Stearns-style protection for its creditors, there was no buyer for Lehman. On September 15, Lehman Brothers filed for bankruptcy. Stock prices declined. The stress in the interbank market rose.

Kenneth Rogoff—Harvard University economics professor, former chief economist of the IMF, and a man who had dropped out of high school to become a chess grand master—was prominent among commentators who welcomed the decision to let Lehman fall. In an op-ed piece for the *Washington Post* on September 16, Rogoff's theme was "The Government is willing to let Wall Street firms fail. That's good." He acknowledged that the financial tumult since the Lehman bankruptcy announcement was unnerving and was likely to continue. But Rogoff insisted that the financial sector had been coddled too long and, as a consequence, had become "badly bloated." Lehman's failure, he said, was necessary to return to a leaner and more effective financial system.

Rogoff was basing his comments on research with Carmen Reinhart, his colleague while at the IMF and now an economics professor at the University of Maryland. They had recently established through careful historical analysis that financial debt crises are followed by prolonged economic distress.[93] Hence, the crucial policy task was to prevent debt from building up in the first place. By allowing Lehman to go bankrupt, the government had signaled it would not rescue reckless lenders. Bankers and investors, Rogoff said, would "think twice before they once again head off to the races." Moreover, disciplining errant financial institutions through the prospect of painful failure would "reduce the political pressure to overregulate the system in the aftermath of the crisis." Pleased though he was with the decision, Rogoff was afraid that, amid the turmoil, this moment of policy clarity might not last. "Let's hope," he ended, "they hang tough for at least a little while longer."[94]

Unfortunately, Paulson had acted impulsively and not on the basis of Rogoff's forward-looking logic. US authorities seemed to lack a strategy. The Lehman bankruptcy had followed Bear Stearns' rescue. The reversal in policy added to the panic in that fast-paced environment. Stock prices plummeted, and interbank stress skyrocketed. The "Lehman moment" became synonymous with policy blunder. The Geithner-Trichet doctrine took deeper hold. Geithner's message was simple: however distasteful it might be to bail out Wall Street fat cats, there was little choice but to do so. He wrote in his memoirs, "After Lehman, I lost whatever minimal tolerance I might have had for letting moral hazard or political considerations impede our efforts to attack the crisis." To keep the system safe, Geithner said, officials needed to help "individuals and institutions that didn't deserve help."[95]

US officials welcomed Trichet's apoplectic reaction to the Lehman decision and his insistence that private creditors should always be bailed out. Bernanke later wrote in his memoirs, "Economics aside, Trichet seemed to view default as inherently dishonorable."[96] The absolute need to avoid another default shadowed policymaking for the rest of the crisis.

The Renewed Rush to Bailout

American International Group (AIG), the world's largest insurance company, had made reckless bets in financial derivatives and was spectacularly vulnerable to the financial turmoil that followed Lehman's failure. Once again, the essential problem was one of regulatory failure, and once again, the signs calling for early action had been all too evident.[97] It was too late now. Amid the panic on September 15 and 16, US authorities rescued AIG, reversing their barely day-old position that irresponsible investors should bear the consequences of their folly.[98] The AIG operation was significant because through it, the government also supported other financial institutions, such as Goldman Sachs, that would have borne significant losses if AIG had been forced to declare bankruptcy.

Sheila Bair, chairman of the Federal Deposit Insurance Corporation (FDIC), did demonstrate that there was a way to prevent a disorderly collapse of a failing bank and at the same time protect the taxpayer. Washington Mutual Bank (WAMU) was another reckless mortgage lender with heavy exposure to the sinking California real estate market. With $300 billion in assets, WAMU was only a little smaller than Bear Stearns. Despite fierce opposition from Geithner, on September 25, the FDIC pushed through a deal under which JPMorgan Chase bought WAMU. Creditors took large losses.[99]

Speculators had bought WAMU's bonds, expecting a bailout. The bonds had traded for 73 cents on the dollar before the FDIC accelerated WAMU's failure; the price of the bonds fell to 25 cents on the day after the operation. The FDIC protected insured depositors. WAMU was the largest-ever FDIC-insured bank to fail, and FDIC officials remain proud of its "textbook" resolution.[100] But Bair and the FDIC were not in sync with the Geithner-led sentiment, and the successful WAMU experiment was largely ignored.

Like WAMU, euro-area banks were also in trouble for an old-fashioned reason: they had made bad lending decisions. The banks with international operations felt the full force of the crisis in the wake of Lehman. The first casualties were the Belgian-Dutch Fortis, the French-Belgian Dexia, and the German Hypo Real Estate along with its Irish subsidiary DEPFA, all of which crashed in the final days of September. All had borrowed short-term funds to invest in the US subprime mess. Some also faced trouble at home, especially Dexia, which had made loans to weak French municipalities. All these banks had survived so far on the ample dollar funds provided by the Fed. Indeed, they were among the largest beneficiaries of the Fed's TAF set up in December 2007.

While US officials were improvising their way forward, their European counterparts were always clear that they would bail out their errant banks. In rescuing Dexia, for example, French Finance Minister Christine Lagarde said that allowing a bank to fail and default on its creditors "would have been dangerous for the stability of the whole system."[101]

However, the troubled euro-area banks were large relative to their national economies (see chapter 4). Truly bailing them out, as US authorities had done for AIG, would have required prodigious sums, which governments did not have or had no appetite to spend. Hence, half measures became the norm, and problems lingered on. The Dexia saga would continue for years, as piecemeal efforts cumulated in sizable use of public funds while ultimately failing to solve the problems.[102] The German government backed a €35 billion liquidity line to keep Hypo Real Estate afloat.[103] Hypo would also require continued government efforts and funds.

Irish authorities faced the most outsized problem, and they made the most impulsive decision to save their banks "on the cheap." Creditors of Irish banks had been fleeing for months. The Central Bank of Ireland had been "printing" money to replace funds withdrawn by private creditors. Anglo Irish was in its final death spiral. Other Irish banks, tempted by Anglo's success over the years, had taken the same foolhardy gambles and were vulnerable now.

Facing the risk that their banks could lose access to new funding the next morning, Irish authorities met for much of the night of September 29.[104]

Kevin Cardiff, the senior Department of Finance official in charge of Irish financial stability, later reported that "very early" in the rolling series of meetings that night, Prime Minister Brian Cowen suggested the possibility of a "blanket guarantee" for all the debt of the six largest Irish banks.[105] A blanket guarantee would say that if Irish banks were unable to repay their creditors, the government would do so; all debt owed by Irish banks would be the responsibility of the Irish taxpayer. Cardiff and his boss, Finance Minister Brian Lenihan, were wary of the enormous financial obligation such a guarantee placed on the government. If it were called on to repay the debt of Irish banks, the government simply did not have the funds to honor that commitment. Cowen later maintained he had not come to the meeting committed to a blanket guarantee. But, as Cardiff tells the story, once Cowen had "suggested" it, others fell in line.[106]

On September 30, the Irish authorities announced the blanket guarantee. Lenihan said, "We are in the eye of the storm. . . . It's time for swift and decisive action."[107] For a while, the guarantee seemed like a clever idea. The government did not have to pay out any money immediately, and if creditors believed the government's word, they would continue to lend to Irish banks. Without spending a single euro, the government would have saved its banks. Indeed, the banks had to pay the government a fee for the guarantee.

Neelie Kroes, European commissioner for competition policy, was upset. She said, "A guarantee without limits is not allowed."[108] Her worry was that the Irish government's generous support might give the country's banks an unfair advantage over banks in other countries. But it was too late to pull Ireland back from its folly without making matters worse. And so the matter was forgotten. At least for a while.

Meanwhile, on October 3, a reluctant US Congress, having initially rejected a proposal by the US Treasury and the Fed but then cowed by the unrelenting financial turmoil, approved $700 billion in spending authority under the Troubled Asset Relief Program (TARP). Paulson and Bernanke had sold the TARP to the Congress as a fund that would buy "toxic" assets and, by thus preventing a precipitous fall in the values of such assets, stabilize struggling financial institutions that were holding these by now nearly worthless securities. But the TARP legislation allowed virtually unconstrained use of funds to protect and revive the financial sector and the economy.[109]

Under pressure to match the protection extended to the US financial system, French President Sarkozy invited key European leaders and officials to meet in Paris on Saturday, October 4. The select group included German Chancellor Angela Merkel, Italian Prime Minister Silvio Berlusconi, British Prime Minister Gordon Brown, the ECB's Trichet, and Jean-Claude Juncker in his role as head of the Eurogroup. Ahead of the meeting, European Commission President José Manuel Barroso encouraged the leaders to work in a spirit of solidarity. "Europe's interest," he wrote to Sarkozy, "requires an intense effort of coordination and convergence."[110]

The rumors were that Sarkozy would propose a fund with TARP-like size and features. But if such an idea ever existed, Merkel quickly squashed it. Indeed, despite later French insistence that there had never been any such proposal for a fund, the Germans took the trouble to publicly spurn the possibility. German Finance Minister Peer Steinbrück made it plain that whereas Germany intended to support its own financial sector, the idea of a European fund was fantasy. "The chancellor and I," he said, "reject a European shield because we as Germans do not want to pay into a big pot where we do not have control and do not know where German money might be used."[111] Steinbrück, a Social Democrat, was among the more "pro-European" German leaders. On the matter of their money, even pro-European Germans drew the line. A European Commission official put it more bluntly: "No German or Estonian is going to accept Brussels spending his money to rescue a failed Greek bank."[112]

At the press conference that followed the failed summit, European leaders continued harping on the "American roots" of the crisis.[113] On their own achievement, Sarkozy said with a straight face, "We have taken a solemn undertaking as heads of states and governments to support the banks and financial institutions in the face of this crisis."[114] That was pretty much what they had done. Taken a solemn oath. Sarkozy ritualistically added, "Europe should exist and respond with one voice."[115]

This episode was the first real test of the "falling forward" thesis, the proposition that the need for coordinated responses in the midst of a crisis would force member states to pool financial resources.[116] Once that threshold was crossed, political unity would follow. Such an expectation had always been far-fetched. Anyone listening to former Chancellor Helmut Kohl would have known that he—the preeminent pro-European—had repeatedly rejected the possibility that German taxpayer funds would pay for others' errors.[117] Many nevertheless believed that in a crunch, Germans would relent. But this belief had no basis. German officials had always acted to defend their national self-interest. If there was a surprise on this occasion, it was the speed and directness with which even the German social democrats scuttled the idea of pooled resources. And while the Germans were the first to reject any pooling of funds, few other member states had an appetite for it either.

Even if clumsily, US authorities were beginning to clean up the mess left by the crisis. They had dealt with many problem banks and had $700 billion of TARP funds to begin fortifying the banking system. In contrast, governments of the euro area's member states had taken half measures in support of their large national banking systems. And even under the pressure of an intense financial crisis, the member states had been unable to come together to mount a common financial defense against further onslaught from the crisis.

These were as yet early days of the crisis, and a monumental task still lay ahead. The worldwide post-Lehman financial meltdown continued. Stock markets remained in free fall. The term premium in the interbank market kept rising. That premium, which had seemed high at around 70 basis points in August 2007 after BNP caused the original fright and disruption, was now approaching 300 basis points in US-dollar markets. The risk that some of the world's prime banks could default on each other was now frighteningly high. A race against time was on. Would self-defeating financial-market pessimism ravage large parts of global financial and economic systems, or could policymakers halt this pessimism in time and begin repairing the damage already wrought?

The World Responds to a Looming Great Depression: October 2008

Global policymakers had already begun mounting more defenses against the rush of the crisis. Starting in late September, Bernanke had appealed to other central bank chiefs to coordinate a reduction in interest rates. Such a move, he said, would "send a powerful signal of international unity," particularly because coordination on that scale had never occurred before.[118] BOE Governor Mervyn King was reluctant at first, but he became an enthusiastic supporter. Trichet was still worried about inflation and needed more "persuasion."

Trichet had refused to acknowledge any merit in the Fed's proactive policy approach. Since the crisis had erupted in July 2007, the Fed had lowered its rate by 3.25 percent while the ECB had raised its interest rate by 0.25 percent. However, sitting on the sidelines while global financial and economic systems sank into an abyss would have brought great ignominy to the ECB. On October 8, 2008, the ECB grudgingly joined other major central banks as each cut its interest rate by 50 basis points.

This was the ECB's first stimulative measure since the crisis had started. Although coordinated with other central banks, the action seemed inadequate to contain the panic. The ECB was beginning to build its shelter while the storm was raging. Global stock prices fell sharply after the October 8 announcement. It was not an auspicious start for the ECB.

The US and European economies were unraveling at such a dizzying speed that the IMF felt compelled to present an updated "World Economic Outlook" on November 6, a month after having released its most recent economic forecast. The IMF now projected that world GDP would increase only by 2.2 percent in 2009, rather than by 3.0 percent as forecast a month earlier and far below the 3.8 percent forecast in April. As the Fed had feared since September 2007, economic and financial conditions had turned "dark." By the IMF's benchmark, when world GDP grows at a rate of less than 3 percent, the global economy is in a recession. The global economy was now in deep recession.

It was time to move beyond the realm of central bankers, protected from the rough and tumble of politics.[119] Two days before the coordinated interest rate reduction, Olivier Blanchard, the IMF's chief economist, had said, "We think that global fiscal expansion is very much needed at this point."[120] It was the IMF's finest moment of the crisis. Traditionally an advocate of fiscal austerity, the IMF was calling for internationally coordinated increases in public spending and lower taxes to prevent a drawn-out recession.

John Maynard Keynes, perhaps the most renowned economist of the twentieth century, had vigorously argued the need for fiscal stimulus to pull an economy out of a recession.[121] The direct beneficiaries of lower taxes and recipients of larger government transfers begin spending more, which creates additional incomes for others, thus activating a "multiplier effect" through a steadily widening circle of consumers and investors. George Akerlof and Robert Shiller, both recipients of the Nobel Prize for Economics, have noted that the mere knowledge that others have increased their spending creates a more optimistic view of the future. Hesitant consumers make purchases that they were postponing; investors take new initiatives. The optimism spreads through a "confidence multiplier."[122] Production increases, and economic recovery gathers momentum.

A fiscal stimulus has especially high value when the economy is in a deep recession. The stimulus puts back to work large numbers of unemployed people and revives the use of idle production facilities. For the size of the economic slump in 2008–2009, the expectation was that the multiplier would be large: one euro of fiscal stimulus could increase GDP by between 1.5 and 2.0 euros, or by an even larger amount.[123] Such a boost to economic growth would bring in additional revenues, which would substantially pay for the stimulus spending and tax cuts.

Moreover, just as the monetary stimulus was coordinated across countries on October 8, it was important to coordinate the fiscal stimulus. Each country's stimulus would increase its imports, which would speed up world trade growth and thus create added benefits for all others.

Britain's Prime Minister Gordon Brown was a prominent political advocate of coordinated fiscal stimulus. But the Germans were not happy. They did not like fiscal stimulus. Hurling words because he had no good arguments, German Finance Minister Steinbrück accused Brown of a "breathtaking shift to crass Keynesianism."[124] Steinbrück and, indeed, most Germans considered it wishful thinking that stepped-up public spending and tax cuts would pay for themselves by pulling an economy out of, or preventing, a recession. A fiscal stimulus, they believed, would merely run up deficits and debts. Instead, they argued, it was best to double down on fiscal austerity. That would reassure people that the government would not levy higher taxes in the future to pay its overdue bills. In the Steinbrück view of the world, austerity and prudence—rather than stimulus—instilled confidence, which induced consumer spending and growth-enhancing investment.

But the resistance was brief. Common sense and the evidence greatly favored an urgent fiscal stimulus. With euro-area industrial production contracting at an annual rate of more than 6 percent, even the German government joined the global fiscal stimulus initiative, just as the ECB had been unable to say no to a globally coordinated interest-rate reduction a month earlier. Merkel overrode her finance minister and backed a European commitment "to provide 1.5 per cent of GDP for the stimulus package."[125] Many observers at the time believed that the planned stimulus was not large enough to deliver the necessary jolt back to growth.[126] But a stunningly large contribution from China complemented the stimulus injected by euro-area and US governments. Thus, together, the world's major economies took a crucial step in the fight against another Great Depression.

Historians will surely look back at the events of those weeks with relief and gratitude to those who came together to stabilize the world economy and financial system. But it is important to understand what was and was not achieved. As Princeton professor and Nobel laureate Paul Krugman wrote, the actions taken had only put out the fires.[127] They had prevented another Great Depression, but much of Europe and the United States would continue in what would soon be called the Great Recession. The strength and speed of measures still to be taken would determine the strength and speed of the recovery from the Great Recession.

The ECB Continues to Lag and Loses Credibility, the Eurozone Economy Suffers

The financial news remained dismal. In late October, the term premium in the interbank US-dollar market, although down from its peak, was at a dangerously high 200 basis points. Stock markets fell through most of October. Although the promised fiscal stimulus was on its way, the rapid-response task still fell on monetary-policy authorities.

The US Federal Reserve once again raced ahead. On October 29, Bernanke favored a 50-basis-point cut but gave the FOMC the option of a 25-basis-point reduction. Some FOMC members advised restraint. They pointed out that the Fed had cut its interest rate by 50 basis points just two weeks earlier and that if the Fed moved hurriedly, its actions, rather than helping, could create uncertainty and erode confidence.[128] They recommended a 25-basis-point rate reduction.

In support of the 50-basis-point cut, Yellen reiterated her philosophy of preemptive action to forestall greater damage. "Frankly," she said, "it is a mistake to act cautiously as the economy unravels. I think the clear lesson from both economic theory and real-world experience is to lower rates as quickly as possible to avoid a deeper and more protracted recession, not to keep our powder dry or to wait to use tools until later if they are available to us now."[129]

Geithner joined Bernanke and Yellen in support of the more aggressive move. Quoting the words of former US President Franklin Delano Roosevelt, Geithner urged "bold experimentation." He acknowledged that over the past several months, there had been disagreements within the FOMC. But Bernanke's strategy of preemptive and escalating monetary stimulus and liquidity provision had proven "largely correct." Bernanke, Geithner said, had made good judgments in weighing the risks. Using unusually emotional words, Geithner added, "I think we all owe him a substantial amount of deference for the judgments he made and his wisdom."[130]

Markets cheered the 50-basis-point cut, and observers interpreted the accompanying statement as promising further monetary easing.[131]

But a month later, the mere promise of more conventional monetary easing was not proving enough. Investors were anxious for a lot more. And, at least some economists concurred. On December 2, 2008, still guided by his analysis that the world was in the middle of a "once-in-a-century financial crisis," Harvard's Ken Rogoff laid out an agenda for "aggressive macroeconomic stimulus." Central banks, he said, must print money and use it to buy their government's debt. Interest rates on government bonds would fall. Such an unconventional measure was needed because the Fed's conventional policy reduces the interest rate only on borrowing for short periods, typically for less than three months. Interest rates on longer-term borrowing, for business investment or home purchases, fall only slowly. By buying the government's long-term debt, the Fed could quickly bring down interest rates on all long-term borrowing. To those who were worried that inflation would flare up if the Fed printed money to buy the government's bonds, Rogoff said that fear of inflation was "like worrying about getting the measles when one is in danger of getting the plague." To the contrary, he explained that setting the goal of raising the inflation rate to 5-6 percent a year was desirable because higher inflation rates would help households and businesses unwind their "epic debt morass."[132]

Note that Rogoff was addressing all central banks. The Fed—although unwilling to raise its inflation target to 5-6 percent—made the big move, thus setting the benchmark for the others.

On Tuesday, December 16, the Fed slashed its policy rate by 75 basis points down to 0–0.25 percent.[133] With no more room to lower rates, the Fed also began "forward guidance," a promise to keep its policy interest rate at "exceptionally low levels for some time."[134] But the most ambitious policy the Fed announced that day was its quantitative easing (QE) program. The Fed would start buying long-term bonds and other securities to help bring down long-term interest rates right away, making it more attractive for households and businesses to borrow and, hence, to spend.[135]

Bloomberg Businessweek commented: "It's a measure of the severity of the financial crisis that there were no dissenters from the Fed vote. Even inflation hawks such as Philadelphia Federal Reserve Bank President Charles Plosser and Dallas Federal Reserve Bank President Richard Fisher voted 'yes' on the measures."[136] Market observers were reassured that with the addition of forward guidance and QE, the Fed was not about to run out of options for stimulating the economy.[137] And the "unusually strong" message left little doubt that countering the economic downturn would receive priority over fighting inflation.[138]

On March 18, 2009, the Fed announced the expansion of its QE program. It would also hold its policy rate at near zero for an "extended period," and not merely for "some time," as it had earlier stated.[139] The Fed was now relying not just on its actions but also on the credibility of its words. The Fed had promised on September 18, 2007, that it would "act as needed." And indeed, it had acted in accordance with its words. There was reason to believe that its word was still good.

The BOE heard the message. Like the ECB, the BOE had initially been slow to use monetary stimulus. Now, however, the BOE was moving at blazing speed. From 5.0 percent before the October 8 decision, the BOE reduced its policy rate down to 0.5 percent by March 2009, a 450-basis-point reduction in five months. At that point, the BOE started its QE program, with the value of long-term assets it purchased, relative to the country's GDP, quickly surpassing that of the Fed (figure 5.6).[140]

Thus, in late 2008 and early 2009, the Fed pushed harder down the path that it believed was working, and the BOE changed course to follow on that path. The narrative at the ECB, however, did not change. The ECB never acknowledged how serious the crisis was. It did reduce its interest rate because it had no other choice. But financial analysts and investors remained deeply skeptical of the ECB's rate cuts, which they viewed as "too little, too late." Making matters worse, ECB rate reductions came with continued expressions of concern about the possible flare-up of inflation. Thus, because the ECB was obviously reluctant to act, investors came to worry that a rate cut was, in fact, the ECB's advance warning of bad news rather than a stimulatory measure.

The ECB continued to provide more liquidity to its banks. On October 15, it opened another long-term financing window. Banks could borrow unlimited amounts, for longer periods, and use a broader set of assets as collateral.[141] Banks quickly stocked up on the funds made available to protect themselves from a renewed seizing up in interbank markets, which could again make private funds scarce and expensive. The ECB's liquidity provision was

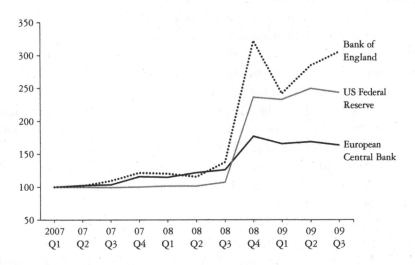

FIGURE 5.6. BOE and the Fed rapidly expand their balance sheets.
(Total central bank assets as a percentage of GDP, 2007 Q1 = 100)
Source: Federal Reserve Bank of St. Louis, codes for assets ECBASSETS, WALCL, UKASSETS; codes for GDP EUNNGDP, GDPMC1, NAEXKP01GBQ652S.

necessary, but it was a passive action. Banks now had easier and more plentiful access to funds. But their more serious problem was that they were weak and urgently needed more capital to operate on a secure basis. Moreover, with euro-area output contracting and no significant policy effort to put money into people's pockets, there were few borrowers.

Hence, the ECB's long-term liquidity mainly facilitated an orderly flight of private sector funds from distressed countries in the periphery to the core euro-area countries. Banks in the core—principally German and Dutch banks—wanted to bring back the money that they had lent to periphery banks. But banks in the periphery member states—Greece, Ireland, Italy, Portugal, and Spain—could not make those large repayments all of a sudden. Thus, the periphery banks borrowed from the ECB to repay the core banks, which deposited the funds received with the ECB. Thus, the core banks accumulated credits at the ECB (in ECB terminology, they had positive Target2 balances), while the periphery banks became more indebted to the ECB. The ECB thus provided a valuable "lender-of-last-resort" function. The arrangement, however, was a temporary safeguard. The more serious question of whether the periphery banks were solvent and could be expected to survive in the long run was not addressed.

Into early November, as the economic contraction quickened, the ECB's interest rate was still 3.75 percent. Its second rate cut, by 50 basis points, came on November 6. Financial markets were disappointed because, pursuing its new strategy of rapid rate reductions, the BOE had announced a "stunning" 150-basis-point cut earlier that day. The BOE's action had raised expectations that the ECB would be more aggressive.[142] Not only did Trichet disappoint on that score, what little he gave with one hand he took away with the other; he continued to highlight the risk that wages and prices might spiral up and, hence, limit the scope for more stimulus.[143]

Executive Board member Lorenzo Bini Smaghi echoed Trichet's message, and then went into denial. "The financial crisis," Bini Smaghi said, had "started on the other side of the Atlantic and has spread rapidly on our side." Literally read, that was a correct statement; importantly though, it refused to acknowledge the deep involvement of euro-area banks in the US subprime crisis. More seriously, Bini Smaghi went on to say that the crisis was "having a bigger impact on the US banking system's capability."[144] This was simply a refusal of euro-area officials to face up to their own reality. Stress in interbank markets was about the same on both sides of the Atlantic, and the euro-area economy was contracting, if anything, faster than the US economy. Observers began to worry that continued denial could only make the euro area's "bad situation decidedly worse."[145]

On December 4, the ECB's bigger-than-expected 75-basis-point rate cut created brief cheer in financial markets. Even so, the commentary was generally skeptical. Analysts and investors read the rate cut as a reaction to more bad economic news rather than a harbinger of a new, more proactive approach. Some observers found the ECB cut tame, considering the "horrific" economic data and the large concurrent rate cuts of 100, 150, and 175 basis points by the BOE, the Reserve Bank of New Zealand, and Sweden's Riksbank, respectively.[146] Moreover, Trichet refused to discuss further easing. "I will say nothing about January," he declared.[147]

The 50-basis-point rate cut on January 15, 2009, also came amid deep anxieties. The ECB's own growth forecast from just the previous month had been marked down.[148] Some had hoped for a cut of 75 basis points, or better still 100 basis points.[149] Analysts accused ECB officials of "dragging their heels" and "being behind the curve."[150] A currency strategist remarked, "Trichet is focused more on inflation, which is not really a concern in the eurozone. The bigger issue at hand is growth prospects."[151]

By now, the pattern was set. Before the March 5 meeting, Thomas Mayer, Deutsche Bank's chief European economist, said, "You suspect the ECB just wants to close its eyes to what's going on. That's not good for the economy."[152] At the press conference following the Governing Council meeting, Trichet finally conceded that poor growth prospects would cause inflation to "remain well below 2% over 2009 and 2010."[153] As many had predicted, inflation was coming down everywhere along with the severe global economic weakness. The ECB had refused to accept this inevitability and, by continuing its phantom fight against inflation, had only managed to hurt the euro area's growth prospects. When, even after recognizing that inflation was no longer a concern over the coming several months, the ECB reduced its policy rate by only 50 basis points, a Goldman Sachs analyst not surprisingly reiterated the market's verdict: "The ECB remains vastly behind the curve."[154]

On May 7, 2009, the ECB reduced its interest rate to 1 percent. The Fed's policy interest rate had been at near zero since the previous December, at which point it had also started its "forward guidance" promise of continued low interest rates and its bond-buying QE program to bring long-term interest rates down quickly.

Altogether, between 2007 and 2009, the ECB achieved little traction with financial markets. The Fed had taken care of the dollar-liquidity shortage of euro-area banks. The ECB's easier supply of euro liquidity helped prop up weak banks, but the ECB and national governments made no effort to restore the banks to good health. Most seriously, the ECB's monetary-stimulus actions came well after the financial economic dislocations had become serious, and when they did come, the actions always appeared to be playing catch-up.

Financial markets can be unreliable guides, but at least in this instance, they were clearly indicating that the ECB had misjudged the nature of the crisis and the risks that came with it. The urgent task, as the Fed had recognized early and the BOE understood after Lehman, was to prevent a psychology of pessimism and low expectations from settling in. The ECB's "too little, too late" approach failed in this task. The ECB stuck with its conviction that the fight against inflation preserved stability. Ritual condemnation of US economic performance and policy—with its implication that economics of crisis prevention and management worked differently on the two sides of the Atlantic—continued. Some observers sensed a German imposition of its ideological position on the euro area. French President Sarkozy seemed to take this view.[155] But the fissures within the euro area were not yet out in the open. For the most part, the stability ideology and the "Europe is different" perspectives were still widely shared in the euro area.

Through 2007 and much of 2008, the US and euro-area stock markets and GDPs had kept pace with each other. However, after the Lehman bankruptcy, the euro-area economy decisively fell behind that of the United States, and it has still not caught up (figure 5.7). That is the irony: even though the Lehman bankruptcy is considered an American crisis, it had longer-lasting consequences on the euro area because the eurozone authorities refused to acknowledge its full force and act decisively.

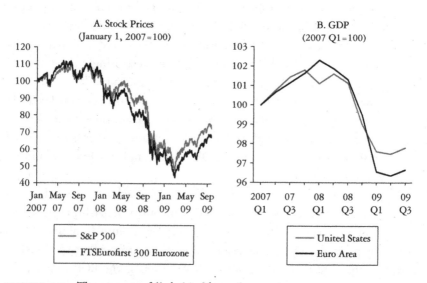

FIGURE 5.7. The euro area falls behind by early 2009.

Eurozone Banks Struggle, Americans Solve Their Banking Problems

The task of stabilizing the financial sector remained, especially in the euro area, where progress had been limited. On January 15, 2009, the Irish government finally nationalized Anglo Irish. Along with recapitalization of the two largest Irish banks—Bank of Ireland and AIB—in February 2009, the burden on public finances was growing intolerably large. Additional obligations would arise if the government's guarantee forced it to repay the banks' creditors.[156] The rapid buildup of the government's debt—and the clear likelihood that the banks would need more support—created widespread concern that the Irish government would not be able to honor all its financial obligations.

Econometric analysis shows that banks and governments became joined at the hip, not just in Ireland but also in several other member countries of the eurozone.[157] As distress in a country's banks added to the likely burden on public finances, investors demanded higher interest rates to lend to government. The higher interest further weakened the government's finances, and investors feared even more that governments would not be able to support the banks, causing them to take fright and dump bank stocks. In this "sovereign-bank doom loop," each seemed to be dragging the other down into a financial abyss.

European initiatives to steady the financial sector went nowhere. Sarkozy's grand plan to create a European fund had died a quick death in October 2008. European Commission President José Manuel Barroso then asked Jacques de Larosière—who had been managing director of the IMF from 1978 to 1987 and governor of the Banque de France from 1987 to 1993—to assess what had gone wrong and what needed to be done. The de Larosière Committee report, released in February 2009, was an indulgent exercise, which refused to confront the difficult issues. As had become customary, the report pointed its finger at the United States for originating the crisis and spreading it to the rest of the world.[158] The report's lack of self-reflection was stunning. It mentioned IKB and Fortis in passing and ignored the problems at BNP, Dexia, Hypo Real Estate, and the German *Landesbanken*. The fact that European banks had leveraged themselves up and had gambled short-term borrowings on the subprime mess barely came up. The report absolved European regulators of blame. Surely, it said, domestic regulators could not have known what their banks were doing abroad. Instead, "US [financial] supervisors should have been able to identify (and prevent) the marked deterioration in mortgage lending standards and intervene accordingly."[159]

The de Larosière Committee's report reached a predictable conclusion: "The way in which the financial sector has been supervised in the EU has not been one of the primary causes behind the crisis."[160] It did recommend enhanced regulatory oversight in Europe, but it did not recommend urgent steps to close, merge, and recapitalize banks. In his assessment, Viral Acharya, a New York University finance professor, said that the report had "notably" ducked a discussion of poorer capitalization of euro-area banks relative to their US counterparts. Acharya darkly warned: "EU banks may have more skeletons in their chest to take out in case the economic malaise persists."[161]

As was the case with monetary policy, US authorities understood the urgency of stabilizing their banks. The FDIC dealt with around two hundred failing banks—with around 6.5 percent of US bank deposits—by either closing them down or merging them with stronger banks.[162] Because the FDIC was a central government body, with its own budget and the backing of the US Treasury, authorities in the states where the failing banks were located bore no financial costs.

The big initiative came soon after Americans elected Barack Obama as their forty-fourth president. When Obama assumed office on January 20, 2009, the pace of economic decline was starting to moderate, but the ranks of the unemployed were still swelling, and many workers had already been out of work for so long that they risked becoming unemployable. On January 27, a week after his inauguration, Obama met with his top economic advisor, Larry Summers, and his treasury secretary, Timothy Geithner. The president's message, as Geithner tells it in his memoirs, was simple: Obama "wanted to rip off the Band-Aid . . . he wanted a strategy to put a quick and definitive end to the crisis."[163] The Obama administration set itself two tasks: push the US Congress to increase the size of the fiscal stimulus and instill renewed confidence in banks.

On banks, Geithner's plan was to conduct "stress tests." Could US banks cope with another financial crisis? Would they, in particular, have enough capital to absorb further losses if the economy went back into a severe recession? If the banks were not likely to have enough capital, the US government would infuse capital into them. On February 10, Geithner announced the initiation of the stress tests (formally, the Supervisory Capital Assessment Program) to assess the condition of the nineteen largest bank groups in the United States.[164] His performance before the TV cameras that day was lampooned. But he had set in motion the decisive step in the US response to the financial crisis.

On May 7, the stress-test results were announced. They hit the sweet spot and transformed the mood in the United States. The federal government had judged that the US banking system was now viable. For banks that needed more capital, TARP funds, authorized in October 2008, were available.[165] The transparently presented findings persuaded financial markets and analysts that banks could withstand considerable stress. Stock prices of the banks that participated in the test jumped.[166] Even the banks that were required by the test results to accept additional capital from TARP funds benefited. A key reason the stress tests succeeded was that they emphasized the principle that investors needed to inject larger amounts of equity into the banks they owned, they needed to have more skin in the game and take greater financial responsibility if their banks did not perform.

The stress tests were Geithner's baby. With justified pride, he later remarked that although there had been lulls in the panic in 2007 and 2008, "there had never been a real sense of stability." After the stress tests, "nearly every financial indicator was heading the right way."[167] For all practical purposes, the US financial crisis was over.

The Legacy

In the summer of 2009, the predominant sense was one of relief.[168] Instead of living through another 1930s-style Great Depression, with its much deeper and more persistent decline in output and rise in unemployment, the world had escaped with merely a Great Recession. Led by US monetary-policy and bank-repair initiatives, policymakers in other countries had followed and pitched in. A global fiscal stimulus was also in the pipeline.

To an important extent, however, the world had also been lucky. The global bounce back owed much to the Chinese authorities, who, having injected a sizable fiscal stimulus, fostered an extraordinary credit boom. In 2009, Chinese banks made *new* loans equal to 30 percent of GDP.[169] Chinese buyers went on a global spending spree. Chinese imports increased from $50 billion a month at the start of 2009 to over $100 billion by the end of the year. Exporters worldwide benefited. Thus, Chinese fiscal and on-steroids credit expansion crucially helped to steady the world economy (figure 5.8).

Among industrialized nations, Germany was the biggest beneficiary of the Chinese impulse. Chinese consumers could not seem to get enough BMWs and Mercedes-Benzes; Chinese factories bought advanced machine tools; and as the Chinese central and local governments rolled out new

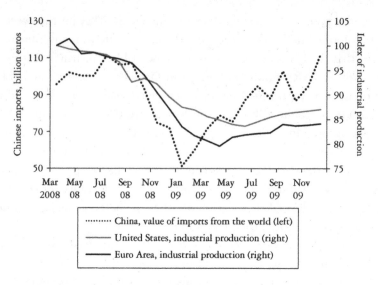

FIGURE 5.8. Chinese stimulus in early 2009 leads the global recovery.
Sources: IMF direction of trade statistics for Chinese imports; World Trade Monitor for US and euro-area industrial production, https://www.cpb.nl/en/data.

infrastructure projects with stunning ambition, German manufacturers sold advanced systems, such as those for high-speed trains. German growth also brought cheer to Eastern European countries that supplied inputs to German manufacturers.

In contrast, the Chinese stimulus did much less for France, Italy, Spain, Portugal, and Greece, which relied for their economic recovery mainly on policy actions closer to home. And because euro-area policy efforts were delayed and tight-fisted, the nascent economic recovery was decidedly weak in these countries. Thus, already from this early phase, performance among euro-area economies began diverging.

Moreover, because the ECB had already hesitated to inject stimulus during the recessionary years between 2001 and 2003, its reputation for a plodding response to economic and financial crises was reinforced during the new, much more severe crisis.[170] That reputation would continue to have perverse consequences. Financial markets came to believe that the ECB would maintain relatively high interest rates. Thus, investors, attracted by the prospect of higher interest rates in the future, kept the euro strong. In May 2009, even though the eurozone's recovery had been slower, one euro bought an already high $1.35; and as the Fed continued its bond-buying QE program to keep US interest rates low, the euro appreciated further through the rest of the year. The euro's strength made economic recovery more difficult for several eurozone member states.

Also, euro-area authorities had made clear that in a crunch, they would bail out banks' creditors. The large and growing government debt burdens in several euro-area countries were bound to test this implicit, and in the Irish case explicit, bailout promise. US authorities, amid much controversy, had bailed out creditors of banks. But US authorities had acted quickly with substantial resources to recapitalize their banks. Investors now considered US banks to be safe. In the euro area, the banks were more fragile than at the start of the crisis.[171] Euro-area banks were protected by ECB liquidity and by government guarantees that promised to repay their creditors. The premise was that the crisis would be short-lived and the banks would recover along with the economy. However, delays in dealing with insolvent banks, which had gambled and lost, were certain to impede the pace of economic recovery and, ultimately, inflict large costs on at least some of the governments and societies.

In its October 2009 "World Economic Outlook" (WEO), the IMF had a generally reassuring message: "the global recession is ending."[172] The WEO also made the right differentiation. It had a hopeful prognosis for the US economy.[173] And it aptly noted that euro-area recovery would be sluggish, pointing to rising unemployment and the need for further financial-sector repair.[174] But the WEO missed the breaking news. Although it was published on October 15, it did not recognize that the euro area's rolling crisis had crossed into Greece. And it certainly did not foresee that a debt-deflation dynamic, propelled by the ideology of monetary and fiscal austerity, would carry the crisis to Italy.

| Delays and Half Measures
Greece and Ireland, 2010

THE DATE WAS October 1, 2009. George Papandreou was campaigning to be the next Greek prime minister. As leader of Greece's socialist party, the Panhellenic Socialist Movement (PASOK), Papandreou had failed to defeat his nemesis, Kostas Karamanlis, in two earlier attempts. To win the favor of a skeptical Greek electorate, Papandreou promised to fight corruption and bring jobs back for the young. At a rally of forty thousand Greeks in Athens, he cried out, "Let's win our dignity back."[1]

Amid the raging global financial crisis between 2007 and 2009, the Greek economy appeared to have held up well. In its most recent annual review of the Greek economy, updated on July 20, 2009, the IMF had concluded that Greek banks were stable and had adequate reserves to deal with more adversities. And while the IMF made its customary pitch for more fiscal belt-tightening, it complimented the government for constructive and "welcome" measures to rein in its budget deficit.[2]

The IMF seemed pleased with Greece's macroeconomic performance, but many Greeks were despondent. Starting in the early 1980s, in the unsparing words of Yale political scientist Stathis Kalyvas, a "virulent strain of populism" had corrupted Greek politicians and institutions. Rather than acting to counter the economic and social corrosion, the EC, and later the EU, had "funded" and "abetted" the "worst excesses of the Greek political system."[3] Pervasive corruption had benefited mainly the powerful and well connected. The young had felt the toll of mismanagement most acutely, especially in the poorly performing educational system. High youth unemployment had become a chronic problem; in 2009, with the election campaign in its last stages, more than 25 percent of the 15–24 years old

Greeks who were looking for a job could not find one. And prospects seemed to be getting worse.

It, therefore, was hard to have much faith in Papandreou's promise to restore Greek dignity. At his Athens rally, an undecided voter said, "I don't know if he can do all he has promised, because the country is in a bad state, but I hope he'll do [the] most [he can]." A thirty-year-old unemployed accountant gloomily remarked, "We vote for hope."[4]

The unemployed accountant had reason to be gloomy. Neither Papandreou nor Karamanlis, offered real hope. Papandreou's father, Andreas Papandreou, had founded PASOK in 1974 and had established Greece's culture of political corruption and fiscal indiscipline during two stints as prime minister, from 1981 to 1989 and then from 1993 to 1996.[5] George Papandreou had been a minister in his father's cabinet during the years when Greek political corruption took root.

Karamanlis, leader of the conservative New Democracy party, had absorbed and adopted Greek norms of political patronage and entitlement.[6] After his comfortable electoral victory over Papandreou in 2004, Karamanlis had "literally spent his way" to a narrow victory in 2007.[7] Upon reelection, the Karamanlis government had, in familiar Greek fashion, cut taxes and run up spending to gain public support. Ministers and their aides were accused of soliciting bribes and were even suspected of fraud and money laundering.[8] Unable to govern, Karamanlis had called for an early election on September 2.

Papandreou won this round. On October 4, he defeated Karamanlis handily, securing 160 of the 300 seats in parliament. In his moment of triumph, he bravely said, "We are a country with great potential. We have the political will to make deep changes in a just and equitable way, to put our country back on a development path, to meet the challenges of a new world."[9] But behind Papandreou's stirring words lay a troubling reality, seamlessly woven into a corrupt political culture.

Lies Fall Apart, a Bankrupt Nation Is Revealed: October 2009

A few months earlier, when the IMF had praised Greece's economic performance, it had also insisted that Greek authorities at the "highest level" give "high priority" to improving their economic statistics.[10] Every informed observer knew that Greece's statistical data were appalling—and too often deliberately misleading. The Greek government had cooked its fiscal accounts to gain entry to the eurozone while the eurozone authorities, anxious to admit Greece as one of their own, had looked the other way.[11] Ever since then, the IMF had complained that poor statistical reporting made it impossible to monitor the Greek economy and assess its performance. When the IMF's board discussed the staff's latest report on July 24, 2009, the executive directors made their displeasure clear. The Swedish director, Jens Henriksson said: "I am just amazed that this continues."[12] Were the Greeks incompetent, Henriksson asked, or were they intentionally making up the numbers? It was a closed-door meeting, and the remarks would not become public for another five years. The IMF economist in charge of Greece, Bob Traa, responded candidly. Incompetence, he said, was not the problem.[13] Greece's leaders consciously chose to mislead, Traa explained, because if they revealed the severe problems they faced, they would invite unwelcome attention and criticism. By fudging the data, Greek governments of all stripes hoped to "control the message."

Those summer ruminations at the IMF's board were quickly forgotten. Certainly, Papandreou after his final ascent to the Greek premiership was not thinking of Greece's chronic statistical misreporting. He was on a mission to reestablish Greek dignity.

On October 8, the governor of the Greek central bank alerted Papandreou that the government's budget deficit—the excess of expenditures over revenues—would not be 6 percent that year, as previously thought, but could reach 10 percent of GDP. The governor then stepped out and spoke to reporters, where he added a hopeful note: "I am optimistic that [the deficit] will not exceed 10 percent."[14] On October 16, Finance Minister George Papaconstantinou acknowledged in an interview with Reuters that the deficit would, after all, be more than 10 percent of GDP.[15] Speaking in the Greek parliament later that day, Papandreou quite simply said, "The situation of our economy is explosive. Today we face an unprecedented fiscal derailment. The deficit must be cut and we must start containing the public debt.[16]

Yields on government bonds rose, although only modestly. From 4.5 percent on October 8, the yield on the ten-year bond rose to around 4.7 percent on October 16. (See box 6.1.) The yield was not notably high. Certainly, investors were not singling Greece out as particularly risky. The spread, the difference between the yields on Greek and German government bonds, held steady at a relatively modest 1.3 percent, often stated as 130 basis points.

Investors were still calm on Monday, October 19, when the Eurogroup (eurozone finance ministers) met in Luxembourg. Papaconstantinou revealed an even deeper fiscal hole.[17] The 2009 deficit would be 12.5 percent of GDP; moreover, the deficit in 2008 had reached 7.7 percent of GDP, and not 5 percent, as earlier reported.[18] The new numbers also showed that the stock of

Greek debt was above 110 percent of GDP, and with large deficits, debt was piling up rapidly.

For Joaquín Almunia, European commissioner for economic and monetary affairs, this was déjà vu all over again. In December 2004, when it had become known that Greece had lied about its fiscal numbers to enter the euro area, Almunia had felt the brunt of the embarrassment. Although he had been appointed commissioner for economic and monetary affairs only after the Greek entry decision had been taken, his staff had vetted the Greek numbers. Almunia had helplessly said, "We had a very sad experience in the case of Greece and we don't want this repeated in the future."[19] But "this" was being repeated, and Almunia's sense of hurt and outrage, then and now, was overdone. He must have—or should have—known. Greek Finance Minister Papaconstantinou said that through the summer of 2009, Almunia's office was fully aware of Greece's dire budget situation. They knew that "things were really off track" and could see that the budget deficit would be closer to 10 percent of GDP rather than the official estimate then of 6 percent.[20] As Traa had explained in July to the IMF's board, every insider knew how Greek political incentives worked. But having once again watched the Greek slow-motion train wreck, Almunia meekly said, "These serious discrepancies will require an open and deep investigation of what has happened." Jean-Claude Juncker, head of the Eurogroup, who also knew of the brewing problems, added more meaningless words: "The game is over, we need serious statistics."[21]

The world began to take note. On Thursday, October 22, the rating agency Fitch downgraded Greece's credit rating from A to A-; the decision came with a "negative outlook," implying that even modest worsening of the fiscal situation would justify another downgrade. A more dangerous connection began to emerge between banking and government financial stress. As the yield on government bonds rose, the Athens stock-price index began to fall, with banking stocks falling faster. This was the sovereign-bank "doom loop" gathering momentum. Along with government-bond yields, higher interest rates were spreading through the economy, causing growth prospects to dim and raising the concern that the banks' borrowers would struggle to repay their debts.

These early financial-market tensions were smothered by the ECB's generous liquidity facilities, which were pacifying banks and bondholders. Banks used their government bonds and other dubious assets as collateral to borrow from the ECB. With those funds, the banks bought more government bonds, which kept a lid on sovereign-bond yields. Greek banks were adept at using the rules to borrow large sums from the ECB.[22] In effect, as Greek problems unfolded, the ECB bought the Greek government's bonds. Thus, yields on the ten-year Greek government bond remained steady until mid-November and then crept up only modestly to around 5 percent by early December.

On December 7, the rating agency Standard and Poor's (S&P) predicted that Greek debt would jump to 125 percent of GDP in 2010, which led it to place Greece's sovereign credit rating on "negative watch."[23] On December 8, Fitch downgraded Greece again, this time to BBB+; and it threatened more downgrades with its continuing "negative outlook."[24] The alarm bells were now ringing in Germany.

As Merkel Waits, Greece Reaches Tipping Point: December 2009

On December 10, two days after the Fitch downgrade, German Chancellor Angela Merkel spoke to reporters in Bonn. "What happens in a member country," she said, "influences all the others, particularly when you have a common currency. That is why we all share a common responsibility."[25] The statement was widely read as an expression of "solidarity," a sense of mutual obligation and support.

On December 16, S&P converted Greece's "negative watch" into a rating downgrade. The next day, Merkel spoke at a Bundestag budgetary debate.[26] Abruptly, her soft words of solidarity disappeared. The German government had enough on its hands, she said. She still needed to focus on the aftershocks from the global financial crisis, which, though diminished in intensity, were still a worry. Germany's economy was fragile. Her government needed to focus on achieving a sustainable recovery at home.

Merkel laid out the markers. "I also say with respect to certain countries with very high deficits: every individual member country is responsible for (maintaining) healthy public finances." She wearily concluded: "We have problem children in Europe."[27] From the initially gracious gesture of "common responsibility," Merkel had pivoted to the theme of national responsibility. Thus, she began guiding Europe through its evolving crisis.

Merkel was born on July 17, 1954, in Hamburg, West Germany.[28] When she was just a few weeks old, her father, a Protestant minister, moved the family to East Germany. Merkel grew up in a decaying, Communist East Germany, but there she led a reasonably privileged life, kept her head down, excelled at Russian and the sciences in school, and went on to receive a doctorate in quantum chemistry. She started her career as a research scientist, writing technical papers with other East German researchers.

In December 1989, a month after the fall of the Berlin Wall, she wandered into the neighborhood offices of a political group called Democratic Awakening and volunteered to help. From that first step onward, it was an astonishing rise. In December 1990, she won a seat as a CDU member of the Bundestag. She then became a resentful cabinet member under an overbearing Chancellor Helmut Kohl. In December 1999, she turned Kohl's political assassin after it became apparent that he had taken illegal campaign contributions. In April 2000, she was elected chairman of the CDU. And following a victory by the narrowest of margins over incumbent Gerhard Schröder, Merkel became German chancellor in November 2005. Through it all, she maintained a low profile and let others take credit.

Even in the first few postwar decades, when Germany needed European legitimacy most pressingly, German chancellors were not shy of placing their national interest ahead of the European interest. Memories of World War II mainly ensured that senior Germans spoke the language of European unity. Helmut Kohl insisted he was promoting the European interest. There was little foundation to his belief that the euro was in the European interest; in any case, he cast the euro in a German mold. Gerhard Schröder, born in 1944, continued to use pro-European language: he gave the green light for Greece to enter the eurozone.[29] Merkel was even more distant than Schröder from the war. And having grown up in East Germany, she had little connection with or interest in the ideology of pro-Europeanism.

After the onset of the global financial crisis in 2007, Merkel mainly stuck to minding her German business. She had no patience for European initiatives, as she made clear at the height of the crisis. In October 2008, the eurozone's leaders were under pressure to create a European financial shield that matched the financial protection that US authorities had set up for their banks. When, in response to that pressure, French President Nicolas Sarkozy proposed grand plans, Merkel spurned them, making clear that German taxpayer money was not available for other countries.[30]

In September 2009, a month before the Greek budget hole came into view, Merkel was reelected German chancellor for a second term. Although she described her victory in glowing terms, she was in the midst of deep domestic political currents. Voter turnout, which had been declining slowly, plummeted in these latest elections. For Merkel, the one solace was that the SPD bore the brunt of voter apathy and anxiety. Social democracy, the melding of material progress and social justice, was fading throughout Europe, both as philosophy and practice. Earlier in the year, the social democratic movement had performed dismally in the elections to the European parliament. Germany's SPD was a victim of the same historical decline, unable to offer a compelling vision of either material progress or of equality and justice. The setback to the self-avowed pro-European SPD was also a warning to Merkel: Germans were wary of more commitment to Europe.

But the problem was broader. All mainstream parties were losing favor and voters were turning to smaller parties. As part of that broader trend, Merkel also lost ground. Her CDU and Bavaria-based sister party, the Christian Social Union (CSU), were returned with a lower vote share than in 2005. Merkel was able to form a coalition only because her other coalition partner, the Free Democratic Party (FDP) did much better than in 2005. Moreover, relations between the coalition partners were tense. The CSU was traditionally euro-skeptic. Horst Seehofer, CSU's leader, famously presented Merkel with a dictionary that translated Bavarian into standard German to help her understand that he and his party members viewed things differently. Meanwhile, the pro-business FDP also had reservations about extending more German financial support to Europe. Merkel herself had no clear mandate. She had smothered political debate, reveling in what observers had described as a boring, indeed banal, campaign. Observers speculated that Merkel's diminished victory was made possible by voters who identified her as "*Mutti*," a stereotypical mother who prudently manages her home.

History, however, was forcing Merkel's hand. A crisis loomed in a euro-zone member country, and it demanded her attention. Her inner circle saw the euro as "a machine from hell," a machine that she was "trying to repair."[31]

To repair the euro reliably, Merkel needed to make a politically risky call for financial sacrifice from German voters. The call was risky not least because the pro-European Kohl—having insisted on imposing the euro on Europe— had repeatedly reassured the German public that they would never pay for the misdeeds of other member states.[32] Every German politician had unfailingly repeated that message.[33] Now the German public needed to hear a new story—and Merkel had to be the one to tell it.

Merkel had survived and succeeded as a politician by waiting. As the Greek crisis unfolded, the German newspaper *Die Tageszeitung* wrote of her: "From the outset, Merkel has remained true to her style of governing. She operates by lying in wait. She does not act but rather avoids action."[34] Her inclination to wait was not necessarily a feature of who she was. It was as much a reflection of the history within which she was placed. In Germany, as in other western democracies, voters were either staying away from the polls or, as in a more recent trend, were seeking alternatives to traditional mainstream parties. Maintaining political hold in this fracturing electoral environment required great caution.

On Greece, waiting was worthwhile to Merkel because there was always a possibility that the problem would helpfully go away; alternatively, if the crisis escalated, it would be easier to knock heads together on her terms to find a way forward. And because Merkel's nod was essential to every major European decision, her wait-and-see approach ensured serial delays and half measures. Thus, she set the plodding pace at which Europe responded to its fast-moving crisis.

To be sure, delays were also costly for Germany. Delays caused the crisis to intensify and raised the eventual price for resolving it. Merkel must have known that. US presidents overseeing the Vietnam War had feared the immediate financial and political costs of decisive action to resolve the conflict; relying on hope and optimistic rhetoric, they had waited while the scale and the cost of the war continued to escalate. In the same manner, Merkel also paused until she was forced to act while the crisis deepened.

Every time she pressed the pause button, she demanded that others do more for themselves. In December 2008, resisting calls for more German fiscal stimulus to relieve the global crisis, Merkel spoke of *Verantwortung*, the German word for "responsibility." To an audience in Stuttgart, she said that the risks of fiscal spending were best understood by the Swabian housewives from that region. Those frugal housewives, Merkel said, "would give us some short and good advice, which would be this: 'You cannot live beyond your means in the long run.'"[35] Merkel's finance minister, Wolfgang Schäuble, repeated that theme. Quoting German writer and polymath Johann Wolfgang von Goethe, Schäuble said, "Let everyone sweep in front of his own door, and the whole world will be clean."[36]

Schäuble believed that countries like Greece, with their undisciplined public finances, did not belong in the euro area. Since 1994, he had promoted his strongly held view that European integration should move forward with only a "hard core" of grown-up countries while the laggards shaped up.[37] In his original conception, even Italy did not fit into Europe's hard core. But when European leaders admitted Greece into the eurozone in 2001, Schäuble and Merkel, then the leaders of the opposition, chose to stay silent. Staying silent was not being neutral. German leaders in opposition routinely criticized the European policies of the government in power. Silence was, at the very least, a signal of "no objection" and could well have been a tacit endorsement. Now, as the rumbles from the Greek crisis were heard throughout Europe, Merkel allowed herself a moment of regret. The decision to bring Greece into the eurozone, she said, "may not have been scrutinized closely enough."[38]

As Merkel waited and watched, Papandreou announced increasingly ambitious fiscal-austerity measures. The hopeful view was that the Greek government's efforts to shrink its fiscal deficit would reassure financial markets. Financial tensions would ease, and the government would have the time to regain control over its finances. The Swabian housewife would have been vindicated. Perhaps Europe would not need to help Greece. Such hope—and accompanying optimistic rhetoric—were essential complements to the wait-and-see approach.

However, despite Papandreou's austerity announcements and even though Greek banks were using the ECB's generous liquidity facilities to buy the Greek government's bonds and were therefore indirectly financing the government's deficit, financial markets were losing patience. By mid-December 2009, the yield on the government's ten-year bond rose to 5.5 percent, up from 4.5 on October 8, when the Greek central bank governor first revealed to the public the depth of the government's fiscal hole.

Greece was about to be trapped in a "vicious spiral." The risk was that higher interest rates on new bonds would not only raise the government's interest burden but would also cause economic growth to weaken. As the economy weakened, the government's revenue inflow would diminish, and borrowers from Greek banks would have greater difficulty repaying their debts. Rating agencies would downgrade the Greek government, which would push interest rates further up, adding to government, banking, and economy-wide stress.

It was time for Merkel and other European leaders to apply the precautionary principle. Just as the US authorities had responded preemptively after the tech bubble had burst in 2000 and then even more aggressively when the financial crisis had threatened to spin out of control between mid-2007 and early-2009, European leaders now needed to create a financial safety net for Greece. Alongside, they needed to begin "restructuring" Greek debt, which required negotiating with Greece's private creditors a schedule of reduced debt repayments. Debt restructuring was essential to set a limit on the extent of fiscal austerity that Greek government would soon need to implement to complete its financial rehabilitation.

But time was of the essence. The history of the IMF's bailout programs showed that they worked best when implemented early, while the country was financially vulnerable but not yet in a full-blown crisis. Once a crisis sets in, the problems become unmanageable.[39] As in well-designed IMF programs, Greece needed a combination of official financial assistance, debt restructuring, and a sensible degree of fiscal austerity.

By the second half of January 2010, yields on the government's bonds were above 6.5 percent. Greece was definitely slipping from vulnerability into crisis. In Washington, on January 21, the IMF announced that its team was in Athens, providing "technical assistance." But the IMF's spokeswoman, Caroline Atkinson, insisted, "We don't expect a request for financial assistance from Greece."[40] European authorities did not want the IMF to provide financial assistance to Greece, fearing the world would view it as a sign of European weakness.[41] IMF Managing Director Dominique Strauss-Kahn, himself a former French finance minister and widely expected to run for the French presidency in 2012, helped make the European case with a curious example: "if it was in California, the Americans would tell us very probably: 'We don't need the IMF.' "[42] The metaphor was catchy, and Eurogroup head Jean-Claude Juncker popularized a pithier version: "If California had a refinancing problem, the United States wouldn't go to the IMF."[43]

By January 26–27, Greece was on the radar screen of the FOMC, the body of the US Federal Reserve System that sets monetary policy. Committee members were worried that the failure of European authorities to act promptly would make Greece's economic problems more intractable and even increase political discord in Europe. The FOMC's vice chairman, William Dudley, predicted: "the circumstances in the EU strike me as likely to get worse before they get better."[44] Michael Palumbo, an economist at the Federal Reserve Board, sketched a more dismal outlook: "If a full-blown debt crisis does erupt in Greece, there seems to be little consensus in Europe as to how it should be managed and, hence, might expose deeper divisions among euro-area countries."[45]

The tipping point seems to have come at the very moment the FOMC was expressing these worries. On January 26, the Greek government spread—the premium that Greek government bonds paid over German bonds—crossed 300 basis points. Over the next few days, as Greek yields touched 7 percent, the spread reached 350 basis points. The Athens stock market was about 25 percent below its level of October 8. Prices of banks' stocks had fallen even faster. Greece needed a bailout program, and it needed one now. The distress in government finances, the banks, and the economy were feeding on one another. Greece was spiraling out of control.

Europeans Indulge in "Cheap Talk," Greece Begins to Implode

By early February, Greek economic indicators painted a grim picture. Industrial production had fallen sharply.[46] The unemployment rate was rising at a rapid pace. Papandreou had promised a more hopeful future, but his deep austerity policies—widespread wage cuts and tax hikes—were pushing the economy into a deepening recession.[47] Public- and private-sector unions were about to go on strike.

Greece's woes would not disappear on their own, and euro-area authorities began making hazy promises of support. On February 10, Schäuble loudly whispered that a financial rescue of Greece had become inevitable.[48] Investors concluded that a Greek bailout was likely to come soon. The pressure on Greek government bonds eased.

Schäuble seemed to have scored an easy victory with a few words, and the seductive strategy of "cheap talk" began to take shape. The European Council, which includes European heads of state or government, met on February 10–11. The council's artfully crafted communiqué said: "Euro area member states will take determined and coordinated action, if needed, to safeguard financial stability in the euro area as a whole."[49] The key phrase was "if needed." Nothing specific was promised, but the prospect of a financial lifeline was dangled before financial markets. The phrase "if needed" was destined to do a lot of heavy lifting in the management of the eurozone crisis.

Cheap talk blended well with Merkel's inclination to wait, an inclination that many others quietly shared. No European leader was keen to incur the domestic political cost of extending financial support to Greece. Thus, in early February, an appealing possibility was that policymakers' reassurances would pacify financial markets, bond yields would fall, and fiscal pressure on the Greek government would decline. A politically difficult financial rescue package would not be necessary.

At first, the strategy seemed to deliver the desired result. In the month after the European Council's February 10–11 meeting, yields on Greek government bonds stayed below 6.5 percent. On March 4, even amid the Greek public's weeklong protests against deepening austerity, the government was easily able to sell €5 billion worth of bonds to private investors at an interest rate of 6.4 percent.[50] The *New York Times* wrote that Greece had taken "a crucial step to pay its bills and contain the euro crisis."[51] A more effusive *Wall Street Journal* report said, "The European Union's strategy for dealing with the Greek crisis by relying on rhetoric instead of direct intervention is working."[52]

Something was working, but it was not private investors expressing confidence in either Greece or the EU. Rather, Greek banks had stepped up their use of ECB funds to buy the Greek government's bonds. That additional demand for Greek government bonds kept the yields from rising. The sums involved were large. In the four months between November 2009 and February 2010, Greek banks drew €12 billion from the ECB. With this new money, it was easy enough to buy the €5 billion worth of bonds sold by the Greek government in early March.

For the banks, this was profitable business. They paid an interest rate of 2 percent or less for the ECB funds, and they earned 6 percent or more on government bonds. Moreover, European regulations treated government bonds as risk-free, and so banks were not required to set aside capital to protect themselves from losses in case the government defaulted. In any case, with the Greek economy slowing down quickly, making new loans to businesses and households was too risky.

But while they kept Greece in a holding pattern for some weeks, these Band-Aids—vague promises of European support and ample ECB liquidity—were unequal to the task. Greece was like a trauma patient. The delay in decisively stemming the blood flow only made it more likely that the patient would continue to hemorrhage. The tax hikes, wage cuts, and freezes in pensions and hiring were causing people's confidence and spending to fall sharply. In March, the Bank of Greece reported that the Greek economy was "in the midst of a deep crisis."[53] Recession had spread to all sectors, employment was falling, many depositors had lost faith that their banks were safe and were withdrawing their savings, and GDP was forecast to fall by at least 2 percent—and possibly much more—over the course of the year.[54]

The euro would unify Europeans, its proponents had promised. Instead, the euro was creating bruising divisions between the German and Greek people. In Germany, the widely read tabloid *Bild* carried the headline "Sell your islands, you bankrupt Greeks—and the Acropolis, too." In Athens, a Greek pensioner who was demonstrating outside the entrance to a German retail franchise lamented, "They're saying we're all criminals, not just our leaders but every Greek."[55]

Greeks were suffering the double humiliation of shrinking livelihoods and insults from the German media. In larger numbers and with increasing intensity, they were demonstrating against the austerity their government was imposing on them. On March 11, an estimated fifty thousand people protested against more spending cuts and tax increases. "Why do the people always have to pay?" asked a Bank of Greece employee. "It is the people always who pay," responded another protester. Masked youth clashed with the police. The strike shut down the government, flights were grounded, and rail and ferry services came to a halt.[56]

Although the severity of Greece's economic and social crisis had become more glaring, some European leaders kept their faith in the power of optimistic rhetoric. In an interview on March 12, 2010, French Finance Minister Christine Lagarde praised the Greek authorities. They had, "for once, over-delivered from what was expected." She was referring to the successful passage of legislation to enable cuts in government spending. These actions, she said, "have demonstrated that [the Greek authorities] are credible and the market [has] responded that way." Greece, Lagarde concluded, did not need a financial bailout.[57]

Schäuble Wants Greece Punished: February–March 2010

On the same day that Lagarde said Greece was managing just fine, Schäuble was deeply worried about the eurozone's future. In an op-ed for the *Financial Times*, he wrote that some eurozone countries lived perpetually beyond their means. Because these countries created a dangerous "disequilibrium" within the eurozone, it was necessary to punish them aggressively.

Schäuble's list of penalties included loss of access to the EU's development funds, suspension of voting rights, and large fines. However, if even these penalties did not persuade the country to "consolidate its budgets," the only option, Schäuble concluded, would be to expel the country from the monetary union.[58] Thus, Schäuble publicly raised the possibility of a Greek exit from the eurozone, a "Grexit."

Lagarde and Schäuble were both narrating good stories, but neither had any touch with reality. Although Lagarde claimed that Greece did not need a bailout, a bailout was already in place through ECB financing. While Schäuble understood that the crisis was severe, his plan to impose financial penalties on countries in fiscal distress was "idiotic," as Merkel quickly pointed out. Speaking to the Bundestag, Merkel brusquely said, "A country that has no money cannot pay money to the Commission. Forcing it to do so we will bring about insolvency particularly fast."[59]

But what did Merkel think of Grexit?

On March 17, Merkel said that the mantra of Europe as a "community of peace" was too fuzzy to guide practical affairs. Instead, it was more appropriate to view Europe as a "community of stability," and it was therefore unwise to pamper unstable member countries with "friendly expressions." The Greeks, she insisted, had "no alternative" but to help themselves. Europe could not "rush" to provide financial aid: such misguided generosity would be "fatal"; it would destroy the foundation of Europe as a "community of rules." Although Merkel dismissed Schäuble's idea of financial penalties on countries with excessive deficits, she agreed with him that if member countries failed "time and again" to live by the rules, they should leave the euro area. These must be the principles, Merkel firmly concluded. "Otherwise," she said, "we cannot work together."[60]

Although Schäuble had made the same suggestion some days earlier, Merkel's willingness to publicly consider the possibility of Grexit made it more real. Throwing Greece out had great emotional appeal.

In a November 2007 essay, Barry Eichengreen, professor of economics at the University of California, Berkeley, had warned that exit of a member country from the euro area was a bad idea: it could cause "the mother of all financial crises."[61] Eichengreen's analysis was straightforward: if a country left the euro area from a position of weakness, its domestic currency would depreciate rapidly, making it extraordinarily hard for the government and residents to repay debts still due in euros. Defaults would lead to more defaults, and the domestic financial system would collapse.

Once Greece exited the eurozone, financial markets would have every reason to bet against other vulnerable countries by, for example, dumping their debt. These countries would then face rising interest rates on their new debt, which would increase the stress on their budgets and push them to the brink of debt default and euro exit. Just as the investor George Soros had for months sold the pound to force Britain out of Europe's ERM on a "Black Wednesday" in September 1992, speculators would have the incentive to scout for governments that could not withstand speculative pressures on their debt. More of the euro-area financial system would come under stress. Thus, a Greek exit could begin a process that ultimately would inflict vast financial and political damage in the euro area and beyond. Grexit was fun to talk about. Its consequences could be severe.

Eichengreen published an extended analysis of his argument in February 2010, a month before Schäuble and Merkel spoke publicly about throwing Greece out of the euro area.[62] The two German leaders must have known—or should have known—that it was not in their interest to trigger a Greek exit. It seemed likely that Schäuble and Merkel were engaged in political theater to pacify German citizens, large numbers of whom were unwilling to pay for Greece's problems. Simon Johnson, back as a professor at MIT after his eighteen-month stint as the IMF's chief economist, certainly felt that way. He said of Merkel's intentions: "She's playing a lot to her domestic audience and presenting the image of [Germany] not getting rolled over by the Greeks."[63]

Merkel Prepares the Ground for a Greek Bailout: Late March 2010

Merkel had hoped that Europe's "problem children"—specifically, the problem child Greece—would grow up. She had many contentious domestic matters to deal with, including tax reform, improvements in the provision of healthcare, and the future of nuclear energy.[64] The domestic policy choices were controversial and had caused her government's standing to drop alarmingly in opinion polls. Conflicts within her governing coalition—her CDU, CSU, and FDP—were out in the open. It looked increasingly likely that she and her coalition partners would lose the May 9 elections in the state of North Rhine-Westphalia, Germany's most populous state, with a quarter of the country's population. This was a state that the coalition had won easily in September 2009 and a loss now would undermine Merkel's personal stature and possibly cause her coalition to lose its majority in the Bundesrat, the German parliament's upper house. There was never a convenient time to discuss the possibility of financial aid to Greece. This was a particularly bad moment.

The press, which had focused on the Grexit comment in Merkel's March 17 speech, took another day to focus on her other, more intriguing, suggestion: perhaps, the IMF should help finance a potential Greek bailout. By inviting the IMF, Merkel was going against the entire European establishment. Just a few days earlier, in an interview with the *Wall Street Journal*, French Finance Minister Lagarde had repeated the popular European line that IMF financing for Greece would be as "odd" as the IMF being called on by the US government to rescue California.[65] In his most recent public position, Schäuble remained strongly opposed to IMF participation. He did not want the IMF muddling around in Europe's problems.[66]

But Merkel had her eyes on domestic politics. The IMF's presence would signal to the German public that the Greek crisis had become acute. Hence, German stability was at risk. Emphasizing the need to maintain stability also helped avoid objections from the powerful German Constitutional Court, which had mandated that German participation in the euro area could continue only if it remained a zone of stability.[67]

It is a commentary on the state of European democracy that Merkel held so much power. At home, she was managing a fractious coalition and dropping in the polls. But on Europe, she had virtually unquestioned authority. Once Merkel spoke, the absolute rejection of IMF participation evaporated. Merkel's close advisors echoed her message, and Dutch and Finnish governments joined in support. Schäuble might have sulked for a few days, but he came out of his corner. This ship had sailed. The IMF was in.

Merkel had spoken, but she was not ready to act. In a radio interview on Saturday, March 21, she pushed back against European leaders who were tiring of the wait and the uncertainty. In preparation for the European Council meeting scheduled for the following Wednesday, Merkel said, "I don't see that Greece needs money at the moment. There's no looming insolvency."[68] Raising premature expectations of a bailout, she warned, would only stir up financial-market turbulence. Merkel was mindful of the relentless campaign led by the *Bild*, which had been railing against the use of German money to bail out Greece.[69] The opinion polls showed the German public strongly opposed financial aid to Greece.

"Just what is the matter with Angela Merkel?" asked Joschka Fischer.[70] Fischer had been German foreign minister and vice chancellor in Schröder's government between 1998 and 2005. He was also a European political philosopher. In May 2000, in a celebrated address at Berlin's Humboldt University, he had charted a path to closer political cooperation among European nations, culminating in a European federation.[71] To Fischer, Merkel's approach to Greece—and hence to Europe—was abhorrent. He complained that she was being "Frau Germania"; she was, he said, pulling Germany "into its shell."[72] Fischer, therefore, called on Merkel to untie German purse strings for Greece; such altruism would profit Germany in the future. In the manner of many European idealists, Fischer's advice to Merkel was that she needed to ignore the German public's opposition to financial aid for Greece.

Fischer's vision of a progression to European federation was a fairy tale. European leaders had rejected the possibility of a European federation immediately after French Foreign Minister Robert Schuman had first proposed it in May 1950.[73] Since then, every brave proponent's latest plan for a European federation had been spurned quickly. Some European leaders kept, however, coming back to it without reflecting on the reasons why the idea had had little traction in the past. As the economics Nobel laureate Thomas Schelling wrote in 1988, in the effort to deny reality, "we can forget and forget that we are forgetting." And forgetfulness, Schelling added, is the essence of drama.[74]

Fischer's further proposition that European leaders should override public opinion was, at the very least, improper. In addition, ever since the agreement on the Maastricht Treaty in December 1991, leaders had increasingly recognized that they could not ignore public opinion on Europe (see chapters 2 and 4). Author and journalist Matthew Lynn was right: "Even if she wanted to, Angela Merkel was going to find it practically impossible to play softball with the Greeks." Not just Merkel, Lynn pointed out, but all European leaders were mindful of public opposition to European ventures. As he pithily wrote, "It was all very well for politicians to talk the language of European solidarity. But on the ground, where votes are won and lost and where the careers of politicians are ultimately made or broken, the rhetoric was meaningless. The voters weren't going to buy it."[75]

Sure enough, the European Council's decision after the March 25–26 summit echoed Merkel's position: all countries must take care of their own finances. The council said that the Greek government was making commendable efforts to put its house in order, the Greek economy was responding to those efforts, and European governments would provide financial assistance—but only "if needed."[76] Herman Van Rompuy, the European Council's first full-time president, in office since November 2009, continued with the "cheap talk." European authorities and the IMF, he declared, would not "abandon" Greece.[77] He predicted that the European promise to stand in solidarity with Greece would give markets reason to calm down, and yields on Greek government bonds would fall.

The End Game Begins: April 2010

Promises by the European Council and Von Rompuy that all would be well failed to impress investors. Greece owed bondholders nearly €9 billion on May 19, and the investors were worried that the Greek government had run out of the cash to make that payment in full. The risk of a Greek debt default was thus increasing, and investors started demanding higher yields as compensation. From 6.2 percent on March 26, the yield on the Greek ten-year bond moved decisively over the next two weeks to above 7 percent. Investors ignored more soothing words from ECB President Jean-Claude Trichet, who said on April 8 that default on Greek debt "was not an issue."[78] For financial markets, the risk of default was very much "an issue."

Finally, on April 11, European governments and the IMF announced a €45 billion financial package to support Greece. In the six months from October 8, 2009, to April 11, 2010, Greek government yields had risen from 4.5 percent to more than 7 percent. Put differently, a ten-year Greek bond that sold for €100 six months earlier now sold for €60. The Greek crisis was evolving eerily according to the script sketched at a late January FOMC meeting in Washington. Economist Michael Palumbo had predicted that divisions among Europeans would hold them back, which would cause the crisis to escalate. Now, in the second half of April, Nathan Sheets, director of the Federal Reserve Board's Division of International Finance, told the members of the FOMC, "What seemed several months ago to be a manageable set of problems is now on the verge of metastasizing, and European authorities still have not been able to marshal a convincing response."[79] The bailout package, Sheets said, had done "little to boost confidence." Financial markets were uncertain what came next, and, in particular, if all member states would ultimately authorize the funds.

Financial markets exerted more pressure on the Greek government. On April 15, the IMF's Strauss-Kahn announced that European officials and an IMF team would meet in Athens to negotiate the details of a financial bailout. But nature added to the delay. Ash with the texture of glass powder poured out of an Icelandic volcano, reaching heights of 36,000 feet into the skies. Fear that the ash would clog jet engines caused widespread flight cancellations, stranding thousands of passengers. To everyone's surprise, however, the Washington-based IMF team was the first to slip through the disruptions, reaching Athens on Monday, April 19.[80]

And "it started well," wrote Matina Stevis, a Greek national and *Wall Street Journal* reporter whose vivid coverage of the Greek crisis through its early years was must reading. The yield on the Greek ten-year bond was galloping toward 8 percent, and options were running out. A European official told Stevis that the arrival of the IMF team in Athens was "almost like the U.S. Marine Corps arriving in a war zone." The fund and its expertise, the official said, were "indispensable."[81]

By April 21, with European teams finally in Athens and the negotiations ready to start, financial markets were in a full-blown panic mode. Making matters worse, on April 22, Greek government authorities announced that the budget deficit for 2009 would be 13.6 percent of GDP and not 12.7 percent as previously projected.[82] The latest estimate of the Greek government's debt-to-GDP ratio stood at above 120 percent, up from the earlier 110 percent. The rating agency Moody's downgraded Greek debt. The yield on the ten-year Greek bond jumped, touching a peak of 8.7 percent, 570 basis points above the German bond. International bailout experts were shuffling numbers in their Excel spreadsheets, and Greece was in a free fall.

The Greek government's anxious private creditors did not necessarily welcome the official financial bailout that was in the works. The plan was for the Greek government to borrow from the IMF and European creditors and use those funds to repay some of the private creditors. While the creditors certainly would receive welcome repayment, as a group, they had a serious concern.[83] Once the Greek government had borrowed from the IMF, the IMF would be the "senior lender." That meant that repayments to the IMF would have priority over those to all other lenders. Since the European governments, as official lenders, would also demand seniority, they would also have priority over private lenders. Thus, after repaying the IMF and the Europeans, the Greek government was unlikely to have enough funds to repay all private creditors. Many would eventually bear large losses.

Greek residents had started withdrawing their bank deposits, both because they needed the money to make up for falling incomes and because they were worried that Greek banks might fail and therefore be unable to repay the deposits.[84] If the deposit withdrawals continued, the banks, in fact, would fail. The officials, however, refused to be rushed. Schäuble explained on Friday, April 23, that the process of approving the Greek bailout would take time, at least another two weeks.[85]

Who Should Pay for the Greek Government's Mistakes, Creditors or Citizens?

On April 24, the editorial board of the *Wall Street Journal* made the earliest and most forceful public case for imposing losses on all of the Greek government's creditors.[86] Their argument was simple. Over the next five years, Greece's government needed to repay its private creditors $240 billion, approximately a year's worth of Greek GDP. The only way the government could make those payments was by first borrowing new money from European governments and the IMF. The government's debt obligations would remain unchanged; instead of owing money to private lenders, the government would owe money to official lenders. Fiscal austerity through tax hikes and spending cuts would not be helpful in reducing the Greek debt burden. As the IMF's past lending programs made clear, deep austerity killed economic growth, and with falling GDP, the burden of repaying debt would go up, not down. There was really no choice, the editorial board concluded: "[Official loans] might delay, but cannot prevent, a radical restructuring of Greek debt."

This was not the cry of a left-leaning editorial board for "burning bondholders." No, it was a simple economic calculation: when debt restructuring is inevitable, it is better to get it done early. Replacing private loans with official loans only makes matters worse. The borrower suffers the agony of prolonged austerity; the weakened borrower repays even less of the debt than if an early restructuring had allowed a fresh start.

But European leaders opposed all calls for debt restructuring with a strangely fierce intensity. Less than a week before the *Wall Street Journal* made its pitch for restructuring Greek debt, the German weekly *Der Spiegel* had interviewed Finance Minister Schäuble while he lay in a hospital bed. Schäuble was recovering from a recurring ailment caused by a 1990 assassination attempt that left him paralyzed below the waist. *Der Spiegel* reporters reminded Schäuble that at Maastricht in 1991, Germany's chief negotiator, Horst Köhler, made clear the German government's position that private creditors would bear losses if a eurozone government could not repay its debts. Hence, the Maastricht Treaty's "no bailout" clause intended that the burden of unsustainable government debts would fall onto the shoulders of private creditors. Schäuble acknowledged that during the Maastricht negotiations, he too had believed in "no bailout," but that this principle was no longer realistic. In words that were to frame the rest of the debate, Schäuble said, "We cannot allow the bankruptcy of a euro member state like Greece to turn into a second Lehman Brothers. Greece is just as systemically important as a major bank."[87] Thus, the assertion was that restructuring of the Greek government's debts would spread chaos in financial markets and again bring the world economy to its knees. Schäuble was raising the specter of financial "contagion," the possibility that financial vulnerabilities would propagate in an uncontrolled manner, causing mayhem.

Aware of Schäuble's prediction of doomsday if Greek debt was restructured, the *Wall Street Journal*'s editors responded: "Greece isn't Lehman." Lehman Brothers was a critical node in a complex global web of interconnected financial nerve centers; the unexpected disabling of the Lehman node had disrupted the entire financial web. Greece had mainly old-fashioned financial arrangements, which experts understood. To the contrary, the editorial warned, if European authorities kept "trying to solve Greece's real debt problems by press release and bailout," Greek financial woes would disrupt an ever-larger portion of the global financial system. Then, matters could, in fact, get out of hand.[88]

Schäuble and the *Wall Street Journal* had made their arguments. What was the evidence? At an FOMC meeting in Washington, Nathan Sheets told anxious committee members that there was no evidence of "wake-up call" contagion from Greece. Greece's problems were not causing investors to "tune in" to the debt problems of a large number of eurozone governments.[89] Irish and Portuguese troubles were homegrown; Spain and Italy remained insulated.[90] Academic studies had also struggled to find evidence of "wake-up call" contagion.[91] Some, such as Karl Otto Pöhl, formerly president of the Bundesbank, believed contagion could occur through banks. French and German banks would be severely hurt if the Greek government did not repay its debts to them.[92] In turn, they would transmit their problems to their creditors. The numbers, however, did not add up. The French and German banks that had poured money into Greece were relatively large and could absorb substantial losses from a Greek default. And if their own capital fell short, they could turn to support facilities set up by their governments in 2008.[93]

But the drummed-up scare of a contagious spread of Greek financial woes continued. As sovereign debt attorney Lee Buchheit remarked, European officials—especially those at the ECB—willed themselves into believing that "demons" lurked around the corner.[94] The chattering classes in the media magnified that narrative of wild contagion. The frenetic number of newspaper articles on the subject portrayed the threat of contagion from Greece as considerably more fearsome than at the time of the Lehman-induced global meltdown in late 2008 and early 2009 (figure 6.1).

Thus, speaking in dark words of the havoc that would follow, European leaders opposed restructuring of Greek debt.[95] French Finance Minister Lagarde said she "rejected the notion."[96] ECB President Trichet was the most passionate and influential foe of Greek debt restructuring. He had been apoplectic when US authorities had failed to rescue Lehman Brothers and, instead, allowed the bank to file for bankruptcy. On Greece, Trichet was firm: "I've always said publicly that default is out of the question."[97]

Merkel understood the crucial financial logic for restructuring the Greek government's debt. But she knew that even after the debt restructuring, the Greek government would need significant financial assistance. To justify that assistance, Germans wanted to see evidence that the Greeks were tightening their belts. Thus, for Merkel, a significantly sized and tightly specified Greek austerity program was a domestic political ally. On April 26, she said she sympathized with German citizens who were upset about bailing out Greeks, and she called on the Greek government to commit to a "rigid deficit-reduction plan."[98] Speaking with an uncharacteristically sharp edge, Merkel continued, "Greece has to accept harsh measures for several years." She hinted that she would hold up the decision on financial aid until she saw evidence that the Greeks were "doing enough."[99] The strategy of playing to her domestic audience by wearing down the Greeks might have appeared politically expedient, but it was causing an economic meltdown.

In that limbo, on April 27, citing a lack of clear European commitment to resolving the Greek crisis, S&P lowered the Greek credit rating to BB+ (or junk status). The yield on the ten-year bond hit 9.8 percent that day. The yield on the two-year bond reached an astonishing 25 percent. The message was sobering: financial markets were saying that with a 60 percent probability, the Greek government would repay only 40 percent of its debts due April 2012.[100]

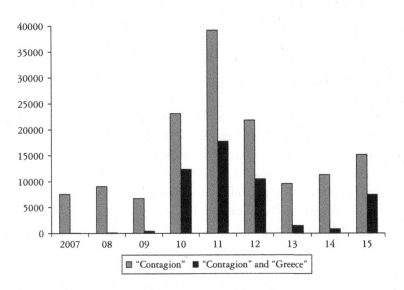

FIGURE 6.1. The drumbeat of Greek contagion.
(Number of Factiva articles with the word "contagion" and the words "contagion" and "Greece")
Source: Factiva Database of Global Newspapers.

The IMF-European creditors' austerity plan would make it even less likely that the Greek government would repay all its debts, as the *Wall Street Journal* had explained some days earlier. Nathan Sheets explained the same logic in somewhat greater detail at the April 27–28 FOMC meeting. If the Greek government could miraculously implement the extraordinary tax increases and spending cuts proposed, businesses and households would spend less, and GDP would fall sharply. Tax revenues would fall along with GDP, and the budget deficit would not shrink as much as anticipated.[101] Because of the decline in GDP and the smaller-than-expected deficit reduction, the debt burden—the debt-to-GDP ratio—would rise from its already high level. Interest rates paid by the government would become intolerable. Sheets concluded that although European authorities considered restructuring of Greek debt "unthinkable," their austerity-centered financial bailout program would make restructuring "unavoidable."[102]

A senior member of Merkel's CDU did raise the possibility of an immediate Greek debt restructuring. On April 27, Norbert Barthle, budgetary spokesman for the CDU contingent in the Bundestag, said that investors holding Greek government bonds should not be fully repaid.[103] Barthle apparently raised the matter the next day with the IMF's Strauss-Kahn and the ECB's Trichet.[104] But that discussion went nowhere.

To Strauss-Kahn, the priority was a faster pace of European decision-making. "Every day that is lost," he said, "the situation is growing worse and worse, not only in Greece but in the European Union."[105] He announced that the size of the financing package needed to go up from the earlier estimate of €45 billion to €120 billion. Strauss-Kahn was impatient for good reason, but his proposal to throw more money at Greece went in the wrong direction. The Greek government did not need ever larger sums of official funds; it needed to negotiate down the debt payments due to private lenders.

The *Wall Street Journal*'s editors felt compelled to weigh in again. They distinguished between a liquidity crisis and a solvency crisis. Greece, they correctly insisted, did not have merely a liquidity problem that could be solved by a temporary infusion of cash from the Europeans and the IMF. "The unhappy reality," they said, "is that Greece is busted and its political-economic model has reached a dead end." By lending to an insolvent Greece, European creditors and the IMF would "end up owning Athens."[106] That, as another journalist politely wrote, would certainly provoke unwelcome political tensions.[107]

As the month of April ended, a virtual consensus existed outside the European establishment and the IMF. Greece could not repay its debts. Excessive austerity would make things worse, not better. The IMF and the

Europeans had reached their own, very different, conclusion: Greeks would tighten their belts and pay back their creditors.

A Bailout Planned in the Shadow of Contagion: May 2010

On May 2, eurozone finance ministers announced that Greece would receive €110 billion, of which €80 billion would be loans from other eurozone member countries and €30 billion would be from the IMF.[108] This would be the largest-ever international bailout package. The IMF measures its loan amount in relation to the country's quota, a number based on various measures of the country's economic size. The Greek loan would be 32 times its quota, another landmark. The first installment of the bailout funds would be available before May 19 so that Greece could pay its private creditors the amount due to them on that day.

Soon after the bailout announcement, the IMF's Poul Thomsen spoke in a conference call with reporters. A Danish economist and veteran of many past bailouts, Thomsen had led the IMF's "marine corps" since the negotiations had started in Athens on April 21. Asked if there were plans for restructuring Greek debt, Thomsen answered: "That was never on the table. It has never been discussed."[109]

Financial markets experienced only short-lived relief. Panic built up, as investors watched the German reaction. A solid majority assured Merkel of easy approval in the Bundestag. But she faced the onslaught of a hostile media and the German public. The *Bild* continued its tirade, with one headline making a play on a common Greek name: "What Will It Costas?" A *Spiegel* headline read, "Euroland Is Burning." The more intellectual *Die Zeit* asked, "What Will Happen to Our Money?" The *Frankfurter Allgemeine Zeitung*, the fastidious voice of German conservatism, said Europe could not continue to solve its problems with German money. More money was not the answer to "the bankruptcy of whole states and the clash of cultures."[110]

No doubt influenced by the media onslaught, the vast majority of the German public opposed financial support for Greece.[111] Partly as a consequence, people were losing confidence in Merkel's leadership. Only two out of five respondents in an opinion poll believed that Merkel had a grip on the Greek crisis.[112] Her popularity rating had fallen from 70 percent in February to 48 percent in early May.[113] And in North Rhine-Westphalia, Merkel's coalition was running neck-and-neck with the opposition.[114]

On May 5, when Merkel opened the three-day Bundestag debate on the decision to finance Greece, she spoke directly to the German people. She had waited, she said, to reassure herself that the Greek government had in place a workable plan to reduce its budget deficit substantially. If she had rushed, others would have been encouraged to demand financial help without first taking care of their own responsibilities. "A good European," Merkel said, "is not necessarily one who comes to the rescue quickly, but one who first considers the rules of the European Union and national law."[115]

However, the time to wait was over. Merkel was now in a hurry, and she invoked the demon of contagion. Failure to act quickly, she said, would set off "a contagious chain-reaction in European and international financial systems." Immediate assistance to Greece was essential "to ensure the financial stability of the eurozone."[116]

Not wishing to leave any stone unturned, Merkel made what was for her a rare appeal to Germany's obligation to Europe. "We owe decades of peace and prosperity to the understanding of our neighbours," she said.[117] Now "Europe is looking to Germany," Merkel admonished her nation's media and public.[118]

Speaking later that afternoon to the Bundestag's budget committee, Bundesbank President Axel Weber returned to Merkel's theme that financial mayhem would surely follow if Germany did not lead Europe to a Greek rescue. "A Greek default in the current very fragile situation," he said, "would pose a substantial risk to the stability of monetary union and the financial system. There is a threat of serious contagion effects for other euro zone countries and increasing negative feedback effects for capital markets."[119] The recently appointed European commissioner for economic and monetary affairs, Olli Rehn, added: "It's absolutely essential to contain the bushfire in Greece so that it will not become a forest fire."[120] European leaders echoed the threat of catastrophic losses all day.[121]

While Merkel reluctantly spoke of Germany's obligations to Europe, and as all European leaders echoed her warning of catastrophe if Greece did not receive immediate financial support, Europe was pulling apart politically, and financial markets were threatening to melt down.

Throughout Greece, millions of citizens rebelled against the fiscal austerity and "structural reforms" demanded by the creditors. In Athens, demonstrations outside the parliament grew increasingly tense. Protesters cried, "Thieves," "Traitors," and "Burn! Let the whorehouse burn!"[122] Riot police and armored vans created a wall to prevent protesters from storming the parliament building. The police hurled tear-gas shells, and the protesters threw back Molotov cocktails. Petrol bombs set a bank branch on fire where employees had continued to work despite the call to strike. A man and two young women, one of them pregnant, died in the blaze.

Just eight months earlier, Greeks had voted for "hope."

Papandreou's PASOK parliamentarians felt cheated. They made a futile effort to soften the austerity, to "make the wage cuts less steep or find less painful alternatives." But Finance Minister Papaconstantinou told them it was too late to make any changes: "It was a take-it-or-leave-it proposition."[123] Thus, on May 6, under the threat of Greek economic and financial collapse, reluctant PASOK members voted to pass the necessary legislation. The New Democracy party under its new leader, Antonis Samaras, voted against the program. Samaras told Papandreou, "you are looking for accomplices and we will not be your accomplices!"[124]

On May 7, the large majority held by Merkel's CDU-led coalition ensured the Bundestag's authorization of German participation in the Greek program. However, the pro-European social democrats (the SPD) abstained from voting, perhaps to score political points against Merkel. More than half of German citizens opposed the Greek bailout.[125] The *Bild* described Germany's contribution to the bailout—€22.4 billion—as the "fattest cheque written in history."[126] A question mark hung over the durability of Germany's commitment to Greece and Europe.

Investors could see the bailout moving ahead, but they could also see Greece placed under greater financial stress and rapidly rising European political tensions. On May 7, the yield on the Greek ten-year bond soared to 12 percent, up from 9 percent on May 3 (and 4.5 percent on October 8, 2009). Through these days, global stock markets swooned and the volatility of the foreign exchange value of the euro against other major currencies spiked up. European leaders had presented an economically and politically incoherent plan to rescue Greece and it had instilled fright among investors.

On the evening of May 7, European leaders met in Brussels to complete the final authorization of the Greek financial-rescue package. The job was not done. They recognized that they required a bigger and more robust defense against more crises. European finance ministers worked through the weekend and on Sunday, May 9 (before markets opened on Monday morning), they announced a €750 billion ($1 trillion) financial "firewall." The centerpiece of this firewall was the €440 billion European Financial Stability Facility (EFSF) set up by eurozone countries to finance bailouts of euro-area countries in financial distress. All EU countries would back a smaller fund of €60 billion, the European Financial Stability Mechanism (EFSM). In addition, through a less clear mechanism, the IMF's shareholders would bolster its lending capacity by €250 billion.

As Merkel worked to secure bailout funds for Greece, voters in North Rhine–Westphalia handed her and her coalition a stinging defeat. Voters paid no attention to Merkel's fleeting message of German obligation to Europe, nor did they seem to care about her stern warning that if Greece failed, Germany would also bear the costs.

For seven months from October 2009, Europe had gone through a stress test of its incomplete monetary union. Greeks had lost dignity and lives. Germans were angry. Europe's bewildered leaders had lost credibility.

A Kabuki Dance: The IMF's Boardroom, May 9, 2010

It was still May 9 in Washington. The IMF's Executive Board met to enact a memorable performance. The performers included First Deputy Managing Director John Lipsky, who chaired the meeting. The executive directors, some in starring roles, were there to discuss the IMF's loan to Greece.[127]

The American executive director, Meg Lundsager, justified the extraordinary IMF support for Greece: "The potential for even more damaging spill-over to other European economies and financial sectors is clear and demands a swift and decisive response."[128]

Timothy Geithner was US Treasury secretary and, as described in chapter 5, he was deeply hostile to debt restructuring. Geithner saw the demons of contagion lurking in the shadows and believed in the show of massive financial strength to scare them away. He would later write in his memoirs that the "devastating" Greek sovereign debt crisis and the accompanying turmoil in Europe "threatened the U.S. financial system." Just "the *possibility* of contagion," Geithner wrote, "was shaking confidence, tightening credit, and depressing growth in the United States." Europe, Geithner said, needed to apply "overwhelming force" to resolve its problems.[129] Not surprisingly, at the IMF board meeting, Geithner's representative, Lundsager, also spoke of the "potential" for damage, which required a "swift and decisive response."

With that, the IMF board meeting was, for all practical purposes, over. European representatives unanimously supported the Greek program. The United States, the Europeans, and their political allies were in favor. The votes to move on were in place. But the IMF's board was a stage, and a brief kabuki presentation was to be part of the day's proceedings.

Chris Legg, Australia's executive director, also represented New Zealand, South Korea, and several Pacific islands. "The comparison with Argentina," he said, "is particularly worrying."[130] Legg was referring to the large sums that the IMF had loaned to Argentina in January 2001. The Argentine economy was then in a dysfunctional state. The government had promised to exchange a peso for a dollar. But with the exchange rate fixed and inflation higher than in the United States, Argentine exports suffered, and growth stalled. As a condition for its loan, the IMF insisted on fiscal austerity, which deepened the economic contraction and, predictably, raised the government's debt burden. As more austerity made matters worse, the country's credit rating spiraled downward. Left with no choice, the IMF kept funding Argentina, essentially to repay private creditors. By the end of 2001, the country was in economic and political turmoil.[131]

Finally, the peso was floated on February 11, 2002. At the outset, currency traders had demanded 1.8 pesos for a dollar, and by late March, they demanded 3 pesos for a dollar. The Argentine economy kept contracting. Restructuring of government debt became unavoidable. The IMF had egg on its face.

Following the Argentine debacle, the IMF did what it does best. In October 2003, it wrote a mea culpa, a retrospective on what had gone wrong.[132] The mea culpa drew all the right conclusions. Argentine growth projections had been too optimistic; the expectation that "structural reforms" would counteract the adverse effects of fiscal austerity had proven illusory. Realistic growth forecasts were important when designing a credible bailout program since even small shortfalls in projected economic growth could lead to rapid increases in debt burdens.

The mea culpa said that the IMF should have nudged Argentina out of its fixed-exchange-rate regime much sooner. Crucially, the report concluded that early debt restructuring is essential; otherwise, problems fester, and everyone—creditors and debtors alike—end up worse off.

Australia's Legg was right. The problems in Greece were decidedly more severe than in Argentina. In 2001, the Argentine government's budget deficit was 5.5 percent of GDP, and its debt-to-GDP ratio was 50 percent of GDP; in 2009, the Greek government's budget deficit was 14 percent of GDP and rising, and its debt-to-GDP ratio was around 130 percent and rising. Argentina had tumbled down a flight of steps, Greece was falling off a cliff. For Argentina, the depreciated peso ultimately had jump-started exports and, thereby, kindled economic growth. Despite the "Grexit" bluster, the currency depreciation option was not open to Greece. Eurozone authorities understood that throwing Greece back to its drachma would start the unravelling of the eurozone.

Tarnished by its grievous errors in the Argentina program, the IMF had special reason to apply the lessons learned from that sorry episode. For Greece, the main lesson from the Argentina debacle was that when the government's debt is too large, it must be restructured without delay.

But the IMF refused to learn that lesson. To deflect focus from the unmistakable need for Greek debt restructuring, the IMF staff's report to the board offered a fudge. The report said that the Greek government's debt was "sustainable"—the government could potentially repay its debt fully—although it was "difficult to state categorically that this is the case with a high probability."[133] In plain language, IMF's staff described an unrealistically benign scenario in which the government's debt burden would eventually begin to decline. Board members were not supposed to focus on the worrying part of the staff's conclusion: very likely, things would go very badly wrong.

In the implausibly happy "everything goes well" scenario, GDP would decline in 2011, but then it would quickly rise again. Rapid economic recovery would occur even though the tax increases and spending cuts required by Greece's creditors would pull out demand equal to 11 percent of GDP between 2010 and 2013.[134] The benign scenario ignored the cascading effects that would follow the austerity measures. The initial reduction in demand would cause profits and incomes to fall throughout the Greek economy, which would further reduce private spending by at least an equal amount. Thus, the austerity schedule as designed was virtually baking in an extraordinary decline of 25 percent in Greek GDP through 2013.

Political preferences had prevailed over the lessons of history and economics. The Americans and Europeans wanted to move ahead without restructuring the Greek government's debt. The Argentina saga was forgotten. And the IMF's chief economist, Olivier Blanchard, apparently had no influence on the design of the Greek program. Blanchard did make the self-evident observation in an internal memo a few days before the board meeting that the draconian austerity proposed for Greece was virtually unprecedented and would crush the economy for a long time.[135]

René Weber, the IMF's executive director for Switzerland, was not privy to Blanchard's internal memo, but the numbers were glaring, and he had reached the same conclusion without the firepower of the IMF's research department. The staff's growth projections, Weber said, were fanciful, and the proposal to proceed without debt restructuring was just not credible. Greece's private creditors, Weber continued, must know that the Greek government has lived way beyond its means for a long time. Surely, they understood that without restructuring its debt, the Greek government will remain overindebted and will ultimately be unable to repay its debts.

Rather than causing panic, the restructuring would "reassure" investors that a fundamental underlying vulnerability was being addressed.[136]

Weber was stating a principle well known to historians and analysts of sovereign debt. When a country has a debt "overhang"—when there is no reasonable prospect that the government will be able to generate enough revenues to repay its debts—early restructuring to reduce the debt burden benefits not just the borrower but also the lender.[137] Following the restructuring, the borrower's economic health improves, and new productive opportunities open up for lenders to renew their business with the government and with the country's residents. In contrast, delays in bringing debt down to manageable levels deepen the borrower's distress, which further undermines the borrower's ability to repay; as a consequence, when the inevitable restructuring does occur, creditors suffer larger losses than they would have borne had the restructuring been carried out at an earlier stage. As economist Ugo Panizza has written, "Delayed defaults can lead to a destruction of value because a prolonged pre-default crisis may reduce both ability and willingness to pay."[138]

Other executive directors continued with Weber's themes. Brazil's Paulo Nogueira Batista described the growth projections as Panglossian. And just as the Fed's Nathan Sheets had done two weeks earlier, India's Arvind Virmani described the plan as internally inconsistent. The "unprecedented" austerity, Virmani said, "could trigger a deflationary spiral of falling prices, falling employment, and falling fiscal revenues that could eventually undermine the program itself."[139]

Poul Thomsen, leader of the IMF's Greek team was beamed in on a video link from Athens. He did not respond to criticisms of the severe fiscal austerity, nor did he defend the unrealistic growth forecasts. He did reject debt restructuring. He repeated his statement from May 2: debt restructuring was "not on the table."[140]

Just before the meeting closed, Switzerland's Weber spoke again. He was puzzled and asked if the IMF's management was changing an important crisis-management policy without seeking the board's authorization.[141] After the Argentine fiasco, the board had decided that the IMF could lend very large amounts (provide "exceptional access" to its funds) only if the staff certified that the debt-to-GDP ratio was likely to decline with "high probability."[142] Whenever debt was not likely to decline with high probability, as the staff acknowledged was the case for Greece, the policy required creditors to bear losses. Thus, not only did the arithmetic warn against proceeding with the proposed program, but current IMF policy also did not permit the "exceptionally" large funding without a strategy for restructuring the Greek government's debt.

The IMF's senior officials, including its legal counsel, acknowledged that they were, indeed, asking the board to authorize a change in policy. Most directors were dismayed, because the policy change had been slipped in without the normal consultation, and executive directors were being confronted by the threat that if they did not approve the change, they could trigger a "systemic crisis." Weber protested that the staff report provided no evidence to support its claim that a large financial package for Greece—with no restructuring of the Greek government's debt—was essential to prevent financial mayhem in global markets.[143]

As he concluded the meeting, Lipsky was annoyed with the repeated calls for debt restructuring, which he felt were utterly irresponsible. Lipsky had started his career as a young economist at the IMF, and then had spent several successful years in investment banking. He returned in 2006 to the IMF as an American political appointee to the position of First Deputy Managing Director, the second-in-command in the institution's hierarchy. "I have been a little disturbed," Lipsky said, "by the suggestion that the Fund program should obviously have involved debt restructuring or even default. I think these kinds of comments in this case not only are not useful, but potentially unhelpful." The proposal before the board was the only way ahead. There was "no Plan B," Lipsky firmly concluded.[144]

Within the IMF, economists understood that a combination of early debt restructuring and less draconian austerity would have improved the outcome of the Greek program. But despite its obligation to take independent decisions based on objective criteria, the IMF now bowed to the wishes of the Europeans and the Americans.[145] The Greek case was a continuation of a long-standing tendency. After examining the history of IMF programs, political scientist Mark Copelovitch has concluded that the IMF acts as a "servant" to its major shareholders, especially when they put up a united front.[146]

On Monday, May 10, financial markets opened knowing that the Greek government would have the €9 billion it needed to pay its creditors on May 19. The ECB further reassured investors by announcing that it would boost its Securities Markets Programme (SMP) to purchase the bonds of euro-area governments and thus bid up their prices and help lower the yields. From a high of 12 percent on Friday, May 7, the yield on Greek bonds fell sharply, reaching 7.25 percent on Wednesday, May 12.

But Greece's problems had not gone away, and the relief was short-lived. The yield started rising again, steadily but relentlessly, to cross 10 percent by the end of June; the stress on Greek banks continued to increase (figure 6.2). Greece was a bankrupt nation before the bailout. It was still a bankrupt nation. After all the sound and fury, that basic problem remained.

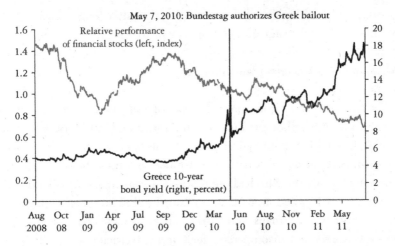

FIGURE 6.2. Greek sovereign and financial stress continues to increase after the bailout.

Note: The relative performance of financial stocks is the ratio of the FTSE/ATHEX banks index and the Athens general index.

Sources: FTSE/ATHEX banks index: Global Financial Data, ticker _FTATBNK. Athens general index: Datastream International, code GRAGENL (PI). Greece 10-Year Bond Yield: Datastream International, code TRGR10T.

In an interview with the *Washington Post* on June 16, 2010 (less than six weeks after the bailout arrangements had been formalized), Lagarde said, "If we had been able to address the Greek problem right from the start, say in February, I think we would have been able to prevent it from snowballing the way that it did."[147] It was easy for Lagarde to see the costs of delayed action when she looked back from the vantage point of June. Three months earlier, she had contributed to the delay. On March 12, she had said that the Greek government's efforts to set its house in order had exceeded expectations; all was well. The cheap talk had not worked. When European leaders finally acted in April and May, they only pushed the problem out into the future.

Did Europe Fall Forward?

In the months that followed, European leaders pointed to their achievement in rescuing Greece from financial disaster; they highlighted the financial bailout mechanisms they had put in place. Time would tell whether the Greek economy regained normalcy and Greek people regained their self-respect. Certainly, the bailout system, with its emphasis on a high degree of austerity, would always, at first, deepen the economic distress. Political tensions would increase.

The real test of falling forward was not whether after long-drawn negotiations European leaders agreed to set up new institutional and financial structures. Rather, falling forward required European citizens to believe that their leaders, and the rules under which they operated, worked to enhance prosperity and justice.

The falling forward question, thus, was whether a eurozone crisis would unleash a groundswell of pro-European sentiment and solidarity, which then would help establish politically legitimate mechanisms that enjoyed widespread support for aiding distressed member countries. In this respect, at its first major test, the euro had unquestionably failed. The Greek crisis and the way it was handled aroused unrestrained public aversion. Antagonism between horrified Germans and Greeks steadily increased. For Germans, Greeks were lazy and incompetent; for Greeks, Germans were bullies. The sense of European identity and common destiny eroded.

Throughout, everyone looked to Merkel to lead. They wanted her to explain to the German people that as Europe's hegemonic power, Germany needed to do much more for Europe. Some of Merkel's harshest critics were Germans. In March, Joschka Fischer had complained that instead of stepping out as "Ms. Europe," Merkel had withdrawn into the shell of "Frau Germania." In late April, sociologist and philosopher Jürgen Habermas warned that German elites were again indulging in nationalistic "narcissism," and he criticized Merkel's "insensitivity" to the plight of other European nations. A true leader, Habermas said, was one who "took domestic political risks for Europe."[148]

On May 5, hours after she had appealed to the Bundestag to authorize the Greek financial bailout package, Merkel joined select guests in the town of Ludwigshafen to celebrate Kohl's eightieth birthday. In his brief remarks, Kohl chided Merkel for not doing enough to help Greece and strengthen Europe. With Merkel looking on, he said he could not understand "people who act as though Greece does not matter."[149] Wheelchair-bound and frail, Kohl—as journalists were quick to point out—was a metaphor for the ailing euro. He repeated his familiar mantra: "the euro is our guarantee of peace."[150]

Two decades earlier, Kohl had not thought through the implications of the euro, which he, as a self-proclaimed "dictator," had foisted on Germany and Europe. He was now, once again, not thinking through his attempt to shame Merkel into doing more for Europe. For Merkel, opening the door for Greece would have raised more questions. After Greece, would Germany need to fund other stressed countries? Would starting down this path create a potentially open-ended financial commitment to Europe? In 1977, the MacDougall Report had calculated that Germany and other euro-area countries each needed to contribute between 5 and 7 percent of GDP to a central budget to achieve a stable euro area.[151] Only with a budget of such size could euro-area authorities deal with inevitable recurring crises.

In a true example of falling forward, in 1933, President Franklin Delano Roosevelt's New Deal program established a sizable central budget, approximately 4 percent of GNP, to support states reeling under the onslaught of the Great Depression.[152] The states received these funds as grants—not loans—and passed them on to those most in need, creating purchasing power and extending economic stimulus. These transfers from better-off to worse-off states were the mechanism for sharing pain; they were crucial to the eventual economic recovery. The US government could set up such a system because it possessed legitimate political authority and the concurrence of sufficient numbers of the country's citizens.

By the time of the Great Recession in 2008–2010, the US federal government's support systems for states had become even more extensive. For example, just before the Great Recession, Nevada paid around 4 percent of its GDP annually as taxes to the federal government; three years into the crisis, Nevada received 6 percent of its GDP.[153] Thus, over a three-year period, the gradual swing in tax revenues in favor of Nevada amounted to almost 20 percent of Nevada's GDP. In addition, the US government launched the American Recovery and Reinvestment Act (ARRA) in 2009, providing additional aid to the states. Approximately a third of ARRA spending substituted federal for state spending or provided direct stabilization funds to the states.[154] The state government of Nevada, for example, received $2.7 billion (around 2 percent of GDP) in direct aid, Medicaid assistance, and other discretionary transfers.[155] This was on top of what were by now substantial ongoing federal transfers of social security and healthcare funds. In addition, the FDIC closed down Nevada's insolvent or unsafe banks and protected the banks' depositors. From 13.5 percent in 2009, Nevada's unemployment rate was down to 4.8 percent in 2017.

In another, older instance of falling forward, the US government had established the "no bailout" principle. After the financial crisis of 1837 and the economic recession that followed, heavily indebted states were unable to repay their debts.[156] By 1842, eight states and the territory of Florida had defaulted.[157] The US Congress refused to pay the British and Dutch creditors, who held much of the states' debts. In the initial messy aftermath, the foreign lenders cried foul. They declared the federal government a rogue debtor for not meeting its "implicit" obligations and cut off its credit.[158] Even the states that had not defaulted had to pay higher interest rates. In his dramatic account, historian Ron Chernow wrote, "when Washington sent Treasury agents to Europe, James de Rothschild had thundered, 'Tell them you have seen the man who is at the head of the finances of Europe, and that he has told you that they cannot borrow a dollar. Not a dollar.' "[159]

Painful though that transition was, the firm stand taken then established a credible "no bailout" regime. Over the next few decades, US states and municipalities experimented with a variety of constitutional arrangements and methods of financing their investments; they achieved greater financial discipline and became more accountable to their populations.[160] State and municipal authorities needed no federal fiscal surveillance and budget rules; instead, they developed their own mechanisms for living within their means. Economists Randall Henning and Martin Kessler said it well: the federal government, by refusing to bail out the states, had given them back their fiscal sovereignty.[161]

Europe was unable to fall forward during its crisis, because sensible collective decisions were impossible. On the matter of "no bailout," a handful of influential, but unaccountable, leaders had ruled it out. The cost of that decision in the form of extended fiscal austerity would be borne not by them or their citizens but by large numbers of Greeks. And, as had been the case since the single currency was first conceived in 1969, national interests ruled out fiscal transfers. Even the loans (which, it is worth repeating, had to be repaid) were opposed by citizens in many countries. Besides the Germans, the Finns were very skeptical of lending to Greece.[162]

Hence, even the system of loans to bail out insolvent (or nearly insolvent) governments was unreliable because it depended on the concurrence of all member states. The most sustained opposition to the bailout theme came from Slovakia. Starting in July 2010, a new Slovak government under Prime Minister Iveta Radičová resisted contributing either to the €440 billion bailout fund, the EFSF, or to the €110 billion loan to Greece.[163] Slovakia's per capita income was less than 60 percent that of Greece. The monthly minimum wage of a Slovak worker was €300, compared with nearly €900 for a Greek worker, and Slovak citizens could expect much smaller pensions.[164] Two-thirds of Slovak citizens opposed any aid for Greece.[165] Fewer than 20 percent of Slovak voters bothered to show up to vote in the European parliamentary elections held in June 2009. The vast majority of Slovaks did not know that a European Parliament existed, and of those who were aware of its existence, most had little idea what it did.

Was it any surprise, then, that the Slovak parliament overwhelmingly rejected financial support for Greece?[166] Prime Minister Radičová called for restructuring Greek debt in an "orderly" way in order to reduce the need for bailout funds.[167] Other leaders who felt the same way but were less forceful for fear of being dubbed "anti-European," quietly cheered Radičová.[168]

Eventually, Radičová grudgingly agreed to contribute to the EFSF, but she demanded tighter rules on further lending, or else Slovakia would exercise its veto on new loans.[169] She waited longer to agree to the Slovak contribution to the Greek loan. The joint governing structure with no accountability to citizens in other countries ensured that individual countries could slow down, or even hold up, the process of providing financial assistance. Delays and half measures were in the DNA of eurozone crisis management. Even when member nations did not explicitly delay decisions and implementation, the recognition of limits beyond which countries were unwilling to go checked the ambition, scale, and timing of initiatives taken.

Key elements of the Greek saga were about to be repeated in Ireland.

Ireland Slips into the "Sovereign-Bank" Doom Loop: January 2009

The Irish crisis had been building since late September 2008. To persuade creditors to continue to fund Irish banks, the government had guaranteed that it would repay the banks' debts.[170] That snap decision annoyed other eurozone governments who feared Irish banks would enjoy an unfair funding advantage. However, creditors were skeptical of the Irish government's word. Irish banks found it ever harder to borrow to keep up their operations and turned to the ECB. In September 2008, Irish banks owed the ECB €19 billion; by November, they owed €40 billion.

But the ECB could only fill a temporary shortfall of cash. Irish banks had made bad lending decisions and had incurred huge losses. If not already bankrupt, they were heading toward bankruptcy as property prices continued to fall and construction projects went sour. In mid-December, the Irish government announced that it would inject capital into the banks to fill the hole on account of the losses. But the worry persisted that this initiative was too late for the troubled Anglo Irish Bank, which had rapidly lost its dazzling reputation and its market value.[171] From €3.84 on September 30, 2008 (the day the government guaranteed the banks' debt repayments), Anglo Irish's share price had fallen to 35 cents.

On January 15, 2009, fearing that depositors would flee with their money, the Irish government nationalized (purchased) Anglo Irish and became its owner. At this point, the government had spent 5 percent of the country's GDP on banks' recapitalization and had guaranteed loans to banks worth 300 percent of GDP. The free fall in property prices and construction activity had also caused a sharp decline in the Irish government's revenues. Thus, in early 2009, the Irish government was making big promises to prop up its banking system, but those promises were looking dubious.

In early 2009, I was responsible for the IMF's relationship with Ireland. It fell on me to ask Irish officials if they wished to discuss the use of a "precautionary" program.[172] Under such a program, a country carries out major economic and financial surgery knowing that the IMF has set aside funds for instant use. With the reassurance of an IMF line of credit for unforeseen expenses, the government can take aggressive corrective measures.

I had special reason to believe in the value of precautionary programs. Such programs, my academic research had showed, helped financially vulnerable countries deal with their problems early and regain market confidence before a crisis set in.[173] A precautionary program worked best when a country was edging toward but not yet in a full-blown financial crisis. A precautionary program was exactly what Ireland needed.

In April 2009, my colleagues and I presented to the Irish authorities our assessment of Ireland's principal vulnerabilities. One research paper showed that taxes and duties on frenzied property transactions had boosted the government's revenues during the years of rising property prices; but not recognizing that those property-related revenues were temporary, the government had made permanent expenditure commitments. Even after the early 2009 effort to rein in the budget deficit, the "structural" hole in the budget was greater than 10 percent of GDP.[174] In other words, even after the economy recovered from its sharp contraction and began operating near its potential, the budget deficit was likely to be around 10 percent of GDP. Moreover, while the government's finances were demonstrably weak, the losses incurred by Irish banks were greater than the authorities believed them to be. IMF estimates at that time suggested that banks' losses were around 20 percent of GDP; these losses, because of the government's guarantee, would likely become the obligations of the Irish government.[175]

During that same visit to Dublin, I presented a research paper to the Irish authorities and their invitees, in which I raised the possibility that Ireland would fall into the vicious "sovereign-bank" doom loop.[176] As the government used more of its limited funds to add capital to banks or repay their creditors, the fear would grow that the government, with its increasingly shaky finances, might not repay its own debts. That would cause the interest rate on government borrowing to rise, creating more stress on public finances. Investors would further question whether the government could keep its promise to support the banks financially. That concern would cause banks' stock prices to fall, and depositors would pull out their savings from the banks. The combination of weak banks and higher interest rates in the economy would depress economic growth, and the circle of distress would keep widening.

Such a sovereign-bank dynamic was a "vicious doom loop," because once it got started, financial and economic conditions could worsen rapidly. As the economy slowed down, banks would suffer more losses, and worried investors would dump stocks of banks and demand higher yields on government bonds. This process would become increasingly difficult to reverse. The policy task was to break the doom loop early before it wreaked extensive damage. The task was either to recapitalize banks heavily, as US Treasury Secretary Geithner had done for several American banks, or to close some banks down and require their creditors to bear large losses, as America's FDIC had done for Washington Mutual and other banks.[177]

A precautionary program would provide the cover to execute these complex transactions. But Irish authorities were not interested in a precautionary IMF arrangement in 2009.

In late May 2009, the government added another €4 billion to Anglo's capital, and Finance Minister Brian Lenihan said at a news conference, "we are getting to the bottom of the problem and we are dealing with it."[178] At that time, Lenihan also reported that buyers had expressed interest in taking over Anglo as a "going concern."[179] The €4 billion in taxpayer funds to recapitalize the bank could, he believed, earn the government a valuable return.[180]

However, the likelihood that Ireland could manage its vulnerability was quickly diminishing. The economy continued to be battered. Irish GDP, which had declined by 2 percent in 2008, seemed set to fall by another 8 percent in 2009 and a further 3 percent in 2010. If these projections held, real GDP would be down by more than 13 percent in three years. The unemployment rate, which had jumped from 6 percent in 2008 to 12 percent in 2009, was expected to continue rising.

Ireland's End Game Begins: May–September 2010

It was now May 2010. European leaders and officials were finalizing the Greek program. Financial markets were in a state of panic, the Greek economy was in a tailspin, the Greek public was revolting against the prospect of harsh austerity, and citizens of creditor European countries were upset that their money would soon flow into a bottomless Greek pit. Few observers were paying attention to Ireland. The IMF, however, remained worried.

Before setting out on the annual trip to Dublin in May 2010, I had called Patrick Honohan, governor of the Irish Central Bank, and again proposed discussion of a precautionary program. I knew Honohan from earlier in our careers, when we had briefly overlapped at the World Bank in Washington. Honohan in his position could best feel the pulse of Ireland's true vulnerability: its fragile banks. The September 2008 guarantee of banks' debt was set to expire at the end of September 2010. Foreign lenders had tailored the duration of their loans to Irish banks to match the period of the guarantee. Irish banks needed to repay their lenders €70 billion (equal to 44 percent of GDP) before the guarantee expired.[181] As Honohan later wrote, "all of Dublin knew" that once those funds were repaid, foreign lenders would not replace them.[182] Irish banks had stepped up their borrowing from the ECB and from the Central Bank of Ireland under a provision that allowed for emergency liquidity.

For this reason, Honohan took my phone call seriously and followed up on it. But Finance Minister Lenihan was still not interested in a precautionary arrangement with the IMF.[183]

By the end of September 2010, the ECB and the Central Bank of Ireland had lent Irish banks €100 billion. To put that number in perspective, it was equal to 60 percent of Irish GDP. Would banks be able to pay this money back? They were hemorrhaging from losses on their commercial property loans. More losses were looming on residential mortgages, as homeowners fell behind on their repayments. If banks failed to pay back the ECB, the government would be on the hook. Thus, as the banks borrowed increasingly large sums from the ECB, the risk that the government would default on its debts rose. The yield on the government's ten-year bond increased along with the banks' ECB borrowing. Starting at around 5 percent in early June, government-bond yields briefly paused in early August and then rose steadily to reach 6 percent in early September, after which the yields raced to nearly 7 percent by the end of the month (figure 6.3).

In Washington on September 21, Nathan Sheets of the Fed briefed FOMC members on global financial developments. Earlier in the year, Sheets had accurately diagnosed the Greek economy's problems. Now, he said, Ireland was becoming the global financial hotspot.[184] Irish banks, he said, had suffered large losses in the first half of the year, and the losses were increasing by the day as borrowers were falling behind on their repayments. Sheets reported that the S&P's estimate of the Irish banking sector's losses had crossed 50 percent of GDP, up from the IMF's estimate of 20 percent of GDP in April 2009.

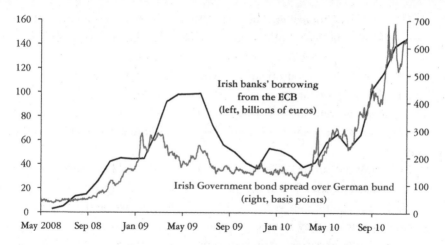

FIGURE 6.3. Irish sovereign stress rises as Irish banks become indebted to the European Central Bank.

Notes: Banks' borrowing from the ECB is the level of Ireland's Target-2 balances. Ireland's ten-year bond spread is the difference between the Irish ten-year bond yield and the German ten-year bond yield. 100 basis points equals 1 percentage point.

Sources: Ireland ten-year bond yield: Datastream International, code S310DE. Germany ten-year bond yield: Datastream International, code S30977. Target 2 balances of Ireland (end-of-month position): ECB Statistical Data Warehouse, key TGB.M.IE.N.A094T.U2.EUR.E

On September 30, Lenihan reported terrifying fiscal numbers to the Dáil (the Irish parliament). Tax revenues were continuing to fall, banks were soaking up more of the government's scarce revenues, and the budget deficit was soaring. Recapitalization of Anglo over the past couple of years had cost the government around €29 billion. For the year 2010, recapitalization funds for Anglo, Bank of Ireland, AIB, and other smaller banks would exceed €30 billion, equal to around 20 percent of GDP.[185] Moreover, even the normal budget deficit (taxes minus conventional expenditures) would be 12 percent of GDP. Thus, after including the unusually high costs of bank recapitalization, the total budget deficit in 2010 would be a shocking 32 percent of GDP. And to keep credit flowing to Irish banks, the government had no choice but to extend the guarantee of repayment to the creditors of Irish banks.

Lenihan had brave words for Irish parliamentarians. The government's finances, he said, were strong enough to handle the stress, and all would be well: "The overall level of State support to our banking system remains manageable and can be accommodated in the Government's fiscal plans in the coming years." He added, "We must continue the fiscal consolidation we have embarked upon. This is the only course to follow if we are to ensure the future economic wellbeing of our society."[186]

Those words of hope offered no solace. To the contrary, the enormity of the scam sank into the Irish public's consciousness. Lenihan's latest elaboration of the sums being spent to cover banks' losses was a jarring juxtaposition to his call for more "fiscal consolidation," which meant higher taxes and reduced government support for those who were losing jobs and homes. At a time when businesses were shutting down and the ranks of the unemployed were growing, the Irish taxpayer was paying bankers and their creditors incredibly large sums.

Reflecting the public's dark mood, the Irish media dubbed September 30, 2010, "Black Thursday."[187] "Burn the bondholders!" became the national cry. If citizens were going to have to pay drastically higher taxes and receive lower wages and benefits, they wanted the banks' bondholders to share the pain.

Lenihan was in a trap. A government guarantee was a magical instrument. If creditors had believed the guarantee, they would have kept funding Irish banks, and normal operations would have quickly resumed. But creditors had ceased believing the Irish government's promise; they wanted to take their money and run before the government ran out of money. Financial stress on the government pushed interest rates up, and the sovereign-bank doom loop played itself out.

Lenihan understood that the guarantee-based financial strategy had gone badly wrong. He also faced a political backlash. And so he introduced another theme in his speech that day, a theme investors focused on. Lenihan said that banks' lenders would need to "share the burden." He pointed specifically to "subordinated debt holders," who were legally first in line, after equity holders, to bear losses. "I expect," Lenihan said, "the subordinated debt holders to make a significant contribution towards meeting the costs of Anglo."[188] During question hour, he said he was also "open" to the possibility that banks' managements would negotiate reduced repayments to their senior creditors.[189] Thus, banks' creditors and other investors were on notice that they could expect to bear losses. They were furious. During a conference call, Lenihan was "drowned out by a deluge of derision."[190] Callers yelled that they would dump Irish government bonds.

The financial crisis continued unabated. On October 5, Moody's placed Irish government bonds "on review for possible downgrade."[191] The rating agency said that the high costs of bank recapitalization revealed by Lenihan on September 30 and rising yields on Irish government bonds would increase the pressure on the government's finances. Moreover, the austerity measures would weaken demand and hold back economic recovery. The next day, rating agency Fitch downgraded Ireland from AA- to A+. The message was the same: the cost of recapitalizing banks was "exceptional and greater-than-expected," and the outlook was negative because of the "uncertainly regarding the timing and strength of economic recovery and medium-term fiscal consolidation effort."[192]

Thus, in early October 2010, Ireland crossed the threshold from financial vulnerability to irreversible crisis. Unlike their Greek counterparts, Irish authorities had not fudged their budget numbers. But, as was true for Greece, the Irish government and European authorities had remained in denial. Indeed, European authorities had not even perceived a looming Irish crisis. To pull back from vulnerability to safety, Irish authorities needed, sometime in 2009, to have closed the worst-performing banks, imposed large losses on the banks' creditors, and used European and IMF funding to tide over a rough transition.

The Ghost of Deauville: October 18, 2010

Although she was late, Merkel finally decided that the eurozone required a true "no bailout" rule. A central budget for relieving financial stress was politically impossible. A credible and enforceable "no bailout" mechanism could serve a similar function. Instead of fiscal transfers from a central fund, reduced payments to creditors would provide breathing room to the government in financial difficulty. The immediate aftermath of a debt default would be messy, but the economy's longer-run performance would be significantly better than if the government and banks continued to labor under the burden of unpayable debt. Neither the economic logic nor the evidence was controversial.[193] The earlier the losses were recognized, the better the outcomes for both debtors and creditors.

October 18 was a pivotal day for the euro's future. The day began in Luxembourg. Finance ministers assembled to discuss a matter of great importance to euro insiders: imposing automatic financial and political sanctions on those who could not keep their budget deficits under control. It was one of those European "Groundhog Day" discussions. Or, as Thomas Schelling may have said, Europeans kept forgetting that they had forgotten. The idea of imposing sanctions for budgetary transactions had started in 1991 during the months when the Maastricht Treaty was drafted, and it had recurred ever since. An impatient Merkel had earlier in the year described automatic sanctions as "idiotic," which I consider the only right way to describe them. But although it was economically silly and politically impossible to enforce, fascination with the idea never seemed to die.

The innovation this time was that, unlike in the past, member states would not have an opportunity to vote on whether to trigger and enforce sanctions. The sanctions would kick in automatically. There was a buzz of excitement among Europe's movers and shakers. Among them were the host, Jean-Claude Juncker, prime minister and finance minister of Luxembourg, and also head of the Eurogroup; Olli Rehn, the European commissioner for monetary affairs, who had replaced Joaquín Almunia earlier in the year and brought his Finnish perspective of fiscal sternness to the discussions; and Jean-Claude Trichet, who attended such meetings in his role as president of the ECB. They were heard commenting that the "moment of truth" had come, and a "new era" was about to begin.[194]

It was the creditor-in-chief's turn to speak. Jörg Asmussen, state secretary in Germany's Ministry of Finance, was sitting in for an unwell Schäuble. Asmussen began predictably, saying that Germany always "favored strict and severe sanctions." Then, without missing a beat, Asmussen said that Germany would not support automatic sanctions. The ministers gathered were incredulous, not quite sure that they had heard correctly. As Der Spiegel reported, "a low murmur filled the room." Juncker was "the first to break the awkward silence that followed." He mockingly commented, "Jörg, considering how you started, you should have finished differently."[195]

For Trichet, automatic sanctions were essential to enforce his concept of fiscal discipline. Asmussen had snatched away that prize, which seemed so tantalizingly close. Trichet was "livid," and "contrary to custom, he switched from English to French and showered his compatriot [Ramon] Fernandez [from the French Ministry of Finance] with verbal insults."[196]

Trichet had reason to direct his anger at the French. He guessed that the French had gutted the idea of automatic sanctions. The French budget deficit was always threatening to exceed 3 percent of GDP, and France did not want to be further embarrassed with sanctions.

Trichet's guess was right: over the preceding few days, French President Sarkozy had won Merkel to his cause.[197] Merkel did not need much persuading. Especially in the form of financial penalties, she understood that sanctions would only make matters worse. Merkel was open to the possibility that a country persistently in deficit would lose its voting rights in European decisions. But she and Schäuble also realized that Germany could one day be under fiscal stress and be subject to the idiocy of fines or the loss of voting rights.[198]

A deeper question worried Merkel and Schäuble. If the EU sanctioned Germany for budgetary transgression, would the Bundestag lose its sovereign authority to tax and spend? The British had worried about this question since 1950.[199] At what point does the national parliament become a meaningless rubber stamp of European decisions? What was the political contract that allowed such evisceration of national democracy?

Merkel was in search of a different solution. In mid-April, Norbert Barthle, budgetary spokesman for Chancellor Merkel's CDU, had raised the possibility of a "haircut" on Greek bondholders. That passing thought, as we know, had gone nowhere. Schäuble had opposed any debt restructuring. In August 2010, Barthle revived the idea, this time with a more precisely stated and forward-looking proposal. The EFSF, the bailout fund, established on the weekend of May 7, 2010, would expire in 2013. A successor, Barthle proposed, would provide financial assistance only if "haircuts" were imposed on the new government bonds issued after it was set up.[200] Announcing such a plan in 2010 would put creditors on notice that governments could default on bonds issued after 2013. Member governments would have a three-year period to bring their finances into better shape, and investors could use that time to assess whether, how much, and at what interest rate they might want to lend to the different eurozone governments.

Barthle said that in contrast to the "unrealistic" insistence on penalties for "budgetary sinners," his plan for "orderly insolvency" was the only "realistic" way to move ahead.[201] He could have pointed out that the procedure he had outlined was exactly the one that the IMF was required to follow before the IMF abandoned its own policy to push through the Greek program under pressure from the Europeans and the United States.

Although Barthle was a senior CDU member and was to become the CDU's leading spokesman on debt restructuring in the years ahead, few took note of his comments in August; euro-area sovereign yields barely moved. Soon, Schäuble, having bought into the idea, was working with his finance ministry officials to refine the proposal.

On October 18, 2010, some hours after European finance ministers began their work in Luxembourg, a second meeting was about to start. Merkel and Sarkozy had traveled to the French resort town of Deauville. The *Wall Street Journal*'s reporters pieced together a romantic account of the Merkel-Sarkozy encounter: "When Ms. Merkel arrived at the Hotel Royal, Mr. Sarkozy embraced the German chancellor and led her into a small salon with views of the English Channel. 'Angela, I'm going to help you,' the French president said, before they set out for the boardwalk. The air chilled, so Mr. Sarkozy ordered an aide to fetch Ms. Merkel's coat. The lights of the palatial casino flickered in the distance."[202]

Merkel and Sarkozy then took their famous "walk on the beach." Merkel again explained that bureaucratic efforts to enforce budget deficits limits did not work. There was only one other option: if a member state could not repay its debts in full, private creditors would need to bear losses. For Merkel, the advantage was clear. She and future chancellors would not need (or would need less) German taxpayer funds to support highly indebted countries. Merkel had domestic political support for her plan from her "pro-business" and investor-friendly coalition partner, the Free Democrats.[203]

With that pitch, Merkel outlined to Sarkozy the same plan that CDU's Barthle had described two months earlier and for which she now had Schäuble's support. Starting in 2013, new debt issued by member states would be subject to restructuring if they wanted support from European financial facilities. Sarkozy agreed. Together, they announced their way forward in a public communiqué.[204]

In Luxembourg, where the ministers were still at work, Asmussen printed out an email he had just received and passed it around the table just after five p.m. The ministers, many of whom had no clue that this was coming, read in the email before them that Merkel and Sarkozy had agreed on an "orderly" insolvency process for eurozone member states.

Trichet was not having a good day. For the second time, he shifted from English to French. For the second time, he yelled at the French delegation. This time, he had a dire message: "You will destroy the euro."[205]

Deauville remains burned into the collective psyche as a moment of grave economic error. Among the many critical voices, two are of particular interest. Simeon Djankov, a reputable scholar who had a ringside view of the European financial crisis as Bulgaria's finance minister, acknowledged in his 2014 memoir that private creditors needed "to pay for their mistakes"; taxpayers could not be expected to shoulder the burden created by irresponsible governments and their lenders. Even so, Djankov severely criticized Merkel's proposal, because it "was introduced without a full assessment of how the financial markets would react."[206]

As evidence that the Deauville decision was misguided, Djankov pointed to Ireland. After Deauville, he insisted, "the crisis in Ireland spread outside the banking sector."[207] He seemed to say that until then, although Irish banks were in a state of crisis, the government's finances were under control. The Deauville declaration was a serious error because it caused the government's borrowing costs to "soar."[208]

This assertion is simply not true. Ireland was in the heart of a banking-fiscal-growth crisis by September 30, as Lenihan's numbers had grimly made clear. Bond investors had demanded nearly 7 percent yield on ten-year government debt. The rating downgrades on October 5 and 6 reflected a widespread belief that the likelihood of Irish government debt default was increasing. Yet, Patrick Honohan, governor of the Central Bank of Ireland at the time, also spoke out against Deauville. Like Djankov, he wrote, "the die was cast by the Merkel-Sarkozy announcement on 18 October at Deauville."

Honohan insisted, "interest rates on all peripheral government debt, but especially Ireland—now clearly seen as next-in-line for a bailout—jumped to insupportable levels."[209]

This repeated claim, which has acquired the status of a deified fact, is wrong both in its logic and in its interpretation of events that unfolded. Consider first the logic. Honohan says that the Deauville decision required bondholders to "contribute to any bailout." That is not correct. The Deauville decision did not affect a single Irish bondholder. However irresponsible we might believe bondholders to be, surely they understood the language of the proposal. Deauville only placed creditors on alert. If, starting in 2013, they continued to lend to governments that lived beyond their means, they could not expect full repayment.

Because current bondholders were not hurt, there is also no evidence of panic in bond markets in the aftermath of Deauville. On the ninth day after the Deauville decision, Greek bond yields were back to where they were nine days before the decision (figure 6.4), Irish bond yields moved in a narrow range during this time window, and Portuguese yields actually fell. Spanish and Italian yields barely moved. Put simply, Deauville did not spark panic or contagion. A more technical analysis reaches the same conclusion. That analysis checks if spreads had been declining in the previous few weeks and Deauville

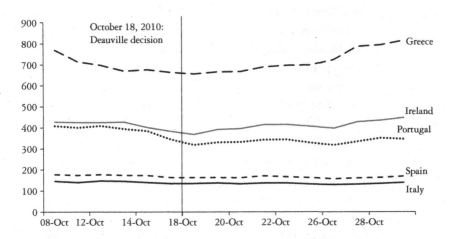

FIGURE 6.4. Except for Greece, bond markets ignore Deauville.
(Government bond spread over German bund, basis points: October 8 to October 29, 2010)
Notes: The ten-year bond spread (basis points) is the difference between the country's ten-year bond yield and Germany's ten-year bond yield. The vertical line represents the date of the Merkel-Sarkozy Deauville decision.
Sources: Datastream International. Spain, code S310Mo; Portugal, code S310KX; Italy, code S310DT; Ireland, code S310DE; Greece, code S3098T; Germany, code S30977.

hurt because it put a halt to that benign tendency. There is no evidence of this either.[210]

Despite this evidence, some continue to believe that Deauville caused the European crisis to flare up. Such critics point to the rise in sovereign yields that began in November 2010 and continued into 2011. It makes no sense to say that bond investors recognized only several days later that Deauville had placed them at risk. The increase in yields in the final two months of 2010 and the first half of 2011 had a perfectly good explanation. Greece and Ireland were becoming increasingly indebted to official creditors: the ECB, the EU, and the IMF. These official debts placed private creditors at a disadvantage. Private creditors understood that governments would first repay their official creditors. For this reason, as official debt levels increased, it became increasingly likely that financially distressed countries would not have enough money left to repay their private creditors. In technical jargon, official creditors were "senior," and private creditors were "junior" or subordinate.[211] To compensate for the higher default risk that private creditors faced, they began charging higher yields on the bonds of the most vulnerable countries.

In Ireland, this "seniority" problem manifested itself primarily through banks' borrowings from the ECB. By the start of October 2010, Irish banks owed nearly €120 billion, a staggering 70 percent of GDP, to the ECB. The Irish government, while not responsible for this entire sum, was on the hook for some significant fraction. Moreover, by November, Ireland was ready to borrow even more from the EU and the IMF. The government's obligations to repay official creditors placed private creditors farther behind in the line to collect on debts. Hence, Irish yields increased rapidly.

The villain was not Deauville. The villain was the strategy of outsize official loans to repay some of the private creditors, while austerity was tasked with bringing the debt burden down. The strategy was unfair to those creditors who eventually did not get repaid. But it was most unfair to Greek and Irish citizens, especially the most vulnerable among them, who had no voice in the decision and yet paid the cost of repaying irresponsible creditors.

In the days that followed the Deauville decision, Merkel, supported by Schäuble, continued to defend their plan to ensure early debt restructuring. At the European Council meeting on October 28, at which time there was no sign of an adverse effect on bond yields, Trichet was the most vocal critic of the proposal. He opposed debt restructuring in any circumstance.[212] Merkel was polite in her response but refused to budge. Sarkozy paid less attention to etiquette and angrily said to Trichet, "You don't realize how serious the situation is." Rubbing it in, Sarkozy told Trichet, "Maybe you're talking to bankers. We are responsible to citizens."[213]

After the meeting, Merkel acknowledged sharp differences with Trichet. Speaking to reporters, she said: "The president of the European Central Bank has the view that he wants to do everything to ensure that markets take a calm view of the euro zone. We are also interested in that, but we also have to keep in mind our people, who have a justified desire to see that it's not just taxpayers who are on the hook, but also private investors. I don't quite share Jean-Claude Trichet's concern."[214]

Bundesbank President Axel Weber supported his chancellor. He repeated that the intent was not to restructure any "current debt." But a timetable needed to be set so that in the near future, bond investors would be "part of the solution rather than part of the problem."[215]

At the G20 summit in Seoul on November 11, Merkel again explained why the eurozone needed the option to restructure debt. "Let me put it very simply," she said. "We cannot keep constantly explaining to our voters and our citizens why the taxpayer should bear the cost of certain risks and not those people who have earned a lot of money from taking those risks."[216] Even French Finance Minister Lagarde, who had in April "rejected the notion" of a Greek debt restructuring, now had words of support for Merkel: "All stake-holders must participate in the gains and losses of any particular situation."[217]

However, over the following months, Trichet managed to wear Merkel down, and Schäuble advised her that it was best to leave this fight for another day.[218] Thus, Merkel abandoned Deauville and walked away from her correct instincts. While she made the big political decisions, she needed the ECB to extend the euro area's financial safety net well beyond what German and other European taxpayers were willing to provide. Merkel needed Trichet.

The IMF, more willingly, threw its lot in with Trichet. In its July 2011 review of the Greek program, just days before European and IMF officials acknowledged that the bankrupt Greek nation would need to restructure its debts, the IMF gratuitously said: "the very public debate on this issue [of imposing losses on private creditors] has been a major problem for secur-ing confidence around the [Greek] program."[219] The IMF had already dam-aged its reputation in an eccentric September 2010 paper, which insisted that restructuring of advanced countries' public debt was "unnecessary and undesirable."[220] The paper's premise was that the euro-area economies were institutionally strong and that a quick resumption of growth would defang the debt crisis. As Lee Buchheit, the sovereign-debt attorney, pointedly said, that IMF study was "spectacularly ill-timed."[221]

Thus, when the Irish bailout was negotiated in late November, the decision was made to fully pay the banks' bondholders. This need not have happened. Lenihan was now passionately committed to "burning the bondholders."[222] For him, every euro taken away from bondholders was a euro saved for Ireland's citizens. During the bailout, Lenihan and I spent a lot of time together. He was battling pancreatic cancer and knew he would soon die. He blamed himself for the blanket guarantee to protect the banks' bondholders. Although he was not the only one to blame for that decision, he spoke ruefully of the "Lenihan guarantee." To him, "burning bondholders" was a litmus test of his legacy. As others have recorded, together we came so very close to turning that idea into reality.[223] Buchheit and a small Irish team reporting to Lenihan quietly put together the legal strategy. It was therefore a shock to the European official creditors when they realized the full extent of readiness to implement the haircut.

Once again, the Geithner-Trichet duo stopped the initiative. Strauss-Kahn, who had talked a good talk until then, fell silent. He later told journalist and author Paul Blustein that when confronted by "Tim [Geithner] plus Trichet, at the end of the day, I was too weak. It was a real pity."[224] Kevin Cardiff, by then the top official in the Irish Department of Finance, has reported that once Geithner and Trichet made their views plain, the IMF "became officially negative" about the idea.[225] He is right to use the phrase "officially negative," since within the team in Dublin, it was clear that we had taken a wrong turn.[226] Lenihan was furious for a few days and bravely told me that he would ignore the Tim-Trichet directives and act on his own. I knew then that it would not be so.

After the European and IMF teams had left, a colleague and I stayed behind to finalize the documents for the IMF's board meeting. Lenihan invited us to lunch, where he told us that the Irish public had forgiven him. He predicted that even though his party, Fianna Fáil, would be crushed in the next election, he would be reelected in his Dublin constituency. Indeed, he was. The only Fianna Fáil Deputy elected out of nearly 50 seats in the Dublin constituencies.

In an Unaccountable Union: Stuck and No Place to Go

The bailout programs for Greece and Ireland were in place but the lid had not yet been put on their financial crises. With Portugal and Spain as the most likely next stops, the eurozone crisis was spreading. On December 5, Luxembourg Prime Minister Juncker and Italian Economy and Finance Minister Giulio Tremonti came up with an enticing idea. "E-bonds," they wrote, "would end the crisis."[227] E-bonds, or eurobonds, they said, would also recommit Europe to economic and political integration and create a new impetus for economic growth.

As always, Merkel quickly put an end to the chatter about eurobonds. The clever idea was that eurozone members would guarantee to pay one another's debts.[228] But since a Greek or Italian guarantee of German debt was of little value, it was easy for Merkel to see that eurobonds would make Germany responsible for the debts of the weaker euro-area countries. The Maastricht Treaty had set up the eurozone as an "incomplete monetary union." The treaty specifically ruled out fiscal support by one member state for another. Eurobonds violated the Maastricht Treaty, and Juncker knew that. Yet he angrily attacked Merkel for being "un-European." Merkel called for calm and said, "This discussion does not help us."[229]

While Merkel was the messenger, she spoke for many others who wished to minimize collective European action and who, instead, emphasized "national responsibility." Among them was Mario Draghi, then the governor of the Banca d'Italia, the Italian central bank. He said that the real problem was that eurozone member countries suffered from "structural misalignments," which required a "national response."[230]

Consistent with the national responsibility theme, Merkel had vigorously pushed a sensibly staggered approach to phase in the "no bailout" provision. A "no bailout" mechanism with a track record would have provided some relief to the incomplete monetary union by forcing losses on to private creditors rather than on to domestic taxpayers in periods of crises. However, under the force of Trichet's vigorous opposition, Merkel backed off.

Thus, despite the addition of the EFSF (the bailout facility) the eurozone retained its fundamentally incomplete structure. It would still have one monetary policy for divergent countries and no compensatory fiscal support in periods of adversity. EFSF loans would be extended on the assumption that crisis countries faced only "liquidity" problems, temporary shortages of cash. No country could be "insolvent." Loans from the EFSF funds (and the IMF) would help repay impatient private creditors. The premise was that fiscal austerity would cure the original fiscal deficit, the crisis countries would repay the EFSF, and no one would suffer any losses. However well-intentioned, decisions under this set up were bound to be delayed, prolonging economic distress, especially for those with the least political voice.

The economic and social failures were obvious, but the subtler political regression was more alarming. Instead of advancing toward greater European democracy and political accountability, Germany emerged as the "reluctant hegemon," and German Chancellor Merkel became de facto European chancellor. Her voice counted more than those of the others—by far. The original French intent—pursued by three French presidents over a quarter century—was to use the monetary union to rein in German power. The opposite had happened. Merkel continued to make a show of consulting with Sarkozy, but she took all the key decisions while France became increasingly marginal. The lack of accountability was even more worrying because Merkel teamed up with a powerful ECB that reported to no one. Merkel with the political clout, and the ECB with its ability to print money.

At the end of 2010, an economic tsunami was about to sweep through the eurozone. The absence of accountability was set to do more damage. Economic and political cleavages were about to widen dangerously.

| Policy Wounds Leave Behind Scar
Tissue, 2011–2013

Tʜᴇ ɢʟᴏʙᴀʟ ғɪɴᴀɴᴄɪᴀʟ and economic turmoil which erupted in July 2007 had largely subsided by October 2009. However, the crisis left two troubling legacies: rising government debt burdens and slower economic growth prospects. In October 2009, debt burdens were surging at about an equal pace in the United States and in the euro area (figure 7.1). Growth prospects, although scaled back on both sides of the Atlantic, looked better in the United States because the Fed had proactively stimulated its economy while the ECB had kept monetary policy needlessly tight.

Policymakers faced a dilemma. Addressing the debt problem required governments to undertake austerity measures—to raise taxes and reduce spending—but austerity would lower the demand for goods and services, which would cause incomes to fall and further set back growth prospects.

Hence, some, including the IMF's Research Department, believed it was important to jump-start economic growth. If feeble growth were allowed to persist, workers who remained continuously unemployed would gradually lose skills, the country's capital stock that lay unused would depreciate, and businesses would cut back their R&D activities. The lingering recessionary or crisis conditions would have permanent effects; the economy's long-term ability to grow would suffer. Economists use the term "hysteresis" to describe such enduring damage to economic prospects.[1] Hysteresis is like scar tissue which continues to debilitate the organ even after its original wound has healed.

Moreover, the rate of price inflation had also declined steeply—in some countries, prices were actually falling. "Deflation pressures," the IMF said, were "expected to remain relatively high over the coming year."[2] Weak

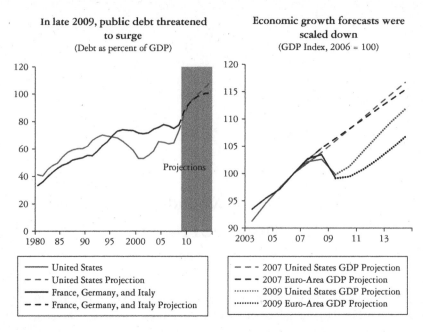

In late 2009, public debt threatened to surge
(Debt as percent of GDP)

Economic growth forecasts were scaled down
(GDP Index, 2006 = 100)

Projections

United States
United States Projection
France, Germany, and Italy
France, Germany, and Italy Projection

− − − 2007 United States GDP Projection
− − − 2007 Euro-Area GDP Projection
·········· 2009 United States GDP Projection
·········· 2009 Euro-Area GDP Projection

FIGURE 7.1. As debt burdens rise, growth outlook becomes bleaker.
Sources: Left panel: International Monetary Fund, World Economic Outlook Database, October 2009. The public debt-to-GDP ratio before 2000 from the IMF's Historical Public Debt Database, available at http://www.imf.org/en/Publications/WP/Issues/2016/12/31/A-Historical-Public-Debt-Database-24332. Right panel: International Monetary Fund, World Economic Outlook Database, October 2007 and October 2009. The 2007 projections are an extrapolation of the average annual GDP growth between 2003 and 2006. The 2009 projections are from the "World Economic Outlook."

economic growth with deflationary tendencies called for more fiscal and monetary stimulus. The stimulus would help increase output and prices, past debts would be easier to repay, and debt-to-GDP ratios would decline.

Writing in the IMF's October 2009 "World Economic Outlook," Chief Economist Olivier Blanchard and Financial Counselor José Viñals were clear: "fiscal stimulus needs to be sustained until the recovery is on a firmer footing." Their message on monetary policy was even stronger. Monetary policy needed to remain "accommodative" (stimulative), all the more so because fiscal stimulus could only do so much.[3]

"No Debate Please, We're Europeans"

The political narrative in favor of fiscal austerity began to gain traction around May 2010, just when the Greek bailout was being finalized. In a press briefing, the new British Chancellor of the Exchequer, George Osborne, said, "Greece is a reminder of what happens when governments lack the willingness to act decisively and quickly, and when problems are swept under the carpet."[4]

The IMF's European Department and European leaders pronounced that much-needed austerity was working in Greece. In August, just three months after the start of the rescue program, Poul Thomsen, head of the IMF's operations in Greece, portrayed the rosy picture of a Greek miracle in the making. Among notable successes, Thomsen pointed to pension reforms, which he said "were a sweeping change in one step." He gave a human face to austerity and won the hearts of many Greeks when he said that the "wealthy will have to pay their share, after pensioners and workers did their bit."[5] Even the stern German finance minister, Wolfgang Schäuble, joined the celebration. He spoke of his "great respect for the Greek government's resolve." That resolve, Schäuble emphasized, was paying dividends. "A few months ago," he said, "hardly anyone would have believed that the Greeks would manage to implement such a drastic austerity program. They're moving in the right direction now."[6]

German authorities had good reason to celebrate austerity. A Chinese import surge had boosted demand for Germany's industrial products, and the German economy was gathering momentum at a stunning speed. In October 2010, the IMF raised Germany's GDP growth forecast for 2010 to 3.3 percent, up from 1.2 percent just a few months earlier.[7] Buoyed by the growth, the German government announced spending cuts and tax increases to accelerate repayment of its debts.[8] German Chancellor Angela Merkel, who had often extolled the Swabian housewife for her frugality, was ready to tighten the German fiscal belt.[9] Merkel and Schäuble ratcheted up pressure on euro-area countries with a much weaker growth outlook than Germany's to also begin ambitious fiscal tightening.[10]

In the United States, President Barack Obama continued to favor fiscal stimulus. Between 2008 and 2010, the stimulus was much larger in the United States than in the euro area (figure 7.2). Schäuble saw fit to mock such recklessness. The American growth model, he said, had relied "on borrowed money for too long" and was now in "deep crisis." The United States, Schäuble advised, needed to reduce its deficit to "curb unrest in the markets."[11] European leaders were on the wrong side of the economic debate and, as they had done between 2007 and 2009, they defended their positions by ridiculing a caricature of US macroeconomic policy.

After the success of Tea Party Republicans in the November 2010 US midterm elections, the economic argument against fiscal austerity was lost. From then on, the mantra everywhere was that fiscal prudence must have

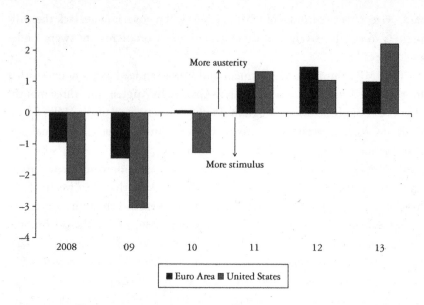

FIGURE 7.2. Between 2008 and 2010, significantly more fiscal stimulus in the United States than in the euro area.

(Change in structural balance as a percentage of potential GDP)

Note: A decrease in the structural fiscal balance represents a fiscal stimulus.

Source: International Monetary Fund, World Economic Outlook Database.

priority over all other economic objectives. The United States also shifted to austerity mode. But euro-area countries practiced extraordinary austerity during these years, relative to their own pasts and relative to what, on average, non-euro-area countries were doing.[12]

To make matters worse, all euro-area members joined the austerity frenzy, even those, such as the Netherlands, which did not need to reduce their public-debt ratios.[13] In fact, Dutch authorities could have used fiscal stimulus to increase incomes and help reduce the heavy debt-repayment burdens of many Dutch households. But whether it was needed or not, as each eurozone country attempted to cut its budget deficit, its own economic growth slowed, which reduced its imports and caused other member-state economies to slow down as well. These cascading effects pushed the eurozone into a collective economic downturn, creating a drag on world economic growth.

Collective eurozone austerity was the result of repetitive, two-decade-long vows of allegiance to the virtues of fiscal discipline. The impetus had come from the Germans, who had agreed to the single European currency only on the condition that all member countries would sign on to a budget rule that prohibited deficits exceeding 3 percent of GDP.[14] Although all member states, including Germany, had disregarded the rule whenever it had pinched, a general acceptance of the virtues of fiscal tightening had become integral to the eurozone's culture.

Indeed, austerity had become part of the eurozone's identity. Economics Nobel laureate George Akerlof and Duke University economist Rachel Kranton explain that in a search for internal coherence and peer esteem, members of a group create rules or norms for "how they and others should behave."[15] Group members protect the rules that define their identity. The eurozone's austerity norms had survived many challenges. During the single-currency negotiations at Maastricht in 1991, European Commission President Jacques Delors complained about Germany's "super-orthodox" standards of fiscal discipline.[16] However, he quickly backed off, fearing that the Germans would walk away from his single-currency dream. In 2002 and 2003, European Commission President Romano Prodi described the "rigid" fiscal rule as "stupid" and argued for flexibility in its use.[17] But he made no headway either. Soon, the norm became a virtue. Despite its bias toward excessive austerity, especially in recessionary conditions, a general European view took hold that some rule, even a bad one, was better than no rule at all. This evolution was an inevitable consequence of the foundational flaw, an incomplete monetary union, one that lacked the safeguard of a fiscal transfer system. That incomplete monetary union came packaged with an ideology: fiscal austerity and commitment to low inflation would establish the required stability.[18] The ideology, by now deeply ingrained, had morphed into Europe's austerity identity.

Everyone agreed that governments that lived beyond their means needed to tighten their belts. Therefore, the debate was not about whether or not to implement fiscal austerity. Instead, it was always about *how quickly* to tighten the belt. In October 2012, the IMF's Blanchard and his colleague Daniel Leigh gave a clear answer: not too quickly while in the midst of a recession.

The caution on excessive and too-rapid austerity rested on a number known as the fiscal multiplier. Blanchard and Leigh estimated that if the economy was already weak and a government cut spending (or raised taxes) by a euro, GDP would fall by nearly two euros; thus, the fiscal multiplier during a recession was close to 2.0 and not 0.5 as the IMF had previously assumed.[19] Quite simply, Blanchard and Leigh were saying that in the conditions prevailing then, aggressive austerity was causing GDP and, hence, tax revenues to fall far too rapidly, and so, paradoxically, austerity was increasing the burden of repaying debt; it was causing the debt-to-GDP ratio to rise. The finding created a media buzz (figure 7.3).

The finding not only carried Blanchard's intellectual authority but also had the backing of the IMF's managing director and its board of executive

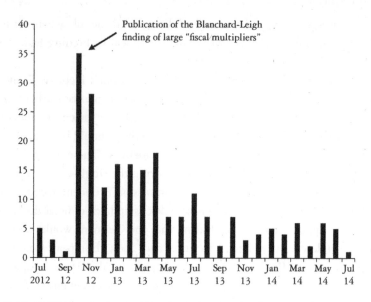

FIGURE 7.3. The costs of austerity—high fiscal multipliers—are brought to public attention.
(Number of articles in Factiva with the phrase "fiscal multiplier")
Source: Factiva.

directors. Blanchard had been consistent since the start of the crisis. In October 2008, when the world economy was on the verge of tipping over into a black hole, he had called for a coordinated global stimulus.[20] That stimulus had proven crucial in stabilizing the world economy. Now, in late 2012, as Europe peered down into its own economic abyss and threatened to drag the world into that void, Blanchard's analysis was the same. While he did not at this time call for more stimulus—that would have been politically unthinkable—he explained why it was important to ease the severity of austerity. "Sharp expenditure cutbacks or tax increases," he said, "can set off vicious cycles of falling activity and rising debt ratios, ultimately undercutting political support for adjustment. The historical record for public debt reduction suggests that a gradual, sustained approach supported by structural changes offers the best chance for success within today's constraints."[21]

Virtually the entire economics profession agreed with the Blanchard-Leigh analysis and recommendations. Over the preceding two years, several other studies had reached the same—or even stronger—conclusions. Based on research first reported in August 2010 and published in a leading peer-reviewed scholarly journal in May 2012, Alan Auerbach and Yuriy Gorodnichenko of the University of California, Berkeley, concluded that fiscal stimulus was particularly helpful—and, by implication, fiscal austerity was particularly damaging—when countries were in recession.[22] Economists Giancarlo Corsetti, André Meier, and Gernot J. Müller reported that the fiscal multiplier was especially high—as high as 2.0—when an economy was struggling to pull out of a crisis.[23] Research papers by several IMF economists reached the same conclusion.[24] One such paper specifically cautioned that if fiscal tightening was deemed essential while an economy was in a recession, then it was important to proceed gradually; the European approach of trying to get it over with quickly risked causing an economic convulsion that would leave behind lasting damage.[25]

Yet, despite the overwhelming scholarly evidence, European authorities reacted furiously to the Blanchard-Leigh estimate of the fiscal multiplier. The estimate could not be correct, they said, because they knew that austerity did not cause a slowdown in growth. To the contrary, they claimed that fiscal restraint by governments helped instill confidence that taxes would be lower in the future and that such confidence encouraged investment and growth. European politicians and technocrats insinuated that Blanchard and Leigh had improperly used the prestige of the IMF to question the deeply held European belief that austerity was always an honorable undertaking.

The most remarkable expression of this conviction was an angry letter, dated February 2, 2013 and posted some days later on the European Commission's website. Addressing European finance ministers, European Commission Vice President Olli Rehn said that not only was the Blanchard-Leigh research wrong, it had certainly "not been helpful." Rehn's choice of words was unusual. He argued that by publicly questioning the virtues of austerity, the IMF had acted to "erode the confidence that we have painstakingly built up over the past years in numerous late-night meetings."[26]

Those who were not in the inner European policy and intellectual circles gasped in disbelief. Soon the Rehn letter became the object of ridicule. "No debate please, we're Europeans," was the title of a particularly trenchant critique authored by Jonathan Portes, director of a London-based think tank, the National Institute of Economic and Social Research. "It just seems bizarre," Portes wrote, that Rehn should be trying to muzzle a "theoretically based and empirically grounded" academic paper on a subject of great contemporary importance. Portes pointed out that Rehn's own economic analysis, which extolled "the excellent policies recommended by the Commission and the European Central Bank," was consistently off the mark.[27] Although Rehn and his European Commission colleagues tried to push back on the criticism, they eventually took the letter off its original link. Those searching for the letter can now only find it in a not easily accessible archive on the European Commission's website.

The Rehn episode is noteworthy because it highlights how deeply the austerity philosophy had come to permeate the European identity. Not only the Germans but all key European decision makers had come to believe that the practice of austerity required by their fiscal rules was necessary and ultimately beneficial.

In his January 2007 presidential address to the American Economic Association, Akerlof pointed out that once an identity is in place, its norms motivate actions that have profound macroeconomic effects.[28] The costs of European fiscal austerity during these years were, indeed, profound. Blanchard and Leigh, along with other scholars, highlighted only the short-term costs: austerity deepened the ongoing economic recession. In addition, and more grievously, economics professors Antonio Fatás at INSEAD and Lawrence Summers at Harvard University believe that eurozone austerity during the years 2011–2012 "permanently" reduced the euro area's "growth potential."[29] Once again, multiple studies reached the same conclusion: prolonged austerity during the eurozone's darkest crisis years inflicted long-term damage.[30] Workers who remained unemployed for long durations lost skills, and businesses delayed the introduction of new technologies into the workplace. The IMF's Research Department had fretted about this hysteresis effect since October 2009.[31] Now the conclusion was that in large parts of the eurozone, several years of excessive austerity had depressed the future path of GDP and tax revenues and, hence, had raised the debt-to-GDP ratio.[32]

In late 2009, the task for policymakers had been to accelerate economic growth and reduce debt burdens. In 2011 and 2012, eurozone policy decisions had achieved the woeful combination of lower long-term growth and higher debt burdens.

The ECB contributed greatly to this unfortunate outcome. The ECB's monetary policy grew out of the other element of the eurozone's identity: a radical commitment to low inflation. The ECB added to the eurozone's scarring. We now turn to that story.

The ECB Goes the Opposite Way: June 2010–June 2011

This monetary policy story begins in mid-2010. China's voracious appetite for industrial, energy, and agricultural commodities had caused their prices to rise, which pushed up global inflation rates. Commodity price inflation was a global phenomenon and, hence, inflation rates in the euro area and the United States were virtually identical. At the ECB, President Jean-Claude Trichet and the Governing Council saw a looming threat of more inflation: rising commodity prices would cause workers to demand higher wages, and such wage demands could cascade into an inflationary spiral.

An Italian journalist pointed out to Trichet that in some of the distressed countries of the eurozone's periphery—Greece, Ireland, Portugal, Italy, and Spain—inflation was rather low and prices were actually threatening to fall.[33] Was it possible, she asked, that these countries could fall into deflation? Could they, in other words, be about to enter a prolonged period of very low inflation with spells of declining wages and prices? Wouldn't that, then, make debts harder to repay? Trichet replied that periphery countries would benefit from a period of deflation since lower prices would help them regain their competitiveness. He insisted, moreover, that persistent deflation was simply not possible, because inflation expectations in the euro area were "remarkably well anchored" at around 2 percent. Trichet's claim was that if inflation fell significantly below the 2 percent threshold, consumers and businesses would anticipate that higher inflation was imminent; they would therefore speed up their purchases, which would bring inflation back to 2 percent.

Trichet believed that the ECB's interest rate was striking the right balance between promoting growth and preventing resurgence of inflation. The ECB's various liquidity facilities were providing funds to banks that could not easily obtain financing from commercial sources. Thus, the ECB held its monetary policy unchanged.

BNP's chief market economist, Ken Wattret, summarized Trichet's message: "We have done all these measures and they appear to be working." In contrast, Wattret said, Fed Chairman Ben Bernanke was focusing on "what the Fed could still do."[34]

Bernanke and his colleagues on the FOMC, the Fed's monetary-policy-setting body, dismissed the specter of an inflationary spiral and saw instead a looming threat of deflation. Thus, as in the years 2001–2003 and 2007–2008, watching the same data unfold, with staff economists trained in the same basic framework, the world's two largest central banks held wildly different views on the risks they faced.

On November 3, 2010, the FOMC announced that the Fed would buy an additional $600 billion of longer-term treasury securities by mid-2011. These purchases, part of its QE program, would bring down long-term interest rates and hence encourage spending on consumption and investment. And the additional spending, FOMC members said, would "help protect against further disinflation and the small probability that the U.S. economy could fall into persistent deflation."[35]

This was our old friend, the stitch-in-time-saves-nine strategy. In 2001–2003 and 2007–2008, the Fed applied the risk-management principle to reining in financial crises; in 2010–2011, it applied the principle to preventing price deflation. The next day, in an opinion piece for the *Washington Post*, Bernanke explained that the high unemployment rate was pushing wages and prices down. "In the most extreme case," he said, "very low inflation can morph into deflation [falling prices and wages], which can contribute to long periods of economic stagnation."[36] Low inflation is, in general, welcome. But very low inflation creates an expectation that inflation might fall further, which causes people to delay expenditures. GDP growth falls, which further reduces the inflation rate. The economy falls into a quagmire of prolonged low growth and low inflation. The economic stagnation makes debts harder to repay, which increases stress in the financial system. Policymakers know— or should know—that they must preempt the deflation scourge.

German Finance Minister Schäuble had no reason for commenting publicly on the Fed's latest decision. Nevertheless, and as always from the wrong side of the policy debate, he could not resist a barb. Referring to the Fed's latest decision to expand its bond-buying program, he said, "I seriously doubt that it makes sense to pump unlimited amounts of money into the markets. There is no lack of liquidity in the US economy, which is why I don't recognize the economic argument behind this measure."[37] Schäuble was setting up a straw man ("lack of liquidity"). The Fed was trying to give people money to spend, so that they would keep the economic recovery going and prevent prices from descending into a deflationary trap.

In early 2011, the Fed and ECB policy positions moved still farther apart. While the Fed continued with its easy monetary policy, the ECB kept its policy interest rate significantly higher and refused to begin its own bond-buying QE program. Even more strangely, the ECB signaled that it was likely to tighten monetary policy.

An important spokesman for the ECB was Banca d'Italia Governor Mario Draghi, who was widely expected to succeed Trichet later in the year as ECB president. In late March, Draghi astonishingly said that ECB monetary policy "has been expansionary for a long time."[38] Draghi's claim was that the current pace of spending in the euro area was high enough to maintain a steady pace of economic growth, which could, in fact, feed inflation. He repeated Trichet's scenario of a wage-price spiral: if people began to expect that inflation would rise, they would negotiate higher prices and wages, causing inflation, in fact, to rise. Thus, while the Fed wanted to encourage people to spend, the ECB wanted to restrain them.

On April 7, 2011, the ECB raised its policy interest rate from 1.0 to 1.25 percent.[39] At his press conference after the announcement of that decision, Trichet repeated three times that the rate hike was necessary to "firmly anchor" inflation expectations. Some reporters expressed concern that higher interest rates would hurt the periphery economies, especially the troubled banking sector in Spain. Trichet responded that the ECB was responsible for seventeen countries with 331 million people. He invoked the ECB mantra that member states needed to keep their fiscal houses in order and undertake more "structural reforms." The fall in stock prices that followed Trichet's announcement reflected investor dismay that monetary policy was so disengaged from worrying economic news.[40]

The ECB Inflicts a Grievous Wound: July 7, 2011

Already in April 2011, multiple crises were brewing within the euro area. By raising its interest rate on April 7 and by threatening more rate hikes, it was as if the ECB was rushing to cause harm.

Despite the IMF's rosy projection just a month earlier, the Greek economy was about to spin out of control. Under the burden of fiscal austerity, Greek citizens were angry and anxious, and there were frequent physical attacks on Greek politicians when they appeared in public places.[41] Finance minister George Papaconstantinou made it clear that the €110 billion bailout funds authorized eleven months earlier, in May 2010, would not be enough for the government to meet its payment obligations.[42] On April 14, IMF Managing Director Dominique Strauss-Kahn and European finance ministers met at the home of the French ambassador in Washington, DC.[43] Strauss-Kahn, who would unceremoniously leave his position a month later on charges of sexual assault, confirmed the Greek finance minister's assessment: to continue repaying its private creditors, the Greek government would need more official funds, virtually immediately.

In Portugal, public discontent and political opposition built up as the minority government of Prime Minister José Sócrates introduced fiscal austerity measures.[44] These domestically unpopular measures did not even appease investors, who understood that the austerity would make the recession worse and would, therefore, raise the debt burden. With investors refusing to lend to the Portuguese government, on May 17, Portugal joined Greece and Ireland as a ward of European official creditors and the IMF.[45]

On May 20, S&P rang a fearsome alarm bell: it placed Italian government bonds on "negative watch" for possible downgrades.[46] The central problem, S&P said, was that Italy seemed stuck in perpetual low productivity growth. Worryingly, this long-standing weakness had become a particularly serious problem because of "intensifying competition in Italy's key export sectors." In other words, Italian producers could no longer compete merely with their "Made in Italy" labels. And since Italian politics seemed unable to deliver the necessary jolt to pull the economy out of its morass, S&P concluded that the government would find it harder to secure the tax revenues needed to repay its huge debt burden. Italian stocks fell by 3.3 percent; banks and insurers, who held substantial quantities of government bonds, took a special beating.[47] Soon enough, another rating agency, Moody's, placed the Italian government and banks on "review for possible downgrade."[48]

All this while, global economic and financial tensions had been rising. On March 11, a monstrous earthquake and tsunami off the northern coast of Japan damaged nuclear reactors, the fallout from which threatened to cause vast additional damage. Amid the human tragedy, the Japanese link in global supply chains broke, disrupting world trade. Torsten Sløk, chief international economist at Deutsche Bank, captured the change in global mood: "the world is rapidly becoming a scarier place."[49] Starting in early April, global stock markets tumbled at a pace not seen since the days following the Lehman Brothers bankruptcy. Chinese and European growth slowed down in May.[50] The US economic recovery seemed to stall; employment fell slightly in May and June, and large numbers of workers stopped looking for jobs. Commodity prices fell. The IMF's Global Financial Stability Report (GFSR) said on June 17, "Global economic recovery may be more fragile than had been thought." The GFSR warned that the "time to address existing vulnerabilities may be running out."[51]

In that scary global economy, the scariest place was the euro area, with the most acute vulnerabilities. At a panel discussion in Vienna on June 26, investor George Soros impatiently said that instead of dealing forcefully with their crisis, authorities in the euro area "are actually engaged in buying time. And yet time is working against them."[52] Soros's comments came amid more pounding of Italian bank share prices. Italian GDP growth was slowing rapidly, creating the worry that Italian borrowers would increasingly default on their bank loans. The five largest Italian banks had lost more than a quarter of their market value since the start of the year. Observing this massive loss in value, the *Wall Street Journal* wrote, "Europe's bruised banking sector welcomed another entrant into the emergency room."[53]

An economic and financial crisis centered on Italy and spreading from there through the rest of the euro area was now a real risk. Trichet, however, continued his unwavering narrative of maintaining "strong vigilance" against inflation, virtually promising another interest-rate hike in his May and June press conferences.[54]

Trichet had an enthusiastic ally. After the uncertainty about whether Merkel would support him had been resolved, Draghi was preparing to succeed Trichet in November as the ECB's president. Draghi made clear that he would stay the course set to tame inflation.

Draghi's credentials were impeccable. He had earned an economics Ph.D. in 1977 from MIT. Contemporaries, such as Ben Bernanke and Olivier Blanchard, thought well of him. One of his professors at MIT, Nobel laureate Robert Solow, said that Draghi "knew his stuff"; another Nobel laureate, Robert Merton, said of him, "he understands risk, and asks the right questions."[55]

Just as Trichet had for France, Draghi had served as Italy's top negotiator at Maastricht in 1991, when the framework for the single currency was established. At Maastricht, Draghi was passionately committed to Italy's early entry into the single-currency zone. As Kenneth Dyson and Kevin Featherstone, the foremost historians of the Maastricht negotiations, say, "in his soul, [Draghi] believed in EMU [European monetary union] as a *vincolo esterno* [an external constraint, an anchor]."[56] Draghi believed that without the deficit limits that were to accompany the single currency, "politicians could not be relied upon to accept long-term budget discipline."[57]

After Maastricht, as a senior finance ministry official, Draghi masterminded Italy's improbable improvement in fiscal numbers that had allowed it to enter the monetary union in January 1999.[58] He had been governor of Italy's central bank, the Banca d'Italia, since 2006.

Presenting himself to the European Parliament on June 14, 2011, Draghi said that the euro had been "a great success, a success that should be preserved for the sake of all the citizens of Europe." With the eurozone stuck in a never-ending crisis, to the parliamentarians who were skeptical of his glowing testimonial, Draghi said, "Let me state that none of the recent events, including the global crisis, call this fact into question." He repeated Trichet's mantra that the euro had succeeded because the ECB had established a reputation for keeping the inflation rate at "just under 2 percent." Draghi said he was "fully committed" to safeguarding that reputation and hard-earned credibility. He repeated his theme from late March: it was time for the ECB to start planning its "exit from the still very accommodative monetary policy stance" and, if necessary, take "preemptive measures" to avoid "deterioration of inflation expectations."[59] Thus, at a time when many observers thought that the euro area desperately needed easier monetary policy, Draghi said that monetary policy was too "accommodative," or too easy, and needed tightening. His message to European parliamentarians was that he would vote for a hike in the interest rate.

The financial crisis kept escalating. On July 6, Moody's downgraded Portuguese government debt to "junk" status.[60] Portuguese bank stocks fell sharply. Spanish banks, with their large exposure to Portugal, were also battered. By now, any news was sufficient to push Italian bank stocks down. Recently released data from the ECB showed that Greek, Irish, and Italian banks had lost deposits; businesses and households were losing confidence in these banking systems and taking their money elsewhere.[61] Portuguese and Spanish deposits were barely holding on.

On the eve of the ECB's July 7 Governing Council meeting, global financial markets were on edge. In the eurozone, investors holding bonds of eurozone governments were anxious, and several banking crises were brewing. In anticipation of a weaker global economy, the commodity price increase had paused. Everything pointed to the need to ease monetary policy. The ECB, however, had promised a rate hike, and Draghi joined Trichet and other members of the Governing Council in a unanimous vote to raise the interest rate by 25 basis points (0.25 percent) to 1.5 percent.

As with fiscal austerity, the European identity had coalesced around the monetary policy norm of fighting any hint of inflation. In the press conference that followed the decision, Trichet acknowledged that economic growth had moderated, but he emphasized that it remained of "paramount importance" to prevent the spread of inflationary pressures."[62] Sticking to his April script, he repeated three times that inflation expectations needed to be kept "firmly anchored." Such anchoring was the only way to maintain the euro area's financial stability and preserve the ECB's credibility.

Identity creates solidarity within a group and incites divisions with outsiders. In a rare departure from his customary reluctance to comment publicly on the decisions of other central banks, Trichet that day said, "Of the big central banks of the advanced economies in the world, we are the only one that is taking a number of decisions that are not generally considered anodyne."[63] "Anodyne" refers to painkillers—such as opium, hemlock, and chloroform—used in the nineteenth century to dull the nervous system. This was the ECB's defensive narrative. Rather than dispense addictive painkillers as the Fed was allegedly doing, the ECB was willing to impose pain, because pain helped focus the mind on the right way ahead.

The next day, Draghi had the same message. In more conventional central bank language, he said, "Expansionary policies have exhausted their margins of maneuver. The need to end the exceptional support to the economies provided by fiscal and monetary policies in the last three years is undisputed."[64] Although not with the abrasive words used by German Finance Minister Schäuble some months earlier to criticize US fiscal and monetary policy, Trichet and Draghi were saying, "We do things differently in Europe—and our way is better."

Market analysts and scholars objected to this European exceptionalism— Europe is different—theme that Europe's leading policymakers were pushing. Speaking for many others, one frustrated analyst remarked, "We are not seeing the inflation risk that the ECB is seeing."[65] Among academic economists, Princeton's Paul Krugman was a consistent critic of the ECB. He impatiently said, "Adding to the [euro area's] problem is the ECB's obsession with maintaining its 'impeccable' record on price stability: at a time when Europe desperately needs a strong recovery, and modest inflation would actually be helpful, the bank has instead been tightening money, trying to head off inflation risks that exist only in its imagination."[66] In a later analysis, but echoing Krugman's contemporary conclusion, Robert Hetzel, senior economist and research adviser at the Federal Reserve Bank of Richmond, painstakingly documented that the ECB rate hikes had come at a moment when the euro-area economy was weak and commodity price inflation was soon to reverse.[67]

Inevitably, a view gained ground that the ECB was responding to German concerns. An article in the Irish edition of the *Sunday Times* noted that Germany was enjoying a "mini boom" and that German inflation had "nudged" above 2 percent. The inference was that the ECB was acting to bring German inflation down, "callously" disregarding "dire" conditions in Ireland, where homeowners were struggling to keep up with their mortgage payments and could not bear these rate hikes.[68]

The ECB's decision on July 7, 2011, to raise its policy interest rate by 25 basis points did not come as a surprise. But when Trichet also implied that still more rate hikes were in the pipeline, financial markets went into a tailspin.[69] Particularly hard-hit were bank stocks, with Italian and Spanish banks taking the worst beating.[70] Milton Friedman might have said that the ECB had just thrown a big-time monkey wrench, which would further damage the eurozone's financial and economic systems. In terms of the medical metaphor I have used, the ECB had inflicted another grievous wound on a body that was already badly injured.

Trichet's Final Months, the Scars Begin to Form: July–December 2011

The yield on the Italian government's ten-year bond, having just recently crossed the 5 percent mark, began rising steadily after the ECB's July 7 decision (figure 7.4). As that yield rose, bank stocks tumbled, extending their downward slide since earlier in the year.

The simultaneous worsening of financial conditions of the banks and the government was not a coincidence. Anticipating lower Italian GDP growth on account of the tight fiscal and monetary conditions, analysts judged that the country's banks would come under greater stress. The costs to the government of supporting and bailing out weak banks would, therefore, rise. With higher bailout costs adding to its already mounting debt, the Italian government's financial condition would become more precarious. As compensation for bearing that greater risk, investors demanded higher yields on Italian government bonds. In turn, the higher government-bond yields

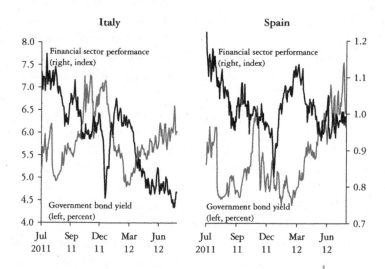

FIGURE 7.4. Sovereigns and banks hurt each other.

Notes: The graph presents the relative performance of financial stocks and the Italian 10-year bond yield from 31 May 2011 to 31 July 2012. The relative performance of financial stocks for Italy is the ratio between the FTSE Italia All-Share Financial Index and FTSE Italia All-Share Index. The relative performance of financial stocks for Spain is the ratio between the Madrid Financial Services index and Madrid SE IBEX-35 index.

Sources: FTSE Italia All-Share Financial Index: Global Financial Data, ticker IT8300 Index; FTSE Italia All-Share Index: Global Financial Data, ticker FTSEMIB Index; Madrid Financial Services Index: Global Financial Data, ticker: _IFNC_MD; Madrid SE IBEX-35: Global Financial Data, ticker _IIBEXD; Italy ten-year bond yield: Datastream International, code S310DT; Spain ten-year bond yield: Datastream International, code S310Mo.

weakened the government's ability to rescue banks. This vicious sovereign-bank doom loop—now operating aggressively in Italy but also in Spain—was familiar from Ireland and Greece.[71]

The fear that European authorities had no plan to either resolve or strengthen their fragile banks added to the market panic. Most observers anticipated that the bank stress-test results due on July 15 would once again fail to distinguish the strong banks from the weak ones.[72] The skepticism proved justified. When the latest results came out, it was immediately apparent that the euro-area authorities had again downplayed the serious risks. The official conclusion was that only nine banks urgently needed more capital to protect themselves from adverse developments, and even those banks would be safe with paltry additional capital of €2.5 billion. The IMF, in contrast, estimated that eurozone banks needed around €200 billion more in capital to create a cushion against the risks they faced.[73] Some scholars suggested that the buffer needed to be even greater, because during a crisis, the risks and associated losses could cascade in unanticipated ways.[74]

One thing was leading to another. With the sovereign-bank vicious spiral on full display in Italy and Spain, and with no sign that anyone was in charge, stress in the interbank market increased. Banks grew increasingly wary of other banks and started charging a steadily higher premium for lending to one another (figure 7.5).[75] This now was a distinctively euro-area crisis. Unlike in 2008, when the financial crisis had besieged banks on both sides of the Atlantic, interbank lending premiums now barely rose in the United States.[76]

The most politically sensitive reflection of the interbank stress was in the ECB's accounts. German banks were unwilling to rollover their loans to troubled Italian and Spanish banks and preferred, instead, to pull out their funds and place them in the safe hands of the ECB. Hence, Italian and Spanish banks, but briefly also French banks, borrowed large sums from the ECB to, in effect, repay the German banks. Just as the ECB had earlier kept Greek, Irish, and Portuguese banks afloat, now it propped up Spanish and Italian banks with an increasing supply of cash.

The ECB was now no longer an arms-length central bank. It was a major creditor to Italian and Spanish banks. Being in that position carried both financial and political risks. What if these banks could not repay the ECB? If so, the ECB would suffer losses and be forced to call on all member countries to replenish its capital. In that case, the Germans, as the largest contributors to the ECB's capital, would bear significant costs.

With that palpable conflict of interest, the financial crisis was turning into a political crisis. To reflect on what came next, the reader should know

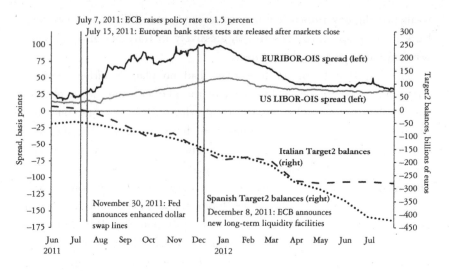

FIGURE 7.5. Market tensions rise after July 7 interest-rate hike and farcical bank stress tests.

Note: 100 basis points is equal to 1 percentage point.

Sources: US LIBOR-OIS spread: Bloomberg, USOOO3M Index—USSOC Curncy; EURIBOR-OIS spread: Bloomberg, EUROO3M Index—EUSWEC Curncy; Target2 balances are end-of-month position from ECB Statistical Data Warehouse.

that while the ECB is responsible for monetary policy, it has no authority over other economic policy matters. True, the ECB had become a major creditor to Italy and Spain. But ECB officials are unelected technocrats and they cannot dictate policy decisions to elected politicians. Yet on August 5, as the 10-year maturity sovereign-bond yields crossed the psychologically worrisome 6 percent barrier, Trichet wrote extraordinary letters to Italian Prime Minister Silvio Berlusconi and Spanish Prime Minister José Luis Rodríguez Zapatero.[77] Elected politicians had failed, and it was time, Trichet decided, for him to instruct the prime ministers what their governments and parliaments should do. Of course, the Italian and Spanish governments had many problems to address. But Trichet and the ECB had made matters much worse by triggering a financial crisis in a misguided pursuit of price stability. From what high ground could the ECB prescribe policy to national governments?

The letter to Berlusconi, signed also by Draghi, laid out a detailed economic program for Italy to follow. Besides the customary call for making it easier to hire and fire workers, the big focus was on more fiscal austerity. The austerity plan adopted just a few weeks earlier was not sufficient, Trichet and Draghi said; the budget deficit needed to be brought down faster, and if the targets were not met, additional expenditure cuts should automatically kick in. The letter even specified parliamentary action and a constitutional amendment to enforce these policies. "We trust the government will take all appropriate actions," the letter sternly concluded.[78] The letter to Zapatero, signed by Trichet and Banco de España Governor Miguel Ángel Fernández Ordóñez, went along similar lines, again calling for far-reaching reforms and more rapid reduction of budget deficits.[79]

The crisis next attacked another vulnerability of euro-area banks, their heavy dependence on US dollar funding. In addition to all the other problems it had created, the ECB's July 7 decision had set off panic among US dollar lenders, who feared that the banks under increasing stress might not be able to honor their debts.[80] On September 22, the premium paid by euro-area banks on 3-month dollar funds crossed 100 basis points, a level not seen since the panic that followed the Lehman bankruptcy in September 2008 (figure 7.6).[81]

In Washington on September 24, 2011, even the IMF's European Department, traditionally an ally of eurozone authorities and generally supportive of ECB policy positions, was getting impatient. The department's director, Antonio Borges, said "even the best European economies are slowing down significantly, which is concerning." Borges went on to say that "inflationary fears are now practically non-existent" and it should be possible to have "a more expansionary monetary policy."[82]

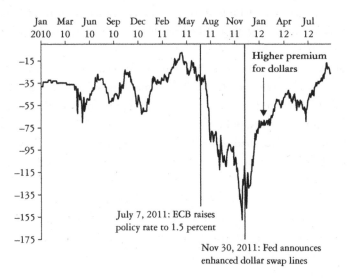

FIGURE 7.6. ECB's July 7 decision creates panicked search for US dollars.
(Euro-dollar swap premium, basis points)
Note: 100 basis points equals 1 percentage point.
Sources: Euro-dollar swap premium: EUR-USD XCCY Basis Swap 3m, Bloomberg.

Would Trichet respond? His final press conference to announce the ECB Governing Council's monetary-policy decision was in Berlin on October 6. Bundesbank President Jens Weidmann, who hosted the ECB's Governing Council that day, praised Trichet for having "delivered price stability for 330 million people."

The narrative and reality were veering in different directions. In lauding Trichet, Weidmann sought protective cover within the eurozone's price stability priority. But the problem lay elsewhere. The euro area was quickly spiraling into an existential crisis. The pressure on Italian and Spanish government bonds remained alarmingly high, and euro-area banks were seizing up. By October, the European Banking Authority assessed that the banks needed more than €100 billion in additional capital, up from the €2.5 billion it had estimated in July but still much lower than IMF estimates. The entire eurozone economy was struggling, unemployment was rising, and the misguided pursuit of price stability was increasing the risk of falling into a deflation trap.

Trichet was leaving the ECB with its main policy interest rate recently raised to 1.5 percent and no QE-style bond-purchase program of the type that the Fed had deployed to speed up economic recovery and fight the risk of deflation. The Fed had, since December 2008, maintained its interest rate at between 0 and 0.25 percent, a range in which it had promised to keep rates for the foreseeable future; in late 2011, the Fed's second round of QE was ongoing. The US economy was recovering, employment was increasing smartly, and banks had long since returned to good health. Despite what Trichet, Draghi, and Schäuble liked to believe, US policy was working, and eurozone policy was not.

After Weidmann concluded his remarks at that October 6 press conference, Trichet acknowledged that financial markets were "tense" and risks had "intensified." But predictably sticking to his script, he said that it remained "essential" for monetary policy to maintain price stability." The Governing Council, he reported, had agreed "by consensus" to keep the policy rate unchanged from July at 1.5 percent.[83] His use of the word "consensus," rather than "unanimity," meant that a tug of war in the Governing Council had begun but that the price stability hawks had held their ground.

After eight years as ECB president, Trichet was ready to bid farewell. He was leaving a stage he had commanded so imperiously. In his farewell speech on October 19, Trichet again took credit for keeping inflation below 2 percent and for firmly anchoring inflation expectations. He spoke with pride of having successfully navigated the eurozone through the financial crisis. Quoting Jean Monnet's refrain, Trichet ended with a flourish: "Continue, continue. There is no future for the people of Europe other than in union."[84]

Thus the official narrative grew in ambition. As keeper of that narrative, Trichet said that "price stability" was the foundation for solidarity among Europeans in "union." There was an alternative narrative. It said that the sense of helplessness that arises when dealing with a hydra-like financial crisis creates political tensions and deepens divisions.

French President Nicolas Sarkozy was among those who were most worried. France's GDP growth had slowed to a crawl. Sarkozy had missed Trichet's speech to be with his wife, who was about to give birth, but at the last minute, "Speedy Sarko" decided to rush to Frankfurt, reaching the Alte Oper just as the concert to honor Trichet was starting. Impatient to speak his mind, Sarkozy pulled Trichet into a side room, where the two of them screamed at each other in French, while Merkel played mediator. Sarkozy was furious with Trichet for not having done more to foster growth. As Trichet defended himself, Merkel stepped in to help him. She reassured Trichet, "You are a friend of Germany's."[85] That was Trichet's reward: as keeper of the official narrative, he had become Germany's friend.

New ECB President, Old Problems: November 2011–July 2012

Draghi succeeded Trichet as the ECB's president on November 1, 2011. On November 3, after chairing his first rate-setting meeting, Draghi announced that the ECB would reduce its interest rate to 1.25 percent. The initial response was favorable. The *Wall Street Journal* commented, "this is a sign that the ECB is finally waking up to the fact that financial conditions are too tight in Europe, and that's good news."[86] But after Draghi's words sank in, stock prices retreated sharply.[87] Draghi had rejected calls for more aggressive monetary stimulus, insisting that there was no risk of deflation.[88] Critical voices quickly gained ground: The latest move, "while welcome, was too modest, given the problems faced by the European economy."[89] ECB policy had fallen so far behind the curve that it had little credibility with financial markets. For Draghi to regain investors' trust and start afresh, he needed to announce bold new measures and make a clean break with the past.

In Italy, and to a lesser extent in Spain, the sovereigns and banks continued to drag each other down. And the eurozone banks' dollar funding difficulties grew more acute; the premium that they needed to pay for dollars was 115 basis points, rising toward levels last seen in the post-Lehman weeks in late 2008. As had been the case at that time, this latest eurozone bank rush for dollars was again creating tensions in US financial markets. On November 11, at a conference in Chicago, Janet Yellen, vice chair of the US Federal Reserve Board, expressed concern that "further intensification of financial disruptions in Europe could lead to a deterioration of financial conditions in the United States."[90] With the ECB unable to contain the financial turmoil, the Fed once again lent a helping hand. On November 30, with the dollar premium around 130 basis points, the Fed announced "enhanced" dollar swap lines, which would provide cheaper dollars to central banks, which, in turn, could lend those dollars to their domestic banks.[91] Investors breathed a sigh of relief and welcomed the "decisive action."[92] Although financial conditions remained delicately balanced, the panic (for now) stopped escalating. The premium on dollar funds stabilized, and so did the spreads on term lending in euro-area interbank markets; yields on Italian and Spanish bonds stopped rising.

The ECB's Governing Council met next on December 8, 2011. The euro area remained in a "perilous" financial condition.[93] The economy was expected to slide into a recession in 2012. But the ECB remained unimpressed and, as in November, lowered its interest rate by merely 25 basis points, to 1 percent. To make matters worse, Draghi acknowledged that at least one member of the Governing Council had resisted even that modest rate reduction, which seemed to imply that no immediate further cuts could be expected. Draghi's ECB, having unwound the two disastrous rate hikes in April and July, seemed ready to pause. Stock markets were disappointed, and all major indices tumbled.[94]

Draghi had still not made the break with the past. In an editorial, the *Financial Times* stated, "Two months into his stint at the helm of the European Central Bank, Mario Draghi has followed a fairly orthodox view of the institution's responsibilities and limitations."[95] ECB orthodoxy was so hard to dislodge because price stability, alongside fiscal austerity, resided at the core of the eurozone's identity.

At that December meeting, the ECB announced two longer-term refinancing operations (LTROs), allowing banks to borrow unlimited amounts for up to three years, rather than for a maximum of one year as permitted so far. The ECB still had the wrong diagnosis of what ailed the eurozone economy. It still believed that the crisis was primarily due to a shortage of liquidity and, therefore, thought of itself as mainly a passive provider of cheap funds to banks. Even at this stage, the ECB did not recognize that the principal problem was that consumer and business confidence had collapsed and its task was to actively help revive the economy. Lower interest rates would give people more money to spend, which would boost confidence. Economic activity would recover and help relieve the financial stresses.

By focusing on a presumed liquidity shortage, the ECB was treating the symptoms rather than the disease, and was thus creating problems for later. Since the very early days of the global financial crisis, banks had used cheap ECB financing to invest in higher-yielding government bonds. This was a handy way for banks to improve their profitability.[96] Once again, upon the availability of the LTRO funds, Spanish and Italian banks grabbed large sums from the ECB's new funding windows and bought bonds issued by their governments (figure 7.7). Superficially, LTRO funds served their purpose. They provided temporary relief. Yields on government bonds came down. Funding for many banks became more secure, the banks stabilized, and financial market tensions eased. But the fundamental tasks of closing or merging insolvent banks and, especially, of reviving economic growth remained unaddressed. The temporary relief brought about by the LTROs, perversely made matters potentially more intractable by binding governments and banks tightly to each other. If either the government or its domestic banks were to stumble, they would come tumbling down together.

But while the risks created by the LTROs lay latent, the ECB misread the reprieve in market tensions and went into a long pause. Throughout the first half of 2012, the ECB was on hold, keeping its interest rate unchanged at 1 percent. At a press conference on April 4, 2012, Draghi gave a cheery

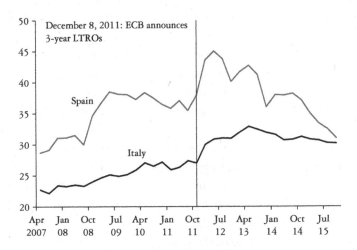

FIGURE 7.7. More ECB liquidity spurs Spanish and Italian banks to load up on government bonds.
(Share of government debt held by domestic banks, percent)
Source: Serkan Arslanalp and Takahiro Tsuda. 2012. "Tracking Global Demand for Advanced Economy Sovereign Debt." IMF Working Paper WP/12/284, Washington, DC, https://www.imf.org/external/pubs/ft/wp/2012/Data/wp12284.zip.

reading of the state of affairs. The LTROs, he said, were "powerful and complex measures." They were providing "relief," for example, by preventing a "credit crunch."[97] In effect, Draghi was saying that eurozone borrowers were desperate for more credit and that the ECB's liquidity facilities had enabled banks to lend more to households and businesses. This analysis, of course, was incorrect. The unemployment rate was climbing to new heights, households had suffered huge income losses, and they had debts to repay. Borrowing new money was far from people's minds. They needed income relief—lower interest rates and, perhaps, more fiscal spending and lower taxes. The ECB had ensured that the banks were flush with funds, but the banks had few borrowers with significant consumption or investment plans. The real problem, of reviving confidence and demand, remained unaddressed.

By early April, even the German economy began to slow. The IMF projected that Italian and Spanish GDPs would contract by 2 percent that year. The ECB's monthly bulletin in April conceded that the eurozone economy as a whole was in recession but summarily concluded that recovery was around the corner; the bulletin asserted that inflation could suddenly surge.[98]

Inflation did not spike, and the recession continued in large parts of the euro area. And when an economy contracts, as it did in Italy and Spain, banks and government finances come under greater stress. In this new, more virulent phase, Italian and Spanish government-bond yields began rising again and banks' stocks took another beating. Worsening prospects for banks placed even greater stress on their governments as the potential costs of bank bailouts rose. And as eurozone governments became more financially vulnerable, their banks faced the risk that their governments might not fully repay the bonds that the banks had bought with the ECB's ill-judged LTRO funds. While they had provided temporary "relief," as Draghi had portrayed, the LTROs had reinforced the sovereign-bank loop, which was now in its vicious mode.[99]

Spain, in particular, was in the throes of a crisis. Spanish banks had pumped up the property bubble through the exuberant years of 2004–2007.[100] These banks were now living through the bust. Spanish authorities had made the bust worse by choosing easy solutions to the severe problems their banks faced. In December 2010, Spanish authorities had "mashed" together seven *cajas*, the regional banks at the heart of the property bubble, to create Spain's third-largest bank, Bankia.[101] Instead of taking decisive measures to resolve troubled banks, they had combined a collective of troubled banks into one troubled new bank. And while they implemented these half measures, government officials had indulged in cheap talk. Finance Minister Elena Salgado had declared that the Spanish banking sector was "prepared to overcome any test it might face in the future."[102] Thus, in late April 2012, even as the IMF called for "swift and decisive measures" to strengthen Spanish banks, especially Bankia, Bank of Spain's chief regulator, José María Roldán, traveled with a slide show to the world's financial centers bearing the message that Spain's banking troubles were over.[103]

The reality of rising government yields and declining bank stock prices did eventually catch up. On June 9, the Spanish government asked the European authorities for €100 billion to bail out the country's failing banks.

In both Spain and Italy, sovereign-bond yields kept rising, and bank stocks kept getting battered. The US economy suddenly stalled, sending tremors through financial markets. The eurozone, already in an economic recession, was slowing down further. The ECB's monetary policy decision on July 5, 2012, came amid these acute financial and economic tensions.

Having waited more than half a year, the ECB lowered its interest rate to 0.75 percent. The ECB also reduced its deposit rate (the rate at which banks place overnight deposits at the central bank) from 0.25 percent to zero: the goal, as always, was to encourage banks to lend to their customers rather than deposit their surplus funds at the ECB. Markets responded adversely. In glaring contrast to the ECB's feeble action, the BOE nearly simultaneously launched its third round of QE. Not surprisingly, one analyst described the ECB's actions as mere "tweaking at the edges."[104] Because the ECB had a reputation for being stodgy, some suspected that it had even worse news, which financial markets were not yet aware of.[105] Draghi himself was skeptical that the ECB could do much more. He said that the eurozone was "fragmented" and the benefits of easier monetary policy would not reach all member countries, especially those viewed as highly risky.[106]

The ECB's July 5, 2012, decision ranks among its worst. A year earlier, the incomprehensible increase in the interest rate had inflicted the big wound. The modest rate reductions since then had done little to undo the damage. Now, with the financial system and the economy under enormous stress, the grudging reduction in the policy rate—with no sense of what might come next—added to the market's anxiety. Italian and Spanish government yields jumped; stock prices of banks in both countries were "pummeled."[107] On July 16, the IMF reported, "Financial market and sovereign stress in the euro area periphery have ratcheted up, close to end-2011 levels."[108]

Along with the financial stress, the political tensions increased. All member states except Finland approved the European bailout of Spain's banks. As the Spanish government waited for the Finnish decision, the stress on public finances increased. The government of the Valencia region needed financial assistance urgently. Valencia was home to some of the most corrupt property deals, to which the *cajas* had lent with great abandon during the wild years before the global crisis began in mid-2007.[109] Property prices in Valencia began falling as early as September 2007, the construction boom turned into a bust, and the regional government's revenues shrank. The likelihood increased that other regional governments would also need help.[110] Spain's central government, however, was running out of cash. Budget Minister Cristóbal Montoro said in parliament, "There is no money in the public coffers. There's no money to pay for public services."[111]

Finland's opposition parties remained opposed to financing the Spanish bailout. They protested that the "floodgates for Finnish taxpayers to support more banking rescues were being opened."[112] The Finnish parliament did eventually vote on July 20 to authorize Finland's €2 billion contribution to the €100 billion loan. The parliament, however, did so on the condition that Spanish authorities would place nearly €800 million in a security deposit as reassurance of repayment to the Finns.

With political fissures widening, European leaders seemed unsure of what they needed to do next. The instinct was to do as little as possible. Richard Barley of the *Wall Street Journal* captured the sentiment when he wrote, "Europe's strategy of buying time for governments to take small steps forward is looking woefully inadequate. Politicians might try to kick the can one more time, but there is little road left ahead of them."[113]

Financial markets ignored the Spanish bailout that had been packaged so agonizingly. Spain's financial implosion continued at its fierce pace. The yield on Spanish government bonds climbed above 7 percent. The Spanish government's debt-repayment burden was rising quickly. However, tax revenues needed to service the debt were contracting along with GDP. Much the same was happening in Italy: yields on government bonds were approaching 6.5 percent; thus, while debt-repayment obligations were increasing, tax revenues were falling along with GDP.

Meanwhile, Spanish and Italian banks had lost access to virtually all sources of private funding. Moody's had lowered the credit ratings of many banks to below the minimum credit quality level required by the internal rules of some investors.[114] In addition, investors were concerned that, with the yields on Spanish and Italian governments bonds soaring to "potentially unsustainable levels," the two governments would not be able to rescue their banks. In fact, even eurozone authorities would find it difficult to mobilize sufficient resources to rescue Spain and Italy if they began tipping into a full-blown sovereign-banking crisis. The Spanish government's debt far exceeded the sum of Greek, Irish, and Portuguese debt. The Italian government's debt was even larger. As the risks mounted, financial shock waves from Spain and Italy rumbled across Europe and the world.

On July 23, Moody's placed a "negative outlook" on the debt of the German, Dutch, and Luxembourg governments, threatening to take away their prized triple-A rating. The agency explained: "The continued deterioration in Spain and Italy's macroeconomic and funding environment has increased the risk that they will require some kind of external support." And "if the euro area is to be preserved in its current form," the scale of "collective support" required for Spain and Italy would place an especially heavy burden on the "more highly rated member states of the euro area."[115] With that eventuality now too close for comfort, their triple-A ratings were justifiably under a cloud. France and Austria had already lost their triple-A ratings in February because of their own shaky finances. Thus, since the major contributors to the EFSF, the eurozone's bailout fund, were all under financial pressure, Moody's placed the EFSF on a "negative watch" as well.[116]

Later on that same day, speaking on PBS, the public broadcasting network, US Treasury Secretary Timothy Geithner criticized European authorities for dithering. The risk of a major financial accident in the eurozone was now too high for his comfort. The problem, he said, lay with German Chancellor Merkel, who instinctively delayed financial relief to the last minute in her bid to force the governments of crisis countries to reform. As if he were speaking directly to Merkel, Geithner said, "If you leave Europe on the edge of the abyss as your source of leverage, your strategy's unlikely to work because you're going to raise the ultimate cost of the crisis."[117]

European authorities, Geithner said, should quickly build a much larger financial defense fund to protect themselves against escalation of financial mayhem. However, Geithner did not appreciate, as Moody's had done, that a bailout of Spain and Italy would stretch German finances. At least as important, Merkel faced political limits on the actions she could take. Many Germans and even leaders of the CSU, the Bavaria-based sister party of Merkel's CDU, were expressing renewed anxiety about the scale of financial commitment that Germany was making to other eurozone member states.[118] Resistance to financial aid was also increasing in the Netherlands, and the Finns had already made clear that they could not be counted on again.[119]

By July 25, Spanish government yields reached 7.5 percent; Italian government yields crossed 6.5 percent. The eurozone-wide fiscal austerity, the tight monetary policy, and the delays in resolving problems had led to this point from which return could become impossible. If the high yields persisted, the Spanish and Italian governments would soon be unable to service their debts. And recognizing that risk, investors would demand even higher interest rates, which would surely lead to the governments defaulting on their debts. The Spanish and Italian governments were no longer just wounded. They—and, by extension, the Spanish and Italian economies—were in trauma. Was there a trauma specialist on the emergency floor?

The clamor for the ECB to step in was growing. Didier Reynders, the Belgian foreign minister, was most direct. The ECB, he said, must run its printing presses to finance member states.[120] Reynders's suggestion was anathema by eurozone norms. The separation of monetary policy from any hint of financial support to member states was the eurozone's most sacrosanct founding principle. But such was the sense of crisis that the unthinkable was being spoken of. Even Draghi, in an interview with the French newspaper *Le Monde*, said that the ECB had "no taboos," although, as always in Draghi's case, he qualified his openness to bold action with the customary "if we see the risks."[121] The question was whether he saw the very real risks to which he and his predecessor, Trichet, had materially contributed, with catastrophic interest-rate increases in 2011 and timid rate cuts ever since.

On July 26, Draghi traveled to London to reassure anxious investors.

ECB Scrambles to Stop the Trauma, Merkel Helps: July–September 2012

"The bumblebee," Draghi began, "is a mystery of nature because it shouldn't fly but instead it does." Thus, his opening salvo to the investors was, "The euro is like a bumblebee. The euro is much, much stronger, the euro area is much, much stronger than people acknowledge today."[122]

But presumably, Draghi quickly realized that these quaint allegories were failing to charm the skeptical and restless audience. Unusually for a central bank chief, Draghi was speaking without a prepared text.[123] "There is another message I want to tell you," he said. "Within our mandate the ECB is ready to do whatever it takes to preserve the euro. And believe me, it will be enough." Tim Geithner, by now former US Treasury secretary, later wrote in his memoirs, "Draghi had not planned to say this, but he was so alarmed by the darkness expressed by hedge funds and bankers at the conference that he ad-libbed an unequivocal commitment to defend Europe."[124]

Investors cheered. They read Draghi's "whatever-it-takes" statement as a guarantee that if a government could not repay its debts, the ECB would do so on the government's behalf. The yield on Italian bonds fell to 6 percent the day after Draghi's speech from 6.5 percent in the days before; Spanish bond yields fell to 6.75 percent from 7.5 percent. Stock prices of banks began to recover.

Draghi had made a promise, but Geithner later noted that the ECB and European authorities had no clear idea what they were "actually prepared to do."[125] The assumption was that the ECB would buy, or promise to buy, the bonds of euro-area governments to prevent interest rates from rising too high. But how would the ECB do that? And would Draghi have the political support to deliver on his promise?

On July 27, the day after Draghi's speech, the Bundesbank announced its opposition to any ECB commitment to buy government bonds. The Bundesbank was worried that such a commitment would dilute the incentives of heavily indebted governments to maintain fiscal discipline and, therefore, would expose the ECB to substantial financial risk.[126]

But also on July 27, Merkel gave Draghi her instant and crucial support. She did not speak specifically about bond purchases, but she echoed Draghi's words. Germany, she said, was "committed to do everything to protect the eurozone."[127] Schäuble welcomed Draghi's intention to "take the necessary measures to secure the euro in the framework of the existing ECB mandate."[128]

Undeterred, Weidmann kept up his powerful opposition. On August 2, at the press conference that followed the ECB's regular rate-setting meeting, Draghi conceded that the decision to move ahead with a bond-purchase program had not been unanimous. And breaking with ECB tradition, he named the dissenter: "it's clear and it's known that Mr. Weidmann and the Bundesbank . . . have their reservations about programmes that envisage buying bonds."[129] Weidmann was an important foe, not just because he was the Bundesbank's president, but also because he gave voice to reservations widely shared in Germany, including by several Bundestag members of Merkel's CDU and coalition partners. Some lawmakers even demanded increased voting rights in the ECB's Governing Council. Germany, they said, would bear a disproportionate financial burden if governments failed to repay fully their bonds purchased by the ECB.[130]

Draghi pushed ahead. After the September 6 rate-setting meeting, he announced that the ECB's Governing Council had agreed to introduce a bond-purchase program, to be called Outright Monetary Transactions (OMTs).[131] At the press conference, journalists were anxious to know if the bond purchases would be "unlimited." Draghi replied there would be "no ex ante [predetermined] limits on amount of Outright Monetary Transactions."

This statement was, of course, not true. As was plain from the start and as Jörg Asmussen, an ECB Governing Council member, later stated unequivocally, "the design of OMTs makes it clear to everyone that the programme is effectively limited."[132] The ECB would purchase only those bonds that were due to mature in more than 1 but in less than 3 years. Even restricted to that pool, there was legal ambiguity about how much the ECB could purchase without violating the Maastricht Treaty.[133] But Draghi's mission was to sell OMTs as a "whatever it takes big bazooka," and so he said at his press conference on September 6, 2012 that the size of purchases would be large enough "to meet our objectives." That was what investors wanted to hear.

Asked if the decision to move ahead was unanimous, Draghi coyly replied, "There was one dissenting view. We do not disclose the details of our work. It is up to you to guess." Weidmann left no one in doubt with his stepped-up public criticism. In a statement the same day, he said that OMTs would be the equivalent of "printing banknotes" to buy government bonds; such largesse, he repeated, would ease the pressure on governments to maintain fiscal discipline.[134] And if the ECB bought the bonds and the governments did not pay the ECB back, German (and other) taxpayers would be asked to make up the ECB's losses.

Investors kept cheering OMTs on. The sense of crisis began to subside. The nonstop complaints from Weidmann seemed needless, indeed irresponsible nitpicking.

The ECB needed an instrument like OMTs. Central banks play a lender-of-last-resort role. When financial markets malfunction, central banks are expected to provide liquidity. The ECB could and did act as a lender of last resort to eurozone banks. But unlike in the United States, where the Fed was also a lender-of-last resort to the US government, the ECB could not perform that function for eurozone governments. The difference lay in the context. In the United States, if the Fed were to end up making losses on the government's bonds that it had purchased, the US Treasury would have an obligation to use taxpayer funds to replenish the Fed's capital. The eurozone, however, was an "incomplete monetary union." It had no fiscal union: there was no "eurozone treasury" to pay for losses that the ECB might incur. Hence, if the ECB ended up losing money on nearly worthless bonds of bankrupt governments, then other eurozone governments would have to pay to top up the ECB's capital.

The political implications were serious, as Christopher Sims, Princeton economics professor and Nobel laureate in economics, had pointed out four months earlier in an essay written for a Banque de France publication. Under the eurozone's rules for capital injection, "Germany would bear a large part of the burden, and it would be clear that German fiscal resources were being used to compensate for ECB losses on other countries' sovereign debts."[135]

Sims said he sympathized with "German skeptics of a lender of last resort role for the ECB." They "have a point," he concluded.[136]

OMTs created a fiscal union by the backdoor. More precisely, they created a *fait accompli* under which some member countries could be forced to contribute fiscal resources if another member state was in financial distress. Thus, notwithstanding the free lunch that Draghi's speech had thus far delivered, OMTs could not be an economically stable and politically legitimate instrument without a clearer political contract.

As Sims had emphasized, an OMT-like instrument needed the transparent backing of fiscal resources managed by a central eurozone institution. Such an institution, with "at least some taxing power" and an independent ability to borrow, would bear the losses after an OMT operation went sour. Most importantly, the central institution's ability to tax and borrow "would of course have to be subject to democratic control."[137]

The ECB's defense of OMTs without a fiscal union was that the governments it assisted would first agree to strictly specified fiscal austerity and structural reforms. Based on that agreement, the government would borrow from the eurozone's bailout fund (the EFSF, and later the soon-to-be inaugurated European Stability Mechanism). Only then would the ECB trigger OMTs. But in that case, the ECB would not be the lender of last resort, standing alert to rapidly prevent systemic financial malfunction.[138] Rather, if it ever triggered OMTs, the ECB would effectively be a "conditional lender," just like the IMF. Like the IMF, the ECB would wade deep into the politics of domestic policy decisions. Poorly designed conditions heaped on a hapless country would make matters worse, as the experience with Greece vividly showed; even with the best intentions, financial distress could intensify. For this reason, not just Weidmann, but other eurozone central bankers were worried.[139]

Draghi offered another argument for OMTs. The ECB, he said, bought and sold bonds and other securities to conduct its routine monetary operations. On some of these transactions, the ECB made profits, and on others, it incurred losses. Normally, the profits and losses balanced out over time, and if they did not, member states had an obligation to replenish the ECB's capital. The OMT operation was also a regular monetary instrument, Draghi said. Its specific purpose, he explained, was to counter speculators betting on the eurozone's breakup. Draghi insisted that speculative craziness, rather than fundamental financial weakness, was driving up government-bond yields, and those higher yields were preventing the transmission of the ECB's low interest rate to Spain and Italy.

Weidmann correctly rejected the claim that OMTs would primarily improve monetary policy operations; rather, he stuck with his theme that OMTs would bail out nearly bankrupt sovereigns. Writing later in his memoirs, former BOE Governor Mervyn King expressed his support for Weidmann's position. King wrote, "It is not easy to see how purchases of the debt of some countries but not others can be construed as solely an act of monetary policy."[140]

But such was Merkel's commitment to the OMT idea that on September 17, she came close to openly contradicting Weidmann even on this highly technical matter. "I acknowledge," Merkel told reporters, "that what the ECB has done is motivated by monetary policy issues. I have no reason to doubt that."[141]

Merkel had good reason to lend her political gravitas to Draghi. She did not have the funds to quell the out-of-control eurozone crisis. With OMTs in place, the need for German taxpayers' support for Europe would greatly diminish. Merkel could keep pushing member states to tighten budgets and implement structural reforms, both of which the ECB endorsed enthusiastically. If all went well, OMTs would be the euro area's financial safety net, leaving Merkel free to direct Europe's economic policy.

From the start of the crisis, Merkel had tried to balance her two competing interests: protecting the German taxpayer while also keeping the euro area together. She had done so by delaying decisions and hoping that she would not actually have to make a choice. This was shortsighted and, as Geithner pointed out, was an extraordinarily costly way of dealing with economic and financial crises. But such was the nature of the Eurosystem. The ECB's rate hike on July 7, 2011 had pushed the eurozone into crisis, and its hesitant and half-hearted stimulus measures since then had let the crisis snowball into an existential threat to the euro area by early July 2012. Merkel had no alternative but to allow OMTs. The pattern had been set: denials and delays, followed by half measures that staved off immediate collapse.

Thus, another falling forward moment was lost. Not even an attempt was made to create a democratically accountable fiscal union. Perhaps, none was possible.

Hence, although celebrated for the relief it had instantly brought, OMTs carried a dangerous risk. If, in the future, a government reaches the point where it needs OMTs, will the ECB's mere promise of a big bazooka again prove to be enough? If not, will the government in trouble be able to negotiate in time the conditionality demanded in return for financial support? The extent of austerity and the nature of reforms called for could prove to be controversial and therefore difficult to agree on. In that case, some members of the ECB's Governing Council might seek to stop, or slow down, the bond purchases. If financial markets sense that the ECB might hesitate, the crisis will escalate: yields on the distressed government's bonds will rise and the country's banks will come under greater pressure. Panicked investors will demand a show of greater bond-buying firepower from the ECB. The Governing Council and national governments will grow even more fearful that the ECB is sinking deeper into the quagmire. There will be more reason to hesitate. A future German chancellor will face greater domestic political resistance to waving OMTs on. Sovereign debt attorney Lee Buchheit and Duke University law professor Mitu Gulati predict that financial markets "will mercilessly test the ECB's resolve."[142] If it does end up buying "unlimited bonds" of a nearly bankrupt government, the ECB could face large potential losses. Political and financial fractures will inevitably follow.

Price Deflation Looms, National Interests Collide: July 2012–2013

For now, the financial wounds had been patched up and the patients were out of intensive care. But the economies were not healing sufficiently quickly, and scars were beginning to form. Left unattended, the build-up of connective scar tissue would create new problems.

Secure in the belief that it had done the hard work, the ECB returned to its shell. For ten months—from July 2012 to May 2013—the ECB kept its policy interest rate unchanged at 0.75 percent. Put differently, from 1 percent before the first rate hike in April 2011 to May 2013, the ECB reduced its interest rate in total by all of 25 basis points. Yes, that is a 0.25 percentage point net reduction in the policy interest rate in the slightly over two years during which several eurozone economies were at first in crisis and then in near-perpetual recession. The Spanish and Italian economies were still contracting, seemingly without an end. The economic weakness was widespread. In mid-2013, even Germany was tipping into recession.

Businesses were locking their doors and the ranks of unemployed workers were dismally large. Not surprisingly, with investment and consumer demand so weak, the euro area's inflation rate began dropping while the US inflation rate stayed stable (figure 7.8). For the first time since the start of the crisis, euro-area and US inflation rates were beginning to diverge. We see this divergence most clearly in the "core inflation" measure, a measure which strips out volatile energy and food prices and is therefore a generally reliable

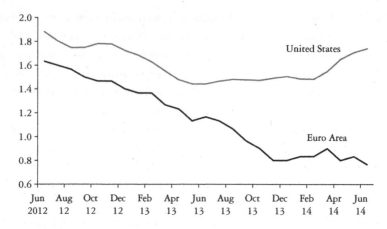

FIGURE 7.8. Euro-area inflation rate continues dropping while US inflation rate stabilizes in mid-2013.

(Three-month moving average of "core" annual inflation rates, percent)
Source: Eurostat: "HICP—All Items Excluding Energy and Food." St. Louis Fed, FRED: "Personal Consumption Expenditures Excluding Food and Energy (Chain-Type Price Index)."

indicator of underlying inflationary pressures as well as a good predictor of future inflation. By early May 2013, core inflation in the euro area was falling toward the 1 percent level; US core inflation, helped by stimulative monetary policy, stayed above 1.5 percent. The divergence reflected the different strategies pursued. The Fed had taken steps, starting in late 2010, to push back deflation risk; the ECB had scoffed at the possibility, insisting that inflation expectations were "anchored" around 2 percent.

The euro area now faced a new danger: low inflation or even deflation. Persistent low inflation, as Bernanke had warned in November 2010, can cause economic stagnation. In a low-inflation environment, people anticipate that inflation may fall further. They therefore reduce current spending, which lowers economic growth and causes inflation to actually fall. Lower growth and minimal inflation make debts harder to repay, and spending declines even more, leading to a high-debt-and-deflation trap.

Finally, on May 2, 2013, the ECB reduced its policy rate by 25 basis points to 0.50 percent.[143] The rate reduction was long overdue, and investors had anticipated it. But the latest measure was too meager to stem the decline in inflation. Part of the problem was that the ECB remained in denial that inflation was drifting downward. This was because the ECB remained focused on "headline" inflation, which includes energy and food prices. Headline inflation had also fallen, but that decline, Draghi said, was mainly due to a fall in energy prices, which would reverse, and inflation would rise again. The ECB still believed there was no real risk that the euro-area inflation rate would fall into dangerously low territory. As Trichet had often done at his press briefings, Draghi repeated three times that "inflation expectations" continued to be "firmly anchored." Do not worry, he was saying; all will be well.

An asymmetry was manifest in the ECB's behavior. The ECB was prepared to act to safeguard price stability only if inflation went up but not when it went down. In 2011, when a temporary surge in energy prices had caused headline inflation rates to increase, the ECB saw fit to raise interest rates twice, almost causing a euro-area systemic financial meltdown. Now, with energy prices falling, the ECB declared that the decline in the headline inflation rate would likely be temporary and would reverse; no urgent action was required. The ECB failed to take note of the core inflation rate, which was also falling and was pointing to deflationary pressures.

In June, Draghi said that the ECB was not in any hurry to take further measures, because the OMT promise had already brought down interest rates in Italy and Spain. In a moment of self-congratulation, Draghi said that the OMT initiative had been "probably the most successful monetary policy measure undertaken in recent time. Before OMT we had some expectations of deflationary risks, and that's over."[144] To reinforce his case, Draghi said that stock prices were rising and that the Italian and Spanish banks were relying less on ECB funds and, instead, were borrowing more from private creditors. The eurozone economy would soon turn the corner; GDP growth would pick up, and so would wages and prices.

The optimism infected other senior European policymakers. On October 10, 2013, five of them—Jeroen Dijsselbloem, Olli Rehn, Jörg Asmussen, Klaus Regling, and Werner Hoyer—wrote in the *Wall Street Journal* that the euro area might have reached a "turning point." Growth, they said, was picking up, and fiscal deficits were lower. Much hard work lay ahead, they acknowledged, but "we will continue on our course. We have everything in place to emerge stronger from the crisis, with more sustainable growth and more jobs."[145]

The ECB stayed on hold, and the inflation rate continued to fall. Draghi was right, of course, that "nominal" interest rates, the rates paid on government bonds and on bank lending, had declined. But to borrowers, what matters when they are making their spending decisions is the "real" interest rate, the nominal interest rate minus the rate of inflation. A higher inflation rate lowers the real interest rate, because inflation does some of the work of repaying past debts and thus creates greater ability and incentive to borrow and spend. And, thanks to the ECB, the inflation rate was low everywhere in the euro area, and in several countries, it was falling.

Thus, despite the decline in nominal interest rates, Italian and Spanish real interest rates had stayed between 3 and 4 percent since late 2012. Those real rates were too high for economies that were contracting. In Italy and Spain, the debt burdens—debt-to-income ratios—for many households and businesses were increasing. In contrast, real interest rates were under 1 percent in Germany, helping to sustain the country's economic recovery. This was the crux of the euro area's problem: a single monetary policy causes member country economies to diverge, helping the stronger countries and handicapping the weaker ones. And as economies diverge, management of monetary policy becomes even harder.

The Italian economy was particularly hard hit. Early signs of deflation—and of the damage it causes—were evident. Although Italy had not had a property price boom before the crisis started, a bust in property prices had begun (figure 7.9). As property prices fell, construction companies fell behind on their debt repayments, hence, "nonperforming loans" of Italian banks—loans not being paid back on time—quickly increased. Economic growth and inflation consistently fell below the optimistic forecasts, and the government's debt-to-GDP ratio rose faster than had been forecast.

The risk now was that a debt-deflation cycle—a continued decline in inflation, feeding into higher debt burdens—could take hold in large parts of the euro area. On November 7, 2013, Draghi finally acknowledged that

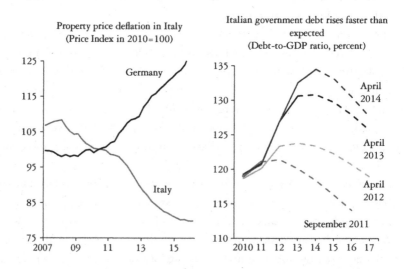

FIGURE 7.9. Italy begins to slide into a debt-deflation cycle.
Note: Dashed lines refer to projections at the time.
Sources: Left panel: OECD, Real House Price Index (2010 = 100). Right panel: International Monetary Fund, World Economic Outlook Database, various editions. (http://www.imf.org/external/ns/cs.aspx?id=28).

undesirably low inflation was, indeed, possible. And, in a move that surprised markets, he announced another small cut in the ECB's main policy rate, down to 0.25 percent.[146] The ECB's policy rate was now down to the level the Fed had reached nearly five years earlier in December 2008.

But back in December 2008, the Fed had also announced a QE program, which it later renewed, because, as Bernanke explained in November 2010, it was important to ward off deflation risk. The ECB was already five years behind in going down this route. And it was not clear if and when it would take that next step.

At the press conference after the Governing Council meeting, a journalist asked Draghi if critics were justified in describing the ECB as a "pea-shooter dealing with an approaching deflationary tank." Draghi remained optimistic that the decline in inflation would be temporary. "Inflation expectations," he said, were "firmly anchored at 2%, or less than 2%." Draghi's claim was that despite falling inflation rates, eurozone citizens "firmly" expected that inflation would soon return to a 2 percent pace and that, in anticipation of higher inflation in the near future, people would step up their purchases, which would, in turn, push up actual inflation. As we have seen often in this story, to be effective, a policy measure must be taken within a time window. The window for aggressive monetary policy action was closing.

In place of a major QE initiative, Draghi offered cheap talk. The ECB, he said, had "a whole range of instruments that we can activate," and which the ECB would deploy "if needed."[147] The phrase "if needed," used previously to delay the urgently needed Greek program, was back on duty. Cheap talk without matching actions had raised the costs of the Greek rescue.

Financial markets were not impressed by the ECB's belated recognition of low-inflation risk or its latest interest-rate decision. Market observers were understandably worried that the ECB would never do the "big stuff."[148] The core inflation rate was below 1 percent and falling. The ECB had consistently acted only when the problem became virulent, and so financial markets interpreted the modest latest action as a harbinger of bad news rather than as a proactive, forward-looking measure.

There was good reason to worry that the ECB would move slowly. The two Germans on the ECB's Governing Council—Jens Weidmann and Jörg Asmussen—and two other northern members, from Austria and the Netherlands, had attempted an internal revolt against the most recent interest-rate reduction.[149] As never before, the north was visibly applying brakes on ECB monetary-policy easing. Their task, they believed, was to preserve the eurozone's price-stability identity.

Not just the German members of the Governing Council but all of Germany, it seemed, opposed easier ECB monetary policy. Even Merkel, who had so eagerly assisted Draghi in creating the OMT program, was not happy. She declared at an election rally that the ECB's interest rate was too low for Germany.[150] German public commentators also applied pressure on the ECB. *Bild*, Germany's largest-circulation daily, accused the ECB of plying "southern" eurozone countries with cheap money.[151] In an op-ed for the Financial Times, the prominent German economist Hans-Werner Sinn said that instead of focusing its mind on monetary policy for the eurozone as a whole, the ECB was carrying out a "regional fiscal policy"—making low-interest-rate funding accessible to governments in southern countries. But this short-term palliative, he averred, was doing them no favor. It was preventing the inevitable and necessary decline of wages and prices which the southern countries needed to regain competitiveness.[152] The attacks became increasingly personal and polemical. The chief economist at the financial weekly *Wirtschaftswoche* described the November 7, 2013, rate cut as a "diktat from a new Banca d'Italia, based in Frankfurt."

Draghi was upset. Speaking at a business conference in Berlin, he said, "Let me react towards what is a nationalistic undertone in some of our countries whereby we [are said to] act against the interests of some countries and in defense of our own countries. We are not German, neither French or Spaniards or Italian, we are Europeans and we are acting for the Eurozone as a whole."[153]

The truth is that despite Draghi's noble and well-intentioned sentiment, the ECB's monetary policy stance could serve only some of the member states and would necessarily neglect the others. Between 2011 and 2013, ECB policy worked mainly for Germany and other northern countries. The southern countries had needed a much more activist monetary policy in order to pull them back from the edge of deflation. There was no solution to this problem. That was the nature of the eurozone tragedy.

The eurozone had been in crisis nearly continuously since July 2007. Eurozone authorities had done little to revive the economy, either in the global phase of the crisis between 2007 and 2009 or since 2010, when the crisis raged mainly in their own backyard. Indeed, throughout, they had made matters worse by not acting quickly enough to heal the economic wounds. The emphasis on fiscal austerity and tight monetary policy had created an economic stranglehold which curtailed economic growth, set off deflationary tendencies, pushed debt burdens up, and left their banks in fragile condition. European leaders repeatedly disregarded evidence, and they remained unwilling to learn from experiences elsewhere. National political interests pulled economic decision-making in opposing directions, and no one was accountable.

And all this while, a larger political drama was unfolding. The extensive economic and financial damage had unleashed powerful political forces that were dividing Europe. To appreciate these far-reaching—possibly irreversible—changes in European politics, we need to take a step back.

Merkel and Other "Unwilling Europeans" Pull in Different Directions

For a long time, Europe's "elites"—national political leaders and technocrats in Brussels and Frankfurt—had run Europe. They had operated under the "Monnet method," named after the venerable Jean Monnet, one of the principal architects of postwar European integration. Monnet believed Europe's tasks and methods of operation were technically complex. According to him, public debate on how Europe should be run was, at best, pointless and could even be counterproductive if adversarial politics created undesirable compromises.[154] The Monnet method worked for just over forty years, from the Schuman Plan in 1950 to the Maastricht Treaty, which was signed in 1992. The task in those decades was to create European institutions for productive dialogue among nation-states and to open borders to trade. Most Europeans saw only a blurred connection between their daily lives and decisions made at the European level. Moreover, since the opening of trade borders had created new business opportunities for many, support for Europe remained high. As Irish political scientist Peter Mair explained, European "elites" had enjoyed a "permissive consensus," a "popular trust," and, hence, a "deference to their decisions" on European matters.[155]

But in 1992, the Maastricht Treaty made the single currency a real possibility. The "permissive consensus" began to break down. The popular public revolt started in Denmark, where, in a June 1992 referendum, citizens rejected the single currency. This revolt continued in France's September 1992 referendum. While a narrow majority of French citizens allowed the single currency to move forward, those who voted against it conveyed a clear message: we, who feel left behind, will not give our uncritical support to Europe. Thus, by the early 1990s, European elites began to lose the people's deference. European projects based on the Monnet method became "vulnerable."[156]

Citizens' distrust reverberated loudly in 2005, when the French and the Dutch voted against the European draft constitution.[157] The pattern of votes was the same: the worse the economic prospects, the more likely a citizen in these countries was to vote against Europe. In 2005, even the young sent the message that Europe was not working for them. Fearing that citizens in other countries would also vote against the constitution, European leaders abandoned the project.

And once the eurozone's economic and financial crisis gathered momentum, the fissure between Europe's public and its ruling class widened dangerously. Especially in the dark days after the ECB's July 2011 interest rate hike, political tensions in the eurozone increased rapidly. Citizens demanded that their national leaders do more to protect and promote national interests, and national leaders responded to these domestic pressures. In the earlier parts of this chapter, I have narrated the economic developments; I now recount the political story—in fact, four concurrently running stories, in Germany, Greece, Italy, and Britain.

MERKEL DISTANCES GERMANY FROM EUROPE

At a Berlin press conference in July 2011, a reporter asked Merkel how she responded to critics who accused her of lacking "passion" for Europe. Merkel frowned and said, "Oh, passion, yes, exactly." A ripple of laughter went through the auditorium. Her approach, she said, was to avoid "spectacular" solutions, which sometimes satisfied "human longing" but were "politically negligent." The only right way forward was to build a strong foundation in small steps. "So, well, that's my passion," she concluded, "Merkel's kind of passion, which is quite intense."[158]

As Germany's chancellor, Merkel gave priority to German financial interests, and she asked that the other member states do more to take care of their own problems. Other German chancellors had behaved the same way. In 1992, Helmut Kohl had stood by while the Bundesbank, acting under authorization from Kohl's predecessor Helmut Schmidt, watched a helpless Italy tumble into a financial crisis. Throughout the 1990s and especially in his April 1998 speech to the Bundestag, Kohl had emphasized to the German people that German taxpayers would not pay for the profligacy of other member-state governments. Merkel was continuing in that tradition.[159]

But Merkel was also Europe's accidental chancellor, its reluctant hegemon, in the midst of a financial crisis that seemed impossible to tame. Former Bulgarian Finance Minister Simeon Djankov, who was privy to the European decision-making process, later wrote in his account of the period between

July 2009 and the spring of 2013, "Germany led all discussions on eurozone issues, sometimes showing token respect for France's views. Germany's main allies—Finland and the Netherlands—played important but secondary roles. No one else mattered much, or at least mattered consistently."[160]

Merkel, therefore, set the strategy for the eurozone's crisis management. She relied on delays and ad hoc, last-minute solutions, which stored up more trouble for the future. She waited until a catastrophic breakdown of the euro loomed, and then rallied the necessary support within her CDU party and in the Bundestag, impressing on those disinclined to go along with her that there was "no alternative" to the politically unpopular rescue measure.[161] Merkel managed the euro crisis just as American presidents had dealt with the Vietnam War. She defused the immediate crisis but could not resolve its underlying causes. The eventual cost of the crisis and financial rescue went up, while resentment and growing animosity drove Europeans apart.

But not just eurozone crisis management, Merkel was shaping the entire economic policy framework of eurozone member states. On November 15, 2011, Volker Kauder, chairman of the CDU/CSU parliamentary faction, somewhat dramatically said, "Now, all of a sudden, Europe is speaking German. Not as a language, but in its acceptance of the instruments for which Angela Merkel has fought so hard."[162] Kauder was speaking at the party's annual conference in Leipzig. He had the unenviable task of persuading CDU party members that German financial support for the eurozone was necessary but that, in return, other eurozone members were following German-style policies.

An immediate example of Kauder's thesis was fiscal policy, which was always of special interest to the German government. At their summit in Brussels on December 8–9, 2011, EU leaders agreed to move forward with the German proposal for a "fiscal compact." Governments of member states would make a commitment, embedded in national law (preferably the constitution), to keep their budgets balanced or in surplus. Automatic mechanisms would quickly eliminate budget deficits. All eurozone member states adopted the fiscal compact by March 2012.

Despite Merkel's minimalist approach and the clear movement by other member states toward German policy ideals, domestic German politics turned increasingly averse to financial assistance for Europe. For Merkel, the opposition crystallized disconcertingly close to her own political base. In September 2012, ahead of the 2013 elections to the Bundestag, long-standing members of Merkel's CDU formed a rebel group, the "Electoral Alternative [*Wahlalternative*] 2013."[163] The rebels said that German taxpayers would never see much of the money their government had poured into

European financial rescues and funding facilities. Playing off Merkel's mantra, they said there *was* an alternative: the euro needed to be steadily unwound.

Notwithstanding this evidence of mounting German opposition to the euro and the financial claims it made on Germany, Europe's "elites," who flitted from capital to capital and met in non-smoke-filled rooms to decide on a pro-European future, remained stuck in the Monnet method. They nursed the hope that Merkel would override shrill German voices against extending a helping hand to those whose needs were great. Drawing on a burst of involutionary energy in late 2012, senior European technocrats prodded Merkel to do something spectacular. On November 30, 2012, European Commission President José Manuel Barroso published his "Blueprint for a Deep and Genuine Monetary Union."[164] Five days later, on December 5, Herman Van Rompuy, president of the European Council, issued his own report, echoing many of Barroso's themes and proposals.[165] Van Rompuy's report carried the suitably original title "Towards a Genuine Economic and Monetary Union," although insiders have ever since described it as the "Four Presidents Report" because it drew on help and ideas from Barroso, Draghi, and Eurogroup head Jean-Claude Juncker.

The Four Presidents Report recommended a "euro area fiscal capacity" to absorb shocks from acute economic and financial crises. Funds from this proposed fiscal "backstop" would rescue European banks in trouble and finance a eurozone unemployment-insurance program.[166] Van Rompuy and the other presidents knew they were pushing into territory where Merkel had refused to tread.

When these proposals came up for discussion at the December 2012 summit of European leaders, Merkel coldly asked, "Where is this money supposed to come from? Can someone explain that to me?" Who, in other words, would fund this "common fiscal capacity"? French President François Hollande, believing that he could smother German opposition with gentle words, told Merkel that she needed to think of the planned facility as a "solidarity mechanism." Merkel replied, "That's all very well." And again she asked, "but where is the money supposed to come from?" Thus, with a few unambiguous rhetorical questions, Merkel gutted the starry-eyed four presidents' proposals.[167] Swedish, Finnish, Danish, and Dutch counterparts gave Merkel their support. Arrayed against them, always at the losing end, were the French, Italians, Portuguese, and Spanish.

The eurozone's political cracks were becoming wider. While many eurozone member states bristled at the German chancellor's influence over their affairs, the German public grew increasingly restive about the obligations it seemed to be taking on. In February 2013, the rebels, who in September

2012 had formed the anti-euro movement *Electoral Alternative*, formed a new political party, called Alternative für Deutschland (AfD). Over the course of the next few months, AfD made gains in several state elections.

On September 17, 2013, five days before the Bundestag elections, a poll showed deep German distrust of Europe.[168] By a large majority, the Germans polled wanted European authority slimmed and, much as in Britain, they wanted powers repatriated to national governments. A large majority of respondents also said that the euro should be restricted to a core group of countries.[169] An even larger majority said that the next German government had no mandate to continue financial aid to European countries, and all new aid should require a public referendum.

Although the AfD's message continued to resonate among Germans, the party received only 4.7 percent of the vote, just shy of the 5 percent threshold needed to claim a seat in the Bundestag. The AfD mainly drained support from the Free Democrats, the FDP, Merkel's pro-business and euro-skeptic-leaning coalition partner.[170]

Merkel's personal popularity and her campaign slogan, "Sie kennen mich [You know me]," carried the day. Germans looked up to her as Chancellor *Mutti*, or Mum. During the 2009 election, Merkel's critics had used *Mutti* as an unflattering epithet for her. But it had turned into an asset. Merkel herself found the characterization annoying, but she understood that the motherly image helped her electorally, and she "embraced it."[171]

During the election campaign, as in 2009, Merkel stayed away from discussing European matters. Indeed, with the slogan, "You know me" and the cover of *Mutti*, she steered clear of any serious policy debate. She bypassed the German citizen. Statistical analysis of postelection surveys showed a distinct "Merkel effect"; she rose above party affiliations.[172] Her Christian Democrats achieved impressive electoral gains, but the FDP's losses required her to scramble for months to assemble a grand coalition with the Social Democrats.

Some observers believed that with the elections out of the way and with a nudge from the Social Democrats, Merkel would open German purse strings to stabilize the euro area. But those with such expectations misunderstood both her and the mood of the German public. To the governments of Greece and other distressed euro-area countries, Merkel conveyed an unchanged message: there was no alternative to fiscal austerity. To the Bundestag, she still said that there was no alternative to modest financial assistance for Europe. Her position as de facto European chancellor was virtually unassailable, and in Germany, she believed she could continue to dodge public debate on Europe with vague promises to keep the Greek bill small.

The political consequences of Merkel's strategy evolved most directly in Greece but also with surprising vigor and antipathy in Italy.

THAT GREXIT QUESTION AGAIN

As noted earlier in this chapter, in August 2010 the IMF's Poul Thomsen had spoken glowingly of the Greek government's efforts to mend its ways. Continuing in that vein, in a March 2011 report, the IMF approvingly reported that "extraordinarily ambitious" austerity measures in 2010 had added up to an astonishing 8 percent of GDP. To achieve this austerity goal, the government had undertaken "socially difficult wage and pension cuts, tax increases, and deep spending cuts," which the IMF said were "by any international comparison, very impressive."[173] Echoing the praise lavished by Schäuble some months earlier, the IMF concluded that the Greek economy would soon turn the corner.

The numbers did not add up. The austerity measures had withdrawn 8 percent of total demand in 2010, and still more austerity was in the pipeline. Yet the IMF predicted that Greek GDP would fall by only 3 percent in 2011. Arithmetic, however, is a hard taskmaster. A few months after the publication of the IMF's report, Greece's economic implosion became starkly evident. In June, Schäuble and other European leaders declared that the Greeks were at fault; the government had not lived up to its end of the bargain.[174]

The Greek economy continued to spiral out of control that summer amid the financial panic triggered by the ECB's rate hikes. On July 21, 2011, European leaders announced that Greece would receive another €109 billion in bailout funds. It was difficult by now to remember how much money the Greeks had already received. European authorities also reduced the interest rate on their loans to the Greek government from 5.5 to 3.5 percent, and they extended the loan-repayment period from seven years to fifteen years. For Greece, this was the beginning of an aid-in-driblets strategy, always enough to keep Greece propped up but never enough to release it from the clutches of its creditors.

The only good news that day was for Ireland, which also received the same concession on the interest rate and the extended repayment time. For Ireland, this was like a "get out of jail free" card. Private lenders to Ireland inferred correctly that there would be more concessions on the repayment terms of official loans. Meanwhile, economic prospects were looking better, in part, because US multinational firms—taking advantage of the low-cor-porate-tax regime—were expanding their operations in Ireland. Yields on

Irish government bonds fell rapidly.[175] The Irish crisis was effectively over in mid-2011.

Greek despair, however, continued. Most Greeks faced some combination of rising taxes and disappearing jobs, alongside falling unemployment benefits and welfare payments. In mid-October, as the Greek parliament voted on new austerity measures, Greek workers went on a two-day general strike; one man died of a heart attack during a rally, and dozens were injured in the protests. There seemed no light at the end of this tunnel.

On October 31, Prime Minister George Papandreou announced he would hold a referendum to ask Greek citizens if they were willing to continue with the austerity that Greece's creditors demanded. Polls showed that even though most Greeks wanted to stay in the eurozone, they rejected the austerity. In essence, the Greek public was pleading, there must be a better way forward, one that allows Greeks some breathing room and keeps them members of the eurozone. Indeed, there was. A slower pace of austerity would have allowed more growth, which would have eased the pain that the Greeks felt and would have helped the Greek government pay off its debts faster. Everyone stood to gain from hearing the plea the Greeks were making.

European leaders, however, were horrified. Merkel faced a German public increasingly hostile to any sign of concession to the Greeks. Merkel and Sarkozy decided that they needed to respond. They were no longer the best of friends, as they briefly had been at Deauville in October 2010. The tensions between them had been apparent at Trichet's farewell event some weeks earlier at the Alte Oper in Frankfurt. On another recent occasion, in conversation with a head of government, Sarkozy was overheard saying of Merkel, "She says she's on a diet then she has a second helping of cheese."[176] Such crude remarks had reached Merkel and she did not think they were funny. However, on the matter of Greece, Merkel and Sarkozy were of the same mind. There could be no concession to Greece. They agreed to kill the referendum. They "summoned" Papandreou to Cannes on November 2, just before the start of the G20 summit of world leaders.[177]

Papandreou arrived late in the evening and walked alone to the Palais des Festivals et des Congrès, where the summit was to begin the next day. The message awaiting him: no more funds for Greece if he heeded the public's call for reduced austerity. On November 3, Papandreou dropped his referendum plan.

Papandreou had become prime minister two years earlier. He had big dreams then. Greece, he had said, was "a country with great potential," a country "with the political will to meet the challenges of a new world."[178] The crisis had smashed these wonderful visions. As the austerity dragged on and the economy continued its dizzying fall, Papandreou rapidly lost the confidence of Greek citizens. In his last speech to parliament, he plaintively said, "I wanted to go beyond the normal approach. I wanted to break taboos for the good of the country."[179] That was not to be.

On November 9, Papandreou resigned. On November 11, Lucas Papademos, formerly vice president of the ECB, became prime minister of a technocratic "crisis coalition," or, as some preferred to call it, a "national unity" government.[180] For European creditors, Papademos was a safe pair of hands. He immediately announced that he stood ready to move ahead with the austerity schedule required by the creditors. In a bid to bring cheer to beleaguered Greek citizens, Papademos said, "I am confident that the country's participation in the eurozone is a guarantee of monetary stability."[181]

In March 2012, Papademos presided over the largest-ever sovereign default, which reduced the debt owed by the Greek government to banks and other private investors from €206 billion to €35 billion.[182] But the default had come nearly two years too late. The draconian austerity demanded by the official creditors to keep rolling over the government's unsustainable stock of debt had sent Greek economic activity into a freefall. Tax revenues had, predictably, shrunk and offset the austerity measures taken to improve the government's finances. Hence, despite substantially reduced debt owed to private creditors after the default, the Greek government in its Alice-in-Wonderland world had borrowed more from European creditors and the IMF to repay its loans to *them*.

With the new official loans, the Greek government's total debt burden, once again, remained virtually unchanged at unsustainable levels.[183] As the Red Queen might have said, "Now, *here*, you see, it takes all the running *you* can do, to keep in the same place. If you want to get somewhere else, you must run at least twice as fast as that."[184]

In April 2012, Papademos concluded that he had completed his task as prime minister. The economy was in chaotic decline. The unemployment rate was racing toward 25 percent. It was time to elect a new government.

Elections held in early May produced a deeply fragmented parliament, reflecting the people's desperate search for alternatives to the crushing economic pain. The biggest beneficiary of the political churn was the anti-austerity and, until then, fringe political party Syriza, which earned 17 percent of the vote and finished a surprising second to New Democracy. Alexis Tsipras, Syriza's leader, was a thirty-seven-year-old ex-Communist student leader who often addressed party members as "comrades." Buoyed by his party's strong showing, he declared, "The Greek people voted for an end to the bailout and barbaric austerity."[185] Tsipras's call for cutting back on unbearable austerity echoed widespread Greek sentiment, but his rhetoric was not welcome in Berlin or Frankfurt. Jörg Asmussen, until recently a minister in Merkel's government and now an ECB Governing Council member, spoke as a German politician rather than as a neutral central banker. He had a tough message for Tsipras: "Greece needs to be aware that there is no alternative to the agreed reform programme if it wants to remain a member of the eurozone."[186]

The bullying tone adopted by Asmussen and others encouraged greater defiance in Greece. When the May elections failed to deliver a governing coalition, Greek citizens gave Syriza an increased vote share of 27 percent in the follow-up election in June. This time around, Antonis Samaras of New Democracy cobbled together a coalition government, and Syriza established itself as the principal voice of the opposition.

Greece's economic collapse continued. Through much of the summer of 2012, Merkel wondered, as she had in 2010, whether Greece was "ballast" that needed to be jettisoned from the eurozone ship.[187] With Greece out of the eurozone, she could better protect her own political credibility and mystique. But after much deliberation, Merkel decided, as she had in 2010, that she could not let Greece go. A Greek exit (Grexit) would be the thin edge of the wedge. It would establish the principle that a country could leave the euro area. Financial markets would be tempted to dump the assets of other weak euro-area countries, which would aggravate their financial distress and force them, ultimately, to leave. Like dominoes, euro-area countries would fall, one knocking down others. While excessive Greek "ballast" in the eurozone was a real problem, Merkel concluded that falling dominoes after Grexit could lead to far graver economic and political consequences.[188]

Once Merkel decided that she could not let Greece go, the costs of keeping Greece on board had to be borne. Greek politics remained "turbulent."[189] The Greek economy continued to nosedive, and the arithmetic of debt burdens continued to work its cruel logic. If GDP falls sharply, the debt-to-GDP ratio—and hence the debt-repayment burden—goes up rapidly. In late 2012, the IMF more plainly than before concluded that Greece's debt was unsustainable.[190] Put simply, there was no real prospect that Greece could ever repay its debt.

Although complicit in causing Greece's debt burden to soar to unsustainable levels, the IMF insisted on being repaid in full and instead called on European authorities to forgive some of the debt that the Greek government owed them.[191] European officials had no choice. They announced on November 27 that they would take more measures to reduce Greece's debt burden, including more interest-rate cuts and extended repayment periods.[192]

As I wrote at the time, it was a bogus deal, which offered trivial relief.[193] Greek debt stood at an extraordinary 200 percent of GDP. IMF and European officials persuaded themselves that the latest concessions would help lower Greece's debt ratio to 124 percent of GDP by 2020. In a, by now, distressing pattern, the officials trotted out wildly optimistic forecasts of Greek economic recovery to justify driblets of debt relief.

In typical fashion, Merkel gained time. She would not need to return to the Bundestag for more money, and there was always a chance that Greece would magically recover. But by early 2013, it was clear that the deal from just a few months earlier had not worked and that Greece needed more debt forgiveness and additional funding. Greece had thus far repaid almost none of the nearly €300 billion in loans that it had received from European governments and the IMF since 2010. To escape from its morass, Greece needed a massive debt write-down. Until that happened, large numbers of Greeks would suffer more pain and their country would continue to be politically humiliated. The creditors, who gave priority to their short-term domestic political considerations, would see less of their money back the longer the Greek economy continued to suffer.

ITALIANS TURN AWAY FROM EUROPE

As in Greece, prolonged economic stress was having a profound impact on Italian politics. By mid-2011, the Italian economy was edging into a debt-deflation cycle. House prices were falling, the government's debt burden was rising faster than forecast, and banks were facing ever-increasing stress.

Italian Prime Minister Berlusconi ignored the August 2011 Trichet-Draghi letter, which had attempted to dictate economic policies that Italy needed to follow. In mid-October, Merkel called Italy's President Giorgio Napolitano. Although the president's job was largely ceremonial, Merkel expressed the hope that he would use his authority to promote reform in Italy.[194] Many interpreted that phone call as an attempt by Merkel to get Napolitano to dismiss Berlusconi; both Merkel and Napolitano denied that charge.

What is true, however, is that on November 8, Berlusconi lost his parliamentary majority, and four days later, Napolitano used the opportunity to appoint Mario Monti, an unelected economist, as Italy's prime minister. Monti, a former European commissioner, was "revered in Brussels."[195] Thus, nearly simultaneously in November 2011, two "Eurocrats" with no domestic democratic mandate—Papademos in Greece and Monti in Italy—became prime ministers of their countries.

Even more so than in Papademos's case, the exercise of raw power to appoint a Eurocrat as Italian prime minister sent an uneasy cheer through Europe. One business leader spoke for many when he said, "What we need, in effect, is a suspension of democracy for 18 to 24 months so difficult decisions can be made."[196] A *Financial Times* editorial acknowledged that "appointing an unelected technocrat is less than ideal," but the action, it said, was justified, because "when the system is dysfunctional, emergency solutions are required."[197] In an editorial entitled "One woman to rule them all," the *Economist* unabashedly applauded Merkel for helping "get rid of clowns like Italy's Silvio Berlusconi."[198]

The "true Europeans" had a more intellectual justification for the removal of elected prime ministers. Sylvie Goulard, a French member of the European Parliament, said concepts of national sovereignty had become quaint. "We are completely interdependent, especially in the euro zone," she said. "We are no longer sovereign in the sense that many people think." It was only right, she believed, that "non-partisan" technocrats, unhampered by domestic political restraints, should push forward essential fiscal austerity and structural reforms.[199]

Draghi would later elaborate on the philosophical basis for direct European intervention in the affairs of member nations. He asserted that sovereign rights belonged not to governments but to the country's citizens. Hence, if the sovereign failed to deliver "essential services that people expect from [their] government," that sovereign "would be a sovereign only in name."[200] In this reading, Berlusconi was not serving the best interests of Italian citizens. Instead, he was violating the people's sovereignty. Senior European leaders and the cheering media believed it was only proper for European technocrats to step in.

In 2012, with Monti as prime minister, the Italian economy contracted by 2.5 percent. The unemployment rate jumped to 11 percent, with the pain most acutely felt by young Italians. While Italy labored under the ECB's tight monetary policy, Monti pushed structural reforms. His major achievement was a politically controversial pension reform, which raised the minimum age at which Italians would be eligible to start receiving pensions.

In December, Berlusconi withdrew parliamentary support for the Monti-led government, Monti stepped down, and elections were scheduled for February 24–25, 2013. The election campaign quickly turned into a contest between the "Europeans" and the large numbers of Italians who were angry at their worsening economic condition and the imposition of austerity by a prime minister with ties to Brussels.

Monti himself jumped into the electoral fray. And as a candidate seeking a political mandate, he continued to believe that the admiration he enjoyed in Europe was an electoral asset at home. During the campaign, he traveled to Brussels and Berlin, claiming that he would reform Europe and reinvent the Italian economy at the same time.[201] Monti was not the only one with this mindset. As secretary of the left-leaning Partito Democratico (the Democratic Party), Pier Luigi Bersani was the man considered most likely to be Italy's next prime minister. Bersani also flaunted his European links. He promised to continue with Monti's domestic reform agenda while working to build a "United States of Europe."[202] Monti and Bersani remained wedded to the idea that a European constraint on Italian politicians—perhaps a softer European constraint than the one applied recently—was essential to guide Italy's economy and people into the future.

Arrayed against Monti and Bersani were the anti-Europe forces. The perennial Berlusconi, who led the center-right People of Freedom party, stoked the public's resentment against Merkel. He asked at one of his rallies: "Who got us into this recessionary spiral? Do you want a government that is subject to the diktats of (German Chancellor Angela) Merkel?" "Nooooo," his charged supporters replied.[203]

Meanwhile, comedian and blogger Beppe Grillo emerged as the dramatic new player on the scene.[204] His Five Star Movement drew younger Italians who faced a bleak future. They were attracted to Grillo's promise to root out corruption in Italian politics, his emphasis on environmental protection, and his promise of greater voice in public affairs through direct democracy.[205] Italy's young joined Grillo's demand for a referendum on whether Italy should stay in the eurozone or leave.

Grillo also gained ground because he shamed Bersani's Democratic Party for its problematic association with the financially fragile and scandal-ridden bank Monte dei Paschi di Siena (MPS). When Grillo said that MPS had become a money machine for the Democratic Party, he struck a chord with many Italians. On this matter, too, Monti was on the wrong side. Financial support from his government had helped MPS stay afloat. Monti had aided MPS with the indefensible claim that Italian banks were the "most solid in the world."[206]

The election held on February 24–25, 2013, sent a ringing anti-Europe message. Grillo and Berlusconi succeeded with their tirades against Europe. Grillo's Five Star Movement gained 25 percent of all votes, and together the two anti-Europe parties won more than half the popular vote. Monti's Civic Choice party and its coalition partner received 10 percent of the votes. Italy's leading daily newspaper, *Corriere della Sera*, wrote that the enthusiasm of European leaders for Monti had not helped him; "rather, it had a negative effect."[207] The Democratic Party did emerge as the single-largest party, but it received only 29 percent of the vote, down from 38 percent in the 2008 election.

Like the Greeks, Italians had also largely withdrawn their support from pro-European parties. Italians were rejecting the "permissive consensus" for European policies and decisions; they wanted a greater say in their country's policy decisions.

German leaders responded impatiently. Foreign Minister Guido Westerwelle insisted that no matter how the Italian public had voted, "politicians in Rome know that Italy still needs a policy of reform, a policy of (budgetary) consolidation." Schäuble echoed those words. German leaders believed they had the right, even an obligation, to dictate policies to other member states. The German press chimed in; having long taunted the Greeks, they now turned on the Italians. One headline asked, "Against Merkel—but for what?" Another exclaimed, "Poor Italy!" The *Bild* wondered, "Will these Italian political clowns destroy the euro?" And, adopting tabloid language, Peer Steinbrück—Schäuble's predecessor as finance minister and leader of the pro-European Social Democrats—said, "I am downright appalled that two clowns won."[208]

In Italy, a post-election political deadlock played out as parties explored various coalitional arrangements.[209] After two months of political wrangling, the Democratic Party's Enrico Letta became prime minister in late April, heading a "grand coalition" of left- and right-leaning parties. President Napolitano, who had himself just been reelected, said that this was "the only government possible" and asked politicians to work quickly and in a spirit of intense cooperation.[210] The economy stayed in recession, and the unemployment rate continued to rise. A new player entered the arena of Italian political sniping. Matteo Renzi, mayor of Florence and aspirant to the leadership of the Democratic Party, accused the fragile Letta government of paralysis, of moving in small steps instead of attempting radical reform.[211]

BREXIT RUMBLINGS

British leaders had always been wary of overreach by European institutions into the domestic policy decision process.[212] The British government had consciously chosen to stay out of the eurozone. Prime Minister Margaret Thatcher had opposed the single currency with all her political energy.[213]

Her successor, John Major, continued that opposition, although in less confrontational style. Tony Blair, Major's successor, was sympathetic to the broader goal of European integration but hedged his position on the single currency.[214] Blair's Chancellor of the Exchequer, Gordon Brown, conducted two rounds of economic assessments on the likely benefits and costs of the single currency, the first in 1997 and another in 2003.[215] On both occasions, Brown decided that the case for joining the eurozone was not "clear and unambiguous." Brown's position, in effect, was, "The euro might eventually be a good idea, but not quite yet."[216]

Hence, Blair's decision to stay out of the eurozone was ultimately a political one. He recognized that the British public strongly opposed the idea and in a referendum would overwhelmingly reject joining the eurozone. The tradition of British euro-skepticism continued. In 2005, Blair also held back from calling a referendum on the European Constitutional Treaty, again knowing that he would lose political capital, since euro skeptics would align themselves to defeat a British endorsement of the treaty.

In 2011, as the euro crisis deepened, British politicians grew concerned that the actions taken by the eurozone's leadership would constrain the conduct of British economic policy. A specific concern was that plans for more intrusive economic surveillance of eurozone member states would extend to—or unwittingly handicap—non-eurozone countries. Prime Minister David Cameron demanded "repatriation of powers" from Brussels back to London. This repatriation demand, Cameron hoped, would pacify euro-skeptical forces among his own Conservative Party members, some of whom were threatening to canvass for a referendum on whether Britain should stay in the EU. Cameron also faced an electoral challenge from the UK Independence Party (UKIP), which was based almost entirely on the proposition that Britain needed to break away from the EU. The rumblings of a British exit (Brexit) from the EU began.

Britain's euro skeptics drew their political sustenance from a growing number of citizens who, beleaguered by the loss of good jobs over the past generation, were placing blame for their plight on the EU. Although nationalist and xenophobic forces often hijacked the public debate on Britain's relationship with the EU, historian Richard Tombs has pointed out that the British public's anxieties about Europe were not "the obsession of an eccentric minority."[217] "Eurobarometer" polls showed that more than half of all Britons believed their country would have a better future outside of the EU than inside it.[218] Cameron, trying to ease unbearable pressure from within his own party—and also to undercut the UKIP—began leaning toward a referendum to decide whether Britain would continue in the EU. Britain seemed on course to recast its always-uneasy relationship with Europe.[219]

European leaders reacted dismissively to Britain's call for repatriation of powers. François Hollande, elected French president in May 2012, was especially brusque. Speaking just after the leaders' summit in Brussels in early December, Hollande declared that Europe was not "à la carte." European rules and bureaucracy, he emphasized, balanced the interests of various member countries and that therefore repatriation of select powers was not possible. A country could not demand authority back from Brussels, Hollande said, adding dramatically, "Europe is for life."[220] In even more memorable words, Italian Prime Minister Monti said, "The EU does not need unwilling Europeans. We desperately need willing Europeans."[221]

No one, however, quite knew what it meant to be a willing European. Even Merkel was not a willing European.

What Did It Mean to Be a Pro-European in 2013?

In late 2009, the goal for policymakers had been to revive growth and reduce government debt burdens. Instead, starting in mid-2011, for more than two years, GDP had contracted in large parts of the eurozone, and debt levels had risen rapidly. The economic wounds inflicted by unrelenting fiscal austerity and zeal for price stability were leaving economic scars. Left untreated, lost growth and low inflation were the connective tissues forming around these scars. They would hobble eurozone states for a long time.

A small group of technocrats and political leaders was running Europe, with Merkel making the key decisions on the eurozone's crisis management and policy priorities. The other consequential decision makers, the ECB's Trichet and Draghi, were accountable to no one. Large numbers of European citizens had fallen into despair, and people of different nations were drawing antagonistic dividing lines between one another. Was this the same Europe that was recently honored by the Nobel Committee for advancement of democracy and reconciliation among nations?[222]

What did it mean to be a European in 2013? Was there a path to a pro-European future? German President Joachim Gauck asked these questions.

Gauck was a former East German pastor, a man admired as a moral authority and a champion of human rights. Churchmen such as he, Merkel said, had "helped bring about East Germany's peaceful revolution."[223] As Germany's president, Gauck spoke passionately for the "European idea." In a much-anticipated speech on February 22, 2013, he said Europe was in the midst of an economic and political crisis:

> Attractive though Europe is, the European Union leaves too many people feeling powerless and without a voice. . . . When I see all the signs of people's impatience, exhaustion and frustration, when I hear about polls showing a populace unsure about pursuing "more" Europe, it seems to me that we are pausing on a new threshold—unsure whether we should really stride out on the onward journey. There is more to this crisis than its economic dimension. It is also a crisis of confidence in Europe as a political project. This is not just a struggle for our currency; we are struggling with an internal quandary too."

The crisis, Gauck said, had undercut Europe's lofty founding principles of peace, freedom, democracy, rule of law, equality, human rights, and solidarity. Brussels had become a distant rule-making machine, and a self-confident, dominant Germany seemed willing to "humiliate its partners." This unfortunate outcome, he said, had one simple cause: Europe had shockingly been "reduced to four letters—euro." While people in some member states "are afraid they are the ones footing the bill in this crisis," in others "there is growing fear of facing ever harsher austerity and falling into poverty." To the "ordinary people of Europe," Gauck lamented, Europe "no longer seems fair."

No senior European leader spoke like that in public. While Gauck emphasized that he remained decidedly pro-Europe, his message was that the euro had sown conflict and distrust and had thus led Europe astray from its true values. Instead of bringing Europe together, the euro had widened the divide across the peoples and nations of Europe.

Gauck said that it was time to pause and reflect. What exactly did the call for "more Europe" mean, and what did it have to offer European citizens? To him, it was clear that Europe could not continue on its current path. A centralized, hierarchical, Germany-dominated control system to manage the euro created power relationships in which some countries were shockingly more equal than others. The euro was steering Europe away from its "timeless canon of values," especially democracy and equality. And while the spirit of solidarity continued to be cynically invoked, the insistent message was that each member state must rely primarily on its own resources.

Gauck said Europe had to regain its true identity based on its founding values. For him, the first step was to break away from an identification of Europe with Brussels and Frankfurt and, instead, create a common "public space," rather like the *agora* of ancient Greece, "a place for public discussion where efforts focused on creating a well-ordered society."[224]

Few took the time to pause and reflect on Gauck's words. He had not spelled out his idealistic alternative, and certainly, his idealism was at odds with the urgency of dealing with the financial crisis. But to those who heard Gauck, his message was unsettling. Columbia University's Mark Mazower wrote that Gauck had presented Europe a stark choice: "give up the euro; or keep it and see the political crisis spin out of control."[225]

Mazower said it dramatically, but he accurately reflected Gauck's more measured words. Europeans had strayed far from their idealistic vision. The euro was sold as a unifying force. That was never a realistic prospect. To the contrary, as many had predicted, the euro caused economic divergence across member countries. Then, amid a fast-paced financial crisis, an unaccountable governance system committed policy errors that persisted and amplified the economic damage, especially in member countries already falling behind.

The financial crisis, in turn, unleashed slow-moving but powerfully divisive political forces. When Mario Monti evocatively criticized the "unwilling European," he was referring, of course, to the perennially irritating British. But, from the crucible of the financial crisis in 2011 and 2012, unwilling Europeans had emerged through much of the euro area. If Europe needed more German funds, then Merkel was also an unwilling European. The Greeks, in the middle of an economic depression were not willing to sign on to a politically unequal relationship. And, as Monti realized quickly enough, Italians, suffering from their own multiple economic and social ailments were turning their backs on Europe. The years 2011 to 2013 marked a radical change in European politics. As before, European leaders asserted their national interests. However for the first time, European citizens, speaking through their national political and electoral processes, said they were weary of Europe.

As 2013 ended, an economic recovery seemed to finally be in sight. Would this recovery last? And would Europe's leaders begin anew the task of building a Europe that did not just bring them together around conference tables but created a greater sense of shared values and common destiny among all its citizens? Or, failing to heed Gauck's warning, would the leaders continue as if nothing had changed while pernicious political divisions continued to widen?

| The ECB Hesitates, the Italian
Fault Line Deepens, 2014–2017

I N EARLY 2014, as the intense years of the economic crisis came to an end, the eurozone entered a new phase, one in which the legacies of the crisis began preying on its long-term weaknesses. The decline in investment during the crisis years reduced the already low growth potential of many eurozone members. The low inflation since mid-2013 could cause growth prospects to worsen. Financial vulnerabilities dogged the large financial sectors: several banks were short of capital to withstand new shocks. And large government debt burdens had become larger in many countries. For many European citizens, standards of living were falling, and the future for them and their children looked uncertain, even gloomy. Growing numbers of citizens were enticed into looking for answers to their problems outside the political mainstream. And, as their trust in eurozone institutions fell, they and their governments shifted into increasingly nationalist positions. The crisis was passing, but the long-term problems had become daunting.

These crisis legacies worked their spell most dangerously in Italy, a country that had no business being in the eurozone. By the early 1990s, Italian economic growth had slowed, the unemployment rate was grinding up toward 10 percent, and the government was running astonishingly large fiscal deficits of around 10 percent of GDP and thereby racking up debt at an alarming pace. Generations of Italian leaders and policymakers—notable among them Mario Draghi, former Banca d'Italia president and now ECB president—had placed their faith in the single currency as Italy's magical path to economic prosperity.[1] They had believed that the single currency would act as Italy's *vincolo esterno*, an external constraint or anchor.

The *vincolo esterno* proposition said that once the escape valve of an ever-depreciating lira was snatched away, Italy's political leaders would be compelled to subdue their self-serving and shortsighted instincts; they would have no option but to enforce sound fiscal and structural policies and thereby secure a better future for Italians.

But first there was the matter of being admitted to the eurozone. Few outside of Italy believed that Italy would qualify for entry in 1999 along with the inaugural batch of members. Its economy was losing international competitiveness and the government's debt rose alarmingly in the early 1990s to more than 120 percent of GDP. Thus, when the numbers showed a surprising improvement in the Italian government's finances in the second half of the 1990s, most observers were intensely skeptical. Almost no one believed that the Italian political system could sustain whatever limited progress the government had made. However, German Chancellor Helmut Kohl, the one person who mattered, insisted that Italy be in at the start. "Not without Italy, please," he said.[2]

After the launch of the euro, the happy *vincolo esterno* proposition failed to work its magic. Italy's fractious political system remained unable to deal with the country's endemic problems. The Italian economy suffered from near-zero productivity growth, the banks eked out meagre profits, and the government's high debt burden rose. The crisis struck ferociously at all of Italy's pre-euro economic and financial fragilities. At the height of the crisis between mid-2011 and mid-2012, a financial collapse (too) often seemed imminent.

In early 2014, where the story of this chapter starts, the worst of the crisis was over, but the destruction left behind was a sight to behold. From the start of the crisis in 2007, per capita (average) Italian incomes had dropped sharply (figure 8.1). As a benchmark, in 2007, the average German had a 10 percent higher income than the average Italian; in 2014, that gap had increased to more than 30 percent. While the 2011–2012 financial crisis was staved off, the Italian economy fell into a near-perpetual recession, starting in the last quarter of 2011 and continuing for nine quarters in a row to the end of 2013. By early 2014, Italy's unemployment rate was 12.7 percent, near its postwar high. Three-fifths of the unemployed had been out of work for over a year.

And that destruction left a legacy. Chronically high unemployment levels, especially among young Italians, the sharp decline in investment, and the slide into low inflation all created further impediments to future growth. These crisis-induced liabilities came on top of the handicaps of a rapidly aging population and a business sector that had lost its vitality decades earlier.

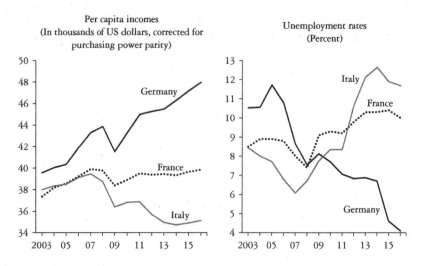

Per capita incomes
(In thousands of US dollars, corrected for
purchasing power parity)

Unemployment rates
(Percent)

FIGURE 8.1. The great divergence in euro-area incomes and employment.
Source: The Conference Board, "Total Economy Database (Adjusted Version)," http://www.conference-board.org/data/economydatabase/; IMF, World Economic Outlook Database, https://www.imf.org/external/pubs/ft/weo/2017/01/weodata/index.aspx.

The crisis also left behind financial vulnerabilities. As people's standards of living had fallen, borrowers had defaulted in increasing numbers on Italian banks. Hence, the banks were teetering. The government's debt burden had risen to 130 percent of GDP, higher than that in all eurozone countries except Greece.

Other than the quarantined Greece, Italy was the eurozone's most troubled member state—and Italy was large. It was the eurozone's third-largest economy, following Germany and France. At the end of 2013, Italian banks held assets worth around €5.6 trillion, compared with around €8.2 trillion in Germany and just over €9 trillion in France. The Italian government's debt, at €2 trillion, was about the same size as the debt owed by the French and German governments. The Italian government's debt was larger than the combined government debt of Spain, Portugal, Greece, and Ireland, the four countries that had needed financial bailouts.

The Greek crisis had been hard enough to deal with. For seven years, eurozone leaders had peered anxiously over every economic, legal, and political cliff edge in their efforts to rein in Greece's crisis. Grexit—a Greek exit from the eurozone—had seemed a real possibility on multiple occasions, but each time, German Chancellor Angela Merkel had pulled Greece back, fearing that if a country left the eurozone, the economic and political consequences could be fearsome. If a Grexit was fearsome, what might an Italexit look like?

Italy's stock of government debt was seven times larger and its economy was nearly nine times larger than Greece's. Italian banks held assets ten times larger than those of Greek banks. If Italy were to have a major economic and financial crisis, credit-rating agencies would almost certainly lower Germany's rating raising its costs of borrowing. The European bailout fund, the ESM—which had replaced the EFSF—would possibly not have sufficient funds to bail Italy out. The ECB would be required to deploy its politically controversial safety net, OMTs. The mere threat of "Italexit" could create incalculable chaos.

Although such concerns were receding because the sense of financial emergency had faded, Italy remained trapped, as former Prime Minister Mario Monti evocatively noted, in an "equally dangerous" emergency of low growth.[3] Monti was quite right to highlight low growth as an "emergency," for that, fundamentally, was Italy's problem when all the drama was stripped off. If growth remained low, rising debt burdens—even at low interest rates—would become steadily unbearable. Defaults on debts due to banks would increase, and the banks themselves would be unable to repay their creditors.

Low growth was also the cause of rising social stress levels. High and rising youth unemployment was leaving a generation behind. Moreover, the Italian education system was failing to deliver needed skills to compete with other advanced nations, and it was doing especially little to help the underprivileged climb the economic and social ladders.[4] Those on the lower rungs tended to remain stuck there, with the grim implication that large numbers of unemployed youth would transmit their distressingly low stations in life to their children.

Mirroring these unforgiving economic and social trends, the Five Star Movement, led by Giuseppe "Beppe" Grillo, had become a significant anti-establishment political force, channeling especially the frustrations of Italian youth. Grillo had tapped into the Italian public's deepening anti-European sentiment. During the February 2013 election campaign, Grillo had even speculated about Italy leaving the eurozone. His Five Star Movement had made big electoral strides.

Another Italian financial and political crisis would simultaneously add to the misery of its citizens and send shock waves through European and global financial systems. European politics could quickly get ugly. The media in Italy and Germany already had traded bitter insults in 2012 and 2013 when it seemed to many Germans that they might be called on to bail out the irresponsible Italian "clowns." Especially if a new crisis seriously undermined

Germany's financial position, the sense of grievance between two of the euro-zone's largest nations could prevent cooperation on sensible solutions.

Thus, at the threshold of 2014, the policy task was to place Italy on a growth path, one that would slowly reduce the country's financial and social stresses. Fiscal stimulus seemed unthinkable because of the fear that it would increase Italy's already large debt burden. Such summary rejection of fiscal stimulus was unfortunate. Higher growth induced by a modest stimulus would have slowed the rise in indebtedness more successfully than the ongoing austerity. In fact, because austerity sucked demand out from the economy, it inhibited growth. And low growth kept the government's debt burden—the debt-to-GDP ratio—high. Low growth also made it harder for businesses and households to repay their debts, which raised the financial pressures on banks.

With or without fiscal stimulus, Italy desperately needed help from mon-etary policy. True, Draghi's "whatever it takes" announcement in late July 2012, followed by the OMT announcement in August, had caused "nominal" interest rates on 10-year maturity Italian and Spanish government bonds to fall to around 4 percent by the end of 2013. But what matters for economic activity is the "real" interest rate—the nominal rate minus the expected rate of inflation. Just as a lower nominal rate reduces the debt-repayment burden, higher inflation makes it easier to repay old debts. Just as a lower nominal rate encourages spending, higher inflation creates an incentive to spend now rather than wait until later.

The immediate problem for Italy, as discussed in chapter 7, was that consumer price inflation was trending down; real estate prices were, in fact, declining. As a result, the Italian real interest rate was 3 percent or even higher, depending on the borrower. For an economy barely beginning to grow again, that real interest rate was too high. It was a hindrance to the revival of growth.

Italy's problem was the direct result of its being in the eurozone. In late 2013, when the Italian real interest rate was around 3 percent, the French real interest rate was around 1.5 percent, and the German close to 0.5 percent.[5] Germans had the double benefit of lower nominal rates and higher inflation rates. Once again, we were seeing reaffirmation of the principle that, within Europe's incomplete monetary union, divergent economies would diverge even more. The weaker the economy was, the tougher it was to recover from a crisis while operating under a single monetary policy and fiscal auster-ity. Quite simply, the weaker the eurozone economy, the higher the nominal interest rate for domestic borrowers and the lower the inflation rate.

The ECB's monetary policy had, for long, been too tight for Italy (and other southern countries). While the FED and the BOE had long since introduced bond-buying, QE programs to bring down long-term interest rates, the ECB had held off from injecting such stimulus. Because of the ECB's tight monetary policy, inflation rates in the eurozone had fallen, and Italy faced the risk of declining prices.

Moreover, reflecting the fact that the ECB's monetary policy was continuously much tighter than the Fed's policy, the euro had remained strong. At the end of 2013, the euro was worth $1.35, around the same value it had at the start of the global crisis in July 2007. The euro should have been much weaker by now, as during the period from July 2007 to December 2013 the eurozone economy had considerably underperformed the US economy. While Germany was doing fine even at the elevated exchange rate, the euro was unbearably strong for Italy. For Italy to grow its exports, the euro's exchange value needed to be close to $1.00.

There was no easy way for eurozone monetary policy to reconcile the divergent interests of strong and weak member states. For Italy to regain reasonable growth momentum, its real interest rate needed to fall from 3 percent to nearly zero, and the euro needed to depreciate substantially. Achieving those objectives would require extraordinary monetary easing, which the Germans, with their more rapid growth and higher inflation, would consider highly inappropriate. Political divisions among member states—reflected in the Governing Council of the ECB—made it much harder to lean in favor of the weaker countries, even if temporarily, to jump-start their growth.

If Italy had stayed out of the eurozone, its central bank, the Banca d'Italia, would have lowered interest rates more rapidly than the ECB did, which would have pushed international financial investors to seek higher returns elsewhere, and the lira's value would have declined. Italian exports and GDP would have received a short-term boost. To be sure, lower interest rates and a cheaper lira would not have solved Italy's serious long-term problems; nevertheless, they would have prevented the Italian economy from falling into an ever-deeper economic and financial hole.

This, then, was the policy dilemma in early 2014. No one could be certain that easier ECB policy would actually pull Italy out of its hole. On the other hand, not doing anything kept alive the risk that Italy could stumble into a financial abyss. A race was on. Perhaps the Italians would reveal a hidden reserve to overcome fiscal austerity and tight monetary policy. If not, would the ECB still hesitate to aggressively ease monetary policy even while knowing that continued economic and political dysfunction along the Italian fault line could send tremors through the rest of the eurozone?

Italy Runs Out of Options

Japan's "lost decade" offers a cautionary tale for Italy. The Japanese financial crisis started in 1990 with a crash in property and stock prices, which triggered a banking crisis. That crisis turned into a lost decade, because Japanese authorities failed to squash it pro-actively. By procrastinating, they allowed financial and economic pathologies to settle in. Perhaps of greatest long-term consequence, the Japanese central bank, the BOJ, repeatedly delayed injecting monetary stimulus and allowed the economy to fall into a price-deflationary trap.

As is always the case, the Japanese deflationary trap worked insidiously. People began to anticipate that prices would increase only slowly or might even start declining, which created an incentive to postpone purchases. Demand and growth therefore remained weak and, exactly as people had feared, prices increased only slowly or actually fell. In this trap, growth and inflation remained persistently low. The longer low-inflation expectations continued, the harder it was for the BOJ to change those expectations. Japanese authorities made matters worse during much of the 1990s by allowing their banks to continue to operate without adequate capital, which further held back resumption of sustained, healthy growth.

In addition to these policy errors, Japan's aging population reinforced the growth slowdown and deflation. The number of people older than sixty-five increased, while the working-age population—those between twenty and sixty-five—stagnated and then slowly declined. The steady shift to an older population reduced consumption and investment demand, which pushed growth and inflation rates further down.

Seen from an Italian perspective, Japan's lost decade was actually an outcome to be envied (figure 8.2). Despite its demographic drag and self-inflicted policy wounds, Japan was able to grow its economy over brief periods. Japan had one great advantage that had prevented the lost decade from turning into outright disaster. A highly educated population and huge investments in R&D kept Japan's "total factor productivity"—the productivity of the bundle of capital and labor inputs—rising at a respectable rate of 1 percent a year. By using machines and workers more efficiently, Japanese firms partly overcame their demographic and policy impediments.

Italy's crisis ran much deeper than Japan's. Italy had all the disadvantages that Japan had and more. Although not as rapidly as Japan's, Italy's population was also aging; the country's working-age population had flattened out. As in Japan, ECB monetary policy had provided little support, causing a

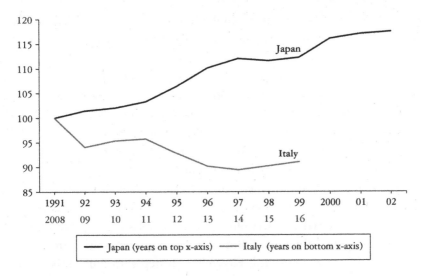

FIGURE 8.2. Italy seen in the mirror of Japan's lost decade.
(Per capita GDP, corrected for purchasing power parity, Japan 1991 = 100, Italy 2008 = 100)
Source: The Conference Board "Total Economy Database (Adjusted Version)," http://www.conference-board.org/data/economydatabase/.

deflationary mentality to set in, and Italy's banks were in increasing trouble as borrowers delayed repayment or defaulted.

Italy had one overarching, debilitating problem: Italian productivity was declining. The efficiency with which Italian businesses were using their machines and workers was falling. Italy's workforce was much less educated than the Japanese workforce, and the Italian R&D rate—at 1.3 percent of GDP—was one-third the Japanese rate. The consequences were predictable.

The once-vibrant industrial corridors of central and northern Italy had become pale shadows of their former selves. Until the early 1980s, Italian electronics pioneer Olivetti had employed fifty thousand people in the town of Ivrea, near Turin.[6] Some thought of Ivrea as "a European Silicon Valley," and Olivetti's workers enjoyed "generous salaries and plush corporate recreational facilities." But by 2014, Olivetti was reduced to "a small machinery company," and its former factories, until a few decades ago considered jewels of Italy's "industrial architecture," had been converted into museums. Olivetti's workers were nearly all gone, and the company's tennis courts lay abandoned. Massimo Benedetto, who had worked at Olivetti's Ivrea facility for thirty years, recalled, "Gradually at first and then suddenly, everything fell apart." In 2014, Ivrea's main employers were a state-run health service and two call centers, which together employed just 3,100 people. The town had little work for its thirty year olds, and many of them lived on their parents' pensions.

Italy's home-appliance producers, renowned until as recently as the 1990s, had been unable to withstand the mounting low-wage competition from Asia and Eastern Europe. Since the launch of the euro in 1999, Italian production of washing machines had fallen by more than 50 percent, while Chinese production soared.[7] Annual refrigerator production had plummeted from ten million in 2001 to two million in 2013.[8]

Iconic Italian home-appliance manufacturer Zanussi, once celebrated for its flair in industrial design, had been unable to survive on its own. In the mid-1980s, Sweden's Electrolux acquired Zanussi, and the arrangement worked until the early 2000s.[9] But as lower-wage competition from China and Eastern Europe intensified, Electrolux, in step with Italy's other home-appliance producers, at first cut back the number of employees and was by 2013 beginning to slash wages.[10] A spokesperson for the company explained that Italian workers earned €24 an hour, while equally skilled Polish workers received only €7 an hour.[11]

Italian industry was in no man's land. Italian businesses did not do enough R&D to compete with advanced global producers, and Italian wages were too high for its companies to compete with sophisticated producers in low-wage locations. Some upscale products with the label "Made in Italy" did flourish; in 2015, of the world's top one hundred "luxury goods" companies, twenty-six were from Italy.[12] However, the high-end luxury goods segment was too small to sustain Italian growth and employment.

University of Chicago economist Luigi Zingales was among the most passionate critics of Italian business management practices and political disorder. Zingales gained academic acclaim for research papers on ways to harness the power of finance to improve people's lives. He coauthored with another distinguished University of Chicago economist Raghuram Rajan an important book, *Saving Capitalism from the Capitalists*.[13] As an Italian, Zingales was fiercely impatient with leaders and officials who, he believed, were unaware that a deep rot had set into the Italian economic system and that this system now spawned grave risks.

In Italy, cronyism trumped merit, Zingales wrote in a 2014 research paper with University of California Los Angeles economist Bruno Pellegrino.[14] Within too many Italian companies, employees earned greater rewards by demonstrating "loyalty" than by doing their jobs well. Company managers, disrespectful of employees' merit and lacking long-term vision, typically tried to get ahead by trading favors with government officials. Pellegrino and Zingales concluded that the culture of cronyism inside companies and in Italian public life discouraged investment in productivity-enhancing technology.

Italy was in a low-growth trap. In comparison with other industrial nations, a relatively small share of Italy's population completed a college education. In 2014, 18 percent of Italians between the ages of twenty-five and sixty-four had finished college; at the high end, the ratio in Sweden was 40 percent.[15] The Italian population's lag in academic achievement had become a severe handicap because education was increasingly essential to benefit from technological advances.[16] Hence, from the early 1980s onward, Italy had been losing ground in the rapidly growing high-technology industries. Sweden, for example, had turned its education advantage into progress in high-end manufacturing and biotechnology-related ventures. As a consequence, since the early 1980s, Swedish per capita income, even though starting from a higher level and therefore with less room to increase further, had grown significantly faster than Italian per capita income.[17]

Making matters worse, bleak economic prospects at home encouraged Italians with college degrees—especially those younger than thirty-five—to seek work abroad (figure 8.3). As they left, Italy's population became, on average, older and less educated. Zingales explained the distressing reason why young, educated Italians were leaving. In an interview with Reuters, he said that many young Italians decided that they could not change the dysfunctional political system and so there was no point in staying at home; with

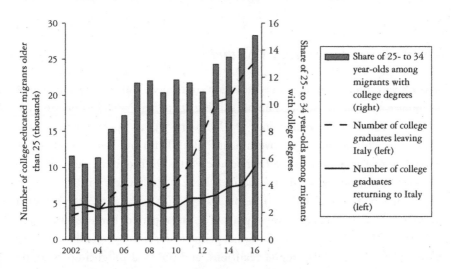

FIGURE 8.3. Young college-educated Italians leave Italy in growing numbers.
Source: Italian National Institute of Statistics.

their departure—and since even those who stayed often had their eyes set elsewhere—the "pressure of protest" was fizzling out, making it increasingly hard to reverse the entrenched cronyism.[18]

This was Italy's true dilemma. Because economic growth had slowed, some of the most qualified were leaving, and because the most qualified were leaving, Italy continued to grow very slowly. Because Italian companies did little R&D, they could not move up the technology ladder, and because they did not move up the technology ladder, the companies were unable to generate growth impulses and so were unable to employ and retain the country's best talent.

Thus, in early 2014, Italy was not dealing merely with the aftermath of a frightening financial crisis. Italy was dealing with its postwar political and economic history. When in the 1990s, Europeans debated whether Italy should join the single currency area, they focused on the dry numbers, deficits and debts. But, as described in chapter 2, a political malaise had begun to form even during the 1950s and 1960s, the decades of the Italian "economic miracle." Political corruption and a fragmented political party structure continued. And, as the postwar reconstruction momentum ran out, it proved impossible to generate a new dynamism. The political and economic traps kept forming. In the hope of anchoring Italy to the euro, Italian and other European leaders created the risk that Italy could bring down the entire edifice.

The reality was simple. A continuation of low growth created grave dangers for the country's large and fragile banking system. If the banks cracked, the shockwaves could quickly overwhelm the government's shaky finances.

Matteo Renzi as Italy's Savior

As Italy's economic and financial attrition continued, Matteo Renzi, mayor of Florence since 2009, stepped up his sniping at Italian Prime Minister Enrico Letta, accusing him of inaction. On February 13, 2014, Renzi raised the stakes by calling for a new government.[19] Both Letta and Renzi belonged to the Partito Democratico, the Democratic Party. On the fourteenth, the party's leadership ousted Letta and anointed Renzi as Italy's next prime minister.

Renzi had engineered an internal party coup to become Italy's fourth prime minister in less than three years. The latest pace of turnover was high, but fit the pattern. Since 1946, Italian prime ministers—plagued by corruption, personal scandals, fragile coalitions, and political infighting—had, on average, lasted around two years. This constant churn of governments had made it nearly impossible to establish policy priorities and follow through on them. Renzi's coup kept that churn going. Letta, who had barely scratched out ten months in office, despondently said to his aides as he prepared to leave, "It is true, Italy does break your heart."[20]

Born on January 11, 1975, Renzi was thirty-nine years old when he became prime minister on February 22. The young Renzi had shown himself to be a master of old-fashioned Italian political infighting. However, he portrayed himself to the world as a modernizer with an upbeat message. "Tonight we are young, so let us set the world on fire," he often exclaimed, using the words of the American pop group Fun; he ran in marathons, rode his bicycle around the city of Florence, and wore black leather jackets.[21] He denounced the Democratic Party's national leaders as "dinosaurs." On Twitter, he used the hashtag #rottamare, a colloquial phrase for junking broken cars and appliances, a not-so-thinly-veiled boast that he would consign to the scrap-heap Italy's aging and corrupt politicians.[22]

Renzi's domestic critics, outraged by his narcissistic power grab, accused him of being "all style and no substance."[23] They alleged that as mayor of Florence, he had inflated his achievements. Many Florentines said that he was quick to make promises but usually failed to deliver; he focused on "communication rather than content."[24] While some admired him for his "speed and decisiveness," a Democratic Party city councilor said of Renzi that he "makes a nice show at first and then wilts." Another councilor, responsible for the city's bookkeeping, said that Renzi "allotted much more time for his Facebook updates than he did for serious discussions of the city's budget."[25]

But with Italy in a never-ending slide and little else to latch on to, international observers were seduced by Renzi's words, and they were dazzled by his youth and expressions of impatience. They hoped he would channel the aspirations and energy of the young and lead Italy to an economic and political renaissance. One foreign commentator described Renzi as "an outsider against the establishment who projects hope of wrenching Italy out of its long decline";[26] another said that his "radical reform agenda" was the "best hope for Italy";[27] and yet another admirer said Renzi was "a rare moment of hope for Italy—and indeed for Europe."[28]

In an editorial, the *Financial Times* wrote, "The best hope lies in a new generation of politicians less tied to the old system with all its compromises and failings. This is why so much hope is invested in Matteo Renzi." The editorial singled out for praise Renzi's "Jobs Act, a 15-point proposal aimed at boosting employment by reforming Italy's labour market."[29] In another editorial some days later, the *Financial Times* said that Renzi's "wide-ranging deal" with Silvio Berlusconi, former prime minister and then a criminally convicted opposition leader, had "rekindled fresh hope for reform."[30] This time, the praise was for a proposal to reform Italy's electoral system. The existing rules allowed many small parties to win parliamentary seats, which led to fragmented and unstable governments; the proposed system would weed out most of the smaller parties and give the winning coalition a working majority. Governments with stable majorities would make the hard decisions needed to reverse Italy's economic decline.

Renzi promised that within one hundred days, with benchmarks assigned for every month until then, he would establish a set of initiatives to overhaul Italy. These initiatives would deliver a leaner and nimbler Italian government, a justice system that worked more rapidly for all, and wide-ranging reforms to revive Italy's failing economy. On his first day in office, he tweeted, "The battle against bureaucracy is the mother of all battles," and "This is the responsibility I feel most strongly: Italy as a land of opportunity, not rentseeking."[31]

Italy's Need—and Renzi's Call—for Less Austerity

Renzi had this part right. Soon after he became prime minister in February 2014, he and his finance minister, Pier Carlo Padoan, pressed Brussels for a relaxation of the fiscal austerity rules and prodded Frankfurt to ease monetary policy. On fiscal policy, Renzi's message was simple: Europe needed to shift its focus away from "budgetary rigour" and begin addressing problems of low growth and youth unemployment. Padoan said that it was time for a "serious, non-ideological debate" on the merits of austerity.[32]

The Italian demands were modest. Italy was in the midst of an "exceptional" economic slowdown, and Renzi and Padoan were asking for an extra year to reach the agreed budget targets.[33] To the European Commission, Padoan wrote that Italy would "deviate temporarily from the budget targets." He tried to reassure them: "we are going in the same direction but at a slower speed." Renzi and Padoan said that they "respected" Europe's budget rules but the European Commission's overseers needed to interpret the rules "flexibly."[34]

For Renzi, the timing of this debate with European technocrats was politically advantageous. He was prime minister only because he was a skilled Democratic Party operative. He had no domestic political mandate. By standing up to Europe, he hoped that he himself would gain national political stature and that his Democratic Party would attract voters in the elections to the European Parliament scheduled for the end of May 2014. The strategy worked. Italians gave Renzi a surprisingly enthusiastic endorsement in the European parliamentary elections. The Democratic Party won the largest share of the Italian vote.

Renzi also gained stature on the European stage. His party's strong performance was a relief to the European establishment. Renzi's radicalism was within the mainstream while many of the new members of the European Parliament—riding on a wave of euro-skepticism—questioned the direction Europe was taking. Some new parliamentarians were openly hostile to the European project. From Italy, Beppe Grillo's Five Star Movement sent a large contingent. In France, Marine Le Pen's anti-Europe National Front received a quarter of the vote, up from 6 percent in the previous election held in 2009. Le Pen's victory was the flip side of a humiliating defeat for French President François Hollande's Socialist Party. France's claim to European leadership received another blow, and Renzi benefited.

An emboldened Renzi stepped up his insistence that the mandarins in Brussels back off from their austerity demands. He compared the European Commission to "an old boring aunt telling us what to do."[35] Now more forcefully asserting his demand for "flexibility," Renzi said that revival of growth, rather than fiscal austerity, should be the priority. The budget-deficit limit should be relaxed when countries undertake structural reforms, and the deficit limit should exclude certain investments, such as those in energy and digital technology.[36]

Hollande fell in with Renzi's message. The French vote for the European Parliament, he said, had voiced a "mistrust towards Europe." "Europe," Hollande dramatically said, "has become illegible, distant, basically incomprehensible, even for governments. This cannot go on."[37] Following Renzi, Hollande said it was time to refocus Europe away from budget deficits and toward growth and employment. The French economy had barely grown in 2012 and 2013. Hence, Hollande's promise in May 2012 to bring France's budget deficit down to 3 percent of GDP by 2013 had become unrealistic, and he had negotiated an extension to reach that target by 2015. Finance Minister Michel Sapin made clear that that too would not happen. France's economy was threatening again to swoon, and European mandarins, Sapin said, must adapt to the "exceptional situation of our Continent."[38]

Europe had had this debate before. It started in 1991, the year during which officials representing different member states negotiated the Maastricht Treaty, which then became the authorizing basis for the single currency.[39] The debate was first replayed in 1997 at the Amsterdam summit, where European leaders fought over the intent and wording of the SGP, the fiscal framework that accompanied the single currency. The

French wanted the framework to emphasize the economic growth objective; the Germans wanted the emphasis to be on austerity-based "stability." The Germans had it their way.[40] The most contentious dispute occurred in 2002–2003, when, after the American tech bubble burst and the 9/11 attacks disrupted world trade, the eurozone economy fell into recession.[41] On this occasion, as before, the terms of the debate were the same: What is the appropriate trade-off between promoting growth and ensuring low budget deficits? How much budget flexibility should there be in making greater allowance to promote growth? What role should "exceptional circumstances" play?

In 2003, the Germans advocated flexibility in interpreting the rules. The German economy was in a long-drawn recession, and German Finance Minister Hans Eichel argued the same case that Renzi and Hollande were now making: fiscal austerity is a bad idea during a recession.[42] But on all other occasions, the German economy did not need fiscal stimulus, and so German officials insisted on faithful commitment to the budget-deficit rule. This dominant German theme continued in 2014.

After Renzi and Hollande expressed their views on the need for more flexibility, Merkel weighed in. Addressing the Bundestag on June 25, she said that the SGP "allows for the necessary flexibility." The SGP, she explained, had an "excellent" balance: "on the one hand clear guard rails and limits, and on the other hand a multitude of instruments for flexibility." If countries stayed within the "guard rails," they could achieve "growth-friendly fiscal consolidation"; thus, for those who stuck to the rules, fiscal austerity would also stimulate growth. In any case, Merkel concluded, lasting growth could "only be achieved via sustainable structural reforms."[43] The evidence—that fiscal austerity and even structural reforms make matters worse during a recession—did not count.

German Finance Minister Wolfgang Schäuble spoke more directly to Renzi. "The Stability and Growth Pact," Schäuble said, "is the foundation for politico-economic cohesion in Europe." He repeated Merkel's message: "The Stability and Growth Pact provides sufficient flexibility." Indeed, precisely because growth had slowed down, it was important for the Italian government to cut its deficit, reduce its debt, and remain focused on ambitious structural reforms.[44]

Draghi echoed the German message. In fact, he went a step further. On July 9, in a lecture in memory of Italian economist Tommaso Padoa-Schioppa, Draghi said that fiscal rules were essential to discipline governments that strayed from prudent management of their finances. Reinforcing Merkel's theme, he said that European rules promoted "growth-friendly fiscal consolidation"; in other words, fiscal austerity could boost growth. Like

Merkel, Draghi emphasized the urgency of structural reforms. He added that it was time to install a centrally administered European disciplining procedure to enforce reforms in laggard member states.[45] Five weeks later, Draghi spoke at the elite central bankers' conference at Jackson Hole, Wyoming. While some heard him as implying that excessive austerity was harmful, his words remained those of the Germans: "We are operating within a set of fiscal rules—the Stability and Growth Pact—which acts as an anchor for confidence and that would be self-defeating to break." He repeated that "the existing flexibility within the rules could be used to better address the weak recovery."[46]

In August, the latest data showed that Italy had fallen back into recession in the second quarter of 2014. Many Italians had been skeptical of Renzi from the start, but they had granted him a brief political honeymoon. Six months had gone by, and the bad news had continued. Renzi's popularity fell. Even his gushing international admirers began to lose hope. The *Financial Times* wrote, "That did not last long."[47] Was there reason to think it would?

Internal Conflict Freezes ECB, Italy Edges toward Deflation

As the stalemate on flexibility in fiscal rules continued, a new pathology was settling in: wage and price deflation. Annarita Licci, a thirty-eight-year-old mother of two, had started working at Electrolux's Porcia factory in the year 2000, when Italy was still the world's largest exporter of home appliances. In early 2014, just about when Renzi became prime minister, Licci's bosses told her that they would reduce her €1,000-a-month salary by €130. Once the wage cut went through, Licci said she would not be able to afford her monthly €600 mortgage payment. "It's a matter of survival," she said.[48]

In Rome, the owner of a small women's shoe shop complained that although she offered steep discounts, she was unable to attract customers and was on the verge of liquidating her shop.[49] Throughout Italy, thousands of businesses like hers were trying to lure customers by reducing prices, but they were ending up with mounting losses and closing down.[50]

Deflation—either an outright decline in wages and prices or, slightly less severely, an inflation rate that tends to remain close to zero—is a macroeconomic scourge, because it creates the expectation of further decline in inflation (or continued low inflation), which leads businesses and households to postpone spending. The lackluster demand holds back economic recovery and increases financial stress.

For this reason, Ben Bernanke throughout his academic and central banking career was an outspoken proponent of early and forceful monetary easing to prevent deflation from settling in. In 1991, then a professor at Princeton University, Bernanke wrote a research paper with his historian colleague Harold James emphasizing that tight monetary policy under the Gold Standard had deepened price deflation during the Great Depression and, hence, had added greatly to the depth and length of the depression.[51]

In 1999, Bernanke impatiently warned the BOJ that its halfhearted attempts at monetary stimulus would be of no value. Bernanke ruthlessly concluded: "To this outsider, at least, Japanese monetary policy seems paralyzed, with a paralysis that is largely self-induced."[52] He predicted that the damage caused by the BOJ's "exceptionally poor monetary policy-making" would persist for many years; the Japanese economy would continue to operate below its potential, while the costs of supporting an aging population would keep rising.[53] In 1998, Paul Krugman, then a professor of economics at MIT, had reached the same conclusion.[54] The BOJ, however, continued to move in baby steps throughout the 2000s, and just as Bernanke and Krugman had predicted, the Japanese economy fell into a deflationary trap. Japanese citizens came to expect that inflation would remain low, they acted on that basis, and so economic growth and inflation did remain low.

In late 2010, as chairman of the Fed and thus the world's most important central banker, Bernanke followed through on the policy lessons he had learned from history. He justified and pushed through an unprecedentedly large monetary stimulus to prevent the American economy from falling into a deflationary trap.[55]

Others reinforced the message. In November 2013, writing what would be published as the lead article in the January 2014 issue of the prestigious *Journal of Monetary Economics*, economists Gauti Eggertsson, Andrea Ferrero, and Andrea Raffo recommended that the ECB pursue an aggressive monetary policy to take deflation risk off the table.[56] They went a step further and warned that the emphasis of eurozone authorities on structural reforms, however well meaning in the long run, would push wages and prices down and, hence, intensify the deflationary tendency.

Yet, despite the ample warnings from economic history, the recent example of proactive Fed policy, and contemporary advice, the ECB was allowing the deflation threat to intensify. Throughout the summer of 2013, eurozone inflation fell faster than the ECB forecast. In November, the "core" inflation rate, which strips out volatile food and energy prices and so is a truer gauge of underlying inflationary pressures than the "headline" or overall inflation rate, had come down to an annual pace of 0.9 percent.[57] Inflation was well short of the ECB's stated goal, a rate below but close to 2 percent.

This is precisely when a "dual" monetary-policy mandate would have made a big difference. Recall that in 1998, Nobel laureates Franco Modigliani and Robert Solow had criticized European leaders for requiring the ECB to single-mindedly pursue price stability. They had recommended that the ECB also give equal consideration to reducing unemployment, just as the Fed did.[58] Even within its price stability mandate, if the ECB had recognized that the inflation rate was falling, it would, by 2014, have long since adopted a much more stimulative policy. Having an unemployment target would have more strikingly highlighted the absurdity of the ECB's policy stance.

The ECB had a political problem. The low average inflation rate obscured an even more worrying divergence in inflation rates across the member countries. The German inflation rate, although also relatively low, was a little above 1 percent (figure 8.4). Germans were quite happy to live with that inflation rate. In contrast, Italian and French inflation rates were falling quite rapidly and were settling in well below Germany's inflation rate. This divergence in inflation rates was not an accident. German per capita incomes were growing, while French incomes were stagnating and Italian incomes were

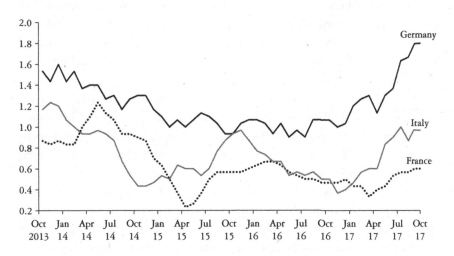

FIGURE 8.4. The euro area's inflation divergence.
(Annual core inflation, three-month moving average, percent)
Note: Core inflation is the annual percentage change in the Harmonized Index of Consumer Prices excluding unprocessed food and energy.
Source: Eurostat.

falling; inflation rates were mirroring the divergence in economic growth trends.

Although Italian inflation rates tended to move around considerably from month to month, their low average level had caused inflation expectations to shift decisively downward. In October 2013, the Banca d'Italia reported that firms expected to keep prices more or less unchanged over the next year.[59] Consumers also came to expect low inflation rates; in surveys, more than half the consumers said they expected prices to remain unchanged or even decline over the next year.[60]

The task for the ECB was not just to raise the eurozone's average inflation rate but also to prevent deflation in Italy, France, and other southern countries—Greece, Portugal, and Spain—where similar forces were at work. The ECB's political problem was that it could not forcefully forestall the looming deflation risk in some of its member countries.

In March 2014, Reza Moghadam and Ranjit Teja, Director and Deputy Director respectively of the IMF's European Department, reinforced the cautionary lesson for the eurozone from Japan's protracted deflation, which they pointed out was a mix of brief periods of outright price declines interspersed with longer phases of "lowflation." Like others before them, they emphasized that it was important "to act forcefully *before* deflation set in." Like others, they repeated that because the BOJ had reacted too slowly, it had to "resort to ever-increasing stimulus once deflation set in. [And] two decades on, that effort is still ongoing."[61] Writing around the same time, Harvard University economist Jeffrey Frankel warned that without easier monetary policy, the eurozone's economic weakness would continue and that some of the member states would be "condemned to suffer painful *deflation*."[62]

Yet the ECB chose to stay put. In early April 2014, Draghi acknowledged that the ECB's projections had by then "underestimated inflation a few times." These errors were not the ECB's fault, he said. The real problem, Draghi insisted, was the steeper-than-expected decline in energy prices, which had pulled down the euro area's "headline" inflation rate. He predicted that energy prices would soon rise again and that the annual inflation rate would return to a more normal range of around 2 percent.

Draghi puzzlingly—and mistakenly—continued to focus on the headline inflation rate, which was indeed being pulled down by falling energy prices. The more relevant "core" inflation rate, while stable, was stuck at an unusually low level of around 0.9 percent. Draghi flippantly dismissed the core-inflation metric and even suggested that the Fed's reliance on that measure was unscientific and led to unreliable policy decisions.[63]

Adding a new phrase to the ECB's lexicon, Draghi said that more action would only be required if inflation remained low for "too prolonged a period." When journalists asked Draghi what he meant by that, his answer revealed more starkly than before the widening rift within the Governing Council. Some members on the Council believed that inflation was already too low and that it was urgent to press ahead with monetary stimulus. Others—and theirs became the official view—believed that inflation expectations were "firmly anchored," and businesses and households would soon bid up prices and bring inflation back to the 2 percent rate.

The national divisions in the ECB's Governing Council emerged in open political debate. Alongside his calls for more flexibility in fiscal rules, Italy's Finance Minister Padoan complained about the ECB's monetary policy. On April 10, 2014, a week after the most recent meeting of the ECB's Governing Council, Padoan said that low inflation was "complicating" his government's efforts to boost its economy. Low inflation was making it harder for the government to repay its debts. A growing number of businesses had simply stopped paying back their banks. More stimulative ECB policy, Padoan said, would have the added benefit of delivering a "slightly less-strong euro," which would help Italian producers increase their exports and bring back some life to the Italian economy.[64]

Padoan was right to complain. Because of ECB inaction, the euro was valued at above $1.35, the extraordinarily high level where it had been stuck for the past six months.[65] The Fed, in contrast, was deploying its third round of QE. Each QE round had acted to reverse the dollar's tendency to strengthen (figure 8.5).[66] Lower interest rates in the United States had boosted domestic consumption and investment, and the weaker dollar helped US exports. In Japan, the BOJ had initiated a massive QE program in January 2013 as the key initiative under the rubric of Abenomics. While the report card on this latest Japanese effort was still awaited, the immediate outcome was a weaker yen. The ECB was the only major central bank not pushing down its exchange rate.

Padoan's effort to "influence" the ECB's decisions was unusual but not unprecedented. Back in 2002, with their economies stumbling in and out of recession, French President Jacques Chirac and German Chancellor Gerhard Schröder had quite rightly disregarded European fiscal rules and had concurrently demanded that the ECB bring interest rates down.[67] Now, in 2014, French President Hollande's cabinet members were badgering the ECB. Outspoken economy minister Arnaud Montebourg complained that the ECB had allowed the euro to become too strong. Euro-area governments, he proposed, should lean on the ECB to ease monetary policy. "The euro's

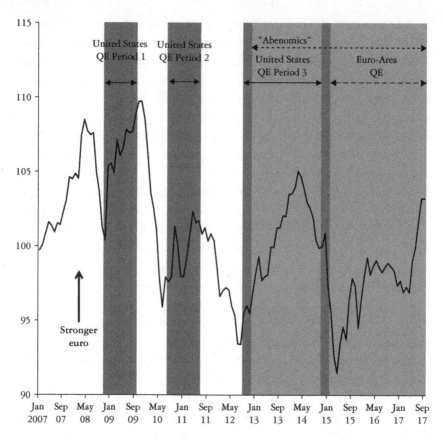

FIGURE 8.5. US and Japanese quantitative easing cause the euro to strengthen.
(Euro nominal effective exchange rate, index 2010 = 100)
Notes: QE1: November 25, 2008 (agency/mortgage-backed securities) to September 23, 2009; QE2:
August 10, 2010 to June 30, 2011; QE3: September 13, 2012, to October 2014; "Abenomics": January
2013 to the present; ECB QE: January 2015 to the present.
Sources: Bank for International Settlements, "Effective exchange rate indices, Narrow indices, Nominal";
Board of Governors of the Federal Reserve System press releases November 25, 2008, September 23,
2009, August 10, 2010, June 22, 2011, September 13, 2012, September 17, 2014; Ben Bernanke,
2013, "The Economic Outlook," testimony before the Joint Economic Committee, US Congress,
Washington, DC., May 22; Shinzo Abe, 2013, "Press Conference by Prime Minister Shinzo Abe," Prime
Minister of Japan and His Cabinet, January 4, ECB press release: January 22, 2015.

strength," he declared, "is a political subject."[68] Some days later, Manuel
Valls, the newly appointed French prime minister, made the same pitch: "We
need a more appropriate monetary policy because the level of the euro is too
high."[69] Valls said that President Hollande would lobby other governments
to push the ECB toward easier monetary policy and a cheaper euro.

The French unemployment rate had crept up above 10 percent, and the
economy seemed stalled. Traditional supporters of Hollande's Socialist Party

were growing weary of poor employment prospects and the simultaneous squeeze they were experiencing due to the government's fiscal austerity; the Socialist Party's electoral prospects were becoming bleaker.[70] Leading French manufacturers were clamoring for a weaker euro.[71]

Of course, just as a monetary boost could not reverse Italy's long-term industrial decline, it could not shake up France's lagging educational system or raise its industrial R&D.[72] European leaders, such as Luxembourg's Prime Minister (and Eurogroup head) Jean-Claude Juncker, chided the French for not doing enough to reinject dynamism into the economy and for demanding instead the crutch of a weak currency.[73] French leaders correctly responded that by lowering economic growth and inflation, tight monetary policy had slowed down the pace of tax revenue inflows; and by pushing up the unemployment rate, it had increased social tensions. Such an environment made it harder to initiate painful structural reforms. The French were making the same argument as Bernanke had used in late 1999 to criticize the BOJ for its continuous harping on structural reform measures instead of providing stepped-up monetary stimulus.

When the ECB's Governing Council met on June 5, 2014, the euro area's core inflation rate had edged down to 0.8 percent, and the Italian rate was falling rapidly. The ECB announced that it would reduce its policy interest rate from 0.25 percent to 0.15 percent. And, to encourage banks to lend out their funds, the ECB announced that it would charge the banks a fee, sometimes described as a "negative interest rate," if they parked their funds at the ECB. The intent of charging the fee was to persuade banks to use their funds for extending loans to consumers and businesses. To further encourage bank lending, the ECB announced it would give the banks plentiful money at low rates so that they could make new loans to their customers. The ECB remained stuck in the mindset that its main task was to get banks to increase the supply of loans. But supply of loans was not the crucial problem. Demand for loans was weak. The Fed had acted primarily at the opposite end of the relationship, by lowering interest rates to boost consumption and investment spending, and hence keep the economic recovery going. Engineering an economic recovery was a superior way of helping banks because it brought in more confident and creditworthy customers. Draghi repeated that the ECB would, in principle, act on the demand side of the borrower-lender relationship. The Governing Council, he said, stood ready to deploy "unconventional instruments," which included the possibility of a bond-buying or QE program. But he also repeated that QE would be used only if "necessary to further address risks of too prolonged a period of low inflation."[74]

French Prime Minister Valls was understandably not impressed. He repeated his concern, "The euro is overvalued, which is bad for our industry and for growth." The ECB's latest interest rate reduction, he said, was a minuscule effort: "my idea of a central bank is one that could go further, including by buying assets on the markets."[75]

In that stalemate, some scholars proposed radical ideas to boost the eurozone economy. Harvard's Frankel suggested that the ECB should buy US government bonds, which would bid up the dollar and weaken the euro. Frankel pointed out that rebooting the eurozone was in the global interest and that the Fed and other monetary authorities should welcome and support ECB efforts to weaken the euro. Christian Odendahl, chief economist of the London-based think tank Centre for European Reform, recommended that the ECB make a public commitment to aggressive QE until the inflation rate was significantly above its 2 percent target, reaching at least a 3 percent annual rate and staying at that level for several years.[76] Odendahl's proposal harked back to a suggestion made independently by Krugman and Bernanke for Japan in 1998 and 1999.[77] In Krugman's terminology, it was time for the ECB to make the "irresponsible" promise that it would act to raise inflation well above its 2 percent norm. Only such an unorthodox strategy stood a chance of persuading the public and financial markets that the ECB was ready to pull the eurozone out of a possible deflationary trap.

In two companion reports issued in July, the IMF joined the chorus of critics. Euro-area inflation, the IMF impatiently said, had been "too low for too long," and deflation risk now was "appreciable."[78] The ECB's failure to revive inflation, the IMF continued, would ultimately undermine the institution's credibility. People would stop believing that inflation would rise anytime soon, and thus, despite Draghi's repeated claims, inflation expectations might become "de-anchored." Businesses would cut back on investment, which would further weaken demand and economic growth—and inflation would fall even more.[79] Just as others had already noted, the IMF was pointing out that the euro area could easily tip into a low-inflation, low-growth, and high-debt trap if the ECB did not aggressively ease monetary conditions.[80] Echoing Frankel, the IMF noted that the stressed economies in the euro area's periphery were especially vulnerable and that they desperately needed relief in the form of a weaker exchange rate and higher inflation.[81]

In early August 2014, Renzi met in "secret" with Draghi. Italian economic output had started falling again, and the core inflation rate—at an annual 0.5 percent—was approaching deflation. The meeting took place in Città della Pieve, a small town in the Umbria region, about halfway between Rome and Florence, where Draghi had his vacation home.[82] As the local newspaper later revealed, Renzi's helicopter landed at a specially cleared strip, and he spent two and a half hours with Draghi. There is no record of what Renzi and Draghi discussed. But some were dismayed at the humiliation of a prime minister apparently traveling as a supplicant to see the ECB president.

On September 4, when the ECB's Governing Council met for its monthly monetary policy decision, the strong euro was still impeding eurozone economic recovery. The Governing Council delicately lowered the main policy interest rate by an additional 10 basis points, from 0.15 percent to 0.05 percent, and it increased the fee charged to banks for depositing their funds at the ECB. The ECB also announced a small program to buy so-called asset-backed securities, such as packages of bank loans. This was yet another step to encourage banks to lend at lower interest rates.

Draghi repeated that inflation expectations "continue to be firmly anchored in line with our aim of maintaining inflation rates below, but close to, 2%." And he said again that the ECB remained committed "to using also unconventional instruments," although only if it became necessary to counter the "risks of too prolonged a period of low inflation."[83]

After having recited his monthly mantra, Draghi made it clear that the Governing Council remained deeply divided on the pace at which the ECB should move. Stock markets took the latest decision poorly.[84] Andrew Balls, a senior executive at bond investor PIMCO, warned that the ECB was playing with fire. "The eurozone," Balls said, "is one shock away from sinking into deflation. There are real costs of acting too late."[85]

The Fed as the World's Central Bank

At this point in history, the Fed had as much or even greater influence on monetary conditions in the eurozone than the ECB did. Hélène Rey, economics professor at the London Business School, has argued that US monetary policy is decisive in setting global financial conditions.[86] The Fed's influence in the eurozone economy was partly the result of the continued dependence of eurozone banks on funding in US dollar money markets. Twice—first in late 2008 after the Lehman Brothers collapse and again in late 2011 after the ECB's rate increases triggered a eurozone crisis—the Fed's added provision of dollars had relieved critical stress faced by eurozone banks.[87] The Fed achieved even greater reach through its large and proactive QE, which had driven down the value of the dollar and had, therefore, exercised a strong influence on the value of other currencies. In contrast, by remaining stodgy throughout the crisis years, the ECB frittered away its global influence, and the eurozone had become more susceptible to Fed policy shifts.

More evidence of the Fed's influence on the eurozone came on September 8, 2014. Researchers at the Federal Reserve Bank of San Francisco reported that financial markets were underestimating the likelihood that the Fed would soon raise rates.[88] Although the research paper presented publicly-available information, investors were jolted. Heightened anticipation of tighter Fed policy caused long-term US interest rates to rise. The dollar strengthened, and the euro finally began to depreciate.[89] As anticipated, in October, the Fed ended its third QE program, i.e., the "tapering" that had commenced a year earlier came to an end. By now, Fed decision makers were getting ready for the next step: an interest rate "lift-off."[90] The dollar continued to strengthen, and the euro helpfully weakened further. Italy's core inflation rate, which had fallen below 0.5 percent a year, clawed its way up to 0.6 percent over the next few months.

Thus, in the final months of 2014, the Federal Reserve was doing more for the euro-area economy than the ECB itself seemed able or ready to do. Yet the signs were not good. Monetary stimulus was coming too late to have a significant impact. It seemed as if the eurozone—or at least large parts of it—had fallen into the Japanese lowflation trap. The euro area's "growth momentum" continued to weaken, as even Draghi acknowledged.[91] Despite the benefit of a depreciating euro, core inflation remained stuck at extremely low levels. In December, Draghi boldly said, "We won't tolerate" a "prolonged" period of low inflation. But it was a weak assurance. Although ECB forecasts now showed that inflation would take longer to rise than had been anticipated earlier in the year, Draghi continued to insist that inflation was "well-anchored."[92] His message was that the ECB had taken several initiatives which needed to be given time to have their full effect.[93]

Popular Protests Add to Pressure On the ECB

Years of financial crisis and high unemployment were fueling popular discontent and euro-skepticism. The scale of protests kept increasing, and the parties that had made gains in the European parliamentary elections—the

National Front in France, the Five Star Movement in Italy, Syriza in Greece, and Podemos in Spain—continued to add to their political strength. In France, opinion polls showed that the National Front's Le Pen would make it to the second-round runoff for the French presidency in 2017.[94] In Italy, the Five Star Movement's Grillo stepped up his campaign for Italy to leave the eurozone.[95]

Whether Draghi liked it or not, the ECB was being sucked into eurozone politics. At his press conferences, journalists asked Draghi if the ECB was responsible for the growing anti-European sentiment. He replied that he was aware that people were enduring hardship, but that the ECB had taken extraordinary measures. Draghi referred specifically to ongoing protests in Italy. He said that the country had long-term problems and that it was wrong to suggest the ECB was "somehow guilty" or "at the origin of this situation."[96] To the question of whether the "radical" parties would compel the ECB to take additional measures, Draghi said he was not sure what more they wanted from the ECB.[97] He reprimanded journalists for their "obsession" with finding dividing lines within the eurozone when in fact, he insisted, there were none.[98]

As political tensions grew, the formerly hazy identities of the opposing camps on the ECB's Governing Council were gradually unveiled. At the December rate-setting meeting, Germany's Jens Weidmann and Sabine Lautenschläger, Luxembourg's Yves Mersch, and even France's Benoît Coeuré amazingly objected to one particular word in Draghi's opening statement at that month's press conference. Draghi, they felt, was making a reckless commitment by announcing that the ECB "intended" to—rather than merely "expected" to—purchase more financial assets to lower the costs of borrowing.[99] That such a minor nuance would cause an open rift raised the question of whether the ECB would ever get to the next stage.

While the Governing Council members from Austria, Estonia, Luxembourg, and the Netherlands quietly opposed QE, Weidmann, who was a member of the ECB's Governing Council by virtue of being Bundesbank president, and Lautenschläger, who had been Bundesbank vice president before she moved full-time to the ECB, launched a public offensive against the measure.[100] Despite all the evidence, they insisted that deflation was not yet a serious risk.[101] They warned that lower interest rates would lift the pressure on member governments to undertake more reforms.[102] The ECB, Weidmann said, could not be the "sweeper" to clean up after national leaders had created a mess.[103]

Lautenschläger added an intriguing question: would QE do the eurozone any good? Unlike the Fed's QE, which had started when interest rates were still high, QE in the eurozone would begin when global interest rates had already fallen sharply. Even Spanish and Italian governments were able to borrow at interest rates close to 2 percent, which was roughly the same as, or even lower than, the rate paid by the US government. The euro had depreciated by around 7.5 percent against the dollar between early September and December 2014. These improved financial conditions should have boosted domestic spending and exports, but the eurozone economy continued to struggle. Without a hint of irony, Lautenschläger, who had held the ECB back for months, asked why the ECB needed to take any further measures.[104]

The answer was that inflation had fallen into dangerously low territory. Low inflation ensured that real interest rates (nominal rates minus the expected inflation rate) remained high, especially in Italy. The Italian real interest rate was still around 1.5 percent, not low enough to spur economic recovery. The Italian economy contracted in 2014 for the third year in a row. Through much of the year, the Italian unemployment rate stood at or above 12.5 percent, a postwar high.[105] In contrast, Germany's real interest rate was turning negative, the economy had rebounded nicely, and the unemployment rate was plummeting. Simply put, the ECB's monetary policy was adding to the pace of economic divergence.

The ECB's purchases of asset-backed securities, intended to boost lending, proved to be a dud. As Felix Blomenkamp and Rachit Jain of PIMCO reported, the ECB mainly bought asset-backed securities from banks in the "core" countries, such as Germany, which did not need the help.[106]

The greater long-term damage was to the ECB's credibility. The ECB had wasted thirteen long months with mainly cheap talk. From November 2013 to December 2014, it had reduced the policy interest rate at a glacial pace by 0.20 percent (one-fifth of one percent). Constrained by the Germans and others for more than a year, Draghi had hinted at more aggressive stimulus to come, but only "if needed" or if inflation remained low for "too prolonged" a period. Despite the worsening deflation outlook, actions had not backed up the cheap talk. And, as Princeton's Alan Blinder reminds us, when actions don't match the words, credibility evaporates.[107]

The ECB was set up as a hyper-independent, unaccountable central bank to keep political influence out of its policy decisions. The result was the worst of both worlds: as intended, the ECB was democratically unaccountable, but political influence seeped into its decision-making in any case. Unaccountability was manifest in its pursuit of a monetary policy that, at first, delayed recovery and then in 2011 did active damage. The ECB was never called on officially to explain the reasons for and defend its actions. Unaccountability was also manifest in the imperious letters that Jean-Claude Trichet, then ECB president, along with the national central bank governors wrote to elected heads of governments in Italy and Spain. And the influence of politics in ECB decision-making was there for everyone to see. In the absence of a due process for establishing accountability, the ECB had become susceptible to aggressive national influences on the ECB's Governing Council.

The irony is that the ECB's independence was intended to free its technical decisions of political taint and hence give those decisions iron-clad credibility. Instead, the ECB's façade of independence hid unregulated national interests, which kept the ECB's actions out of step with the eurozone's economic needs and undermined its credibility.

Renzi's Jobs Act Makes Him Loved in Europe—and Hated at Home

Renzi had the right instincts on the need for easier fiscal and monetary policy to help revive growth. However, he fell in with the European mantra of "more structural reforms." All European leaders believed in the virtues of structural reforms. ECB officials lost no opportunity to sing their praises, and European Commission President José Manuel Barroso made them a central theme of his State of the Union addresses.[108]

In European discourse, the benign phrase "structural reforms" nearly always meant weakening the bargaining power of workers. The thesis was that employers would be more willing to hire workers whom they could fire easily. Workers would be forced to accept lower wages, and cheaper workers would help lower the costs of production and thus sell products at reduced, more competitive prices, both domestically and in international markets.

Renzi's Jobs Act was faithful to that thesis. Under one of its key provisions, a company found to have wrongfully dismissed an employee would no longer have to rehire that worker. The Jobs Act also gave employers incentives to hire workers on "open-ended" contracts. These contracts were a response to the reality that the vast bulk of new employment, especially of younger workers, was occurring in the form of temporary contracts, and such contracts created a pervasive sense of job insecurity. In principle, "open-ended" contracts were more secure than temporary contracts. But they also made it easier to fire workers. Moreover, the Jobs Act encouraged a particularly egregious form of temporary contract, under which workers received vouchers as payment; this system existed mainly as a way to curtail workers' benefits and rights. The Jobs Act raised the limit of allowed compensation through vouchers from €5,000 per year to €7,000 per year.[109]

The Jobs Act was a continuation of successive Italian government efforts over the preceding quarter century to reduce labor market "rigidities" and to increase "flexibility." But such reforms, however sensible they sounded, were a little bit like the drunk man looking for his lost keyes under the lamppost because that is where the light was. With advances in labor-saving technology and increased "outsourcing" by companies to low-wage locations, workers' had lost much of their bargaining leverage and it was easy to push through such labor market reforms. The reforms further reduced workers' leverage. The task completed, policymakers had a sense of accomplishment.

But what did the historical evidence show on how valuable labor market reforms were? What could they do for Italy?

For one thing, putting a lid on wages—and, possibly, even pushing them down—reinforced the deflationary tendency in the near term. Thus, the timing of the reforms was particularly bad. Moreover, even when viewed through the lens of improved competitiveness, the gap between Italian and eastern European wages was so large that it would take an extraordinary decrease in Italian wages to materially influence competitiveness. Italian wages would need to go at least halfway down to Romanian wages, which would presumably help Italian manufacturers become more competitive in low-value-added, labor-intensive products. Such a strategy was bound to have its limits. For long-term growth, Italy needed to transition to high-end manufacturing or into emerging fields such as biotechnology. In such high-value-added activities, employers pay premium wages to skilled workers.

In fact, the Jobs Act could have adverse long-term consequences. The Italian economy's already low productivity growth rate would almost certainly fall. Well-established international evidence showed that companies made little effort to train workers whom they could easily fire. Hence, economy-wide labor productivity suffered.[110] Recent Italian experience exactly matched the international experience. In a 2010 study, economists Federico Lucidi and Alfred Kleinknecht noted that, over the past several years, Italian governments had steadily reduced "rigidities" and increased "flexibility" in the Italian labor market. As a result, businesses had hired more workers, but mainly on short-term contracts. While employment had increased, productivity growth of Italian workers had fallen.[111] Making matters worse, with access to cheap labor, Italian firms had reduced their investments in R&D and in actively seeking export markets.[112] The Italian economy's total factor productivity growth rate, the comprehensive measure for efficiency enhancements, was in continual decline.[113]

Part of the European mythology of structural reforms grew out of an incorrect interpretation of the so-called Hartz reforms, which were introduced by German Chancellor Gerhard Schröder's administration between January 2003 and January 2005. The Hartz reforms made it easier for employers to hire temporary workers, reduced restrictions on firing workers, and increased the pain on the unemployed if they did not look harder for work.[114] These measures worked no special magic in Germany. They had the same effects as observed elsewhere in the world. Unemployed workers returned to look for jobs sooner than was the case before the reforms, and they accepted the lower wages on offer.[115] More workers could find jobs, but on short-term contracts, and their wages grew slowly, if at all.[116]

A popular view took hold that the slow wage growth induced by the Hartz reforms had made German companies more internationally competitive and thus sparked Germany's economic revival in the mid-2000s.[117] German politicians, keen to see other countries adopt similar reforms, perpetuated this view.

However, the reasons for Germany's economic renewal had little to do with the Hartz reforms.[118] German producers increased their competitiveness, in part, by shifting some of their manufacturing operations to lower-wage European economies. More important, German producers invested in developing innovative products and in improving manufacturing efficiency.[119] In the product categories they dominated, German companies were world leaders in research and patent registration. They maintained the high traditions of Germany's vocational training and worker participation in management decisions. German labor productivity in manufacturing increased steadily by 1 percent a year from the early 1980s through the early 2000s, a rate comfortably above that in US manufacturing. And Germany's highly productive manufacturing workers largely maintained their privileged, high-wage positions. In contrast, much of the short-term German employment at low wages was in service sectors, where productivity growth fell behind the productivity growth in German manufacturing and relative to the service sectors of other advanced economies.[120]

Italian manufacturing companies invested little in innovation and worker training. The Jobs Act took them off the hook once again, since the firms now had the option of muddling along by paying lower wages to their workers.

In October 2014, soon after Renzi announced the outline of his Jobs Act, European leaders enthusiastically welcomed this shift to a less "rigid," more "flexible" job market. Merkel and European Commission President Barroso were among the first to applaud the initiative.[121] Once the legislative process for the Jobs Act concluded, Merkel continued her praise. In a press conference with Renzi in Berlin, she said, "It's quite impressive how things have been implemented—from the institutional reforms to the so-called Jobs Act."[122] The head of the Paris-based Organisation for Economic Co-operation and Development (OECD), José Ángel Gurría, described the Jobs Act as one of Italy's "most important transformations."[123] Traditional Italian leaders, such as the Democratic Party's Pier Luigi Bersani, supported the Jobs Act.[124] Italian employers were pleased.[125]

Under the Jobs Act, phased in between January and March 2015, employers grabbed Renzi's temporary tax incentives for open-ended contracts and hired workers they would have hired in any case to meet their business needs.[126] The Jobs Act reinforced the tendency toward increased use of temporary contracts. Thirty-three-year-old Alessandro Giuggioli, who produced a television series highlighting the plight of young Italians surviving on temporary work, said, "The situation is dramatic. We are all precarious. I am and all my friends are."[127] Especially in the prime working-age group, ages twenty-five to fifty-four, the share of temporary employment continued to rise.[128]

The Jobs Act was deployed alongside fiscal austerity, which weakened social safety nets. The combination fed anti-government and anti-European sentiment.[129] Italian workers protested.[130] Grillo linked his criticism of the Jobs Act with a renewed call to exit the eurozone.[131] Thus, as the eurozone "elite" and Italian employers cheered, large segments of the Italian population positioned themselves on the other side of the political debate. To those who were economically vulnerable, the Jobs Act was more evidence that the European establishment was pursuing a "neoliberal" agenda that took away economic security but offered little hope in return.

Renzi's real task was harder: to give people greater opportunities to increase their skills, with which they would be more likely to get well-paying jobs. European politicians speak often and glowingly of this alternative. However, only Scandinavian nations have made significant headway toward the objective. Especially in southern Europe, politicians have remained unwilling or unable to invest sufficient energy in setting up the infrastructure and establishing the incentives to expand educational and skill-development options commensurate with evolving international standards. Certainly, southern European nations fell well short of the high benchmarks being set in some of the advanced East Asian economies. Even among the laggards, Italy was at the back of the pack.

Thus, for too many Italians, insecurity in the job market was an immediate reality, while the government's modest efforts to raise the quality of education and vocational training were grossly inadequate to meeting people's aspirations for themselves and for their children.

The Government Keeps Dying Banks Alive

As Italy was sliding into a low-growth deflationary trap, in another parallel with Japan, Italian banks were threatening to die. Italy has more bank branches per capita than any other European country.[132] Indeed, as one wit remarked, Italy has more bank branches than it has pizzerias.[133] Even during the years before the global financial crisis, banks struggled to return a profit in a slow-growing economy. After the crisis started, Italian banks did not go up in flames; rather, they began a slow burn. Italy's already low GDP growth rate took a beating. Except for a brief spell in 2010, when a rising world economic tide had lifted even the Italian boat, GDP stayed flat or fell. And when GDP stays flat or falls, many borrowers are not able to repay their debts.

Italian officials denied that their banking system had a problem. To the contrary, the officials took pride in the banks. Italian banks, they said, had not been seduced by US subprime securities and had therefore admirably survived the global financial crisis. On July 13, 2011, just days after the ECB gratuitously raised its policy interest rate and thus set in motion what was to be the gravest phase of the eurozone crisis, Draghi gave a glowing report on Italian banks. Still the governor of the Banca d'Italia but already slated to be the next ECB president, he said, "Italian banks have shown and continue to show an ability to resist and react in times of difficulty."[134]

The truth, however, was that the nonperforming loans of Italian banks— loans that were not being repaid on time—had risen every year since 2007. The banks' problems had steadily become more acute, and almost on the very day of Draghi's upbeat assessment in July 2011, the IMF warned that with many businesses unable to repay their debts, Italian banks were falling into a deeper financial hole.[135] Nonperforming loans of Italian banks had reached the dangerous level of 10 percent, up from 5.25 percent in 2007. Over the year 2011, the Italian banking system suffered a loss.

Italian banks had become a danger to others. If they collapsed, they could quickly overwhelm the government's shaky finances and send tremors through the euro-area and global financial systems. Ultimately, Italian banks were the country's true hotspot. The eurozone's fault line ran through Italy, and Italy's fault line ran through its banks.

Italy's banking malaise was most starkly visible in Banca Monte dei Paschi di Siena (MPS), Italy's fifth-largest bank. The bank was established in 1472, and it is considered by some to be the world's oldest still-operating bank. The bank's main shareholder, the Fondazione Monte dei Paschi di Siena, was described as a "charitable" foundation but was, in effect, a cash machine for the city of Siena.[136] Over the past fifteen years, the foundation had doled out nearly €2 billion to Siena on projects ranging from a biotech facility to train-ing of horses for the historic Palio horse races.[137] To some observers it seemed that Siena's residents fell into three groups: those who received a pension from MPS, those who worked at MPS and expected to draw a pension, and those who aspired to work at MPS one day so that they too would draw a generous pension. The "charitable" foundation, which owned the majority stake in MPS, was closely associated with Renzi's Democratic Party. So close was the association that many, including the Five Star Movement's Grillo, accused MPS of being a funding machine for the Democratic Party.

In November 2007, with the bank's traditional lending business making losses, MPS began to gamble. It bought a competitor bank, Antonveneta, for €9 billion, a sum most analysts believed was far above market value—a sum, moreover, that MPS could ill afford.[138] However, Italian Prime Minister Romano Prodi, until recently president of the European Commission, welcomed the Antonveneta purchase, which he said was "something to be considered positively."[139] A year later, in November 2008, Prodi was gone in the perennial Italian shuffle. With the vener-able Siena bank "under pressure since it bought rival Antonveneta," Prime Minister Silvio Berlusconi's government felt compelled to prop up MPS with an infusion of cash.[140]

Around the same time, MPS began entering into exotic derivative deals, with alluring names such as "Alexandria," "Santorini," and "Nota Italia."[141] In 2010, inspectors at the Banca d'Italia alerted their management—then under Governor Draghi—about "potentially critical" risks embedded in these transactions. But no evident restraint was applied.[142] In January 2013, MPS disclosed to the public that the derivatives-based bets had turned badly sour.[143] Later that month, the Banca d'Italia, now under Governor Ignazio Visco, said it had a "favourable opinion" of MPS and approved Prime Minister Monti's plan to infuse another round of cash to cover MPS's mount-ing losses.[144] "There is no question that the bank is stable," Visco said.[145] Vittorio Grilli, minister of economy and finance, said that MPS was a "solid" bank and that the government's cash was "not a bailout of an insolvent bank" but a mere "reinforcement of its capital."[146]

In March, the head of MPS's communication department was found dead at the bank's headquarters; he was believed to have committed suicide.[147] Investigations for fraud and corruption in the Antonveneta and derivative transactions were now closing in on MPS's senior management.

In September 2013, the IMF concluded that MPS was in a near-terminal state. More than 22 percent of MPS's loans were nonperforming. Because of "junk" ratings from major international credit rating agencies, MPS found it difficult to borrow in the interbank market; cheap ECB funds kept the bank barely functioning.[148] The IMF described MPS as a "systemic," or "systemically important," bank.[149] In other words, if MPS keeled over, it could bring the entire Italian banking system down with it. Hence, the IMF concluded that urgent measures were required to "rehabilitate" MPS.

The IMF's diagnosis was right, but the prescribed cure was not. It was too late to rehabilitate MPS. The bank needed to die. Yet over the next few years, even as it failed every European stress test, successive Italian governments kept the tottering bank on life support.

With endless tragic monotony, first the Italian and then also European authorities continued with denials, delays, and half measures. The role of European authorities in national banking systems was a recent development. All these years, national supervisors had been responsible for monitoring and disciplining the banks operating in the country. But the Irish and Spanish credit and property bubbles had led many observers to conclude that national supervisors were likely to become too cozy with their own banks and would, therefore, allow irresponsible banks to take on too much risk. The verdict was that a single eurozone-wide bank supervisor, detached from national politics and pressures, would ensure prudent bank behavior.

The single supervisor was the first of three steps toward the grander idea of a European "banking union."[150] Under an authority granted by European leaders to the ECB, the Single Supervisory Mechanism (SSM) began operating in November 2014. Starting in January 2016, a Single Resolution Board (SRB) stood ready to "resolve" and restructure banks based on a rulebook, the Bank Recovery and Resolution Directive (BRRD). With continuing disrespect for words, Europeans called this collective—the SSM and SRB—their "banking union." The practice of attaching the word "union" to every European intitiative gave it symbolic gravitas. But the European Union is not a union, the much-touted "political union" was never a serious idea, and Europe did not have a monetary union—it had an incomplete monetary union.

The so-called "banking union" was not a "union." Each member state was still responsible for the costs incurred when closing down a troubled bank or merging it with another bank. No eurozone government was willing to finance cleaning up another member state's banking systems.

A true banking union was not possible for the same reason that a fiscal union was not possible: sovereign states would not share their tax euros with other member states which had fallen into recessionary or crisis conditions. European leaders did agree to set up a resolution fund to which European banks would contribute. But, as *Financial Times* columnist Wolfgang

Münchau wrote, even at its peak, the resolution fund would be so tiny "that it could not resolve a medium-sized casino."[151] When all was said and done, the Italian government would still be responsible for cleaning up the mess that its banks made.

In October 2014, to create a benchmark for the SSM, which was about to begin its supervisory activities, the European Banking Authority (EBA)—the agency responsible for conducting banks' stress tests—reported updated estimates of additional capital that banks needed to raise in order to protect themselves in "adverse scenarios."[152] Analysts had lampooned previous European stress tests, conducted between 2009 and 2011, for their ridiculously low estimates of banks' capital requirements.[153] After the October 2014 test, the EBA reported that of the 123 banks it had reviewed, 24 banks needed around €24 billion in additional capital. Nine of the capital-deficient banks were from Italy; MPS alone, the EBA said, needed €4 billion more capital.

Most analysts found these latest estimates of capital shortfalls to be plausible. However, some financial experts remained skeptical. Viral Acharya, finance professor at New York University, and Sascha Steffen, finance professor at the Frankfurt School of Finance and Management, concluded that the EBA had overestimated the actual capital held by banks, especially French, German, and Italian banks.[154] The problem, they noted, was that the EBA used the "book values" of capital, which were often out of date; the much lower, but probably also more realistic, "market values" of banks' equity implied considerably larger capital shortfalls. The EBA also treated government bonds held by banks as risk-free, and so it had underestimated the risks of default faced by banks. Thus, by overestimating capital and underestimating risks, the EBA formed a view of banks' health that was more optimistic than was warranted.

For Italy, even the EBA estimates were dire enough to cause a scare. After the stress results were announced, stock prices of Italian banks nosedived, and in a well-worn pattern, Italian leaders rushed out to talk up their banks. "There is a strength, a solidity, in the Italian banks," Renzi said. He added that the MPS challenge had to be "tackled with determination, without underestimating it but without thinking the problems can't be resolved."[155] Finance Minister Padoan said that Italian banks were healthy and would not need any more public money, because private investors would gladly fill in the capital shortfalls. Fabrizio Viola, chief executive of MPS, echoed Padoan's statement: the perpetually distressed MPS would "categorically" not need another government bailout.

The unfortunate parallels with Japan were growing. Like Japan, Italy was falling into the dangerous price-deflation zone. Japanese authorities had also failed, for seven long years between 1991 and 1998, to acknowledge that their banks were in distress. Even when they finally accepted that there was a problem, they tried to make do with half measures. Recapitalization of banks in February 1998 had proven insufficient, as had another attempted capital infusion in March 1999; even in 2002, some banks were operating with insufficient capital. Only after a substantial recapitalization in June 2003 were the banks finally placed on a sound financial footing.[156]

The Japanese lesson was that denials and delays have a cost. While the Japanese government waited, the country's troubled banks faced mounting losses as more borrowers threatened to stop repaying their loans.[157] Lacking sufficient capital to absorb the losses, banks chose to pretend that the losses did not exit. They "evergreened" the loans: when borrowers did not repay, the banks just extended the repayment period. As could be expected, banks particularly short of capital were the most active in playing this "extend and pretend" game.[158]

Low interest rates made this cozy "extend and pretend" arrangement especially convenient for "zombie" borrowers, the borrowers who were de facto bankrupt but continued operating simply because their creditors chose not to foreclose on them. Unfortunately, the low interest rates came too late to kick-start the Japanese economy and, in particular, they did little to revive the zombie borrowers. Such borrowers stayed on life support, happy to have their loans renewed at low interest rates and play along with the fiction that they would eventually repay their debts. The distressed banks, having given priority to keeping zombie companies alive, chose to cut back on loans to productive companies.[159] This incentive to allocate credit to unproductive rather than to productive companies further damaged economic growth and steadily raised the eventual cost of bailing out the distressed banks. The Japanese approach to dealing with problem banks was a tutorial in how to make a bad banking crisis even worse.

The same story, except with more severe consequences, repeated itself in Italy. Interest rates paid by governments and businesses started falling after the ECB announced its OMT program in August–September 2012. However, as in Japan, the interest-rate reductions came too late. By mid-2013, inflation rates also started falling, and the Italian real interest rate (the nominal interest rate applied to borrowers in Italy, corrected for Italy's rate of inflation) was too high to revive growth. Just as Japanese banks had done two decades earlier, Italian banks chose to keep alive the zombie companies so they could delay acknowledging the losses they had already incurred and were continuing to make.[160] For example, although the large Italian bookseller Feltrinelli was racking up losses, it continued to secure more credit from some of Italy's top banks, at "an interest rate below what top-rated companies in Europe were paying."[161] Because the banks had limited capital, which they needed to protect themselves against losses on loans made to their zombie customers, banks cut back on credit to healthy firms. Thus, in tandem, the zombie banks and firms perpetuated Italian economic distress.

Despite Padoan's boast, few private investors were willing to risk their money to recapitalize nearly bankrupt Italian banks. The government had two choices. It could put a large amount of its own money into the banks to raise their capital sufficiently to restore them to normal functioning. Or, instead of using taxpayer money to "bail out" the banks and their creditors, the government could "bail in" banks' creditors, or, as the Irish might have said, the government could "burn the bondholders." Burning the bondholders would give taxpayers a break, and banks' creditors would bear greater responsibility for the mess they had helped create.

For some banks, it was time to burn all the bondholders. As the head European bank supervisor Danièle Nouy dramatically said, several European banks had "no future," and needed to "die."[162] It would be wrong, she said, even to merge them with other institutions. The eurozone's banking sector was too large; there was simply not enough business to go around.

Nouy's no-nonsense conclusion that some banks needed to die applied with particular force to Italy. Many banks made virtually no profits even in good times, which placed them at risk whenever their borrowers experienced stress. Eighteen percent of all Italian bank loans were nonperforming. The losses on those nonperforming loans could cause several banks to fail and spread financial instability. If only it could be shrunk to two-thirds of its current size, the Italian banking sector would better serve Italy.

On November 22, 2015, the Italian government tried the gentlest form of the "bail-in"—the "burning bondholders"—option. The option was tested in the resolution of four small banks: Banca Marche, Banca Popolare dell'Etruria e del Lazio, Cassa di Risparmio di Chieti, and Cassa di Risparmio di Ferrara.[163] Together these banks held less than 1 percent of the deposits of the Italian banking system. The bail-in was restricted to "subordinated" or "junior" bondholders, the first in line after equity holders to take losses; senior bondholders were spared.[164] To prevent a more draconian bail-in, Italian authorities had persuaded "healthier" banks to inject capital into the four ailing banks and buy some of their nonperforming loans. This was a short-sighted arrangement since the "healthier" banks were themselves operating in a weak economy and so were not particularly healthy.

However, the government quickly backed off even from its modest step in the right direction. Just a bit more than two weeks after the bail-in announcement, a sixty-eight-year-old pensioner hanged himself, fearful of the prospect of losing over €100,000 of savings that he had placed in the junior bonds of one of the four banks.[165] His was not an isolated case. Several other small and financially vulnerable bondholders woke up to the possibility that their lifetime savings could disappear.

A public uproar followed. The Banca d'Italia officials reacted defensively. Having failed in their obligation to warn small bondholders (so-called retail investors) of the risks they were taking, the officials attacked the bail-in rules. Carmelo Barbagallo, head of financial supervision and regulation at the Banca d'Italia, said, "bail-in can exacerbate—rather than alleviate—the risks of systemic instability . . . It can undermine confidence."[166] This was the habitual scaremongering that imposing losses on creditors inevitably created the risk of financial disruption. At least for Italy, the opposite was true. As long as the weakest banks were kept functioning, they would undertake more zombie lending, and their increasing reported and unreported losses would heighten systemic financial risk. The eventual cost of cleaning up the mess would continue to rise.

The economic rationale for bail-in was strong. Renzi, however, had little option but to pull back. To him, the public backlash was politically toxic. He blamed the banks for not having made clear to bondholders that they could lose their money. Padoan scrambled to compensate retail bondholders on "humanitarian" grounds. "We don't want people dying of hunger," a senior Italian official said. The Italian government set up a €100 million fund to repay some of the ten thousand bondholders likely to be bailed in.[167]

The decision to compensate financially vulnerable bondholders was clearly politically motivated, but it could have been justified as an appropriate policy measure. The compensation amount—€100 million—was not large. But Italian policymakers drew the wrong inference and went the wrong way; they backed off from the bail-in option. Padoan gingerly said, "The bail-in is a new regime that needs to be introduced with sensitivity and at the right pace."[168]

Next came the tortured story of two Veneto-region banks, Banca Popolare di Vicenza and Veneto Banca. In the October 2014 stress tests, the EBA estimated that these two banks needed additional capital of around €250 million.[169] The Acharya-Steffen estimates suggested that the banks might need ten times as much. The two banks tried to raise equity capital so that they would not default on their creditors. Not surprisingly, no investor was willing to inject new equity in these loss-making enterprises. This placed Italy's two largest banks, UniCredit and Intesa Sanpaolo, in a bind because they had underwritten the equity-raising efforts of the failing Veneto banks. Being themselves in a financially fragile condition, and trying to spread the pain, UniCredit and Intesa Sanpaolo joined with other Italian banks and insurance companies to create the Atlante Fund in April 2016. And Atlante then injected equity funds into the two Veneto banks to make them, at least in principle, financially viable once again.

The entire idea of the Atlante Fund was bizarre. UniCredit, the largest Italian bank, was itself groaning under a huge burden of nonperforming loans. It incurred large losses in 2016, extending its repeated bouts of losses over the previous five years. Even Intesa Sanpaolo, the strongest Italian bank, had lost money in 2013 and, as Moody's said, could not insulate itself from Italy's weak economy.[170] The low interest rates that Italian banks were able to charge further squeezed their profits. Intesa Sanpaolo was profitable in 2016 but was still recovering from the difficult crisis years. Insurance companies were also stressed by the country's general economic weakness. Why would these financial institutions waste precious resources to bail out insolvent banks?

One speculative answer is that to limit the use of the Italian government's funds, European officials applied pressure on weak financial institutions to support the weakest banks.[171] The public testimonials were certainly clear. Draghi said that Atlante was a "small step in the right direction."[172] His comment followed an endorsement by European Competition Commissioner Margrethe Vestager, who said, "I think [the Italian government is] trying to find the best way for the Italian banking sector to move forward."[173] Even former ECB President Jean-Claude Trichet, no longer basking in the spotlight he once relished, came out in support of Atlante.[174]

The University of Chicago's Luigi Zingales noted that newspapers which were most heavily indebted to banks played up the official testimonials, and a consensus emerged on the virtues of the Atlante Fund. To be sure, newspapers less beholden to banks saw that this emperor had no clothes. One paper carried an article with the headline "Too many NPLs [nonperforming loans] but too little money: The weight that crushes Atlante." But such lone voices were powerless against the groupthink. Zingales despondently concluded that Atlante was the channel through which Italian banks transferred some of their losses on to insurance companies—and hence to unsuspecting pensioners and other retirees.[175]

In mid-2016, Atlante raised €4.25 billion and reportedly spent €2.5 billion to rescue the Veneto banks, well above the €250 million capital shortfall that the EBA had projected in October 2014 but fairly close to the larger sum that Acharya and Steffen had believed was likely. Briefly, hope flickered that Atlante could turn around and sell the banks to other investors. That hope was always illusory; virtually everyone understood that the banks had big financial holes. That realization came late to Alessandro Penati,

Atlante Fund's manager. Penati said he was shocked when he looked into the banks' books. "I had never looked at banks from the inside," he said. "I was stunned they are run in this way."[176] Penati discovered that Banca Popolare di Vicenza's former bosses had not just mismanaged the bank for years but had also engaged in "illicit conduct."[177] The bank's operations, he said, seemed like a "horror film."

Atlante quickly reached its limit. It had also bought nonperforming loans of three banks—Banca Etruria, Banca Marche, and CariChieti—that had been rescued in November 2015. With that additional investment, Atlante had placed nearly all its money in distressed assets. In February 2017, Penati said he needed another €4 billion and three more years to get those assets working again.[178] The Veneto banks needed even more capital than the amount Atlante had originally pumped in. But by now, the banks that had invested in Atlante had had enough. Penati had promised them a 6 percent return on their investment.[179] Instead, the two largest investors, Intesa Sanpaolo and UniCredit, each with a contribution of €1 billion to the Atlante Fund, believed they would likely lose almost 80 percent of their investment.[180]

Carlo Messina, Intesa's chief executive, said he had done enough, and it was time for the Italian government to use its own money to rescue the country's bankrupt banks.[181] The European Commission insisted that government funding would unfairly help the Veneto banks and they should first raise more funds from private investors before the government could step in with its support.

But where was the additional private money to come from? As the rating agency S&P had warned, even the stronger Italian banks had their own problems and their creditworthiness would be hurt if they continued to support the most troubled banks.[182] Moreover, although the Italian government seemed willing to assist, could it possibly afford to increase its large debt burden to support the rogue banks? Perhaps it was time to reflect on Danièle Nouy's proposition from nearly three years earlier. Continued efforts to keep the troubled banks alive would ultimately do great damage to the Italian banking system. Their problems would only grow, and the eventual cost of the cleanup would keep increasing. As a senior Italian banker said, "You can keep kicking the can down the road, but suddenly the road turns uphill and the can comes back and hits you in the face."[183]

Eventually, in June 2017, the Italian government and the European Commission worked their way through the convoluted maze of European rules. The European Commission gave the green light for the government to use its own money to settle the Veneto banks' problems. Some bondholders were bailed in but were promised that they would be compensated. In the main transaction, the government paid—yes, *paid*—Intesa Sanpaolo €4.8 billion to fold the "good assets" of the Veneto banks into its operations. The government also guaranteed that if losses continued to mount on even these "good assets," the government would pay Intesa Sanpaolo a further €12 billion.[184] From an anticipated €250 million in October 2014, the cost of handling just these two banks had grown to a possible €17 billion. There were also the "bad assets" of the two banks, which the government could be billed for in the future.

The kicking-the-can-down-the-road strategy faced its real test with MPS. Recall that in October 2014, the EBA estimated that MPS would need additional capital of around €4 billion.[185] The bank raised that amount and more. But in July 2016, the EBA concluded that MPS needed yet another €5 billion in capital.[186] Acharya and Steffen, this time joined by Diane Pierret of the University of Lausanne, reported that by the standards of US stress tests, MPS needed close to €9 billion.[187] As in past stress tests, the EBA methodology underestimated the risks banks faced and overestimated the capital they held.

For some months, the hope was that a JPMorgan-led consortium would help MPS raise €5 billion in additional capital and sell €30 billion of the bank's bad loans. If such a transaction were possible, MPS would have an opportunity for a fresh start. But MPS's financial hole was much deeper, and its business and political connections were much murkier than at the Veneto banks—banks that no private sector investor had been willing to touch.

By December 2016, with no white-knight investor in sight, the Italian government understood that it would need to use substantial taxpayer funds to recapitalize MPS. By now, European authorities had concluded that MPS would need almost €9 billion of additional capital, as Acharya and his colleagues—with their consistent track record—had already estimated. Action was delayed for several months, because European rules required creditors to be bailed in before a bank received government financial support, and the Italian government remained unwilling to bail in creditors. Thus, European authorities and the Italian government agreed on the fiction that MPS was a "solvent" bank and, if given the additional capital, would reemerge as a productive financial institution. Finally, in early July 2017, the government was ready to inject between €6 billion and €8 billion.[188] The exact numbers are unclear. Of the nearly €9 billion needed, MPS contributed a small amount from its reserves. Junior debt holders—first in line to absorb losses after equity holders—were bailed in (holders of such debt would receive the bank's shares); however, a third of the junior debt, owed to retail investors, would be repaid through a special government compensation system.[189]

In the end, the central government became 70 percent owner of MPS. With ownership came the burden of losses on MPS's loans. The Atlante Fund had "committed" to buying €25 billion of MPS's nonperforming loans at 21 cents on the euro.[190] That seemed a generous price, since the stronger UniCredit had also sold its nonperforming loans at a similar discount.[191] Moreover, Atlante had little money left in its own pot and would need to attract other investors to complete the purchase. The bigger problem, as any historian of banking crises knew, was that initial estimates of financial holes left by banking crises almost always proved to be embarrassingly inadequate. For the Veneto banks, the government had acknowledged that possibility and guaranteed Intesa Sanpaolo a further €12 billion to cover more losses. Zingales pointed out in an interview with Bloomberg that MPS and other troubled banks had been evergreening their troubled loans, in which case the true size of their nonperforming loans was possibly substantially larger than reported.[192]

The risk was that Italian officials, lulled by a stabilization of nonperforming loans, would declare their task done (figure 8.6).[193] In December 2016, the government set aside €20 billion to stabilize the banking system, a large part of which it quickly used for the Veneto banks and MPS. Drawing on the recent history, Zingales, in another interview, predicted that the full cleanup of Italian banks would require €50 billion.[194] And even this amount could prove too little if the sources of mismanagement and fraud in Italian banks were not identified and fixed. It was time, Zingales said, for an independent commission of international experts to propose a fundamental restructuring of the Italian banking system. But Italy's political leaders apparently did not have the self-confidence to open up a public discussion of the future of Italian banking, and without such a transparent assessment, problems would continue, and more mistakes would certainly occur.

The Italian Economy Gets a Breather—a Brief One

A new source of optimism emerged. Italian GDP, which had crawled out of recession in 2014 and had increased at an annual rate of around 1 percent in 2015 and 2016, started growing at a pace close to 1.5 percent in 2017. That stepped-up pace was just about the average that the Italian economy had achieved in the decade before joining the euro. This was still a very low

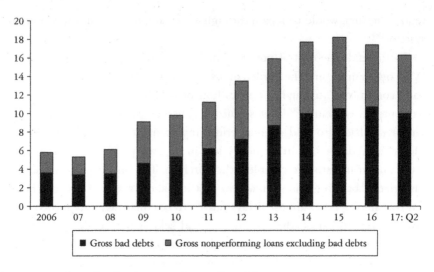

20
18
16
14
12
10
8
6
4
2
0

2006 07 08 09 10 11 12 13 14 15 16 17: Q2

■ Gross bad debts ■ Gross nonperforming loans excluding bad debts

FIGURE 8.6. Italian banks struggle to collect debts.
(Nonperforming loans as a percentage of all loans)
Note: "Nonperforming loans" are the loans on which scheduled payments are late by more than 90 days.
"Bad debts" are a category of nonperforming loans whose full repayment is highly uncertain because the
debtors are either legally insolvent or are in an essentially similar situation.
Source: Banca d'Italia. "Financial Stability Report." November 2017, https://www.bancaditalia.it/
pubblicazioni/rapporto-stabilita/2017-2/index.html. The complete data series is in: "Data for charts,"
Section 2. Financial system risks, Figure 2.11. Non-performing loan ratios, per cent.

growth rate, especially after such a prolonged downturn. But any sign of
Italian growth deserved celebration. The question was whether the growth—
and the celebration—would continue.

Italy's welcome breather in growth was in part due to a revival of global
trade in mid-2017. The breather was also helped by a shift away from the
severe fiscal austerity of 2012–2013 to a small fiscal stimulus in 2014–2015
and even more stimulus in 2016–2017. Italy was experiencing a relief rally.
As several studies have shown, the fiscal multiplier—the amplification of
fiscal stimulus into GDP growth—is particularly high when an economy is
in or near recessionary conditions. With the squeeze of the past years partly
lifted, people who had postponed consumption were now catching up on
purchases they had long delayed.

Renzi deserved credit for fighting the good fight against fiscal austerity.
Italy's need for fiscal relaxation was real, and Renzi had economics on his side.
However, the process and the accompanying debates were agonizing. To any
outsider, these debates would seem an exercise in absurd precision. Padoan
argued—pleaded—that the European Commission needed to see sense. The
government's spending had increased to deal with multiple earthquakes and

migrants arriving by boat across the Mediterranean Sea. And the Italian economy remained sluggish. The commission seemed aware that its "politically toxic" demands for more fiscal belt-tightening were shoring up support for the anti-euro Five Star Movement.[195] And yet the commission dragged its feet, repeating the mantra that Italy needed to stay focused on deficit reduction. Thus, despite recent experience which unambiguously showed that, in a recession, austerity hurts and stimulus helps, the eurozone did not achieve the necessary change to a sensibly responsible fiscal policy. Rather, a new narrowly discretionary policy regime emerged. The commission would modestly ease its earlier adherence to fiscal austerity. However, the impression gained ground that Italy and, even more so, France would receive special leeway in this new regime.[196]

For Italy, the question was what would happen when the fiscal stimulus ended, as was projected to occur in 2018. The IMF reported that Italian investment had "collapsed." Investment spending had fallen sharply in 2012 and 2013 at the onset of the draconian fiscal austerity drive and since then it had either fallen further or stayed stable . The IMF estimated that Italy's potential growth had declined to about 0.5 percent a year.[197] On top of Italy's long-term problems, including a working-age population that had stopped increasing and near-zero productivity growth, the intense austerity had further damaged long-term growth prospects.

And if Italian GDP growth remained at around the IMF's potential growth rate estimate, Italy's financial vulnerabilities would remain worrisome. The recent descent into low inflation made growth harder to revive and added to the risk that debt burdens would remain elevated.

Could the ECB help revive inflation?

The ECB's QE: Not Too Little, but Too Late

The ECB's QE came on January 22, 2015. Draghi announced that the ECB would "add the purchase of sovereign bonds to its existing private sector asset purchase programmes," with combined monthly purchases amounting to €60 billion.[198] Purchases were to start in March and continue at least until September 2016.

The tensions remained. Jens Weidmann was not shy in opposing QE publicly. In an interview with *Bild*, Weidmann rightly said that QE would make the ECB the principal creditor to eurozone governments.[199] Having gone down this route, the ECB would have little choice but to hold government debt at low interest rates for a long time, and it would become a pawn in the political process.[200] German media, business interests, and politicians echoed Weidman's views.[201]

Merkel, as always, was more circumspect. She had not confronted the ECB thus far, and she did not do so now. She did wonder why QE was needed when the world was already "well supplied with liquidity"; the "real growth impulses," she said, "must come from conditions set by [domestic] politicians."[202] But the ECB was an independent organization, she added, and its decision would probably help economic recovery, although only if the countries carried out their own reforms.[203]

Starting in January 2015, over the next three years, the ECB bought large quantities of government bonds, extending the program beyond the original terminal date of September 2016. The ECB's balance sheet more than doubled from €2 trillion in January 2015 to about €4.5 trillion in late 2017. But here's the rub: the ECB laid out all this money, and the eurozone's average inflation rate remained stubbornly unchanged, moving in a small range below 1 percent until mid-2017, before rising slightly above 1 percent for technical and temporary reasons (figure 8.7).[204] The German rate remained above the average rate; Italian and French inflation rates remained below the eurozone average. ECB staff continued, each year, to predict that inflation would return to near 2 percent, but the inflation rate did not respond.

A student of the BOJ's experience could have predicted the lack of response to the ECB's QE. The BOJ had steadily pushed its balance sheet up over several years. Yet during these years, Japanese inflation rose only for brief spells, soon to fall back again. In January 2013, recently elected Prime Minister Shinzo Abe announced that the government and the BOJ, working "in close cooperation" would pursue "bold monetary policy" to fight entrenched low inflation.[205] The initiative, popularly labeled "Abenomics," created a flurry of popular interest and excitement. In April 2013, the BOJ unfurled a historically unprecedented QE program.[206] By early 2014, the BOJ was buying considerably more than the net amount of new bonds issued by the Japanese government.[207] By this metric, the BOJ's QE was much larger than the Fed's. The Fed did not come close to buying the net issuance of US government bonds.[208] The BOJ's QE pushed down the exchange value of the yen. In fact, starting in December 2012, in anticipation of a big monetary stimulus, and continuing through mid-2015, the yen depreciated (relative to the dollar) by about 20 percent. The yen's depreciation tended to raise the prices of goods imported into Japan, which temporarily raised the domestic inflation rate. However, despite that boost, by early 2014, the inflation rate began coming down. The BOJ's extraordinary effort had little to show by way of sustained increase in inflation.[209]

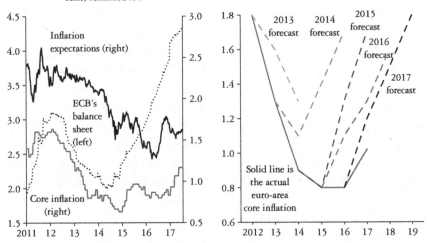

The ECB's balance sheet (left-hand scale, trillion euros) increased rapidly, but the annual inflation rate (right-hand scale) remained low

Despite ECB forecasts of rise in inflation, inflation remained at a low level

FIGURE 8.7. ECB's quantitative easing fails to move inflation.

Note: The ECB's balance sheet and inflation expectations are plotted at weekly frequency; the core inflation rate for the week is the same as the year-on-year monthly inflation during the month in which the week falls.

Sources: Left panel: ECB Balance Sheet, Bloomberg's weekly "EBBSTOTA Index" at weekly frequency; inflation expectations are measured by Bloomberg's daily FWISEU55 index (five-year, five-year inflation swaps); core inflation is the three-month moving average of Eurostat's annual change in the monthly "HICP—All-items excluding energy and food" index.

Right panel: ECB's Macroeconomic Projections made in March of the year, https://www.ecb.europa.eu/pub/projections/html/index.en.html.

In March 2014, Paul Krugman, by then professor of economics at Princeton and the 2008 recipient of the Nobel Prize in Economics, commented on the disappointing results from Abenomics. His message was simple: the BOJ had lost credibility.[210] It had been timid for too long, and people were no longer sure that it would see its new promises through. To restore its credibility, the BOJ needed an even bolder QE to display an even firmer commitment to raising inflation substantially. Only then would people believe that inflation was likely to rise. Japanese QE was faltering, Krugman said, because—despite its unprecedented scale—it was not bold enough. Japanese policymakers, he said, were still stuck in a "timidity trap." If implemented a decade earlier, the QE could well have been productive, even decisive. Now it was only a "half-measure."[211] In June 2017, researchers at the University of Tokyo found support for Krugman's interpretation of the Japanese problem. Unlike in the United States, where producers increase their prices by an average of 2 percent every year, Japanese producers do not change their prices. Because of "prolonged deflation," the norm for Japanese firms is to "keep prices unchanged."[212] Thus, price-setting behavior has become disengaged from monetary policy. The lesson was that a policy not taken in time is a policy not taken. The ECB was relearning that lesson.

The ECB's QE, coming as late as it did, was considerably larger than the BOJ's. The ECB's bond purchases reached seven times governments' net bond issuance.[213] In other words, for every euro of net new bonds issued by eurozone governments, the ECB bought €7 worth of bonds. Thus, the ECB was gobbling up the inventory of bonds issued in the past. The ECB was becoming a major creditor to eurozone governments. But despite that massive effort, like the BOJ, the ECB seemed a victim of its timidity trap. For too long, the ECB had not followed up on its many promises to take measures bold enough to register a firm message of resolve; hence, deflationary forces appeared to have settled into large parts of the eurozone.

Moreover, QE would soon need to be scaled down. Purchases of government bonds were approaching the ECB's self-imposed limit of 33 percent of the share of a country's outstanding bonds.[214] In anticipation of gradual QE reduction, the euro strengthened.

In late October 2017, Draghi announced that from January 2018, the ECB would reduce bond purchases to €30 billion a month, down from €60 billion every month since January 2015.[215] QE tapering had begun. In the days after Draghi's press conference, one euro was worth between $1.16 and $1.18, about the same level as in early January 2015, when QE seemed imminent. Thus, unlike the yen, which remained below its pre-Abenomics level, the euro was back to its starting point before QE. The eurozone QE's boost to growth and inflation through a weaker exchange rate was, therefore, limited.

The implications are sobering. In Japan, despite potentially open-ended aggressive monetary policy, the hoped-for increase in inflation did not materialize. In the eurozone, where the large QE was always known to be time bound, the impact is likely to be even weaker. As in Japan, eurozone member countries will experience brief spells of renewed inflation in the coming years, but these episodes will relapse into low inflation.[216] Already, expecting inflation to remain low, businesses have adapted their price setting behavior. In Italy over the last few years, a large number of producers have raised their prices by less than 1 percent a year.[217] If such lowflation tendency persists, debt burdens will remain high and, with weak productivity growth, GDP growth will remain sluggish. In that case, financial stresses will linger.

Thus, the eurozone's—and Italy's—sweet spot in the second half of 2017 appeared likely to end. Fiscal stimulus seemed set to stop, interest rates seemed likely to rise, and the euro was already stronger. Unless world trade stayed unexpectedly strong, there would have been too little time in the sweet spot to resume investment for long-term growth. For the Italian government's creditors and for Italy's fragile banks, this was not good news.

Although its benefits were questionable, QE left a troubling legacy. As Harald Benink and Harry Huizinga, professors of economics and finance at Tilburg University, wrote, "too little attention has been paid to how the details of the new quantitative easing run the risk of undermining the credibility of other ECB programs in ways that could make a future crisis harder to resolve."[218] For QE, each national central bank would buy its own government's bonds and hold 92 percent of the risk of those bonds; the ECB would bear only 8 percent of the risk. If the Italian government defaulted on its bonds, the Banca d'Italia would need to draw on its capital and reserves to absorb 92 percent of the loss; all member states would share the other 8 percent of the losses. The ECB had designed its QE program to protect the Germans, who had opposed the plan to the very end.

As a result of the decisions taken on the matter of QE, a potentially serious precedent has been set for the controversial OMT program described in chapter 7. Only the ECB can print money to buy a member country's bonds in potentially "unlimited quantities" and thus squash fears of default on those bonds. National central banks do not have capital and reserves large enough to promise credibly that they will buy "unlimited quantities" of their own government's bonds. Although Draghi has reaffirmed that the ECB will bear the entire risk in an OMT operation, the likelihood has grown that politicians would demand that national central banks also bear the risk in an OMT operation and thus fatally undermine that program.

The original conundrum remains. A single monetary policy for diverse countries cannot operate effectively without a mechanism to share risks in crisis conditions. Eurozone leaders cannot agree to a risk-sharing mechanism based on a democratically legitimate political contract. Under pressure during the crisis years, they agreed on technical arrangements to share risks. These arrangements can be undone politically at an inopportune moment.

Italy, the Theater for EuroTragedy

In his book *Collapse: How Societies Choose to Fail or Succeed*, biologist, ecologist, anthropologist, and Pulitzer Prize-winning author Jared Diamond writes that some societies slip into what at first is an imperceptible decline. The decline goes unnoticed, he explains, because "If the economy, schools, traffic congestion, or anything else is deteriorating only slowly, it's difficult to recognize that each successive year is on the average slightly worse than the year before that." The decline begins to appear normal. Or, as Diamond puts it, because the slide is not evident, a sense of "creeping normalcy" settles in. Hence, it can take decades of "slight year-to-year changes before people realize, with a jolt," that conditions have deteriorated greatly.[219]

A creeping national economic decline is the essence of the Italian story. Italian productivity growth, which had been slowing since the early 1970s, ground to a halt after Italy entered the fold of the single currency. Sadly, but some would say predictably, the euro failed to act as the "external anchor" that would tame Italy's unruly politics. Once the global financial crisis started in mid-2007, Italy remained either in crisis or in a state from which it could quickly relapse into another crisis. During these crisis years, the euro area's macroeconomic policies—operating with the twin norms of fiscal austerity and price stability at all costs—constrained Italian opportunities for economic recovery. Those constraints operated most viciously between 2011 and 2013, and they pushed Italy close to the economic and financial cliff edge. The easing of interest rates—through the promise of OMTs in July 2012 and QE since 2015—was too late to help stimulate a robust recovery and pull Italy out of a potential deflationary trap.

The tragedy is that inside the eurozone, Italy experienced the worst of all worlds. The euro and its governance structures did not create a positive impulse for change, and neither did they provide a "jolt" to shake Italians out of their sense of "creeping normalcy." The eurozone's financial support systems created a safety net, which helped the country survive in near-crisis conditions. Italy did not undergo a much-needed economic and political catharsis.

Italian and European authorities alike kept hoping that Italy would soon turn the corner. Perhaps the next recapitalization would save MPS, and it would become a real bank again. Instead, the bill for rescuing MPS continued to increase. Perhaps the unelected technocrat Monti would implement structural reforms. But Monti barely left an impression.

The ultimate great hope was Renzi. Perhaps Renzi would upend the old and corrupt political order, which he said was engaged merely in "rent-seeking." Then Italy would make a truly new start. Renzi correctly identified Italy's core problem to be its entrenched networks of patronage, which had long flourished beneath the cacophony of Italian politics. In the early and mid-1990s, the *mani pulite* ("clean hands") judicial inquiries had exposed leading Italian politicians and weakened centralized corruption.[220] However, corruption merely spread to regional and municipal governments, where it continued as a plague. And as the Italian government extended its regulatory and administrative reach, more opportunities for corruption opened up in seeking preferential deals and padded procurement contracts. The threshold of public tolerance for corruption increased along with the emergence of Berlusconi as a national leader. Italians elected Berlusconi as their prime minister in 2001 and 2008, even though he had been under investigation in multiple corruption cases. Berlusconi gained license to undermine the fight against corruption with his defiance of the judicial system.

The IMF, which rarely comments on corruption in advanced economies, had remained pessimistic; Italy's epidemic of corruption and money laundering seemed set to continue.[221] These corrosive networks created entitlements in the public sphere and undermined merit in the private sphere. They nudged Italians to diminish their own aspirations and their expectations of others. Italy settled into a "normal" of reduced expectations.

But while Renzi talked the good talk of fighting long-standing corruption in Italian politics and public affairs, he lacked the endurance to follow through. He even cynically gutted an ongoing effort essential in the fight against corruption, an attempt to streamline Italy's notoriously inefficient public administration and unprofitable government-owned companies. His predecessor, Enrico Letta, had appointed Carlo Cottarelli, a former IMF official, as a special commissioner of public spending to suggest ways of downsizing the government and saving operational costs. When Cottarelli had proposed sweeping cuts, Renzi had balked.

Renzi's minister for public administration, Marianna Madia, mournfully said, "When things remain the same for a very long time, they become set in stone and that makes change slow and difficult."[222] Indeed, things had remained the same for a very long time in Italy, and Renzi was not going to be the man to change that. His youthful zeal faded. Having started with a promise to "set the world on fire," he meekly concluded, "There is a sense of worry, fatigue, lack of confidence in Italy."[223] The fatigue of a nation beaten down by long years of economic and political disarray seeped into Renzi.

And so Renzi raced down yet another path that Italian politicians had traversed before without success. He sought to curb the powers of the senate (the upper house of parliament) and to reduce the authority of regional and municipal governments. In combination with his plan to change the electoral law so that it would favor single-party or strong coalition governments, Renzi attempted to create an electoral system that would concentrate more executive authority in the prime minister. This may have been a worthy goal; perhaps this was how the Gordian knot needed to be cut.

But in December 2016, when Renzi asked Italian citizens in a national referendum to ratify his plan, the country's accumulated economic anxiety and humiliation had its say. Renzi desperately played the anti-Europe card to win over the Italian public.[224] He removed the European Union flag from his desk, leaving six Italian flags on display. Sandro Gozi, Renzi's Undersecretary of State for European Affairs, dramatically said, "We're very tired of a Europe that is petty in what matters and overbearing in what is petty, and we're convinced that if Europe doesn't change, we're looking at the onset of European disintegration." Not to be outdone, Grillo also wrapped himself in the Italian flag. "I will be waiting for you tomorrow in Rome," he tweeted. "We'll meet at 1:30 at the Basilica di San Paolo fuori Le Mura (St. Paul's Outside the Walls). If you can, bring an Italian flag."[225]

Nearly 60 percent of Italians voted to reject the proposed changes. Italians rejected the changes to the electoral system not because they had thought very deeply about the changes proposed but, rather, because the referendum gave them an opportunity to vent their economic and political frustrations. For many, the referendum was on whether or not the Italian political establishment was willing to stand up to Europe. Renzi's defiant last-minute call for Europe to reform was neither impressive nor credible.

As had by now become the norm in European referendums, the protest vote came from those who were poorly educated and who lived in districts where hope of economic revival was ebbing. Italy's young, who had borne the brunt of the country's economic woes, voted even more angrily: around 80 percent of those between the ages of eighteen and twenty-four voted against the changes Renzi had proposed.

Renzi was young in age, but he had stayed tightly trapped in the machinations of the old political order. From within that trap, it was hard for him to make a connection with the needs and aspirations of Italy's dispirited youth.

Renzi had promised that he would resign if Italians rejected his proposal, and he did so immediately. He had held the prime minister's office for two years and ten months, around the average tenure of a postwar Italian prime minister. In his brief moment in the Italian and European spotlight, Renzi further splintered Italian politics and badly divided his own Democratic Party. And as people looked for alternatives, Grillo's Five Star Movement and euro-skepticism took deeper root in Italy.

The Italian public, which had at one time so wanted to believe in Europe, appeared to have abandoned hope that European "discipline" would help achieve a more hopeful future. In 2016, only 36 percent of Italians trusted the EU, down a precipitous 38 percentage points from 74 percent in 2001 (figure 8.8). This stunning decline in Italians' trust in Europe mirrored their own economic sense of hopelessness.

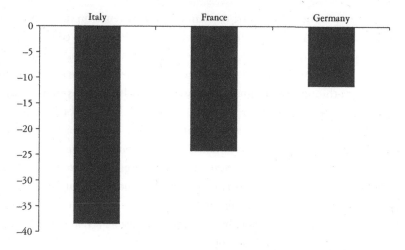

FIGURE 8.8. Italians lose their trust in Europe.
(Decrease in percentage of respondents who trust the European Union, 2016 relative to 2001)
Note: Respondents answered the following question: "I would like to ask you a question about how much trust you have in certain institutions. For each of the following institutions, please tell me if you (Tend to trust it; Tend not to trust it) The European Union." The chart presents the change in share of people who said they trusted the EU. For each year, 2001 and 2016, responses for the two available quarters are averaged.
Source: Standard Eurobarometer survey, available at http://zacat.gesis.org.

More remarkable, although not surprising, was the extraordinarily low trust that young Italians now placed in Europe. Ever since such surveys began, the youngest Europeans had been the most idealistic and had supported and trusted Europe more than previous generations had done. But that gap narrowed in many European countries, as the plague of youth unemployment chewed away at the idealism of the young. In Italy, this tendency went a step further: Italian millennials—those born after 1991—trusted Europe far less than their parents and grandparents did.[226] Italy's youth, who had given up on Renzi, were giving up on Europe.

The combination of economic stress and political disarray led to murmurs of Italexit, the possibility that Italy would need to leave the eurozone. If that happened, the new lira would depreciate quickly, and in the ensuing panic, it is entirely possible that Italians would need between three and four new liras to buy a euro.[227] With such large depreciation, debts denominated in euros would become hard, if not impossible, to repay. In January 2017, analysts at Mediobanca Securities wrote a widely read report in which they concluded that with the passage of every year, it was becoming more expensive for Italy to drop the euro and return to the lira.[228] Under some existing debt contracts, legal loopholes appear to allow Italian borrowers to repay 100 liras in place of the €100 they earlier owed. But the eurozone's insistence on new debt contracts make such a ruse more difficult; Italians would need to come up with the lira equivalent of the €100 and they would thus find it harder to repay their debts. Widespread defaults would follow, whose knock-on effects would send tremors through world financial markets.[229] If Italexit has to happen, it had better be soon. The longer the wait, the bigger Italy's debt burden will be and, hence, the larger the debt defaults will be. The damage from such defaults to European and global financial systems could be extensive.

In early July 2017, the Five Star Movement organized a seminar in the European Parliament on the costs of Italexit.[230] The Five Star Movement's leadership was cautious about taking a position on the matter. But the fact that a high-profile seminar was held in the European Parliament was itself noteworthy. This genie had come out of the bottle.

CHAPTER 9

The Final Act

A Declining and Divided Europe

SINCE THE EURO'S launch in 1999, eurozone economies have fallen steadily behind in the league of the world's major economies. The eurozone's most serious and persistent infirmity is its low productivity growth. This handicap was compounded over the past decade, initially by the hesitant monetary and fiscal policy response to the global financial crisis that began in mid-2007 and then by disastrous policy errors in dealing with the eurozone's own rolling crises between late 2009 and early 2014. While the eurozone economy stumbled from one crisis to another, the US economy recovered slowly but surely, bolstered by forceful monetary stimulus and aggressive efforts to revive the financial system (figure 9.1). Even the US recovery was weak when compared with its own standards of postwar recoveries from economic crises. This was so in part because the government withdrew fiscal stimulus too quickly. But the US response was sufficiently proactive to quickly banish the specter of its 1930s Great Depression. Eurozone economies as a group did worse even relative to their own performance after the Great Depression.

Indeed, since the onset of the global crisis in 2007, no eurozone economy has performed better than Japan did in its "lost decade." As described in chapter 8, after Japan's property-banking bubble burst in late-1990, Japanese policymakers made the mistake of keeping monetary policy too tight, which not only slowed down economic growth but also pushed prices down into a low-inflation zone. Persistent lowflation created expectations of possible price declines and, hence, delay of planned purchases, increasing the drag on growth. The Japanese economy did not suffer more because it had important strengths. Many decades of investment in education, R&D, advanced

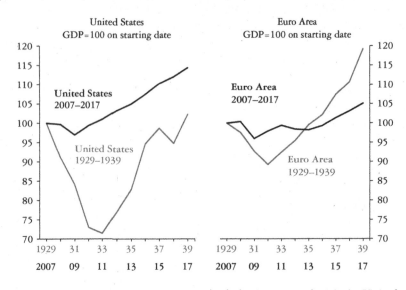

United States
GDP=100 on starting date

Euro Area
GDP=100 on starting date

United States
2007–2017

Euro Area
2007–2017

United States
1929–1939

Euro Area
1929–1939

FIGURE 9.1. The crisis sets the euro area back, both compared with the United States and relative to its own pace after the Great Depression.
Sources: Angus Maddison, "Historical Statistics of the World Economy 1-2008AD," http://www.ggdc.net/maddison/oriindex.htm; International Monetary Fund, World Economic Outlook Database October, http://www.imf.org/external/pubs/ft/weo/2014/02/weodata/index.aspx, series "Gross Domestic Product, constant prices," 2007–2016.

production machinery, and innovative shop-floor management imparted a resilience that helped Japanese businesses make modest progress despite the policy errors. The eurozone's crisis hit the southern economies—France, Greece, Italy, Portugal, and Spain—particularly hard. These countries had, to varying degrees, the double disadvantage of an incipient Japanese-style lowflation and meager investments in sources of long-term growth.

Moreover, the eurozone's decline in the global economic league is set to continue. On top of the historically low productivity growth, stingy monetary stimulus through 2014 and fiscal austerity through 2013 inflicted damage not just at the time but also to future growth potential.[1] Some workers who were unemployed for long periods might never catch up with ever more demanding skill requirements, and it will take years for companies to make up for protracted cutbacks in investment and research during the long-drawn crisis. Looking ahead, even with monetary and fiscal policy brakes taken off, eurozone economies will very likely grow at a significantly slower average pace over the next decade than they did in the decade before the crisis began.

The long-term productivity-growth lag, made worse by the setback of the prolonged crisis, practically ensures that eurozone economies will fall farther behind the world's most dynamic economies. The United States, despite its many political problems and, even at the best of times, messy governance process, remains a hub of frontier technology. Asian nations are leaving Europe behind in the technology race at a dramatic pace (figure 9.2). If China continues to invest in its educational system and R&D at its recent rate, most European nations will descend permanently to second- and even third-tier technological status.

Protracted low eurozone growth will be a particularly serious problem because financial vulnerabilities remain elevated and widespread. Economic growth is the most potent antidote to financial stresses. Growth helps borrowers reduce their debt burdens and financially stronger borrowers help restore the banking sector's health. The eurozone's combination of high government-debt burdens, banking fragility, and low growth creates the classic conditions for rapid loss of investor confidence that could tip the region back into a crisis and once again send tremors through European and, indeed, world financial markets.

A further consequence of the crisis is that the economic disparities between the north and south have increased. Unlike the southern countries, the northern eurozone countries—the most financially secure of which are Austria, Finland, Germany, and the Netherlands—have emerged from the

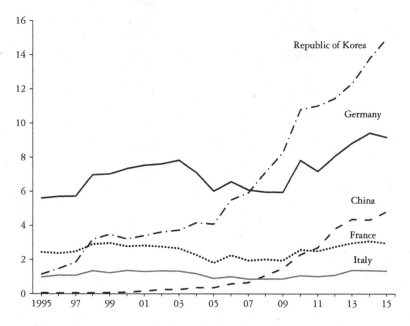

FIGURE 9.2. Asia surges ahead of Europe in the technology race.
(US patents granted annually to companies in different countries, numbers in thousands)
Source: World Intellectual Property Statistics Database, https://www3.wipo.int/ipstats/index.htm.

crisis bruised but not battered. This economic divergence within the euro-zone has had political consequences. Through the course of the crisis, the north has remained wary of having to finance the south. Political tensions among the leaders of these two groups of countries, and among the peoples of these two country groups, have grown. These tensions are here to stay and they limit the prospect of finding collective solutions to Europe's problems.

North and South Eurozone on Divergent Paths

In the north, government debt burdens—debt-to-GDP ratios—initially rose after the onset of the global financial crisis, but then either declined or remained comfortably below 100 percent of GDP, the threshold beyond which public debt becomes a serious financial risk (figure 9.3).[2] In the south, debt ratios

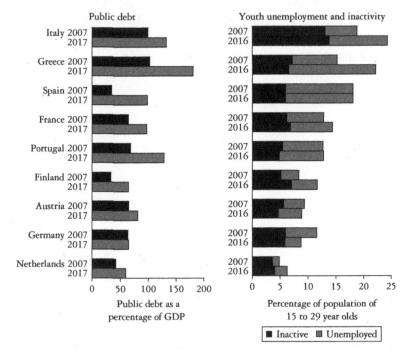

FIGURE 9.3. The great euro-area north-south divergence: public debt and youth distress.

Note: Countries on the left side correspond to the countries on the right side. The "unemployed" are those who are looking for a job but are unable to find one; the "inactive" are not looking for a job and neither are they in an educational or training program. The sum of the unemployed and inactive is known as "neither in employment, education or training" (NEET).

Source: IMF, "World Economic Outlook" Database; Eurostat (edat_lfse_20).

rose almost continuously during the extended eurozone crisis and now are close to or above the risky 100 percent of GDP threshold.

The more troubling disparity between the north and the south is in the fortunes of the young. The best measure to assess the economic conditions and prospects of young people is not the conventional unemployment rate, which focuses only on those who are in the labor force (and, hence, either working or looking for a job); a more comprehensive measure takes account of the entire population of young people. While some in the population are unemployed, those who are classified as "inactive" also experience severe stress; indeed, their numbers point to economic hopelessness. The inactive are not in school or college, have no formal work, and have stopped looking for a job; they have given up in despair. By this metric, which sums the unemployed and the inactive, northern countries, with their better-performing economies, have better catered to the needs of their young citizens. The problem of youth unemployment and inactivity has actually declined in the past decade in Austria and Germany; in Finland and the Netherlands, despite a modest increase, it has remained low.

The southern countries have unfortunately failed to give their young hope for the future. Their acute youth distress either has remained unchanged, as in Portugal and Spain, or has increased, as in France, Greece, and Italy. Italy stands out. Around 10 percent of all Italians between the ages of fifteen and twenty-nine are unemployed. An additional 14 percent are inactive. Thus, nearly a quarter of all young Italians and around one-fifth of young Spaniards have big question marks hanging over their future economic security.

The euro was bound to create north-south divergence. Economists Nicholas Kaldor in 1971 and Alan Walters in 1986 predicted that a single currency, with its single monetary policy and uniform fiscal policy, would amplify differences between the stronger and weaker member nations.[3] European leaders chose to defy economics. Economics is exacting its revenge.

In fact, the problem is more serious than Kaldor and Walters anticipated. Economic growth is highly nonlinear. Critical moments in history create opportunities for some countries to flourish and, at the same time, they can push other countries into a low-growth trap. One such critical juncture was the onset of the Industrial Revolution in the late eighteenth century, when some European economies set off on an explosive growth path, while many formerly advanced economies in Latin America and Africa fell into long-term decline.[4] Scholars have described this eighteenth-century bifurcation in the economic fortunes of nations as the "Great Divergence." Even at less dramatic critical junctures, the same phenomenon repeats: the hardy survive and even flourish; the weak do not just suffer a temporary setback, but they lose the reserves to regroup and regain even their earlier modest performance.[5]

The twin blows of the global and eurozone crises created another such critical juncture. At that juncture, north and south eurozone countries, using the same currency, set off on different economic trajectories. While the weaker southern members suffered wounds and carry long-lasting scars, the stronger northern eurozone members seem to have emerged with minor injuries. The divergence between the hobbled south and largely healed north will, I expect, persist—and it will further test the functioning and integrity of the eurozone.

The Eurozone's South Lacks Domestic Resilience

Every economy needs mechanisms to cope with adversity. A country's exchange rate is one such mechanism. But eurozone countries do not have their own currencies, which they can let depreciate during a recession or a crisis. Depreciation helps stimulate exports, which creates jobs in the domestic economy.

While all eurozone countries gave up their national currencies, the southern member states have the additional disadvantage that they also suffer from particularly low productivity growth. Robust productivity growth can act as a coping mechanism, because it engenders confidence among borrowers that economic growth will soon resume despite the adversity and they will, therefore, be able to repay their debts. In contrast, when productivity growth is low, recessions and crises place borrowers and their creditors under severe financial stress. Those stresses reduce spending and weaken confidence in the future. Crisis-like conditions persist and recovery takes longer. Thus, the eurozone's authorities' preference for tight monetary and fiscal policies had a more severe impact in the south. The tight policy stance left the southern countries with no realistic option to grow out of the crisis, and the extended period in recession or crisis, further lowered their potential to grow.

In the early discussions on membership of the eurozone, many questioned the wisdom of including Greece, Italy, Portugal, and Spain in the single currency area. There were big question marks on whether these countries were ready for the rigors of operating without their own currencies and monetary policies.[6] The decision to go ahead and include them in the eurozone was based on the belief that these countries would take active policy measures to strengthen their economies so that they could better withstand economic shocks. That optimistic belief proved unfounded. Once they were inside the eurozone, their economies performed even worse than in earlier years. Crucially, through much of the euro's first decade, their productivity growth rates were close to zero—and, for extended stretches, were even negative. Such poor productivity performance reflected weak educational and R&D systems and, hence, the inability to produce a range of high-quality products needed to compete with advanced nations in international markets.[7]

Even France's total factor productivity growth in the eurozone's first ten years—between 1999 and 2008—was close to zero. While French R&D rates were a notch above those in other southern countries, the French educational system had fallen behind those of other advanced economies; technological output, as measured by patents, languished.

The deeper causes of the southern eurozone's low productivity growth lay in endemic institutional deficiencies. In the Greek and Italian cases, the deficiencies manifested themselves in pervasive corruption, which sucked up creative energies.[8] In all southern countries, institutional weaknesses were evident in the significant incentives for people to work in the "shadow" economy, where those unable to find gainful employment in the formal economy worked at the edges of the law to earn a livelihood. Intriguingly, France, in keeping with the recent manifestation of its decline, was one of the few European countries where the share of the shadow economy increased after 2013.[9]

A comprehensive World Bank indicator of national governance and institutional quality tells a worrisome story for the southern countries (figure 9.4). They all rank low on this measure; Greece and Italy rank strikingly low; all except France have fallen further behind since they joined the eurozone.

Thus, the north-south divide in debt and youth unemployment noted earlier in this chapter is not a surprise. Countries with weak governance and institutions, on average, grow more slowly, as a recent ECB study confirmed.[10] Because they grow more slowly, they tend to build up debt burdens (their debt-to-GDP ratios) more quickly, and they tend to leave their youth struggling. It is an unforgiving trap: poor governance and institutions diminish the incentives to invest in growth, which elevate the debt burdens and youth stress.

Emerging from this trap has been difficult because social inequalities make it hard to reach political consensus. And inequalities have remained high because educational systems failed to create sufficient opportunities for children to lead better lives than their parents did. Large groups of citizens, therefore, have had reason to believe that they would remain stuck in their low stations in life. Austerity and structural-reform policies during the crisis heightened these social inequalities by placing the greatest burden of

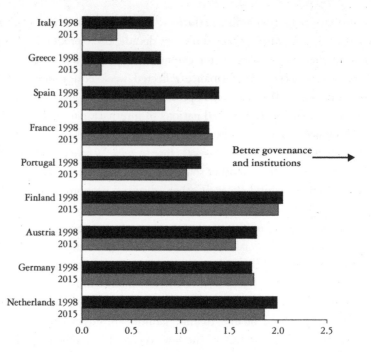

FIGURE 9.4. Southern euro area suffers from weak governance and institutions.
Note: The overall index presented is an average of measures for government effectiveness, regulatory quality, rule of law, and control of corruption. Each individual measure is normally distributed, with a mean of zero, a standard deviation of 1, and an approximate range of -2.5 to 2.5. Larger values indicate better governance.
Source: World Bank, Worldwide Governance Indicator.

economic adjustment on those who were least able to bear it. The task of reaching political consensus on the way forward became that much harder.

These long-term concerns about the eurozone's south seemed to recede somewhat starting in mid-2017. A mood of optimism spread through much of Europe. GDP growth picked up in virtually every country, which also helped increase government revenues and, hence, eased budgetary pressures. Newspaper reports echoed statements by officials who spoke of a "broad-based" recovery, one that was "resilient" and "gathering pace."

In part, the improved sentiment in Europe reflected broader global bullishness. As Nobel laureate Robert Shiller wrote, newspapers were incessantly repeating how stock markets were reaching "record highs."[11] Starting around mid-2017, the global bullishness appeared in world trade growth. Eurozone economies, with their heavy dependence on world trade, benefited from the trade renewal.

Southern eurozone countries were also benefiting from a phenomenon that economists call mean reversion: after a sharp fall or prolonged underperformance, an economy briefly recovers some of its lost ground. In all southern countries, the easing of austerity, and even a fiscal stimulus in some instances, helped the economies revert closer to their means. People were catching up with purchases they had long postponed. However, mean reversion effects are temporary. And the gains from mean reversion were blunted, in part, by hysteresis effects, the legacy of diminished skills and low investment due to extended underperformance during the long crisis.[12] The recovery, therefore, was disappointing by historical standards. But it had been so long in coming and growth expectations had been set so low that it was easy for officials and commentators to hail the recovery as a significant step forward.

The dangers of premature optimism were once again great, as was made clear with the unhelpful reaction of financial markets to comments by ECB President Mario Draghi. In June 2017, at the ECB's annual conclave of central bankers in Sintra on the Portuguese Riviera, Draghi said, "All the signs now point to a strengthening and broadening recovery in the euro area." And even though inflation was still stuck at undesirably low levels, Draghi insisted, "Deflationary forces have been replaced by reflationary ones." He was "confident," he emphasized three times, that inflation would return close to the ECB's 2 percent benchmark by 2019.[13]

Financial markets read Draghi's words as a signal that the ECB was declaring victory and would soon "taper" (reduce) its monthly bond purchases.[14] Because tapering implied tighter monetary policy earlier than anticipated, the value of the euro rose quickly. For the eurozone's southern members, the stronger euro risked putting a brake on their export growth and depressing their inflation rates by making imports cheaper. Once again, eurozone authorities were getting ahead of themselves. If a strong euro persisted, the recovery would stumble, and the lowflation tendency would intensify.

In a longer perspective, the eurozone's south faces years of low growth. In addition to the crisis-induced hysteresis effects, aging populations will chip away at their growth potentials. Outside of Japan, the countries with the most rapidly aging populations are Spain, Italy, Greece, and, to a slightly lesser extent, Portugal.[15] Families are having fewer children; hence, as older citizens retire, the size of the working-age population will decline.

Thus, southern eurozone countries face multiple economic and political problems. It is in Italy, however, that these problems come together in their most aggressive form. The Italian economy's productivity came to a stubborn halt after Italy joined the eurozone. Italian banks are large and fragile. Other than Greece's, the Italian government's debt ratio is the highest in the eurozone. In Italy's deeply fragmented political system, politicians are perennially preoccupied with forming coalitions and ensuring their own survival. Generating consensus to deal with the country's severe problems is hard, particularly since social inequalities persist and the Italian education system provides only limited help in climbing the economic ladder.[16] Among those who do receive high-quality education, many leave the country, having concluded that they can do little to change the system that provides them with only meager payoffs.[17] The constituency for political and economic change, therefore, remains weak. Economic and financial erosion continue. Italy will remain the eurozone's fault line.[18]

Italy's pathologies work with varying intensities in the other southern eurozone countries.

FRANCE MOVES DECISIVELY TO THE SOUTH

France's shift from the north to the eurozone's south since the onset of the global crisis was of particular significance: it accentuated Europe's economic and political divide and made it increasingly less likely that Europe can regroup as a cohesive economic and political force.

Perhaps France was always in the south and its earlier northern status was an illusion. That illusion had conveniently kept alive another fiction that Germany and France, acting as equals, would together drive European integration forward. However, for long, France has had a weak economy and a divided society. Economic historian Charles Kindleberger argued as early as 1978 that France had lost economic vitality; influential "vested interests" made privileged demands on the French government's budget.[19] An expanding range of such vested interests—the agricultural lobby, workers in state enterprises, public servants, better-off retirees, the rich (who have access to tax breaks for the upkeep of chateaux, wine collections, works of art)—gradually created fortresses of claims on the government's financial support, which came to be justified as necessary to maintain social consensus.

Government expenditures crossed the 50 percent of GDP mark in the early 1980s and rose to the extraordinary level of 56 percent of GDP by 2017. The rising expenditures failed to build social consensus. Instead, in the manner of performance-enhancing drugs, they boosted French GDP growth through much of the 1980s and again through much of the euro's first decade.[20] Such fiscal-stimulus-driven growth helped disguise France's steadily declining international competitiveness.

The financial crisis exposed the inability of a large number of French firms to compete with international rivals. Without the help of a devalued franc, as in pre-euro years, businesses faced shrinking profits and held investment back.[21] The government's debt ratio reached around 100 percent of GDP, and France's chronic youth unemployment problem became worse.

Observing the alarming rise in the French government's debt alongside deteriorating international competitiveness of the French economy, straight-speaking European Commission President Jean-Claude Juncker remarked, "We have a real problem with France. The French spend too much money and spend it on the wrong things."[22]

The French still do some things stunningly well. France, like Italy, is and will remain a global leader in high-fashion luxury goods. French officials, trained by the country's elite institutions, are a dazzling presence in international institutions and discussion forums. But the French economy has too many "weak links."[23]

The most critical of France's weak links is an educational system unable to prepare a large number of its citizens for an honorable living. In the Program for International Student Assessment (PISA) tests conducted by the thirty-five-member Organisation for Economic Co-operation and Development (OECD), French schools lag especially in science and mathematics. French students' tests scores are considerably lower than in the northern eurozone countries and well behind the pack of leading Asian nations.[24] These relatively low French PISA scores reflect particularly high shares of "low-performing" students. Studies show that such weakness in the quality of school education stunts economic growth prospects.[25]

More shockingly, France does worse than all OECD countries in meeting the needs of students with economic, social, and cultural disadvantages.[26] After the publication of the PISA results in December 2016, Annie Genevard, who served on the French parliament's committee for cultural affairs and education and who in 2009 received France's highest civilian award, the Légion d'honneur, tweeted, "France retains its sad title as champion of social inequalities at school."[27] The French university system perpetuates these inequalities by promoting a social elite rather than contributing to growth and equal opportunity. The elites go to the "grandes écoles," which receive disproportionately high funding, while everyone else goes to underfunded and crowded universities.[28]

The consequences have been grave. Children of high-earning and highly educated parents have had the best educational opportunities, and in a globalizing world with rapid technological change, they have gained the most from the rising education "skill premium." Therefore, those on the higher rungs of the economic ladder with their superior skills have had the opportunity to move up ever faster, while the education system has done little to make the climb any easier for those on the lower rungs.[29] Inevitably, inequalities have increased over recent generations.[30] French children born in disadvantaged circumstances still have the least opportunities for economic and social advancement and carry the legitimate fear that they might do worse than their parents.[31] The tendency of French youth to drop out of the job market and to stop educating themselves is but one manifestation of this social dysfunction. The French political system created vast fiscal entitlements, ostensibly, to promote social cohesion. But the failure to increase equality in educational opportunities has entrenched social fragmentation.

Alarmed by France's lackluster economic performance and budgetary problems, the Germans were anxious to offer their patented structural reforms and fiscal austerity advice to revive the French economy and help close France's perennial budget deficit. In November 2012, Reuters reported that German Finance Minister Wolfgang Schäuble's advisers were preparing policy recommendations for France.[32] The Germans denied that this was ever the case, but French pride was hurt. Prime Minister Jean-Marc Ayrault traveled to Berlin to meet with Merkel. At the press conference after the meeting, Ayrault insisted that the French government's policy would rely on "the profound values that make France what it is. The job that is under way is constructing the new French model."[33] In December 2014, when German leaders, including Merkel, continued their monotonous criticism of France's perennial budget overruns, Finance Minister Sapin repeated the familiar French response: "I take steps I think are good for the country. I think people have to be careful from the outside on how they express views on France."[34] Sapin then predicted that German criticism of French policies would only stoke populist fires in France, which could propel the far-right Front National leader Marine Le Pen to the second and final round of the French presidential election in 2017.

Sapin turned out to be prescient. Le Pen, who campaigned on an anti-Europe and even anti-euro platform, reached the second round of the election, where her unexpected opponent was thirty-nine-year-old Emmanuel Macron.

In the May 2017 election, Macron defeated Le Pen handily to become French president. Macron was a political newcomer who had never held elected office. His background and career could be viewed as exemplifying, to an almost caricatural degree, the French elite. Among his way stations was the ultra-selective Ecole Nationale d'Administration (ENA), which is the entry path into the uppermost echelons of France's governing caste. From there he went into the Inspection générale des finances, which each year recruits the most highly ranked of ENA's graduates. His next stop was Rothschild & Cie Banque, where he led several lucrative mergers and acquisitions. He briefly served as deputy chief of staff to President François Hollande before being appointed minister of economy and finance in August 2014. Rivalry between him and Prime Minister Manuel Valls, and Hollande's growing conviction that Macron was disloyal, created tensions that led to his resignation in late August 2016. While still in his ministerial position, in April 2016, he had created his own political party or "movement," En Marche! ("Onward!" or "On the Move!").

Macron's dizzying ascent to the French presidency was celebrated by the many who were worried that France might turn to an extreme form of nationalism. In June 2017, Macron achieved yet another striking political victory. His party, now called La République En Marche (LREM), won a clear majority in the French National Assembly. With his decisive wins, Macron achieved astonishing political power to put France on a new course. Whether he also had the legitimacy to set that course was, however, unclear.

Macron's victory was a continuation of two historical trends common to all Western democracies.[35] The two candidates in the final runoff—Macron and Le Pen—were outsiders. The Socialist Party candidate, Benoît Hamon, finished fifth in the first round of the election. The party was "dead," former prime minister Valls said. Thus, a traditional "pro-European" force in French politics seemed ready to disappear. The party, which espoused the social democratic agenda of social justice, had failed to address the fears of growing numbers of citizens. François Fillon, the conservative Republican candidate, although initially the favorite to win the presidential race, fizzled out when he was charged with misusing public funds to pay his wife large sums for a fake job as his parliamentary assistant. Thus neither of the two traditional mainstream parties had a candidate in the final round. Voters were anxious for change. Macron certainly fit that bill.

The other continuing trend, however, sent a more worrying signal. Large numbers of French citizens, frustrated that all politicians were self-serving and unresponsive, had given up on the political process. They chose to not vote. In the presidential race, three-quarters of French voters showed up at polling booths, the lowest turnout in decades; moreover, a large number left their votes blank, and hence, only two-thirds voted for a candidate. In the parliamentary elections, voter turnout imploded, down from nearly 80 percent in 1986 to well below 50 percent in 2017. Those who chose not to vote typically had limited education and low incomes, and they worked in dead-end jobs. This abstention pattern reflected the sullen anger of citizens who were born into disadvantaged circumstances and to whom the French education system failed to give a helping hand.

The prism for understanding French fears and anger lay in the country's young citizens. While Macron crushed Le Pen in the presidential race, his vote shares were the least among younger population groups. In another display of lack of enthusiasm for Macron, young French citizens stayed away from the polls. While voter turnout fell sharply in all age groups, only 26 percent of those between the ages of eighteen and twenty-four bothered to vote in the second round of the parliamentary election; even in the next-higher age group, twenty-five to thirty-four, only 30 percent voted.[36]

There were striking parallels between Italy's former prime minister Matteo Renzi and Macron. Both were thirty-nine years old when they became leaders of their countries. Renzi failed to connect with young Italians, who delivered him a humiliating defeat in the December 2016 referendum on a new electoral law.[37] In France, Macron's youth failed to excite the young French.

What did Macron have to offer? He campaigned as a pro-European, and for that, he won the admiration of international commentators. In Macron, the international community saw new hope, a new beginning, for Europe and for the global community.

Macron's election victory came less than a year after "Brexit," Britain's decision in June 2016 to leave the EU, and just six months after Donald Trump's election as US president. Brexit and Trump challenged the postwar institutional framework of international trade and governance. Macron gave hope that he would save the old European and world order and that he would strengthen it. Greg Ip of the *Wall Street Journal* pronounced Macron "Globalism's Great Hope." Ip wrote, "For global elites left dispirited by Britain's vote to leave the European Union and Donald Trump's presidency, France has provided a shot of adrenaline."[38] The *Handelsblatt* said, "There is renewed hope for the European project, owing to Emmanuel Macron's election as president of France."[39] The *Guardian* described the result of the French election as "a win for Macron and for hope."[40] Not to be outdone, the *Economist* showed a montage of Macron walking on water and asked if he would be the savior Europe had been waiting for.[41]

Again, the parallel with Renzi was remarkable. Virtually the same group of international commentators had greeted Renzi's ascent to the position of Italian prime minister with repeated expressions of "hope."

From citizens at home, however, the message to Macron was deeply euroskeptical, even anti-European. French voters had rejected Le Pen's belligerent nationalism, but they had by no means endorsed a pro-European agenda. In the first round of the presidential election, two outspoken anti-European candidates—the far-left Jean-Luc Mélenchon and the far-right Le Pen—together received 40 percent of the votes. These candidates representing the political extremes attracted voters who were worried about their futures, who believed they were not getting a fair chance, and who anticipated more job losses to foreign competition and immigrants. Another 20 percent of the votes went for Fillon, a self-avowed Gaullist who emphasized the goal of a strong and sovereign France and took a hard-line position on immigration.[42] In the second round of the presidential race, Le Pen received one-third of the vote (almost twice the share of votes her father received when he contested the incumbent Jacques Chirac for the presidency in 2002). In the parliamentary election, not only did a large number feel too dispirited to vote, but in economically distressed regions, such as the department of Seine Saint-Denis and the northern rust belt, voters preferred Mélenchon's leftist party La France Insoumise or Le Pen's Front National over Macron's LREM.[43]

The French public had long been trying to convey to its leaders that Europe offered no easy solutions for France's deep-rooted domestic problems. In 1992, French citizens came very close to rejecting the Maastricht Treaty and the single European currency. Reflecting on the result at the time, French Prime Minister Pierre Bérégovoy recognized that French citizens "most exposed to the harshness of existence" had voted against further integration with Europe. Bérégovoy added that with their focus on Europe, France's leaders had failed to comprehend the harsh lives that many citizens lived, and that failure had caused "a rupture between the people and their representatives."[44] But few other French leaders heard that message. Instead, relieved that they could move ahead with plans for the single currency, they ignored citizens' anguish, and the rupture with the people continued. In 2005, French citizens again scorned Europe, rejecting this time the largely symbolic European constitution.[45] In that vote, young French citizens opposed the constitution with particular vehemence. Those who had voiced antipathy to Europe in the two European referendums—people with low education, low incomes, and pessimism about their futures—were now the ones least impressed by Macron.

The French who voted against Europe in the referendums and held their votes back from Macron were not necessarily anti-European; they were mainly trying to redirect the attention of French leaders back to the many domestic problems that Europe could not solve. French presidents had tried for too long to make Europe work for France. But the pursuit of such hope was a dangerous distraction. Meanwhile, French economic, social, and political problems had become more acute.

After he won his sweeping victories, Macron persisted in his European crusade. Europe, he said, had "lost its way." Macron talked about launching "democratic conventions" aimed at "refounding Europe."[46]

But he got off to a curious start by launching a complaint against "posted" workers. These include Bulgarian truck drivers, Lithuanian bricklayers, and iconic Polish plumbers posted by Eastern European companies to perform jobs in richer Western European countries.[47] Posted workers, although subject to minimum wage laws in the host country, receive a compensation package set by the lower Eastern European standards; in particular, their bonuses, overtime compensation, and holidays are based on their domestic norms. Eastern European companies set great importance on being able to post their workers in other European countries, and, with some justification, they complained that Macron was contesting an important feature of free trade in services within Europe.

But Macron continued to kick up a fuss. The large pay gap between Eastern European and French workers, he said, undermined the "idea of Europe" and fed extremism.[48] Seeking symbolic solidarity with French workers, he described posted workers as a form of "social dumping."[49]

Such characterization of posted workers, Zsolt Darvas of the Brussels-based Bruegel think tank says, is bogus. The total numbers of posted workers is trivially small. They do not in any noticeable way hurt the incomes and prospects of workers in the host country.[50] The most charitable explanation of Macron's fuss was that he had fallen prey to the traditional French protectionist instinct and was cynically using the politically salient issue to claim that he was protecting the French worker.

Macron proposed other actions that chipped away at free-trade principles. He proposed a Buy European Act, which would give preference to European producers in bidding for government contracts. And he called for more intense screening of foreigners planning to invest in Europe. Despite his youth and endorsement of globalization, Macron was rooted in French dirigiste instincts, which placed faith in a benevolent, activist government. Speaking for many Germans who believed in a more limited role for government, Thomas Mayer, former Deutsche Bank chief economist, warned in his regular *Frankfurter Allgemeine Zeitung* column that Macron was a "dangerous partner."[51]

Setting his sights on major changes in the eurozone, Macron quickly urged Merkel to join him in establishing a budget that would help member states when their economies were in recessions or crises. Merkel, predictably and cautiously replied yes, "if it makes sense."[52] Domestic political resistance to a eurozone budget gave Merkel little room for maneuver. She had been firm all these years: Germany would not extend an open-ended financial safety net to others. Merkel wanted all eurozone member states to be "independent," to stand on their own feet.[53]

At home, Macron set about creating a regal presidency. His display of "pomp and monarchical authority" surprised even his supporters, who had thought of him as a "champion of liberal democracy."[54] The display failed to impress the French press, which described his ninety-minute speech delivered to members of both chambers of parliament at the Palace of Versailles as "seemingly endless" and a "string of platitudes."[55]

Just as Renzi had done, Macron began his substantive agenda with an initiative to reduce the number of lawmakers and "speed up lawmaking by shortening procedures and simplifying voting processes."[56] On economics, too, Macron began labor-market "reforms" that were similar to Renzi's Jobs Act.[57] Macron's reforms would also strengthen the hands of employers and, in particular, would make it easier for them to fire workers. The goal, as in Italy, was to give French companies more "flexibility" to "adapt to the marketplace." As described in chapter 7, such reforms increase workers' sense of insecurity and reduce long-term productivity growth. For this reason, Macron's reform package included enhanced unemployment insurance and more training in the workplace. However, enhanced insurance came with a bill and stalled because Macron also promised to cut the government's budget deficit. The proposal to boost training remained tied up in bureaucratic tangles. Creating job insecurity is easy, but compensating workers for heightened insecurity is always hard. Macron's labor-market reforms seemed set to deliver the same outcomes as other such European reforms had done: more employment on short-term contracts while the French economy's productivity growth rate would remain low and possibly fall.

Macron's proposals for tax and spending cuts appeared likely to benefit the rich and hurt the poor. Thomas Piketty, the celebrity economist and author of *Capital in the 21st Century*, was one of Macron's earliest critics. In the days before the presidential election, Piketty had predicted that Macron, a former banker, would favor policies that enriched bankers and other wealthy French citizens. Macron lived up to that stereotype.[58] His budget for 2018 abolished the Impôt de solidarité sur la fortune, a tax on wealth, and reduced the tax on dividends, interest, and capital gains. In contrast, although government spending on higher education had fallen by 10 percent since 2008 on a per-student basis, the budget did nothing to reverse that trend. Macron also made no effort to reduce the imbalance between public universities and the "Grandes Ecoles." Moreover, with his reduction of a housing subsidy, which many students relied on to pay their rent, and his comment that striking workers were lazy and cynical, Macron was soon regarded as "president of the rich" by a majority of French citizens. Even Macron's advisers, economists Jean Pisani-Ferry and Philippe Martin, were worried that the new president had done little for working and middle-class citizens and his tax cuts would benefit only the richest segment of the population.[59]

Thus, Macron's economic reforms gave little hope that they would jump-start growth and seemed almost certain to increase politically perilous social inequalities. And the news that in his first three months as president, the thirty-nine-year-old Macron had spent €26,000 of taxpayer funds for makeup services was a source of both amusement and consternation.

To make political—and hence eventually economic—progress, Macron needed to recognize the urgency of reversing the polarizations in French society. His task was to create consensus for a new social contract that led to more broadly inclusive growth. The risk is that without such a contract, even sensible policies will remain jammed. In that case, economic drift will continue, and France will remain in the eurozone's south. Certainly, the goal of parity with Germany in a dynamic Europe—the goal that had set off the French ambition for a single European currency—will remain a vain dream.

PORTUGAL AND SPAIN SUFFER FROM LOW GROWTH POTENTIAL

Briefly, it appeared as if Portugal would emerge stronger from its crisis. In September 2012, German Finance Minister Schäuble praised the Portuguese government for implementing "painful" reforms at a "faster-than-expected" pace.[60] In November, Schäuble was even more enthusiastic. "Portugal is doing extraordinary work in a difficult situation," he said to reporters. "Portugal is on the right path. Portugal will continue along the path, I have no doubt about that."[61]

Optimistic rhetoric and cheap talk are in the DNA of every good policy-maker. But as we have seen throughout this book, eurozone authorities rely to an unusual extent on words rather than deeds. Constrained by their inability to act, they never lose hope that words will do the task that only deeds can accomplish. Since it is impossible to dig a country out of an economic and financial hole by imposing fiscal austerity and structural reforms, leaders repeatedly declare success in the hope that financial markets will believe that a new dawn is indeed beckoning.

The reality was that heavy austerity was taking its toll in Portugal. While Schäuble was trying to talk up the Portuguese economy, higher taxes and cutbacks in welfare payments had shrunk disposable incomes of many households. Borrowers were falling behind on their debt repayments, and banks faced a "bleak" outlook.[62] In July 2013, Finance Minister Vítor Gaspar resigned, saying that his repeated inability to deliver on promises had "undermined" his "credibility as finance minister."[63]

Yet less than a year later, in May 2014, when the Portuguese government decided it was time to end the "bailout," Schäuble again said, "Steadfast programme implementation has allowed Portugal to bring its economy back on track, put public finances on a path to sustainability, and reduce imbalances that had been building up before the crisis." He added that the Portuguese decision to exit from the bailout was proof that "the European crisis resolution strategy is working."[64] Schäuble rooted for Portuguese success in the hope that he could lay the blame for the growing Greek disaster on the Greek government rather than on European economic policies.

Other than Schäuble, most analysts were cautious about Portugal's path forward. In its first "post-program review," in November 2014, the IMF wrote, "Portugal still faces a pressing growth challenge. Labor market slack [unemployment] remains at historically unprecedented levels, and under-investment is eroding the country's capital stock."[65] Investment was low because Portuguese companies, having gorged themselves on debt before the crisis began, still labored under a heavy debt burden. The IMF did manage to strike a note of hope, predicting that the annual GDP growth rate would tick up from around 1 to 1.5 percent, and the government's debt ratio would decline steadily from its 130 percent of GDP level. Even that flicker of optimism faded. By September 2016, the IMF said that the brief economic recovery was "running out of steam," the banking system was "plagued by low profitability and rising NPLs [nonperforming loans]," and the government's finances were under great pressure.[66] GDP growth had not risen; the debt burden had remained virtually unchanged.

When Portuguese GDP did perk up in the first quarter of 2017, Schäuble once again saw the glimmer of a Portuguese economic renaissance. This time, he described Portuguese Finance Minister Mário Centeno as "the Ronaldo of the ECOFIN" (the group of EU finance ministers), comparing Centeno to the Portuguese football star.

Perhaps Schäuble's optimism will eventually prove prescient. In the meantime, Portugal has a treacherous course to navigate. Despite progress, Portuguese banks have a high burden of nonperforming loans; only Italian banks face a more severe nonperforming-loan problem. Profitability of Portuguese banks is low, their asset quality is poor, and the capital they hold could prove insufficient to buffer the next crisis.[67] In 2017, Portuguese per capita GDP was at around the same level as in 2001. Since 2011, the level—and not just the growth rate—of total factor productivity has fallen. In other words, the Portuguese economy is using resources less efficiently than in the past.[68] Thus, in a vicious circle, anemic growth has kept debt burdens high and banks weak, which has kept growth low.

Through the course of the crisis, economic inequalities have grown as the share of workers either relying on involuntary part-time jobs or working on temporary contracts has increased sharply. These trends have taken their heaviest toll on younger Portuguese. The cruelest indicator of that toll is the dramatic rise of the "persistent-at-risk" poverty rate among Portuguese between the ages of eighteen and twenty-four, from 10 percent in 2007 to more than 20 percent in 2015. During the same period, persistent poverty has declined among those older than sixty-five.[69]

These grim outcomes are the consequence of long-term constraints on Portuguese growth. In its 2017 review, the OECD noted that only around 45 percent of the Portuguese population between the ages of 25 and 64 have completed the final years of high school education, a lower rate than for all OECD countries other than Mexico and Turkey.[70] In Poland and the Czech Republic, for example, the completion rate is 90 percent. Portuguese children frequently repeat grades and drop out of school early. How can they compete with Eastern European workers who are much better educated and earn much lower wages? Portugal's vocational training system is fragmented and ineffective. As in Italy, low education has persisted from one generation to another.[71] And austerity-enforced cuts in public expenditures have reversed even the modest efforts made before the crisis to help the economy break out of its low-growth trap. Without the necessary human capital, Portuguese business does little research and has few connections with university researchers. In a world that is racing ahead to adopt increasingly sophisticated technologies, Portugal has fallen farther behind.

Spain bounced back impressively from its crisis. Since early 2015, GDP has grown at a smart pace, more than 3 percent a year. From a peak of 26 percent in 2013, the unemployment rate fell to 18 percent by early 2017. These welcome gains mainly reflected the Spanish economy's particularly large scope for mean reversion. Because of the sharp economic collapse that followed the country's real estate and banking crash, the economy had considerable room to bounce back from its fall. And brushing aside warnings from European authorities, the Spanish government sensibly injected a relatively large fiscal stimulus between 2014 and 2016 to regain some of the lost ground.

But the post-crisis recovery is a self-limiting process, which will run its course. Looking ahead, the IMF estimates that Spain's potential growth rate is around 1.5 percent; the OECD is more concerned that Spanish productivity growth will not compensate for the expected decline in working-age population and therefore estimates a lower potential growth at 0.9 percent a year.[72] Spain's fundamental growth constraint is the same as in Italy and

Portugal: education and R&D capabilities are deficient. Generational inequities in access to education persist, which precludes inclusive growth.

As in Italy and Portugal, the Spanish economy carries deep scars from the crisis. While the unemployment rate has fallen, it remains extraordinarily high at 18 percent. Of those who have been unemployed for an extended duration, many have previously worked in the once-buoyant construction sector. Such workers have often not completed high school and now appear to be unemployable. Around 10 percent of those in the labor force said that they were working part-time because they could not find full-time jobs.[73]

Moreover, following the European template, so-called labor-market reforms have made it easier for employers to fire workers; hence, new jobs are mainly temporary. Large numbers of workers face the risk that they might spend much of their lives in "permanently" low-end temporary jobs. OECD analysis shows that Spanish workers employed in temporary jobs struggle to make the transition to more permanent work.[74] As elsewhere in the southern eurozone, the young face the most difficult labor-market conditions; nearly 70 percent of those employed work on temporary contracts.[75] Thus, the reforms implemented during the crisis exacerbated the already large inequities of opportunity. The reforms also reduced employers' incentives to invest in their workers and, thus, increased the risk that Spain's productivity growth will remain low.[76] On this path, the IMF said, "pockets of over-indebtedness" and financial vulnerabilities will persist.[77]

Spanish authorities made good use of European bailout funds to deal with their deeply troubled banks. Spanish banks steadily improved their financial condition. However, question marks still hovered over their futures. In July 2016, the EBA indicated concerns about Banco Popular Español, but otherwise gave Spanish banks a clean bill of health. Financial-risk expert Viral Acharya and his colleagues, as was their custom, painted a grimmer picture.[78] They warned that the value of the assets held by Spanish banks was likely less than that stated by the banks on their books; moreover, if the banks came under stress, they would suffer substantially greater losses than the regulators estimated.[79]

Acharya and company had been right on Italian banks, and their grimmer warning proved all too true for Spain's Banco Popular. It suffered a loss of €3.6 billion in 2016. Recognizing the bank's fragility, depositors started withdrawing their money in September 2016. The stress continued in 2017. Curiously, in early June, even as a run on the bank's deposits began, Banco de España Governor Luis María Linde insisted that Banco Popular was "solvent."[80] However, on the evening of June 6, when it seemed that the run on deposits would not stop, the Single Resolution Mechanism, Europe's bank-resolution authority, finally stepped in to engineer a sale.[81] Under the terms of the sale, existing shareholders and subordinated debt holders lost much of their investments, making it possible for Santander, the Spanish bank with deep pockets, to buy Banco Popular for €1. The purchase price was superficially low, but Santander's shareholders were also now responsible for the losses on nearly €8 billion worth of Banco Popular's nonperforming loans.[82]

In October 2017, the IMF reported that although the stock of troubled loans had fallen significantly from its peak, banks held foreclosed property, which was not earning any return. Banks profits were also being squeezed because the low interest rates induced by the ECB's QE had placed a cap on the interest rate that banks could charge. Steady economic growth for some years was needed for banks to return to good health. In the meantime, Spanish authorities faced some unanswered questions: were there more hidden problems, and could strong banks continue to absorb some of the losses of bankrupt banks?

Perhaps the most worrying sign for Spain, Portugal, and Italy was that foreign investors were leaving with their money. When international investors pull out of a eurozone country, the country's central bank ends up paying on behalf of the nation by borrowing from the ECB. The sums that the Banca d'Italia, the Banco de España, and the Banco de Portugal borrowed from the ECB grew to be very large, which indicated that a lot of money had left these three southern countries (figure 9.5). This latest bout of capital flight started in early 2015, soon after the onset of the ECB's bond-purchase QE program.[83] As part of the overall bond-purchase operation, the central banks—the Banca d'Italia, the Banco de España, and the Banco de Portugal—bought their governments' bonds from investors, but the investors decided they did not want to reinvest their funds in any other assets in Italy, Spain, or Portugal. Thus, the three central banks had to borrow from the ECB to pay departing investors. The extent of this borrowing, which largely mirrors the capital flight, was a stark reminder of how little confidence international investors had in these three southern countries.

The Alternative Greek Narrative

When historians narrate the Greek saga, they will tell one of two stories. The commonly told one will be that the Greeks refused to take the necessary painful medicine and so turned their critical illness into a near-terminal condition. This story is simply not true. Between 2009 and 2014,

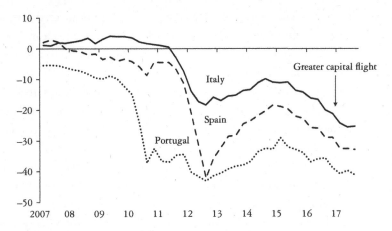

FIGURE 9.5. Flight of foreign investors from Italy, Spain, and Portugal.
(Capital flight financed by ECB funds, percent of GDP)
Note: The figure shows each country's Target2 balance with the ECB. The negative Target2 balance
implies that the national central bank had to borrow from the ECB to buy their government's bonds
from investors. The investors who sold the bonds did not reinvest the funds in the country.
Sources: Target2: ECB Statistical Data Warehouse (compiled by Euro Crisis Monitor, Institute of
Empirical Economic Research, Osnabrück University); GDP figures from Eurostat.

Greek governments undertook austerity measures—raised taxes or reduced expenditures—equivalent to over 15 percent of GDP. Even Poul Thomsen, the IMF's man in charge of Greece acknowledged in October 2014, "Greece has probably done more than anybody, no doubt about that."[84] Greek governments also implemented "structural reforms," which allowed Greece to climb up in the World Bank's "Ease of Doing Business" global ranking.[85]

Greek authorities should—and could—have done more to improve tax collection, which required greater administrative streamlining and eliminating pockets of corruption. A dark stain will forever remain on Prime Minister Alexis Tsipras and his government for egregiously prosecuting Andreas Georgiou. As head of the Greek statistical agency Elstat, Georgiou revealed in late 2010 that the true size of the government's debt was significantly greater than reported at the time.[86] The Tsipras government absurdly blamed him for the austerity enforced by the creditors.

But some will tell another story to explain Greece's economic depression and its gloomy consequences for the country's future. In that story, told in a hushed tone, the Greeks had economic logic firmly on their side, but the eurozone's politics inflicted unnecessary misery on them. Here is how the alternative goes.

The voice for sensible economics came from the ground up, from the people of Greece. Starting with elections in May and June 2012, Greek citizens pleaded that wage cuts and austerity imposed by European creditors and the IMF were causing unbearable pain. To make their message clear, Greeks voted in increasing numbers for Syriza, the party that promised to reverse the creditors' policies (see chapter 7).

Paradoxically, an IMF staff report in March 2012 echoed the Greek people's voice. Based on an extensive survey of the international experience, IMF staff wrote that relying on wage cuts to restore a country's competitiveness had "proved to be a difficult undertaking with very few successes."[87] Wage cuts were particularly damaging, the IMF report said, when accompanied by fiscal austerity and tight monetary policy, as was the case for Greece at the time. Recalling the Argentina experience between 1998 and 2002, the report warned that the mix of policies being prescribed for Greece could cause a "downward spiral," leading to eventual debt default and exit from the eurozone.

Thus, the IMF staff report supported the contemporaneous instinct of Greek citizens that the creditors' policy program could only do great harm. Other IMF analyses, including that by its chief economist, Olivier Blanchard, documented the perils of never-ending fiscal austerity.[88]

But, despite this fine staff analysis, the IMF as a creditor kept faith with Europe's official lenders. Together, they continued with the policy package that could only make matters worse. Evidence that the policy was not working mounted. Greek GDP continued to fall, and the government's debt-to-GDP ratio continued to mount. European authorities began a process of debt relief in driblets, which was self-defeating because the creditors did not pull back from the ill-advised strategy of more wage cuts and fiscal austerity.[89] By December 2014, it appeared that the Syriza party, with its promise to lighten the burden of austerity, was on its way to a parliamentary victory.

In a warning relayed to Greek voters, German Finance Minister Schäuble announced from Berlin, "New elections change nothing."[90] The Greek government, he said, must stick to the program in place. On January 25, 2015, Greek citizens responded by electing Syriza to power with a comfortable parliamentary majority. Tsipras became prime minister with a mandate to negotiate debt relief and dial down the austerity. European leaders—fiery advocates of democratic ideals—were aghast at the Greek people's revolt against policies dictated from Berlin, Brussels, and Frankfurt. The international media faithfully echoed dire predictions for Greece's fate.

Stripped of the drama, Syriza's demand was simple: debt relief and less austerity. This demand had overwhelming support in both the scholarly economics literature and the practice of economic policy. Scholars for decades had emphasized that excessive debt—"debt overhang"—reduces the ability and incentive to invest, slows economic growth, causes lowflation or even deflation to set in, and makes debts harder to repay.[91] Excessive austerity makes matters worse by further reducing economic growth and deepening deflation.

On policy practice, legendary British economist John Maynard Keynes made the most famous statement on the wisdom of debt forgiveness. In his 1919 book, *The Economic Consequences of the Peace*, written during the negotiations for the Versailles Treaty in the aftermath of World War I, Keynes argued for canceling Germany's debts and limiting the war reparations owed to the victorious Allied governments. Enforcing those payments would impoverish Germany, Keynes said, in which case, he famously warned, "vengeance, I dare say, will not limp."[92]

Keynes' passionate call for debt forgiveness was controversial then, and scholars still debate whether the failure to follow his advice contributed to the resurgence of German nationalism. However, the victorious allies after World War II did not risk making the same mistake: under the London Debt Agreement in 1953, they wrote off about half of German prewar and postwar debt. That debt write-off created the fiscal space for the German government to increase expenditures on public health, education, and housing, and by lowering default risk, the write-off reduced the interest rates the government had to pay on its debt to private creditors.[93] Economists Carmen Reinhart and Christoph Trebesch have documented that such benefits of debt forgiveness have applied in a large number of cases. They report that in the 1920s, the United States and the United Kingdom wrote off substantial portions of debt owed to them by several European countries, providing much-needed growth impetus to the countries receiving relief.[94]

Tsipras and Syriza had influential supporters, such as Columbia University economist Jeffrey Sachs and US President Barack Obama. In an opinion piece, Sachs wrote that the Greek government's debt at 170 percent of GDP was intolerable by any imaginable metric. An effort to repay it, he said, would inflict "a level of pain that is simply beyond the tolerance of democratic societies."[95] Speaking to CNN's Fareed Zakaria, Obama more forcefully said, "You cannot keep on squeezing countries that are in the midst of depression." Obama recognized that "the Greek economy was in dire need of reform." But, he said, "it's very hard to initiate those changes if people's standards of living are dropping by 25 percent over time; eventually the political system, the society can't sustain it." To reinforce his theme, Obama repeated, it was simply not possible "to squeeze more and more out of a population that is hurting worse and worse."[96]

Greece's creditors espoused a different philosophy. Speaking for the creditors, IMF Managing Director Christine Lagarde told the *Irish Times*: "A debt is a debt, and it is a contract. Defaulting, restructuring, changing the terms has consequences."[97]

Greek Finance Minister Yanis Varoufakis proposed a sensible solution: the use of GDP-linked debt repayment. When the Greek economy grew rapidly, the Greek government would pay more, and when the economy slowed down, it would pay less. With the ability to repay debt in the years when the economy was doing well, Greek authorities could scale back austerity. The Greek government offered to maintain its primary budget surplus (the surplus not counting interest payments) at 1.5 percent of GDP rather than the ridiculously high 4.5 percent of GDP that creditors demanded.

Varoufakis was instantly controversial, for both his flashy style and the demands he was making. But his proposal was economically sound. Reduced austerity would have given the Greek economy breathing room to grow; over time, the government would have become more capable of repaying its creditors. The details needed discussion, debate, and negotiation, but it was an excellent starting point.

On January 31, 2015, barely six days after the Syriza government had taken over, Erkki Liikanen, governor of Finland's central bank and in that capacity a member of the ECB's Governing Council, threatened that the ECB would stop funding Greek banks if the Greek government did not agree to the terms of the creditors.[98] And on February 4, the ECB decided Greece's fate. In an aggressive move that took everyone by surprise, the ECB cut off funding to Greek banks, preemptively immobilizing the Greek government before it could begin negotiations with its creditors. The ECB withdrew an earlier arrangement under which Greek banks used their government bonds as collateral (security) to obtain funds for running their day-to-day operations. Although Greek government bonds had a junk rating and normally only higher-rated bonds qualified as collateral, the ECB had waived that requirement to help the banks stay afloat. With its February 4 decision, the ECB revoked that waiver.[99] Greek banks could now only borrow from the Greek central bank under an Emergency Liquidity Arrangement (ELA), but ELA funds carried a higher interest rate and, moreover, could be turned off at any time and thus choke the Greek financial system.

Stock prices of Greek banks fell sharply, and two days later, S&P pushed the Greek government's rating further into junk territory. With continuing deposit flight from Greek banks and the threat of a financial meltdown, the Syriza government rapidly lost any leverage even before it could use its economic argument in a political negotiation.

With their February 4 decision, unelected ECB officials stepped into the political arena and determined Greece's economic and political trajectory. Newspaper reports suggested—and public statements later confirmed—that northern representatives on the Governing Council had pushed through the decision, overcoming the opposition of those who had argued to allow time for a proper discussion of the best way ahead.[100] No one was accountable for the ECB decision; certainly, no one was accountable to the Greek people, who had asked through their elected representatives for relief but now faced the prospect, as Obama might have said, of being squeezed "worse and worse."

On February 5, Varoufakis traveled to Berlin to meet with Schäuble. Schäuble had nothing to offer; he could wait while deposits leaked out of Greek banks. At the press briefing after the meeting, Schäuble said, "We agreed to disagree." Varoufakis gloomily responded that an agreement was "never on the cards."[101]

Schäuble's was the voice that refused the much-needed debt relief, but virtually every member state other than Italy and France opposed any concession to the Greeks. As the Irish *Sunday Business Post* wrote, even Ireland, which had only recently emerged from its own sense of shame and humiliation at the hands of European creditors, turned into "one of the harshest critics of the new Greek government, pushing as hard and uncompromising a line as Germany."[102] Eastern European member states, reveling, as described a little later in this chapter, in their self-confident role as northern nations, joined in public ridicule of the Greek government.[103]

One senior European did express alarm at the uncompromising policy stance and the harsh tone of the creditors. On February 18, European Commission President Juncker said, "We have sinned against the dignity of the people of Greece, Portugal, and sometimes Ireland." He added, "Everything that's called austerity policy is not necessarily austerity policy. Because often those austerity policies end up being excessive." Previously, as Luxembourg's finance minister, Juncker had himself been part of the collective creditors' decisions on the Greek program. Recalling his complicity in the formulation and enforcement of the policies he was now criticizing, Juncker added, "I seem stupid for saying this but we need to learn lessons from the past and not repeat the same mistakes." He even questioned the "democratic legitimacy" of European creditors and of the IMF in their unaccountable rush to impose punitive policies.[104]

Juncker's remorse did not fit the official narrative, and since the media had invested itself in that narrative, only a couple of little-known journalists even bothered to report the comments. After all, Juncker often made emotional and extravagant statements. But ten days later, and now with a special focus on Greece, Juncker repeated to a German newspaper, "Every single Greek person feels that his or her dignity was violated, because every single Greek person feels like something unfair is happening here."[105]

The IMF, in principle, represented the interests of the global community and was the only possible neutral arbiter in the ruinous European power play. But through the first half of 2015, the IMF stood firmly on the side of the European creditors. While the northern members of the ECB's Governing Council—supported by France's Benoît Coeuré and President Draghi—kept up threats of halting disbursement of ELA funds to Greek banks, the IMF added to the pressure on Greece.[106] It did so by remaining silent on the matter of debt relief and by reinforcing the demand for a primary budget surplus of 4.5 percent of GDP, insisting especially and repeatedly on wage and pension cuts. The IMF's management was acting, as it often does, in step with its major shareholders' preferences.[107] Obama could have restrained the IMF. But despite having talked a good game, he was unwilling to lend his political weight to the Greeks. The German position held sway on the IMF's management and board.

We do not know what transpired beyond the public spotlight, but an account by Landon Thomas of the *New York Times* is revealing.[108] On June 25, five months after Syriza came to power, Varoufakis brought up the question of debt relief again at a meeting of European finance ministers. Repeatedly rebuffed by the ministers, he turned to the IMF's Lagarde, who also attended these meetings, and said, "I have a question for Christine: Can the IMF formally state in this meeting that this proposal we are being asked to sign will make the Greek debt sustainable?" Lagarde knew the answer to that question. In an analysis just completed, IMF staff had concluded that without substantial debt relief, the Greek government's debt would remain "unsustainable"; the government would never be able to repay its debts. But before Lagarde could respond, Dutch Finance Minister Jeroen Dijsselbloem told Varoufakis, "It is a take it or leave it offer, Yanis."

In the late evening on Friday, June 26, Tsipras announced that on July 5 Greek citizens would vote in a referendum whether they were willing to accept the creditors' terms. Speaking to the nation in a televised address, Tsipras said that his government had tried to find "a viable agreement that respects democracy." That effort had failed and "the people must decide free of any blackmail."[109]

Another Greek prime minister, George Papandreou, had announced a similar referendum in November 2011. Merkel and Sarkozy had responded angrily and had told Papandreou that conducting a referendum would be tantamount to Greek exit from the eurozone.[110] Papandreou had pulled back, and had resigned shortly thereafter. Tsipras faced similar pressure, but held on. Hence, on Saturday morning, June 27, eurozone "partners" assembled in Brussels to deny Greece extension of the financial assistance program due to expire on Tuesday. Depositors in Greek banks panicked and began withdrawing their money. On Sunday, as cash machines ran dry, the ECB froze the level of ELA that the Greek central bank could provide its banks. The panic escalated, and the government imposed controls on the amount of cash withdrawals. Greek banks would not open on Monday morning.

On Thursday, July 2, the IMF's report, which made clear that the Greek government's debt was unsustainable, was leaked.[111] Greek citizens went into the referendum knowing that their government could not repay its debts and, facing limits on how much money they could withdraw, they could foresee possibly months of hardship.

Yet, on July 5, 61 percent of Greeks voted *oxi*, a resounding no. In fact, a student said she had voted "*Oxi, oxi, oxi*."[112] "What you have heard," she exclaimed, "is the voice of the people, the rage of the gods." According to one estimate, 85 percent of those between the ages of eighteen and twenty-four voted *oxi*.[113] A student who had just completed her master's degree said, "I have absolutely no chance of work; basically I am being told to emigrate."[114] Young and adult alike voted *oxi* if they were unemployed, had no college education, and were in "financial difficulty." A small majority of even those who said they were "living comfortably" voted *oxi*. The *oxi* voters understood that their vote was possibly a vote to give up the euro, a vote for Grexit. While they had no wish to leave the eurozone, they insisted they were proud to be Greeks.

Tsipras had campaigned for the *oxi* vote, but faced with the dark Grexit threat, he fell in line with the demands of European creditors. The Greek public tried one more time. When Tsipras called another election to seek a fresh mandate in September 2015, Greek citizens elected him and Syriza again, believing perhaps that they offered the greatest prospect of a dignified outcome. Nothing came of that hope. Over the next two years, the debt-relief kabuki continued, the creditors made no material concession, and the economy remained in a recessionary state.

After the July 2015 referendum, the IMF did change its public tune and made increasingly strident noises about the urgency of debt relief for Greece. Judging from the timing of its change in public stance, the IMF seemed to have the go-ahead from the Americans.[115] But the Germans remained unwilling to budge. The German finance ministry's calculations showed that following another round of debt relief, Germany might receive €100 billion less than the amount Greece originally owed.[116] The numbers were approximate, but for German leaders, more debt relief to Greece risked attracting the wrath of their taxpayers. And the IMF was not prepared to fight the Germans.

The IMF could have forgiven the debt owed to it by the Greeks. This dramatic gesture would have created international pressure on the Germans and other European creditors to do the right thing. The IMF had a moral obligation to take such a drastic step, if for no other reason than to make amends for its complicity in the tragedy. At the time of the original bailout in May 2010, IMF management had prevented the Greek government from defaulting on its private creditors, an action that several members of the IMF's Executive Board and the vast majority of external analysts then and later believed was essential to reduce Greece's debt burden.[117] Even in retrospect, the IMF's management refused to acknowledge that grievous error. In June 2013, by which time the average Greek was 20 percent poorer than at the start of the bailout program, the IMF's Poul Thomsen said, "If we were in the same situation, with the same information at that time, we would probably do the same again."[118] Having left Greece saddled with a mountain of debt to repay, the IMF insisted that the Greek government implement a historically unmatched level of fiscal austerity, compressed in an extraordinarily short period. When the Greeks undertook that austerity, Thomsen did acknowledge their heroic effort.[119] However, the IMF pushed for more, unwilling to recognize that the austerity was trapping Greece in an endless economic depression.

Instead of continuing with a failed strategy, at the very least, the IMF could have walked out of the program in mid-2017. That step would have deeply embarrassed the Germans and perhaps required the German government to seek a contentious reauthorization from the Bundestag. Instead, the IMF agreed to continue its participation in the program that it believed would not work. To protect itself, the IMF, for now, would not lend Greece any more money. German authorities got their way. They did not care about the IMF's money; they merely needed to report to the Bundestag that the IMF was still part of the deal. The Greek bailout strategy, which had not worked all these years, would continue. Debt relief in driblets since 2012 had not materially reduced the Greek debt burden, but the driblets-of-relief approach would stay in place. Austerity had hampered economic recovery. More austerity would be required of Greece, with the goal of an incredibly high 3.5 percent of GDP primary budget surplus, only somewhat lower than the earlier ridiculously high target of 4.5 percent of GDP.

Through these months, Tsipras tried to work the margins, hoping for minor concessions. When the European finance ministers responsible for the terms of the program refused to budge, Tsipras called Merkel. And for doing so, Schäuble portrayed him as a whimpering fool. "He keeps calling the whole time," Schäuble told an audience in Berlin, "and the chancellor says again and again, 'Alexis, this issue is for the finance ministers.'"[120] Former Greek Finance Minister George Papaconstantinou has written that in closed-door meetings, European finance ministers often indulged in "hazing" Greek finance ministers.[121] Schäuble made the hazing public.

Schäuble's self-confidence in his economic-policy prowess was remarkable. He was among the key decision makers who stopped the necessary Greek debt default in 2010.[122] He mocked the Fed's successful monetary policy.[123] From all eurozone nations, Schäuble demanded counterproductive fiscal austerity. At home, he insisted on shortsighted austerity rather than rebuilding the country's infrastructure and thereby pushed the German current account surplus to more than 8 percent of GDP, creating a source of global trade friction. Germany's surplus was mirrored in the deficits run by several countries, including the United States, all of whom blamed Germany for not buying more of their goods.

In Greece, the Schäuble-inspired strategy of minuscule doses of debt relief alongside deeper and deeper austerity was set up to fail, as the Reinhart and Trebesch study predicted. For German and other official creditors, the strategy had the short-term attraction of avoiding politically unpopular decisions at home. The long-term consequence was that everyone would be worse off: Greeks would suffer more pain, and European creditors would eventually see less of their money.

By 2017, Greek GDP was down by 25 percent since the bailout program began; the unemployment rate remained stuck above 20 percent. An IMF staff report, in its matter-of-fact style, reported that severe austerity had "tested the social and political fabric" of the country and had "taken a large toll on society, with unemployment and poverty levels without precedent in the euro zone."[124] The OECD predicted that high and persistent youth unemployment, pervasive insecurity in temporary jobs, a sharp increase in overall poverty, and a troubling increase in child poverty "will have permanent effects on employability and prosperity, and might impede intergenerational mobility and long-term opportunities for the younger generations."[125]

One-third of Greek students who had graduated from college since 2011 were unemployed, and a quarter of those had stopped bothering to look for a job; of those who were employed, three-quarters earned less than €800 euros a month.[126] Nearly half of all Greeks between the ages of eighteen and thirty-five said their parents supported them financially.[127] An April 2017 Pew survey of global attitudes found that only 2 percent of Greek citizens believed their current economic situation was good (by far the most pessimistic country response in the survey), and only 21 percent thought their children would do better (with only the French and the Japanese more fearful of the future).[128]

The die seems cast. Greece will be a poorer economy and a more unequal society. As we look down the passage of time, we can see a Greece that is older, from which scientists, doctors, and entrepreneurs have gradually out-migrated, while many of those who have stayed behind have nowhere else to go.

The official story remained unchanged. In June 2017, European Commission Vice President Valdis Dombrovskis and Commissioner Pierre Moscovici said that European authorities had protected Greece from "even more serious harm."[129] The European leadership's unwillingness to recognize the costs borne by the Greek economy and its people was a dismal reminder of their self-serving refuge in groupthink.

The Eurozone's North Is "Insulated" from the Eurozone

Compared with the southern member states, the northern countries had economic strengths that made them resilient to economic shocks and to the errors in eurozone monetary and fiscal policy. Crucially, the northern countries had higher long-term productivity-growth rates based on more extensive and advanced R&D capabilities and better educational systems. Thus, while the crisis did hurt the northern countries, and excessive fiscal austerity and tight monetary policy did delay their recovery, they better withstood the crisis. The curious lesson is that the best recipe for success in the eurozone is to make the eurozone largely irrelevant, to become economically insulated from the eurozone. However, the lesson of the past decade is also that a eurozone member's economic strength weakens its political commitment to Europe.

ECONOMICALLY INSULATED, GERMANS DRIFT POLITICALLY FROM EUROPE

Germany's technological assets helped it overcome the adverse effects of ECB policy decisions. In 2010, when ECB policy was too tight and the euro was strong, German exports nevertheless boomed, because China was importing goods at a frenzied pace. Over the next four years, even as world trade slowed down, Germany maintained steady export growth. Especially between 2011 and 2014, while the eurozone stumbled from crisis to crisis, German exporters found willing buyers for their wares in America and Asia. In turn, this reliable buffer of export growth created spillover activity in the domestic economy. Factories in the export businesses sought domestically produced machinery and other inputs; workers in these factories spent on consumption goods and services.

Germany's export success paradoxically diminished its commercial and political interests in the eurozone. Because several eurozone countries have been growing slowly and incomes have been growing faster in other parts of the world, German companies have increasingly looked to sell their products abroad (figure 9.6). For years now, Germany's most vibrant export markets have been in three EU countries not in the eurozone: the Czech Republic, Hungary, and Poland. Exports to China have boomed. In contrast, France and Italy have become steadily less important customers for German businesses. If current trends continue, soon the Czech Republic, Hungary, and Poland will buy more German goods than France and Italy combined. So much for the thesis that the euro is needed to promote trade.

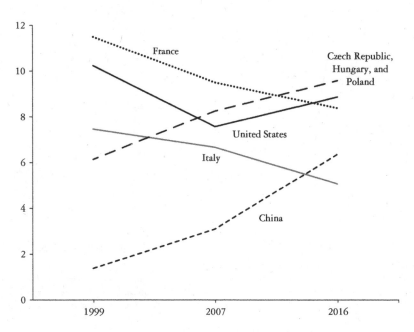

FIGURE 9.6. German exporters shift their sights away from the euro area.
(Percent of total German exports to the various countries)
Source: IMF Data, http://data.imf.org/regular.aspx?key=61013712.

As the evidence of nearly a half century shows, popular support for and trust in Europe rises and falls with the intensity of commercial relationships with other European countries. This is true for Germany and for all European countries (figure 9.7).[130] The long years of the eurozone's economic and financial crisis have reinforced a quarter-century-long tendency of slowly declining trade relationships within Europe. With that, Germany's support for Europe has declined, and probably would have declined even faster had it not been for growing trade relationships with non-euro eastern European countries. However, since it is almost certain that, over the next few decades, eurozone economies will grow at a slower pace than high-performing economies elsewhere, the share of trade with eurozone economies will decline and public willingness to support the eurozone financially will diminish.

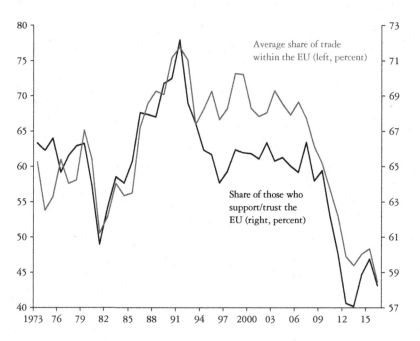

FIGURE 9.7. Support for and trust in the European Union has declined along with the reduced share of trade with EU partners.

Note: The data presented are the average for the following eleven countries: France, Germany, Italy, Netherlands, Spain, Portugal, Greece, Belgium, United Kingdom, Ireland, and Denmark. From 1973 to 2009, the series for "support for (membership in)" the EU is used. Since the support series was discontinued in 2011, the series for "trust" in the EU is used from 2009 onward. During the three years of overlap, 2009–2011, the support and trust series are very close to each other.

Sources: Eurobarometer survey data on support for and trust in the EU, reported twice a year in the second and fourth quarters, http://zacat.gesis.org/webview/; International Monetary Fund, Direction of Trade Statistics.

On September 24, 2017, the German population signaled it was ready to move further away from commitments to the eurozone. In the election to the Bundestag, the big loser was the pro-European SPD, a member of the outgoing "grand coalition" with the CDU and the CSU. SPD won only 20.5 percent of the vote, its lowest vote share in the postwar years. Europe's social democratic movement received another setback.

There were two broader themes in the SPD's collapse. In a tendency first noted in 1965 by Yale University political theorist Robert Dahl, the differences among mainstream parties had narrowed. Merkel had moved her policy agenda toward greater social inclusion, and the SPD had moved, as social democratic parties around the world had done, toward conservative economic positions. The SPD had also tempered its apparently pro-European stance in acknowledgment of the reality that the German public was only willing to go so far.[131] Thus, the SPD offered little that was distinctive. In the general shift toward a more nationalistic view, the SPD lost out.

Merkel's CDU and her electoral partner, the Bavaria-based CSU, were also rebuked by voters. Together, they received 33 percent of the vote, their lowest vote share since the 1949 elections and down from 41.5 percent in 2013. The winners were AfD and FDP, which together received 23.3 percent of the vote (12.6 percent for AfD and 10.7 for FDP), up from less than a combined 10 percent in 2013.

AfD, which had emerged from the nucleus of an anti-euro movement in September 2012, had failed in 2013 to gain the threshold of 5 percent of votes cast necessary for admission to the Bundestag. However, the AfD's electoral appeal shot up starting in late August 2015, when Merkel made a generous commitment to accept desperately fleeing Syrian refugees into Germany.[132]

Hundreds of thousands of refugees poured in. While many Germans welcomed them, others expressed anxiety and anger at the large numbers that were entering the country. Merkel was under pressure at home to stem the inflow, and other European leaders were concerned that her open-door policy was attracting into Europe an unchecked flow of refugees fleeing conflict and prosecution along with economic migrants. But Merkel held to her decision. When Hungarian Prime Minister Viktor Orbán suggested to Merkel that she build a fence to discourage refugees and migrants, she showed a rare flash of emotion. Recalling her East German upbringing, she said, "I lived a long time behind a fence. It is not something I wish to do again."

But at home, opposition to Merkel's policy continued to increase. Critics blamed the policy for sexual assaults committed in Cologne on New Year's Eve by men believed to be refugees.[133] The AfD used that incident to appeal to nationalistic and xenophobic sentiments and gained ground in regional elections. And although Merkel strengthened border controls and stepped up deportations of failed asylum seekers, AfD continued to ride the wave of anti-immigrant sentiment and received nearly 13 percent of the vote in the 2017 election. Juxtaposed against SPD's losses, AfD's gains were another sign of Germany's shift to more nationalistic and euro-skeptic politics.

Many AfD voters had not cast a vote in 2013, believing that mainstream parties would not hear their voices. In 2017, these voters reentered the political process, looking for alternatives. Those who voted for AfD had one very specific German feature: many were East Germans. Aside from that, however, the AfD vote manifested a pattern observed elsewhere in Europe and in the United States. In East and West Germany, low-income men with only "basic" school education or with vocational training voted in large numbers for AfD.[134] Most AfD voters were between the ages of 30 and 59; they worked in blue-collar jobs, often with little job security. They lived in small cities and rural areas.

Economic protest and anti-immigrant sentiment overlapped in AfD voters. Even prosperous Germany had left behind many of its citizens. Marcel Fratzscher, president of the research institute DIW Berlin, explains in his forthcoming book that the country's economic gains in the last few decades have not percolated to the bottom half of the German population.[135] In this bottom half, real incomes have barely grown; few are able to save for a rainy day. Political alienation and conflict within society have increased.

FDP voters were generally affluent professionals, who typically lived in urban areas. A pro-business party, FDP had, often in the past, been a member of CDU-led coalitions. In recent years, the party had developed a euro-skeptic edge.

Christian Lindner, the FDP's head, had campaigned for dismantling the eurozone's financial safety net. He wanted to wind down the ESM, the eurozone's bailout fund. That would also disable the ECB's rescue bazooka, OMTs. Lindner wanted to throw the Greeks out of the eurozone. While he seemed willing to pull back from these extreme positions, he was unwilling to agree with Merkel's limited agenda of financial support for the eurozone. "Nothing would be worse," Lindner said, "than having a new government . . . that carries on as the previous [one]," he said. "This would drive voters into the arms of protest parties."[136]

AfD and FDP peeled away the most conservative voters from the CDU-CSU bloc. For Seehofer, CSU's leader, the clear message was that he had left his "right flank open." In a bid to regain the favor of voters who had abandoned the CSU, Seehofer called for a ceiling on the number of refugees Germany would admit.

Even Merkel was worried. She had long been reluctant to acknowledge AfD's existence in public. Now she said, "We want to win back AfD voters by solving problems, by taking account of their concerns and fears, and above all with good policies."[137] Merkel also had trouble within the CDU. The more conservative CDU parliamentarians were fretting. Her close confidant Volker Kauder faced unexpected resistance in his reelection as the head of the CDU's Bundestag contingent.

Germany changed on September 24, 2017. German chancellors had long assumed they could override domestic public opinion on Europe and so had consciously chosen to keep Germany's European policy stance out of debates leading up to national elections. As she had done in 2009 and 2013, Merkel made that play again in 2017. But this time, German voters sent their message in any case. From here on, nationalism and euro-skepticism will play a bigger role in German politics. In words similar to Lindner's, Seehofer said, "Continuing with business as usual is, we believe, not possible."[138]

The new Bundestag will almost certainly create much stronger restraints on German financial support for Europe. Whether in or out of government, FDP's Lindner has made it clear that he plans to take a hard-line approach to financial assistance for crisis countries, and that he will demand strict adherence to European fiscal austerity rules. The CDU/CSU leadership will be wary of initiatives that require greater financial engagement with Europe. They cannot afford to lose more support to euro-skeptics. The SPD is a spent political force.

On September 26, Emmanuel Macron gave another big speech at the Sorbonne in Paris. He restated his call for a more ambitious Europe. He said Europeans were in a "civil war," and the only way to end it was by constructing a "European sovereignty."[139]

Wolfgang Schäuble, the outgoing finance minister, quickly rejected Macron's call for a large eurozone budget to help countries in trouble.[140] Such a budget, Schäuble declared, was "economically not necessary for a stable monetary union." Instead, Schäuble wanted to create a European authority that would exercise tighter control over budgetary policies of member states. The reality is simple. Any German leader will find it incredibly hard from now on to justify sacrifices for Europe.

There was also a question of whether Germany could maintain its economic dynamism, which made it possible for others to demand that Germany do more for Europe. The German economy has its Achilles heels. In September 2015, the US Environmental Protection Agency concluded that the giant automaker Volkswagen (VW) had installed "defeat devices" in its cars.[141] These devices lowered the nitrogen oxide emissions of VW's diesel-fueled cars in lab tests, but once on the road, the cars' emissions far exceeded allowed limits. German regulators, however, resisted an initiative by the European Commission to establish a more comprehensive emissions-testing system in the EU.[142] That resistance continued even after VW revealed that it had engaged in a cartel-like arrangement with other automakers—Audi, Porsche, BMW, and Daimler—to develop "defeat devices" together.[143] German carmakers have invested heavily in diesel technology and have fallen behind in petrol-fueled and electric cars. However, the German authorities' effort to protect the car producers with their increasingly obsolete technologies is bound to be frustrated. The shift to electric cars is well under way. Indeed, German city administrators have ambitious plans to reduce use of all types of cars.[144] A failure by Germany's fabled car manufacturers to respond with new ideas could disable a critical German growth engine.

The other German weakness lies in its banks. Germany still has too many banks, and for years, they have chewed away at one another's profits. Many German banks gambled for easy profits in the heady days of US subprime craziness.[145] With massive government support, the banks worst hit by the financial crisis have largely recovered. However, a question mark hangs over the giant Deutsche Bank, which has engaged in several irregular transactions.[146] It misrepresented the risks in the mortgage-backed securities it sold before the global financial crisis began; in 2008–2009, it engineered derivative contracts to hide losses at the troubled Italian bank MPS.[147] In January 2017, UK and US authorities fined Deutsche Bank $630 million for facilitating transactions that very likely were used to launder money out of Russia.

For now, the German economy appears to be absorbing these worrying domestic tendencies without disruption. However, if Germany's domestic weaknesses intensify, not only would its insulation from the eurozone diminish, but Germany would be even less willing than now—and, indeed, less able—to aid other eurozone countries.

FINLAND'S ECONOMIC SETBACK REINFORCES EURO-SKEPTICISM

In the north, Finland fell on bad days in 2012. The main causes of Finland's problems were unrelated to the eurozone. Star company Nokia had taken a big knock in the global technology race, and the country's highly efficient paper industry had suffered from falling demand.[148] At such a time, having its own currency to devalue would have been particularly helpful in preventing, or at least limiting the severity of, an economic recession. Instead, stuck with the euro, the Finnish economy went into a prolonged recession.

Despite this setback, the Finnish economy's long-term prospects remain bright. Finland has many strengths, including schools that are the envy of the world. Because of the school system's commitment to "fight against the failure" of children, Finland has among the highest social-mobility rates in the Western world; large numbers of children can expect to earn more over their lifetimes than their parents did.[149] Finland is among the world's leaders in densities of engineers and scientists. Finnish firms excel in worker training and advanced research. The public-debt ratio did rise through the crisis, but it remained relatively low. Recent data show that Finland is beginning a strong economic recovery. Finland's historical advantages, rather than the eurozone's monetary and fiscal policies, will determine the country's economic progress. In this sense of long-term economic insulation from the eurozone's policy errors, Finland is, for now, firmly in the north.

In the northern group of eurozone nations, Finnish public opinion was among the earliest to turn against financial aid to the southern states. In 2011, the True Finns, a right-wing nationalist party, made large electoral gains. Responding to that rise and to the broader public unease about the direction Europe was taking, the Finnish government resisted paying for bailouts of eurozone countries in financial crises.[150] Although the government did not ultimately veto any bailout, it delayed the process and demanded and received collateral for the loans it extended.

In 2015, the True Finns, by now known simply as the Finns, became members of the governing coalition. Domestic political anxiety was redirected toward inflows of economic migrants and refugees. In June 2017, the Finns who took a hard line on admitting refugees left the governing coalition, while the more moderate members, calling themselves Blue Reform, stayed on in government.[151] Thus, although the political process marginalized extreme voices, economic nationalism established itself in Finland's ideological mainstream.

DUTCH NATIONALISM TAKES DEEPER ROOTS

The Dutch government, in keeping with the eurozone's stability ideology, pursued excessive austerity in 2011 and 2012, which caused an unnecessarily long downturn.[152] But that phase was soon over. Even in the worst days, the government's debt levels and unemployment rates remained firmly in financial and political safe zones.

On the single currency, the Dutch—always sympathetic with the Germans—distrusted countries that they believed were fiscally irresponsible. A former Dutch central bank president described Germany as the prudent ant and France as the irresponsible cricket. Dutch Finance Minister Gerrit Zalm bitterly opposed Italian entry into the eurozone.[153]

Dutch nationalistic forces, drawing on euro-skepticism and anti-immigrant sentiment, grew through the crisis. To ensure their own political survival, mainstream parties steadily adopted that skepticism. In December 2016, conservative Dutch Prime Minister Mark Rutte cautioned that the drive for "more Europe" could be counterproductive. It would alienate the population, fan more populism, and, thus, push the European project "over the edge."[154] During the March 2017 Dutch parliamentary election campaign, Rutte fought back the challenge from far-right, ultra-nationalist Geert Wilders by co-opting elements of Wilders's anti-immigrant language; Rutte offered "his own, gentler version of anti-immigrant populism."[155] In the final days of the campaign, Rutte said, "If you don't like it here, you can leave."[156] Most observers interpreted that remark as a threat to immigrants and even to second- and third-generation descendants of immigrants. Although Rutte's center-right, conservative party lost vote share compared to the previous election (held in September 2012), his "soft" nationalism seemed to have worked in the limited sense that Wilders's electoral gains fell short of the large advances predicted by the polls. Rutte defensively declared that he had halted the "wrong kind of populism," implying that he was now the standard bearer of "good populism."[157]

The "pro-European," social democratic Labor party was crushed. A nativism seemed to take hold in Dutch politics. In the days before a new Rutte-led government was formed, the Labor party's Jeroen Dijsselbloem, who continued in that period as caretaker finance minister and had no democratic legitimacy to speak even on behalf of the Dutch people, gave gratuitous advice to governments and citizens in southern countries: "You cannot spend all the money on women and drinks and then ask for help."[158] In the outrage that followed, Dijsselbloem defended his statement. European "solidarity," he said, requires adherence to budget rules on debt and deficit limits. He was just being "stern," he added. The conservative Merkel had earlier used the metaphor of problem child for Greece, and the social democrat Dijsselbloem emphasized stern parenting. When it came to safeguarding national taxpayer funds, political ideology did not matter. National interests and power relationships trumped the goal of European unity of equal nations.

IRELAND MOVES FROM THE PERIPHERY
TO THE NORTH

Ironically, Ireland also established its claim to membership in the "northern club." In the not-so-distant past, at the height of the global and eurozone crises between 2008 and 2011, Ireland was designated a member of the eurozone's periphery, along with Greece, Italy, Portugal, and Spain. To avert a financial collapse, the Irish government received, in per capita terms, a larger dose of official funds than any of the other periphery countries. Ireland's banks survived on virtually unlimited liquidity support from the ECB. Although Ireland benefited from European support, Irish citizens acutely resented their loss of sovereignty; their sense of national humiliation was palpable when former ECB President Jean-Claude Trichet dictated decisions to Irish officials.[159] Like citizens of other eurozone periphery countries, the Irish felt trapped, fearing that they would remain dependent on their rescuers for years to come.

Hence, when the Irish economy quickly and impressively recovered, European leaders were anxious to chalk up a victory for their austerity and structural-reform strategy. Merkel repeatedly praised Ireland for following the European economic recipe. In November 2011, she described Ireland as a "superb example" of a country that had succeeded by doggedly implementing austerity.[160] In September 2013, at a press conference in Berlin just after she was reelected chancellor for the third time, Merkel singled out Irish Prime Minister Enda Kenny for praise: "I'm grateful to my colleague Enda Kenny for implementing the reforms so passionately."[161] Six months later, at a press conference in Dublin, Merkel told Kenny, "I would like to pay you respect and admiration for what you have achieved."[162] ECB Governing Council member Benoît Coeuré and European Commission Vice President Valdis Dombrovskis repeated Merkel's message but with charts and figures.[163]

It was tempting to present Ireland as the poster child of European austerity and structural-reform policies. This story was also wrong.

Ireland recovered not because of but despite eurozone-imposed strictures and policies.[164] Ireland implemented virtually no "structural reforms"; the Irish economy did not grow out of the crisis because of policies to reduce workers' wages as a way to regain international competitiveness. A group of Irish scholars has emphatically concluded that Ireland was not the euro area's poster child; Ireland was, at best, a "beautiful freak."[165]

Ireland's special advantage arose from its nearly three-decades-old corporate-tax regime, which combined a low corporate tax rate with assorted additional side deals to attract foreign investors.[166] For years, other European countries had loudly complained about the unfair advantage Ireland had carved out for itself. But Irish authorities steadfastly held on to their prized competitive edge. To be sure, the low tax regime had its unseemly side, as Irish blogger Michael Hennigan tirelessly pointed out: multinationals booked their international profits in Ireland, which led to ludicrously high reported GDP growth rates in some years and therefore exaggerated the speed of Ireland's economic recovery.[167]

But the tax regime also helped Ireland maintain a genuine connection with American multinationals, especially with companies that delivered computer services and manufactured pharmaceuticals and biotechnology products.[168] The global demand for these products and services remained steady even during the crisis years. Thus, the multinationals provided Ireland with a vent for export growth, which helped overcome the contractionary effect of austerity and allowed Ireland to escape from the eurozone trap. Moreover, as exports grew, the multinationals, with their deep pockets, raised the already-generous wages they paid to their Irish employees. Higher wages helped raise demand for, and hence supported production of, domestic goods and services.

Thus, Ireland managed to insulate itself from the harmful effects of the eurozone's policy framework and, in this sense, became a member of the zone's "northern club."

Ireland's transition from the eurozone's periphery to the northern club was accompanied by a remarkable change in Irish leaders' attitudes toward financial assistance to eurozone member countries in distress. As late as January 2015, when Ireland stood on the edge of the periphery, Irish government officials called for a "debt conference" to forgive debts owed by periphery countries to their European creditors.[169] However, when it became clear that any hope of forgiveness of Irish debts was a pipe dream, Irish leaders quickly changed tack and turned into increasingly strident critics of debt relief for Greece.

Although they are now self-consciously aligned with the leaders of the northern countries, Irish authorities' confidence that the country stands on its own feet could prove premature. Ireland's freakish advantage could well end. The European Commission's recent conclusion that the Irish government has given the US tech giant Apple unusually favorable tax treatment, along with the stepped-up international scrutiny of tax havens, will require Ireland to create a new growth model, one that does not rely so heavily on low corporate taxes.[170] Ireland is not well prepared to deal with the challenge of that shift. Ireland's domestic companies do little R&D. The damage from the crisis continues: fiscal austerity forced a decline in public-education expenditures, and large numbers of young Irish citizens with college degrees left for the United Kingdom, other "Anglo-Saxon" countries, and the Gulf

States.[171] Without its low-tax regime, Ireland will find it hard to sustain economic momentum. Ireland cannot take for granted its insulation from eurozone policies.

EASTERN EUROPEANS AS MEMBERS OF THE EUROZONE'S NORTH

The principle of insulation from the eurozone also applies, at least for now, to four Eastern European eurozone members: Estonia, Latvia, Lithuania, and Slovakia. These countries have their own special economic dynamic. They emerged battered from the Soviet Union's planned-economy system with low per capita incomes in the early 1990s and began a painful transition to market economies. With their well-educated populations, they rapidly made up for lost ground by establishing a modern institutional infrastructure and investing in up-to-date technologies. Joining the EU in 2004 helped immeasurably in these efforts. But being in the EU, they also were sucked into the financial exuberance of those years and inevitably experienced a severe economic and financial shock at the peak of the global crisis in 2008 and 2009. They were not in the eurozone at the time, but their fixed exchange rates with the euro placed them effectively under the ECB's monetary policy and prevented their central banks from lowering interest rates and allowing currency depreciation to match their needs. That tie to the eurozone deepened their crises.

Propelled, however, by the still significant opportunities to catch up with advanced economies, Eastern European member states resumed robust growth in 2010. They kept up strong growth performances despite the eurozone's tight monetary policy and commitment to fiscal austerity. With their optimistic outlook, these countries chose to enter the eurozone: Slovakia adopted the euro in 2009, Estonia in 2011, Latvia in 2014, and Lithuania in 2015. As long as their catch-up growth impulse lasts, eurozone monetary and fiscal policies will exert only modest influence on these member countries. Few have thought through the challenges that will arise when Eastern Europe's high-inflation tendencies begin to bite.

In line with their economic optimism, Eastern European members of the eurozone joined the northern political coalition. They allied themselves with the north in resisting financial support or policy initiatives that favored southern member states. In 2011, Slovak authorities refused at first to make their full contribution to the European bailout fund, mainly because they believed that the financial aid to Greece was excessive.[172] In 2014, Estonia supported northern countries that opposed easier ECB monetary policy.[173]

The Stage Is Set

This is where my story ends. It ends at a moment when the worst of the last crisis is over and a mood of optimism prevails. The European narrative, on the defensive for the past few years, is regaining strength and confidence. Jean-Claude Juncker's words from his September 2016 State of the Union address are a rallying cry: "Being European, for most of us, also means the euro." Through the crisis, Juncker asserted, "the euro stayed strong and protected us from even worse instability." Thus, he said, Europeans must always remember that the euro "brings us huge, often invisible benefits." He concluded grandiosely: "We can be united even though we are diverse."[174] Virtually every European leader believes this uplifting story.

However, through the veil of short-term optimism, it is possible to see alarming long-term forces. On the economics, the recovery could go on for some years and take the edge off the financial vulnerabilities. However, if the short-term boost from fiscal stimulus and world trade fades too quickly, the eurozone's economic prospects will be weighed down by low productivity growth, which had been slowing down even before the crisis and has slowed further since then. The eurozone could fall into an extended period of slow growth, which would keep government debt levels high and banks under pressure. Global economic and financial accidents could then trigger another round of financial tensions.

The risks to the eurozone's political future are most saliently observed in the decline of the social democratic movement. To a large extent, such decline was inevitable. As a political ideology, social democracy was born "as a solution to the injustice of the industrial system."[175] While promoting the interests of the industrial labor force, it was more broadly a movement to achieve social equality in peaceful ways. With time, the original rationale for social democracy started to disappear. Globalization and technical change steadily eroded the economic and political role of traditional industrial workers. Other political ideologies absorbed the values and priorities of social justice. Losing their moorings, social democrats themselves moved to market-oriented, "neo-liberal" policy positions and so ceased to protect economically vulnerable population groups.

Against this background of long-term decline, social democrats imploded in the 2017 electoral cycle because they had little to offer in response to the eurozone's crisis. Especially the acute crisis years, 2011–2012, demanded a political response. But social democrats had no new ideas at home and, while they claimed to champion pro-Europeanism, they had no new ideas for Europe. In December 2017, in a particularly absurd demonstration of how lost the social democratic movement was, Martin Schulz, leader of Germany's Social Democrats, called for a new European constitution. All member states, he said, would be required to adopt the constitution; and if they refused to do so, they would be ejected from the EU. This comically vain gesture was void of all sense of European history. Europe had repeatedly refused to go down this road before. With time, achieving this goal had become much harder.

Thus, the 2017 elections were not an event in a normal electoral cycle. There was no reason to believe that the past political configurations could be recreated. Rather, the financial crisis speeded up a historical political trend. Just as it was an economic critical juncture, which intensified the north-south eurozone divergence, the crisis was also a political critical juncture. The space vacated by social democrats was occupied, in part, by nationalist parties. Mainstream conservative parties, in a defensive response to their own declining electoral fortunes, continued to promise stability and justice but also moved to a "soft nationalism." Reflecting that change, Mark Rutte, the conservative Dutch prime minister claimed that he was a guardian of "good populism." Others will surely make similar claims.

Macron's bid to rejuvenate an old-fashioned pro-European agenda cheers many who fear that no one else will lead that cause. But history seems to have moved ahead of Macron. To succeed, he needs to bring the French people along on his proposed trip back to the future. Moreover, he faces powerful forces arrayed against "more Europe." Northern nations resent the financial burden that the south has imposed on them. Even Jeroen Dijsselbloem, the Dutch Labour Party politician and outgoing finance minister, speaks disparagingly of southern member states. Some years of economic growth could create a new willingness to cooperate. But growth did not help between 2004 and 2007. And the next crisis will severely test the financial Band-Aids applied during the one that has just passed. A new crisis will certainly test the political willingness to hold the European project together.

For now, though, many European leaders inertially repeat the conventional narrative of a united Europe. In his September 2017 State of the Union address, Juncker proposed measures to strengthen the roles of the European Commission and the European Parliament.[176] But, as always, the bid to create suprastate-like features at the European level and thus downgrade the authority of the nation-state, met with instant resistance. The FDP's Christian Lindner reacted bluntly. He said that the first order of business had to be strict enforcement of budget-deficit limits and creation of an orderly process allowing default by overly indebted countries. Dutch Prime Minister Rutte dismissed Juncker's proposals as "romantic." He himself, Rutte added, was a "when you have visions, go see a doctor kind of guy."[177]

It is a heady mix. In January 2018, as this manuscript goes to the printer, the "united in diversity" narrative lives on, but it is at odds with the reality of increasing economic and political divergence among countries. European leaders cannot agree on how to reverse the divergence and what, if anything, the "united in diversity" slogan means. It is awkward, therefore, that the curtain on this historical drama comes down just when the story is getting interesting. How will the conundrums be resolved? Is there a happy ending? We do not know the answers. But we can sketch some possibilities for how this ninth act might conclude.

| The Future Ain't What It
Used to Be

I DESCRIBE HERE two scenarios, two possible ways in which this final act plays out. In the first scenario, which I label "more of the same," there are dawns and periods of optimism, as between 2004 and 2007, but setbacks and crises recur to test the euro and its accompanying political vision. European authorities remain confident that they are essentially on the right track, and they continue to make modest course corrections, which they believe will ensure a brighter European future. But history contests this vision. Europe's decline as a once great economic and political power continues in steps that are immeasurable to the eye but that cumulate over time. The "united in diversity" slogan does not work. The forces that have caused economic divergence remain undiminished. The elusive and frustrating pursuit of deeper economic and financial integration causes more economic and political damage. The euro struggles to survive.

In the second scenario, European authorities recognize the important truth that "more Europe" will not solve Europe's most pressing economic and social problems. They recognize that fine-tuning European institutions and processes is mainly an involutionary effort, which relabels and rearranges while adding little value. They dismantle the economically counterproductive and politically corrosive system of administratively supervised fiscal rules and instead rely increasingly on financial markets to enforce fiscal discipline. Nation-states reclaim more of their sovereignty, and the apparent "fragmentation" of Europe becomes a source of creative energy. National leaders turn their attention to the critical task at home of rebuilding a technological base rooted in educational systems that provide an impetus to long-term growth and to reducing social inequalities. As each nation makes its best effort, a vibrant competitive decentralization plays itself out. This is my pro-European vision. It offers, I believe, the best hope for Europe to regenerate itself and to create an identity that relies not on coordinated governance but on a new European Republic of Letters.

More of the Same: A Dangerous Drift

The "more of the same" scenario is founded on the groupthink splendidly articulated by Jean-Claude Juncker in his 2016 State of the Union Address: the euro delivers "huge" even if "often invisible benefits." Others have echoed the sentiment in more pedestrian language. In a May 2017 "Reflection Paper," European Commission Vice President Valdis Dombrovskis and Commissioner Pierre Moscovici wrote that the benefits of the euro are "clear-cut."[1] Dombrovskis and Moscovici recognized that eurozone member states have diverged since the launch of the euro. They acknowledged that if left "unaddressed," the forces pulling the countries of the eurozone apart would probably "weaken citizens' support for the euro."[2] Dombrovskis and Moscovici proposed a eurozone budget to help member states during recessions and crises, although in order to blunt the predictable storm of opposition from Germany and other northern states, they described their proposal as a mechanism to express "solidarity." The Four Presidents Report, published in December 2012, similarly appealed to a sense of "fiscal solidarity."[3] Dombrovskis and Moscovici repeated the obligatory call for "democratic accountability" in European decision-making. In September 2017, speaking from Pnyx Hill in Athens, with the magnificent Acropolis in the background, France's President Emmanuel Macron made his own call for a common eurozone budget, although his speech was "otherwise short of specifics."[4]

In this maze of sanitized words, the sharply divergent interests of northern and southern countries are finessed. The decisive sovereignty impediment remains. However, the message remains unwavering. More of the same.

In this first scenario, then, the eurozone's south remains under economic and financial stress. As the boost from world trade and easing of fiscal austerity wears off, each country's GDP increases at close to its potential growth rate. The Italian economy grows at a post-World War II low around the IMF's estimated potential growth rate of 0.5 to 0.75 percent per year, although it sometimes seems that the OECD's even lower projection is more realistic.[5] Similarly, Portugal's potential growth rate stays at or below 0.5 percent a year.[6] Even Spain and France grow only around an average of 1 percent a year.

For short periods, renewed world trade growth lifts eurozone GDP growth rates in a pattern that has recurred over the past 150 years (figure 10.1). However, the dividend from world trade has diminished over the years as several eurozone economies, especially those in the south, have lost competitiveness. Moreover, significant and extended pickups in world trade have become less frequent, confirming researchers' views that the era of hyperglobalization is over.[7] Global supply chains—set up to source materials, parts, and equipment from low-cost locations around the world—are now largely in place. Compared with the blistering 9 percent growth rate in the pre-global-crisis years between 2004 and 2007, the rate of world trade growth now stays, generally, in the range of 3 to 5 percent a

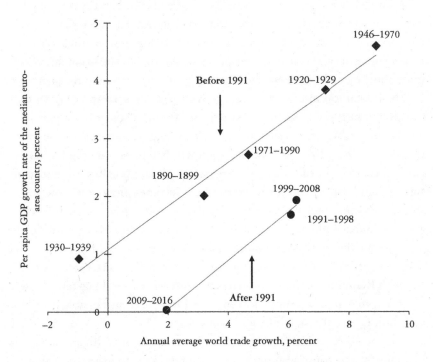

FIGURE 10.1. Euro-area growth marches to the drum of world trade growth.
Note: Eurozone countries in this chart include Austria, Belgium, Finland, France, Germany, Ireland, Italy, Netherlands, Portugal, Spain. The periods 1914–1919 and 1940–1945 are missing due to a lack of wartime trade data.
Sources: *Real per capita GDP growth rates:* Angus Maddison, "Historical Statistics of the World Economy 1-2008AD," http://www.ggdc.net/maddison/oriindex.htm; Penn World Tables 8.0, http://www.rug.nl/ggdc/; International Monetary Fund, "World Economic Outlook" Database, http://www.imf.org/external/pubs/ft/weo/2014/02/weodata/index.aspx. *World trade:* League of Nations, Monthly Bulletin of Statistics; CPB Netherlands Bureau for Economic Analysis, World Trade Monitor, https://www.cpb.nl/en/data.

year, rarely reaching even a 6 percent pace. Thus, world trade does not do enough to raise European growth rates.

Financial stress continues because of low GDP growth and because of the lowflation unleashed by tight monetary policy between 2011 and 2014. The core inflation rate—which strips out volatile energy and food price movements and hence measures underlying price pressures—remains close to 1 percent for the entire eurozone and is even lower in the eurozone's south. The inflation rate does rise for brief periods, moved by unusual domestic and international factors. But that rise only lulls ECB officials into believing they have solved the low-inflation problem. The lesson from Japan is that once inflation falls below a psychological threshold, any increase is short-lived. People postpone their spending because they expect inflation to decline again. Such postponement reinforces the low-growth and low-inflation tendency.

A crucial consequence of these developments is that the real interest rate—the difference between the nominal interest rate and the inflation rate—remains high in the eurozone's south. While low nominal rates do help repay debts and encourage people to spend, the low inflation rate offsets those gains by making debts harder to repay and by discouraging spending.

The Italian real interest rate stays above 1 percent, somewhat higher than the growth rate of its real (inflation-adjusted) GDP. Thus, interest payments on existing debts grow faster than economic output, adding to the country's debt burden. Even in good years, growth barely pays off the interest on past debts. Debt burdens therefore remain high and possibly rise for many small manufacturers and for workers whose incomes grow only slowly. The arithmetic is as cruel to Portugal. For France and Spain, the arithmetic is only somewhat kinder, and debt burdens fall, but they do so only slowly. Throughout the south, the combination of low growth and high debt levels leaves countries vulnerable to "real-life stress tests," as Harvard economist Kenneth Rogoff predicted. Each stress test further reduces long-term growth potential, making the countries even more prone to unsustainable debt burdens and, hence, at risk of financial "convulsions."[8]

The paradox is that while for some governments, businesses, and households, the nominal interest rates are too high, they are too low from the perspective of banks. Banks make their profits mainly on the interest-rate margin, the difference between the interest rate they charge their customers and the interest rate they pay depositors and other creditors. Since the ECB has brought nominal interest rates down through its bond-purchase QE program, banks can charge only low rates, especially to their best customers. Indeed, low interest rates for customers was the whole point of the ECB's bond purchases. But custom has not allowed banks to equally decrease the interest rates they pay their depositors.[9] Hence, banks' interest-rate margins have narrowed. And since business has not increased commensurately, QE has extended the historically low profitability of many fragile eurozone banks.

Banks' profitability is further constrained by international regulatory pressure to "deleverage." This pressure emerged soon after the global financial crisis began, when regulators worldwide agreed that investors should be required to hold more equity capital in banks—placing more of their skin in the game—to absorb the losses that banks incur and thus minimize the government's financial obligation to rescue them. Most eurozone banks have increased their equity holdings. At the same time, relatively meagre GDP growth, low interest-rate margins, and the continued need to make provisions for past losses have put a lid on the banks' profits. Hence, the profit rates earned by banks' equity investors are near historically low levels. Consequently, market valuations of banks are low relative to the book value of their assets. These low valuations reflect the added concern in financial markets that, under renewed stress, banks' borrowers may not be able to repay their debts.

Thus, the medium-term economic and financial outlook for the eurozone has many worrying features. Slow GDP growth and low inflation keep debt burdens elevated. Banks are unable to generate significant volumes of new business to compensate for low interest-rate margins and are unable to offer adequate equity returns needed to attract sufficient capital shock absorbers. Economic and financial conditions stay in a fragile zone.

The ECB has steadily become less effective. ECB officials insist that low nominal interest rates, engineered by the extensive bond purchases, aided the eurozone's economic recovery and prevented a further decline in inflation rates. That claim is hard to validate. The recovery benefited more directly from reduced austerity and the step up in world trade growth. In contrast, it is clear that the ECB acted too slowly to bring down nominal rates, allowing a deflationary psychology to become entrenched in southern countries. Workers have now lived for several years in an environment of low wage increases; and with many of them either unemployed or stuck in precarious, low-productivity and low-wage jobs, most expect that their wages will increase only slowly, if at all. Fearful of international competition, businesses have held back price increases.[10] Eurozone inflation expectations have "de-anchored" as they did in Japan, and stubbornly stay well below 2 percent. The Bank of Japan, despite its open-ended Abenomics monetary stimulus, has been unable to raise the inflation rate. The ECB is hemmed in by a weaker commitment. Hence, southern eurozone real interest rates remain positive, which inhibits spending and rises in inflation.

To make matters worse, Germany and other northern countries are ready for higher interest rates, while the countries in the south are not. The German preference is clear. Higher nominal rates will do little to dent Germany's growth, nor will they increase debt service costs significantly since government and private debt burdens are fairly low. And Germans do not worry about a decline in inflation. In contrast, German banks, deeply constrained by low nominal rates, stand to gain significantly from higher rates.

Eventually, the tug for higher rates from Germany and other northern eurozone members leads episodically to speculation that the ECB might taper bond purchases more rapidly than anticipated, causing interest rates to rise. As happened briefly after the ECB's Sintra Forum in June 2017, when Mario Draghi suggested that economic recovery was well on its way and "reflationary forces" had set in, speculation that monetary policy will be tightened gains momentum. Although ECB officials hedge their words, their eagerness to emphasize that monetary policy has worked to restore growth and, hence, inflation will soon rise, adds to the expectation that the ECB is about to cut back its bond purchases and guide nominal interest rates upward. In any event, the ECB has set itself a technical limit of holding at most one-third of all outstanding bonds issued by a country. This limit begins to bite, slowing down the bond purchases.

This expectation of slowing bond purchases and higher interest rates causes the euro to appreciate. From the euro's earliest days, financial markets have understood that the ECB maintains tighter monetary policy than other central banks do. Early expected tightening now fits that experience. The euro remains too strong for the southern countries, which makes their exports less competitive and pushes domestic inflation down, reinforcing deflationary psychology.

Hope lurks that a global wave of scientific and technological change will usher in a new era of global prosperity. Breakthroughs in biotechnology and information-communications technologies and in the production and delivery of renewable energy could revolutionize economic and social structures worldwide. Such breakthroughs could sweep away the eurozone's—indeed, the world's—economic and financial stresses, until, that is, human beings mess things up again.

But the promised tantalizing breakthroughs have not yet come. Robert Gordon, economics professor at Northwestern University, has long been pessimistic that such breakthroughs will come anytime soon. In an exhaustive study, he has argued that modern technologies, despite their continual promise, will not match the technological advances achieved in the late nineteenth and early twentieth centuries.[11] Those earlier transformative advances included the development and spread of electricity, telephony and other communications technologies, the internal combustion engine, running water and sanitation, and chemicals, plastics, antibiotics, and other modern medicines. They delivered far-reaching economic benefits until around 1970, and once their potential was exhausted, the new generation of technological advances has been unable to generate comparable gains. Thus, notwithstanding the commonly perceived sense that technological breakthroughs are already paying dividends, productivity growth in advanced economies had been falling for a few decades before the global crisis started, and this fall has continued ever since.[12] Gordon makes the bold prediction that productivity growth will continue to fall.

Looking forward, Gordon's bleak prediction of weak productivity growth proves well founded for several years. In addition, fear of the future places a cap on consumer and investment demand and, hence, on global growth. Memories of the global and eurozone financial crises do not fade quickly, and worries about living through another wrenching experience remain.[13] Many workers are afraid of losing their jobs to the spread of automation in service sectors. Because of such fears, consumers everywhere spend only in brief bursts, businesses invest cautiously, and aggregate demand does not gather sufficient momentum to spur sustained growth.

Without a sudden burst of technologically driven global optimism, global trade provides only an occasional and limited lift. Positive real interest rates persist and the countries in the southern eurozone continue, at best, in a benign drift. Their debt ratios, banking stress, and unemployment rates stay high, declining slowly in some phases but rising back again. The southern eurozone countries also lose more ground in the international marketplace, unable to compete either with advanced Asian producers or with low-cost regions of Europe. The young and best qualified in the eurozone's south see little value in mounting domestic dissent and instead seek opportunities abroad, which makes domestic growth revival harder. Domestic politics remain fragmented; saviors briefly stir hope, only to disappoint.

European leaders seek answers to their problems in "more" Europe. Macron and, after him, like-minded national leaders continue to promote a pro-European agenda. Not surprisingly, given the diversity of interests—east versus west and south versus north—plans for a European budget and finance minister, as has happened so many times in the past, go nowhere. The sovereignty barrier remains intact. Eurozone member states still cannot agree to share even 2 or 3 percent of their tax revenues in a common pool. Member-state governments find it unacceptable that a European finance minister in charge of this pool of funds would have the right to tax European citizens and issue bonds backed by national government guarantees. Macron himself kills the financial transactions tax—a tax on transactions such as buying and selling of stocks and bonds—which he had campaigned for as a possible source of central funds.[14] Macron is concerned that such a tax would diminish the prospects of Paris emerging as an international financial hub. Other ideas that go nowhere include the apparently modest proposal to unify national unemployment insurance schemes: several governments find it unacceptable that they might end up subsidizing other governments for far too long.

Views also differ on the role of the proposed finance minister. Would he, as Macron seemed to suggest, have authority to spend money as he saw fit, or would he, as former German Finance Minister Wolfgang Schäuble wanted, merely enforce Europe's budget rules with greater determination?[15] To whom would a European finance minister be accountable, to the heads of government or to representatives elected to the European Parliament? These questions have not been resolved for more than half a century, and they will not now be resolved in a hurry.

The great danger is an ill-thought-out compromise that creates a false sense of financial protection and establishes yet another unaccountable eurozone authority. Amid the buzz, it is always important to remember the wise words of former Dutch central banker André Szász. European compromises are not sensible intermediate positions that accommodate the interests of various parties. Rather, compromises are carefully crafted words that allow each government to interpret the agreement in line with its own preferences.[16] "European budget," "European finance minister," and "fiscal union" mean completely different things to the Germans and to the French. The Germans are clear: they merely want to tighten the screws on those who depart from the eurozone's norms of fiscal austerity. Nobody knows—perhaps not even the French know—what the French believe is truly needed to create and sustain a robust eurozone architecture. Thus, if in order to notch up a victory for "European integration," French and German leaders ram through another half-baked attempt under a cloud of words, the structure will fail during the next episode of financial distress.

To breach the sovereignty barrier, Europe needs a genuinely workable political framework. Europe's only democratic institution, the European Parliament, holds some promise as the foundation for political accountability. However, the Parliament suffers from several ills in common with the broader European project. Trust in the European Parliament has steadily fallen. From a relatively high 62 percent for the first election to the European Parliament in 1979, voter turnout fell steadily to 43 percent in 2014. The low European voter turnout in 2014 was remarkable, because citizens were angry and had reason to make their voices heard, but they evidently did not believe that the European Parliament had much to offer them. In countries where trust in European institutions fell the most, voter turnout for European parliamentary elections also declined the most.[17] In Italy, for example, support for and trust in Europe was stratospherically high in 1979, and 86 percent of eligible voters cast their votes in the election that year. By 2014, Italian trust in the EU had fallen sharply, and only 57 percent of voters bothered to go to the polls. Much of Eastern Europe has always been disengaged from the European Parliament. In Slovakia, just 13 percent of eligible voters voted in 2014.

Members of the European Parliament (MEPs) generally vote according to their ideological dispositions, but on crucial matters, ideologies take a back seat and national interests take precedence.[18] Often, national interests are very special; the French want to maintain the European Parliament's wasteful outpost in Strasbourg rather than consolidate all activity in Brussels, and the Irish have successfully pressed for recognition of Irish Gaelic as an official European language.[19] But national interests also dominate political ideology on key economic and financial matters; votes on agricultural policy are overwhelmingly influenced by nationality, an especially salient fact since one-third of the EU budget is spent on agricultural subsidies.[20] Similarly, German MEPs across ideological lines tend to vote in line with the German government's opposition to initiatives such as eurobonds—bonds that would carry the financial guarantee of all eurozone member states and hence could create a potential fiscal claim on the German government.[21]

The European Parliament is an institution in limbo. MEPs often come with personal agendas. All too frequently, they misuse funds allocated to them for their expenses. Sylvie Goulard, an avowed pro-European, was forced out of her position as Macron's defense minister when an investigation began into the conditions under which parliamentary funds were used for hiring her assistants.[22] The sense is widespread that many MEPs treat their sojourn at the European Parliament as a well-paid sinecure. While these facts are widely known, only Juncker has been willing to say that this emperor has no clothes. "You are ridiculous," he has chided MEPs.[23] Juncker was in parliament to participate in a debate and was upset because only around 30 of the 751 MEPs bothered to show up. Alexander Stubb, then Finland's minister for European affairs and once an MEP himself, has said that the European Parliament exercises power but is itself not accountable.[24] Influential Germans want to pull back power from the European Parliament. National parliaments, they say, should have the right to stop the European Parliament from passing a bill.[25]

On the surface, Europe's economic and political drift seems benign. The economic and financial crisis between 2007 and 2013 was a severe shock but is now seen mainly in the rearview mirror. Voices, such as Rogoff's, warning of more real-life stress tests and debt convulsions are not heeded. German Chancellor Angela Merkel, in her customary style, chooses to stall. Despite simmering political tensions and vast differences in national perspectives, the sense is that new technocratic initiatives to strengthen the eurozone are on their way. But such initiatives always lack the essential political glue.

Pulitzer Prize-winning author Jared Diamond has written that societies collapse in the same way as forests lose their tree cover from one year to another. "One incredible act of stupidity" does not destroy a forest. Rather, "we cut down a few trees over there, but saplings are beginning to grow back again [over] here." The erosion is hard to discern. Only those who have a sense of history recognize that the trees are "fewer, smaller, and less important."[26]

The system becomes weak and struggles to cope with new shocks. A crisis may come from a sharp correction in US financial markets or from the bursting of the Chinese property-cum-banking bubble or from investor flight from Italian banks and government debt. Panic spreads through global financial markets, and world trade falls sharply. European exports take a hit. Because of Europe's heavy dependence on trade, European GDP contracts rapidly, and the weakest banks come under unbearable pressure. Those weakest banks are in Italy. Cracks in a few of these banks radiate tremors to other fault lines within Italy and throughout Europe.[27]

As the financial earthquakes spread from their Italian epicenter, only the ECB—using the might of its OMTs—can prevent financial devastation. The first step in triggering OMTs is an agreement between Italy and the European bailout fund, the ESM, on a policy and funding program. The discussions are fractious. Moreover, it is not clear that the ESM has sufficient money to bail out Italy. Even if these hurdles are crossed, others remain. In principle, OMT powers extend beyond QE rules and authorize the ECB to buy "unlimited quantities" of a member country's bonds to prevent bond yields from rising too high. But the legal definition of "unlimited quantities" has been left vague.[28] These ambiguities come to haunt ECB officials.

Market participants know that since 2015, the ECB and the Banca d'Italia have purchased large quantities of Italian government bonds under the QE program. The European System of Central Banks is heavily exposed to Italian risk. Is the ECB willing to take on more Italian risk?

Fearing that European authorities might not be able to get their act together, investors start dumping Italian bonds. As a result, bonds purchased earlier through the QE program lose market value, creating immediate accounting losses for the ECB. The Governing Council wavers. Italian government bond prices fall further, and yields correspondingly creep up entering a danger zone; Italian bank stocks are battered, and the risk of bank runs increases.[29] By now, Governing Council members are worried that the ECB's and the Banca d'Italia's exposure to the risk of financial defaults in Italy is growing too large and that if the Italian government—unable to bear the pressure of higher interest rates and banking stress—defaults on its debt, the accounting losses will become all too real and will need to be shared by all member states. As the finance professors Harald Benink and Harry Huizinga predicted, political murmurs grow that the Banca d'Italia, not the ECB, should be bearing the risk of an Italian government default.[30]

But the risk is too large for the Banca d'Italia to bear.

For the Italians, exit from the eurozone is tempting. Some scholars and analysts say that returning Italy to the lira is the best way out. The lira's value, they note, would fall, Italian producers would become more competitive, the Italian economy would enjoy a burst of growth and inflation would emerge from its deflation trap as higher prices for imported goods push up the general price level. Together, these favorable outcomes would help reduce unemployment and bring down the debt-to-GDP ratio.[31]

But if it were so simple, Italy would not have waited so long to exit the eurozone. For upon exit, the Italian government and Italian businesses and households will receive revenues in liras and will still need to repay debts denominated in euros. If it takes two, three, or even more liras to buy one euro, the government's debt burden will become intolerable, and the government will surely default. Italian banks that have borrowed in euros or in US dollars will be unable to repay their debts. Creditors to the Italian government and banks will be unable to repay their own debts. Fearing that such defaults are likely to spread, speculators will dump Greek, Portuguese, Spanish, and possibly French bonds. Well before the beneficial influence of a weaker lira kicks in to revive Italian growth, Italy's earthquake could bring the global financial system to its knees.

No, it would not be a good idea to reach the point where triggering OMTs becomes a real possibility, for in that case, OMTs could crack.

The euro will have a happier ending at that point if Germany leaves the euro area.[32] There really will be no losers. A German return to the deutschmark will cause the value of the euro to fall immediately. If, as is likely, the Netherlands, Austria, Finland, and Belgium follow Germany's lead, perhaps to form a new currency bloc, the euro will depreciate even further. Those who stay in the smaller eurozone will continue to pay their debts in the new cheaper euro, which will also give them a much-needed boost in competitiveness and a chance to jump-start growth.

Global financial disruption from a German exit will be minor. Because a new deutschmark will buy more goods and services in Europe (and in the rest of the world) than a euro does today, Germans will become richer in one stroke. Germany's assets abroad will be worth less in terms of the pricier deutschmarks, but German debts will be easier to repay.

Some Germans worry that a rising deutschmark will render their exports less competitive abroad. That is actually a desirable outcome for the world—and eventually for Germany, too. For years, Germany has been running a large current account surplus, meaning that it sells a lot more than it buys. The gap has only increased since the start of the crisis, reaching a new record of nearly $300 billion in 2016. Insufficient German demand for international goods weakens world growth, which is why both the US Treasury and the IMF continually prod the country to save less and buy more from abroad. Even the European Commission has concluded that Germany's current account surplus is "excessive."

Germans know how to live with a stronger exchange rate. Before the introduction of the euro, the deutschmark appreciated almost continuously. German companies adapted to that appreciation by producing higher-quality products. If German authorities reintroduce the deutschmark now, German manufacturers will have a more urgent incentive to raise their own productivity to stay competitive. Domestic service providers will also be under greater pressure to improve their lagging productivity.

Perhaps the greatest gain will be political. Germany plays the role of a hegemon in Europe but is unwilling to bear the cost of being a hegemon. All too often, it acts like a bully with a moral veneer, doing the region a disservice. Rather than helping build "an ever closer union" in Europe, German authorities endanger its delicate fabric. Germany in the eurozone is keeping Europe on its tragic course.

A Republic of Letters for Europe: A Modern Agora

The second scenario begins after the optimism from the 2017 recovery has receded. The longer-term challenges are in clearer focus, but no new crisis has erupted. In Germany, there is little appetite for more financial engagement in Europe.

The worrying signs, however, do not go away. The southern economies, their governments' finances, and their banks are not healing at a sufficiently rapid pace; they remain vulnerable to new shocks. If the eurozone experiences a new crisis, Merkel is concerned that Germany might not be able to play the expected leadership role. Domestic politics will hold her back, and the scale of the crisis could be so large that Germany might not be able to mobilize sufficient financial resources to mount a credible response. Things could get messy. Despite her instinct to wait, the time to act, she finally decides, is now.

In this scenario, I visualize that Merkel intuitively understands that for too long, pro-Europeanism has been a set of unchanging slogans, which do nothing to counter growing economic disparities. Instead, they deepen political fissures. She decides it is time to change the conception and direction of a pro-European future. Addressing other heads of government at a European Council meeting, Merkel announces that she has something to say. Her European colleagues take note. They sense that she is about to make an unusual statement. But no one anticipates the radical changes she is about to propose. Her remarks, "Merkel's Exit Monologue," become a turning point in the European drama.

An era of European history has run its course. We have achieved much. Through the wisdom of our postwar leaders, we stopped fighting each other on battlefields more than seventy years ago. We transferred our energies to conference tables around which—sometimes in the spirited pursuit of national interests—we found common interests. We opened our trade borders to one another, and the prosperity that followed strengthened the peace.

Through these years, we fought hard to preserve the values of human dignity, tolerance, and freedom, but we increasingly gave primacy to the economic purpose of Europe. The euro became the focal point of the economic purpose. The promise was that the euro would deliver economic gains, in the pursuit of which European leaders and citizens would redouble their commitment to form a closer political union.

Many economists have said over the years that the euro adds little value other than the convenience of personal travel across Europe. Certainly, countries that chose to stay out of the eurozone—Britain, Sweden, Poland, and the Czech Republic—have done well with their own currencies. Among those that joined the eurozone, some were hit hard by the shock of the financial crisis, in part, because they no longer had the safety valve of a domestic currency that they could devalue to cushion the shock. As Europeans, we did our best to help the hard-hit countries, but the contentious process of delivering that financial help created acute political divisions. Instead of spirited but constructive exchanges across conference tables, our debates degenerated into acrimony. And preoccupied by taming the financial crisis, we lost sight of the fact that Europe was falling farther behind in the global competitive race.

Tomorrow I will ask the Bundestag to forgive two-thirds of the debt that Greece owes the German government. I understand that this violates European treaties and possibly oversteps the German Constitution. But the Greek public has endured much. European Commission President Juncker is right: through our actions, we have violated Greek dignity. This is not how we build a European community, and it is time for a fresh start. I hope other member states will follow the German lead and let Greece stand, once again, on its own feet.

I need, at the same time, to promise the German people that they will not bail out Greece again. With Greek debt largely written down and the Greek primary budget (the budget net of interest payments) close to balance, private creditors should be willing to lend to the Greek government. Greek government-bond contracts must make clear that if the government's finances reach critical stress points, private creditors will receive delayed or reduced repayments.[33] Greece will pay appropriately high interest rates for such contracts, which will ensure that the current and future governments live within their means.

Indeed, all eurozone countries must provide a risk warning and default triggers in the new bonds they issue, starting five years from now. The five-year window to make the transition to this new regime should give enough time for governments and investors to adjust their expectations. In October 2010, I made a similar proposal after meeting then French President Nicolas Sarkozy at Deauville. Many at the time incorrectly concluded that that call spread panic among investors, who then preemptively raised interest rates on eurozone bonds. There is simply no evidence that the Deauville announcement caused interest rates to rise.[34] But if now, investors do briefly take fright, then it is the ECB's legitimate role to stanch the panic. Above all, we need to move to a more sustainable financial structure supporting the euro. Remember, in the nineteenth century, the US monetary union operated without federal funding to help states in recessions or financial crises; if the states could not repay their debts, private creditors bore losses.[35] That is the only way we can work.

To the heads of government gathered today, I also urge that we abolish the fiscal rules that have governed Europe for so long. For too long, we Germans have obsessively insisted on these rules even though it has been obvious that they cause economic disruption and breed political discord. Former European Commission President Romano Prodi was right in observing that the fiscal rules are stupid.[36] Amazingly, we still maintain the fiction that countries that violate the rules will pay fines or face other sanctions. But we have never once levied fines or applied sanctions.

The very idea of sanctions, as I have said before, is "idiotic."[37] By what economic or moral principle do you impose financially costly sanctions on a country that is already under financial stress?

We tried governing together. We saved the eurozone from disintegrating, but during the drawn-out process, we made many errors. We therefore grew weaker and moved farther apart from one another.

The three steps I have outlined today—forgiveness of Greek debt, new government debt issued five years from now to carry clear warnings of risk to private creditors, and the dismantling of fiscal rules—will loosen the ties that bind us all too tightly. Each of these steps draws on sound economic principles and makes eminent political sense. By returning full fiscal responsibility to national governments, we will respect a central tenet of national sovereignty. At the European level, we will free ourselves of a vast amount of essentially unproductive—often counterproductive—tasks, and we will no longer need bitter and endless negotiations that drag on from one fruitless, late-night summit to another.

Managing the euro's crisis and its ongoing governance has sucked up too much of our time; it has become an alibi for not attending to urgent tasks at home. I have concluded that European leaders have overreached in attempting to govern Europe together. A small group of leaders, especially in a crisis when national interests are clearly different, cannot objectively decide what is best for Europe. Certainly, as German chancellor, having to make crucial decisions during the crisis, I was aware of the widely diverging perspectives. In the way we now operate, no one is ultimately accountable.

Those in power, political scientist Karl Deutsch once said, often choose not to learn.[38] If we fail to learn the lesson that European leaders cannot govern together on matters that lie at the heart of member nations' sovereignty, then we will make more mistakes, and history will not judge us kindly. For this reason, it would be foolish to go down the path of more financial "union" through eurobonds and a common European budget to support the single currency. If, by some miracle, we did implement such arrangements, there would be no way to administer them in a fair and accountable manner. Who would judge if a European finance minister's decision was fair?

As former German President Joachim Gauck tried to tell us in 2013, we cannot continue to be "swept along by events" without the essential anchor of political accountability and legitimacy.[39] How many of us paused to heed President Gauck's warning? We must pause now. The single currency will never create the momentum to fall forward into a more politically united Europe. An unthinking pursuit of deeper European financial commitments will only breed more resentments and conflicts within Europe. Wisdom requires us to step back from that ill-advised rush and change course.

To be clear, while I believe we need to stop building a fragile financial superstructure for the single currency—and, indeed, we need to unwind some of that superstructure—we do need to advance the European common market, especially to create technical and pricing standards for digital networks and to share energy resources. I hope we can also agree on a fair method to share the burden of refugees and develop joint approaches to European security, fighting terrorism, and fighting climate change.

But it is time also to forge a new path on our European journey, a path that does not rely on "more Europe" to solve Europe's essential problems. Our work now lies at home.

We Europeans are losing the global technology race. The United States retains its technological lead. Now Asian nations are running ahead of us. They are educating their children better, they are building world-class universities, and they are harnessing their workforce's skills in the development of next-generation technologies. At this rate, Europeans will soon be technological also-rans.

Europe must respond with its own genius. In April 2010, in a lecture to the Royal Society in London, I recalled that we owe our "contemporary way of life" to the astonishing scientific progress made during Europe's Age of Enlightenment in the seventeenth and early-eighteenth centuries.[40] That progress occurred, as economic historians have reminded us, within a politically fragmented Europe but one that was united in the marketplace of ideas.[41] Indeed, political fragmentation was a source of creative energy as nations sought to gain the intellectual and scientific lead. Nations promoted and competed for the best minds. Galileo Galilei, Johannes Kepler, and Isaac Newton were among the intellectual giants. Universities, academies, and learned societies "sprang up all over Europe," which created a ferment of innovative excitement.[42] Europe was successful then as a republic of letters, not as a political organization that tried to coordinate European nations through rules and committees. Europe must again be a republic of letters invigorated by competition among its nation-states.

It is time for Europeans to come together once again in the marketplace for ideas. In this marketplace, the currency must be the willingness to pursue excellence, and spirited intellectual exchange must advance the next generation of scientific methods and technologies.

The question we need to ask today is how we can build a new republic of letters. A vibrant marketplace for ideas—one that is adequate to the call of our time—requires as building blocks much higher-quality schools and universities. Because our schools and universities have fallen woefully behind those of global leaders, some of our best minds prefer to work in more stimulating environments abroad.[43] The challenge now is for all sovereign nations—and states and provinces and communities within nations—to run this competitive race, to create egalitarian access to education that matches and exceeds the best in the world. Such a network of educational institutions will be the engine of European growth, it will pull the despondent young we are leaving behind into a creative and optimistic future, and it will be the modern agora, the meeting place where all Europeans—not just the privileged few—gather to reaffirm their cultural identity and their commitment to our timeless values.

Let me be clear. From the time of the industrial revolution in the mid-eighteenth century to today, the only consistent source of growth has been the quality of education that the citizens of a nation have received.[44] The United States claimed global leadership from Europe by establishing a network of public schools and universities. Today, although US schools have their problems, the United States still has incomparable research universities. Creative minds can tap a deep pool of capital to finance risky new technologies. For the past few decades, Asian nations have positioned themselves to become the world's leading economic powers. A centerpiece of their strategy has been to create some of the best schools in the world and advance their universities to compete with the finest in the world.[45] I can see that China is trying to recapture the global scientific preeminence it held in the tenth century.[46] Make no mistake: today, more so than ever, a nation's schools and colleges will win the race for the future.

As I emphasized in my London remarks, knowledge has "a very short sell-by date," for which reason, I said, German prosperity must "be sought through investment in research, education and science, and this to a disproportionate degree." The German government has committed "a lot of resources" to education, and we will continue to do so. We need more motivated students and teachers. "We must empower every young person, through education, to contribute his or her skills to the community."[47] And I invite all European nations to make their own commitments so that we can join in competition and spur one another to greater effort.

Education, moreover, is not just a source of economic growth, but it is also the great equalizer. It is the only consistent and reliable path for children to have a better life than their parents did. For the past quarter century at least, the fear of remaining trapped in low economic and social status has caused deep anxiety. Those who feel trapped in their bleak circumstances blame Europe for their plight. In the French referendum on the Maastricht Treaty in 1992, in the French and Dutch referendums on the European constitution in 2005, and in the recent Greek referendum on continued austerity under the European financial bailout program, the country's weakest citizens have always voted against Europe.[48] This pattern repeated itself in the June 2016 British referendum on Brexit, the decision to leave the EU. Citizens who have fallen off the education ladder voted in large numbers to leave.[49] As former Prime Minister Gordon Brown wrote in the days after the Brexit referendum, unable to face Asian competition, British manufacturing has "collapsed," and industrial towns have "hollowed out," leaving semiskilled workers "on the wrong side of globalisation."[50] Such workers and their families blame their economic woes and poor prospects on globalization and on the EU.

Although the EU does not deserve the blame for the inequalities generated by globalization and technological change, we need to recognize that the fear is real and that it has long been building up across large parts of Europe. And yes, unprincipled xenophobes and nationalists have often hijacked the votes of vulnerable citizens.[51] But I worry that over a long time span and across a range of member-states, the same people have justifiably lost faith in Europe. For the sake of Europe, we need to take actions that give them hope and renew their faith that someone is listening to them and working on their behalf.

Education offers the best prospect for generational advance, laying a firm foundation for a Europe that is respectful and fair to all its people and where the knowledge that the system is fair creates a sense of self-confidence, which becomes a vibrant source of growth.[52]

And not just for growth's sake. For those of us who care about Europe, education offers the best prospect of keeping us together, united in a common identity. Today a common European purpose and identity cannot rely on a European promise of material prosperity. At best, Europe can deliver small economic gains. That is also the perception of European citizens, as the European Commission's surveys show. At least since the early 2000s, steadily fewer Europeans believe that Europe will bring them economic benefits. For this reason, popular support for Europe has fallen. But the surveys also point us to a more hopeful sign. Since 2013, a modestly increasing number of European citizens, although skeptical of economic benefits on offer, have reaffirmed faith in the European values of an "open society": democracy, social protection, freedom of travel, and cultural diversity.[53]

A modern agora, rooted in a network of educational institutions, creates the best prospect for fostering such open-society values. Such values are especially attractive to younger Europeans, and they therefore generally offer greater support to Europe than their parents or grandparents do. But we cannot take the support of young Europeans for granted. I am thinking especially of Italian youth, whose trust in Europe has fallen distressingly.

So let us each, according to our national genius, build our own outstanding schools and colleges. These will become the modern agora, the network within a new European Republic of Letters, where vast numbers of self-confident European youth meet. The agora will be the foundation of a consistent and creative affirmation of European values, rooted in respect and fairness. The agora and the values it promotes will become the European identity. Our youth will be better prepared to face the forces of globalization, and they will be proud Europeans.

Quite simply, if we create a European Republic of Letters, economic dynamism and political goodwill will give us the reserves to deal with financial and political crises. If we shrink now and stay preoccupied with minor changes to European governance, we will struggle to achieve progress, and new crises will continue to overwhelm us.

People often ask me, "Chancellor Merkel, do you have passion for Europe?"[54] This is my passion. This is the Merkel passion for Europe. It is for a vision of Europe in which each nation invests in its young and prepares, in its own way, to meet the economic and social challenges we face. In that Europe, all Europeans meet in common spaces to reaffirm their universal values.

I do not know if Merkel will say these words, or whether she will even be around as chancellor long enough to command the attention that the words deserve. But she is uniquely positioned to redirect Europe. She is under pressure at home to change the relationship with Europe. Germans have refused to give her a mandate to lay out more resources for Europe. She has never tried to seek such a mandate and, given her weaker position today, it is too late for her to do so. She can, however, sell to the German public a strategy for financial disengagement from Europe while simultaneously articulating a new philosophy of pro-Europeanism. Only a German chancellor can achieve these twin objectives of breaking from the past and pointing Europe in a new direction. And the next German chancellor will take years to gain the stature Merkel has, and, in fact, may never do so.

In their magisterial 1963 *Monetary History of the United States*, University of Chicago economist Milton Friedman and monetary scholar Anna Schwartz wrote that "great events have great origins," and therefore, "something more than the characteristics of the specific person" is required to explain shifts in history.[55] But, as they also wrote, individuals in key positions can and do direct the traffic at the crossroads of history. Once the traffic begins moving along its new path, cumulative forces build up to help continue that journey. One of Merkel's predecessors, Helmut Kohl, stood at such a crossroads in the 1990s, when, for reasons that only he could reveal, he directed Europe into the euro. Alone among European politicians, Merkel has an opportunity to undo much of that legacy and begin a new one.

The undoing part of the task is straightforward. The fiscal rules have never worked. The claim that "bad rules are better than none" has been repeatedly proven untrue. Bad rules are bad rules, bad economics, and bad politics. Besides undoing the rules, there is one other step which, even in my flight of fancy, I could not imagine Merkel demanding. That step is to change the ECB's mandate away from a single-minded focus on price stability to giving equal weight to an employment objective.

A new framework for the eurozone also requires an innovative debt restructuring mechanism for its sovereign governments. A floating exchange rate is valuable because it acts as a shock absorber. In a gush of hubris, eurozone nations gave up that shock absorber. Within the eurozone, a sovereign debt contract that allows automatic and incremental reductions in debt repayments—well before a crisis becomes unmanageable—gives member nations the only other option for a shock absorber. Banks are beginning to use such "contingent" debt contracts, where the payment is tied to specific contingencies—well-specified future risks. Eurozone nations can lead the way on redefining contracts and markets in sovereign debt.

And the final bit of the undoing—forgiving Greek debt—is an essential step toward restoring European democracy. For nearly a decade, the Greek parliament has rubber-stamped decisions made by outsiders. That subservience will continue, even if with a lighter touch, as long as Greece owes a mountain of debt to its official creditors. It is time to let the Greeks make their own decisions, knowing that, as they regain that authority, they are also subject to limits set by financial investors and markets. Merkel understands, I believe, that Germany's disengagement from intrusion into the affairs of other countries is desirable for all. She grew up in East Germany.

And because she grew up in East Germany, she has little attachment—possibly even an aversion—to the mythology of pro-Europeanism. Her statements and actions have insistently focused on national responsibility, a belief in a more decentralized Europe.

A focus, then, on education as the central guiding theme for revitalizing Europe also comes naturally from Merkel's background and priorities. And, as Shakespeare might have said, education is thrice blessed. It promotes growth, reduces inequalities, and offers the best prospect of creating a new European identity. Important for economic growth since the start of the industrial revolution, education today is essential for material progress. On reducing inequalities, as Nobel laureate Robert Solow recently said, the urgent need is to respond to the "so many, so many" who despair that life is not fair to them, who believe "that they're being treated like dirt."[56] High quality education offers the best—perhaps, only—antidote to the hopelessness that breeds disaffection and a sense of unfairness.

And European identity cannot continue to be defined by fiscal and monetary rules which, while emphasizing prudence and stability, are administered by officials who can never be held accountable for their decisions. Instead, a modern European Republic of Letters can create an identity based on collective aesthetic and intellectual aspirations that emerge through spontaneous interactions.

The republic of letters scenario holds great promise. But even in this more hopeful Europe, the single currency area will always be subject to the one risk that finally undid the US monetary union as it existed before the Great Depression. That system survived with no central fiscal resources and relied instead on the states and their creditors sharing the costs of crises. But even that arrangement proved unequal to the force of the Great Depression. Under the New Deal initiatives, sizeable fiscal transfers to the states began and, ever since, have buffered the states during recessions and crises. Thus, even with a new growth momentum in a benign European scenario, the risk of another deep and unmanageable crisis will remain.

Hence, it is possible to visualize the ultimate disengagement, perhaps, preemptively. In a replay of a January morning in 1999, on another January morning, at 5:00 a.m. Sydney time, when world financial markets open, the deutschemark trades against the dollar and the euro. The euro depreciates against the other major currencies. And when the German stock exchange rings its opening bell that morning, the screens display share prices in deutschmarks. It is a new start. "The future," as Yogi Berra might have said, "ain't what it used to be."

Epilogue

LOGICALLY, THE EURO could do no economic or political good. It could do a lot of harm. The warnings were sounded. It need not have been. It almost wasn't. The rest followed. It could get worse, much worse. That is the EuroTragedy.

The euro defied the principles of economics. The early proponents understood that a single currency came with serious risks. Member nations of the single currency area would live under a single European monetary policy and so they would be deprived of national currencies and monetary policies to respond to domestic economic adversity. While the single currency took away these valuable domestic monetary policy tools, it came without the compensating alternative of a pooled fiscal fund to ease the economic and financial stress that member nations would surely face.

Against these risks, the proponents saw benefits. Governments of member countries would behave in a more disciplined way. They would build economic resilience and thus avoid periods of financial stress. Member countries would trade more with one another and so help the entire eurozone grow faster.

Most importantly the single currency came with an implied political promise, the falling forward promise. Necessity, especially during crises, would bring forth goodwill among member nations and eventually ensure the creation of shared fiscal resources for all to use. Such a coming together would draw European nations closer to a United States of Europe.

Critics—outsiders and insiders—warned that the economic benefits would be meagre, if any. In contrast, the serious risks that lay ahead could not be easily overcome. They warned that because the economic risks were great, the political promise would prove to be false. Instead of generating goodwill, the euro would create resentment, even antagonism. From the moment the single currency idea came into political consciousness in 1969, events repeatedly validated these warnings. There were many opportunities to walk away before creating a bond so tight that it would be almost impossible to loosen.

Instead of walking away, European leaders wrapped themselves in obsessive groupthink and portrayed the single currency as a pro-European enterprise, a concept that was maddeningly vague and had no evident culminating point. Europeans wanted to do some things together, but they did not want to merge into a single nation. No one knew where, in between the nation-state and the United States of Europe, lay the marker at which Europe would rest.

In that haziness, unwilling to commit to sharing fiscal resources, member states converged on an economic stability ideology, whose rules allowed little flexibility in macroeconomic management and which, if enforced, critics warned once again, would amplify economic booms and busts. Making matters worse, the governance system that accompanied the stability ideology lacked political accountability.

Thus, through a torturous, nearly three-decades-long negotiating process, eleven European countries abandoned their own currencies and adopted the euro in January 1999.

The tragedy played itself out relentlessly. The euro delivered no economic benefits, as was predicted. The idea that the euro would be an external anchor, a disciplining device, proved utterly misguided. The "southern" countries—Greece, Italy, Portugal, and Spain—which were most expected to benefit from the discipline, did not become more resilient to economic shocks and they did not move into higher and more stable growth trajectories. The promised benefits in terms of more trade within the eurozone did not materialize either. Even before the global financial crisis began in 2007, the share of within-eurozone trade had started to decline, and that tendency accelerated as the crisis persisted.

The inevitable adversity that would test the eurozone came as the global financial crisis in 2007 and then continued as multiple rolling eurozone banking and sovereign debt crises through to 2013. During these years, the euro caused the most damage in the weakest eurozone countries, widening existing income disparities between member nations. Without their own currencies to devalue, the southern countries struggled to recover from the repeated economic shocks. The crises left even France hobbled with high debt and youth unemployment problems familiar to the southern group of countries. In contrast, the strongest survived the best. The German economy came out virtually unscathed.

Growing economic disparities across nations led to greater imbalance in political power. Germany became Europe's undisputed economic leader, with veto power over the most important decisions for the whole of Europe. The German chancellor became the de facto European chancellor, albeit without the instruments that would make for effective and democratic decisions. Thus, the eurozone's governance system became even less accountable than it had been at the start.

A handful of European leaders became responsible for the welfare of many, but this handful was not accountable to the people whose lives they influenced. Since national elections downplayed European matters, European citizens had no mechanism to voice their opposition to the way in which the eurozone was being managed. This sense of disenfranchisement was particularly acute in the countries of the south, where economic prospects were dim to start with and where the crises caused their greatest damage. Social tensions were also high in these southern countries because the ability to make economic and social progress from one generation to another had weakened alarmingly. In the northern countries, the political instinct of governments and citizens was to insulate themselves from demands made by the south. The north-south political rift widened. In the war of words, German politicians and media disparaged the Greeks as lazy problem children and the Italians as clowns; the Greeks and the Italians responded, understandably but unhelpfully, with references to Germany's dark past.

And, in one of the great ironies of history, the single-currency venture, which the French pushed to blur the economic gap between themselves and the Germans, ended up emphasizing that gap. Inescapably, the much-vaunted but largely mythical Franco-German postwar friendship became an economically lopsided and politically grouchy relationship. Germany's press and its leaders had begun publicly expressing contempt for France's lagging economic performance as early as the 1960s. With the passage of time, there was little reason to shrink back from such expressions of disdain. Responding to German growling in December 2014, then French Finance Minister Michel Sapin complained about "certain extreme comments in Germany" intended to ridicule the French. In measured but angry words, Sapin said, "We really need to be careful, to respect each other and to respect each other's history, national identity and points of sensitivity, because otherwise it will help extreme parties to grow." He called for an end to "outdated" stereotyping of countries.

Thus, among the euro's many tragedies, not only did the German and French compromises in creating the single currency do great harm to large parts of Europe, but the euro also drove a deeper wedge between these two great European nations.

Today, European leaders have little more to offer than an assurance that the euro is a force for good. European Commission President Jean-Claude Juncker insists that the euro "brings us huge, often invisible benefits."[1] The benefits it is alleged to deliver elevate the euro to the core of Europe's identity. "Being European, for most of us," Juncker says, "also means the euro."[2]

Insiders who protested were ignored. In February 2013, then German President Joachim Gauck lamented the reduction of Europe to "four letters—euro."[3] The euro, he warned, was associated with "growing fear of facing ever harsher austerity and falling into poverty"; to many "ordinary people in Europe," a Europe centered on the euro "no longer seems fair." But while Gauck said it was time to "pause," to "rethink the situation," Juncker sees the euro as Europe's guiding light. He urges all European nations to adopt the euro and charge ahead on a mission to achieve more unity.

Other western democracies share the eurozone's problems. But the eurozone faces the greatest risk of economic decline and erosion of democracy. Productivity growth in the eurozone has been lower than in other advanced democracies and, from that lower base, is now slowing as elsewhere. Democratic processes to voice dissent are weaker in the eurozone than in most advanced democracies. While everywhere national governments have tied their hands to some extent through international agreements, this process has gone much further in the eurozone, where national fiscal and labor market policies are increasingly constrained by European directives and ideologies. Hence, the role of national parliaments has weakened but the European Parliament has not created an alternative channel for European citizens to pin responsibility and demand accountability.

As eurozone nations gaze in sometimes-horrified fascination at this, their pro-European venture, they continue their slide in global economic standing. Asian economies have steadily gained ground. The US economy, despite its troubles, has thus far managed to reinvent itself periodically. More so than ever, countries of the eurozone seem set to fall further behind in the global economic race.

The eurozone's recent crises have passed. But the legacy of low growth, high debt burdens, and weak banks leaves the southern eurozone countries in a more vulnerable position today than they were in 2007, at the onset of the global financial crisis. A new crisis—and there always will be a new crisis—will test the eurozone severely, especially if, as is likely, Italy is the epicenter of the crisis. Political divisions will deepen as financial tensions unfold, and the crisis could tear through the eurozone's financial safety nets.

Can this EuroTragedy end? Can there be a happy ending? Whether and how the EuroTragedy ends will depend on the choices European leaders make. Along the present course, the muddle will continue. The national sovereignty barrier remains strong. National interests differ widely. While leaders may agree on notions such as "European finance minister" and "European budget," they all have wildly different and mutually incompatible interpretations of what these words mean. Even apparently modest efforts such as common unemployment schemes and a banking union backed by taxpayer funds repeatedly run into the sovereignty barrier. Discussions on these proposals have acquired a *Groundhog Day* flavor. Interspersed with periods of hope, more disappointment and crises remain inevitable.

The evidence in this book points insistently to specific measures to improve the functioning of the eurozone. These include scrapping the fiscal rules, creating mechanisms for predictable and orderly default on public debt to instill greater discipline in debtor governments and their creditors, and changing the ECB's mandate to require that reducing unemployment be an objective of monetary policy on a par with maintaining price stability.

Whatever the fortunes of the euro, it is time to foster a new pro-Europeanism, one that is not tied to its shared currency. Ultimately, there is no alternative but to renew the wellsprings of economic growth. A new European Republic of Letters, forged as part of a renewed commitment to competitive decentralization, a race among nations to build new frontiers of knowledge, will, I believe, best serve the effort to regenerate and sustain growth. But it will do more. For those being left behind, it will create more opportunities for climbing the economic and social ladder. It will give new hope to many of Europe's young who face the prospect of long durations of unemployment and insecure, poorly paying jobs. It will restore voice and vigor in European democracies. Above all, it will anchor the European values of an open society. A march to that pro-European vision will be an inspiration to the entire world.

MAIN CHARACTERS IN THE EURO DRAMA

Konrad Adenauer (1876–1967). German politician (Christian Democratic Union). Chancellor of Federal Republic of Germany [known commonly then as "West Germany"] (1949–1963). As German chancellor, Adenauer welcomed Schuman's plan to place Germany's coal and steel industry under a joint European umbrella. For him, sharing German sovereignty over coal and steel production was a small price to pay for reintegration into Europe and the international community.

José Manuel Barroso (1956–). Portuguese politician (Social Democratic Party) and Eurocrat. Minister of foreign affairs (1992–1995), prime minister (2002–2004), president of European Commission (2004–2014). As European Commission president, he presented proposals for centralized euro-area governance and financial capacity.

Olivier Blanchard (1948–). French-born American economist. Chief economist of the IMF (2008–2015). He made the case for a global fiscal stimulus in November 2008 and repeatedly advised against excessive fiscal austerity.

Willy Brandt (1913–1992). German politician (Social Democratic Party). Mayor of West Berlin (1957–1966), minister for foreign affairs and vice chancellor (1966–1969), chancellor of West Germany (1969–1974). Brandt was skeptical of Georges Pompidou's idea of a European monetary union. However, to gain French support for *Ostpolitik* (closer ties with East Germany and reconciliation with Poland), he allowed the monetary union discussion to continue. Germany joined the first step toward monetary union, the "snake in the tunnel" arrangement, in 1972.

Jacques Chirac (1932–). French politician (Union for a Popular Movement). Mayor of Paris (1977–1995), prime minister (1974–1976, 1986–1988), president (1995–2007). After jostling with German Chancellor Gerhard Schröder on the issue of voting rights in the council of ministers, Chirac joined Schröder to set up a common front in 2003: together, they successfully opposed the European Commission's effort to impose sanctions on their governments for exceeding the budget deficit limit set by the SGP.

Jacques Delors (1925–). French politician (Socialist Party) and Eurocrat. Member of European Parliament (1979–1981), minister of finance (1981–1984), president of European Commission (1985–1995). While president of the European Commission, he headed the Delors Committee, which revived the moribund Werner Committee proposal. The report prepared by the Delors Committee became the basis for drafting the Maastricht Treaty, which, in turn, was the basis for the single currency eventually introduced in January 1999.

Mario Draghi (1947–). Italian economist. Governor of the Banca d'Italia (2006–2011), president of the ECB (2011–). Draghi followed Jean-Claude Trichet as ECB president. Through the year 2014, the ECB under Draghi lowered interest rates at a pace that disappointed financial markets. He is best known for his announcement in July 2012 that the ECB would do "whatever it takes" to save the euro. Two months later, the ECB followed up on Draghi's promise by launching the OMT program, a step that defused the eurozone's financial crisis. Draghi announced the ECB's QE program in January 2015.

Wim Duisenberg (1935–2005). Dutch economist and politician (Labor Party). Finance minister (1973–1977), governor of Dutch central bank (1982–1997), president of the ECB (1998–2003). Since French president Jacques Chirac demanded that a Frenchman be ECB president, Duisenberg agreed to step down before his eight-year term was complete to make way for Jean-Claude Trichet.

Charles de Gaulle (1890–1970). French general and politician (Union for the New Republic). President (1958–1969). Although he was an advocate of reconciliation between France and Germany, de Gaulle only reluctantly accepted that the Treaty of Rome, which reduced trade barriers within Europe, would generate economic benefits. Wedded to France's national sovereignty, he disrupted the functioning of the EEC and twice (in 1963 and 1967) vetoed British entry.

Timothy Geithner (1961–). American government official and central banker. President of the Federal Reserve Bank of New York and vice chairman of the FOMC (2003–2009), Secretary of the Treasury (2009–2013). On the FOMC, Geithner was an advocate of aggressive monetary stimulus to prevent the financial crisis from gathering momentum. As president of the Federal Reserve Bank of New York, he oversaw the rescue of Bear Stearns. He was a fierce opponent of efforts to impose losses on creditors of financially stressed banks and governments.

Valéry Giscard d'Estaing (1926–). French politician (Republican Independents). Finance minister (1962–1966, 1969–1974), president (1974–1981). Giscard d'Estaing shared with Georges Pompidou the conviction that monetary union was the best way to achieve French economic parity with Germany. After the first step toward monetary union, the "snake in the tunnel," collapsed, Giscard d'Estaing and Chancellor Helmut Schmidt revived it in March 1970 as the EMS. Giscard d'Estaing also led the effort to prepare the Draft Constitutional Treaty for the EU, which Dutch and French citizens eventually rejected in referendums held in 2005.

Jean-Claude Juncker (1954–). Luxembourgian politician (Christian Social People's Party) and Eurocrat. Minister of employment (1984–1999), minister of finance (1989–2009), minister of the treasury (2009–2013), prime minister (1995–2013), president of Eurogroup (2005–2013), president of European Commission (2014–). Together with other leaders of the European institutions, he presented a number of proposals for centralized euro-area governance, such as eurobonds and a common fiscal capacity, both as president of the Eurogroup and later as president of the European Commission.

Helmut Kohl (1930–2017). German politician (Christian Democratic Union). Minister-president of Rhineland-Palatinate (1969–1976), chancellor of the Federal Republic of Germany, before (1982–1990) and after (1990–1998) reunification. After the unanticipated fall of the Berlin Wall in November 1989, Kohl used the historic moment to reunify East and West Germany. Although he was aware of the economic disadvantages of a single currency, as the chancellor of a unified Germany, Kohl ensured the creation of the euro.

Christine Lagarde (1956–). French lawyer and politician (Union for a Popular Movement). Commerce minister (2005–2007), agriculture minister (2007), finance minister (2007–2011), managing director of the IMF (2011–). Lagarde continued with the European view on fiscal austerity and no debt relief for Greece until July 2015; then, while her public posture changed, she and the IMF seemed unable to influence the European position.

Emmanuel Macron (1977–). French civil servant and banker before entering politics (Socialist Party, La République En Marche). Minister of economy (2014–2016), president (2017–). An adviser and minister under President François Hollande, Macron founded the political movement En Marche! (later a political party, La République En Marche), which he rode to victory in the presidential election. He campaigned as a pro-European, defeating Marine Le Pen, leader of the Front National.

Robert Marjolin (1911–1986). French economist, international civil servant, and Eurocrat. Secretary General of the Organisation for European Economic Co-operation (1948–1955), vice president of the European Commission (1958–1967). He was a strong advocate of the Treaty of Rome but opposed monetary union. He led the Marjolin Committee, which in its 1975 report concluded that political willingness to subordinate national interests was absent, and thus no plan for a monetary union was credible.

Angela Merkel (1954–). German politician (Christian Democratic Union). Minister for women and youth (1991–1994), minister for the environment, conservation, and nuclear safety (1994–1998), chancellor (2005–). Merkel was brought up in East Germany and thus was a latecomer to European politics. From the onset of the Greek crisis in October 2009, she balanced the competing objectives of protecting German fiscal resources and preserving the euro area. With veto power over every major decision, she emerged as de facto European chancellor.

François Mitterrand (1916–1996). French politician (Socialist Party). Various cabinet positions (1947–1957), president (1981–1995). Following his predecessors Pompidou and Giscard d'Estaing, he renewed the French demand for a European single currency. He kept up this demand until the agreement on the Maastricht Treaty in December 1991, after which German Chancellor Helmut Kohl became the principal advocate of the single currency.

Jean Monnet (1888–1979). French civil servant. Deputy secretary-general of the League of Nations (1919–1923), president of the High Authority set up to oversee the ECSC (1952–1955) and believed to have been the author of the 1950 "Schuman Declaration," which led to its creation. As president of the High Authority, Monnet became controversial for attempting to take on responsibilities traditionally reserved for national governments. Well after he ceased holding an official position, he continued to promote European integration.

Mario Monti (1943–). Italian economist, Eurocrat, and politician (Civic Choice). European commissioner (1995–2004), prime minister (2011–2013). Amid the swirling Italian financial crisis in November 2011, President Giorgio Napolitano appointed the unelected Monti to replace the scandal-ridden Silvio Berlusconi as prime minister.

Lucas Papademos (1947–). Greek economist. Vice president of the ECB (2002–2010), prime minister (2011–2012). The unelected Papademos became prime minister of a technocratic "crisis coalition" in November 2011. He implemented the austerity program demanded by European and IMF creditors. In April 2012, he presided over Greece's inevitable sovereign default, the largest on record.

George Papandreou (1952–). Greek politician (Panhellenic Socialist Movement). Foreign minister (1999–2004), prime minister (2009–2011). Within days after Papandreou became prime minister in October 2009, the governor of the Greek central bank revealed that the government's fiscal deficit was much larger than earlier reported. A financial crisis quickly engulfed Greece. In May 2010, European governments and the IMF bailed out Papandreou's government with a large loan. The conditions of the bailout—no Greek debt default, deep austerity instead—sent Greece into an extraordinarily deep and prolonged depression. Papandreou resigned in November 2011.

Georges Pompidou (1911–1974). French conservative politician (Union for the New Republic, Union of Democrats for the Republic). Prime minister (1962–1968), president (1969-1974). Pompidou persuaded himself that a European monetary union would create an impression of French economic parity with Germany. He called for a summit of European heads of state and government at The Hague in December 1969 to initiate steps toward European monetary union.

Romano Prodi (1939–). Italian politician and Eurocrat. Prime minister (1996–1998, 2006–2008), president of the European Commission (1999–2004). In October 2002, Prodi famously described European fiscal rules as "stupid." When he nevertheless pushed to apply the rules to France and Germany, he was unable to break the common front put up by German Chancellor Gerhard Schröder and French President Jacques Chirac.

Matteo Renzi (1975–). Italian politician (Democratic Party). Mayor of Florence (2009–2014), prime minister (2014–2016). The thirty-nine-year-old

Renzi engineered an internal party coup to become prime minister in February 2014. International commentators hailed him as the great Italian and European hope. Domestically, he enjoyed less success. In a December 2016 referendum, the Italian public, especially young Italians, decisively rejected his proposals for reforming the political system. Renzi resigned immediately.

Nicolas Sarkozy (1955–). French politician (Union for a Popular Movement). Minister of the interior (2002–2004, 2005–2007), minister of finance (2004), president (2007–2012). He gained German Chancellor Angela Merkel's support in stopping an initiative to impose automatic sanctions for breaching European fiscal rules. In October 2010, in the French town of Deauville, he agreed with Merkel to create an orderly method for restructuring unsustainable government debts. That debt-restructuring plan was soon abandoned.

Wolfgang Schäuble (1942–). German politician (Christian Democratic Union). Minister of the interior (2005–2009), minister of finance (2009–2017). In 1994, he proposed the idea of "multispeed" Europe, which would allow countries to integrate with one another in flexible ways. As finance minister during the euro crisis years, Schäuble reinforced the German preference for national fiscal austerity and opposed initiatives that would add to the burden on the German taxpayer.

Helmut Schmidt (1918–2015). German politician (Social Democratic Party). Finance minister (1972–1974), chancellor (1974–1982). Although Schmidt was at first against the idea of fixing exchange rates, he became an advocate of the EMS advanced by French President Valéry Giscard d'Estaing. Schmidt sought, in return, an elusive European cooperation in defense.

Gerhard Schröder (1944–). German politician (Social Democratic Party). Prime minister of Lower Saxony (1990–1998), chancellor (1998–2005). As Germany's first chancellor with no personal memories of World War II, he fought hard for German interests in Europe's governance. His most pro-European act was to ensure Greek entry into the euro area. His administration's Hartz reforms had questionable value for Germany, but European politicians and bureaucrats quickly embraced such reforms as essential elements of good policymaking.

Robert Schuman (1886–1963). French politician (Popular Republican Movement). Prime minister (1947–1948), foreign minister (1948–1952), president of the European Parliamentary Assembly (1958–1960). In May 1950, he read the famous "Schuman Declaration." The declaration's proposal that France and Germany operate their coal and steel industries under unified supervision began the process of post-World War II European integration.

Dominique Strauss-Kahn (1947–). French economist and politician (Socialist Party). Minister of industry (1991–1993), minister of finance (1997), managing director of the IMF (2007–2011). Once German Chancellor Angela Merkel concluded that she needed the IMF in the Greek bailout program to signal to the German public that Greece really needed help, Strauss-Kahn fell in line with the American-European preference for no restructuring of Greek government debt. Thus, the IMF also became an advocate for extraordinary Greek fiscal austerity.

Margaret Thatcher (1925–2013). British politician (Conservative Party). Secretary of state for education and science (1970–1974), prime minister (1979–1990). She played a constructive role in negotiations of the SEA but fiercely opposed European monetary union.

Jean-Claude Trichet (1942–). French civil servant. Governor of the Banque de France (1993–2003), president of the ECB (2003–2011). As a director at the French treasury, he led the French delegation during the Maastricht negotiations in 1991. As ECB president, Trichet kept monetary policy too tight, setting off a financial panic in July 2011. Together with US Treasury Secretary Timothy Geithner, he consistently opposed restructuring of debts owed by financially distressed governments and banks to private creditors.

Alexis Tsipras (1974–). Greek politician (Syriza). Prime minister (2015–). An ex-Communist, Tsipras led the Syriza party on a platform to end austerity imposed by official creditors (the European governments, the European bailout fund, and the IMF). As prime minister, Tsipras made little headway in persuading official creditors to dial down austerity and provide debt relief. On July 5, 2015, he held a referendum to ask Greek citizens if they would tolerate continued austerity. Although a large majority voted against austerity, Tsipras backed off and, however reluctantly, accepted the creditors' demands.

Jens Weidmann (1968–). German economist. Head of the Department for Economic and Fiscal Policy in the German Chancellery (2006–2011), president of the German Bundesbank (2011–). Among ECB governors, the strongest opponent of the ECB's OMT program in 2012, maintaining his opposition even though he had been one of Chancellor Merkel's closest advisors at the Chancellery and knew that she was anxious to see the ECB's protective financial shield deployed quickly. In 2013 and 2014, Weidmann refused to acknowledge the risk of price deflation in the eurozone and was a strong and vocal opponent of the ECB's QE program.

Pierre Werner (1913–2002). Luxembourgian politician (Christian Social People's Party). Prime minister (1959–1974, 1979–1984). In 1970, he presided over the Werner Committee, which produced the first design of a European monetary union. The Werner Committee recognized that European politics permitted only an "incomplete" monetary union, one that lacked the necessary backing of a fiscal union. However, the committee predicted (hoped) that the incomplete monetary union would induce European nations to gradually form a political and fiscal union.

TIMELINE OF KEY EVENTS: HOW IT UNFOLDED

Before the Euro

May 9, 1950: Schuman Declaration. French Foreign Minister Robert Schuman announced in Paris that France and Germany had agreed to operate their coal and steel industries under unified supervision. This first "leap in the dark" marks the beginning of post-World War II European integration.

April 18, 1951: Treaty of Paris. Leaders from the "original six"—France, West Germany, Italy, Belgium, Luxembourg, and the Netherlands—signed the Treaty of Paris, formally the "Treaty Establishing the European Coal and Steel Community" (ECSC). The ECSC came into effect in 1952 under the supervision of the High Authority. Jean Monnet was the High Authority's first president.

May 27, 1952: European Defense Community. The "original six" signed the "Treaty Establishing the European Defense Community" (EDC). It would have created a European army with its own budget, a big first step toward a "United States of Europe." The German Bundestag ratified the treaty, but the French National Assembly rejected it in August 1954. The treaty, therefore, never came into force, and the momentum toward a politically united Europe fizzled.

March 25, 1957: Treaty of Rome. This was the second "leap in the dark." Seeking to redirect Europe away from political to economic goals, the "original six" signed the Treaty of Rome, formally the "Treaty Establishing the European Economic Community" (EEC), which set up the EEC. The signatory states formed a customs union and agreed on a plan to reduce trade barriers. The French were reluctant participants and, as part of the deal, insisted on a Common Agricultural Policy (CAP) to protect farmers. The Treaty of Rome replaced the High Authority—which, many European governments felt, encroached on their sovereign rights—with a scaled-down executive institution, the European Commission.

December 1–2, 1969: Summit of European Heads of State and Government, The Hague. French President Georges Pompidou called on European leaders to explore the idea of a European monetary union, and the summit authorized a committee to present a blueprint for such a union. Pierre Werner, Luxembourg's prime minister, would chair the committee. Thus began the third "leap in the dark."

October 8, 1970: Werner Committee Report. The Werner Committee presented its report, which recommended development of the monetary union in stages. The first stage—a training ground for monetary union—was a fixed-exchange-rate regime, the "snake in the tunnel" system. Thus, just as the postwar global arrangement of fixed-but-adjustable exchange rates—the Bretton Woods system—was collapsing, Europeans doubled down on an effort to fix the rate at which their currencies exchanged. To no one's surprise, the snake died a quick death.

March 13, 1979: European Monetary System. French President Valéry Giscard d'Estaing persuaded German Chancellor Helmut Schmidt to reestablish a commitment to fixed exchange rates. Together, they created the European Monetary System (EMS) within which the Exchange Rate Mechanism (ERM) attempted to revive the snake. In its first several years, the ERM survived only by allowing frequent exchange-rate changes.

April 17, 1989: Delors Committee Report. With the ERM still struggling, the Delors Committee was set up to propose a way forward to monetary union. Chaired by European Commission President Jacques Delors, this new committee made assertive claims about the benefits of a European monetary union but otherwise repeated the Werner Committee's plan. The Delors Committee completed its report in April 1989, and European leaders agreed to use it as a basis for further action at a summit in Madrid in late June that year.

November 9, 1989: The Berlin Wall falls. Although a series of events had undermined the regimes of Eastern Europe, it was ultimately a miscommunication on this day that led many East Germans to rush to a checkpoint in the Berlin Wall, which led to its fall. Later the same month, Chancellor Kohl presented a ten-point plan for reunification. After Kohl reassured the Americans that the German commitment to NATO would remain steadfast, the reunification received the blessing of US President George H. W. Bush.

December 8–9, 1989: Summit of European Heads of State or Government, Strasbourg. Chancellor Kohl resisted the idea of an intergovernmental conference to begin considering the form and timetable of a potential European monetary union. Only days before the Strasbourg summit, Kohl wrote to Mitterrand that a "basis" for monetary union still did not exist. However, at the Strasbourg summit, he withdrew his insistence on the need for "complete and adequate" preparations before the project could proceed. And thus, Kohl seemed to concede that it should go ahead. Why he changed his mind remains unclear to this day.

February 7, 1992: Maastricht Treaty. By now, the EEC had twelve member states; Denmark, Ireland, the United Kingdom, Greece, Spain, and Portugal had joined the original six. The Maastricht Treaty, the "Treaty on European Union," renamed the EEC the European Union (EU). Despite advice from the Bundesbank and the German Finance Ministry, Chancellor Helmut Kohl, at the urging of French President François Mitterrand, agreed that the signatories of the treaty would introduce the single currency by January 1, 1999. A centerpiece of the Maastricht Treaty was the fiscal rule that required governments of member states to keep their fiscal deficits below 3 percent of GDP. Britain received an "opt-out," which exempted it from the requirement to join the single-currency zone.

June 2, 1992, May 18, 1993: Danish referendums on Maastricht Treaty. Danish voters rejected the Maastricht Treaty in 1992 by a 51–49 percent margin. In 1993, as in the case of Britain, Denmark received an exemption from the single-currency requirement. In a new referendum, Danish citizens accepted the Maastricht Treaty.

September 20, 1992: French referendum on Maastricht Treaty. French citizens accepted the Maastricht Treaty by a 51–49 percent margin. The unexpectedly large vote against the treaty reflected a deep anxiety among economically vulnerable French citizens, who feared that the euro—and the further intrusion of Europe into their lives—would make their lives even harder. The popular unease about the single currency added to the fragility of the fixed-exchange-rate system in the ERM, which led de facto to the floating of European currencies after August 1993.

June 16–17, 1997: Stability and Growth Pact. At a European Council meeting in Amsterdam, European leaders signed on to the Stability and Growth Pact (SGP), which Germany had championed and which established procedures for monitoring and enforcing the fiscal rule agreed to in Maastricht.

April 23, 1998: Bundestag authorizes Germany's participation in euro area. As a condition for Germany joining the euro area, the German Constitutional Court required the Bundestag to reaffirm that other member states would follow sound fiscal policies. In his speech to the Bundestag, Kohl twice said that German taxpayers would not have to pay the bills for other member states, since the fiscal rules limiting budget deficits were in place.

May 2–3, 1998: European Council agrees on first set of eurozone members and on European Central Bank president. Kohl had ensured agreement on Italy's inclusion in the first set of eleven eurozone members. However, the choice of the first president of the European Central Bank (ECB) proved highly controversial and dragged on into the early hours of May 3. French President Jacques Chirac insisted on Frenchman Jean-Claude Trichet, while the Germans supported the Dutch central bank governor, Wim Duisenberg. The compromise was that Duisenberg would be the first ECB president but would "voluntarily" step down before his eight-year term was over.

After the Euro, Before the Crisis

January 1, 1999: Launch of the euro. The single currency, agreed to at Maastricht and named the euro in December 1995, replaced the national currencies of eleven of the fifteen member states. Britain and Denmark had received exemptions. From among the countries that had joined the EU since the signing of the Maastricht Treaty, Austria and Finland were in the inaugural batch of eurozone members. Sweden (on technical grounds) and Greece (for good reason) did not qualify under the entry standards. New euro banknotes and coins only became legal tender on January 1, 2002, but from January 1999, eleven eurozone member states, having "irretrievably" fixed their exchange rates with one another, operated under the monetary policy set for all by the ECB.

September 28, 2000: Danish referendum on the euro. In spite of the exemption from monetary integration received after Danish citizens rejected the Maastricht Treaty in 1992, the government held a new referendum on whether Denmark should, after all, join the euro area. Danes voted by a bigger margin, 53–47 percent, to stay out.

January 1, 2001: Greece becomes twelfth member of eurozone. German Chancellor Gerhard Schröder expressed his strong support for Greece's entry to the eurozone, and ECB president Duisenberg noted the "remarkable progress" made by Greece to meet the entry criteria. In 2004, three years after Greece's euro entry, an audit of Greek fiscal accounts revealed that Greece's fiscal deficit around the time of the euro entry decision was well above the entry criteria.

September 14, 2003: Swedish referendum on the euro. Swedes voted to stay out of the single currency by a 56–42 percent margin (2 percent of the ballots were blank).

October 29, 2004: Constitution for Europe. EU member states signed a "Treaty Establishing a Constitution for Europe." By now, the EU had twenty-five member states, having grown significantly following the inclusion of Eastern European nations. The Constitutional Treaty sought mainly to streamline procedures for European decision-making.

May 29, 2005: French referendum on European Constitution. French voters rejected the European Constitution by a 55–45 percent margin. As they did in the Maastricht referendum, voters feeling economically left behind voted emphatically against the referendum. In a new development, young French voters also rejected the referendum.

June 1, 2005: Dutch referendum on European Constitution. The Dutch literally scorned the constitution by a 62–38 percent margin. As with the French vote, economically disadvantaged and young voters were most opposed to the idea. After the French and Dutch rejections, European leaders abandoned the idea of a European Constitution. Instead, they amended existing treaties, leading in 2007 to the Treaty of Lisbon, formally the "Treaty on the Functioning of the European Union," which became the basis for the operation of the EU.

The Global Financial Crisis, July 2007–June 2009

July 30, 2007: IKB Deutsche Industriebank announces expected large losses on subprime investments. The IKB announcement triggered the collapse of the US asset-backed commercial paper (ABCP) market, marking the start of the global financial crisis.

August 9, 2007: ECB makes unlimited funds available to banks. Following an announcement by the French bank BNP Paribas that it would halt investor withdrawals from investment funds with heavy exposure to US subprime assets, the interbank market (within which banks lend to one another for short durations) threatened to seize up. The ECB stepped up liquidity provision to banks in the eurozone. The next day, the US Federal Reserve (Fed) followed the ECB and authorized increased liquidity to banks operating in the United States.

September 18, 2007: Fed lowers interest rates. In response to the financial-market turbulence, the Fed reduced its policy interest rate by 50 basis points (100 basis points equal 1 percentage point). The Fed thus embarked on aggressive monetary easing to "forestall" adverse effects from the financial-market disruptions.

March 14–16, 2008: Fed rescues Bear Stearns. JPMorgan Chase agreed to buy Bear Stearns, with the Fed agreeing to pay JPMorgan Chase up to $29 billion in case Bear Stearns's losses turned out to be larger than anticipated. By promising to bear the burden of unanticipated losses, the Fed "bailed out" Bear Stearns's creditors. That action established a presumption that the Fed would continue to bail out other distressed financial institutions.

June 2, 2008: Trichet celebrates euro's first decade. Well into a full-blown global financial crisis, with several eurozone banks in distress and euro-area industrial output beginning to fall, Trichet celebrated the success of the euro. "The euro has been a remarkable success," he said, adding that he did not want to "name and shame" those who had predicted the euro would fail.

July 3, 2008: ECB raises its policy interest rate. The ECB, which had kept its policy interest rate unchanged since the start of the crisis in July 2007, now raised the rate by 25 basis points. Thus, while the Fed was easing, the ECB decided to tighten monetary policy. At the press conference, ECB president Trichet said the measure would control the increase in inflation and wage pressures.

September 15, 2008: Lehman Brothers files for bankruptcy. After the US government's rescue of Bear Stearns and then of mortgage finance giants Fannie Mae and Freddie Mac in early September 2008, the US political establishment unexpectedly allowed Lehman Brothers to fail, triggering a global financial panic.

October 3, 2008: US Congress approves Troubled Asset Relief Program. The Troubled Asset Relief Program (TARP) gave the US Treasury a $700-billion spending authority, in principle to buy "toxic" (mainly subprime) securities and thereby support financial institutions holding those securities. However, once approved, the Treasury could use TARP funds for a wide variety of purposes.

October 8, 2008: Major central banks coordinate interest-rate cuts. Amid global panic, Fed Chairman Ben Bernanke urged major central banks to announce a coordinated reduction of their policy interest rates. The ECB reluctantly reduced its rate by 50 basis points, its first interest-rate reduction since the start of the crisis.

November 6, 2008: ECB cuts policy rate again. For the second time since the start of the crisis, the ECB cut its policy rate by 50 basis points. Coming after a "stunning" 150-basis-point cut by the Bank of England (BOE) earlier that day, the ECB's limited move disappointed financial markets.

December 16, 2008: Fed reduces interest rates to near zero, begins forward guidance, and announces quantitative easing. The Fed lowered its interest rate to the 0.0–0.25 percent range, publicly committed itself to keeping interest rates low for "some time" (forward guidance), and initiated quantitative easing (QE), which is the purchase by the central bank of long-term bonds and other securities to bring down long-term interest rates.

March 5, 2009: BOE reduces interest rates and launches QE. With the BOE reducing its interest rate to 0.5 percent, British rates had fallen by 450 basis points since the coordinated rate cut of October 2008. The BOE also launched its QE program. In contrast, while the ECB continued to reduce its interest rates, it did so much more slowly, acquiring a reputation for doing "too little, too late." An ECB QE was not even under consideration.

May 7, 2009: Results of US stress tests published. The transparently presented findings of the Supervisory Capital Assessment Program persuaded financial markets and analysts that banks were resilient. The US Treasury used TARP funds to inject capital into banks that needed topping up. With US banks recapitalized, the US financial crisis was effectively over, allowing the American economy to begin recovering from its deep recession.

Euro Crisis, 2009–2012

October 8–19, 2009: Greece announces budget deficit will be much larger than projected. Starting with a statement on October 8 by the governor of the Bank of Greece, Greek authorities steadily raised their estimate of the government's budget deficit in 2009. On October 19, at a meeting in Luxembourg of eurozone finance ministers (the Eurogroup), Greek Finance Minister George Papaconstantinou raised the estimate for the 2009 budget deficit to 12.5 percent of GDP; he also noted that the 2008 deficit was higher than previously reported.

April 11, 2010: Eurozone countries and International Monetary Fund agree, in principle, to give financial assistance to Greece. Eurozone governments and the International Monetary Fund (IMF) agreed that they would provide the Greek government €45 billion to help it repay private lenders. With the situation rapidly deteriorating, on May 2 the creditors raised the total size of the bailout funds to €110 billion.

May 7, 2010: German Bundestag approves Greek bailout. The Bundestag approved Germany's financial contribution to the Greek bailout, and later that evening, eurozone authorities authorized their full rescue package.

May 9, 2010: European Financial Stability Facility announced. In the midst of heightened financial tensions, the European Financial Stability Facility (EFSF) was a financial firewall, a €440-billion bailout fund set up by eurozone countries to support other euro countries in financial distress. All EU countries would back a smaller fund of €60 billion, the European Financial Stability Mechanism (EFSM).

May 9, 2010: IMF Executive Board authorizes contribution to Greek bailout. Several IMF executive directors objected to the design of the bailout program. Some specifically demanded a partial default on debt owed by the Greek government to private creditors. Such a default would help scale back the unrealistically intense fiscal austerity proposed. But the United States, reflecting Treasury Secretary Timothy Geithner's hostility to forcing losses on private creditors, and EU member states opposed default by the Greek government on its debt. Given that the crippling debt burden would remain, fiscal austerity appeared to be the only way forward.

May 10, 2010: ECB announces Securities Markets Programme. Announced amid rising financial market worries about Greece, the Securities Markets Programme (SMP) would purchase bonds of eurozone governments, thereby bidding up their prices and helping to lower the interest rates the governments paid.

October 18, 2010: Merkel and Sarkozy meet in Deauville. In a famous walk on the beach, French President Nicolas Sarkozy agreed with German Chancellor Angela Merkel's plan for an orderly method that would impose losses on the private creditors of heavily indebted governments that were also seeking financial assistance from the European bailout fund and European governments.

November 28, 2010: Financial assistance program for Ireland. With Ireland's banks on the verge of collapse, both the EU and IMF estimated that Ireland needed a financial package of €85 billion euros. Irish authorities used €17.5 billion from the nation's cash reserves and other liquid assets. The EU and IMF agreed to provide the rest of the needed funding.

April 7, 2011: ECB increases policy interest rate. The ECB Governing Council decided to raise its policy rate by 25 basis points. ECB President Trichet said the rate hike was necessary to "firmly anchor" inflation expectations. When asked by reporters if higher interest rates could hurt periphery economies, Trichet underlined that member states needed to keep their fiscal houses in order and undertake more structural reforms.

May 17, 2011: Financial assistance program for Portugal. EU finance ministers and the IMF agreed on the terms of a €78 billion financial assistance package.

July 7, 2011: ECB increases rates again. Amid an escalating euro crisis, Governing Council members decided unanimously to raise the ECB's interest rate for the second time in three months. Financial markets went into a tailspin, setting off the most intense phase of the euro crisis.

July 15, 2011: European bank stress-test results released. As the crisis continued to escalate, observers feared that the stress-test results would fail to identify weak banks. The skepticism was justified; while the European Banking Authority (EBA) estimated that banks would be safe with merely €2.5 billion in extra capital, the IMF estimated that they needed about €200 billion more in capital to create a cushion against current risks. Banks grew increasingly wary of other banks and started to charge steadily higher premiums for lending to one another.

July 21, 2011: Europe's official creditors reduce interest rates and extend repayment periods on loans to Greece, Ireland, and Portugal. In a bid to dampen spreading financial panic, European leaders reduced the interest rates and extended the repayment periods for loans to the three countries. Although intended primarily to ease the repayment burden of the Greek government, the concessions mainly benefited Ireland. Investors quickly concluded that the Irish government could now repay its debts. For Greece, and even for Portugal, investors judged the same concessions to be too little to improve repayment prospects materially.

August 5, 2011: Trichet sends policy instructions to Italian and Spanish prime ministers. As financial-market panic increased and Italian and Spanish government-bond yields crossed the psychological 6 percent barrier, Trichet and Banca d'Italia president Mario Draghi wrote a letter to Italian Prime Minister Silvio Berlusconi specifying the policy reforms that Italy needed to undertake. Trichet and the Banco de España president Miguel Ángel Fernández Ordóñez wrote a similarly intrusive letter to Spanish Prime Minister José Luis Rodriguez Zapatero. The act of writing these letters and the list of reforms they specified went well beyond the ECB's mandate. Unelected eurozone central bankers were attempting to override democratic decision-making in member countries.

October 31–November 3, 2011. After an ultimatum from Merkel and Sarkozy, Papandreou drops planned Greek austerity referendum. On October 31, with the scale of the budget cuts required by the Greek government's official creditors weighing heavily on the country's population, Prime Minister George Papandreou announced that a referendum would be held asking voters to approve further austerity. Merkel and Sarkozy summoned Papandreou to Cannes, where they were to attend a G20 summit. In the late evening of November 2, they told him that Greece needed to either accept the austerity required by the official creditors or leave the eurozone. Faced with that choice, Papandreou called off the referendum on November 3.

November 11–16, 2011: Papademos and Monti appointed prime ministers. Following Papandreou's resignation on November 9, Lucas Papademos, formerly vice president of the ECB, became the Greek prime minister of a "crisis coalition" on November 11. In Italy, Berlusconi lost his parliamentary majority on November 8, and four days later, President Giorgio Napolitano invited Mario Monti, a former European commissioner, to lead a new government. Monti was sworn in as Italian prime minister on November 16.

December 8–9, 2011: European leaders agree to the fiscal compact. At a European Union summit, euro-area leaders agreed to move forward with the German proposal for a "fiscal compact." Governments of member states would make a commitment, embedded in national law (preferably in the constitution), to keep their budgets balanced or in surplus. Automatically triggered tax and spending measures would quickly eliminate budget deficits. By March 2, 2012, all euro-area member states signed the fiscal compact, officially "Treaty on Stability, Coordination and Governance in the Economic and Monetary Union" (also called the Fiscal Stability Treaty). Other than Britain and the Czech Republic, non-euro-area countries also agreed to abide by the fiscal compact.

June 9, 2012: Financial assistance announced for the Spanish banking sector. In response to a request from the Spanish government, the Eurogroup announced it would provide a €100 billion loan to the Spanish government. The funds provided were intended to stabilize Spanish banks.

July 5, 2012: ECB lowers interest rate by 25 basis points. Markets were disappointed with the meager interest-rate reduction and believed the ECB was not acting with a sense of purpose. Yields on Italian and Spanish government bonds started to rise.

July 26, 2012: Draghi announces ECB will do "whatever it takes" to save euro. At a conference of panicked international investors in London, ECB president Draghi promised that the ECB would take extraordinary measures—"do whatever it takes"—to ease the financial distress. Italian and Spanish government-bond yields started declining, and the pressure on the banks' stocks eased.

September 6, 2012: ECB announces Outright Monetary Transactions. After Draghi's July statement and the ECB's announcement in August that it was preparing a new initiative, Draghi presented the Outright Monetary Transactions (OMT) program, under which the ECB would buy "unlimited quantities" of bonds of a eurozone government in financial distress. However, the ECB would buy the bonds only after the government had agreed to a financial assistance program with the eurozone's bailout fund, the European Stability Mechanism (ESM), which was soon to be set up. Thus, OMT was not a traditional central bank lender-of-last-resort instrument. Rather, it was IMF-style lending based on policy conditionality.

September 27, 2012: European Stability Mechanism set up. Member states agreed to fold the earlier financial bailout funds, the EFSF and the EFSM, into the ESM.

October 8, 2012: IMF reports that during recession, fiscal multipliers are much larger than previously believed. In its semiannual "World Economic Outlook," the IMF's chief economist, Olivier Blanchard, in a study with IMF economist Daniel Leigh, reported that fiscal multipliers in the eurozone were close to 2, rather than 0.5 as the IMF had earlier assumed. The implication was that fiscal austerity enforced in eurozone countries was causing GDPs to contract severely, with the perverse effect that austerity was causing debt burdens—the debt-repayment obligations relative to GDPs—to rise. Eurozone authorities dismissed these findings.

November 4, 2014: Single Supervisory Mechanism. Under an authority granted to the ECB, the Single Supervisory Mechanism (SSM) would directly oversee the 120 largest banks, with 80 percent of the assets of all eurozone banks. The SSM would also have "broad oversight" of 3,500 other banks, which would continue to be supervised by national authorities.

The Political Fraying of Europe

February 24–25, 2013: Italian parliamentary election sees rise of anti-European sentiment. Italy had been in nearly continuous recession since

2011, and the unelected government of Prime Minister Monti continued to implement fiscal austerity policies. With high and rising unemployment, especially among young Italians, the anti-Europe Five Star Movement, led by comedian and blogger Beppe Grillo, gained ground, receiving around a quarter of all votes. Berlusconi had also campaigned on an anti-Europe, specifically anti-Merkel, platform; his party, the center-right People of Freedom, received 29 percent of the vote. After protracted negotiations, an unstable coalition led by Enrico Letta of the Democratic Party hung on to power for less than a year; on February 22, 2014, the ambitious and rising Matteo Renzi, also of the Democratic Party, displaced Letta to become prime minister.

June 5, 2014: ECB introduces negative interest rates. Because of insufficient monetary-policy stimulus, very low rates of inflation—and the risk of deflation—had set in for some eurozone member states. While reducing the main policy rate to 0.15 percent, the ECB announced "negative interest rates" on bank deposits at the ECB, in effect, a fee to park money there, so as to encourage banks to lend their funds rather than deposit them at the ECB.

January 22, 2015: ECB announces quantitative easing. In addition to purchases of private securities initiated earlier, the ECB announced that it would also purchase eurozone government bonds to help lower the interest rates on those bonds. Total bond purchases amounting to €60 billion per month would start in March 2015. However, the inflation rate remained stuck in a low range.

January 25, 2015: Tsipras becomes Greek prime minister. The Syriza party, led by Alexis Tsipras, had steadily gained electoral ground ever since the unelected Papademos stepped down from his brief tenure as prime minister in May 2012. Distress among Greek citizens remained acute. Tsipras promised Greeks that he would ease austerity, and in the January 2015 election, the Greek public gave Tsipras the opportunity to lead the next government.

July 5, 2015: Greeks say *oxi* (no) to more austerity. Under pressure from the official creditors—the ECB, European governments, and the IMF—to undertake more fiscal austerity, Tsipras called a referendum. The question asked of Greek citizens was whether they accepted the austerity required by the creditors. Greeks voted *oxi* (no) with an overwhelming 61–39 percent margin. In a pattern familiar since the September 1992 French referendum on the single currency, low-income, poorly educated citizens living outside big cities overwhelmingly voted *oxi*. Young Greeks, who faced crippling rates of unemployment, voted *oxi* in large numbers. Tsipras, fearful of the consequences of rejecting the creditors' demands, ignored the *oxi* vote and agreed to the austerity demanded.

January 1, 2016: Single Resolution Mechanism begins operating. The Single Resolution Mechanism (SRM) was set up to "resolve" and restructure banks based on a rulebook, the Bank Recovery and Resolution Directive (BRRD).

June 23, 2016: British public votes to leave EU. By a margin of 52–48 percent, the British public voted to leave the EU. As had become the norm, the "leave" vote was strongest among those with low incomes and limited education. Rural areas and former industrial towns, which had lost manufacturing jobs to low-wage international competitors, also voted disproportionately to leave.

December 4, 2016: Italian citizens reject changes in constitution. Prime Minister Renzi had proposed constitutional changes that would have potentially reduced Italy's chronic dependence on weak and unstable coalition governments and allowed instead the formation of stronger central governments. Italians rejected the proposals by a huge 59–41 percent margin. The rejection reflected the continuing frustrations of low-income and poorly educated citizens and especially the anger of younger Italians with what they saw as the self-absorbed ruling political elite.

May 7, 2017: French citizens elect Macron as their president. In the second round of the French presidential election, Emmanuel Macron easily defeated the Front National's Marine Le Pen. In the second round of the parliamentary election on June 18, Macron's La République En Marche (Republic on the Move) emerged as the largest electoral winner. Commentators around the world welcomed Macron's victory over nationalistic forces in France. But the French elections also saw a sharp fall in voter turnout. As in European referendums, Macron and his party did least well among those who felt economically vulnerable, and despite his youth, Macron struggled to win the favor of and give hope to young French citizens.

September 24, 2017: Anti-Europe forces gain in Bundestag elections. The mainstream German parties—Chancellor Merkel's Christian Democratic Union, its sister party the Bavaria-based Christian Social Union, and the Social Democrats—received an electoral shellacking in the Bundestag elections. Together these parties received 53 percent of the vote, down from a combined 67 percent in 2013. The big gainer was Alternative für Deutschland (AfD), which won 12.6 percent of the vote, up from 4.7 percent in 2013. AfD, born as an anti-euro political movement in September 2012 at the height of the eurozone's economic and political crisis, by now had turned into a nationalistic and xenophobic party. AfD supporters shared the low-income, low-education features of protest voters in European referendums and elections. The Free Democrats, representing voters with a more economically successful profile and euro-skeptical views, received 10.7 percent of the vote, more than double their 2013 vote share.

NOTES

Introduction

1. Timmermans 2017.
2. Friedman 1968.
3. Friedman 1968, 12.
4. Kenen 1969.
5. Janis 1972.
6. Akerlof and Shiller 2009.
7. The 1971 article was published in a collection of essays, Kaldor 1978.
8. Prabhavananda and Isherwood 1981, 131.
9. Juncker 2016.
10. Barroso 2013; Macron 2017b.
11. Guirao and Lynch 2016, 532.
12. Schelling 1988, 182.
13. Geertz 1963.

Chapter 1

1. Monnet 1978, 303–304. Written in 1976, the memoirs were translated into English in 1978. The references here are from the translation.
2. Schuman 1950.
3. Adenauer 1966, 314–315; Monnet 1978, 303.
4. Judt 2006, locations 3766–3771.
5. Duchêne 1988, 727, column 1.
6. Duchêne 1994, 30, 49, 61.
7. Monnet 1978, 305.
8. Monnet 1978, 308.
9. Duchêne 1988, 729.

10. Van Middelaar 2013, 42. The Treaty was signed on April 18, 1951, and came into force on July 23, 1952.
11. Van Middelaar 2013, 16, 333.
12. Monnet 1978, 340.
13. Monnet 1978, 340.
14. Duchêne 1994, 228.
15. Duchêne 1994, 228.
16. Duchêne 1994, 229; Adenauer 1966, 346.
17. Duchêne 1994, 230.
18. Adenauer 1966, 426.
19. Duchêne 1994, 254.
20. Judt 2006, locations 5736–5740.
21. Duchêne 1994, 256.
22. Judt 2006, location 5744.
23. Duchêne 1994, 241.
24. Duchêne 1994, 245–246.
25. Duchêne 1994, 239–240.
26. Duchêne 1994, 256. In almost identical words, Marjolin (1989, 280) wrote: "Everyone realized that the political and military avenues were now closed."
27. Spaak Committee 1956, 2.
28. Hegre, Oneal, and Russett 2010; Martin, Mayer, and Thoenig 2012; Dafoe and Kelsey 2014.
29. Marjolin 1989, 281, italics in original: Erhard "was a universalist, a fervent advocate of total freedom of trade on a world scale. . . . *France at that time was essentially protectionist.*" See also Judt 2006, locations 7134–7138.
30. Moravcsik 2008, 160.
31. Duchêne 1994, 257.
32. http://europa.eu/about-eu/institutions-bodies/european-commission/index_en.htm.
33. Macmillan 1961, 68.
34. De Gaulle 1970, 181.
35. Judt 2006, location 7121.
36. Marjolin 1981, 48.
37. Peyrefitte 1994, 159; Vanke 2001, 96.
38. Teasdale 2016, 11; Parsons 2003, 132–135; Marjolin 1989, 329.
39. Macmillan 1961, 67–68.
40. Vanke 2001, 100.
41. Vanke 2001, 98.
42. Marjolin 1989, 350.
43. Marjolin 1989, 347.
44. Marjolin 1981, 47.

45. Garton Ash 1998, 52, 62.
46. Garton Ash 1998, 63.
47. Duchêne 1994, 335.
48. Kindleberger 1978, 416, 419.
49. Kindleberger 1978, 419.
50. Eichengreen 2007b, 100–105.
51. Emminger 1977, 18.
52. International Monetary Fund 1969, 7.
53. Emminger 1977.
54. Tanner 1968b.
55. Emminger 1977, 22.
56. Tanner 1968a; Tanner 1968b.
57. Tanner 1968c.
58. Dyson and Featherstone 1999, 105.
59. Tanner 1968a.
60. Tanner 1968a.
61. Quoted in Szász 1999, 25.
62. Tanner 1968a.
63. Tanner 1968c; Tanner 1968a.
64. Tanner 1968a.
65. Tversky and Kahneman 1973.
66. Szász 1999, 25.
67. Werner 1970, annex 1, 31.
68. Parsons 2003, chapter 4.
69. Dyson and Featherstone 1999, 106.
70. Roussel 2004, 337.
71. Védrine 1996, 433.
72. Bordo 1981, 7.
73. Eichengreen and Temin 2010, 370.
74. Eichengreen 1992.
75. Eichengreen and Temin 2010; Haberler 1976, 17.
76. Friedman 1953, 163.
77. Taylor 2001, 128; Friedman 1953.
78. Bordo 1993, 83.
79. Bordo 1993.
80. Tobin 1978, 443.
81. Johnson 1969, 12–13.
82. Hetzel 2002, 30.
83. Roussel 2004, 336.
84. Farnsworth 1969.
85. Hofmann 2013.
86. Binder 1992.

87. Hofmann 2013.

88. Brandt 1992, 200.

89. https://www.nobelprize.org/nobel_prizes/peace/laureates/1971/press.html.

90. Brandt 1978, 239.

91. Brandt 1978, 247.

92 Brandt 1978, 247.

93. Garton Ash 1994, 129–130.

94. Szász 1999, 27.

95. Duchêne 1994, 335, 338.

96. Brandt 1978, 247; Maes and Bussière 2016, 32.

97. Maes 2004, 14.

98. Duchêne 1994, 335.

99. Brandt 1978, 247.

100. Tombs 2014, 798.

101. Tombs 2014, 798.

102. Tombs 2014, 798.

103. Brandt 1978, 160.

104. *Financial Times* 1969.

105. In the appendix to this chapter, I discuss other factors that may have exerted some influence on the monetary union negotiations.

106. European Council 1969, 15; Werner 1970.

107. Mundell 1961.

108. Decressin and Fatás 1995; Obstfeld and Peri 1998.

109. Kenen 1969.

110. Sala-i-Martin and Sachs 1991.

111. Asdrubali, Sørensen, and Yosha 1996.

112. Werner 1970, 8, 10–11, 13.

113. Werner 1970, 12.

114. Werner 1970, 12, 26.

115. Monnet 1978, 417. Written in 1976, the memoirs were translated into English in 1978. The references here are from the translation.

116. Marsh 2009a, 56.

117. Marsh 2009a, 62.

118. Werner 1970, 24–25.

119. Werner 1970, 25, emphasis added.

120. Werner 1970, 10, 12, emphasis added.

121. Werner 1970, 24.

122. Werner 1970, 26.

123. Werner 1970, 14. For Pompidou's remark, see Roussel 2004, 341.

124. Tietmeyer 1994, 24.

125. Szász 1999, 34.

126. Brittan 1970.

127. Kaldor 1978, 204. The citations of Kaldor's 1971 article are from his 1978 collection of essays.
128. Kaldor 1978, 205.
129. Kaldor 1978, 206.
130. Campbell 2012.
131. Campbell 2012, 337.
132. Greif and Laitin 2004.
133. Dyson and Featherstone 1999, 107.
134. Dyson and Featherstone 1999, 109.
135. Dyson and Featherstone 1999, 107.
136. Dyson and Featherstone 1999, 108–109.
137. Dyson and Featherstone 1999, 110.
138. Marsh 2009, 61–63
139. Campbell 2012, 337.
140. Gerth and Mills 1961, 280.
141. Janis 1972, 9–10; see also psychologist and Nobel laureate Daniel Kahneman's interview in Schrage 2003.
142. Sunstein and Hastie 2017, locations 217–222.
143. Akerlof 2017; see also Janis 1972.
144. Krugman 1995, 36.
145. Rutherford 1971.
146. Schiller 1971, 195.
147. That theme persisted in German economic advocacy. On November 11, 1988, Helmut Schlesinger (1988, 1), then vice president of the Bundesbank, said that whenever there was a conflict between the fixed exchange rate and domestic policy goals, governments "usually decide in favor of their national priorities." This, he said, was appropriate, "since the stability of exchange rates is no end in itself."
148. Marjolin 1989, 311.
149. *New York Times* 1971.
150. Farnsworth 1972.
151. Wittich and Shiratori 1973, 11–12.
152. André Szász email, January 28, 2015.
153. Hetzel 2002, 41; Silk 1972.
154. Hetzel 2002, 42–43.
155. This sketch of Giscard is from Farnsworth 1974.
156. *Le Monde* 1974 ; Mathieu 1974.
157. Marjolin 1989, 281.
158. Marjolin 1975, 4.
159. Marjolin 1981; the lectures were delivered in September 1980. The memoirs, Marjolin 1989, 65–67, appeared in French in 1986; the English translation was published as Marjolin 1989.
160. Marjolin 1989, 363.

161. Marjolin 1989, 226.

162. MacDougall 1977, 20.

163. MacDougall 1977, 21. Wallis and Oates (1998, 166) describe the ramp-up in US fiscal transfers to states between 1931 and 1934 for relief during the Great Depression. In 1934, transfers for grants and social insurance equaled 4 percent of national GDP and therefore constituted much larger shares of state GDPs.

164. Solomon 1982, 293–297, chapter 18.

165. Marjolin 1981, 60–63; Eichengreen 2007b, 3–8.

166. Szász 1999, 41, 51.

167. Masson and Mussa 1995.

168. Marjolin 1981, 62.

169. Marjolin 1981, 63.

170. Friedman 1968, 5, 11. For its citation as one of the most influential papers of the past one hundred years, see Arrow et al. 2011; for the German view, see Schlesinger 1988, 2.

171. Giscard d'Estaing 1988, 136. See also Szász 1999, 52.

172. Ludlow and Spaventa 1980; Solomon 1982, 295.

173. *Le Monde* 1978.

174. Giscard repeated this theme many times, including in *Der Spiegel* 1979.

175. Ludlow 1982, 32; Dyson and Featherstone 1999, 110–116.

176. *Times* 1980; Giavazzi and Pagano 1988; Dyson and Featherstone 1996.

177. Szász 1999, 56, 233.

178. Ludlow 1982, 58.

179. Solomon 1982, 295.

180. Szász 1999, 52.

181. Giscard d'Estaing 1988, 136. See also discussion in Szász 1999, 52.

182. Szász 1999, 56.

183. Szász 1999, 53–66.

184. *Le Monde* 1978.

185. Szász 1999, 64–65.

186. Eichengreen and Wyplosz 1993, 56.

187. Eichengreen and Wyplosz 1993, 56, table 1.

188. *Le Monde* 1978.

189. Thatcher 2013, locations 11734–11735.

190. Milward 1992.

191. Szász 1999, 214.

192. Szász 1999, 8–12.

193. Judt 2006, location 7208; Judt 2011, 22.

194. Fitchett 1998.

195. Solomon 1982, 360.

196. Solomon 1982, chapter 18.

197. Fischer 2001.

198. *Akten zur Auswärtigen Politik der Bundesrepublik Deutschland* 2002, 1064.

Chapter 2

1. Eichengreen and Wyplosz 1993, 56, table 1.
2. Szász 1999, 59.
3. Schwarz 2012, 44–45.
4. Schwarz 2012, 47. In 1963, Kohl named his firstborn son Walter.
5. Schwarz 2012, 47.
6. Clemens 1998a, 2.
7. Schwarz 2012, 352; also Védrine 1996, 290.
8. Küsters 1998, 28.
9. Marjolin 1981, 59.
10. Agreement on the SEA was achieved at the Luxembourg summit December 2–3, 1985; the act had to be signed twice, on February 17 and February 28, 1986 (for an explanation, see http://www.cvce.eu/obj/the_signing_of_the_single_european_act-en-d29e6c74-ba4d-4160-abc0-1f1d327bfaae.html). It came into effect on July 1, 1987.
11. Thatcher 2013, location 10015.
12. Moravcsik 1991, 41.
13. Moravcsik 1998, 318, 327, 330;. Schwarz 2012, 417.
14. Sachs and Wyplosz 1986, 263.
15. See chapter 1.
16. Hodson 2016; Sachs and Wyplosz 1986.
17. See chapter 1.
18. Sachs and Wyplosz 1986, 276; Cameron 1992.
19. Schabert 2009, 177, 353.
20. Dyson and Featherstone 1999, 368.
21. Grant 1994, 119.
22. Schabert 2009, 184.
23. Blair 1999, 151. The Delors report was completed in April 1989.
24. Delors 1989, paragraph 26.
25. Binyon 1989.
26. Reuters News 1989.
27. *Financial Times* 1989.
28. Mann 1989.
29. Buchan, Stephens, and Dawkins 1989.
30. Buchan, Stephens, and Dawkins 1989.
31. Védrine 1996, 420.
32. Védrine 1996, 420.
33. European Council 1989, 11.
34. Thatcher 2013, location 10023.
35. Marsh and Fisher 1989.
36. *Economist* 1988b.
37. Guigou 2000, 77–78.

38. Sarotte 2014a.

39. Plender 1989.

40. Küsters and Hofmann 1998, 565–566; letter from Kohl to Mitterrand, Bonn, November 27, 1989.

41. Savranskaya, Blanton, and Zubok 2010; see also http://nsarchive.gwu.edu/NSAEBB/NSAEBB296.

42. Former US Secretary of State Henry Kissinger (1999, 617) emphasized the NATO interest: "History will surely give high marks to the tour de force of achieving the unification of Germany while remaining anchored in its Atlantic relationships."

43. Sauga, Simons, and Wiegrefe 2010; Guigou 2000, 78–79.

44. Garton Ash 2012, 5.

45. Wiegrefe 2010.

46. *New York Times* 1989.

47. Cornwell 1985.

48. See chapter 1.

49. Giscard d'Estaing 1995, 4.

50. Küsters and Hofmann 1998, 599; emphasis added.

51. Küsters and Hofmann 1998, 596–597.

52. Sarotte 2014b, 78–79.

53. Sarotte 2014b, 78–79.

54. Küsters and Hofmann 1998, 641; and commentary by Schabert 2009, 234; Binyon, Murray, and Jacobson 1989; and Riding 1989.

55. Küsters and Hofmann 1998, 641.

56. *Frankfurter Allgemeine Zeitung* 1989.

57. *Times* 1989.

58. *New York Times* 1989.

59. Riding 1989.

60. Szász 1999, 135–136; *Times* 1989.

61. Sarotte 2009.

62. Sarotte 2014b, 48–49.

63. Sarotte 2009, 188–192.

64. *Deutsche Welle* 2012a; Judt 2006, location 5657.

65. Védrine 1996, 417–419.

66. Aeschimann and Riché 1996, 51.

67. Schabert 2009, 248.

68. Küsters and Hofmann 1998, 638.

69. Sarotte 2014b, 49.

70. Schabert 2009, 240.

71. Pulzer 1999, 135. On the autonomy achieved from the government and the party, see also Helms 2002, 154.

72. Marsh 1992, 209.

73. Marsh 1992, 209–210.

74. Waigel, in his capacity as a leader of the Christian Social Union, had fiercely opposed Pöhl's appointment and renewal as Bundesbank president; but on this matter, the two were of like mind (Marsh 1992, 210).

75. Eisenhammer 1990b; Protzman 1990.

76. Andrews 2000.

77. Akerlof, Rose, Yellen, and Hessenius 1991, 1.

78. Even in his "glass half full" assessment, Humboldt University's Michael Burda (2009) is clear that the conversion rate created a severe burden. University of Chicago economist Harald Uhlig (2008) is harsher. He concluded that East Germany had settled into a steady state of low labor productivity, high unemployment, and high emigration. With its young and best qualified leaving, he described the East as a dying region turning into a wasteland. By 2014, a quarter century after the fall of the Berlin Wall, migration out of the former East Germany finally stopped but possibly only "because everybody who wanted to go west has gone" (Wagstyl 2014). Unemployment rates remained about twice as high, and productivity was still only about three-quarters that of the West.

79. Allen-Mills 1990.

80. Allen-Mills 1990.

81. Kinzer 1990.

82. Eisenhammer 1990a.

83. Allen-Mills 1990.

84. Dyson and Featherstone 1999, 375.

85. Whitney 1994b.

86. Whitney 1994b.

87. Clemens 1998b, 91.

88. Laughland 2000.

89. Paul 2010, 48.

90. Dyson and Featherstone 1999, 449.

91. Lakoff 2017.

92. Dyson and Featherstone 1999, 444.

93. Marsh 1991; Marsh 1992, 221.

94. Usborne 1991.

95. Marsh 1991; Marsh 1992, 222.

96. Quoted in Marsh 1991.

97. Marsh 1992, 236.

98. Peel 1991.

99. Paul 2010, 293.

100. Schwan and Jens 2014, location 2823.

101. Ellsberg 1972, 75.

102. Lamont 1999, 134.

103. Lamfalussy 1989, 108.

104. Lamfalussy, Maes, and Péters 2014, 136–137.

105. Szász 1999, 13.

106. Fleming 2011.

107. Szász email, November 20, 2014.

108. Henning and Kessler 2012, 12.

109. Delors 1989, 20.

110. See chapter 1.

111. The reference to binding limits appears several times; see, for example, Delors 1989, 14.

112. Buchan, Stephens, and Dawkins 1989.

113. Deutsche Delegation 1993.

114. Schubert 2013.

115. Aeschimann and Riché 1996, 92–93.

116. Aeschimann and Riché 1996, 92–93.

117. Mazzucelli 1997, 67, 108.

118. Tirole 2012.

119. Grant 1994, 183–184; Blair 1999, 185–186.

120. Grant 1994, 184.

121. Lamont 1999, 119.

122. Delors 2004, 429.

123. Bernanke 2016.

124. Volcker 1997, 256.

125. Modigliani et al. 1998, 347.

126. Modigliani and La Malfa 1998.

127. See chapter 1.

128. Dyson and Featherstone 1999, 439, 442–443.

129. Lamont 1999, 126.

130. Bundesverband der Deutschen Industrie 1991.

131. Védrine 1996, 472.

132. Grant 1994, 200.

133. Védrine 1996, 472.

134. Védrine 1996, 472.

135. Parsons (2000, 61) adds that Mitterrand had also been advised against agreeing to a definite introduction date; thus, like their German counterparts, "even many French participants were surprised when he made the deadline his principal demand."

136. Guigou 2000, 103.

137. Schwarz 2012, 701; Grant 1994, 200.

138. Védrine 1996, 472.

139. Trean 1992.

140. Moravcsik 1998, 265; Judt 2006, locations 16932–16933.

141. Kohl 1991, 5798.

142. Kohl 1991, 5799.

143. Kohl 1991, 5780.

144. Masson and Mussa 1995.
145. Eichenberg and Dalton 2007.
146. James 1992.
147. Monnet 1978, 367; Parsons 2000, 64.
148. Védrine 1996, 298–299.
149. Védrine 1996, 298–299.
150. Lamont 1999, 123.
151. Austin 1992; Brock 1992; Follett 1992.
152. Raifberger 1992; Allaire 1992.
153. Criddle 1993, 229.
154. Buchan 1992.
155. Walters 1986, 125-132.
156. L. Svensson 1994. Detailed analyses of the "unstable" nature of the ERM are in Eichengreen and Wyplosz 1993 and Higgins 1993.
157. Eichengreen and Wyplosz 1993, 58.
158. Criddle 1993, 234.
159. Blankart 2013, 519.
160. Szász, email, October 15, 2014; see also Szász 1999, 178.
161. Marsh 2009a, 160–161.
162. Marsh 2009a, 160–161; Eichengreen and Wyplosz 1993, 109.
163. Brulé 1992.
164. Ferenczi 1992.
165. Brehier 1992.
166. Paris 1992.
167. Ferenczi 1992.
168. Sachs and Wyplosz 1986.
169. Lee 2004.
170. Séguin, Vernet, and Servent 1993.
171. Dornbusch's comment accompanying Eichengreen and Wyplosz 1993, 135.
172. Marsh 1993.
173. Agence Europe 1992.
174. Peel 1992b.
175. Peel 1992b; Eisenhammer 1992.
176. Eisenhammer, Jackson, Chote, and Marshall 1992; Palmer, Tomforde, and Kelly 1992.
177. Kohl 1992, 9219.
178. Kohl 1992, 9220.
179. Eichengreen and Wyplosz 1993, 58.
180. Hagerty 1992.
181. Redburn 1992.
182. Smith 1993.
183. Smith 1993.
184. Norman 1993.

185. Peel 1992a; Peel 1992b; Toomey 1993.

186. Schlesinger 1992, 3.

187. German Federal Constitutional Court 1993, 2.

188. Boyes 1993.

189. Dominguez 2006, 70.

190. Schäuble and Lamers 1994, 72.

191. Schäuble and Lamers 1994, 77.

192. Donnelly 2004, 38–41.

193. Murphy 1994; Agence France-Presse 1994; *Times* 1994.

194. Agence France-Presse 1994; *Times* 1994.

195. Giscard d'Estaing 1995, 2.

196. Schäuble and Lamers 1994, 75–76.

197. Frankland 1994.

198. Crawshaw 1994.

199. International Monetary Fund 1994a, 3.

200. International Monetary Fund 1994a, 3.

201. Crawshaw 1994.

202. Heneghan 1994.

203. Schwan and Jens 2014, location 1893.

204. Barber 1996.

205. Whitney 1994a.

206. Agence Europe 1994.

207. *Financial Times* 1995. In this interview, Schäuble also predicted, "Britain will recognize relatively soon that its interest lies in participation [in the monetary union], not in keeping its distance."

208. Agence Europe 1996.

209. Dornbusch 1996.

210. Barber 1996.

211. Agence Europe 1996; Barber 1996.

212. That invited the predictable response from Jacques Santer, the largely forgotten European Commission president: "Stopping the clocks will not prevent the 21st century arriving." See Bremner 1996.

213. Whitney 1996.

214. Agence Europe 1996.

215. Kohl 1996.

216. Kamm 1996.

217. Mortimer 1996.

218. Swardson 1997.

219. Taylor 1997.

220. Marshall 1997a.

221. Dow Jones Online News 1997.

222. Judt 1997.

223. Jukes 2010.

224. Drohan 1997.

225. Eichengreen and Wyplosz 1998, 67.

226. Stephens 1997.

227. Kirschbaum 1997.

228. Drozdiak 1997.

229. Gallagher 1997.

230. Stoiber belonged to the mainly Bavaria-based Christian Social Union (CSU). The CSU and the much larger Christian Democratic Union (CDU) formed the German conservative coalition.

231. Norman 1997.

232. Marshall 1997b.

233. Noble 1998.

234. Keohane 1986.

235. Sutherland 1997.

236. Feldstein 1997, 23.

237. See chapter 1.

238. Friedman 1997.

239. Carli 1993, 259.

240. Carli 1993, 5, 166.

241. Carli 1993, 13.

242. Ferrero and Brosio 1997; Fabbrini 2000.

243. Judt 2006, locations 6071–6072.

244. Carli 1993, 341.

245. Masson and Mussa 1995.

246. Ford and Suyker 1990, 7–8, 51.

247. Shleifer and Vishny 1998, chaps, 3 and 4.

248. Fabbrini 2000, 174.

249. Fabbrini 2000, 187.

250. Judt 2006, locations 6076–6078.

251. Tanzi 1998, 580.

252. Carli 1993, 265, 320, 374.

253. Maastricht Treaty 1992, article 104c.

254. Blitz 1998.

255. Delhommais 1998; Cook 1998.

256. Cook 1998.

257. Cook 1998; *Financial Times* 1998.

258. *Financial Times* 1998.

259. Böll, Reiermann, Sauga, and Wiegrefe 2012.

260. Kohl 1998, 21054.

261. Kohl 1998, 21051.

262. Barber 1998.

263. https://www.svtplay.se/video/1263369/ordforande-persson/del-1-794?start=auto, minutes 46:30 to 50:20.

264. Barber 1998.

265. Boyes 1998b.

266. Helm 2000; Kohl 2014, location 453.

267. Grey 2000 has a colorful account; Laughland 2000 is an angry description.

268. Dow Jones International News 1999.

269. Kirschbaum 1999.

270. Merkel 1999; translation from Packer 2014.

Chapter 3

1. Schmid 1998; Boyes 1998a.

2. *Berliner Zeitung* 1998; *Der Spiegel* 1998; Musolff 2003.

3. Cohen 1998.

4. Cohen 1998.

5. Boyes 1998a.

6. Didzoleit, Aust, and Koch 1999.

7. Harrison 1998.

8. Lichfield 1998.

9. Butler 1998.

10. Nash 1998.

11. Notes and coins would not come until January 1, 2002; until then, the old national currencies would exchange at fixed rates vis-à-vis the euro.

12. Graham and Münchau 1999.

13. Graham and Robinson 1999.

14. European Central Bank 1999a, 16.

15. Associated Press 1999.

16. Associated Press 1999.

17. Wheatley 1999.

18. See chapter 2.

19. Didzoleit, Aust, and Koch 1999.

20. Sesit 2000a.

21. Gordon 2004; Cette, Fernald, and Mojon 2016.

22. Gordon 2004, 34.

23. European Central Bank 1999a, 40.

24. International Monetary Fund 1999a, 39.

25. International Monetary Fund 1999a, 4, 24, 37–38.

26. International Monetary Fund 1999c, 1.

27. International Monetary Fund 1999c, 4-5.

28. Andrews 1998.

29. Hughes 1999.

30. International Monetary Fund 1999b, 12.

31. International Monetary Fund 1999b, 33.

32. International Monetary Fund 1999b, 24–25.

33. European Central Bank 1999a, 16.

34. Cohen 1999. Earlier, on April 19, the Bundestag had resumed its meeting place in the renovated Reichstag building, burned down in 1993 by a mysterious fire, see http://news.bbc.co.uk/2/hi/europe/322934.stm.

35. Kalyvas 2015, 126; Karamouzi 2014.

36. European Commission 1976, 12–13.

37. European Commission 1976, 13.

38. Dale 1976; Hornsby 1976.

39. European Commission 1976, 5.

40. *Times* 1977.

41. Kalyvas 2015, 126.

42. Judt 2006, locations 12240–12242.

43. Reuters News 1979.

44. International Monetary Fund 1983.

45. International Monetary Fund 1983, 6.

46. Kalyvas 2015, 127.

47. For a graphic account of the failings of the Greek state under Papandreou and fostered by European funds, see Kalyvas 2015, especially 142–147.

48. These figures are from the IMF's World Economic Outlook Database in April 2015. The data at that time showed even worse performance.

49. International Monetary Fund 1990, 1. The report describes stagnant manufacturing output and investment, inability to compete in international markets, and unbridled growth of the public sector (International Monetary Fund, 1990, 2, 16). Steep devaluation of the drachma provided a brief respite in 1986–87.

50. Kalyvas 2015, 142.

51. Murphy, Shleifer, and Vishny 1993.

52. McDonald 1991.

53. Paris 1991.

54. International Monetary Fund 1994b, 2.

55. Gaunt 1999.

56. Reuters News 1999a.

57. *Frankfurter Allgemeine Zeitung* 1999.

58. Boer 1999.

59. Market News International 1999.

60. *Handelsblatt* 2000.

61. Winestock 2000. At the same time, the commission concluded that Sweden was not ready for adopting the euro (Norman 2000). Over the next fifteen years, Sweden would turn out to be one of the best-performing and most resilient of European economies.

62. Dow Jones Business News 2000.

63. European Council 2000.

64. Barber 2000.

65. Agence Europe 2000.

66. The two German conservative parties—the Christian Democratic Union (CDU) and the Christian Social Union (CSU)—are traditional allies. Because the CDU is so much larger, its leader is normally the candidate that represents the two parties for the chancellor's position. However, Angela Merkel, after becoming the CDU chairman in June 2000, agreed that Stoiber would lead the conservatives in the 2002 election. Although ahead in the polls until the very end, the conservative coalition lost to the Schröder-led socialist-green coalition.

67. *Frankfurter Allgemeine Zeitung* 2000.

68. *Berliner Zeitung* 2000.

69. Hope 2000.

70. Dow Jones Newswires 2001.

71. Featherstone 2003, 932, 936.

72. Hanreich 2004.

73. Quinn 2004.

74. Bowley 2004.

75. See chapter 2.

76. P. Svensson 1994.

77. Cowell 2000; Marcussen and Zølner 2003.

78. Brown-Humes and MacCarthy 2000.

79. Winestock and Champion 2000.

80. Winestock and Champion 2000.

81. *Financial Times* 2000.

82. Winestock and Champion 2000; Cowell 2000.

83. Brown-Humes 2000.

84. Buerkle 2000.

85. Cited in Winestock and Champion 2000.

86. Buerkle 2000.

87. L. Barber 2000.

88. L. Barber 2000.

89. Evans-Pritchard 2000.

90. Norris 2000.

91. Sesit 2000b; Norris 2000.

92. BBC News 2000.

93. CNN Money 2000; Hofheinz and Sesit 2000.

94. Oddly, the ECB press release mentioned only the "monetary authorities of the United States and Japan," failing to acknowledge the participation of Canadian and UK counterparts, see https://www.ecb.europa.eu/press/pr/date/2000/html/pr000922.en.html.

95. https://www.ecb.europa.eu/press/pr/date/2000/html/pr001103.en.html.

96. Duisenberg and Noyer 2000.

97. Duisenberg and Noyer 2000.

98. Federal Reserve System 2001, 13.

99. Duisenberg and Noyer 2001b.

100. Duisenberg and Noyer 2001c.

101. Duisenberg and Noyer 2001b.

102. Duisenberg and Noyer 2001b.

103. Friedman 1968.

104. Friedman 1968, 12, 14.

105. Bernanke 1999, 2–3.

106. Duisenberg and Noyer 2001b.

107. International Monetary Fund 2001c.

108. International Monetary Fund 2001d, 1.

109. International Monetary Fund 2001d, 9.

110. Duisenberg and Noyer 2001a.

111. Sims 2001.

112. International Monetary Fund 2001e, 4.

113. See International Monetary Fund 2001a, 3.

114. Rhoads and Hofheinz 2001.

115. Rhoads and Hofheinz 2001; Schmid 2001a.

116. Schmid 2001a.

117. International Monetary Fund 2001b, 33.

118. International Monetary Fund 2002b, 5.

119. Agence Europe 2001.

120. Rhoads and Hofheinz 2001.

121. Rhoads and Hofheinz 2001.

122. International Monetary Fund 2001b, 22 this report was published in November.

123. International Monetary Fund 2001b, 22.

124. L. Barber 2001; *Economist* 2001.

125. Economist Intelligence Unit 2002.

126. Crossland 2001; Schmid 2001b.

127. Economist Intelligence Unit 2002.

128. Hofheinz and Boston 2002.

129. Mallet 2002; Alderman 2002.

130. Agence France-Presse 2002.

131. Alderman 2002.

132. International Monetary Fund 2002d, 25.

133. International Monetary Fund 2002b, 11, 24.

134. Elliott and Denny 2002.

135. In principle, Germany would have been required to make a non-interest-bearing deposit, which would be confiscated if deficits continued to exceed 3 percent of GDP.

136. Leparmentier and Zecchini 2002.

137. *Times* 2002.

138. Righter 2002.

139. Righter 2002.
140. https://www.ecb.europa.eu/press/pr/date/2002/html/pr021024_1.en.html.
141. Egan 2002.
142. *Economist* 1999.
143. Landler 2003.
144. Sinn 2003, 22.
145. International Monetary Fund 1995, 11.
146. Carlin and Soskice 2007; Carlin and Soskice 2009.
147. See box 2.2.
148. Boyes 2002.
149. Sciolino 2003.
150. Council of the European Communities 2003.
151. Council of the European Union 2003b, 21.
152. Cook 2003.
153. Reuters News 2003.
154. Gowers, Major, and Williamson 2003; Major and Williamson 2003.
155. Schwammenthal and Echikson 2003; *Irish Examiner* 2003.
156. Council of the European Union 2003a.
157. Eastham 2003; Sciolino 2003.
158. Harding, Henley, and Black 2003.
159. Eichel 2003.
160. Council of Economic and Financial Affairs 2003, 16, 21.
161. Thurston and Joshi 2003.
162. Thurston and Joshi 2003.
163. Thurston and Joshi 2003.
164. Thurston and Joshi 2003.
165. https://www.ecb.europa.eu/press/pr/date/2003/html/pr031125.en.html.
166. Parker and Crooks 2003.
167. European Court of Justice 2004; Dutzler and Hable 2005.
168. Posen 2005, 8.
169. Mascolo and Schwennicke 2011.
170. Posen 2005, 8.
171. See chapter 2.
172. Parker 2003.
173. European Commission 2003.
174. Werner 1970, 12.
175. Tietmeyer 2003, 30.
176. Cohen 1998.
177. Boyes 2002.
178. Rhoads and Winestock 2001; *Wall Street Journal Europe* 2002; Guerrera 2003; Mortished 2004.
179. Parker 2003.

Chapter 4

1. International Monetary Fund 2004a, 1.
2. International Monetary Fund 2004a, 3.
3. International Monetary Fund 2004a, 3, 27.
4. Greenspan 1996.
5. Greenspan 1996.
6. Shiller 2015, xix.
7. See chapter 2.
8. Gorton and Ordoñez 2016.
9. Summers (2005) is an example of such a study.
10. Greenspan 2002.
11. The ECB president does report to the European Parliament. But the parliament has no authority over the ECB.
12. Padoa-Schioppa 2004.
13. Reuters News 1999b.
14. Corsetti and Pesenti 1999, 295–296, 325.
15. Kindleberger 1964, 48.
16. Zysman 1983, 83, and discussion that precedes, 81–83.
17. Gerschenkron 1962, 15, 88–89, 139. Zysman 1983, 289–290, has a good summary of Gerschenkron's argument.
18. Battilossi, Gigliobianco, and Marinelli 2013.
19. Eichengreen 2007b, 6.
20. Battilossi, Gigliobianco, and Marinelli 2013.
21. Robinson 1952, 86.
22. Some authors report that European per capita income peaked at 75 percent of US GDP. The exact peak seems to depend on the country composition and the averaging method. But all estimates fall in the 70–75 percent range.
23. Eichengreen 2007b, 6.
24. Megginson 2005, 1936.
25. La Porta, Lopez-de-Silanes, and Shleifer 2002; Barth, Caprio, and Levine 2004; Zysman 1983, 150–151.
26. Zysman 1983, 113, 117–179; Sachs and Wyplosz 1986, 273.
27. Hall 1986, 190.
28. Battilossi, Gigliobianco, and Marinelli 2013, 491–492.
29. Battilossi, Gigliobianco, and Marinelli 2013, 513.
30. Van Ark, O'Mahony, and Timmer 2008, 26, 30.
31. Piketty and Zucman 2014.
32. Gennaioli, Shleifer, and Vishny 2014; Philippon 2015.
33. Rajan and Zingales 2003, 247; Kindleberger 1984, 128.
34. Thomas 2012, 16–17.
35. Pagano et al. 2014, 2; Belaisch, Kodres, Levy, and Ubide 2001, 12.
36. Belaisch, Kodres, Levy, and Ubide 2001, 10.

37. Belaisch, Kodres, Levy, and Ubide 2001, 41.
38. Belaisch, Kodres, Levy, and Ubide 2001, 52.
39. Belaisch, Kodres, Levy, and Ubide 2001, 55.
40. Belaisch, Kodres, Levy, and Ubide 2001, 43.
41. Belaisch, Kodres, Levy, and Ubide 2001, 21–22.
42. Belaisch, Kodres, Levy, and Ubide 2001, 56.
43. Belaisch, Kodres, Levy, and Ubide 2001, 12, 41–42; Langfield and Pagano 2016a, 91.
44. Tarullo 2008, locations 806–807, 1861–1863, 1867–1869; Aggarwal and Jacques 2001. Canadian regulators also set more stringent regulatory practices than required by Basel; Bordo, Redish, and Rockoff 2015, 218, 238.
45. Bair 2012, 28–29. Admati and Hellwig 2013 have made the most forceful case for banks to hold more equity.
46. Greenspan 1998, 167; Tarullo 2008, locations 397–398; Bair 2012, 16, 27.
47. Labaton 2008; Bair 2012, 369.
48. Financial Crisis Inquiry Commission 2011, 155.
49. Bair 2012, 27.
50. Tarullo 2008, locations 3460–3462; Bair 2012, 33–36.
51. Caprio 2013, 17.
52. Shin 2012, 161; Langfield and Pagano 2016b, 16–17.
53. International Monetary Fund 2015b, 21. Belaisch, Kodres, Levy, and Ubide 2001, table 12, had also reported similar differences in profitability.
54. Gordon 2004.
55. Van Ark, O'Mahony, and Timmer 2008.
56. Van Ark, O'Mahony, and Timmer 2008; Cette, Fernald, and Mojon 2016; Poirson 2013.
57. European Council 2000a.
58. Mettler 2004.
59. Geertz 1963.
60. Tabellini and Wyplosz 2004, 34.
61. Blanchard 2004, 3.
62. Rose 2000, 9, 12, 31.
63. Rose 2000, 10.
64. Rose 2000, 32.
65. Rose 2000, 10, 33.
66. Bennett and Shrimsley 2000; Reuters News 2001.
67. Crooks 2003; Reuters News 2001.
68. Bernanke 2004.
69. Santos Silva and Tenreyro 2010; Glick and Rose 2015.
70. Gordon 2004.
71. Sapir et al. 2003, ii.
72. Goldin and Katz 2008.
73. Shin 2012.

74. Shin 2012, 155.

75. Obstfeld 2013, 15–16.

76. Padoa-Schioppa 2004.

77. Trichet 2005; Trichet 2006.

78. Rogoff 2004, 97.

79. For Sinn's remarks, see chapter 3; Bernanke 2004.

80. Walters 1986, 126.

81. Bruno and Shin 2013.

82. See chapter 3.

83. Lane 2006, 47.

84. Malkin and Nechio 2012.

85. Chen, Milesi-Ferretti, and Tressel 2012, 4.

86. L. Svensson 1994.

87. *Economist* 1988a.

88. O'Mahony 2000.

89. Honohan and Walsh 2002, 8, 39–41.

90. *Irish Times* 1996.

91. McManus 1996.

92. *Irish Times* 1996.

93. International Monetary Fund 1997b, 12, 23, 25.

94. International Monetary Fund 1996, 10; International Monetary Fund 1997b, 25.

95. Pogatchnik 2005.

96. *Irish Times* 2006; Ginsberg 2006; O'Toole 2012.

97. *Irish Times* 2006; Byrne 2012, 200.

98. Honohan 2000, 20.

99. Honohan and Walsh 2002, 24.

100. International Monetary Fund 2003b, 15.

101. International Monetary Fund 2003b, 16.

102. International Monetary Fund 2003b, 15.

103. International Monetary Fund 2003b, 16 and the Executive Board's Assessment in the Public Information Notice.

104. Kindleberger and Aliber 2005, 13.

105. Murray 2003.

106. McEnaney 2006.

107. *Sunday Business Post* 2009.

108. Nyberg 2011, iv.

109. Nyberg 2011, 4, 61–62.

110. Nyberg 2011, 31.

111. International Monetary Fund 2006b.

112. International Monetary Fund 2006a.

113. Nyberg 2011, 66.

114. Shiller 2015, 226.

115. International Monetary Fund 2004c, 7–8.

116. International Monetary Fund 2004c, 8.

117. Fernández Ordóñez 2003a; Fernández Ordóñez 2003b.

118. Bank of Spain 2005, 8, 10.

119. Kindleberger and Aliber 2005, 188.

120. Crawford 2005.

121. Crawford 2006.

122. Owen, Adams, and Bale 2006.

123. Santos 2014, 2.

124. Santos 2014, 3.

125. Association of the Bank of Spain Inspectors 2006.

126. International Monetary Fund 2006c, 3.

127. Crawford 2007.

128. Association of the Bank of Spain Inspectors 2006.

129. *El País* 2007c.

130. *El País* 2007b.

131. *El País* 2007a.

132. International Monetary Fund 2007c, 1, 15, 26.

133. Blanchard and Giavazzi 2002, 154.

134. Blanchard and Giavazzi 2002, 148.

135. Blanchard and Giavazzi 2002, 186.

136. Gourinchas 2002, 206.

137. Comments at the end of Blanchard and Giavazzi 2002, 204–205.

138. Reinhart, Rogoff, and Savastano 2003, 1.

139. Reinhart, Rogoff, and Savastano 2003, 1–2.

140. See chapter 3.

141. International Monetary Fund 2003a, 8.

142. International Monetary Fund 2003a, 4.

143. International Monetary Fund 2005, 17; International Monetary Fund 2007b, 17.

144. Artavanis, Morse, and Tsoutsoura 2015.

145. Artavanis, Morse, and Tsoutsoura 2015, 4.

146. International Monetary Fund 2005, 16.

147. International Monetary Fund 2008c, 1.

148. International Monetary Fund 2003d, 3.

149. International Monetary Fund 2002c, 24.

150. The paper, written in 2006, was published a year later; Blanchard 2007, 1.

151. Reis 2013, 156.

152. Gopinath, Kalemli-Ozcan, Karabarbounis, and Villegas-Sanchez 2015, 4.

153. Frankel and Schreger 2013, 247.

154. See chapter 2.

155. See chapter 3.

156. Rose 2005a.

157. European Communities 2004, 9.

158. Sciolino 2005; Moravcsik 2006, 219.

159. Moravcsik 2006, 219–221.

160. Rose 2005a; Thornhill 2005; Agence France-Presse 2005.

161. De Boissieu and Pisani-Ferry 1995; see chapter 2.

162. Sciolino 2005.

163. European Commission 2005a, annex table 12; Ivaldi 2006, 57.

164. Rose 2005b.

165. Youth unemployment data are from the World Bank, see http://data.world-bank.org/indicator/SL.UEM.1524.ZS.

166. Moïsi 2005.

167. Lorentzsen 2005.

168. European Commission 2005a, annex tables 1, 12.

169. Arnold and Thornhill 2005.

170. Campbell 2005.

171. Helm 2005; *Irish Times* 2005; Thorpe 2005.

172. Thornhill 2005b; Walker 2005.

173. Rennie 2005.

174. Sage 2005.

175. European Commission 2005a, annex table 12; European Commission 2005b, annex table 14.

176. Sage 2005.

177. Hollinger and Thornhill 2005; Moïsi 1995; Moïsi 2005.

178. Norris 2005.

179. Landler 2005.

180. Mair 2007, 12.

181. Mair 2007, 7.

182. Dahl 1965, 22.

183. Syal et al. 2005.

184. Jenkins 2005.

185. International Monetary Fund 2007a, 1, 25.

186. International Monetary Fund 2007a, Public Information Notice, 3.

187. International Monetary Fund 2007a, 13, 26.

188. International Monetary Fund 2007a, 25.

189. European Central Bank 2007b.

190. Trichet 2007.

191. Trichet 2008.

192. Orwell 1961, 211.

193. Bordo and James 2008, 19–23.

Chapter 5

1. Financial Crisis Inquiry Commission 2011, 246.

2. Kjetland 2007.

3. Financial Crisis Inquiry Commission 2011, 247.

4. Financial Crisis Inquiry Commission 2011, 246–247.

5. Bernanke 2015, 140–143.

6. Acharya and Schnabl 2010, figure 1.

7. Financial Crisis Inquiry Commission 2011, 248.

8. Mollenkamp and Taylor 2007; Simensen 2007b.

9. *Euroweek* 2007; Buck 2007; Simensen 2007a. On August 17, Sachsen LB would be the first of the German *Landesbanken* to fall. For the troubled history of *Landesbanken*, see Fischer, Hainz, Rocholl, and Steffen 2011; *Economist* 2015.

10. http://www.bnpparibas.com/en/news/press-release/bnp-paribas-investment-partners-temporaly-suspends-calculation-net-asset-value-fo. See also Bank for International Settlements 2008b, 95.

11. Armantier, Krieger, and McAndrews 2008, 2.

12. Bernanke 2015, 139–140.

13. The premium is measured as the LIBOR-OIS spread. LIBOR (the London Interbank Offered Rate) indicates the rate that a large bank pays to borrow from another large bank. The OIS (Overnight Indexed Swap) contract entitles the borrowing bank to receive payments at close to the overnight federal funds rate, the policy rate set by the Fed. Because an OIS is a hedging contract, with no actual lending, it carries no default risk. Hence, the LIBOR-OIS spread reflects the default risk over the term of the loan. For a helpful explanation, see Sengupta and Tam 2008. In Europe, Euro Overnight Index Average (EONIA) is the rate at which banks lend to one another overnight. Hence, the EONIA swap spread is the relevant hedging contract, which ensures a stream of interest payments over the agreed term at close to the overnight rate when no principal is at risk.

14. Normally, the ECB makes available a fixed amount of funds, for which the banks bid. But that day, and on other occasions during the crisis, a bank could borrow as much as it wanted at the prevailing policy interest rate. In ECB terminology, this was "full allotment."

15. European Central Bank 2007a.

16. http://www.federalreserve.gov/newsevents/press/monetary/20070810a.htm.

17. Federal Reserve System 2007a, 11.

18. Federal Reserve System 2007b, 15.

19. Observation by William Dudley, then executive vice president at the Federal Reserve Bank of New York, where he was responsible for the Fed's open market operations; Federal Reserve System 2007b, 11.

20. International Monetary Fund 2008b, 80.

21. Blinder 2013, 94.

22. Personal communication, December 23, 2014. See also Hetzel 2012, chapter 14.

23. Akerlof and Shiller 2009.

24. Blinder 2013, 93.
25. Federal Reserve System 2007c, 112.
26. Federal Reserve System 2007c, 96, 104.
27. http://www.federalreserve.gov/newsevents/press/monetary/20070918a.htm.
28. Kang, Ligthart, and Mody 2015, 25.
29. Kang, Ligthart, and Mody 2015, 6–7.
30. Steelman 2011.
31. King 2016, 168; Svensson 1999.
32. Svensson 1999, 83, 96, 107.
33. Blinder 2013, 94; Bank for International Settlements 2008b, 64.
34. Bank for International Settlements 2008b, 64.
35. Trichet and Papademos 2007.
36. Federal Reserve System 2001, 13; see also chapter 3.
37. See chapter 3.
38. Bernanke 2015, 184.
39. Banks bid simultaneously to pay a common interest rate determined through the auction. The intent was that this would prevent "stigma" associated with a bank's need to borrow from the central bank; Cecchetti 2009, 66.
40. Federal Reserve System 2008a, 12.
41. Federal Reserve System 2008b, 16.
42. Bernanke 2015, 194.
43. http://www.federalreserve.gov/newsevents/press/monetary/20080122b.htm.
44. Interest-rate reductions of this size were last seen in 1981–82, when rates were being brought down from the 18–20 percent level.
45. Isidore 2008.
46. The ECB started publishing "accounts" of its monetary-policy meetings starting in February 2015.
47. Trichet and Papademos 2008a.
48. Trichet and Papademos 2008b.
49. In January 2008, the International Monetary Fund (2008e, table 1) projected that the United States and the euro area would both grow their GDPs by about 1.5 percent in 2008; both forecasts had been lowered by around half a percentage point since October 2007.
50. Trichet and Papademos 2008b.
51. See Barber 2008 for European politicians' characterization of America's economic problems. Among European commentators, Tigges (2007) and Buiter (2007) asserted that the Fed's rate cuts in September and November 2007 were intended to appease financial markets. Buiter (2008) described the unscheduled January 22, 2008, rate cut as a sign of panic.
52. http://www.reuters.com/article/us-bearstearns-chronology-idUSN1724031920080317.
53. Grant 2008.

54. Curran 2008.

55. Reinhart 2011, 76.

56. Cecchetti 2009.

57. Craig 2008.

58. Federal Reserve System 2008b, 4.

59. Wessel 2009, location 2716.

60. Bernanke 2015, 197.

61. Geithner 2014, locations 2507–2511.

62. Geithner 2014, locations 2489–2490.

63. Geithner 2014, location 2492.

64. Geithner 2014, locations 2507–2511.

65. Dungey, Fry, Gonzalez-Hermosillo, and Martin 2006; Pinto and Ulatov 2010.

66. Volcker 2008, 2.

67. Ip 2008; Reinhart 2011, 88.

68. Carswell 2011, 143.

69. Beesley 2008.

70. Beesley 2008.

71. International Monetary Fund 2009e, 29.

72. Federal Reserve System 2008d, 30.

73. Federal Reserve System 2008d, 91.

74. International Monetary Fund 2008d, XV, 1.

75. International Monetary Fund 2008d, XVI.

76. Trichet and Papademos 2008c.

77. Hetzel 2009, 213–214.

78. International Monetary Fund 2008f.

79. Hetzel 2009.

80. Bernanke 2015, 238–239.

81. Trichet and Papademos 2008c.

82. Stark 2008.

83. Trichet and Papademos 2008d.

84. Wiesmann 2008.

85. International Monetary Fund 2008a, 12; Based on more careful retrospective analysis, Robert Hetzel 2014 later reached the same conclusion.

86. Bank for International Settlements 2008b, 143.

87. *Bloomberg Businessweek* 2008; Gow 2008.

88. Landler 2008; *Bloomberg Businessweek* 2008.

89. Financial Crisis Inquiry Commission 2011, 327.

90. Sloan and Boyd 2008.

91. Nocera 2009.

92. Wessel 2009, location 315. Ball 2016 sorts through many competing arguments as to why US authorities allowed Lehman to fail, and he also concludes

that Paulson, sensitive to political criticism for coddling bankers, forced the decision.

93. Reinhart and Rogoff 2008.

94. Rogoff 2008.

95. Geithner 2014, locations 3307–3310.

96. Bernanke 2015, 266, 350, 479, 507.

97. Financial Crisis Inquiry Commission 2011, 350–352.

98. http://www.federalreserve.gov/newsevents/press/other/20080916a.htm; Financial Crisis Inquiry Commission 2011, 350.

99. Geithner 2014, locations 3353–3354.

100. Bovenzi 2015, 178.

101. Shah, Schaefer Muñoz, Stein, and Ramstad 2008.

102. Shah, Schaefer Muñoz, Stein, and Ramstad 2008; Pisani-Ferry and Sapir 2010, 354.

103. *Financial Times Deutschland* 2008; Benoit and Wilson 2008.

104. Cardiff 2016, chapter 4.

105. Cardiff 2016, 41.

106. Cardiff 2016, 41.

107. Shah, Schaefer Muñoz, Stein, and Ramstad 2008.

108. Rogers 2008.

109. Blinder 2013, 178, 198–199.

110. Love 2008.

111. Pylas 2008.

112. Taylor 2008.

113. Schwartz and Bennhold 2008.

114. Love and Willard 2008.

115. Schwartz and Bennhold 2008.

116. See chapter 2.

117. See chapter 2.

118. Bernanke 2015, 326, 347.

119. Rogoff 1985; Alesina and Summers 1993.

120. https://www.imf.org/external/pubs/ft/survey/so/2008/NEW110608A.htm.

121. Keynes 1973 [1936].

122. Akerlof and Shiller 2009, 14–16.

123. Jordà and Taylor 2016.

124. Smyth 2008.

125. Smyth 2008.

126. On the limits of the German stimulus, see Carare, Mody, and Ohnsorge 2009. For the United States, see Krugman 2012, 111.

127. Krugman 2012, 111.

128. Federal Reserve System 2008c, 144–145.

129. Federal Reserve System 2008c, 121–122.

130. Federal Reserve System 2008c, 145–146.

131. Ydstie 2008; NPR 2008.

132. Rogoff 2008b.

133. Coy 2008.

134. Federal Reserve System 2008d.

135. http://www.federalreserve.gov/newsevents/press/monetary/20081216b.htm. The Term Asset-Backed Lending Facility (TALF), to which the December 16 announcement also referred, was set up earlier in November. Under this facility, the US Treasury took on significant credit risk to induce banks to lend. See Akerlof and Shiller 2009, 91–95.

136. Coy 2008.

137. Elliott and Seager 2008.

138. Andrews and Calmes 2008; Coy 2008.

139. http://www.federalreserve.gov/newsevents/press/monetary/20090318a.htm.

140. Fawley and Neely 2013 for details on QE programs of major central banks.

141. http://www.ecb.europa.eu/press/pr/date/2008/html/pr081015.en.html. Instead of lending funds to banks for two weeks, as it normally did under its main refinancing operations, the ECB extended its longer-term refinancing operations (LTROs), which provided funds to banks for longer periods of time. Banks, therefore, reduced reliance on short-term ECB funds and shifted to long-term borrowing. But they had every reason to believe that the ECB's short-term funds would continue to be rolled over. So the value added of the long-term funds was unclear. Moreover, just because banks had longer-term funds from the ECB, that did not mean that the banks were lending more to their customers.

142. Trotta 2008; CBS News 2008.

143. Trichet and Papademos 2008e.

144. Bini Smaghi 2008.

145. CBS News 2008.

146. Strupczewski 2008.

147. Trichet and Papademos 2008f.

148. Suoninen 2009; Gow 2009.

149. Suoninen 2009; Meier 2009.

150. Rooney 2009; Gow 2009.

151. Rooney 2009.

152. Kennedy 2009.

153. Trichet and Papademos 2009.

154. Kennedy 2009.

155. Marsh 2009b.

156. International Monetary Fund 2015c, 7.

157. Mody and Sandri 2012, 204–207.

158. De Larosière et al. 2009, 6.

159. De Larosière et al. 2009, 10.

160. De Larosière et al. 2009, 39.

161. Acharya 2009.

162. Aubuchon and Wheelock 2010.

163. Geithner 2014, locations 4285–4286.

164. https://www.treasury.gov/press-center/press-releases/Pages/tg18.aspx.

165. http://www.federalreserve.gov/newsevents/press/bcreg/20090507a.htm.

166. Bayazitova and Shivdasani 2012, 397.

167. Geithner 2014, locations 5455–5457.

168. Eichengreen and O'Rourke 2010a.

169. International Monetary Fund 2010a, 4.

170. See chapter 2 for the pace of the ECB between 2001 and 2003.

171. See chapter 4.

172. International Monetary Fund 2009f, 1.

173. International Monetary Fund 2009f, 67.

174. International Monetary Fund 2009f, 75.

Chapter 6

1. Melander 2009.

2. International Monetary Fund 2009b, 1, 21.

3. Kalyvas 2015, 150–151.

4. Melander 2009.

5. See chapter 3.

6. Kalyvas 2015, 142.

7. Kalyvas 2015, 156.

8. Reuters News 2009i.

9. Kyriakidou 2009.

10. International Monetary Fund 2009b, 35.

11. See chapter 3.

12. International Monetary Fund 2009d, 55.

13. International Monetary Fund 2009d, 57.

14. Reuters News 2009g.

15. Reuters News 2009h.

16. Reuters News 2009h.

17. Athens News Agency 2009.

18. Reuters News 2009e.

19. Pattanaik 2004.

20. Papaconstantinou 2016, locations 391–395, 541–542.

21. Reuters News 2009b.

22. Kaminska 2009a; Kaminska 2009b.

23. Agence France-Presse 2009b.

24. Reuters News 2009d.

25. Agence France-Presse 2009a; Reuters News 2009f.

26. Merkel 2009.

27. Merkel 2009, 905–906; Reuters News 2009c.

28. This account of Merkel's life is mainly from Packer 2014.

29. See chapter 3.

30. See chapter 5.

31. Packer 2014.

32. See chapter 2.

33. On Steinbrück, see Reuters News 2009a; on Schäuble, see Dow Jones International News 2009 and Cohen 2010.

34. Spiegel Online International 2010e.

35. Rees-Mogg 2008.

36. Spiegel Online International 2011a.

37. See chapter 2.

38. Reuters News 2010d.

39. Mody and Saravia 2006.

40. International Monetary Fund 2010d.

41. Cohen 2010.

42. Reuters News 2010d.

43. Thomson 2010.

44. Federal Reserve System 2010a, 148.

45. Federal Reserve System 2010a, 105.

46. Hadoulis 2010.

47. Hadoulis 2010; Reguly 2010.

48. Crawford, Karnitschnig, and Forelle 2010.

49. European Council 2010a.

50. Thomas and Jolly 2010; Mollenkamp and Bryan-Low 2010.

51. Thomas and Jolly 2010.

52. Mollenkamp and Bryan-Low 2010.

53. Bank of Greece 2010b, 4.

54. Bank of Greece 2010b, 5.

55. Saunders 2010.

56. Dow Jones Institutional News 2010.

57. Casey 2010.

58. Schäuble 2010.

59. Merkel 2010b, 2719.

60. Merkel 2010b, 2719.

61. Eichengreen 2007a.

62. Eichengreen 2010.

63. Pylas 2010.

64. Spiegel Online International 2010e.

65. Casey 2010.

66. Walker and Forelle 2010.

67. See chapter 3.

68. Walker 2010.

69. Lynn 2010, 136–138.

70. Fischer 2010.
71. Fischer 2000.
72. Fischer 2010.
73. See chapter 1.
74. Schelling 1988, 182.
75. Lynn 2010, 138.
76. European Council 2010b.
77. Forelle and Walker 2010.
78. Phillips 2010.
79. Federal Reserve System 2010c, 66–67.
80. Agence France-Presse 2010.
81. Stevis 2013.
82. Barley 2010.
83. Barley 2010.
84. Bank of Greece 2010a, 19.
85. Market News International 2010.
86. *Wall Street Journal* 2010b; for other contemporary advocates of Greek debt restructuring, see International Monetary Fund 2013a, 29, n. 17.
87. Spiegel Online International 2010c.
88. *Wall Street Journal* 2010b.
89. Federal Reserve System 2010b, 38.
90. Federal Reserve System 2010c, 84.
91. Forbes 2012.
92. Spiegel Online International 2010b.
93. International Monetary Fund 2011a; Glover and Richards-Shubik 2014.
94. Bases 2012.
95. International Monetary Fund 2013a, 29, n. 17.
96. Thomas and Paris 2010b; Karnitschnig, Fidler, and Lauricella 2010.
97. Thomas and Paris 2010b; Karnitschnig, Fidler, and Lauricella 2010.
98. Thomas and Paris 2010a.
99. Thomas and Paris 2010a; William Dudley in Federal Reserve System 2010c, 83.
100. William Dudley in Federal Reserve System 2010c, 83.
101. Federal Reserve System 2010c, 68.
102. Federal Reserve System 2010c, 68.
103. Reuters News 2010b.
104. Reuters News 2010f.
105. Walker and Shah 2010.
106. *Wall Street Journal* 2010c.
107. Kaminski 2010.
108. Eurogroup 2010.
109. Reuters EU Highlights 2010.
110. Walker and Karnitschnig 2010.

111. Paterson 2010.

112. Peel 2010b.

113. Paterson 2010.

114. Paterson 2010.

115. Merkel 2010a, 3722; *Deutsche Welle* 2010.

116. Merkel 2010a, 3724; Evans-Pritchard 2010; Reuters News 2010e.

117. Merkel 2010a, 3727.

118. Merkel 2010a, 3722.

119. Reuters News 2010e.

120. Reuters News 2010e.

121. Reuters News 2010e.

122. Papaconstantinou 2016, locations 2158–2160.

123. Papaconstantinou 2016, locations 2155–2157.

124. Papaconstantinou 2016, locations 2206–2207.

125. Sturdee 2010.

126. Sturdee 2010.

127. International Monetary Fund 2010b.

128. International Monetary Fund 2010b.

129. Geithner 2014, locations: 6763–6767, 6812, 6846–6848.

130. International Monetary Fund 2010d, 61.

131. Dow Jones International News 2001.

132. International Monetary Fund 2003c.

133. International Monetary Fund 2010c, 20.

134. International Monetary Fund 2010c, 10, 13.

135. Reported in Blustein 2016, 123.

136. International Monetary Fund 2010c, 65.

137. Krugman 1988; Grossman and Van Huyck 1988; Jorgensen and Sachs 1989; Kovrijnykh and Szentes 2007; Drelichman and Voth 2011.

138. Panizza 2013, 6; Buchheit 2011.

139. International Monetary Fund 2010c, 49 and 14.

140. International Monetary Fund 2010c, 78.

141. International Monetary Fund 2010c, 92.

142. International Monetary Fund 2002a, 15, 17, 32; Schadler 2013.

143. International Monetary Fund 2010c, 96.

144. International Monetary Fund 2010c, 102, 103.

145. Thacker 1999; Copelovitch 2010.

146. Copelovitch 2010.

147. Schneider and Faiola 2010.

148. Jeffries 2010.

149. Walker and Karnitschnig 2010.

150. Walker and Karnitschnig 2010; Peel 2010b; Fletcher 2010.

151. See chapter 1.

152. Wallis and Oates 1998, 166.

153. Eichengreen, Jung, Moch, and Mody 2014.

154. See Blochliger, Charbit, Pionero Campos, and Vammalle 2010.

155. http://www.recovery.gov/Transparency/RecoveryData/Pages/RecipientReportedDataMap.aspx?stateCode=NV&PROJSTATUS=NPC&AWARDTYPE=CGL.

156. Henning and Kessler 2012, 11.

157. Sylla and Wallis 1998, 269.

158. Henning and Kessler 2012.

159. Chernow 1990, 5–6.

160. Wallis and Weingast 2008.

161. Henning and Kessler 2012, 12.

162. Djankov 2014, locations 4206–4207.

163. Winning and Horobin 2010.

164. Santa and Strupczewski 2010.

165. Santa 2010.

166. *Wall Street Journal* 2010a.

167. Rousek 2010.

168. Rousek 2010; Djankov 2014, location 2182.

169. Rousek 2010.

170. See chapter 5.

171. See chapter 5.

172. Such discussions with country authorities are considered confidential, but the IMF has allowed public acknowledgment of these discussions, first in an authorized description of how the IMF works (Ahamed 2014, 111) and then in testimony to the Irish parliament (Chopra 2015).

173. Mody and Saravia 2006.

174. International Monetary Fund 2009c, 22; Kanda 2010 gave a more detailed explanation of these numbers a year later.

175. International Monetary Fund 2009c, 24.

176. International Monetary Fund 2009a, 18. The original findings in Mody 2009 were extended in Mody and Sandri 2012.

177. See chapter 5.

178. Murray Brown 2009.

179. *Irish Examiner* 2009.

180. Murray Brown 2009.

181. International Monetary Fund 2010c, 16.

182. Honohan 2014, location 1344.

183. Honohan 2014, locations 1332–1338.

184. Federal Reserve System 2010d, 24.

185. Lenihan 2010a.

186. Lenihan 2010a.

187. Shah and Enrich 2010.

188. Lenihan 2010a.

189. Lenihan 2010b.

190. Forelle, Gauthier-Villars, Blackstone, and Enrich 2010.

191. Moody's Investors Service 2010.

192. Murray Brown 2010.

193. Mody 2013 summarizes the evidence. See especially Panizza, Sturzenegger, and Zettelmeyer 2009; Levy Yeyati and Panizza 2011.

194. Ludlow 2010, 12.

195. Müller, Reiermann, and Schult 2010.

196. Müller, Reiermann, and Schult 2010.

197. Ludlow 2010, 10–11.

198. Müller, Reiermann, and Schult 2010.

199. See chapter 1.

200. Graham 2010.

201. Graham 2010.

202. Forelle, Gauthier-Villars, Blackstone, and Enrich 2010.

203. Müller, Reiermann, and Schult 2010.

204. Franco-German Declaration 2010.

205. Forelle, Gauthier-Villars, Blackstone, and Enrich 2010.

206. Djankov 2014, locations 2129–2131.

207. Djankov 2014, locations 331–332.

208. Djankov 2014, location 2145.

209. Honohan 2014, locations 1359–1362.

210. Mody 2014d.

211. Chamley and Pinto 2011; Steinkamp and Westermann 2014; Mody 2014c.

212. Ludlow 2010, 20, 22.

213. Forelle, Gauthier-Villars, Blackstone, and Enrich 2010.

214. Castle 2010.

215. Castle 2010.

216. Spiegel and Oakley 2010.

217. Spiegel Online International 2010a.

218. Forelle, Gauthier-Villars, Blackstone, and Enrich 2010; Walker and Forelle 2011.

219. International Monetary Fund 2011d, 32–33.

220. Cottarelli, Forni, Gottschalk, and Mauro 2010.

221. Buchheit, Gulati, and Tirado 2013, 194.

222. Ahearne 2014, locations 431–432, 548–549; MacSharry 2014, locations 1899–1908; Ryan 2014, locations 3866–3870.

223. Chopra 2015; Cardiff 2015; Blustein 2016.

224. Blustein 2016, 175.

225. Cardiff 2015.

226. Chopra 2015.

227. Juncker and Tremonti 2010.

228. Reuters News 2010a for the contemporary discussion; Claessens, Mody, and Vallee 2012 for a description of the many proposals.
229. Peel 2010d.
230. Atkins, Barber, and Barber 2010.

Chapter 7

1. International Monetary Fund 2009f, 32, 130–131.
2. International Monetary Fund 2009f, 29–30.
3. International Monetary Fund 2009f, xi.
4. Wardell 2010.
5. Skrekas 2010.
6. Spiegel Online International 2010d.
7. International Monetary Fund 2010e, 2.
8. Peel 2010a.
9. Peel 2010c; Beste, Reiermann, and Theile 2010.
10. Weisman 2010.
11. Spiegel Online International 2010d.
12. Mody 2015c, 4, table 1, figure 4.
13. Mazzolini and Mody 2014.
14. See chapter 2.
15. Akerlof and Kranton 2010, 4.
16. See chapter 2.
17. See chapter 3.
18. See chapter 2.
19. Blanchard and Leigh 2012, 41–43; International Monetary Fund 2012f, 21. Over the next year, Blanchard and Leigh (2013a and 2013b) published additional research to establish the robustness of their findings.
20. See chapter 5.
21. International Monetary Fund 2012f, 21.
22. Auerbach and Gorodnichenko 2012. The research continued. Two years later, economists Daniel Riera-Crichton, Carlos Vegh, and Guillermo Vuletin (2014) went a step further: during a recession, austerity hurt even more than stimulus helped.
23. Corsetti, Meier, and Müller 2012, 525.
24. Batini, Callegari, and Melina 2012; Baum, Poplawski-Ribeiro, and Weber 2012.
25. Baum, Poplawski-Ribeiro, and Weber 2012, 3–4.
26. Rehn 2013.
27. Portes 2013.
28. Akerlof 2007.
29. Fatás and Summers 2015.
30. Blanchard and Leigh 2013a; Gechert, Horn, and Paetz 2017.
31. International Monetary Fund 2009f, 130.

32. Fatás and Summers 2015, 27.

33. Polidori 2010.

34. Kennedy and Lanman 2010.

35. Federal Reserve System 2010e, 8.

36. Bernanke 2010a.

37. Spiegel Online International 2010d.

38. Koeppen and Blackstone 2011.

39. Trichet and Constâncio 2011a; Carrel 2011.

40. Kang, Ligthart, and Mody 2015.

41. Melander 2011.

42. Forelle and Froymovich 2011.

43. Forelle and Walker 2011.

44. Kowsmann 2011.

45. Banca d'Italia 2011, 14–15.

46. Standard and Poor's Global Ratings 2011; Banca d'Italia 2011, 15.

47. Kollmeyer and Tryphonides 2011.

48. Banca d'Italia 2011, 15.

49. Barta and Whitehouse 2011.

50. Kollmeyer and Tryphonides 2011.

51. International Monetary Fund 2011c, 5.

52. Schneeweiss 2011.

53. Cohen 2011.

54. Trichet and Constâncio 2011b.

55. Thomas and Ewing 2011.

56. Dyson and Featherstone 1996, 279.

57. Dyson and Featherstone 1996, 289.

58. Chapter 2 describes Italy's path to the euro.

59. Draghi 2011b, 2–5.

60. Dowsett and Aguado 2011.

61. Reuters News 2011b.

62. Trichet and Constâncio 2011c.

63. Trichet and Constâncio 2011c.

64. Draghi 2011c, 3; Robinson 2011.

65. Ewing and Werdigier 2011.

66. Krugman 2011.

67. Hetzel 2014.

68. Lyons 2011.

69. Kang, Ligthart, and Mody 2015.

70. Kollmeyer 2011.

71. See chapter 6.

72. Nixon 2011.

73. International Monetary Fund 2011b, 18–21.

74. Acharya, Schoenmaker, and Steffen 2011.

75. Enrich 2011.
76. Chapter 5 tracks the stress in the interbank market during 2008.
77. Kenna 2011.
78. Trichet and Draghi 2011.
79. Trichet and Fernández Ordoñez 2011.
80. See chapters 4 and 5.
81. The premium on dollars is measured by the "cross-currency basis swap spread." See Bank for International Settlements 2008a, 73–86; Chang and Lantz 2013.
82. http://www.imf.org/external/np/tr/2011/tr092311a.htm.
83. Trichet and Constâncio 2011d.
84. Trichet 2011.
85. Samuel 2011; Walker, Forelle, and Meichtry 2011.
86. Gongloff 2011.
87. Kang, Ligthart, and Mody 2015, 45.
88. Draghi and Constâncio 2011.
89. Isidore 2011.
90. Yellen 2011, 11.
91. Federal Reserve System 2011.
92. White 2011.
93. International Monetary Fund 2012g, 1.
94. Conway 2011; Rodrigues and Demos 2011; Kang, Ligthart, and Mody 2015, 46.
95. *Financial Times* 2011b.
96. See chapter 5.
97. Draghi and Constâncio 2012a.
98. European Central Bank 2012, 5.
99. International Monetary Fund 2012d, 5, 6.
100. See chapter 4.
101. Schaefer Muñoz, Enrich, and Bjork 2012.
102. Schaefer Muñoz, Enrich, and Bjork 2012.
103. International Monetary Fund 2012c; Schaefer Muñoz, Enrich, and Bjork 2012.
104. Maatouk and Kollmeyer 2012; Morgan 2012.
105. Maatouk and Kollmeyer 2012.
106. Draghi and Constâncio 2012b.
107. Maatouk and Kollmeyer 2012.
108. International Monetary Fund 2012h, 1.
109. See chapter 4.
110. Chaturvedi 2012; Brat, Román, and Forelle 2012.
111. Bjork, Forelle, and Dalton 2012.
112. Wall 2012.
113. Barley 2012.
114. Shrivastava 2012.

115. Moody's Investors Service 2012b.

116. Moody's Investor Services 2012a.

117. July 23, 2012. The interview transcript is at https://charlierose.com/videos/17697.

118. Chambers 2012a.

119. Dinmore 2012.

120. Fontanella-Khan and Wilson 2012.

121. Izraelewicz, Gatinois, and Ricard 2012.

122. Draghi 2012.

123. King 2016, 227.

124. Geithner 2014, locations 7415–7418.

125. Geithner 2014, locations 7427–7429.

126. Agence France-Presse 2012a.

127. *Deutsche Welle* 2012b.

128. *Deutsche Welle* 2012b.

129. Draghi and Constâncio 2012c.

130. Chambers 2012b.

131. Draghi and Constâncio 2012d.

132. Asmussen 2013.

133. Mody 2014b.

134. Steen 2012

135. Sims 2012, 221; for a virtually identical statement, see also Sims 1999.

136. Sims 2012, 221.

137. Sims 2012, 217–218.

138. Mody 2014b, 13–15.

139. Jones, Atkins, and Wilson 2012.

140. King 2016, 386.

141. Boston 2012.

142. Buchheit and Gulati 2013, 6.

143. Draghi and Constâncio 2013a.

144. Draghi and Constâncio 2013b.

145. Dijsselbloem, Rehn, Asmussen, Regling, and Hoyer 2013.

146. Draghi and Constâncio 2013c.

147. Draghi and Constâncio 2013c.

148. Kennedy and Riecher 2013.

149. Spiegel and Wagstyl 2013.

150. Spiegel and Wagstyl 2013.

151. Spiegel and Wagstyl 2013.

152. Sinn 2013.

153. Wagstyl 2013.

154. Mair 2013, 110–114; Ross 1995, 232–233.

155. Mair 2013, 114.

156. Mair 2013, 114.

157. See chapter 4.

158. Fischer 2011.

159. See chapter 2.

160. Djankov 2014, locations 551–553.

161. Moeller 2012.

162. Spiegel Online 2011 and Molony 2011.

163. DAPD Landesdienste 2012; BBC Monitoring European 2013; Peel 2012.

164. Barroso 2012a.

165. Van Rompuy 2012.

166. Van Rompuy 2012, 7–11; Stevis 2012.

167. Spiegel Online International 2012a.

168. Open Europe 2013b.

169. Open Europe 2013a.

170. Weiland 2013.

171. Packer 2014.

172. Mader and Schoen 2015.

173. International Monetary Fund 2011d, 22.

174. Traynor and Elliott 2011.

175. Mody 2014b.

176. *Times* 2014.

177. Papaconstantinou 2016, 224.

178. See chapter 6.

179. Hope 2011.

180. Reuters News 2011a.

181. Barber 2011.

182. Zettelmeyer, Trebesch, and Gulati 2013, 34–35.

183. Zettelmeyer, Trebesch, and Gulati 2013, 35.

184. Carroll 1899, 33; italics in original.

185. Agence France-Presse 2012c; Papachristou and Graff 2012; Hope and Stevenson 2012.

186. Hope and Stevenson 2012.

187. Spiegel Online International 2012b; von Hammerstein and Pfister 2012.

188. Von Hammerstein and Pfister 2012.

189. Charlemagne 2012.

190. International Monetary Fund 2013b, 30.

191. International Monetary Fund 2012e; International Monetary Fund 2013b, 31.

192. International Monetary Fund 2012e; Eurogroup 2012; International Monetary Fund 2013b, 84.

193. Mody 2012.

194. Ehlers 2011; Walker, Forelle, and Meichtry 2011.

195. Barber 2011; Dinmore, Sanderson, and Spiegel 2011.

196. Dinmore, Sanderson, and Spiegel 2011.

197. *Financial Times* 2011a.

198. *Economist* 2013c.
199. Taylor 2011.
200. Draghi 2013a.
201. Milasin 2013; Thuburn 2013.
202. Agence France-Presse 2013a; Milasin 2013.
203. Ide 2013b.
204. Ide 2013a.
205. Agence France-Presse 2013d.
206. Herenstein 2013.
207. Agence France-Presse 2013c.
208. Aronssohn 2013.
209. Doggett 2013.
210. Donadio 2013.
211. *Economist* 2013b.
212. See chapter 1.
213. See chapter 2.
214. Rentoul 2017.
215. Rentoul 2017.
216. Cottarelli and Escolano 2004.
217. Tombs 2014, 867.
218. European Commission 2013, 70.
219. Tombs 2014, 867.
220. Roland 2012.
221. Agence France-Presse 2013b.
222. https://www.nobelprize.org/nobel_prizes/peace/laureates/2012/announce-
ment.html.
223. Marsh 2012.
224. Gauck 2013.
225. Mazower 2013.

Chapter 8

1. See chapter 2; Dyson and Featherstone 1996, 274, 278.
2. See chapter 2.
3. Walker and Ball 2014.
4. Eurofound 2017, 44; Corak 2013, 82.
5. Kang, Ligthart, and Mody 2015, figure 10.
6. The description in this paragraph is from Jones and Mackenzie 2014.
7. DPA International 2014; Masoni and Piscioneri 2014.
8. Masoni and Piscioneri 2014.
9. Masoni and Piscioneri 2014.
10. *La Stampa* 2012.
11. DPA International Service 2014.

12. Deloitte 2017, 35.

13. Rajan and Zingales 2003.

14. Pellegrino and Zingales 2017.

15. OECD Educational Attainment and Labour Force Status statistics, https://stats.oecd.org.

16. Ang, Madison, and Islam 2011; Goldin and Katz 2008.

17. Mody and Riley 2014.

18. Jones and Mackenzie 2014.

19. BBC News 2014.

20. Dinmore and Segreti 2014.

21. Segreti and Dinmore 2012; Kadri 2013.

22. Yardley, Povoledo, and Pianigiani 2014.

23. Yardley, Povoledo, and Pianigiani 2014.

24. Segreti 2014.

25. Mayr 2014.

26. Dinmore 2013.

27. Münchau 2013.

28. Emmott 2013.

29. *Financial Times* 2014b.

30. *Financial Times* 2014a.

31. Bone 2014.

32. Mackenzie 2016.

33. Dinmore and Fontanella-Khan 2014.

34. Giugliano and Barber 2014.

35. Jones, Segreti, and Dinmore 2014.

36. Spiegel, Wagstyl, and Carnegy 2014.

37. John and Melander 2014.

38. Horobin 2014.

39. See chapter 2.

40. See chapter 2.

41. See chapter 3.

42. See chapter 3.

43. Merkel 2014, 3294–3295.

44. Thomas 2014.

45. Draghi and Constâncio 2014a.

46. Draghi and Constâncio 2014b.

47. *Financial Times* 2014a.

48. Masoni and Piscioneri 2014.

49. Politi 2014.

50. Sanderson 2014a.

51. Bernanke and James 1991, 33.

52. Bernanke 1999, 25.

53. Bernanke 1999, 2–3.

54. Krugman 1998.

55. See chapter 7.

56. Eggertsson, Ferrero, and Raffo 2014, 2.

57. To even out monthly fluctuations, this is the three-month moving average of the annual inflation rate.

58. Modigliani et al. 1998, 13.

59. Banca d'Italia 2013, 29.

60. Banca d'Italia 2015a, 28; Banca d'Italia 2017a, 29.

61. Moghadam, Teja, and Berkmen 2014.

62. Frankel 2014; italics in original.

63. Draghi and Constâncio 2014a.

64. Blackstone 2014b.

65. Mody 2014a.

66. Glick and Leduc 2013; Rosa and Tambalotti 2014.

67. See chapter 3.

68. Reuters News 2014a.

69. Carnegy 2014b; Reuters News 2014c.

70. Carnegy 2014a; Carnegy 2014b.

71. Carnegy 2014a.

72. Aghion, Cette, and Cohen 2014.

73. Barkin 2014; Carnegy 2014a.

74. Draghi and Constâncio 2014b.

75. Reuters News 2014b.

76. Odendahl 2014.

77. Krugman 1998, 139, 161; Bernanke 1999, 17.

78. International Monetary Fund 2014b, 12, 24.

79. International Monetary Fund 2014b, 8, 13.

80. International Monetary Fund 2014a, 27.

81. International Monetary Fund 2014a, 20.

82. Polleschi 2014.

83. Draghi and Constâncio 2014c.

84. Kang, Ligthart, and Mody 2015, 50.

85. Balls 2014.

86. Rey 2013.

87. See chapters 5 and 7.

88. Christensen and Kwan 2014, 4.

89. Pattanaik 2014.

90. Reuters News 2014e.

91. Draghi and Constâncio 2014d; Draghi and Constâncio 2014e.

92. Draghi and Constâncio 2014f.

93. Draghi and Constâncio 2014e.

94. Spiegel 2014.

95. ANSA 2014.

96. Draghi and Constâncio 2014d.

97. Draghi and Constâncio 2014f.

98. Draghi and Constâncio 2014e.

99. Münchrath, Osman, and Cermak 2014.

100. Seith 2014.

101. Dow Jones Institutional News 2014; Münchrath, Osman, and Cermak 2014.

102. Seith 2014; Dow Jones Institutional News 2014.

103. Seith 2014.

104. Blackstone 2014a.

105. International Monetary Fund 2014c, 6.

106. Blomenkamp and Jain 2015.

107. Blinder 2000.

108. Barroso 2012b, 5; Barroso 2013, 5.

109. Piscioneri 2017; Jones 2016.

110. Gordon 2004; Dew-Becker and Gordon 2008.

111. Lucidi and Kleinknecht 2010, 526; Boeri and Garibaldi 2007.

112. Lucidi and Kleinknecht 2010, 539.

113. Hassan and Ottaviano 2013.

114. Engbom, Detragiache, and Raei 2015, 8–10.

115. Engbom, Detragiache, and Raei 2015, 4.

116. Dustmann, Fitzenberger, Schönberg, and Spitz-Oener 2014, 171.

117. Dustmann, Fitzenberger, Schönberg, and Spitz-Oener 2014, 168.

118. Carlin and Soskice 2007, 2.

119. Carlin and Soskice 2007, 1.

120. Poirson 2013, 66.

121. Jones 2014.

122. Barkin 2015.

123. Koranyi and Nasr 2017.

124. ANSA 2017.

125. Aloisi and Pollina 2015.

126. Politi 2015.

127. Politi 2015.

128. "Incidence of Permanent Employment," https://stats.oecd.org.

129. See chapter 4.

130. Sanderson 2014b.

131. Mackenzie 2014.

132. International Monetary Fund 2013c, 35.

133. Sanderson, Barker, and Jones 2016.

134. Draghi 2011a, 5.

135. International Monetary Fund 2011f, 5.

136. Crimmins 2013

137. Aloisi 2013; Crimmins 2013.

138. Reuters News 2007; Michelson 2007.

139. Piscioneri 2007.

140. Dey 2008.

141. Jones 2013.

142. Aloisi, Bernabei, and Ognibene 2013.

143. Jones 2013.

144. Jones and Aloisi 2013.

145. Aloisi and Bernabei 2013.

146. Bone 2013; Agence France-Presse 2013e.

147. Ognibene 2013.

148. International Monetary Fund 2013c, 15.

149. International Monetary Fund 2013c, 13, 15.

150. For helpful details on the banking union, see Baglioni 2016.

151. Münchau 2014.

152. European Banking Authority 2014.

153. See chapter 7.

154. Acharya and Steffen 2014, 3.

155. Politi 2014.

156. Gianetti and Simonov 2013, 139.

157. Hoshi and Kashyap 2015, 119–120.

158. Gianetti and Simonov 2013.

159. Peek and Rosengren 2005; Caballero, Hoshi, and Kashyap 2008.

160. Acharya, Eisert, Eufinger, and Hirsch 2015; Schivardi, Sette, and Tabellini 2017.

161. Thomas 2016.

162. *Financial Times* 2014a.

163. Banca d'Italia 2015b.

164. Unmack 2015.

165. Politi and Sanderson 2015.

166. Reuters News 2015a.

167. Neumann, Kowsmann, and Legorano 2016.

168. Neumann, Kowsmann, and Legorano 2016.

169. European Banking Authority 2014.

170. Moody's Investors Service 2013.

171. Sanderson and Arnold 2016.

172. Longo 2016.

173. Longo 2016.

174. Occorsio 2016; Zingales 2016.

175. Zingales 2016.

176. Za 2017.

177. Paolucci 2017.

178. Za 2017.

179. Za 2017.

180. Bernabei 2017.

181. Reuters News 2017a.

182. *Banker* 2016.

183. Sanderson, Barker, and Jones 2016.

184. Merler 2017.

185. European Banking Authority 2014.

186. European Banking Authority 2016.

187. Acharya, Pierret, and Steffen 2016a; Acharya, Pierret, and Steffen 2016b.

188. Bloomberg Government Disclosure 2017.

189. Bloomberg Government Disclosure 2017; Armellini 2017.

190. Bloomberg Government Disclosure 2017.

191. Sanderson and Hale 2017.

192. https://www.bloomberg.com/news/videos/2016-12-30/zingales-italy-has-to-stick-to-the-rules.

193. Banca d'Italia 2017b, 10.

194. *Libero Quotidiano* 2017.

195. Brunsden and Khan 2017.

196. Mody 2014a; Spiegel 2015.

197. International Monetary Fund 2017c, 12.

198. Draghi and Constâncio 2015.

199. *Deutsche Welle* 2015.

200. Zampano 2015.

201. *Deutsche Welle* 2015.

202. Stewart 2015.

203. Reuters News 2015f; Zampano 2015.

204. Nagle 2017.

205. Abe 2013.

206. Watanabe and Watanabe 2013, 2.

207. "Net bond issuance" equals the value of the new bonds issued minus the value of bonds maturing. International Monetary Fund 2017a, 18.

208. International Monetary Fund 2017a, 18–19.

209. Watanabe and Watanabe 2017, 2.

210. Krugman 2014b.

211. Krugman 2014a.

212. Watanabe and Watanabe 2017, 1.

213. International Monetary Fund 2017a, 18–19.

214. Ducrozet 2016.

215. Draghi and Constâncio 2017.

216. Moghadam, Teja, and Berkmen 2014.

217. Banca d'Italia 2017c.

218. Benink and Huizinga 2015.

219. Diamond 2005, 425.

220. The rest of this paragraph draws on Vannucci 2009.

221. International Monetary Fund 2014c, 15–16.

222. Zampano 2014.

223. Zampano 2014.

224. Evans-Pritchard 2016.

225. ANSA - English Media Service 2016.

226. Becheau 2017, 62–64.

227. When the Argentine "currency-board" arrangement was broken in January 2002, the peso went from parity with the US dollar to 3.4 pesos by the end of the year; International Monetary Fund 2004b, 8.

228. Guglielmi, Suárez, and Signani 2017.

229. Eichengreen 2010.

230. Eurointelligence Professional Edition, July 4, 2017.

Chapter 9

1. See chapters 5, 7, and 8.

2. International Monetary Fund 2012a.

3. See chapter 1.

4. Jones 1981; Acemoglu, Johnson, and Robinson 2002.

5. Pritchett 2000; Jerzmanowski 2006; and Jones and Olken 2008.

6. See chapters 2 and 3.

7. See chapters 4 and 8.

8. See chapter 3 for Greece and chapters 2 and 8 for Italy.

9. Schneider 2016, 48.

10. Masuch, Moshammer, and Pierluigi 2017.

11. Shiller 2017.

12. See chapters 7 and 8.

13. Draghi 2017.

14. Unmack 2017.

15. OECD 2008, 19.

16. Corak 2013, 82; Eurofound 2017, 44.

17. On low returns to college education, see Corak 2013, 87. On emigration of college-educated Italians, see chapter 8.

18. See chapter 8.

19. See chapter 1.

20. The French government's structural balance as a share of potential GDP rose from -1.3 percent in 1999 to -3.8 percent in 2008.

21. International Monetary Fund 2015a, 4–5.

22. Saeed 2017.

23. Hirshleifer 1983.

24. OECD 2016b, 44.

25. Hanushek and Woessmann 2015.

26. OECD 2016b, 46, 218.

27. France 24 2016.

28. Aghion, Cette, and Cohen 2014.

29. Autor 2014, 849.

30. Eurofound 2017; Corak 2013, 82.

31. Aghion, Cette, and Cohen 2014, 80–81.

32. Brown and Barkin 2012.

33. Brown and Barkin 2012.

34. Spiegel 2014.

35. See chapter 4.

36. http://m.ipsos.fr/sites/default/files/doc_associe/ipsos_sopra_steria_sociologie_
    des_electorats_18_juin_20h45.pdf.

37. See chapter 8.

38. Ip 2017a.

39. Leonard 2017.

40. *Guardian* 2017.

41. https://www.economist.com/na/printedition/2017-06-17.

42. Jackson 2017.

43. *New York Times* Editorial Board 2017.

44. See chapter 2.

45. See chapter 4.

46. Agence France-Presse 2017.

47. Macdonald and Rose 2017; Batsaikhan 2017.

48. Macdonald and Rose 2017.

49. Macron 2017a.

50. Darvas 2017.

51. Mayer 2017.

52. Dalton and Troianovski 2017.

53. Horobin 2017.

54. Meichtry 2017.

55. BBC Monitoring 2017.

56. Chassany 2017.

57. See chapter 8.

58. Piketty 2017.

59. Pisani-Ferry and Martin 2017.

60. Agence France-Presse 2012b.

61. Kissler and Angelos 2012.

62. Brierley 2012.

63. Cabral 2013.

64. Reuters News 2014d.

65. International Monetary Fund 2014d.

66. International Monetary Fund 2016d, 21.

67. International Monetary Fund 2017d, 8.

68. International Monetary Fund 2017d, 5, 27, 35.

69. International Monetary Fund 2017d, 32.

70. OECD 2017b, 10.
71. Eurofound 2017, 44.
72. OECD 2017c, 27; International Monetary Fund 2017e, 4.
73. International Monetary Fund 2017d, 35.
74. OECD 2017c, 33.
75. International Monetary Fund 2017d 35.
76. International Monetary Fund 2017e, 23.
77. International Monetary Fund 2017e, 23.
78. See chapter 8.
79. Acharya, Pierret, and Steffen 2016b.
80. Eurointelligence Professional Edition, June 21, 2017.
81. Bloomberg View 2017.
82. Buck and Brunsden 2017; *Fortune* 2017.
83. For earlier episodes of similar capital flight, see chapters 5 and 7.
84. https://www.imf.org/en/News/Articles/2015/09/28/04/54/tr101014d.
85. Darvas 2015.
86. Ip 2017b.
87. International Monetary Fund 2012b, 48.
88. See chapter 7.
89. See chapter 7.
90. Torry 2014; Agence France-Presse 2014.
91. For a summary of the literature, see Mody 2013.
92. Keynes 1920, 268.
93. Galofré-Vilà, McKee, Meissner, and Stuckler 2016.
94. Reinhart and Trebesch 2016.
95. Sachs 2015.
96. Mody 2015d.
97. Mody 2015a.
98. Reuters News 2015d.
99. European Central Bank 2015.
100. Jones and Giugliano 2015.
101. Millar 2015.
102. *Sunday Business Post* 2015.
103. Rankin 2015.
104. http://www.eesc.europa.eu/?i=portal.en.members-former-eesc-presidents-henri-malosse-videos, around minute 55. For a transcript, see *New Europe* 2015.
105. Wettach 2015.
106. Reuters News 2015b; Reuters News 2015c; Reuters News 2015e; Donnellan 2015; O'Donnell and Koutantou 2015; Agence France-Presse 2015.
107. Mody 2016.
108. Thomas 2015.
109. Jackson and Duperry 2015.

110. See chapter 7.

111. Taylor 2015; Alderman and Ewing 2015.

112. Smith 2015.

113. http://www.publicissue.gr/en/2837.

114. Smith 2015.

115. Mody 2015b.

116. Hildebrand, Koch, and Häring 2017.

117. See chapter 6.

118. Thomsen 2013.

119. https://www.imf.org/en/News/Articles/2015/09/28/04/54/tr101014d.

120. Karnitschnig 2017.

121. Papaconstantinou 2016, 212.

122. See chapter 6.

123. See chapter 7.

124. International Monetary Fund 2017b, 28.

125. OECD 2016a, 14.

126. MacroPolis 2017.

127. Kokkinidis 2017.

128. http://www.pewglobal.org/2017/06/05/global-publics-more-upbeat-about-the-economy.

129. Dombrovskis and Moscovici 2017, 10.

130. Becheau 2017, 8, 22–25.

131. See chapter 7.

132. EurActiv.com 2015.

133. *Deutsche Welle* 2017.

134. Roth and Wolff 2017.

135. Fratzscher 2018.

136. Troianovski and Thomas 2017.

137. Charter 2017.

138. Troianovski and Thomas 2017.

139. Macron 2017a.

140. http://media2.corriere.it/corriere/pdf/2017/non-paper.pdf.

141. Reuters News 2017b; Ewing 2017.

142. Scally 2017.

143. Dohmen and Hawranek 2017.

144. Scally 2017.

145. See chapter 5.

146. Williams-Grut 2017.

147. See chapter 8.

148. International Monetary Fund 2016a, 1.

149. Corak 2013, 81; Aghion, Cette, and Cohen 2014, 155; Aghion, Akcigit, Hyytinen, and Toivanen 2017.

150. Moen 2011; BBC Monitoring 2012; Stothard 2012; and see chapter 7.

151. Solletty 2017.

152. See chapter 7.

153. See chapter 2.

154. Robinson 2016.

155. Thal Larsen 2017; Pop and Walker 2017.

156. Walker 2017.

157. Mudde 2017.

158. Khan and McClean 2017.

159. See chapter 6.

160. Bushe 2011.

161. Blaney 2013; Scally 2013.

162. Smith 2014.

163. Coeuré 2013; European Commission 2015.

164. For a detailed account, see Roche, O'Connell, and Porthero 2017.

165. Roche, O'Connell, and Porthero 2017, 1.

166. See chapter 4.

167. http://www.finfacts.ie; Central Bank of Ireland 2017, 13.

168. Regan 2015.

169. Minihan 2015.

170. http://ec.europa.eu/competition/elojade/isef/case_details.cfm?proc_code=3_SA_38373.

171. Kinsella 2017; Glynn and O'Connell 2017.

172. See chapter 6.

173. See chapter 8.

174. Juncker 2016.

175. Judt 2006, location 8497.

176. Juncker 2017.

177. Khan 2017.

Scenarios

1. Dombrovskis and Moscovici 2017, 8.

2. Dombrovskis and Moscovici 2017, 3.

3. Van Rompuy 2012, 9.

4. Kitsantonis 2017.

5. International Monetary Fund 2016c, 12; OECD 2017a, 82.

6. OECD 2017b, 61.

7. International Monetary Fund 2016b; Krugman 2017.

8. Rogoff 2017.

9. Di Lucido, Kovner, and Zeller 2017; Coimbra and Rey 2017.

10. Auer, Borio, and Filardo 2017; Hamilton 2017.

11. Gordon 2016.

12. Gordon 2016; Fernald, Hall, Stock, and Watson 2017. Syverson 2017 confirmed that the long-term decline in productivity growth was real and not due to poor measurement.
13. Shiller 2017.
14. Proaño and Theobald 2017.
15. Mussler 2017.
16. See chapter 1.
17. McDougall and Mody 2014.
18. Cicchi 2013; Słomczyński and Stolicki 2014.
19. Słomczyński and Stolicki 2014, 13.
20. Cicchi 2013, 38, 59.
21. Cicchi 2013, 105.
22. Willsher 2017.
23. Rankin 2017.
24. *Economist* 2014.
25. Clement, Dulger, Issing, Stark, and Tietmeyer 2016.
26. Diamond 2005, 426.
27. Bak 1996.
28. Mody 2014.
29. Buchheit and Gulati 2012, 6; and see chapter 7.
30. See chapter 8.
31. Bagnai, Granville, and Mongeau Ospina 2017.
32. Mody 2015a.
33. Mody 2014e.
34. See chapter 6.
35. See chapter 6.
36. See chapter 3.
37. See chapter 6.
38. Deutsch 1963, 111.
39. Gauck 2013.
40. Merkel 2010c.
41. Mokyr 2016, chapters 11, 12.
42. Mokyr 2016, 173.
43. Aghion, Dewatripont, Hoxby, Mas-Colell, and Sapir 2008.
44. Easterlin 1981; Autor 2014.
45. Aghion Dewatripont, Hoxby, Mas-Colell, and Sapir 2008.
46. Merkel 2010c.
47. Merkel 2010c.
48. See chapter 2 on the 1992 French referendum, chapter 4 on the 2005 referendums, and pages XXX-XXX on the Greek referendum.
49. Becker, Fetzer, and Novy 2016; Colantone and Stanig 2016a, 2016b, 2016c; Autor, Dorn, and Hanson 2013.

50. Brown 2016.

51. Brown 2016; Rodrik 2017.

52. Akerlof and Shiller 2009, 12–13, 25.

53. Becheau 2017, 53–55.

54. See chapter 7.

55. Friedman and Schwartz 1993, 419.

56. Boushey 2017.

Epilogue

1. Juncker 2016.

2. Juncker 2016.

3. See chapter 7.

REFERENCES

Acemoglu, Daron, Simon Johnson, and James Robinson. 2002. "Reversal of Fortune: Geography and Institutions in the Making of the Modern World Income Distribution." *Quarterly Journal of Economics* 117, no. 4: 1231–1294.

Acharya, Viral. 2009. "Some Steps in the Right Direction: A Critical Assessment of the De Larosière Report." VoxEU, March 9. http://voxeu.org/article/critical-assessment-de-larosiere-report.

Acharya, Viral V., Tim Eisert, Christian Eufinger, and Christian Hirsch. 2015. "Whatever It Takes: The Real Effects of Unconventional Monetary Policy." Paper presented at the 16th Jacques Polak Annual Research Conference, International Monetary Fund, Washington, DC, November 5–6. https://www.imf.org/external/np/res/seminars/2015/arc/pdf/Eisert.pdf.

Acharya, Viral V., Diane Pierret, and Sascha Steffen. 2016a. "Capital Shortfalls of European Banks since the Start of the Banking Union," July 29. http://www.sascha-steffen.de/uploads/5/9/9/3/5993642/shortfalls_v28july2016_final.pdf.

Acharya, Viral V., Diane Pierret, and Sascha Steffen. 2016b. "Introducing the 'Leverage Ratio' in Assessing the Capital Adequacy of European Banks," August 1. http://www.sascha-steffen.de/uploads/5/9/9/3/5993642/benchmarking_august2016.pdf.

Acharya, Viral, and Philipp Schnabl. 2010. "Do Global Banks Spread Global Imbalances? Asset-Backed Commercial Paper during the Financial Crisis of 2007–09." *IMF Economic Review* 58, no. 1: 37–73.

Acharya, Viral, Dirk Schoenmaker, and Sascha Steffen. 2011. "How Much Capital Do European Banks Need? Some Estimates." VoxEU, November 22. http://voxeu.org/article/how-much-capital-do-european-banks-need.

Acharya, Viral V., and Sascha Steffen. 2014. "Benchmarking the European Central Bank's Asset Quality Review and Stress Test—A Tale of Two Leverage Ratios."

http://www.sascha-steffen.de/uploads/5/9/9/3/5993642/benchmarking_ceps_
v18nov2014_va_ss.pdf.

Adenauer, Konrad. 1966 [1965]. *Konrad Adenauer: Memoirs, 1945–53*.
Chicago: Henry Regnery.

Admati, Anat, and Martin Hellwig. 2013. *The Bankers' New Clothes: What's Wrong
with Banking and What to Do about It*. Princeton: Princeton University Press.

Aeschimann, Eric, and Pascal Riché. 1996. *La Guerre de Sept Ans: Histoire secrete du
franc fort 1989–1996* [The Seven Year's War: The Secret Story of the Franc Fort
1989–1996]. Paris: Calmann-Levy.

Agence Europe. 1992. "Maastricht—The French Approve the Treaty with 51.05%
'Yes' Votes," September 22.

Agence Europe. 1994. "Stances of Foreign Ministers on 'Hard Core' within the
Union," September 14.

Agence Europe. 1996. "Texts of the Week," January 27.

Agence Europe. 2000. "EP/EMU/Convergence," May 4.

Agence France-Presse. 1994. "Kohl Defends Two-Tier EU, EU Unimpressed."
September 7.

Agence France-Presse. 2002. "France Takes Heat on Deficit Position," May 14.

Agence France-Presse. 2005. "France Rejects EU Constitution, Plunging Europe
into Crisis," May 29.

Agence France-Presse. 2009a. "EU Shares Responsibility for Crisis-Hit
Greece: Merkel," December 10.

Agence France-Presse. 2009b. "Standard & Poor's Places Greek Credit on Negative
Watch," December 7.

Agence France-Presse. 2010. "IMF Team Arrives in Athens: Finance Ministry,"
April 19.

Agence France-Presse. 2012a. "Bundesbank Remains Opposed to ECB Bond
Purchases." July 27.

Agence France-Presse. 2012b. "Germany Says Portugal's Economic Reforms
'Encouraging,'" September 19.

Agence France-Presse. 2012c. "Greek Leftist Leader Begins Government Talks with
President," May 8.

Agence France-Presse. 2013a. "Italian Front-Runner Vows to Continue Monti
Reforms," February 5.

Agence France-Presse. 2013b. "Italy's Monti 'Confident' Britain Would Vote to
Stay in EU," January 23.

Agence France-Presse. 2013c. "Mario Monti: From Crisis Hero to Election's Big
Loser," February 26.

Agence France-Presse. 2013d. "Thousands in Rome for Blogger's Election Rally,"
February 22.

Agence France-Presse. 2013e. "Troubled Italian Bank Is 'Solid': Ministry,"
January 29.

Agence France-Presse. 2014. "Greece Must Pursue Reforms after New Elections," December 29.

Agence France-Presse. 2015. "Bundesbank Opposes More Emergency Funding for Greece: Report," March 27.

Agence France-Presse. 2017. "Macron Says Europe Has 'Lost Its Way,'" July 3.

Aggarwal, Raj, and Kevin Jacques. 2001. "The Impact of FDICIA and Prompt Corrective Action on Bank Capital and Risk: Estimates Using a Simultaneous Equation Model." *Journal of Banking and Finance* 25: 1139–1160.

Aghion, Philippe, Ufuk Akcigit, Ari Hyytinen, and Otto Toivanen. 2017. "Living the American Dream in Finland: The Social Mobility of Inventors." Harvard University, January 6. https://scholar.harvard.edu/files/aghion/files/living_american_dream_in_finland.pdf.

Aghion, Philippe, and Benedicte Berner. 2017. "The Two Pillars of French Economic Reform." Project Syndicate, September 1.

Aghion, Philippe, Gilbert Cette, and Élie Cohen. 2014. *Changer de modèle: De nouvelles idées pour une nouvelle croissance* [Changing the Model: New Ideas for New Growth]. Paris: Odile Jacob.

Aghion, Philippe, Mathias Dewatripont, Caroline Hoxby, Andreu Mas-Colell, and André Sapir. 2008. "Higher Aspirations: An Agenda for Reforming European Universities." Bruegel Blueprint 5, Brussels.

Ahamed, Liaquat. 2014. *Money and Tough Love: On Tour with the IMF*. Bristol: Visual Editions.

Ahearne, Alan. 2014. "The Doctor on Duty." In *Brian Lenihan: In Calm and Crisis*, edited by Brian Murphy, Mary O'Rourke, and Noel Whelan, chapter 1. Kildare: Merrion. Kindle edition.

Akerlof, George. 2007. "The Missing Motivation in Macroeconomics." *American Economic Review* 97, no. 1: 5–36.

Akerlof, George, and Rachel Kranton. 2010. *Identity Economics: How Our Identities Shape Our Work, Wages, and Well-Being*. Princeton: Princeton University Press.

Akerlof, George A., Andrew K. Rose, Janet L. Yellen, and Helga Hessenius. 1991. "East Germany In From the Cold: The Economic Aftermath of Currency Union." *Brookings Papers on Economic Activity* 1: 1–87.

Akerlof, George, and Robert Shiller. 2009. *Animal Spirits: How Human Psychology Drives the Economy, and Why It Matters for Global Capitalism*. Princeton: Princeton University Press.

Akerlof, Robert J. 2017. "Value Formation: The Role of Esteem." *Games and Economic Behavior* 102: 1–19.

Akten zur Auswärtigen Politik der Bundesrepublik Deutschland 1971 [Documents concerning Germany's Foreign Policy [1971]. 2002. Vol. 2, document 228, July 5 meeting. Munich: Oldenbourg.

Alderman, Liz. 2002. "France Reverses Budget Stance, Paris Vows to Meet Deadline." *International Herald Tribune*, May 16.

Alderman, Liz, and Jack Ewing. 2015. "I.M.F. Agrees with Athens That Greece Needs Debt Relief." *New York Times*, July 2.

Alesina, Alberto, and Lawrence H. Summers. 1993. "Central Bank Independence and Macroeconomic Performance: Some Comparative Evidence." *Journal of Money, Credit and Banking* 25, no. 2: 151–162.

Allaire, Marie-Benedicte. 1992. "Mitterrand Launches Maastricht Referendum Campaign." Reuters News, June 5.

Allen-Mills, Tony. 1990. "Touch of Magic Sets Kohl Fair for Poll Triumph." *Sunday Times*, December 2.

Aloisi, Silvia, Stefano Bernabei, and Silvia Ognibene. 2013. "Downfall of the World's Oldest Bank." Reuters News, March 9.

Aloisi, Silvia, and Elvira Pollina. 2015. "Businesses Hail Renzi's Reforms, Urge More to Speed Italy's Upturn." Reuters News, September 7.

Andrews, Edmund. 1998. "Hard Money for a Softer Europe; Leftist Politics Complicates the Job of the Euro's Banker." *New York Times*, November 4.

Andrews, Edmund, 2000. "In the Midst of Upheaval, Yet Out of Public Sight: Horst Köhler." *New York Times*, March 15.

Andrews, Edmund, and Jacky Calmes. 2008. "Fed Cuts Key Rate to a Record Low." *New York Times*, December 16.

Ang, James, Jakob Madsen, and Md. Rabiul Islam. 2011. "The Effects of Human Capital Composition on Technological Convergence." *Journal of Macroeconomics* 33: 465–476.

ANSA. 2014. "Grillo Presses for Euro Exit after 'Migrants Out' Call," October 21.

ANSA. 2017. "Bersani Calls for Government Action on Jobs Act," January 11.

Armantier, Olivier, Sandy Krieger, and James McAndrews. 2008. "The Federal Reserve's Term Auction Facility." Federal Reserve Bank of New York, *Current Issues in Economics and Finance* 14, no. 5. 1–11 https://www.newyorkfed.org/research/current_issues/ci14-5.html.

Armellini, Alvise. 2017. "Italy's MPS Bank to Shed 5,500 Jobs, Close 600 Branches after Bailout." DPA International, July 5.

Arnold, Martin, and John Thornhill. 2005. "Discontent with Government Colours French Vote." *Financial Times*, May 29.

Aronssohn, Daniel. 2013. "Italy's Anti-Austerity Vote Provokes Unease in Germany." Agence France-Presse, February 27.

Arrow, Kenneth J., B. Douglas Bernheim, Martin S. Feldstein, Daniel L. McFadden, James M. Poterba, and Robert M. Solow. 2011. "100 Years of the American Economic Review: The Top 20 Articles." *American Economic Review* 101: 1–8.

Artavanis, Nikolaos, Adair Morse, and Margarita Tsoutsoura. 2015. "Measuring Income Tax Evasion Using Bank Credit: Evidence from Greece." Chicago Booth Research Paper 12-25; Fama-Miller Working Paper, September. http://dx.doi.org/10.2139/ssrn.2109500.

Ascarelli, Silvia. 2001. "Outlook 2001: Bull or Bear, Investors Will Get Another Wild Ride in 2001; In Europe, Some Analysts Are Warning of Economic Turbulence Ahead; Most Tell Investors to Stick with Defensive Plays." *Wall Street Journal Europe*, January 2.

Asdrubali, Pierfederico, Bent Sørensen, and Oved Yosha. 1996. "Channels of Interstate Risk Sharing: United States 1963–1990." *Quarterly Journal of Economics* 111, no. 4: 1081–1110.

Associated Press. 1999. "Euro Trading Begins in Dawn of New Era for World currencies." January 4.

Association of the Bank of Spain Inspectors. 2006. "Letter to the Deputy Prime Minister and the Minister of the Economy and Finance," Madrid, May 26. http://estaticos.elmundo.es/documentos/2011/02/21/inspectores.pdf.

Athens News Agency. 2009. "FinMin [Finance Minister] Briefs ECOFIN on Greek Econ Situation; 'Concerns' Aired by Almunia." October 20.

Atkins, Ralph, Lionel Barber, and Tony Barber. 2010. "Interview with Mario Draghi: Action on the Addicts." *Financial Times*, December 9.

Aubuchon, Craig P., and David C. Wheelock. 2010. "The Geographic Distribution and Characteristics of U.S. Bank Failures, 2007–2010: Do Bank Failures Still Reflect Local Economic Conditions?" *Federal Reserve Bank of St. Louis Review* 92, no. 5: 395–415.

Auer, Raphael, Claudio Borio, and Andrew Filardo. 2017. "The Globalisation of Inflation: The Growing Importance of Global Value Chains." BIS Working Papers 602, Basel, January.

Auerbach, Alan J., and Yuriy Gorodnichenko. 2012. "Measuring the Output Responses to Fiscal Policy." *American Economic Journal: Economic Policy* 4, no. 2: 1–27.

Austin, Tony. 1992. "Danes Voted No from Anxiety over National Identity." Reuters News, June 3.

Autor, David. 2014. "Skills, Education, and the Rise of Earnings Inequality among the 'Other 99 Percent.'" *Science* 344, no. 6186: 843–850.

Autor, David, David Dorn, and Gordon H. Hanson. 2013. "The China Syndrome: Local Labor Market Effects of Import Competition in the United States." *American Economic Review* 103: 2121–2168.

Baglioni, Angelo. 2016. *The European Banking Union: A Critical Assessment*. London: Palgrave Macmillan.

Bagnai, Alberto, Brigitte Granville, and Christian A. Mongeau Ospina. 2017. "Withdrawal of Italy from the Euro Area: Stochastic Simulations of a Structural Macroeconometric Model." *Economic Modelling* 64: 524–538.

Bair, Sheila. 2012. *Bull by the Horns: Fighting to Save Main Street from Wall Street and Wall Street from Itself*. New York: Free Press.

Bak, Per. 1996. *How Nature Works: The Science of Self-Organised Criticality*. New York: Copernicus.

Banca d'Italia. 2011. "Economic Bulletin," Rome, July. https://www.bancaditalia.it/pubblicazioni/bollettino-economico/2011-0003/en_boleco_61.pdf?language_id=1.

Banca d'Italia. 2013. "Economic Bulletin," Rome, October.

Banca d'Italia. 2015a. "Economic Bulletin," Rome, January.

Banca d'Italia. 2015b. "Information on Resolution of Banca Marche, Banca Popolare dell'Etruria e del Lazio, Cassa di Risparmio di Chieti, and Cassa di Risparmio di Ferrara Crises," November 22. https://www.bancaditalia.it/media/approfondimenti/2015/info-soluzione-crisi/info-banche-en.pdf?language_id=1.

Banca d'Italia. 2017a. "Economic Bulletin," Rome, July.

Banca d'Italia. 2017b. "Financial Stability Report," Rome, April.

Banca d'Italia. 2017c. "Survey on Inflation and Growth Expectations," Rome, July.

Banker. 2016. "Italy Makes Its NPL Move," July 1.

Bank for International Settlements. 2008a. "BIS Quarterly Review," March. http://www.bis.org/publ/qtrpdf/r_qt0803h.pdf.

Bank for International Settlements. 2008b. "78th Annual Report." June 30.

Bank of Greece. 2010a. "Financial Stability Report." Athens, July. http://www.bankofgreece.gr/BogEkdoseis/fstability201007_en.pdf.

Bank of Greece. 2010b. "Monetary Policy, 2009–2010." Athens, March. http://www.bankofgreece.gr/BogEkdoseis/NomPol20092010_en.pdf.

Bank of Spain. 2005. *Economic Bulletin*, April. http://www.bde.es/bde/en/secciones/informes/boletines/Boletin_economic/index2005.html.

Barber, Lionel. 1996. "When the Countdown Faltered." *Financial Times*, January 27.

Barber, Lionel. 1998. "The Euro: Single Currency, Multiple Injuries." *Financial Times*, May 5, 2.

Barber, Lionel. 2000. "Late Nights in Nice—Old-Fashioned Power Politics Are on Display at the EU." *Financial Times*, December 9.

Barber, Lionel. 2001. "Eichel's Second Thoughts" *Financial Times*, August 21, 17.

Barber, Tony. 2000. "Euro-Zone Welcome for Greece Overrides Bundesbank Doubts." *Financial Times*, December 20, 8.

Barber, Tony. 2008. "Europe Blames Market Turmoil on US Fiscal Policy." *Financial Times*, January 22.

Barber, Tony. 2011. "Eurozone Turmoil: Enter the Technocrats." *Financial Times*, November 11.

Barkin, Noah. 2014. "Juncker Says France Shouldn't Blame Its Woes on Euro." Reuters News, May 9.

Barkin, Noah. 2015. "Pace of Italian Reforms Is 'Impressive,' Merkel Tells Renzi." Reuters News, July 1.

Barley, Richard. 2010. "Aid Package or No, Big Questions Remain about Greece." *Wall Street Journal*, April 23.

Barley, Richard, 2012, "Bailing on Spain's Bailout," Wall Street Journal, July 21.

Barroso, José Manuel. 2012a. "A Blueprint for a Deep and Genuine Economic and Monetary Union: Launching a European Debate." Brussels, November 30.

http://ec.europa.eu/archives/commission_2010-2014/president/news/archives/
2012/11/pdf/blueprint_en.pdf.

Barroso, José Manuel. 2012b. "State of the Union 2012 Address," September 12.
http://europa.eu/rapid/press-release_SPEECH-12-596_en.htm.

Barroso, José Manuel. 2013. "State of the Union Address 2013," September 11.
http://europa.eu/rapid/press-release_SPEECH-13-684_en.htm.

Barta, Patrick, and Mark Whitehouse. 2011. "Crisis Adds New Risk to Global
Recovery." *Wall Street Journal*, March 16.

Barth, James, Gerard Caprio Jr., and Ross Levine. 2004. "Bank Regulation
and Supervision: What Works Best?" *Journal of Financial Intermediation*
13: 205–248.

Bases, Daniel. 2012. "The Governments' Man When Creditors Bay." Reuters
News, May 23.

Batini, Nicoletta, Giovanni Callegari, and Giovanni Melina. 2012. "Successful
Austerity in the United States, Europe and Japan." IMF Working Paper 12/190,
Washington, D.C.

Batsaikhan, Uuriintuya. 2017. "EU Posted Workers: Separating Fact
and Fiction." Bruegel Blog, August 31. http://bruegel.org/2017/08/
eu-posted-workers-separating-fact-and-fiction.

Battilossi, Stefano, Alfredo Gigliobianco, and Giuseppe Marinelli. 2013. "Resource
Allocation by the Banking System." In *The Italian Economy since Unification*,"
edited by Gianni Toniolo. New York: Oxford University Press.

Baum, Anja, Marcos Poplawski-Ribeiro, and Anke Weber. 2012. "Fiscal
Multipliers and the State of the Economy." IMF Working Paper 12/286,
Washington, D.C.

Bayazitova, Dinara, and Anil Shivdasani. 2012. "Assessing TARP." *Review of
Financial Studies* 25, no. 2: 377–407.

BBC Monitoring. 2012. "Finnish Finance Minister Defends Demand for Greek,
Spanish Collateral," July 25.

BBC Monitoring. 2017. "French Press Unimpressed by 'Vague' Macron Speech," July 4.

BBC Monitoring European. 2013. "German Paper Profiles New Anti-Euro Party,"
April 4.

BBC News. 2000. "IMF Calls for Euro Intervention," September 19.

BBC News. 2014. "Italy PM Letta's Rival Renzi Calls for New Government,"
February 13.

Bean, Charles R. 1992. "Economic and Monetary Union in Europe." *Journal of
Economic Perspectives* 6, no. 4: 31–52.

Becheau, Quentin. 2017. "Legitimacy under Threat: 25 Years of Declining Support
for the European Union." Senior thesis, Woodrow Wilson School of Public and
International Affairs, Princeton University.

Becker, Sascha, Thiemo Fetzer, and Dennis Novy. 2016. "Who Voted for Brexit?
A Comprehensive District-Level Analysis." University of Warwick Working
Paper Series 305, October.

Beesley, Arthur. 2008. "Regulator Starts Inquiry into 'False Rumours' about Banks." *Irish Times*, March 21.

Belaisch, Agnès, Laura Kodres, Joaquim Levy, and Angel Ubide. 2001. "Euro-Area Banking at the Crossroads." IMF Working Paper WP/01/28, Washington, D.C.

Benink, Harald, and Harry Huizinga. 2015. "QE Undermines the ECB's Crisis-Fighting Ability." *Wall Street Journal Europe*, March 13.

Bennett, Rosemary, and Robert Shrimsley. 2000. "Britain 'Could Triple Its Trade with Euro-Zone.'" *Financial Times*, June 26.

Benoit, Bertrand. 2003. "Surprise over Eichel's 'Emotional' Response." *Financial Times*, November 26.

Benoit, Bertrand, and James Wilson. 2008. "State and Banks Bail Out HRE." *Financial Times*, September 29.

Berliner Zeitung. 1998. "Schröder nennt Euro 'kränkelnde Frühgeburt'" [Schröder Calls Euro a "Sickly Premature Baby"], March 27. http://www.berliner-zeitung. de/archiv/Schröder-nennt-euro--kraenkelnde-fruehgeburt-,10810590,9413742. html.

Berliner Zeitung. 2000. "BDI-Chef Henkel: Verheerendes Signal: Wirtschaft warnt vor Beitritt Griechenlands zur Währungsunion" [President of the Federation of German Industries Henkel: Devastating Signal: Industry Warns about Greece's Entry to Monetary Union], May 4, 4, 37.

Bernabei, Stefano. 2017. "Italy's Intesa Fed Up with Bailing Out Weaker Rivals—Update 1." Reuters News, May 24.

Bernanke, Ben. 1999. "Japanese Monetary Policy: A Case of Self-Induced Paralysis?" Princeton University, December. http://www.princeton.edu/ ~pkrugman/bernanke_paralysis.pdf.

Bernanke, Ben. 2004. "The Euro at Five: An Assessment." Peterson Institute of International Economics, Washington, D.C., February 26. https://www. federalreserve.gov/boarddocs/speeches/2004/200402262/default.htm.

Bernanke, Ben S. 2010a. "Aiding the Economy: What the Fed Did and Why." *Washington Post*, November 4.

Bernanke, Ben S. 2010b. "Monetary Policy Objectives and Tools in a Low-Inflation Environment." Speech at "Revisiting Monetary Policy in a Low-Inflation Environment" Conference, Federal Reserve Bank of Boston, October 15. https:// www.federalreserve.gov/newsevents/speech/bernanke20101015a.htm.

Bernanke, Ben S. 2015. *The Courage to Act: A Memoir of a Crisis and Its Aftermath.* New York: W.W. Norton.

Bernanke, Ben. 2016. "'Audit the Fed' Is Not about Auditing the Fed." January 11, https://www.brookings.edu/blog/ben-bernanke/2016/01/11/ audit-the-fed-is-not-about-auditing-the-fed.

Bernanke, Ben, and Harold James. 1991. "The Gold Standard, Deflation, and Financial Crisis in the Great Depression: An International Comparison." In *Financial Markets and Financial Crises*, edited by R. Glenn Hubbard, 33–68. Chicago: University of Chicago Press. http://www.nber.org/chapters/c11482.

Beste, Ralf, Christian Reiermann, and Merlind Theile. 2010. "Plans for Sweeping Cuts—Germany Tries to Plug Gaping Hole in Its Budget." Spiegel Online, May 26.

Binder, David. 1992. "Willy Brandt Dead at 78; Forged West Germany's Reconciliation with the East." *New York Times*, October 9.

Bini Smaghi, Lorenzo. 2008. "Economic Policies on the Two Sides of the Atlantic: (Why) Are They Different?" Collegio Carlo Alberto, Moncalieri, November 7. https://www.ecb.europa.eu/press/key/date/2008/html/sp081107.en.html.

Binyon, Michael. 1989. "New Push for Monetary Union." *Times*, April 15.

Binyon, Michael, Ian Murray, and Philip Jacobson. 1989. "Kohl Breaks with Paris on Delors Plan." *Times*, December 7.

Bjork, Christopher, Charles Forelle, and Matthew Dalton. 2012. "Spain Bond Sale Sends Chill." Wall Street Journal Online, July 20.

Blackstone, Brian. 2014a. "ECB's Lautenschläger Opposes Government Bond Purchases—Update." Dow Jones Institutional News, November 29.

Blackstone, Brian. 2014b. "Italy Finance Minister Says Low Inflation Complicating Economic Reforms; Pier Carlo Padoan Says ECB Should Consider More Steps to Boost Growth." Wall Street Journal Online, April 10.

Blair, Alasdair. 1999. *Dealing with Europe: Britain and the Negotiation of the Maastricht Treaty*. Aldershot: Ashgate.

Blanchard, Olivier. 2004. "The Future of Europe." *Journal of Economic Perspectives* 18, no. 4: 3–26.

Blanchard, Olivier. 2007. "Adjustment within the Euro: The Difficult Case of Portugal." *Portuguese Economic Journal* 6: 1–21.

Blanchard, Olivier, and Francesco Giavazzi. 2002. "Current Account Deficits in the Euro Area: The End of the Feldstein-Horioka Puzzle?" *Brookings Papers on Economic Activity* 2: 147–186.

Blanchard, Olivier, and Daniel Leigh. 2012. "Are We Underestimating Short-Term Fiscal Multipliers?" In International Monetary Fund, "World Economic Outlook: Coping with High Debt and Sluggish Growth," Box 1.1. Washington, D.C., October.

Blanchard, Olivier, and Daniel Leigh. 2013a. "Fiscal Consolidation: At What Speed?" VoxEU, May 3. http://www.voxeu.org/article/fiscal-consolidation-what-speed.

Blanchard, Olivier, and Daniel Leigh. 2013b. "Growth Forecast Errors and Fiscal Multipliers." IMF Working Paper 13/1, Washington, D.C.

Blaney, Ferghal. 2013. "Merkel Hails Ireland and Austerity Policy." *Irish Daily Mail*, September 24.

Blankart, Charles. 2013. "Oil and Vinegar: A Positive Fiscal Theory of the Euro Crisis." *Kyklos* 66, no. 3: 497–528.

Blinder, Alan. 2013. *After the Music Stopped: The Financial Crisis, the Response, and the Work Ahead*. New York: Penguin.

Blitz, James. 1998. "Italy's Picture of Health: The Extraordinary Transformation of the Country's Prospects of Joining Europe's Single Currency." *Financial Times*, January 21, 21.

Blöchliger, Hansjörg, Claire Charbit, José Maria Pinero Campos, and Camila Vammalle. 2010. "Sub-Central Governments and the Economic Crisis: Impact and Policy Responses." OECD Economics Department Working Paper 752, Paris.

Blomenkamp, Felix, and Rachit Jain. 2015. "The ECB's ABS Purchases—Catalyst or Dud?" PIMCO Viewpoints Blog, October. https://www.pimco.com/insights/viewpoints/viewpoints/the-ecbs-abs-purchases-catalyst-or-dud.

Bloomberg Businessweek. 2008. "The ECB Pulls the Rate-Hike Trigger," July 3.

Bloomberg Government Disclosure. 2017. "Banca Monte dei Paschi di Siena SpA 2017–2021 Restructuring Plan Approved by the European Commission Call—Final," July 5.

Bloomberg View. 2017. "Europe (Finally) Shows How to Deal with a Failing Bank," June 8.

Blustein, Paul. 2016. *Laid Low: Inside the Crisis That Overwhelmed Europe and the IMF*. Waterloo, Canada: Center for International Governance and Innovation.

Boer, Martin. 1999. "EU Removes Greece from Deficit List." *Wall Street Journal Europe*, November 30.

Boeri, Tito, and Pietro Garibaldi. 2007. "Two Tier Reforms of Employment Protection: A Honeymoon Effect?" *Economic Journal* 117, no. 521: F357–F385.

Böll, Sven, Christian Reiermann, Michael Sauga, and Klaus Wiegrefe. 2012. "New Documents Shine Light on Euro Birth Defects." Spiegel Online, August 5. http://www.spiegel.de/international/europe/euro-struggles-can-be-traced-to-origins-of-common-currency-a-831842-druck.html.

Bone, James. 2013. "Draghi 'Not to Blame' for Scandal." *Times*, January 29.

Bone, James. 2014. "Italy's Youngest Prime Minister Promises Revolution on Twitter." *Times*, February 23.

Bordo, Michael. 1981. "The Classical Gold Standard: Some Lessons for Today." *Federal Reserve Bank of St. Louis Review* 63, no. 6: 1–17.

Bordo, Michael. 1993. "The Bretton Woods International Monetary System: A Historical Overview." In *A Retrospective on the Bretton Woods System: Lessons for International Monetary Reform*, edited by Michael D. Bordo and Barry Eichengreen. Chicago: University of Chicago Press. http://www.nber.org/chapters/c6867.

Bordo, Michael, Angela Redish, and Hugh Rockoff. 2015. "Why Didn't Canada Have a Banking Crisis in 2008 (or in 1930, or 1907, or . . .)?" *Economic History Review* 68, no. 1: 218–243.

Boston, William. 2012. "WSJ: Merkel Backs ECB Bond Buying." Dow Jones News Service, September 17.

Boughton, James M. 2012. *Tearing Down Walls: The International Monetary Fund 1990–1999*. Washington, D.C.: International Monetary Fund.

Boushey, Heather. 2017. "Equitable Growth in Conversation: Robert Solow." Washington Center for Equitable Growth, July 20, http://equitablegrowth.org/research-analysis/equitable-growth-in-conversation-robert-solow/.

Bovenzi, John F. 2015. *Inside the FDIC: Thirty Years of Bank Failures, Bailouts, and Regulatory Battles*. Hoboken: Wiley.

Bowley, Graham. 2004. "EU Warns on Deficit of Greece Commission Seeks New Eurostat Powers." *International Herald Tribune*, December 23.

Boyes, Roger. 1993. "Strict Speed Limits Imposed on Bonn's Road to Maastricht." *Times*, October 13.

Boyes, Roger. 1998a. "Germans Turning Green with Anxiety." *Times*, December 29, 10.

Boyes, Roger. 1998b. "Kohl Risks Being Booed Off Stage If Euro-Juggling Act Falters." *Times*, January 19.

Boyes, Roger. 2002. "The Euro Chancellor." *Times*, February 22.

Braithwaite, Tom. 2014. "Alternative Stress Tests Find French Banks Are Weakest in Europe." *Financial Times*, October 27.

Brandt, Willy. 1978. *People and Politics: The Years 1960–1975*, London: Collins.

Brandt, Willy. 1992. *My Life in Politics*. New York: Viking.

Brat, Ilan, David Román, and Charles Forelle. 2012. "Spanish Worries Feed Global Fears." Wall Street Journal Online, July 20.

Brehier, Thierry. 1992. "The Results of the French Referendum on the European Union." *Le Monde*, September 22.

Bremner, Charles. 1996. "Santer Tells Euro Doubters 'Clock Cannot Be Stopped.'" XXXXXX, January 25.

Brierley, David. 2012. "Portugal's Banks Take Pounding." *SNL European Financials Daily*, December 6.

Brittan, Samuel. 1970. "The Politics of Monetary Union." *Financial Times*, November 16, 29.

Brock, George. 1992. "War Hero Resists New Conquest—Maastricht Highlights National Dilemma." *Times*, June 1.

Brown, Gordon. 2016. "The Key Lesson of Brexit Is That Globalisation Must Work for All of Britain." *Guardian*, June 29.

Brown, Stephen, and Noah Barkin. 2012. "France's German-Speaking PM Tries to Reassure Berlin—Update 1." Reuters News, November 15.

Brown-Humes, Christopher. 2000. "Swedish Support for Euro Dims." *Financial Times*, October 2.

Brown-Humes, Christopher, and Clare MacCarthy. 2000. "Denmark Rejects Joining Euro: Referendum Deals Blow to Single Currency." *Financial Times*, September 29.

Brulé, Michel. 1992. "France after Maastricht." *Public Perspective*, November/December: 28–30.

Bruno, Valentina, and Hyun Song Shin. 2013. "Capital Flows, Cross-Border Banking and Global Liquidity." National Bureau of Economic Research Working Paper 19038, May. http://www.nber.org/papers/w19038.

Brunsden, Jim, and Mehreen Khan. 2017. "Brussels Warns Rome to Cut Record Debt." *Financial Times*, February 23.

Buchan, David. 1992. "Mutiny Rocks EC Ship of State: Denmark's Rejection of the Maastricht Treaty Poses a Grave Threat to Hopes." *Financial Times*, June 4.

Buchan, David, Philip Stephens, and William Dawkins. 1989. "EC Moves on Monetary Union; Delors First Stage Agreed, Thatcher Opposes Further Steps." *Financial Times*, June 28, 1.

Buchheit, Lee. 2011. "Six Lessons from Prior Debt Restructurings." Paper prepared for "Resolving the European Debt Crisis" conference hosted by Peterson Institute for International Economics and Bruegel, Chantilly, France, September 13–14. https://piie.com/publications/papers/buchheit20110913.pdf.

Buchheit, Lee, and Mitu Gulati. 2012. "The Eurozone Debt Crisis: The Options Now." *Capital Markets Law Journal* (December): 1–8.

Buchheit, Lee C., and G. Mitu Gulati. 2013. "The Gathering Storm: Contingent Liabilities in a Sovereign Debt Restructuring." August 21. Duke Law Scholarship Repository, https://scholarship.law.duke.edu/faculty_scholarship/3112/

Buchheit, Lee, G. Mitu Gulati, and Ignacio Tirado. 2013. "The Problem of Holdout Creditors in Eurozone Sovereign Debt Restructurings." *Butterworths Journal of International Banking and Financial Law* (April): 191–194.

Buck, Tobias. 2007. "National Reputation Hangs on IKB Rescue." *Financial Times*, August 2.

Buck, Tobias, and Jim Brunsden. 2017. Emergency Funds Failed to Save Banco Popular from Death Spiral." *Financial Times*, June 8.

Buerkle, Tom. 2000. "Euro Unscathed by Danish 'No' but Vote Sharpens Divisions in EU over Its Currency Policy." *International New York Times*, September 30.

Buiter, Willem. 2007. "Should the Fed Raise Interest Rates?" Willem Buiter's Mavercon Blog, November 30. http://blogs.ft.com/maverecon/2007/11/should-the-fed-html/#axzz3kCcMg3th.

Buiter, Willem. 2008. "The Bernanke Put: Buttock-Clenching Monetary Policymaking at the Fed." Willem Buiter's Mavercon Blog, January 22. http://blogs.ft.com/maverecon/2008/01/the-bernanke-puhtml/#axzz3kysaxFzY.

Bundesverband der Deutschen Industrie. 1991. "BDI: Wirtschafts- und Währungsunion nicht um jeden Preis" [BDI: Economic and Monetary Union Not at Any Cost]. Press release on the occasion of the hearing of the Finance Committee of the Bundestag, September 18, Cologne.

Burda, Michael. 2009. "Half-Empty or Half-Full: East Germany Two Decades Later." VoxEU, May 9. http://www.voxeu.org/article/half-empty-or-half-full-east-germany-two-decades-later.

Bushe, Andrew. 2011. "Austerity-Hit Ireland Is Poster Boy for Euro Bailout Success." Agence France-Presse, November 26.

Butler, Kathlerine. 1998. "Countdown to the Euro: View from Ireland," *Independent*, December 29.

Byrne, Elaine. 2012. *Political Corruption in Ireland, 1922–2010: A Crooked Harp?* Manchester: Manchester University Press.

Caballero, Ricardo, Takeo Hoshi, and Anil Kashyap. 2008. "Zombie Lending and Depressed Restructuring in Japan." *American Economic Review* 98: 1943–1977.

Cabral, Thomas. 2013. "Portugal Destabilised by Shock Finance Minister Exit." Agence France-Presse, July 2.

Cameron, David. 1992. "The 1992 Initiative: Causes and Consequences." In *Euro-Politics: Institutions and Policymaking in the "New" European Community*, edited by Alberta M. Sbragia. Washington, D.C.: Brookings Institute.

Campbell, Andrea Louise. 2012. "Policy Makes Mass Politics." *Annual Review of Political Science* 15: 333–351.

Campbell, Matthew. 2005. "France Scoffs As Chirac Places His Faith in a Noble Saviour; Euro Crisis." *Sunday Times*, June 5.

Caprio, Gerard Jr. 2013. "Financial Regulation after the Crisis: How Did We Get Here, and How Do We Get Out?" LSE Financial Markets Group Special Paper 226, November. http://www.lse.ac.uk/fmg/workingPapers/specialPapers/PDF/sp226.pdf.

Carare, Alina, Ashoka Mody, and Franziska Ohnsorge. 2009. "The German Fiscal Stimulus in Perspective." VoxEU, January 23. http://www.voxeu.org/article/german-fiscal-stimulus-package-perspective.

Cardiff, Kevin. 2016. *Recap: Inside Ireland's Financial Crisis*. Dublin: The Liffey Press.

Carli, Guido. 1993. *Cinquant'anni di vita italiana* [Fifty Years of an Italian Life]. Rome and Bari: Editori Laterza.

Carlin, Wendy, and David Soskice. 2007. "Reforms, Macroeconomic Policy, and Economic Performance in Germany." Centre for Economic Policy Research Discussion Paper 6415. www.cepr.org/pubs/dps/DP6415.asp.

Carlin, Wendy, and David Soskice. 2009. "German Economic Performance: Disentangling the Role of Supply-Side Reforms, Macroeconomic Policy and Coordinated Economy Institutions." *Socio-Economic Review* 7, no. 1: 67–99.

Carnegy, Hugh. 2014a. "France Steps Up Campaign to Weaken Euro." *Financial Times*, May 8.

Carnegy, Hugh. 2014b. "France Urges Action to Lower Euro's Value." *Financial Times*, April 29.

Caron, Jules. 2011. "Switzerland Pegs Franc to Euro, Analysts Say Defence Risky." Agence France-Presse, September 6.

Carrel, Paul. 2011. "ECB Hikes Rates, Ready to Move Again if Necessary." Reuters News, April 7.

Carroll, Lewis. 1899. *Alice's Adventures in Wonderland*. New York: M. F. Mansfield and A. Wessels.

Carswell, Simon. 2011. *Anglo Republic: Inside the Bank That Broke Ireland*. London: Penguin.

Casey, Michael. 2010. "No Need for Greek Bailout Now, France's Lagarde Says." Wall Street Journal Online, March 13.

Castle, Stephen. 2010. "E.U. Splits on Plan for Handling Crises; Differences on Demands That Investors Share Pain Cloud Accord on Action." *International Herald Tribune*, October 30.

CBS News. 2008. "Big Rate Cuts As Stock Markets Sink," November 6.

Cecchetti, Stephen G. 2009. "Crisis and Responses: The Federal Reserve in the Early Stages of the Financial Crisis." *Journal of Economic Perspectives* 23, no. 1: 51–76.

Central Bank of Ireland. 2017. "Q2 Central Bank Quarterly Bulletin." Dublin, April.

Cette, Gilbert, John Fernald, and Benoit Mojon. 2016. "The Pre-Great Recession Slowdown in Productivity." Banque de France Working Paper 586, March. https://ssrn.com/abstract=2758506 or http://dx.doi.org/10.2139/ssrn.2758506.

Chambers, Madeline. 2012a. "Moody's Warning Fuels German Resentment over Euro Bailouts." Reuters News, July 24.

Chambers, Madeline. 2012b. "UPDATE 1—German lawmakers demand ECB voting reform, oppose bond buying." Reuters News, August 16.

Chamley, Christophe, and Brian Pinto. 2011. "Why Official Bailouts Tend Not to Work: An Example Motivated by Greece 2010." The Economists' Voice, February. www.bepress.com/ev.

Chang, Michael, and Carl Lantz. 2013. "Credit Suisse Basis Points: Cross-Currency Basis Swaps." New York: Credit Suisse, April 19 https://doc.research-and-analytics.csfb.com/docView?language=ENG&format=PDF&source_id=csplusresearchcp&document_id=1014795411&serialid=mW557HA4UbeT5Mrww553YSwfqEwZsxUA4zqNSkp5JUg%3D.

Charlemagne. 2012. "Greek Debt: A Bail-Out by Any Other Name." *Economist*, November 27.

Charrel, Marie. 2017. "Les mesures fiscales du gouvernement pourraient creuser les inégalités" [The Government's Fiscal Measures Could Increase Inequality]. Le Monde Economie, July 12.

Chassany, Anne-Sylvaine. 2017. "Macron Pledges to Give Louder Voice to Smaller Parties." *Financial Times*, July 4.

Chaturvedi, Neelabh. 2012. "Spanish Bond Yields Reach Euro-Era High." Wall Street Journal Online, July 20.

Chen, Ruo, Gian Maria Milesi-Ferretti, and Thierry Tressel. 2012. "External Imbalances in the Euro Area." WP/12/236, Washington, D.C., September.

Chernow, Ron. 1990. *The House of Morgan*. New York: Simon & Schuster.

Chopra, Ajai. 2015. "Joint Committee of Inquiry into the Banking Crisis: Witness Statement of Ajai Chopra." House of the Oireachtas, Dublin, September 10. https://inquiries.oireachtas.ie/banking/wp-content/uploads/2015/09/Ajay-Chopra-Opening-Statement.pdf.

Christensen, Jens, and Simon Kwan. 2014. "Assessing Expectations of Monetary Policy." FRBSF Economic Letter 2014-27, September 8.

Cicchi, Lorenzo. 2013. "The Logic of Voting Behaviour in the European Parliament: New Insights on Party Group Membership and National Affiliation As Determinants of Vote." IMT PhD thesis, Lucca. http://e-theses.imtlucca.it/124/

Claessens, Stijn, Ashoka Mody, and Shahin Vallee. 2012. "Making Sense of Eurobond Proposals." VoxEU, August 17. http://voxeu.org/article/making-sense-eurobond-proposals.

Clemens, Clay. 1998a. "Introduction: Assessing the Kohl Legacy." *German Politics* 7, no. 1: 1–16.

Clemens, Clay. 1998b. "Party Management As a Leadership Resource: Kohl and the CDU/CSU." *German Politics* 7, no. 1: 91–119.

Clement, Wolfgang, Rainer Dulger, Otmar Issing, Jürgen Stark, and Hans Tietmeyer. 2016. "Zurück zur Eigenverantwortung" [Back to Self-Responsibility]. *Frankfurter Allgemeine Zeitung*, October 21.

CNN Money. 2000. "New IMF Chief Talks Tough," September 20.

Coeuré, Benoît. 2013. "Adjustment and Growth in the Euro Area Economies." Nova School of Business and Economics and the Banco de Portugal, Lisbon, February 22. https://www.ecb.europa.eu/press/key/date/2013/html/sp130222.en.html.

Cohen, Adam. 2010. "Two EU Ministers: No Bailout for Greece." Wall Street Journal Online, January 18.

Cohen, Roger. 1998. "Kohl and His Story: New Chapter, or History?" *New York Times*, August 14.

Cohen, Roger. 1999. "Schröder Moves to Germany, and So Does Germany's Center of Gravity." *New York Times*, August 24. http://www.nytimes.com/1999/08/24/world/schroder-moves-and-so-does-germany-s-center-of-gravity.html.

Cohen, Sabrina. 2011. "Italy's Banks Sail in Choppy Waters." *Wall Street Journal Asia*, July 5.

Coimbra, Nuno, and Hélène Rey. 2017. "Financial Cycles with Heterogeneous Intermediaries." National Bureau of Economic Research Working Paper 23245.

Colantone, Italo, and Piero Stanig. 2016a. "Global Competition and Brexit." BAFFI CAREFIN Centre Research Paper 2016-44, November 16. https://papers.ssrn.com/sol3/papers.cfm?abstract_id=2870313.

Colantone, Italo, and Piero Stanig. 2016b. "The Real Reason the U.K. Voted for Brexit? Job Losses to Chinese Competition." *Washington Post*, July 7.

Colantone, Italo, and Piero Stanig. 2016c. "The Trade Origins of Nationalist Protectionism: Import Competition and Voting Behavior in Western

Europe." Bocconi University, Milan, July 8. https://drive.google.com/file/d/0B3QouNVpd9TfSGZ5VHBUcnAwSE0/preview.

Conway, Brendan. 2011. "Stocks Find Little Solace in Europe; Dow Industrials Sink 198 Points after Euro-Zone Summit Hits Bumps; Banks Suffer Heavy Losses." Wall Street Journal Online, December 8.

Cook, Lorne. 2003. "Germany Cannot Respect EU Budget Constraints: Eichel." Agence France-Presse, May 11.

Cook, Peter. 1998. "What Italian Renaissance?" Globe and Mail, February 2, B2.

Copelovitch, Mark S. 2010. "Master or Servant? Common Agency and the Political Economy of IMF Lending." International Studies Quarterly 54: 49–77.

Corak, Miles. 2013. "Income Inequality, Equality of Opportunity, and Intergenerational Mobility." Journal of Economic Perspectives 27, no. 3: 79–102.

Corcoran, Jody. 2011. "Our EU Masters Will Make Us a Vassal State." Sunday Independent (Ireland), July 24.

Cornwell, Rupert. 1985. "Kohl Sets Out Goals for West Germany at Milan EEC." Financial Times, June 8, 2.

Corsetti, Giancarlo, André Meier, and Gernot J. Müller. 2012. "What Determines Government Spending Multipliers?" Economic Policy 27: 521–565.

Corsetti, Giancarlo, and Paolo Pesenti. 1999. "Stability, Asymmetry, and Discontinuity: The Launch of European Monetary Union." Brookings Papers on Economic Activity 1999, no. 2: 295–372.

Cottarelli, Carlo, and Julio Escolano. 2004. "Assessing the Assessment: A Critical Look at the June 2003 Assessment of the United Kingdom's Five Tests for Euro Entry." IMF Working Paper WP/04/116, Washington, D.C., July.

Cottarelli, Carlo, Lorenzo Forni, Jan Gottschalk, and Paolo Mauro. 2010. "Default in Today's Advanced Economies: Unnecessary, Undesirable, and Unlikely." IMF Fiscal Affairs Department, Washington, D.C.

Council of Economic and Financial Affairs. 2003. "2546th Council Meeting: Press Release." Brussels, November 25. http://ec.europa.eu/economy_finance/economic_governance/sgp/pdf/11_council_press_releases/2003-11-25_council_press_release_en.pdf.

Council of the European Communities. 2003. "Recommendation for a Council Decision." SEC 1316 final, November 18. http://ec.europa.eu/economy_finance/economic_governance/sgp/pdf/30_edps/104-08_commission/2003-11-18_de_104-8_commission_en.pdf.

Council of the European Union. 2003a. "2480th Council Meeting—Economic and Financial Affairs." C/03/15, 5506/3 (Presse 15), Brussels, January 21. http://europa.eu/rapid/press-release_PRES-03-15_en.htm?locale=en.

Council of the European Union. 2003b. "Council Decision of 3 June 2003 on the Existence of an Excessive Deficit in France—Application of Article 104(6) of the Treaty Establishing the European Community." 2003/487/EC, Brussels.

http://ec.europa.eu/economy_finance/economic_governance/sgp/pdf/30_edps/
104-06_council/2003-06-03_fr_104-6_council_en.pdf.

Cowell, Alan. 2000. "Britain Winces at Denmark's Rejection of the Euro."
New York Times, September 30.

Coy, Peter. 2008. "Bernanke Attacks the Recession with Force." *Bloomberg
Businessweek*, December 16.

Craig, Susanne. 2008. "Lehman Finds Itself in Center of Storm." *Wall Street Journal*,
March 18.

Crawford, David, Matthew Karnitschnig, and Charles Forelle. 2010. "Europe
Weighs Rescue Plan for Greece; Germany Leads Talks on Backing Greek
Debt; Markets Cheer Bid to Stave Off Crisis." Wall Street Journal Online,
February 10.

Crawford, Leslie. 2005. "Hot Money Pays for Boom on Spain's Costa del
Crime: Spanish Police Blow Whistle on Silent Invasion of the Mafia and Its
Links to the Construction and Property Industries." *Financial Times*, March 23.

Crawford, Leslie. 2006. "Spanish Mayor Held over Property Graft." *Financial Times*,
March 30.

Crawford, Leslie. 2007. "'Bubble' Fears Hit Spanish Property." *Financial Times*,
April 20.

Crawshaw, Steve. 1994. "Europe, a Matter for the Heart." *Independent*,
September 30.

Criddle, Byron. 1993. "The French Referendum on the Maastricht Treaty
September 1992." *Parliamentary Affairs* 46, no. 2: 228–238.

Crooks, Ed. 2003. "The Five Tests—If Gordon Brown Says 'No' to the Euro Now,
Can Britain Say 'Yes' in a Few Years' Time?" *Financial Times*, May 3.

Crossland, David. 2001. "Germany May Reshape Economic Policy As Growth
Slows." Reuters News, October 19.

Curran, Rob. 2008. "US Stocks Down As Bear Stearns Stirs Market Panic—
Update." Dow Jones News Service, March 14.

Dafoe, Allan, and Nina Kelsey. 2014. "Observing the Capitalist Peace: Examining
Market-Mediated Signaling and Other Mechanisms." *Journal of Peace Research*
51: 619–633.

Dahl, Robert. 1965. "Reflections on Opposition in Western Democracies."
Government and Opposition 1, no. 1: 7–24.

Dale, Reginald. 1976. "Greece Not Ready for Full Membership, Says EEC."
Financial Times, January 30, 5.

Dalton, Matthew, and Anton Troianovski. 2017. "Angela Merkel Shows
Willingness to Join France in Bolstering EU." Wall Street Journal Online,
May 16.

DAPD Landesdienste. 2012. "Wissenschaftler wollen mit Euro-Themen
Bundestagswahlkampf Machen" [Academics Want the Euro to Be Debated in
the Election Campaign], September 21.

De Boissieu, Christian, and Jean Pisani-Ferry. 1995. "The Political Economy of French Economic Policy and the Transition to EMU." CEPII, no. 1995-9, Paris, October. http://www.cepii.fr/PDF_PUB/wp/1995/wp1995-09.pdf.

Decressin, Jörg, and Antonio Fatás. 1995. "Regional Labor Market Dynamics in Europe." *European Economic Review* 39, no. 9: 1627–1655.

De Gaulle, Charles. 1970. *Memoires d'espoir: Le renouveau, 1958–1962* [Memoirs of Hope: The Revival, 1958–1962]. Paris: Plon.

De Larosière, Jacques, et al. 2009. "The High-Level Group on Financial Supervision in the EU." Brussels, February 25. http://ec.europa.eu/internal_market/finances/docs/de_larosiere_report_en.pdf.

Deloitte. 2017. "Global Powers of Luxury Goods 2017: The New Luxury Consumer." https://www2.deloitte.com/content/dam/Deloitte/global/Documents/consumer-industrial-products/gx-cip-global-powers-luxury-2017.pdf.

Delors, Jacques. 1989. "Report on Economic and Monetary Union in the European Community." Office for Official Publications of the European Communities, Luxembourg. http://aei.pitt.edu/1007/1/monetary_delors.pdf.

Delors, Jacques. 2004. *Memoires*. Paris: Plon.

Der Spiegel. 1979. "Wir sind ein junges, entschlossenes Land: Der französische Staatspräsident Valéry Giscard d'Estaing über Frankreich und das Europa-Jahr 1979" [We Are a Young Resolute Country: French President Valéry Giscard D'Estaing on France and Europe 1979]. January 1. http://www.spiegel.de/spiegel/print/d-40350800.html.

Der Spiegel. 1998. "Den Druck erhöhen" [Increase the Pressure]. March 30. http://www.spiegel.de/spiegel/print/d-7852349.html and http://magazin.spiegel.de/EpubDelivery/spiegel/pdf/7852349.

Deutsch, Karl. 1963. *The Nerves of Government*. New York: Free Press.

Deutsche Delegation. 1993. "Bei den WWU-Verhandlungen: Vorschlag einer Änderung des EWG-Vertrages im Hinblick auf die Errichtung einer Wirtschafts- und Währungsunion [Proposal for Changes of the EEC Treaty with Regard to the Establishment of an Economic and Monetary Union]. Document 58 in *Europäische Wirtschafts und Währungsunion: Vom Werner-Plan zum Vertrag von Maastricht. Analysen und Dokumentation* [European Economic and Monetary Union: From the Werner Report to the Treaty of Maastricht. Analyses and Documentation], edited by Henry Krägenau and Wolfgang Wetter, 331–334. Baden-Baden: Nomos.

Deutsche Welle. 2010. "Merkel Cites 'Future of Europe' As Reason for Greek Bailout," May 5.

Deutsche Welle. 2012a. "The Élysée Treaty: A Model for Other Old Enemies," September 23.

Deutsche Welle. 2012b. "German-French Statement for Eurozone Integrity," July 27.

Deutsche Welle. 2015. "German Financial and Political Leaders Critical of ECB Stimulus Plan," January 23.

Deutsche Welle. 2017. "Two Years since Germany Opened Its Borders to Refugees: A Chronology," September 4.

Dew-Becker, Ian, and Robert Gordon. 2008. "The Role of Labor Market Changes in the Slowdown of European Productivity Growth." National Bureau of Economic Research Working Paper 13840, March. http://www.nber.org/papers/w13840.

Dey, Iain. 2008. "Italy Next to Bail Out Banks." *Sunday Times*, November 9.

Diamond, Jared. 2005. *Collapse: How Societies Choose to Fail or Succeed*. New York: Penguin.

Didzoleit, Winfried, Stefan Aust, and Dirk Koch. 1999. "Uns die Last erleichtern" [We Lighten the Load]. *Der Spiegel*, January 4, http://www.spiegel.de/spiegel/print/d-8337662.html and http://magazin.spiegel.de/EpubDelivery/spiegel/pdf/8337662.

Dijsselbloem, Jeroen, Olli Rehn, Jörg Asmussen, Klaus Regling, and Werner Hoyer. 2013. "Europe's Crisis Response Is Showing Results." *Wall Street Journal*, October 9.

Di Lucido, Katherine, Anna Kovner, and Samantha Zeller. 2017. "Low Interest Rates and Bank Profits." Liberty Street Economics Blog, Federal Reserve Board of New York, June 21. http://libertystreeteconomics.newyorkfed.org/2017/06/low-interest-rates-and-bank-profits.html.

Dinan, Desmond. 2005. *Ever Closer Union: An Introduction to European Integration*. 3rd ed. Boulder: Lynne Reinner.

Dinmore, Guy. 2012. "Italy Stands Firm in Face of Markets Crisis." *Financial Times*, July 25.

Dinmore, Guy. 2013. "Italy: Matteo Renzi Rocks Boat ahead of Democratic Leadership Vote." *Financial Times*, December 5.

Dinmore, Guy, and James Fontanella-Khan. 2014. "Italy Request to Push Back Budget Targets Dismays Brussels." *Financial Times*, April 14.

Dinmore, Guy, Rachel Sanderson, and Peter Spiegel. 2011. "Straight-Talking Monti Boosts Italy's Hopes." *Financial Times*, November 10.

Dinmore, Guy, and Giulia Segreti. 2014. "Italy's Prime Minister Letta Resigns." *Financial Times*, February 14.

Djankov, Simeon. 2014. *Inside the Euro Crisis: An Eyewitness Account*. Washington, D.C.: Peterson Institute for International Economics. Kindle edition.

Doggett, Gina. 2013. "Italy at Impasse after Vote, Rattling Markets." Agence France-Presse, February 26.

Dohmen, Frank, and Dietmar Hawranek. 2017. "The Secret Cartel of the German Car Makers." Spiegel Online, July 21.

Dombrovskis, Valdis, and Pierre Moscovici. 2017. "Reflection Paper on the Deepening of the Economic and Monetary Union." European Commission, Brussels, May 31.

Dominguez, Kathryn. 2006. "The European Central Bank, the Euro, and Global Financial Markets." *Journal of Economic Perspectives* 20, no. 4: 67–88.

Donadio, Rachel. 2013. "Italy Forms New Coalition Government to End Months of Political Stalemate." *New York Times*, April 28.

Donnellan, Aimee. 2015. "10 Days to Save Greece before Crucial ECB Vote." *Sunday Times*, February 7.

Donnelly, Shawn. 2004. *Reshaping Economic and Monetary Union*. Manchester and New York: Manchester University Press.

Dornbusch, Rudi. 1996. "Euro Fantasies." *Foreign Affairs* 75, no. 5: 110–124.

Dow Jones Business News. 2000. "EU Finance Ministers Support Greece's Bid to Join Euro Zone," June 5.

Dow Jones Institutional News. 2010. "Violence As Greek Unions Hold 24-Hour Strike—Update 2," March 11.

Dow Jones Institutional News. 2011. "Finland Approves EFSF Expansion," September 28.

Dow Jones Institutional News. 2014. "Grand Central: Rising Joblessness Could Pressure Eurozone Leaders to Do Some Rethinking," December 1.

Dow Jones International News. 1999. "Kohl's Own Party Secretary Demands He Identify Donors," December 21.

Dow Jones International News. 2001. "Argentina Searches for a Savior As IMF, World Bank Wait," December 31.

Dow Jones International News. 2009. "German Fin Min: Greece Must Pursue Deficit Cut Itself—Update," December 10.

Dow Jones Newswires. 2001. "Greek Think-Tank Urges Privatization, Structural Changes," January 4.

Dow Jones Online News. 1997. "Kohl Warns against Delay of EU Single-Currency Debut," June 4.

Dowsett, Sonya, and Jesus Aguado. 2011. "Peripheral Euro Zone Banks Hit by Portugal Downgrade—Update 2." Reuters News, July 6.

DPA International. 2014. "Electrolux Under Fire in Italy for Plan to Cut Workers' Salaries," January 28.

Draghi, Mario. 2011a. "Address by the Governor of the Bank of Italy Mario Draghi." Italian Banking Association Annual Meeting, Rome, July 13. https://www.bancaditalia.it/pubblicazioni/interventi-governatore/integov2011/en-draghi-130711.pdf?language_id=1.

Draghi, Mario. 2011b. "Opening Statement by Mario Draghi: Candidate for President of the ECB to the Economic and Monetary Affairs Committee of the European Parliament." Brussels, June 14. https://www.bancaditalia.it/pubblicazioni/interventi-governatore/integov2011/draghi_parl_eu.pdf?language_id=1.

Draghi, Mario. 2011c. "Tensions and New Alliances: The Currency Wars."
Les Rencontres Économiques d'Aix-en-Provence, July 8–10. https://www.
bancaditalia.it/pubblicazioni/interventi-governatore/integov2011/en_draghi_
080711.pdf?language_id=1.

Draghi, Mario. 2012. "Verbatim of the Remarks Made by Mario Draghi." Global
Investment Conference, London, July 26. http://www.ecb.europa.eu/press/key/
date/2012/html/sp120726.en.html.

Draghi, Mario. 2013. "Europe's Pursuit of 'a More Perfect Union.'" Harvard
Kennedy School, Cambridge, October 9. https://www.ecb.europa.eu/press/key/
date/2013/html/sp131009_1.en.html.

Draghi, Mario. 2014a. "Memorial Lecture in Honour of Tommaso Padoa-
Schioppa," July 9. https://www.ecb.europa.eu/press/key/date/2014/html/
sp140709_2.en.html.

Draghi, Mario. 2014b. "Unemployment in the Euro Area." Jackson Hole,
August 22. https://www.ecb.europa.eu/press/key/date/2014/html/sp140822.
en.html.

Draghi, Mario. 2017. "Accompanying the Economic Recovery." European Central
Bank, June 27. https://www.ecb.europa.eu/press/key/date/2017/html/ecb.
sp170627.en.html.

Draghi, Mario, and Vítor Constâncio. 2011. "Introductory Statement to the Press
Conference (with Q&A)." European Central Bank, November 3.

Draghi, Mario, and Vítor Constâncio. 2012a. "Introductory Statement to the Press
Conference (with Q&A)." European Central Bank, April 4.

Draghi, Mario, and Vítor Constâncio. 2012b. "Introductory Statement to the Press
Conference (with Q&A)." European Central Bank, July 5.

Draghi, Mario, and Vítor Constâncio. 2012c. "Introductory Statement to the Press
Conference (with Q&A)." European Central Bank, August 2.

Draghi, Mario, and Vítor Constâncio. 2012d. "Introductory Statement to the Press
Conference (with Q&A)," European Central Bank, September 6.

Draghi, Mario, and Vítor Constâncio. 2013a. "Introductory Statement to the Press
Conference (with Q&A)." European Central Bank, May 2.

Draghi, Mario, and Vítor Constâncio. 2013b. "Introductory Statement to the Press
Conference (with Q&A)." European Central Bank, June 6.

Draghi, Mario, and Vítor Constâncio. 2013c. "Introductory Statement to the Press
Conference (with Q&A)." European Central Bank, November 7.

Draghi, Mario, and Vítor Constâncio. 2014a. "Introductory Statement to the Press
Conference (with Q&A)." European Central Bank, April 3.

Draghi, Mario, and Vítor Constâncio. 2014b. "Introductory Statement to the Press
Conference (with Q&A)." European Central Bank, June 5.

Draghi, Mario, and Vítor Constâncio. 2014c. "Introductory Statement to the Press
Conference (with Q&A)." European Central Bank, September 4.

Draghi, Mario, and Vítor Constâncio. 2014d. "Introductory Statement to the Press
Conference (with Q&A)." European Central Bank, October 2.

Draghi, Mario, and Vítor Constâncio. 2014e. "Introductory Statement to the Press Conference (with Q&A)." European Central Bank, November 6.

Draghi, Mario, and Vítor Constâncio. 2014f. "Introductory Statement to the Press Conference (with Q&A)." European Central Bank, December 4.

Draghi, Mario, and Vítor Constâncio. 2015. "Introductory Statement to the Press Conference (with Q&A)." European Central Bank, January 22.

Drelichman, Mauricio, and Hans-Joachim Voth. 2011. "Serial Defaults, Serial Profits: Returns to Sovereign Lending in Habsburg Spain, 1566–1600." *Explorations in Economic History* 48: 1–19.

Drohan, Madelaine. 1997. "France, Germany Intensify Feud over Unemployment: War of Words between Countries Heats Up on Eve of EU Summit." *Globe and Mail*, June 16.

Drozdiak, William. 1997. "Unity Drive Is Faltering in W. Europe; Defense, Money Plans Raise New Concerns." *Washington Post* Foreign Service, July 4.

Duchêne, François. 1988. "Jean Monnet: L'initiateur" [Jean Monnet: The Initiator]. *Commentaire* 3, no. 43: 724–735.

Duchêne, François. 1994. *Jean Monnet: The First Statesman of Interdependence.* New York and London: W. W. Norton.

Duisenberg, Willem F. and Christian Noyer, 2000, "Introductory Statement," European Central Bank, Frankfurt am Main, December 14. https://www.ecb.europa.eu/press/pressconf/2000/html/is001214.en.html.

Duisenberg, Willem F., and Christian Noyer. 2001a. "Introductory Statement." Frankfurt am Main, February 1. https://www.ecb.europa.eu/press/pressconf/2001/html/is010201.en.html.

Duisenberg, Willem F., and Christian Noyer. 2001b. "Introductory Statement." Frankfurt am Main, April 11. https://www.ecb.europa.eu/press/pressconf/2001/html/is010411.en.html.

Duisenberg, Willem F., and Christian Noyer. 2001c. "Introductory Statement." Dublin, Frankfurt am Main, June 21. https://www.ecb.europa.eu/press/pressconf/2001/html/is010621.en.html.

Dungey, Mardi, Renee Fry, Brenda Gonzalez-Hermosillo, and Vance Martin. 2006. "Contagion in International Bond Markets during the Russian and the LTCM Crises." *Journal of Financial Stability* 2, no. 1: 1–27.

Dustmann, Christian, Bernd Fitzenberger, Uta Schönberg, and Alexandra Spitz-Oener. 2014. "From Sick Man of Europe to Economic Superstar: Germany's Resurgent Economy." *Journal of Economic Perspectives* 28, no. 1: 167–188.

Dutzler, Barbara, and Angelika Hable. 2005. "The European Court of Justice and the Stability and Growth Pact—Just the Beginning?" European Integration Online Papers 9, no. 5. http://eiop.or.at/eiop/texte/2005-005a.htm.

Dyson, Kenneth, and Kevin Featherstone. 1996. "Italy and EMU as a 'Vincolo Esterno': Empowering the Technocrats, Transforming the State." *South European Society and Politics* 1, no. 2: 272–299.

Dyson, Kenneth, and Kevin Featherstone. 1999. *The Road to Maastricht: Negotiating Economic and Monetary Union.* Oxford: Oxford University Press.

Easterlin, Richard. 1981. "Why Isn't the Whole World Developed?" *Journal of Economic History* 41, no. 1: 1–19.

Eastham, Paul. 2003. "Schroeder-Chirac Pact Sidelines Blair." *Daily Mail*, October 16, 15.

Economist. 1988a. "Poorest of the Rich: A Survey of the Republic of Ireland," January 16.

Economist. 1988b. "Twinset and Pöhl Join Battle against Europe's Federalists." October 29, 113.

Economist. 2001. "Eichel Rocks (and Rolls)," August 25, 68.

Economist. 2013a. "Italian Manufacturing: A Washout," August 10, http://www.economist.com/news/business/21583283-years-crisis-have-reinforced-pressure-italys-once-envied-industrial-base-washout.

Economist. 2013b. "Italian Politics: Monti's Threat," July 2.

Economist. 2014. "European Parliament: Elected, Yet Strangely Unaccountable," May 14.

Economist. 2015. "German Landesbanken: Lost a Fortune, Seeking a Role," January 10. http://www.economist.com/news/finance-and-economics/21638143-seven-german-landesbanken-survived-financial-crisis-are-still.

Economist Intelligence Unit. 2002. "Germany Economy—No Early Warning." EIU Viewswire, February 12.

Editorial Board. 2017. "For Macron, Triumph and a Warning," New York Times, June 20.

Egan, Mark. 2002. "IMF Cuts Euro Growth Forecasts, Urges Easing Bias." Reuters News, October 29.

Eggertsson, Gauti, Andrea Ferrero, and Andrea Raffo. 2014. "Can Structural Reforms Help Europe?" *Journal of Monetary Economics* 61: 2–22.

Ehlers, Fiona. 2011. "Absent in the Euro Crisis: Political Paralysis Prevails in Italy." Spiegel Online, November 1.

Eichel, Hans. 2003. "The Stability Pact Is Not a Blunt Instrument." *Financial Times*, November 17.

Eichenberg, Richard C., and Russell J. Dalton. 2007. "Post-Maastricht Blues: The Transformation of Citizen Support for European Integration, 1973–2004," *Acta Politica* 42: 128–152.

Eichengreen, Barry. 1992. *Golden Fetters: The Gold Standard and the Great Depression, 1919–1939.* Oxford: Oxford University Press.

Eichengreen, Barry. 1993. "European Monetary Unification." *Journal of Economic Literature* 31, no. 3: 1321–1357.

Eichengreen, Barry. 2007a. "The Euro: Love It or Leave It?" VoxEU, November 17, republished May 4, 2010. http://voxeu.org/article/eurozone-breakup-would-trigger-mother-all-financial-crises.

Eichengreen, Barry. 2007b. *The European Economy Since 1945*. Princeton: Princeton University Press.

Eichengreen, Barry. 2010. "The Breakup of the Euro Area." In *Europe and the Euro*, edited by Alberto Alesina and Francesco Giavazzi. Chicago: University of Chicago Press.

Eichengreen, Barry, Verena Jung, Stephen Moch, and Ashoka Mody. 2014. "The Eurozone Crisis: Phoenix Miracle or Lost Decade?" *Journal of Macroeconomics* 39: 288–308.

Eichengreen, Barry, and Kevin O'Rourke. 2010a. "A Tale of Two Depressions." VoxEU, March 8. http://voxeu.org/article/tale-two-depressions-what-do-new-data-tell-us-february-2010-update.

Eichengreen, Barry, and Kevin O'Rourke. 2010b,. "What Do the New Data Tell Us?" VoxEU, March 8. http://voxeu.org/article/tale-two-depressions-what-do-new-data-tell-us-february-2010-update#apr609.

Eichengreen, Barry, and Peter Temin. 2010. "Fetters of Gold and Paper." *Oxford Review of Economic Policy* 26, no. 3: 370–384.

Eichengreen, Barry, and Charles Wyplosz. 1993. "The Unstable EMS." *Brookings Papers on Economic Activity* 1: 51–143.

Eichengreen, Barry, and Charles Wyplosz. 1998. "The Stability Pact." *Economic Policy* (April): 66–113.

Eisenhammer, John. 1990a. "Germany's Well-Behaved Start." *Independent*, October 5, 10.

Eisenhammer, John. 1990b. "Kohl Gives Way over Currency Union Rate." *Independent*, April 24, 1.

Eisenhammer, John. 1992. "Kohl Blinded by His Visions—Unification and European Integration." *Independent*, September 27.

Eisenhammer, John, Tim Jackson, Robert Chote, and Andrew Marshall. 1992. "'Little Europe' May Proceed without UK." *Independent*, September 25.

Elliott, Larry, and Charlotte Denny. 2002. "Do They Want to Join This Club?" *Guardian*, October 10.

Elliott, Larry, and Ashley Seager. 2008. "Federal Reserve Slashes Interest Rates to Nearly Zero." *Guardian*, December 17.

Ellsberg, Daniel. 1972. "The Quagmire Myth and the Stalemate Machine." In Daniel Ellsberg, *Papers on the War*. New York: Simon & Schuster.

El País. 2007a. "Bank of Spain Backs Local Lenders to Ride Out Turbulence," September 19.

El País. 2007b. "Central Bank Chief Predicts Soft Landing for Property," June 15.

El País. 2007c. "Share Prices Plunge on Fears Housing Bubble Could Burst," April 25.

Emminger, Otmar 1977. "The D-Mark in the Conflict between Internal and External Equilibrium, 1948–1975." Essays in International Finance 122. Princeton University, Princeton, June.

Emminger, Otmar. 1982. *Exchange Rate Policy Reconsidered*. Occasional Papers 10. New York: Group of 30.

Emmott, Bill. 2013. "Let Us Hope Renzi Will Become an Italian Blair." *Financial Times*, December 9.

Engbom, Niklas, Enrica Detragiache, and Faezeh Raei. 2015. "The German Labor Market Reforms and Post-Unemployment Earnings." IMF Working Paper WP/15/162, Washington, D.C., July.

Enrich, David. 2011. "European Banks Grow Weary of Lending." *Wall Street Journal*, July 12.

EurActiv.com. 2015. "Germany Suspends Dublin Agreement for Syrian Refugees," August 26.

Eurofound. 2017. "Social Mobility in the EU." Publications Office of the European Union, Luxembourg.

Eurogroup. 2010. "Statement by the Eurogroup." Brussels, May 2. http://www.consilium.europa.eu/uedocs/cmsUpload/100502-%20Eurogroup_statement.pdf.

Eurogroup. 2012. "Statement on Greece," November 27. https://www.bundesregierung.de/ContentArchiv/EN/Archiv17/_Anlagen/2012-11-27-statement-griechenland_en.html.

European Banking Authority. 2014. "Results of 2014 EU-Wide Stress Test," October 26. https://www.eba.europa.eu/documents/10180/669262/2014+EU-wide+ST-aggregate+results.pdf.

European Banking Authority. 2016. "EU-Wide Stress Tests," July 29. http://www.eba.europa.eu/documents/10180/1532819/2016-EU-wide-stress-test-Results.pdf.

European Central Bank. 1999a. *Monthly Bulletin*. Frankfurt, January. https://www.ecb.europa.eu/pub/pdf/mobu/mb199901en.pdf.

European Central Bank 1999b. "Possible Effects of the EMU on the EU Banking System in the Medium to Long Term." Frankfurt, February.

European Central Bank. 2007a. "Box 3: The ECB's Additional Open Market Operations in the Period from 8 August to 5 September 2007." *Monthly Bulletin*, Frankfurt, September.

European Central Bank. 2007b. *Monthly Bulletin*. Frankfurt, July.

European Central Bank. 2012. "Monthly Bulletin." Frankfurt, April. https://www.ecb.europa.eu/pub/pdf/mobu/mb201204en.pdf.

European Central Bank. 2015. "Eligibility of Greek Bonds Used As Collateral in Eurosystem Monetary Policy Operations," February 4. http://www.ecb.europa.eu/press/pr/date/2015/html/pr150204.en.html.

European Commission. 1976. "Opinion on Greek Application for Membership." *Bulletin of the European Communities* 2/76, January 20. http://aei.pitt.edu/961.

European Commission. 1990. "One Market, One Money: An evaluation of the potential benefits and costs of forming an economic and monetary union." *European Economy* 44: 1–341.

European Commission. 2003. "President Prodi Statement at the IGC Final Press Conference." IP/03/1728, Brussels, December 13. http://europa.eu/rapid/press-release_IP-03-1728_en.htm.

European Commission. 2005a. "The European Constitution: Post-Referendum Survey in France." Fieldwork, May 30–31. Published in Flash EB171, Brussels, June. http://ec.europa.eu/public_opinion/flash/fl171_en.pdf.

European Commission. 2005b. "The European Constitution: Post-Referendum Survey in the Netherlands." Fieldwork, June 2–4. Published in Flash EB172, Brussels, June. http://ec.europa.eu/public_opinion/flash/fl172_en.pdf.

European Commission. 2013. "Standard Eurobarometer 79: Public Opinion in the European Union," Spring. http://ec.europa.eu/public_opinion/archives/eb/eb79/eb79_publ_en.pdf.

European Commission. 2015. "Speech by Vice-President Dombrovskis at the Humboldt University: The Euro and the Future of Europe." Berlin, September 21. http://europa.eu/rapid/press-release_SPEECH-15-5687_en.htm.

European Communities. 2004. "Treaty Establishing a Constitution for Europe." Office for Official Publications of the European Communities, Luxembourg, October 29. https://europa.eu/european-union/sites/europaeu/files/docs/body/treaty_establishing_a_constitution_for_europe_en.pdf.

European Council. 1969. "Meeting of the Heads of State or Government." The Hague, December 1–2. http://aei.pitt.edu/1451/1/hague_1969.pdf.

European Council. 1989. "European Council [Madrid Summit]: Madrid 26 and 27 June." Reproduced from *Bulletin of the European Communities* 6. http://aei.pitt.edu/1453.

European Council. 2000a. "Lisbon European Council 23 and 24 March 2000: Presidency Conclusions." http://aei.pitt.edu/43340.

European Council. 2000b. "Santa Maria da Feira European Council, Conclusions of the Presidency, 19–20 June 2000." http://aei.pitt.edu/43325.

European Council. 2010a. "Statement by the Heads of State or Government of the European Union." Brussels, February 11. http://www.consilium.europa.eu/en/european-council/euro-summit/documents-2010-2013.

European Council. 2010b. "Statement by the Heads of State or Government of the European Union." Brussels, March 25. http://www.consilium.europa.eu/en/european-council/euro-summit/documents-2010-2013.

European Court of Justice. 2004. "Judgment of the Court of Justice in Case C-27/04 Commission of the European Communities v. Council of the European Union." Press Release no. 57/04, July 13. http://curia.europa.eu/jcms/upload/docs/application/pdf/2009-02/cp040057en.pdf.

Euroweek. 2007. "Fire Brigade Called to IKB but Losses Hidden in Smoke," August 3.

Evans-Pritchard, Ambrose. 2000. "Nice Summit—Germany Becomes First among Equals: Big and Small Nations Engage in Epic Power Struggle." *Daily Telegraph*, December 12.

Evans-Pritchard. Ambrose. 2010. "Merkel Plea to Save Europe As Contagion Hits Iberia." *Daily Telegraph*, May 6.

Ewing, Jack. 2017. *Faster, Higher, Farther: The Volkswagen Scandal*. New York: W. W. Norton.

Ewing, Jack, and Julia Werdigier. 2011. "European Central Bank Raises Rates As Expected." *New York Times*, July 7.

Fabbrini, Sergio. 2000. "Political Change without Institutional Transformation: What Can We Learn from the Italian Crisis of the 1990s?" *International Political Science Review* 21, no. 2: 173.196.

Farnsworth, Clyde. 1969. "French Expected to Press for Closer Ties." *New York Times*, November 30, 9.

Farnsworth, Clyde. 1972. "Talks Aim at Common Market Monetary Union in '72." *New York Times*, February 11, 47.

Farnsworth, Clyde. 1974. "Valéry Giscard d'Estaing." *New York Times*, May 7, 14.

Fatás, Antonio, and Lawrence Summers. 2015. "The Permanent Effects of Fiscal Consolidations." Centre for Economic Policy Research, Discussion Paper 10902, October.

Fawley, Brett, and Christopher Neely. 2013. "Four Stories of Quantitative Easing." *Federal Reserve Bank of St. Louis Review* 95, no. 1: 51–58. https://research. stlouisfed.org/publications/review/13/01/Fawley.pdf.

Featherstone, Kevin. 2003. "Greece and EMU: Between External Empowerment and Domestic Vulnerability." *Journal of Common Market Studies* 41, no. 5: 923–940.

Federal Reserve System. 2001. "Federal Open Market Committee Conference Call," January 3. https://www.federalreserve.gov/monetarypolicy/files/ FOMC20010103ConfCall.pdf.

Federal Reserve System. 2007a. "Conference Call of the Federal Open Market Committee," August 10. http://www.federalreserve.gov/monetarypolicy/files/ FOMC20070810confcall.pdf.

Federal Reserve System. 2007b. "Conference Call of the Federal Open Market Committee," August 16. http://www.federalreserve.gov/monetarypolicy/files/ FOMC20070816confcall.pdf.

Federal Reserve System. 2007c. "Meeting of the Federal Open Market Committee," September 18. http://www.federalreserve.gov/monetarypolicy/files/ FOMC20070918meeting.pdf.

Federal Reserve System. 2008a. "Conference Call of the Federal Open Market Committee," January 21. http://www.federalreserve.gov/monetarypolicy/files/ FOMC20080121confcall.pdf.

Federal Reserve System. 2008b. "Meeting of the Federal Open Market Committee," March 18. http://www.federalreserve.gov/monetarypolicy/files/ FOMC20080318meeting.pdf.

Federal Reserve System. 2008c. "Meeting of the Federal Open Market Committee," October 28–29. https://www.federalreserve.gov/monetarypolicy/files/ FOMC20081029meeting.pdf.

Federal Reserve System. 2008d. "Press Release," December 16. https://www.federalreserve.gov/newsevents/press/monetary/20081216b.htm.

Federal Reserve System. 2010a. "Meeting of the Federal Open Market Committee," January 26–27. https://www.federalreserve.gov/monetarypolicy/files/FOMC20100127meeting.pdf.

Federal Reserve System. 2010b. "Meeting of the Federal Open Market Committee," March 16. https://www.federalreserve.gov/monetarypolicy/files/FOMC20100316meeting.pdf.

Federal Reserve System. 2010c. "Meeting of the Federal Open Market Committee," April 27–28. https://www.federalreserve.gov/monetarypolicy/files/FOMC20100428meeting.pdf.

Federal Reserve System. 2010d. "Meeting of the Federal Open Market Committee," September 21. https://www.federalreserve.gov/monetarypolicy/files/FOMC20100921meeting.pdf.

Federal Reserve System. 2010e. "Minutes of the Federal Open Market Committee," November 2–3. https://www.federalreserve.gov/monetarypolicy/files/fomcminutes20101103.pdf.

Federal Reserve System. 2011. "Press Release," November 30. https://www.federalreserve.gov/newsevents/press/monetary/20111130a.htm.

Feldstein, Martin. 1997. "The Political Economy of the European Economic and Monetary Union: Political Sources of an Economic Liability." *Journal of Economic Perspectives* 11, no. 4: 23–42.

Ferenczi, Thomas. 1992. "The Results of the Referendum on the European Union." *Le Monde*, September 22.

Fernald, John, Robert Hall, James Stock, and Mark Watson. 2017. "The Disappointing Recovery of Output after 2009." Brookings Papers on Economic Activity, conference draft, Washington, D.C., March 23–24.

Ferrero, Mario, and Giorgio Brosio. 1997. "Nomenklatura Rule under Democracy: Solving the Italian Political Puzzle." *Journal of Theoretical Politics* 9, no. 4: 445–475.

Fernández Ordoñez, Miguel Ángel. 2003a. "El legado de Rato" {Rato's Legacy]. *El País*, September 11. http://elpais.com/diario/2003/09/11/economia/1063231210_850215.html.

Fernández Ordoñez, Miguel Ángel. 2003b. "Un presupuesto sin futuro" [A Budget That Disregards the Future]. *El País*, October 1. http://elpais.com/diario/2003/10/01/economia/1064959221_850215.html.

Financial Crisis Inquiry Commission. 2011. "Financial Crisis Inquiry Report: Final Report of the National Commission on the Causes of the Financial and Economic Crisis in the United States." Washington, D.C.: US Government Publishing Office, January.

Financial Times. 1969. "France Seeks to Dispel Doubts," December 4, 29.

Financial Times. 1989. "An EMU for the EC," April 18.

Financial Times. 1995. "The FT Interview: Kohl's Loyal Lieutenant, Wolfgang Schäuble," March 21.

Financial Times. 1998. "EMU May Shake Up Dutch Election," January 16, 2.

Financial Times. 2000. "Leader: Implications of the Danish No," September 29.

Financial Times. 2011a. "Leaders Needed, Not Just Managers," November 10.

Financial Times. 2011b. "The Silent Bazooka; ECB's Move Leaves the Heavy Lifting to Europe's States," December 9.

Financial Times. 2014a. "The End of Renzi's Italian Honeymoon; Rome Needs Europe's Help to Haul Itself out of Stagnation," August 9.

Financial Times. 2014b. "Renzi's Gamble Is a Dice Worth Rolling," January 13.

Financial Times Deutschland. 2008. "Hypo Real Estate Rescued by German Government," September 30.

Fischer, Joschka. 2000. "From Confederacy to Federation—Thoughts on the Finality of European Integration." Humboldt University, Berlin, May 12. https://www.cvce.eu/en/obj/speech_by_joschka_fischer_on_the_ultimate_objective_of_european_integration_berlin_12_may_2000-en-4cd02fa7-d9d0-4cd2-91c9-2746a3297773.html.

Fischer, Joschka. 2010. "Ms. Europe or Frau Germania?" Project Syndicate, March 23.

Fischer, Markus, Christa Hainz, Jörg Rocholl, and Sascha Steffen. 2011. "Government Guarantees and Bank Risk Taking Incentives." AFA 2012 Chicago Meetings Paper, February 4. https://ssrn.com/abstract=1786923 or http://dx.doi.org/10.2139/ssrn.1786923.

Fischer, Sebastian. 2011. "Merkel macht Urlaub—Tschüss, Krise!" [Merkel Is on Holiday—Bye, Bye Crisis!]. Spiegel Online, July 22.

Fischer, Stanley. 2001. "Exchange Rate Regimes: Is the Bipolar View Correct?" *Journal of Economic Perspectives* 15, no. 2: 3–24.

Fitchett, Joseph. 1998. "Europe's Journey to a Single Currency—Giscard d'Estaing Retraces Steps That Led to Monetary Union." *International Herald Tribune*, December 10.

Fitoussi, Jean Paul, et al. 1993. *Competitive Disinflation: The Mark and Budgetary Politics in Europe*. Oxford: Oxford University Press.

Fleming, Stewart. 2011. "Of Ants and Crickets: A Fable for Our Times." *European Voice*, March 9. http://www.europeanvoice.com/article/of-ants-and-crickets-a-fable-for-our-times.

Fletcher, Martin. 2010. "'The Greeks Retire Early—But Here in Germany We Have to Work till We Fall Over'; Martin Fletcher Finds That the Bailout Is Not Popular on the Streets of Ludwigshafen." *Times*, May 25.

Follett, Christopher. 1992. "Politicians Receive Snub—Maastricht Referendum." *Times*, June 3.

Fontanella-Khan, James, and James Wilson. 2012. "Free ECB's Hand to Aid States, Says Minister." *Financial Times*, July 25.

Forbes, Kristin J. 2012. "The 'Big C': Identifying and Mitigating Contagion." Paper prepared for Jackson Hole Symposium hosted by Federal Reserve Bank of Kansas City, September 6.

Ford, Robert, and Wim Suyker. 1990. "Industrial Subsidies in the OECD Countries." OECD Department of Economics and Statistics Working Paper 74. http://www.oecd.org/tax/public-finance/2002580.pdf.

Forelle, Charles, and Riva Froymovich. 2011. "Doubts on Europe Plan; Trichet Calls Sanctions 'Insufficient' after Being Weakened." Wall Street Journal Online, March 16.

Forelle, Charles, David Gauthier-Villars, Brian Blackstone, and David Enrich. 2010. "Europe on the Brink; As Ireland Flails, Europe Lurches across the Rubicon." Wall Street Journal Online, December 27.

Forelle, Charles, and Marcus Walker. 2010. "Europeans Agree on Bailout for Greece." Wall Street Journal Online, March 26.

Forelle, Charles, and Marcus Walker. 2011. "EU Dithering Gives Crisis Global Reach." Wall Street Journal, December 30.

Fortune. 2017. "Spain's Santander Bank Rescues Banco Popular from Collapse," June 7.

France 24. 2016. "French Students Most Affected by Social Inequality, OECD Finds," December 14.

Franco-German Declaration. 2010. "Statement for the France-Germany-Russia Summit," Deauville, October 18. http://www.eu.dk/~/media/files/eu/franco_german_declaration.ashx?la=da.

Frankel, Jeffrey. 2014. "The ECB Should Buy American." Project Syndicate, March 13. https://www.project-syndicate.org/commentary/jeffrey-frankel-urges-the-ecb-to-buy-us-treasuries-to-expand-the-monetary-base.

Frankel, Jeffrey, and Jesse Schreger. 2013. "Over-Optimistic Official Forecasts and Fiscal Rules in the Eurozone." Review of World Economics 149: 247–272.

Frankfurter Allgemeine Zeitung. 1989. "Vor dem Straßburger Gipfel Gespräche über Regierungskonferenz: Die Verwirklichung der Wirtschafts und Währungsunion/'Wir müssen vorwärts gehen'" [Before the Strasbourg Summit, Conversations about the Intergovernmental Conference: The Realization of the Economic and Monetary Union/"We Must Move Forward"], December 6.

Frankfurter Allgemeine Zeitung. 1999. "Schröder lobt die 'sehr guten' Beziehungen zu Griechenland" [Schröder Praises "Excellent" Relations with Greece], October 6, 7.

Frankfurter Allgemeine Zeitung. 2000. "Stoiber: Euro-Einführung in Griechenland 'falsches Signal'" [Stoiber: Introduction of the Euro in Greece "Wrong Signal"], May 5, 7.

Frankland, Mark. 1994. "Bonn's Federal Dreamer Tries Selling Delights of Hard Core." Observer, November 13.

Friedman, Milton. 1953. "The Case for Flexible Exchange Rates." In Milton
    Friedman, *Essays in Positive Economics*, 157–203. Chicago: University of
    Chicago Press.

Friedman, Milton. 1968. "The Role of Monetary Policy." *American Economic Review*
    58, no. 1: 1–17.

Friedman, Milton. 1997. "Why Europe Can't Afford the Euro." *Times*, November
    19, 22.

Friedman, Milton, and Anna Schwartz. 1993 [1963]. *A Monetary History of
    the United States, 1857–1960*. 9th paperback ed. Princeton: Princeton
    University Press.

Gallagher, Terence. 1997. "Kohl Says EMU Basis for Political Union." Reuters
    News, July 6.

Galofré-Vilà, Gregori, Martin McKee, Christopher M. Meissner, and David
    Stuckler. 2016. "The Economic Consequences of the 1953 London Debt
    Agreement." National Bureau of Economic Research Working Paper 22557,
    Cambridge.

Garton Ash, Timothy. 1994. *In Europe's Name: Germany and the Divided Continent*.
    New York: Vintage.

Garton Ash, Timothy. 1998. "Europe's Endangered Liberal Order." *Foreign Affairs*
    77, no. 2: 51–65.

Garton Ash, Timothy. 2012. "The Crisis of Europe." *Foreign Affairs* 91, no.
    5: 2–15.

Gauck, Joachim. 2013. "Speech on the Prospects for the European Idea." Schloss
    Bellevue, Berlin, February 22. http://www.bundespraesident.de/SharedDocs/
    Reden/EN/JoachimGauck/Reden/2013/130222-Europe.html.

Gaunt, Jeremy. 1999. "Greece May Need Help to Meet EMU Inflation." Reuters
    News, March 30.

Gechert, Sebastian, Gustav Horn, Christoph Paetz. 2017. "Long-Term Effects of
    Fiscal Stimulus and Austerity in Europe." Hans-Böckler-Stiftung Working
    Paper 179, May.

Geertz, Clifford. 1963. *Agricultural Involution: The Processes of Ecological Change in
    Indonesia*. Berkeley: University of California Press.

Geithner, Timothy F. 2014. *Stress Test: Reflections on Financial Crises*.
    New York: Crown/Archetype. Kindle edition.

Gennaioli, Nicola, Andrei Shleifer, and Robert Vishny. 2014. "Finance and the
    Preservation of Wealth." *Quarterly Journal of Economics* 129, no. 3: 1221–1254.

German Federal Constitutional Court (Bundesverfassungsgericht). 1993.
    "Judgment on the Maastricht Treaty," October 12. Full text in German reported
    in *Official Court Reports* [BVerfGE] 89, 155.

Gerschenkron, Alexander. 1962. *Economic Backwardness in Historical Perspective*.
    Cambridge: Harvard University Press.

Gerth, Hans, and Charles Wright Mills, eds. 1961. *From Max Weber: Essays in
    Sociology*. Oxford: Oxford University Press.

Gianetti, Mariassunta, and Andrei Simonov. 2013. "On the Real Effects of Bank Bailouts: Micro Evidence from Japan." *American Economic Journal: Macroeconomics* 5, no. 1: 135–167.

Giavazzi, Francesco, and Alberto Giovannini. 1989. *Limiting Exchange Rate Flexibility*. Cambridge: MIT Press.

Giavazzi, Francesco, and Marco Pagano. 1988. "The Advantage of Tying One's Hands: EMS Discipline and Central Bank Credibility." *European Economic Review* 32: 1055–1082.

Ginsberg, Jodie. 2006. "Irish PM Says Did Nothing Wrong in Accepting Loans." Reuters News, September 26.

Giscard d'Estaing, Valéry. 1988. *Le pouvoir et la vie* [Power and Life],Vol. 1. Paris: Compagnie 12.

Giscard d'Estaing, Valéry. 1995. "Manifeste pour une nouvelle Europe fédérative [Proposal for a New Federal Europe]." Le Figaro, January 11.

Giugliano, Ferdinando, and Tony Barber. 2014. "Italy's Finance Minister Criticises EU over Jobs and Growth." *Financial Times*, April 30.

Glick, Reuven, and Michael Hutchison. 1992. "Budget Rules and Monetary Union in Europe." FRBSF Weekly Letter 92-32, September 18.

Glick, Reuven, and Sylvain Leduc. 2013. "The Effects of Unconventional and Conventional U.S. Monetary Policy on the Dollar." Economic Research Department, Federal Reserve Bank of San Francisco.

Glick, Reuven and Andrew Rose. 2015. "Currency Unions and Trade: A Post-Emu Mea Culpa." National Bureau of Economic Research Working Paper 21535, September, Cambridge, MA.

Glover, Brent, and Seth Richards-Shubik. 2014. "Contagion in the European Sovereign Debt Crisis." National Bureau of Economic Research Working Paper 20567. http://www.nber.org/papers/w20567.

Glynn, Irial, and Philip O'Connell. 2017. "Migration." In *Austerity and Recovery in Ireland: Europe's Poster Child and the Great Recession*, edited by William Roche, Philip O'Connell, and Andrea Porthero. Oxford: Oxford University Press.

Goldin, Claudia, and Lawrence Katz. 2008. *The Race between Technology and Education*. Cambridge: Harvard University Press.

Gongloff, Mark. 2011. "ECB Cuts Rates, in Surprise Move." *Wall Street Journal*, November 3.

Gopinath, Gita, Sebnem Kalemli-Ozcan, Loukas Karabarbounis, and Carolina Villegas-Sanchez. 2015. "Capital Allocation and Productivity in South Europe." National Bureau of Economic Research Working Paper 21453, August.

Gordon, Robert J. 2004. "Why Was Europe Left at the Station When America's Productivity Locomotive Departed?" National Bureau of Economic Research Working Paper 10661, August. http://www.nber.org/papers/w10661.

Gordon, Robert J. 2016. *The Rise and Fall of American Growth: The U.S. Standard of Living since the Civil War*. Princeton: Princeton University Press.

Gorton, Gary, and Guillermo Ordoñez. 2016. "Good Booms, Bad Booms." National Bureau of Economic Research, Working Paper 22008, Cambridge, February.

Gourinchas, Pierre-Olivier. 2002. "Comments on 'Current Account Deficits in the Euro Area: The End of the Feldstein-Horioka Puzzle?' by Olivier Blanchard and Francesco Giavazzi." *Brookings Papers on Economic Activity* 2: 196–206.

Gow, David. 2009. "ECB Cuts Eurozone Interest Rate to 2%." *Guardian*, January 15.

Gowers, Andrew, Tony Major, and Hugh Williamson. 2003. "Schroder Urges ECB Action on Euro." *Financial Times*, July 11.

Graham, Dave. 2010. "Interview: Future EMU Debt Needs Haircut Option— German CDU." Reuters News, August 25.

Graham, George, and Gwen Robinson. 1999. "Euro Trading Off to Cautious Start." *Financial Times*, January 4, 1.

Graham, George, and Wolfgang Münchau. 1999. "Euro Conversion Is Off to a Flying Start." *Financial Times*, January 4, 2.

Grant, Charles. 1994. *Delors: Inside the House That Jacques Built*. London: Nicholas Brealey.

Grant, Justin. 2008. "Stocks Sink As Bear Stearns Reignites Credit Fears." Reuters News, March 14.

Greenspan, Alan. 1996. "The Challenge of Central Banking in a Democratic Society," Speech, Washington, D.C., December 5. https://www.federalreserve. gov/BOARDDOCS/SPEECHES/19961205.htm.

Greenspan, Alan. 1998. "The Role of Capital in Optimal Banking Supervision and Regulation." *Federal Reserve Bank of New York Economic Policy Review* 4, no. 3: 163–168.

Greenspan, Alan. 2002. "Regulation, Innovation, and Wealth Creation." Speech, Society of Business Economists, London, September 25. http:// www.federalreserve.gov/BoardDocs/Speeches/2002/20020925/default. htm.

Greif, Avner, and David Laitin. 2004. "A Theory of Endogenous Institutional Change." *American Political Science Review* 98, no. 4: 633–652.

Grey, Stephen. 2000. "Loadsamoney: Once the Friendship of Helmut Kohl and François Mitterrand Was the Symbol of All That Was Best about the New Europe." *Sunday Times*, January 30.

Grossman, Herschel I., and John B. Van Huyck. 1988. "Sovereign Debt As a Contingent Claim: Excusable Default, Repudiation." *American Economic Review* 78, no. 5: 1088–1097.

Guardian. 2017. "The Guardian View on France's Election: A Win for Macron and Hope," April 23.

Guerrera, Francesco. 2003. "EU to Sue Germany over Volkswagen Takeover Law." *Financial Times*, February 26.

Guglielmi, Antonio, Javier Suárez, and Carlo Signani. 2017. "Redenomination Risk Down As Time Goes By." Milan: Mediobanca Securities, http://marcello. minenna.it/wp-content/uploads/2017/01/Italy-2017-01-19.pdf.

Guigou, Elisabeth. 2000. *Elisabeth Guigou: A Woman at the Heart of the State* [Elisabeth Guigou: Une femme au coeur de l'etat]. Paris: Fayard.

Guirao, Fernando, and Frances Lynch, eds, 2016. *Alan S. Milward and Contemporary European History*. New York: Routledge.

Haberler, Gottfried. 1976. *The World Economy, Money, and the Great Depression 1919–1939*. Foreign Affairs Study 30. Washington, D.C.: American Enterprise Institute.

Hadoulis, John. 2010. "Greece Hikes Pension Age, Calls on Strikers to Accept Bonus Cuts." Agence France-Presse, February 9.

Hagerty, Bob. 1992. "Delors Urges EC to Make a Dash toward Union." *Asian Wall Street Journal*, September 25.

Hall, Peter. 1986. *Governing the Economy: The Politics of State Intervention in Britain and France*. New York: Oxford University Press.

Hamilton, James. 2017. "Are We in a New Inflation Regime?" Econbrowser, July 2. http://econbrowser.com/archives/2017/07/are-we-in-a-new-inflation-regime.

Handelsblatt. 2000. "Berlin will raschen Euro-Beitritt Griechenlands" [Berlin Wants Euro Entry of Greece Quickly], January 18, 12.

Hanreich, Gunther. 2004. "Eurostat Takes Issue with former Greek PM on Reasons for the Revision of Economic Data." *Financial Times*, December 28.

Hanushek, Eric, and Ludger Woessmann. 2015. *The Knowledge Capital of Nations: Education and the Economics of Growth*. Cambridge: MIT Press.

Harding, Luke, Jon Henley, and Ian Black. 2003. "Schröder and Chirac Flaunt Love Affair in Brussels." *Guardian*, October 16. http://www.theguardian.com/world/2003/oct/16/france.germany.

Harrison, Stuart. 1998. "Limerick." *Daily Mail*, December 29, 54.

Hassan, Fadi, and Gianmarco Ottaviano. 2013. "Productivity in Italy: The Great Unlearning." VoxEU, November 30. http://voxeu.org/article/productivity-italy-great-unlearning.

Hegre, Håvard, John Oneal, and Bruce Russett. 2010. "Trade Does Promote Peace: The Perils of Simultaneous Estimation of the Reciprocal Effects of Trade and Conflict." *Journal of Peace Research* 46, no. 6: 763–774.

Helm, Toby. 2000. "Backing the Euro Cost Me Election, Says Kohl." *Daily Telegraph*, November 20, 4.

Helm, Toby. 2005. "European Leaders About to Fall off the Bike." *Daily Telegraph*, July 17.

Helms, Ludger. 2002. "'Chief Executives' and Their Parties: The Case of Germany." *German Politics* 11, no. 2: 146–164.

Heneghan, Tom. 1992. "Kohl Backs Maastricht, Critics See Multi-Track Europe." Reuters News, September 25.

Heneghan, Tom. 1994. "Kohl Fights Impression He Would Quit in Midterm." Reuters News, October 7.

Henning, C. Randall, and Martin Kessler. 2012. "Fiscal Federalism: US History for Architects of Europe's Fiscal Union." Peterson Institute for International Economics Working Paper 2012-1.

Herenstein, Amelie. 2013. "Protests As Shareholders of World's Oldest Bank Meet in Italy." Agence France-Presse, January 25.

Hetzel, Robert. 2002. "German Monetary History in the Second Half of the Twentieth Century: From the Deutsche Mark to the Euro." *Federal Reserve Bank of Richmond Economic Quarterly* 82, no. 2: 29–64.

Hetzel, Robert. 2009. "Monetary Policy in the 2008–2009 Recession." *Economic Quarterly* 95, no. 2: 201–233.

Hetzel, Robert. 2012. *The Great Recession: Market Failure or Policy Failure?* New York: Cambridge University Press.

Hetzel, Robert. 2014. "Contractionary Monetary Policy Caused the Great Recession in the Eurozone: A New Keynesian Perspective." Federal Reserve Bank of Richmond Working Paper Series, August 22.

Higgins, Byron. 1993. "Was the ERM Crisis Inevitable?" *Federal Reserve Bank of Kansas City Economic Review*, Fourth Quarter: 27–40.

Hildebrand, Jan, Moritz Koch, and Norbert Häring. 2017. "Greek Debt Showdown." *Handelsblatt*, June 6.

Hirshleifer, Jack. 1983. "From Weakest-Link to Best-Shot: The Voluntary Provision of Public Goods." *Public Choice* 41, no. 3: 371–386.

Hodson, Dermot. 2016. "Jacques Delors: Vision, Revisionism, and the Design of EMU." In *Architects of the Euro: Intellectuals in the Making of European Monetary Union*, edited by Ivo Maes and Kenneth Dyson. Oxford: Oxford University Press.

Hofheinz, Paul, and Bill Boston. 2002. "EU Commission Appears Set to Lose Battle with Germany." *Wall Street Journal Europe*, February 11.

Hofheinz, Paul, and Michael R. Sesit. 2000. "IMF Head Steps Up Intervention Push." *Wall Street Journal Europe*, September 21.

Hofmann, Sarah. 2013. "Willy Brandt: German, European and Cosmopolitan." December 18. http://www.dw.com/en/willy-brandt-german-european-and-cosmopolitan/a-17300003.

Hollinger, Peggy, and John Thornhill. 2005. "Chirac's Record on Europe Hampers Yes Campaign: EU Treaty." *Financial Times*, April 14.

Honohan, Patrick. 2000. "Ireland in EMU: Straitjacket or Skateboard?" *Irish Banking Review*, 15–32.

Honohan, Patrick. 2014. "Brian Lenihan and the Nation's Finances." In *Brian Lenihan: In Calm and Crisis*, edited by Brian Murphy, Mary O'Rourke, and Noel Whelan, chapter 5. Kildare: Merrion. Kindle edition.

Honohan, Patrick, and Brendan Walsh. 2002. "Catching Up with the Leaders: The Irish Hare." *Brookings Papers on Economic Activity* 2002, no. 1: 1–74.

Hope, Kerin. 2000. "Greece Labours to Change." *Financial Times*, June 20, 21.

Hope, Kerin. 2011. "Debt Crisis Brings Humiliating End for PM." *Financial Times*, November 7.

Hope, Kerin, and Alexandra Stevenson. 2012. "Greek Left Demands End to 'Barbarous' Austerity Plans As It Seeks a Coalition." *Financial Times*, May 9.

Hornsby, Michael. 1976. "Qualified Welcome by EEC Falls Far Short of Greek Hopes." *Times*, January 30, 8.

Horobin, William. 2014. "France Gives Up on Deficit Goal." *Wall Street Journal Europe*, August 15.

Horobin, William. 2017. "Macron Pushes Germany to Commit More to Eurozone; German Chancellor Angela Merkel Has Expressed Cautious Openness to Ideas." Wall Street Journal Online, July 13.

Hoshi, Takeo, and Anil Kashyap. 2015. "Will the U.S. and Europe Avoid a Lost Decade? Lessons from Japan's Postcrisis Experience." *IMF Economic Review* 63, no. 1: 110–163.

Hughes, David. 1999. "As Red Oskar Resigns, the Euro's Value Is Sent Soaring." *Daily Mail*, March 12, 2.

Ide, Ella. 2013a. "Beppe Grillo: The Live Wire of Italy's Election." Agence France-Presse, February 16.

Ide, Ella. 2013b. "Berlusconi the Showman Fires Up Rome Election Rally." Agence France-Presse, February 7.

International Monetary Fund. 1969. "Minutes of Executive Board Meeting." EBM/69/14, Washington, D.C., March 7.

International Monetary Fund. 1983. "Greece: Staff Report for the 1982 Article IV Consultation," SM/83/37, Washington, D.C., February 23.

International Monetary Fund. 1990. "Greece: Staff Report for the 1990 Article IV Consultation." SM/90/76, Washington, D.C., April 26.

International Monetary Fund. 1994a. "Germany—Staff Report for the 1994 Article IV Consultation." SM/94/203, Washington, D.C., August 2.

International Monetary Fund. 1994b. "Greece: Staff Report for the 1994 Article IV Consultation." SM/94/151, Washington, D.C., June 20.

International Monetary Fund. 1995. "Germany—Staff Report for the 1995 Article IV Consultation." SM/95/183, July, Washington D.C.

International Monetary Fund. 1996. "Ireland: Staff Report for the 1996 Article IV Consultation." SM/96/126, Washington, D.C., June.

International Monetary Fund. 1997a. "Excerpts of a Speech by Managing Director Michel Camdessus at the EMU Conference on March 18." *IMF Survey* 26, no. 7 (April 7): 102–103.

International Monetary Fund. 1997b. "Ireland: Staff Report for the 1997 Article IV Consultation." SM/97/138, Washington, D.C., June.

International Monetary Fund. 1999a. "Monetary and Exchange Rate Policies of the Euro Area (In the Context of the 1999 Article IV Discussions with Euro-Area Countries)." SM/99/61, Washington, D.C., March 5.

International Monetary Fund. 1999b. "Monetary and Exchange Rate Policies of the Euro Area (In the Context of the 1999 Article IV Discussions with Euro-Area Countries)." SM/99/212, Washington, D.C., August 23.

International Monetary Fund. 1999c. "The IMF Concludes Article IV Consultation with Germany." Public Information Notice no. 99/101, Washington, D.C., November 3.

International Monetary Fund. 2001a. "France: Staff Report for the 2001 Article IV Consultation." SM/01/287, Washington, D.C., September.

International Monetary Fund. 2001b. "Germany: 2001 Article IV Consultation-Staff Report; Staff Supplement; and Public Information Notice on the Executive Board Discussion." IMF Country Report No. 01/202, November, Washington D.C.

International Monetary Fund. 2001c. "Press Conference on the World Economic Outlook." Washington, D.C., April. https://www.imf.org/external/np/tr/2001/tr010426.htm.

International Monetary Fund, 2001d. "World Economic Outlook," Washington, D.C., May.

International Monetary Fund. 2001e. "World Economic Outlook," Washington, D.C., October.

International Monetary Fund, 2002a, "Access Policy in Capital Account Crises," July, Washington, D.C.

International Monetary Fund. 2002b. "Germany: 2002 Article IV Consultation-Staff Report; Staff Supplement; and Public Information Notice on the Executive Board Discussion." IMF Country Report No. 02/239, October, Washington D.C.

International Monetary Fund. 2002c. "Portugal: 2001 Article IV Consultation—Staff Report and Public Information Notice on the Executive Board Discussion." IMF Country Report 02/90, Washington, D.C., April.

International Monetary Fund. 2002d. "World Economic Outlook." Washington, D.C., September.

International Monetary Fund. 2003a. "Greece: 2003 Article IV Consultation—Staff Report; Staff Statement; Public Information Notice on the Executive Board Discussion; and Statement by the Executive Director for Greece." IMF Country Report no. 03/156, Washington, D.C., June.

International Monetary Fund. 2003b. "Ireland: 2003 Article IV Consultation—Staff Report; Staff Supplement; and Public Information Notice on the Executive Board Discussion for Ireland." IMF Country Report no. 03/242, Washington, D.C., August.

International Monetary Fund. 2003c. "Lessons from the Crisis in Argentina." Washington, D.C., October 8. https://www.imf.org/external/np/pdr/lessons/100803.htm.

International Monetary Fund. 2003d. "Portugal: 2002 Article IV Consultation—Staff Report." IMF Country Report 03/99, Washington, D.C., April.

International Monetary Fund. 2004a. "Economic Prospects and Policy Issues." "World Economic Outlook," chapter 1, Washington, D.C., September.

International Monetary Fund. 2004b. "The IMF and Argentina, 1991– 2001: Evaluation Report." Independent Evaluation Office, Washington, D.C.

International Monetary Fund. 2004c. "Spain: 2003 Article IV Consultation—Staff Report; Staff Supplement; Public Information Notice on the Executive Board Discussion; and Statement by the Executive Director for Spain." IMF Country Report no. 04/89, Washington, D.C., March.

International Monetary Fund. 2005. "Greece: 2004 Article IV Consultation—Staff Report; Public Information Notice on the Executive Board Discussion; and Statement by the Executive Director for Greece." IMF Country Report no. 05/43, Washington, D.C., February.

International Monetary Fund. 2006a. "Ireland: Financial System Stability Assessment Update." IMF Country Report 06/292, Washington, D.C., August. https://www.imf.org/external/pubs/ft/scr/2006/cr06292.pdf.

International Monetary Fund. 2006b. "Ireland: 2006 Article IV Consultation— Staff Report; Staff Supplement; and Public Information Notice on the Executive Board Discussion." IMF Country Report 06/293, Washington, D.C., August.

International Monetary Fund. 2006c. "Spain: 2006 Article IV Consultation—Staff Report; Staff Supplement; Public Information Notice on the Executive Board Discussion; and Statement by the Executive Director for Spain." IMF Country Report 06/211, Washington, D.C., June.

International Monetary Fund. 2007a. "Euro Area Policies: 2007 Article IV Consultation—Staff Report; Staff Supplement; Public Information Notice on the Executive Board Discussion; and Statement by the Executive Director for Member Countries." IMF Country Report 07/260, Washington, D.C., July.

International Monetary Fund. 2007b. "Greece: 2006 Article IV Consultation—Staff Report; Public Information Notice on the Executive Board Discussion; and Statement by the Executive Director for Greece." IMF Country Report no. 07/26, Washington, D.C., January.

International Monetary Fund. 2007c. "Spain: 2007 Article IV Consultation—Staff Report; Staff Statement; and Public Information Notice on the Executive Board Discussion." IMF Country Report no. 07/175, Washington, D.C., May.

International Monetary Fund. 2008a. "Euro Area Policies—Staff Report for the 2008 Article IV Consultation with Member Countries." August. http://www.imf.org/external/pubs/ft/scr/2008/cr08262.pdf.

International Monetary Fund. 2008b. "Global Financial Stability Report." Washington, D.C., October. http://www.imf.org/external/pubs/ft/gfsr/2008/02.

International Monetary Fund. 2008c. "Greece: 2007 Article IV Consultation— Staff Report; Public Information Notice on the Executive Board Discussion; and Statement by the Executive Director for Greece." IMF Country Report no. 08/148, Washington, D.C., May.

International Monetary Fund. 2008d. "World Economic Outlook." Washington, D.C., April. https://www.imf.org/external/pubs/ft/weo/2008/01/pdf/text.pdf.

International Monetary Fund. 2008e. "World Economic Outlook Update." Washington, D.C., January 29. http://www.imf.org/external/pubs/ft/weo/2008/update/01.

International Monetary Fund. 2008f. "World Economic Outlook Update." Washington, D.C., July 17. http://www.imf.org/external/pubs/ft/weo/2008/update/02.

International Monetary Fund. 2009a. "Germany—Staff Report for the 2008 Article IV Consultation." Washington, D.C., January 22. https://www.imf.org/external/pubs/ft/scr/2009/cr0915.pdf.

International Monetary Fund. 2009b. "Greece: 2009 Article IV Consultation—Staff Report; Staff Supplement; Public Information Notice on the Executive Board Discussion; and Statement by the Executive Director for Greece." IMF Country Report 09/244, Washington, D.C., August.

International Monetary Fund. 2009c. "Ireland: 2009 Article IV Consultation—Staff Report; and Public Information Notice on the Executive Board Discussion." IMF Country Report 09/195, Washington, D.C., June.

International Monetary Fund. 2009d. "Minutes of Executive Board Meeting 09/80-3, 4:30 p.m., July 24, 2009." Washington, D.C., November.

International Monetary Fund. 2009e. "Spain—Staff Report for the 2008 Article IV Consultation." Washington, D.C., February 3. https://www.imf.org/external/pubs/ft/scr/2009/cr09128.pdf.

International Monetary Fund. 2009f. "World Economic Outlook." Washington, D.C., October. https://www.imf.org/external/pubs/ft/weo/2009/02/pdf/text.pdf.

International Monetary Fund. 2010a. "China—Staff Report for the 2010 Article IV Consultation." Washington, D.C., July 9. https://www.imf.org/external/pubs/ft/scr/2010/cr10238.pdf.

International Monetary Fund. 2010b. "Greece: Staff Report on Request for Stand-By Arrangement." IMF Country Report 10/110, Washington, D.C., May 5.

International Monetary Fund. 2010c. "Minutes of Executive Board Meeting 10/45-1, 10:00 a.m., May 9, 2010: Greece - Request for Stand-By Arrangement; Rule K-1 Report on Breach of Obligations Under Article VIII, Section 5 of the Articles of Agreement." Washington D.C., September 20.

International Monetary Fund. 2010d. "Transcript of a Press Briefing by Caroline Atkinson, Director, External Relations Department International Monetary Fund." Washington, D.C., January 21. http://www.imf.org/external/np/tr/2010/tr012110.htm.

International Monetary Fund. 2010e. "World Economic Outlook." Washington, D.C., October. https://www.imf.org/external/pubs/ft/weo/2010/02.

International Monetary Fund. 2011a. "Germany: 2011 Article IV Consultation—Staff Report; Public Information Notice on the Executive Board Discussion;

and Statement by the Executive Director for Germany." IMF Country Report no. 11/168, Washington, D.C., July 12.

International Monetary Fund. 2011b. "Global Financial Stability Report." Washington, D.C., September 21. https://www.imf.org/external/pubs/cat/longres.aspx?sk=24745.

International Monetary Fund. 2011c. "Global Financial Stability Report: Market Update." Washington, D.C., June 17. http://www.imf.org/external/pubs/ft/fmu/eng/2011/02/pdf/0611.pdf.

International Monetary Fund. 2011d. "Greece: Fourth Review under the Stand-By Arrangement and Request for Modification and Waiver of Applicability of Performance Criteria." IMF Country Report 11/175, Washington, D.C., July 13.

International Monetary Fund. 2011e. "Greece: Third Review under the Stand-By Arrangement—Staff Report; Informational Annex; Press Release on the Executive Board Discussion; Statement by the Staff Representative on Greece; and Statement by the Executive Director for Greece." IMF Country Report 11/68, Washington, D.C., March 16. https://www.imf.org/external/pubs/cat/longres.aspx?sk=24708.0.

International Monetary Fund. 2012a. "The Good, Bad, and Ugly: 100 Years of Dealing with Public Debt Overhangs." "World Economic Outlook," Washington, D.C., October. https://www.imf.org/external/pubs/ft/weo/2012/02.

International Monetary Fund. 2012b. "Greece: Request for Extended Arrangement under the Extended Fund Facility—Staff Report; Staff Supplement; Press Release on the Executive Board Discussion; and Statement by the Executive Director for Greece." IMF Country Report 12/57, Washington, D.C., March.

International Monetary Fund. 2012c. "Spain: Financial Sector Assessment, Preliminary Conclusions by the Staff of the International Monetary Fund," April 25. https://www.imf.org/en/News/Articles/2015/09/28/04/52/mcs042512.

International Monetary Fund. 2012d. "Spain 2012 Article IV Consultation." IMF Country Report 12/202, Washington, D.C., July 27. https://www.imf.org/external/pubs/ft/scr/2012/cr12202.pdf.

International Monetary Fund. 2012e. "Statement on Greece by IMF Managing Director Christine Lagarde." Press Release 12/458, November 26. https://www.imf.org/en/News/Articles/2015/09/14/01/49/pr12458.

International Monetary Fund. 2012f. "World Economic Outlook: Coping with High Debt and Sluggish Growth." Washington, D.C., October. https://www.imf.org/external/pubs/ft/weo/2012/02/pdf/text.pdf.

International Monetary Fund. 2012g. "World Economic Outlook Update." Washington, D.C., January 24. https://www.imf.org/external/pubs/ft/weo/2012/update/01/pdf/0112.pdf.

International Monetary Fund. 2012h. "World Economic Outlook Update." Washington, D.C., July 16. http://www.imf.org/external/pubs/ft/weo/2012/update/02/pdf/0712.pdf.

International Monetary Fund. 2013a. "Greece: Ex Post Evaluation of Exceptional Access under the 2010 Stand-By Arrangement." IMF Country Report no. 13/156, Washington, D.C., June.

International Monetary Fund, 2013b. "Greece: First and Second Reviews under the Extended Arrangement under the Extended Fund Facility, Request for Waiver of Applicability, Modification of Performance Criteria, and Rephasing of Access—Staff Report; Staff Supplement; Press Release on the Executive Board Discussion; and Statement by the Executive Director for Greece." IMF Country Report 13/20, Washington, D.C., January.

International Monetary Fund. 2013c. "Italy: Financial System Stability Assessment." IMF Country Report 13/300, Washington, D.C., September.

International Monetary Fund. 2014a. "Euro Area Policies: 2014 Article IV Consultation—Staff Report; Press Release; and Statement by the Executive Director." IMF Country Report 14/198, Washington, D.C., July 14.

International Monetary Fund. 2014b. "IMF Multilateral Policy Issues Report: 2014 Spillover Report." Washington, D.C., July 29. https://www.imf.org/external/np/pp/eng/2014/062514.pdf.

International Monetary Fund. 2014c. "Italy 2014 Article IV Consultation—Staff Report; Press Release; and Statement by the Executive Director for Italy." IMF Country Report 14/283, Washington, D.C., September.

International Monetary Fund. 2014d. "Portugal: Concluding Statement of the First Post-Program Monitoring Discussion," November 5. http://www.imf.org/external/np/ms/2014/110514.htm.

International Monetary Fund. 2015a. "France: 2015 Article IV Consultation—Press Release; Staff Report; and Statement by the Executive Director for France." IMF Country Report 15/178, Washington, D.C., July.

International Monetary Fund. 2015b. "Global Financial Stability Report," Washington, D.C., October. https://www.imf.org/external/pubs/ft/gfsr/2015/02/pdf/text.pdf.

International Monetary Fund. 2015c. "Ireland—Ex Post Evaluation of Exceptional Access under the 2010 Extended Arrangement." IMF Country Report no. 15/20, Washington, D.C., January. https://www.imf.org/external/pubs/ft/scr/2015/cr1520.pdf.

International Monetary Fund. 2016a. "Finland: 2016 Article IV Consultation—Press Release; Staff Report, and Statement by the Executive Director for Finland." IMF Country Report 16/368, Washington, D.C., December.

International Monetary Fund. 2016b. "Global Trade: What's Behind the Slowdown?" "World Economic Outlook," Washington, D.C., October. http://www.imf.org/external/pubs/ft/weo/2016/02.

International Monetary Fund. 2016c. "Italy: 2016 Article IV Consultation—Press Release; Staff Report; and Statement by the Executive Director for Italy." IMF Country Report 16/222, Washington, D.C., July.

International Monetary Fund. 2016d. "Portugal: 2016 Article IV Consultation—Press Release; Staff Report; and Statement by the Executive Director for Portugal." IMF Country Report 16/300, Washington, D.C., September.

International Monetary Fund. 2017a. "Global Financial Stability Report." Washington D.C., October.

International Monetary Fund. 2017b. "Greece: 2016 Article IV Consultation—Press Release; Staff Report, and Statement by the Executive Director for Greece." IMF Country Report 17/40, Washington, D.C., February.

International Monetary Fund. 2017c. "Italy: 2016 Article IV Consultation—Press Release; Staff Report; and Statement by the Executive Director for Italy." IMF Country Report 16/222, Washington, D.C., July.

International Monetary Fund. 2017d. "Portugal: Selected Issues." IMF Country Report 17/279, Washington, D.C., September.

International Monetary Fund. 2017e. "Spain: 2016 Article IV Consultation—Press Release; Staff Report, and Statement by the Executive Director for Spain." IMF Country Report 17/23, Washington, D.C., January.

Ip, Greg. 2017a. "Globalism's Great French Hope; French President Emmanuel Macron Has Exposed a Hole in the Nationalist Agenda." Wall Street Journal Blogs, June 20.

Ip, Greg. 2017b. "In Defense of the Dismal Science." *Wall Street Journal*, August 26.

Irish Examiner. 2003. "France and Germany under Cosh over Deficit," September 12.

Irish Examiner. 2009. "Lenihan: Allowing Bank to Fail Was Not an Option," May 30.

Irish Times. 1996. "Main Conclusions of ESRI Report," July 27.

Irish Times. 2005. "The Great Unravelling," June 4.

Irish Times. 2006. "'Friends Would Assist a Politician in Difficulty.'" December 20.

Isidore, Chris. 2008. "Fed Delivers Another Rate Cut." CNN Money, January 30.

Isidore, Chris. 2011, "European Central Bank Cuts Rates." CNN Wire, November 3.

Ivaldi, Gilles. 2006. "Beyond France's 2005 Referendum on the European Constitutional Treaty: Second-Order Model, Anti-Establishment Attitudes and the End of the Alternative European Utopia." *West European Politics* 29, no. 1: 47–69.

Izraelewicz, Erik, Claire Gatinois, and Philippe Ricard. 2012. "Interview with *Le Monde* Mario Draghi, President of the ECB," conducted July 18, published July 21. https://www.ecb.europa.eu/press/inter/date/2012/html/sp120721.en.html.

Jackson, Guy. 2017. "France's Fillon Bowed but Not Broken in Presidential Race." Agence France-Presse, April 16.

James, Steve. 1992. "Sell European Union Harder, Germany's Kinkel Says."
Reuters News, June 3.

Janis, Irving. 1972. *Victims of Groupthink: A Psychological Study of Foreign-Policy Decisions and Fiascoes*. Boston: Houghton Mifflin.

Jeffries, Stuart. 2010. "What the Philosopher Saw: Jürgen Habermas on Europe, Democracy and Public Debate." *Financial Times*, April 30.

Jenkins, Simon. 2005. "The Peasants' Revolt." *Sunday Times*, June 5.

Jerzmanowski, Michal. 2006. "Empirics of Hills, Plateaus, Mountains, and Plains (A Markov-Switching Approach to Growth)." *Journal of Development Economics* 81: 357–385.

John, Mark, and Ingrid Melander. 2014. "France's Hollande Wants to Change EU Focus after Far-Right Win—Update 4." Reuters News, May 26.

Johnson, Harry. 1969. "The Case for Flexible Exchange Rates, 1969." *Federal Reserve Bank of St. Louis Review*, June: 12–24. http://research.stlouisfed.org/publications/review/article/588.

Jones, Benjamin, and Benjamin Olken. 2008. "The Anatomy of Start-Stop Growth." *Review of Economics and Statistics* 90, no. 3: 582–587.

Jones, Claire, and Ferdinando Giugliano. 2015. "ECB Split Points to Sensitivity of Greek Liquidity Curbs." *Financial Times*, February 5.

Jones, Claire, Giulia Segreti, and Guy Dinmore. 2014. "Renzi Likens Europe to 'Old Boring Aunt.'" *Financial Times*, June 24.

Jones, Eric L. 1981. *The European Miracle: Environments, Economies and Geopolitics in the History of Europe and Asia*. Cambridge: Cambridge University Press.

Jones, Gavin. 2014. "Italy's Renzi Wins Plaudits for Vague Labour Reform Proposals." Reuters News, October 10.

Jones, Gavin. 2016. "Italy Pushes Labour Flexibility to Limit with Job Vouchers." Reuters News, March 11.

Jones, Gavin, and James Mackenzie. 2014. "Special Report: How Italy Became a Submerging Economy." Reuters News, July 14.

Jones, George, and Ambrose Evans-Pritchard. 2000. "Nice Summit—A Marathon with Jostling All the Way: Europe's Leaders Wrestle for Power and Influence." *Daily Telegraph*, December 11.

Jordà, Òscar, and Alan M. Taylor. 2016. "The Time for Austerity: Estimating the Average Treatment Effect of Fiscal Policy." *Economic Journal* 126: 219–255.

Jorgensen, Erika, and Jeffrey Sachs. 1989. "Default and Renegotiation of Latin American Foreign Bonds in the Interwar Period." In *The International Debt Crisis in Historical Perspective*, edited by Barry Eichengreen and Peter Lindert, 48–85. Cambridge: MIT Press.

Judt, Tony. 1997. "Continental Rift." *New York Times*, June 5.

Judt, Tony. 2006. *Postwar: A History of Europe since 1945*. New York: Penguin Group US. Kindle edition.

Judt, Tony. 2011 *A Grand Illusion? An Essay on Europe*. New York: New York University Press. Kindle edition.

Jukes, Peter. 2010. "Tony Judt: The Last Interview." *Prospect*, July 21. http://www.prospectmagazine.co.uk/magazine/tony-judt-interview.

Juncker, Jean-Claude. 2016. "State of the Union Address 2016: Towards a Better Europe—A Europe That Protects, Empowers and Defends." Strasbourg, September 14. https://ec.europa.eu/commission/state-union-2016_en.

Juncker, Jean-Claude. 2017. "State of the Union Address 2017." Brussels, September 13. https://ec.europa.eu/commission/state-union-2017_en.

Juncker, Jean-Claude, and Giulio Tremonti. 2010. "E-Bonds Would End the Crisis." *Financial Times*, December 5.

Kadri, Françoise. 2013. "Italy's Renzi: Web-Savvy Politician Who Looks to Obama." Agence France-Presse, December 8.

Kaldor, Nicholas. 1978 [1971]. "The Dynamic Effects of the Common Market." In Nicholas Kaldor, *Further Essays on Applied Economics*. New York: Holmes and Meier.

Kalyvas, Stathis. 2015. *Modern Greece: What Everyone Needs to Know*. New York: Oxford University Press. Kindle edition.

Kamil, Herman. 2012. "How Do Exchange Rate Regimes Affect Firms' Incentives to Hedge Currency Risk? Micro Evidence for Latin America." IMF Working Paper 12/69, March.

Kaminska, Izabella. 2009a. "ECB Secret QE, or Not?" FT Alphaville, September 9. https://ftalphaville.ft.com/2009/09/08/70336/ecb-secret-qe-or-not.

Kaminska, Izabella. 2009b. "The Return of Widening Sovereign Credit Spreads." FT Alphaville, November 23. https://ftalphaville.ft.com/2009/11/23/84666/the-return-of-widening-sovereign-credit-spreads.

Kaminski, Matthew. 2010. "Europe's Other Crisis; the Bailout of Greece Threatens the Very Integrity of the European Union." Wall Street Journal Online, April 30.

Kamm, Thomas. 1996. "End to Strike May Not Halt Juppe's Slide." *Wall Street Journal Europe*, December 2.

Kanda, Daniel. 2010. "Asset Booms and Structural Fiscal Positions: The Case of Ireland." IMF Working Paper WP/10/57, Washington, D.C., March.

Kang, Dae Woong, Nick Ligthart, and Ashoka Mody. 2015. "The European Central Bank: Building a Shelter in a Storm." Griswold Center for Economic Policy Studies Working Paper 248, December. https://www.princeton.edu/ceps/workingpapers/248mody.pdf.

Karamouzi, Eirini. 2014. *Greece, the EEC and the Cold War, 1974–79: The Second Enlargement*. New York: Palgrave Macmillan.

Karnitschnig, Matthew. 2017. "Why Greece Is Germany's 'De Facto Colony': The Debt Relief Athens Desperately Wants Is Hostage to Berlin's Election Politics." *Politico*, June 14.

Karnitschnig, Matthew, Stephen Fidler, and Tom Lauricella. 2010. "Crisis Spreads in Europe—Debt Downgrades in Portugal, Greece Sow Fear of Contagion; World Markets Hit." *Wall Street Journal*, April 28.

Kenen, Peter B. 1969. "The Theory of Optimum Currency Areas: An Eclectic View." In *Monetary Problems of the International Economy*, edited by Robert Mundell and Alexander Swoboda, 41–60. Chicago: University of Chicago Press.

Kenna, Armorel. 2011. "Trichet Sends Letters to Berlusconi, Zapatero, *Corriere* Reports." Bloomberg, August 6.

Kennedy, Simon. 2009. "ECB Interest-Rate Cuts May Fail to Rescue Economy—Update 1." Bloomberg, March 5.

Kennedy, Simon, and Scott Lanman. 2010. "Bernanke, Trichet Economic Paths May Diverge at Jackson Hole." Bloomberg, August 27.

Kennedy, Simon, and Stefan Riecher. 2013. "Draghi Cuts ECB Rates to Combat 'Prolonged' Inflation Weakness." Bloomberg, November 7.

Keohane, Robert O. 1986. "Reciprocity in International Relations." *International Organization* 40, no. 1: 1–27.

Keynes, John Maynard. 1920 [1919]. *The Economic Consequences of Peace*. New York: Harcourt, Brace, and Howe.

Keynes, John Maynard. 1973 [1936]. *The General Theory and After: Defence and Development*, edited by Donald Edward Moggridge. New York: Macmillan.

Khan, Mehreen. 2017. "Jean-Claude Juncker Pushes His Integrationist Vision." *Financial Times*, September 14.

Khan, Mehreen, and Paul McClean. 2017. "Dijsselbloem Under Fire for Saying Eurozone Countries Wasted Money on 'Alcohol and Women.'" *Financial Times*, March 21.

Kindleberger, Charles. 1964. *Economic Growth in France and Britain, 1851–1950*. Cambridge: Harvard University Press.

Kindleberger, Charles P. 1978. "The Aging Economy." *Weltwirtschaftliches Archiv* 114, no. 3: 407–421. http://www.jstor.org/stable/40438527, accessed November 11, 2014.

Kindleberger, Charles. 1984. *A Financial History of Western Europe*. London: George Allen and Unwin.

Kindleberger, Charles P., and Robert Z. Aliber. 2005. *Manias, Panics, and Crashes: A History of Financial Crises*. 5th ed. Hoboken: John Wiley.

King, Mervyn. 2016. *The End of Alchemy: Money, Banking, and the Future of the Global Economy*. New York: W. W. Norton.

Kinsella, Stephen. 2017. "Economic and Fiscal Policy." In *Austerity and Recovery in Ireland: Europe's Poster Child and the Great Recession*, edited by William Roche, Philip O'Connell, and Andrea Porthero. Oxford: Oxford University Press.

Kinzer, Steven. 1990. "Evolution in Europe: Kohl Is Savoring 'This Happy Hour.'" *New York Times*, November 25, 16.

Kirschbaum, Erik. 1997. "Kohl Confident Euro Coming Despite Doubts." Reuters News, June 27.

Kirschbaum, Erik. 1999. "German CDU Mulls Putting 'Warhorse' Kohl to Grass." Reuters News, December 21.

Kissinger, Henry. 1999. *Years of Renewal*. New York: Simon & Schuster.

Kissler, Andreas, and James Angelos. 2012. "Germany's Schäuble: No Doubt Portugal Will Continue Reforms." Dow Jones Institutional News, November 21.

Kitsantonis, Niki. 2017. "Emmanuel Macron, in Greece, Calls for 'Rebuilding' E.U." *New York Times*, September 7.

Kjetland, Ragnhild. 2007. "Germany's IKB Issues Profit Warning, CEO Resigns As U.S. Subprime Lending Crisis Is Felt." Associated Press, July 30.

Koeppen, Nina, and Brian Blackstone. 2011. "Trichet Signals Rate Rise Still Likely." *Wall Street Journal Europe*, March 22.

Kohl, Helmut. 1991. "Helmut Kohl's Speech in the German Parliament on December 13, 1991." Deutscher Bundestag: Stenographischer Bericht 68, Sitzung, Plenarprotokoll 12/68, 5797–5803.

Kohl, Helmut. 1992. "Current Developments in European Politics." Deutscher Bundestag: Stenographischer Bericht 108, Sitzung, Bonn, Plenarprotokoll 12/108, September 25, 9219–9221.

Kohl, Helmut. 1996. "Speech by Chancellor Helmut Kohl on the Occasion of the Conferral of His Honorary Doctorate by the Catholic University in Leuven, Belgium, February 2." http://germanhistorydocs.ghi-dc.org/pdf/eng/Ch9Doc03FIN.pdf.

Kohl, Helmut. 1998. "Helmut Kohl's Speech in the German Parliament on April 23, 1998." Deutscher Bundestag: Stenographischer Bericht 230, Sitzung, Plenarprotokoll 13/230, S. 21050–21058.

Kohl, Helmut. 2014. *Aus Sorge um Europa: Ein Appell* [Out of Concern for Europe: An Appeal]. Munich: Droemer. Kindle edition.

Kokkinidis, Tasos. 2017. "Half of Greeks between 18–35 Financially Supported by Family." Greek Reporter, July 17.

Kollmeyer, Barbara. 2011. "European Banks Tumble." Wall Street Journal Online, July 8.

Kollmeyer, Barbara, and Andrea Tryphonides. 2011. "Europe's Banks, Insurers, Airlines Lead Selloff." Wall Street Journal Online, May 23.

Koranyi, Balazs, and Joseph Nasr. 2017. "Italy Would Be Unwise to Reverse Labour Market Reform: OECD." Reuters News, March 17.

Kovrijnykh, Natalia, and Balázs Szentes. 2007. "Equilibrium Default Cycles." *Journal of Political Economy* 115, no. 3: 403–446.

Kowsmann, Patricia. 2011. "Political Turmoil Grows in Portugal." Wall Street Journal Online, March 15.

Krugman, Paul. 1995. "Dutch Tulips and Emerging Markets." Foreign Affairs 74, no. 4: 28–44.

Krugman, Paul. 1988. "Financing vs Forgiving a Debt Overhang." *Journal of Development Economics* 29: 253–268.

Krugman, Paul. 1998. "It's Baaack: Japan's Slump and the Return of the Liquidity Trap." *Brookings Papers on Economic Activity* 2: 137–205.

Krugman, Paul. 2011. "An Impeccable Disaster." *New York Times*, September 11.

Krugman, Paul. 2012. *End This Depression Now!* New York: W. W. Norton.

Krugman, Paul. 2014a. "Timid Analysis." Conscience of a Liberal, New York Times Blogs, March 21. http://krugman.blogs.nytimes.com/2014/03/21/timid-analysis-wonkish/?_r=0.

Krugman, Paul. 2014b. "The Timidity Trap." *New York Times*, March 20. https://www.nytimes.com/2014/03/21/opinion/krugman-the-timidity-trap.html

Krugman, Paul. 2017. "A Finger Exercise on Hyperglobalization," June 14. https://krugman.blogs.nytimes.com/2017/06/14/a-finger-exercise-on-hyperglobalization.

Küsters, Hanns Jürgen. 1998. "Entscheidung für die deutsche Einheit" [Decision for German Unity]. In *Deutsche Einheit: Sonderedition aus den Akten des Bundeskanzleramtes, 1989/90* [German Unity: Special Edition of the Documents of the Federal Chancellery, 1989/90], edited by Hanns Jürgen Küsters and Daniel Hofmann. Munich: Oldenbourg Verlag.

Küsters, Hanns Jürgen, and Daniel Hofmann. 1998. *Deutsche Einheit: Sonderedition aus den Akten des Bundeskanzleramtes, 1989/90* [German Unity: Special Edition of the Documents of the Federal Chancellery, 1989/90]. Munich: Oldenbourg Verlag.

Kyriakidou, Dina. 2009. "Papandreou Fought Long, Hard Battle to the Top." Reuters News, October 4.

Labaton, Stephen. 2008. "U.S. Regulator's 2004 Rule Let Banks Pile Up New Debt." *International Herald Tribune*, October 3.

Lakoff, George. 2017. "#ProtectTheTruth." https://georgelakoff.com/2017/02/18/protectthetruth.

Lamfalussy, Alexandre. 1989. "Macro-Coordination of Fiscal Policies in Economic and Monetary Union in Europe." In *The Report on Economic and Monetary Union in the European Community: Collection of Papers Submitted to the Committee for the Study of Economic and Monetary Union*, Office for Official Publications of the European Communities, Luxemboourg, 91–125. http://aei.pitt.edu/1008/1/monetary_delors_collected_papers.pdf.

Lamfalussy, Christophe, Ivo Maes, and Sabine Péters. 2014. *Alexandre Lamfalussy: The Wise Man of the Euro*. Leuven: LanooCampus.

Lamont, Norman. 1999. *In Office*. London: Little, Brown.

Landler, Mark. 2003. "On a Sickbed, Is Germany Too Weak for Cure?" *New York Times*, March 3.

Landler, Mark. 2005. "Euro Bruised by Rejection of New Pact by France." *New York Times*, May 31.

Landler, Mark. 2008. "ECB Raises Key Rate to 4.25%." *New York Times*, July 3.

Lane, Philip. 2006. "The Real Effects of European Monetary Union." *Journal of Economic Perspectives* 20, no. 4: 47–66.

Langfield, Sam, and Marco Pagano. 2016a. "Bank Bias in Europe: Effects on Systemic Risk and Growth." *Economic Policy* 31, no. 85: 51–106.

Langfield, Sam, and Marco Pagano. 2016b. "Financial Structure." In *The Palgrave Handbook of European Banking*, edited by Thorsten Beck and Barbara Casu. London: Palgrave Macmillan.

La Porta, Rafael, Florencio Lopez-de-Silanes, and Andrei Shleifer. 2002. "Government Ownership of Banks." *Journal of Finance* 57, no. 1: 265–301.

La Stampa. 2012. "Household Appliance Makers Struggle to Survive," August 9.

Laughland, John. 2000. "Many Key Players Who Forced the Euro on to the Statute Book Were Crooks." *Times*, January 25.

Lee, Jae-Seung. 2004. "The French Commitment to European Monetary Integration: A Review of the Two EMS Crises (1981–83, 1992–93)." *Global Economic Review* 33, no. 2: 39–56.

Le Monde. 1974. "M. Valéry Giscard d'Estaing répond aujourd'hui à nos questions" [Mr. Valéry Giscard d'Estaing Answered Our Questions Today]. May 3.

Le Monde. 1978. "La conférence de presse du président de la république" [Text of statements by Valéry Giscard d'Estaing at a press conference on November 21 at the Maison de Radio-France]. November 23.

Lenihan, Brian. 2010a. "Minister's Statement on Banking," Dublin: Department of Finance, September 30, https://web.archive.org/web/20170420171433/http://www.finance.gov.ie/news-centre/press-releases/minister%E2%80%99s-statement-banking-30-september-2010.

Lenihan, Brian. 2010b. "Other Questions—Bank Guarantee Scheme," September 30. http://oireachtasdebates.oireachtas.ie/debates%20authoring/debateswebpack.nsf/takes/dail2010093000013?opendocument.

Leonard, Mark. 2017. "French-German Leaders; Can Merkron Save Europe?" *Handelsblatt Global*, July 5.

Leparmentier, Arnaud, and Laurent Zecchini. 2002. "Prodi: 'La France doit s'engager advantage en Europe'" [Prodi: "France Must Engage More with Europe"]. *Le Monde*, October 18, 1, 5.

Levy Yeyati, Eduardo, and Ugo Panizza. 2011. "The Elusive Costs of Sovereign Defaults." *Journal of Development Economics* 94, no. 1: 95–105.

Libero Quotidiano. 2017. "Mps e banche, l'allarme dell'economista: 'Italia a fondo, non ha senso restare nell'Ue'" [MPS and Banks, the Economist's Warning: "Italy in a Deep Hole, Makes No Sense to Stay in the EU"], January 3. http://www.liberoquotidiano.it/news/economia/12264845/mps-banche-luigi-zingales-italia-fondo-rischio-uscita-ue-.html.

Lichfield, John. 1998. "Countdown to the Euro—View from France—Europe United by Apathy and Ignorance." *Independent*, December 29.

Longo, Morya. 2016. "Draghi: The New Atlante Fund 'Is a Small Step in the Right Direction.'" ItalyEurope24, April 22.

Lorentzsen, Erika. 2005. "Chirac Defends E.U. Constitution on TV." *Washington Post*, April 15.

Love, Brian. 2008. "Paris Summit Seeks European Response to Crisis." Reuters News, October 3.

Love, Brian, and Anna Willard. 2008. "European Leaders Vow to Fight Financial Crisis." Reuters News, October 4.

Lucidi, Federico, and Alfred Kleinknecht. 2010. "Little Innovation, Many Jobs: An Econometric Analysis of the Italian Labour Productivity Crisis." *Cambridge Journal of Economics* 34: 525–546.

Ludlow, Peter. 1982. *The Making of the European Monetary System: A Case-Study of the Politics of the European Community*. London: Butterworth Scientific.

Ludlow, Peter. 2010. "The Euro Crisis Once Again: The European Council of October 28–29, 2010." Eurocomment Briefing Note 8 (3), Brussels, December.

Ludlow, Peter, and Luigi Spaventa. 1980. "The Political and Diplomatic Origins of the European Monetary System: July 1977–March 1979." Johns Hopkins University, Joint Bologna Center, European University Institute Conference, November 16–17, 1979.

Lynn, Matthew. 2010. *Bust: Greece, the Euro and the Sovereign Debt Crisis*. Hoboken: John Wiley.

Lyons, Tom. 2011. "Noonan Must Do Battle on Interest Rate Rise." *Sunday Times*, July 10.

Maastricht Treaty. 1992. "Treaty on European Union," signed February 7, effective November 1, 1993. https://europa.eu/european-union/law/treaties_en.

Maatouk, Michele, and Barbara Kollmeyer. 2012. "Spanish Stocks, Bonds Pummeled." Wall Street Journal Online, July 5

Macdonald, Alastair, and Michel Rose. 2017. "France's Macron Urges EU to Curb Cheap East European Workers." Reuters News, May 25.

MacDougall, Donald. 1977. Report of the Study Group on the Role of Public Finance in European Integration." Office for Official Publications of the European Communities, Luxembourg. http://www.cvce.eu/content/publication/2012/5/31/c475e949-ed28-490b-81ae-a33ce9860d09/publishable_en.pdf.

Mackenzie, James. 2014. "Italy's Grillo Attacks Renzi Reform, Seeks Referendum on Euro." Reuters News, October 12.

Mackenzie, James. 2016. "Italy Economy Ministry Calls for Change of Approach in EU—Update 1." Reuters News, March 28.

Macmillan, Harold. 1961. "Memorandum by the Prime Minister." Written between December 29, 1960, and January 3, 1961. PREM 11/3325, 57–88. Prime Minister's Office, London.

Macron, Emmanuel. 2017a. "Speech by the President of the French Republic." September 7, Athens. https://newyork.consulfrance.org/Speech-by-the-President-of-the-French-Republic-in-Greece.

Macron, Emmanuel. 2017b. "Initiative for Europe." Sorbonne University, Paris, September 26.

MacroPolis. 2017. "Greeks Graduating after 2011 Encountered Limited Opportunities, Low Pay," July 6. http://www.macropolis.gr/?i=portal.en.society.5825.

MacSharry, Ray. 2014. "The Poisoned Chalice." In *Brian Lenihan: In Calm and Crisis*, edited by Brian Murphy, Mary O'Rourke, and Noel Whelan, chapter 8. Kildare: Merrion. Kindle edition.

Mader, Mattias, and Harold Schoen. 2015. "Chancellor Merkel, the European Debt Crisis and the AFD: An Analysis of Voting Behaviour in the 2013 Federal Elections." In *Germany after the 2013 Elections: Breaking the Mould of Post-Unification Politics*. Farnham, England: Ashgate.

Maes, Ivo. 2004. "Macroeconomic and Monetary Policy-Making at the European Commission, from the Rome Treaties to the Hague Summit." National Bank of Belgium Working Paper 58, Brussels, August.

Maes, Ivo, and Eric Bussière. 2016. "Robert Triffin: The Arch Monetarist in the European Monetary Integration Debates?" In *Architects of the Euro: Intellectuals as Policy-Makers in the Process of European Monetary Integration*, edited by Kenneth Dyson and Ivo Maes. London: Oxford University Press.

Mair, Peter. 2007. "Political Opposition and the European Union." *Government and Opposition* 42, no. 1: 1–17.

Mair, Peter. 2013. *Ruling the Void: The Hollowing of Western Democracy*. London: Verso.

Major, Tony, and Hugh Williamson. 2003. "Rift Widens As ECB Holds Firm over Interest Rates." *Financial Times*, July 12.

Malkin, Israel, and Fernanda Nechio. 2012. "US and Euro-Area Monetary Policy by Regions." FRBSF Economic Letter 2012-02, February 27. http://www.frbsf.org/economic-research/files/el2012-06.pdf.

Mallet, Victor. 2002. "France Wants to Break Balanced Budget Pledge." *Financial Times*, May 13.

Mann, Siegfried. 1989. *European Monetary Policy: From Convergence to an Institution*. Cologne: Bundesverband der Deutschen Industrie.

Marcussen, Martin, and Mette Zølner. 2003. "The Danish EMU Referendum 2000: Business As Usual." *Government and Opposition* 36, no. 3: 379–402.

Marjolin, Robert. 1975. "Report of the Study Group: Economic and Monetary Union, 1980." Directorate General of Economic and Financial Affairs, Commission of the European Communities. Brussels, March 8. http://www.cvce.eu/content/publication/2010/10/27/93d25b61-6148-453d-9fa7-9e220e874dc5/publishable_en.pdf.

Marjolin, Robert. 1981. "Europe in Search of Its Identity." Russell C. Leffingwell Lectures. Council on Foreign Relations. New York, September 1980.

Marjolin, Robert. 1989 [1986]. *Architect of European Unity: Memoirs, 1911–1986*. London: Weidenfield and Nicolson.

Market News International. 1999. "Duisenberg Sees Good Chance for Greece to Join EMU by 2001," December 21.

Market News International. 2010. "Germany FinMin Expects Decision on Greek Aid in Two Weeks," April 23.

Marsh, David. 1991. "Monday Interview; Navigating in Turbulent Waters." *Financial Times*, April 29, 32.

Marsh, David. 1992. *The Bundesbank: The Bank That Rules Europe*. London: Heineman.

Marsh, David. 1993. "Caught Out by a Turning Tide." *Financial Times*, April 8, 19.

Marsh, David. 2009a. *The Euro: The Battle for the New Global Currency*. New Haven: Yale University Press.

Marsh, David. 2009b. "France, Germany and Fissures in the Eurozone." *Financial Times*, January 11.

Marsh, David and Andrew Fisher. 1989. "Man in the News: Sceptical Champion of EC Monetary Integration—Karl Otto Pohl." *Financial Times*, July 1, 7.

Marsh, Sarah. 2012. "Former Rights Activist Gauck to Become German President." Reuters News, February 19.

Marshall, Matt. 1997a. "Bonn Abandons Gold-Revaluation Plan." *Asian Wall Street Journal*, June 4.

Marshall, Matt. 1997b. "Tribal Taboo: Bavarian Politicians Prepare to Challenge Bonn on EMU Policy." *Wall Street Journal Europe*, June 26.

Martin, Philippe, Thierry Mayer, and Mathias Thoenig. 2012. "The Geography of Conflicts and Regional Agreements." *American Economic Journal: Macroeconomics* 4, no. 4: 1–35.

Mascolo, Georg, and Christoph Schwennicke. 2011. "Interview with Gerhard Schröder: Europe Needs to Wake Up." Spiegel Online, September 5. http://www.spiegel.de/international/europe/spiegel-interview-with-gerhard-Schröder-europe-needs-to-wake-up-a-784357.html.

Masoni, Danilo, and Francesca Piscioneri. 2014. "A Washing Machine Factory Tests Italy's Industrial Future." Reuters News, March 2014.

Masson, Paul, and Michael Mussa. 1995. "Long-Term Tendencies in Budget Deficits and Debt." IMF Working Paper 95/128. Presented at the Federal Reserve Bank of Kansas City Symposium on "Budget Deficits and Debt: Issues and Options," September. http://papers.ssrn.com/sol3/papers.cfm?abstract_id=883274##.

Masuch, Klaus, Edmund Moshammer, and Beatrice Pierluigi. 2017. "Institutions, Public Debt, and Growth in Europe." *Public Sector Economics* 41, no. 2: 159–205.

Mathieu, Gilbert. 1974. "Une opération en deux temps" [A Two-Step Operation]. *Le Monde*, June 4, 5.

Mayer, Thomas. 2017. "Macron ist ein gefährlicher Partner" [Macron Is a Dangerous Partner]. *Frankfurter Allgemeine Zeitung*, June 24.

Mayr, Walter. 2014. "Italy's New Prime Minister Promises Radical Reform." Spiegel Online, March 6.

Mazower, Mark. 2013. "Italy Exposes Wider Crisis of Democracy." *Financial Times*, February 28.

Mazzolini, Giulio, and Ashoka Mody. 2014. "Austerity Tales: The Netherlands and Italy." Bruegel Blog, October 26. http://bruegel.org/2014/10/austerity-tales-the-netherlands-and-italy.

Mazzucelli, Colette. 1997. *France and Germany at Maastricht: Politics and Negotiations to Create the European Union*. New York: Garland.

McDonald, Robert. 1991. "Greece Struggles to Rescue Economy." *Toronto Star*, August 21.

McDougall, Owen, and Ashoka Mody. 2014. "Will Voters Turn Out in the 2014 European Parliamentary Elections?" VoxEU, May 17. http://voxeu.org/article/turnout-european-parliament-elections.

McEnaney, Tom. 2006. "Fast Growth Is the Property of the Niche Player Banking on Collateral." *Irish Independent*, December 7.

McManus, John. 1996. "EMU Plan Faces Irish Backlash." *Sunday Times*, October 20.

Megginson, William L. 2005. "The Economics of Bank Privatization." *Journal of Banking and Finance* 29: 1931–1980.

Meichtry, Stacy. 2017. "French President Assumes Royal Bearing in Office." *Wall Street Journal*, July 14.

Meier, Simone. 2009. "ECB Cuts Key Rate As Recession Forces Trichet's Hand—Update 1." Bloomberg, January 15.

Melander, Ingrid. 2009. "Papandreou Woos Undecided Greeks ahead of Vote." Reuters News, October 1.

Melander, Ingrid. 2011. "Greek Recession Helps Put Lid on Corruption—Survey." Reuters News, March 17.

Merkel, Angela. 1999. "Die von Helmut Kohl eingeräumten Vorgänge haben der Partei Schaden zugefügt" [The Party Has Suffered Harm from the Deeds That Helmut Kohl Has Admitted To]. *Frankfurter Allgemeine Zeitung*, December 22 (the article has a Berlin, December 21 dateline).

Merkel, Angela. 2009. "Government Statement" [Regierungserklärung]. December 17, 904–908. http://dipbt.bundestag.de/doc/btp/17/17012.pdf.

Merkel, Angela. 2010a. "Government Statement" [Regierungserklärung]. May 5, 3721–3727. http://dip21.bundestag.de/dip21/btp/17/17039.pdf.

Merkel, Angela. 2010b. "Herculean Budgetary Consolidation and Higher Growth: Speech in the General Debate on the Federal Budget" [Herkulesaufgabe Haushalt konsolidieren und Wachstum schaffen: Rede in der Generaldebatte zum Bundeshaushalt]. March 17, 2711–2720, http://dip21.bundestag.de/dip21/btp/17/17030.pdf.

Merkel, Angela. 2010c. "Speech by the Federal Chancellor on Being Awarded the Royal Society's King Charles II Medal," April 1. https://royalsociety.org/news/2010/german-chancellor.

Merkel, Angela. 2014. "Rede vor dem Bundestag" [Parliament Speech]. June 25, 3691–3697. http://dip21.bundestag.de/dip21/btp/18/18042.pdf.

Merler, Silvia. 2017. "A Tangled Tale of Bank Liquidation in Venice." Bruegel Blog, June 26. http://bruegel.org/2017/06/a-tangled-tale-of-bank-liquidation-in-venice.

Mettler, Ann. 2004. "Brussels Needs a New Vocabulary of Reform." *Wall Street Journal Europe*, June 24.

Milasin, Ljubomir. 2013. "Europe Takes Key Role in Italy's Elections." Agence France-Presse, February 8.

Millar, Kate. 2015. "Greek Finance Minister Met with 'Scepticism' in Bruising Berlin Debt Talks." Agence France-Presse, February 5.

Milward, Alan. 1992. *The European Rescue of the Nation-State*. London: Routledge. Kindle edition.

Minihan, Mary. 2015. "Burton Says Debt Conference Idea 'Has Merit'; Tánaiste Says Ireland Will Look for Any Further Relief That May Be Obtainable." *Irish Times*, January 15.

Modigliani, Franco, and Giorgio La Malfa. 1998 "Perils of Unemployment." *Financial Times*, January 16.

Modigliani, Franco, Jean-Paul Fitoussi, Beniamino Moro, Dennis Snower, Robert Solow, Alfred Steinherr, and Stefano Sylos Labini. 1998. "An Economists' Manifesto on Unemployment in the European Union." *BNL Quarterly Review* 51, no. 206: 327–361.

Mody, Ashoka. 2009. "From Bear Stearns to Anglo Irish: How Eurozone Sovereign Spreads Related to Financial Sector Vulnerability." IMF Working Paper WP/09/108, Washington, D.C., May.

Mody, Ashoka. 2012. "Greece's Bogus Debt Deal." Project Syndicate, December 12.

Mody, Ashoka. 2013. "Sovereign Debt and Its Restructuring Framework in the Eurozone." *Oxford Review of Economic Policy* 29, no. 4: 715–744.

Mody, Ashoka, 2014a. "Are the Eurozone's Fiscal Rules Dying—If So, Good Riddance." Bruegel Blog, October 29. http://bruegel.org/2014/10/are-the-eurozones-fiscal-rules-dying.

Mody, Ashoka. 2014b. "Did the German Court Do Europe a Favour?" *Capital Markets Law Journal* (December): 1–17.

Mody, Ashoka. 2014c. "Europhoria Once Again." February 10. http://www.bruegel.org/nc/blog/detail/article/1242-europhoria-once-again.

Mody, Ashoka. 2014d. "The Ghost of Deauville." VoxEU, January 7. http://www.voxeu.org/article/ghost-deauville.

Mody, Ashoka. 2014e. "Making Argentina's Debt Debacle a Rarity." Bloomberg View, October 2.

Mody, Ashoka. 2015a. "Germany, Not Greece, Should Exit the Euro." Bloomberg View, July 17.

Mody, Ashoka. 2015b. "Living (Dangerously) without a Fiscal Union." Bruegel Working Paper 2015/03, March.

Mody, Ashoka. 2015c, "Obama Joins the Greek Chorus." Project Syndicate, February 5.

Mody, Ashoka. 2015d. "Professor Blanchard Writes a Greek Tragedy." Bruegel Blog, July 13. http://bruegel.org/2015/07/professor-blanchard-writes-a-greek-tragedy/.

Mody, Ashoka. 2016. "Saving the IMF." Project Syndicate, April 9.

Mody, Ashoka, and Emily Riley. 2014. "Why Does Italy Not Grow?" Bruegel Blog, October 10. http://bruegel.org/2014/10/why-does-italy-not-grow.

Mody, Ashoka, and Damiano Sandri. 2012. "The Eurozone Crisis: How Banks and Sovereigns Came to Be Joined at the Hip." *Economic Policy* 27: 199–230.

Mody, Ashoka, and Diego Saravia. 2006. "Catalysing Private Capital Flows: Do IMF Programmes Work As Commitment Devices?" *Economic Journal* 116 (July): 843–867.

Moeller, Almut. 2012. "Angela Merkel's Real Nightmare." CNN, June 30. http://www.cnn.com/2012/06/30/opinion/opinion-moeller-merkel-nightmare/index.html.

Moen, Arild. 2011. "Finland PM: Expects Collateral Deal with Greece in Few Days or Weeks." *Dow Jones Institutional News*, August 31.

Moghadam, Reza, Ranjit Teja, and Pelin Berkmen. 2014. "Euro Area—'Deflation' versus 'Lowflation.'" IMF Blog, March 4. https://blogs.imf.org/2014/03/04/euro-area-deflation-versus-lowflation.

Moïsi, Dominique. 1995. "Chirac of France: A New Leader of the West?" *Foreign Affairs*, November–December: 8–13.

Moïsi, Dominique. 2005. "Handing the 21st Century to Asia: The EU Constitution III." *International Herald Tribune*, May 26.

Mokyr, Joel. 2016. *A Culture of Growth: The Origins of the Modern Economy*. Princeton: Princeton University Press.

Mollenkamp, Carrick, and Cassell Bryan-Low. 2010. "Greece Leaps Crucial Hurdle with Debt Sale" *Wall Street Journal*, March 5.

Mollenkamp, Carrick, and Edward Taylor. 2007. "Subprime Troubles Hit Commerzbank and IKB." *Wall Street Journal Europe*, July 31.

Monnet, Jean. 1978 {1976}. *Memoirs*. London: William Collins Sons.

Moody's Investors Service. 2010. "Moody's Places Ireland's Aa2 Rating on Review for Possible Downgrade." Press release, October 5.

Moody's Investors Service. 2012a. "Moody's Changes Outlook on the EFSF's (P)Aaa Rating to Negative." Press release, July 24.

Moody's Investors Service. 2012b. "Moody's Changes the Outlook to Negative on Germany, Netherlands, Luxembourg and Affirms Finland's Aaa Stable Rating." Press release, July 23.

Moody's Investors Service. 2013. "Moody's Affirms Intesa Sanpaolo's Baa2/P-2 Ratings; Lowers BCA to Baa3." Press release, July 24.

Moravcsik, Andrew. 1991. "Negotiating the Single European Act: National Interests and Conventional Statecraft in the European Community." *International Organization* 45, no. 1: 19–56.

Moravcsik, Andrew. 1998. *The Choice for Europe: Social Purpose and State Power from Messina to Maastricht*. Ithaca: Cornell University Press.

Moravcsik, Andrew. 2006. "What Can We Learn from the Collapse of the European Constitutional Project?" *Politische Vierteljahresschrift* 47, no. 2: 219–241.

Moravcsik, Andrew. 2008. "The European Constitutional Settlement." *World Economy* 31, no. 1: 158–183.

Morgan, Simon. 2012. "ECB Trims Rates, but Markets Pound 'Timid' Response." Agence France-Presse, July 5.

Mortimer, Edward. 1996. "Journey to EMU's Heartland." *Financial Times*, December 23.

Mortished, Carl. 2004. "VW Cannot Be Special." *Times* January 28.

Mudde, Cas. 2017. "'Good' Populism Beat 'Bad' in Dutch Election." *Guardian*, March 19.

Müller, Peter, Christian Reiermann, and Christoph Schult. 2010. "Merkel Caves In to Sarkozy—Germany's Allies Shocked by Euro Zone Backdown." Spiegel Online, October 25.

Münchau, Wolfgang. 2013. "A Perilous Time to Switch Italy's Voting System." *Financial Times*, December 8.

Münchau, Wolfgang. 2014. "Once Again National Interests Undermine Europe." *Financial Times*, March 10.

Münchrath, Jens, Yasmin Osman, and Christopher Cermak. 2014. "At Loggerheads: Man with an Iron Will." *Handelsblatt Global*, December 17.

Mundell, Robert. 1961. "A Theory of Optimum Currency Areas." *American Economic Review* 51: 657–665.

Murphy, Kevin, Andrei Shleifer, and Robert Vishny. 1993. "Why Is Rent-Seeking So Costly to Growth?" *American Economic Review* 83, no. 2: 409–414.

Murphy, Richard. 1994. "Kohl Distances Himself from Party's EU Reform Idea." Reuters News, September 5.

Murray, Michael. 2003. "Fund Managers Missed the Anglo Irish Boat." *Sunday Business Post*, November 30.

Murray Brown, John. 2009. "Lenihan Sees Bail-Out As Key for Republic's Revival." *Financial Times*, May 29.

Murray Brown, John. 2010. "Fitch Downgrades Ireland's Debt Rating." *Financial Times*, October 6.

Musolff, Andreas. 2003. "Metaphor Corpora and *Corporeal* Metaphors." Paper Presented at Interdisciplinary Workshop on Corpus-Based Approaches to Figurative Language, Lancaster University, March 27. Revised version published in *Proceedings of the Interdisciplinary Workshop on Corpus-Based Approaches to Figurative Language*, edited by John Barnden, Sheila Glasbey, Mark

Lee, Katja Markert, and Alan Wallington. University Centre for Computer Corpus Research on Language, Technical Papers 18. Lancaster: Lancaster University, 48–57, http://ucrel.lancs.ac.uk/papers/techpaper/vol18.pdf.

Mussler, Werner. 2017. "Schäuble erteilt Eurohaushalt eine Abfuhr Brüsseler Ideen zur Vertiefung der Währungsunion 'nicht realistisch'/EU-Finanzminister gegen Bad Bank" [Schäuble Rejects EU Budget: Ideas regarding the Further Integration of the Monetary Union "Not Realistic"/EU Finance Minister Opposes Bad Bank]. *Frankfurter Allgemeine Zeitung*, April 9.

Nagle, Peter. 2017. "Global Macro Views: Euro Area Inflation Still a Headache for the ECB." Institute for International Finance, Washington, D.C., September 7.

Nash, Elizabeth. 1998. "Countdown to the Euro: View from Portugal." *Independent*, December 29.

Neumann, Jeannette, Patricia Kowsmann, and Giovanni Legorano. 2016. "European Banks Buffeted by Bond Investors' Fears; Central Banks Are Wary of Suffering a Political and Financial Backlash if They Force Losses on a Bank's Individual Investors." *Wall Street Journal*, February 15.

New Europe. 2015. "Jean Claude Juncker Questions Troika's 'Democratic Legitimacy,'" February 19. https://www.neweurope.eu/article/jean-claude-juncker-questions-troikas-democratic-legitimacy.

New York Times. 1971. "2 Constellations Pull Together," January 15, 55.

New York Times. 1989. "Upheaval in the East," December 7, A21.

Nixon, Simon. 2011. "Will the Stress Be Stressful Enough?" Wall Street Journal Online, January 27.

Noble, Christopher. 1998. "France Qualifies for EMU As Economy Rebounds." Reuters News, February 27.

Nocera, Joe. 2009. "Lehman Had to Die, It Seems, So Global Finance Could Live." *New York Times*, September 12.

Norman, Peter. 1993. "EC Interest Rates Puzzle—Why Germany Pushed at an Open Door on Monetary Policy." *Financial Times*, August 17.

Norman, Peter. 1997. "Defender of a Decimal Point." *Financial Times*, July 7.

Norman, Peter. 2000. "Brussels Proposes Greece Should Join Euro-Zone." *Financial Times*, May 4.

Norris, Floyd. 2000. "Rise in Rates Is Not Stemming the Euro's Slide." *New York Times*, September 7.

Norris, Floyd. 2005. "A New Fall Guy Emerges in Europe: The Euro." *International Herald Tribune*, June 8.

NPR. 2008. "Fed Cuts Interest Rate by Half Point to 1 Percent." October 29.

Nyberg, Peter. 2011. "Misjudging Risk: Causes of the Systemic Banking Crisis in Ireland." Report to the Commission of Investigation into the Banking Sector in Ireland, March. http://www.bankinginquiry.gov.ie/Documents/Misjuding%20Risk%20-%20Causes%20of%20the%20Systemic%20Banking%20Crisis%20in%20Ireland.pdf.

Obstfeld, Maurice. 2013. "Finance at Centre-Stage: Some Lessons of the Euro Crisis." Economic Papers 493, European Commission, Brussels, April.

Obstfeld, Maurice, and Giovanni Peri. 1998. "Asymmetric Shocks: Regional Non-Adjustment and Fiscal Policy." *Economic Policy*, April: 206–259.

Occorsio, Eugenio. 2016. "La Ue dica sì al piano italiano" [Let the EU Say Yes to the Italian Plan"]. *La Repubblica*, April 20.

Odendahl, Christian. 2014. "Quantitative Easing Alone Will Not Do the Trick." Centre for European Reform, April 28. http://www.cer.org.uk/insights/quantitative-easing-alone-will-not-do-trick#sthash.YWU9YtaD.dpuf.

O'Donnell, John, and Angeliki Koutantou. 2015. "Draghi Ties ECB's Greek Funding to Bailout Compliance." Reuters News, March 5.

OECD. 2008. "Ageing OECD Societies" Paris. https://www.oecd.org/berlin/41250023.pdf.

OECD. 2016a. "OECD Economic Surveys: Greece 2016." Paris, March.

OECD. 2016b. "PISA 2015 Results: Excellence and Equity in Education," December. http://dx.doi.org/10.1787/9789264266490-en.

OECD. 2017a. "OECD Economic Surveys: Italy," February.

OECD. 2017b. "OECD Economic Surveys: Portugal," February.

OECD. 2017c. "OECD Economic Surveys: Spain," March.

Ognibene, Silvia. 2013. "Police Investigate Death of Monte Paschi Spokesman—Update 3." Reuters News, March 7.

O'Mahony, John. 2000. "A Tiger by the Tail." *Guardian*, August 18. http://www.theguardian.com/books/2000/aug/19/books.guardianreview.

Open Europe. 2013a. "German Voters Reject All Forms of Further Financial Support to the Eurozone," September 17. http://openeurope.org.uk/wp-content/uploads/2014/10/German_voters_reject_all_forms_of_further_financial_support_to_the_eurozone.pdf.

Open Europe. 2013b. "German Voters Say Next Chancellor Should Back Efforts to Devolve EU Powers Back to Member States," September 17. http://openeurope.org.uk/wp-content/uploads/2013/09/German_voters_say_next_chancellor_should_back_efforts_to_devolve_EU_powers_back_to_member_states.pdf.

Orwell, George. 1961. "Looking Back on the Spanish War." Reprinted in *Collected Essays*. London: Mercury.

O'Toole, Fintan. 2012. "Giving the People of Ireland a Chance Not Chancers." *Irish Times*, March 27.

Owen, Ed, Lucia Adams, and Joanna Bale. 2006. "Thousands of Second Homes Face Bulldozer in Costa Scam." *Times*, April 3.

Packer, George. 2014. "The Quiet German: The Astonishing Rise of Angela Merkel, the Most Powerful Woman in the World." *New Yorker*, December 1. http://www.newyorker.com/magazine/2014/12/01/quiet-german.

Padoan, Pier Carlo. 2015. http://www.ilsole24ore.com/art/notizie/
2016-12-28/padoan-basta-l-opacita-vigilanza-bce-232343.
shtml?uuid=AD66RoLC&refresh_ce=1.

Padoa-Schioppa, Tommaso. 2004. "Building on the Euro's Success." Speech
at conference "The Euro at Five: Ready for a Global Role?" Institute of
International Economics, Washington, D.C., February 26. https://www.ecb.
europa.eu/press/key/date/2004/html/sp040226.en.html.

Pagano, Marco, Sam Langfield, Viral Acharya, Arnoud Boot, Markus
Brunnermeier, Claudia Buch, Martin Hellwig, André Sapir, and Ieke van den
Burg. 2014. "Is Europe Overbanked?" European Systemic Risk Board Advisory
Scientific Committee, Report 4, June. https://www.esrb.europa.eu/pub/pdf/asc/
Reports_ASC_4_1406.pdf.

Palmer, John, Anna Tomforde, and Ruth Kelly. 1992. "'Fast Track' EC Monetary
Union Closer." *Guardian*, September 25.

Panizza, Ugo. 2013. "Do We Need a Mechanism for Solving Sovereign Debt
Crises? A Rule-Based Discussion." Graduate Institute of International
and Development Studies Working Paper 03/2013, Geneva. http://repec.
graduateinstitute.ch/pdfs/Working_papers/HEIDWP03-2013.pdf.

Panizza, Ugo, Federico Sturzenegger, and Jeromin Zettelmeyer. 2009. "The
Economics and Law of Sovereign Debt and Default." *Journal of Economic
Literature* 47, no. 3: 651–698.

Paolucci, Gianluca. 2017. "Il film dell'orrore di Popolare Vicenza. 'Da Zonin
& C. danni per 2 miliardi'" [The Horror Film of Popolare Vicenza. 'Zonin
and Company Face Damages of 2 Billion Euros]. La Stampa Economia, April
7. http://www.lastampa.it/2017/04/07/economia/il-film-dellorrore-di-popolare-
vicenza-da-zonin-c-danni-per-miliardi-eMXEcYjSVBSHsQxmkSFk5O/pagina.
html.

Papachristou, Harry, and Peter Graff. 2012. "Poll Shows Greece Electing Pro-
Bailout Government." Reuters News, May 17.

Papaconstantinou, George. 2016. *Game Over: The Inside Story of the Greek Crisis*.
CreateSpace. Kindle edition.

Paris, Costas. 1991. "Greek Economy in Crisis until 1997—Bank Governor."
Reuters News, November 11.

Paris, Gilles. 1992. "The Results of the Referendum on the European Union: A
Rich and Urban Yes." *Le Monde*, September 22.

Parker, George. 2003. "Brussels Says Good-bye to Annus Horribilis." *Financial
Times*, December 18.

Parker, George, and Ed Crooks. 2003. "Breaking the Pact." *Financial Times*,
November 26.

Parsons, Craig. 2000. "Domestic Interests, Ideas, and European Integration."
Journal of Common Market Studies 38, no. 1: 45–70.

Parsons, Craig. 2003 *A Certain Idea of Europe*. Ithaca: Cornell University Press.

Paterson, Tony. 2010. "Merkel Woos the State She Cannot Afford to Lose."
  Independent, May 7.

Patnaik, Ila, and Ajay Shah. 2010. "Does the Currency Regime Shape Unhedged
  Currency Exposure?" *Journal of International Money and Finance* 29: 760–769.

Pattanaik, Swaha. 2004. "EU Tests Budget Disciplining Power with Greek Step—
  Update 2." Reuters News, December 22.

Pattanaik, Swaha. 2014. "'Hike Huff' Could Disrupt Markets." Reuters News,
  September 15.

Paul, Jens Peter. 2010. "Bilanz einer gescheiterten Kommunikation.
  Fallstudien zur deutschen Entstehungsgeschichte des Euro und ihrer
  demokratietheoretischen Qualität" [Records of Failed Communication: Case
  Studies from the German Genesis of the Euro and Its Relation to Democratic
  Theory]. Dissertation, Goethe-Universität Frankfurt, Frankfurt am Main.

Peek, Joe, and Eric Rosengren. 2005. "Unnatural Selection: Perverse Incentives and
  the Misallocation of Credit in Japan." *American Economic Review* 95: 1144–1166.

Peel, Quentin. 1991. "Bundesbank Urges Tough Emu Line," Financial Times,
  September 19.

Peel, Quentin. 1992a. "German Poll Shows Support for Referendum." *Financial
  Times*, June 9, 3.

Peel, Quentin. 1992b. "Kohl Struggles to Land His Catch: The Debate in Germany
  on European Economic and Monetary Union Could Last until December."
  Financial Times, March 17.

Peel, Quentin. 2010a. "Germans Poised for €10bn Yearly Budget Cuts." *Financial
  Times*, May 23.

Peel, Quentin. 2010b. "Germany: Merkel's Moment." *Financial Times*, May 7.

Peel, Quentin. 2010c. "Hefty Stimuli Dent Germany's 'Swabian' Habit." *Financial
  Times*, June 21.

Peel, Quentin, 2010d. "Merkel Seeks Calm after Juncker E-Bond Attack."
  Financial Times, December 8.

Peel, Quentin. 2012. "Germany's Eurosceptics Build Case against Merkel."
  Financial Times, October 8.

Pellegrino, Bruno, and Luigi Zingales. 2017. "Diagnosing the Italian Disease."
  Stigler Center for the Study of the Economy and the State, University of Chicago
  Booth School of Business New Working Paper Series 14, Chicago, October.

Peyrefitte, Alain. 1994. *C'etait de Gaulle* [It Was about de Gaulle]. Paris: Fayard.

Philippon, Thomas. 2015. "Has the US Finance Industry Become Less Efficient?
  On the Theory and Measurement of Financial Intermediation." *American
  Economic Review* 105, no. 4: 1408–1438.

Philippon, Thomas, and Ariell Reshef. 2013. "An International Look at the
  Growth of Modern Finance." *Journal of Economic Perspectives* 27, no. 2: 73–96.

Phillips, Matt. 2010. "Can Words Still Soothe the Market's Greece Worries?" Wall
  Street Journal Blogs, April 9.

Pictet Wealth Management. 2016. "Bond Scarcity under New ECB QE Rules—It Ain't Over Till It's Over," December 14. http://perspectives. pictet.com/wp-content/uploads/2016/12/Flash-Note-FD-ECB-QE-bond-scarcity-14-December-2016-1.pdf.

Piketty, Thomas, and Gabriel Zucman. 2014. "Capital Is Back: Wealth-Income Ratios in Rich Countries 1700–2010." *Quarterly Journal of Economics* 129, no. 3: 1255–1310.

Pinto, Brian, and Sergei Ulatov. 2010. "Financial Globalization and the Russian Crisis of 1998." World Bank Policy Research Working Paper 5312, Washington, D.C. https://openknowledge.worldbank.org/bitstream/handle/10986/3797/WPS5312.pdf?sequence=1.

Pisani-Ferry, Jean, and Andre Sapir. 2010. "Banking Crisis Management in the EU: An Early Assessment." *Economic Policy*. (April): 341–373.

Piscioneri, Francesca. 2017. "Italy to Curb Labour Flexibility, Bowing to Trade Union Pressure." Reuters News, March 16.

Plender, John. 1989. "Thatcher Backed by Pöhl on EMS." *Financial Times*, November 20, 26.

Pogatchnik, Shawn. 2005. "Ireland's Former Justice Minister Sent to Prison for Tax Evasion." Associated Press, January 24.

Poirson, Helene. 2013. "German Productivity Growth: An Industry Perspective." In *Germany in an Interconnected World Economy*," edited by Ashoka Mody. Washington, D.C.: International Monetary Fund.

Polidori, Elena. 2010. "Jean-Claude Trichet Interview with *La Repubblica*." European Central Bank, Frankfurt, June 24. https://www.ecb.europa.eu/press/inter/date/2010/html/sp100624.en.html.

Politi, James. 2014. "Italian Shoe Shop Struggles to Find Best Fit for Boosting Growth." *Financial Times*, September 14.

Politi, James. 2015. "Workers Test the Long-Term Effect of Italy's Middle Way; Doubts Raised over Renzi Reform That Offers More Job Security but Fewer Rights." *Financial Times*, August 13.

Politi, James, and Rachel Sanderson. 2015. "Renzi Faces Political Backlash over Italian Banks' Rescue." *Financial Times*, December 10.

Polleschi, Ilaria. 2014. "Italy's Renzi, ECB's Draghi Hold 'Secret' Meeting As Economy Slides—Update 2." Reuters News, August 13.

Pop, Valentina, and Marcus Walker. 2017. "Dutch Voters Rebuff Anti-Immigration Candidate." *Wall Street Journal*, March 15.

Portes, Jonathan. 2013. "No Debate Please, We're Europeans." National Institute of Economic and Social Research, February 15. http://www.niesr.ac.uk/blog/no-debate-please-were-europeans#.WAkjhvkrLIW.

Posen, Adam. 2005. "Why the Pact Has No Impact." *International Economy* (Winter): 8–11.

Prabhavananda, Swami, and Christopher Isherwood. 1981 [1953]. *How to Know God: The Yoga Aphorisms of Patanjali*. Hollywood, CA: Vedanta Press.

Pritchett, Lant. 1997. "Divergence, Big Time." *Journal of Economic Perspectives* 11, no. 3: 3–17.

Pritchett, Lant. 2000. "Understanding Patterns of Economic Growth: Searching for Hills among Plateaus, Mountains, and Plains." *World Bank Economic Review* 14, no. 2: 221–250.

Proaño, Christian, and Thomas Theobald. 2017. "Macron and the EU Financial Transaction Tax." Social Europe, August 11.

Protzman, Ferdinand. 1990. "Bonn Offers East a Generous Rate in Unifying Money." *New York Times*, April 24, 1.

Pulzer, Peter. 1999. "Luck and Good Management: Helmut Kohl As Parliamentary and Electoral Strategist." *German Politics* 8, no. 2: 126–150.

Pylas, Pan. 2008. "European Governments Go Own Way on Deposit Guarantees and Crisis Strategy As Stocks Plunge." Associated Press, October 6.

Pylas, Pan. 2010. "Cure or Curse? Europeans Mull Option of Bailing Out of Euro—But Experts See Dangers." Associated Press, March 18.

Quinn, Patrick. 2004. "Greek Finance Minister Says EU May Give Greece till End of 2006." Associated Press, November 17.

Raifberger, François. 1992. "France Calls Maastricht Referendum, Rules Out Renegotiation." Reuters News, June 3.

Rajan, Raghuram, and Luigi Zingales. 2003. *Saving Capitalism from the Capitalists: How Open Financial Markets Challenge the Establishment and Spread Prosperity to Rich and Poor Alike*. New York: Crown. Kindle edition.

Rankin, Jennifer. 2015. "Eurozone Crisis: Which Countries Are for or against Grexit." *Guardian*, July 12.

Rankin, Jennifer. 2017. "Jean-Claude Juncker Criticises 'Ridiculous' European

Redburn, Tom. 1992. "EC Leaders Vow Unity, Charting Separate Paths." *International Herald Tribune*, September 22.

Rees-Mogg, William. 2008. "Listen to Prudence, the Swabian housewife; . . . Hers Is the True Voice of German Opinion, Whatever the Declarations of European Unity May Suggest to the Contrary." *Times*, December 15.

Regan, Aidan. 2015. "Debunking Myths: What Really Explains the Irish Economic Recovery." Dublin European Institute, May 22. http://europedebate. ie/what-explains-the-irish-economic-recovery.

Reguly, Eric. 2010. "EU Set to Pull Greece from the Brink; Move Led by Germany to Bail Out Debt-Laden Member an Attempt to Prop Up Euro, Calm Markets." *Globe and Mail*, February 10.

Rehn, Olli. 2013. "Letter to Michael Noonan and Other European Finance Ministers." Brussels, February 10. http://ec.europa.eu/archives/commission_ 2010-2014/rehn/documents/cab20130213_en.pdf.

Reinhart, Carmen, Kenneth Rogoff, and Miguel Savastano. 2003. "Debt Intolerance." *Brookings Papers on Economic Activity* 1: 1–74.

Reinhart, Carmen, and Christoph Trebesch. 2016. "Sovereign Debt Relief and Its Aftermath." *Journal of the European Economic Association* 14, no. 1: 215–251.

Reinhart, Vincent. 2011. "A Year of Living Dangerously: The Management of the Financial Crisis in 2008." *Journal of Economic Perspectives* 25, no. 1: 71–90.

Reis, Ricardo. 2013. "The Portuguese Slump and Crash and the Euro Crisis." *Brookings Papers on Economic Activity* 46 (Spring): 143–193.

Rentoul, John. 2017. "Ed Balls: Tony Blair Never Really Wanted to Join the Euro." *Independent*, March 3.

Reuters EU Highlights. 2010. "Euro Zone Finance Ministers' Meeting on Greece," May 2.

Reuters News. 1979. "Greece Signs Treaty to Join as 10th Member of EEC." *Globe and Mail*, May 29.

Reuters News. 1989. "Efficient Single Market Needs One Currency, French Say," April 18.

Reuters News. 1999a. "Dutch Tell Greeks EMU CPI Rule Can Be Discussed," February 19.

Reuters News. 1999b. "ECB—No Need Yet for Europe-Wide Bank Supervisor," February 9.

Reuters News. 2001. "US Academic Says EMU Good for Swedish Trade, Growth," November 12.

Reuters News. 2003. "Policymakers' Comments about Euro," July 11.

Reuters News. 2009a. "After Hardball, Greece Gets EU Solidarity Pledges," December 11.

Reuters News. 2009b. "EU Blasts Greece over Statistical Discrepancies," October 20.

Reuters News. 2009c. "Euro Members Responsible for Own Finances—Merkel," December 17.

Reuters News. 2009d. "Fitch Rating Cut Latest Blow to Troubled Greece," December 8.

Reuters News. 2009e. "Greece Must Slash Budget Gap in 2 Yrs—Cbank [Central Bank]," October 20.

Reuters News. 2009f. "Greece's Fate Is Joint Euro Zone Responsibility—Merkel," December 10.

Reuters News. 2009g. "Greek GDP, Deficit Seen Worsening—Officials," October 8.

Reuters News. 2009h. "New Greek PM Papandreou Says Economy 'Explosive,'" October 16.

Reuters News. 2009i. "Scandals Rock Greece's Conservative Government," April 29.

Reuters News. 2010a. "France Seen Warming to E-Bonds over Time," December 10.

Reuters News. 2010b. "German CDU to Push Greek Debt Haircuts with IMF, ECB—Update 1," April 27.

Reuters News. 2010c. "IMF Would Not Be Right Body for Greek Aid," January 14.

Reuters News. 2010d. "Merkel Says Talks with Greece Must Be Speeded Up," April 28.

Reuters News. 2010e. "Policymakers' Comments on Greek Rescue Package," May 6.

Reuters News. 2010f. "Trichet, Strauss-Kahn to Speak on Greece at 1230 GMT—Update 1" April 28.

Reuters News. 2011a. "Greece's Debt Crisis," December 1.

Reuters News, 2011b. "Private Sector Deposits in Euro Zone Banks," July 6.

Reuters News. 2014a. "French Economy Minister Urges Talks over Euro Strength—Update 1," April 16.

Reuters News. 2014b. "French PM Says Euro Overvalued, Urges ECB Asset Purchases," July 2.

Reuters News. 2014c. "French PM Valls Says Euro Too Strong—Update 1," May 3.

Reuters News. 2014d. "Germany's Schäuble Congratulates Portugal on Bailout Exit," May 17.

Reuters News. 2014e. "Recent Remarks by US Federal Reserve Officials," October 20.

Reuters News. 2015a. "Bail-In Rules May Undermine Confidence in Banking—Bank of Italy Official." December 9.

Reuters News. 2015b. "Bundesbank Chief Warns Greece against Emergency Funding for Banks," February 5.

Reuters News. 2015c. "ECB Divided over Extra Emergency Funds for Greek Banks—Sources," February 18.

Reuters News. 2015d. "ECB's Liikanen: No Lending to Greek Banks If No Deal by End of February," January 31.

Reuters News. 2015. "ECB Won't Agree to Greece Issuing More Short-Term Debt—Coeure," DonnellanMarch 7.

Reuters News. 2015f. "Merkel—Reform Drive Everywhere Must Continue after ECB Move," January 23.

Reuters News. 2015g. "Weidmann Fears ECB Bond-Buying Will Take Pressure off Italy, France." January 23.

Reuters News. 2017a. "EU Refuses to Lower Size of Private Cash Injection for Veneto Banks' Rescue—Sources," May 24.

Reuters News. 2017b. "Timeline: Volkswagen's Long Road to a U.S. Dieselgate Settlement," January 11.

Reuters News. 2017c. "World Leaders Bid Farewell to Germany's Kohl As Force for European Unity," July 1.

Rey, Hélène. 2013. "Dilemma, Not Trilemma: The Global Financial Cycle and Monetary Policy Independence." Proceedings of the Economic Policy

Symposium, Federal Reserve Bank of Kansas City, Jackson Hole, 285–333. https://www.kansascityfed.org/publicat/sympos/2013/2013rey.pdf.

Rhoads, Christopher, and Paul Hofheinz. 2001. "Euro Zone Is Caught in Tug-of-War on Policy: Fiscal-Monetary Standoff Could Weaken Economy." *Wall Street Journal Europe*, October 17.

Rhoads, Christopher, and Geoff Winestock. 2001. "The Euro: Cash in Hand—The Euro Facade: A Single Currency but Many Markets—Reason for Its Sorry State: A Lack of Common Rules—Real Financial Integration Remains Elusive." *Wall Street Journal Europe*, September 10.

Riding, Alan. 1989. "Mitterrand Backs Europe Integration." *New York Times*, December 8.

Riera-Crichton, Daniel, Carlos A. Vegh, and Guillermo Vuletin. 2014. "Fiscal Multipliers in Recessions and Expansions: Does It Matter Whether Government Spending Is Increasing or Decreasing?" World Bank Policy Research Paper 6993, Washington, D.C.

Righter, Rosemary. 2002. "Romano Was Right, but It Is the Currency, Stupid." *Times*, October 24, 24.

Robinson, Duncan. 2016. "Pushing for 'More Europe' Risks Fanning Populism, Warns Rutte." *Financial Times*, December 11.

Robinson, Frances. 2011. "ECB's Draghi: Currency Controls Conflict with Price Stability." Dow Jones International News, July 8.

Robinson, Joan. 1952. *Rate of Interest*. London: Macmillan.

Roche, William, Philip O'Connell, and Andrea Prothero, eds. 2017. *Austerity and Recovery in Ireland: Europe's Poster Child and the Great Recession*. Oxford: Oxford University Press.

Rodrigues, Vivianne, and Telis Demos. 2011. "Stocks and Euro Hit by Dented ECB Hopes." *Financial Times*, December 9.

Rodrik, Dani. 2017. "Economics of the Populist Backlash." VoxEU, http://voxeu.org/article/economics-populist-backlash.

Rogers, Iain. 2008. "German Government to Guarantee Deposit Accounts—Ministry." Reuters News, October 5.

Rogoff, Kenneth. 1985. "The Optimal Degree of Commitment to an Intermediate Monetary Target." *Quarterly Journal of Economics* 110: 1169–1189.

Rogoff, Kenneth. 2004. "Globalization and Global Disinflation." In *Monetary Policy and Uncertainty: Adapting to a Changing Economy*, Federal Reserve Bank of Kansas City, 77–112.

Rogoff, Kenneth. 2008. "No More Creampuffs." *Washington Post*, September 16.

Rogoff, Kenneth. 2017. "The Eurozone Must Reform or Die." Project Syndicate, June 14.

Roland, Denise. 2012. "Debt Crisis: As It Happened." Telegraph Online, December 17.

Rooney, Ben. 2009. "Dollar Mixed in Narrow Range." CNN Money, January 15.

Rosa, Carlo, and Andrea Tambalotti. 2014. "How Unconventional Are Large-Scale Asset Purchases?" Liberty Street Economics Blog, Federal Reserve Board of New York, March 3. http://libertystreeteconomics.newyorkfed.org/2014/03/how-unconventional-are-large-scale-asset-purchases.html#.U1_YTPldVDC.

Rose, Andrew. 2000. "One Money, One Market: The Effect of Common Currencies on Trade." *Economic Policy* 15, no. 30: 7–45.

Rose, Charlie. 2005a. "Conversation with Valéry Giscard d'Estaing, Former President of France; Interview with Actress Joan Allen." *Charlie Rose*, PBS, March 7.

Rose, Charlie. 2005b. "European Constitution; Richard Reeves; 'Who's Afraid of Virginia Woolf?'" *Charlie Rose*, PBS, June 6.

Ross, George. 1995. *Jacques Delors and European Integration*. Oxford: Polity.

Rousek, Leos. 2010. "Slovak Premier Slams Euro Bailouts." Wall Street Journal Online, September 2.

Roussel, Eric. 2004. *Georges Pompidou, 1911–1974*. Rev. ed. Paris: Perrin.

Rutherford, Malcolm. 1971. "French and Germans Argue on about Floating Rates." *Financial Times*, July 6, 7.

Ryan, Eamon. 2014. "Unprecedented Circumstances." In *Brian Lenihan: In Calm and Crisis*, edited by Brian Murphy, Mary O'Rourke, and Noel Whelan, chapter 17. Kildare: Merrion. Kindle edition.

Sachs, Jeffrey. 2015. "Let Greece Profit from German History." *Guardian*, January 21.

Sachs, Jeffrey, and Charles Wyplosz. 1986. "The Economic Consequences of President Mitterrand." *Economic Policy* 1, no. 2: 261–322.

Saeed, Saim. 2017. "Juncker: 'The French Spend Too Much Money.'" *Politico*, May 18.

Sage, Adam. 2005. "Discontented Dutch Seize on Chance to Deliver Protest Vote; EU Constitution." *Times*, June 2.

Sage, Adam. 2017. "Macron's Ratings Slump As Left Urges Protest." *Times*, August 27.

Sala-i-Martin, Xavier, and Jeffrey Sachs. 1991. "Fiscal Federalism and Optimum Currency Areas: Evidence for Europe from the United States." National Bureau of Economic Research Working Paper 3855, Cambridge.

Samuel, Henry. 2011. "Sarkozy's 30-Minute Visit to His Wife in Labour: Media." Postmedia News, October 19.

Sanderson, Rachel. 2014a. "Italian Business Grows Restless with Matteo Renzi." *Financial Times*, September 24.

Sanderson, Rachel. 2014b. "Renzi Protest: Italy's Services Suffer during General Strike." *Financial Times*, December 13.

Sanderson, Rachel, and Martin Arnold. 2016. "Italy Agrees €5bn Fund to Rescue Weaker Lenders." *Financial Times*, April 12.

Sanderson, Rachel, Alex Barker, and Claire Jones. 2016. "Italian Banks: Essential Repairs." *Financial Times*, July 10.

Sanderson, Rachel, and Thomas Hale 2017. "UniCredit Finalises Sale of Bad Loans to Pimco and Fortress." *Financial Times*, July 17.

Santa, Martin. 2010. "Slovak Vote Poses Test for EU Unity, Support for Greece." Reuters News, June 11.

Santa, Martin, and Jan Strupczewski. 2010. "ECB Outraged by Slovak Refusal to Aid Greece—Sources." Reuters News, September 2010.

Santos, Tanos. 2014. "Antes del Diluvio: The Spanish Banking System in the First Decade of the Euro." March. https://www0.gsb.columbia.edu/mygsb/faculty/research/pubfiles/6162/Santos-March-2014.pdf.

Santos Silva, J. M. C., and Silvana Tenreyro. 2010. "Currency Unions in Prospect and Retrospect." *Annual Review of Economics* 2: 51–74.

Sapir, André, et al. 2003. "An Agenda for a Growing Europe: Making the EU Economic System Deliver." Report of an Independent High-Level Study Group Established on the Initiative of the President of the European Commission, Brussels. http://citeseerx.ist.psu.edu/viewdoc/download?doi=10.1.1.620.4948&rep=rep1&type=pdf.

Sarotte, Mary Elise. 2009. "Enlarging NATO, Expanding Confusion." *New York Times*, November 29, http://www.nytimes.com/2009/11/30/opinion/30sarotte.html.

Sarotte, Mary Elise. 2014a. "How the Fall of the Berlin Wall Really Happened." *New York Times*, November 6.

Sarotte, Mary Elise. 2014b. *1989: The Struggle to Create Post-Cold War Europe*. Princeton: Princeton University Press.

Sauga, Michael, Stefan Simons, and Klaus Wiegrefe. 2010. "The Price of Unity: Was the Deutsche Mark Sacrificed for Reunification?" *Der Spiegel*, September 30. http://www.spiegel.de/international/germany/0,1518,719940,00.html.

Saunders, Doug. 2010. "Europe's New Divide: Greek Bailout Drives Rift in 'Brotherhood.'" *Globe and Mail*, March 5.

Savranskaya, Svetlana, Thomas Blanton, and Vladislav Zubok, eds. 2010. *Masterpieces of History: The Peaceful End of the Cold War in Eastern Europe, 1989*. Budapest and New York: Central European University Press.

Scally, Derek. 2013. "Merkel Offers 'Gratitude' to Irish and Says Reforms Are Paying Off." *Irish Times*, September 24.

Scally, Derek. 2017. "Berlin Gets the Better of Brussels in Dieselgate Row." *Irish Times*, May 2.

Schabert, Tilo. 2009. *How World Politics Is Made: France and the Reunification of Germany*. London and Columbia: University of Missouri Press.

Schadler, Susan. 2013. "Unsustainable Debt and the Political Economy of Lending: Constraining the IMF's Role in Sovereign Debt Crises." CIGI Papers 19, Waterloo, Canada: Center for International Governance and Innovation, October.

Schaefer Muñoz, Sara, David Enrich, and Christopher Bjork. 2012. "Spain's Handling of Bankia Repeats a Pattern of Denial." *Wall Street Journal Online*, June 11.

Schäuble, Wolfgang. 2010. "Why Europe's Monetary Union Faces Its Biggest Crisis." *Financial Times*, March 12.

Schäuble, Wolfgang, and Karl Lamers. 1994. "Reflections on European Foreign Policy." Document by the CDU/CSU Group in the German Bundestag. Reprinted in *The European Union: Readings on the Theory and Practice of European Integration*, edited by Brent Nelsen and Alexander Stubb, Basingstoke: Macmillan.

Schelling, Thomas. 1988. "The Mind as a Consuming Organ." In *Decision Making: Descriptive, Normative, and Prescriptive Interactions*, edited by David E. Bell, Howard Raiffa, and Amos Tversky. Cambridge: Cambridge University Press.

Schiller, Karl. 1971. "Statement by the Governor of the Bank for Germany." *Summary Proceedings of the Twenty-Sixth Annual Meetings, September 27–October 1, 1971*. Washington, D.C.: International Monetary Fund.

Schivardi, Fabiano, Enrico Sette, and Guido Tabellini. 2017. "Credit Misallocation during the European Financial Crisis." VoxEU, July 18. http://voxeu.org/article/credit-misallocation-during-european-financial-crisis.

Schlesinger, Helmut. 1988. "Zur weiteren Entwicklung der währungspolitischen Kooperation auf internationaler und europäischer Ebene" [Concerning the Further International and European Development of Monetary Policy Cooperation]. Anläßlich der Mitgliederversammlung des Verbandes öffentlicher Banken, München, Deutsche Bundesbank: Auszüge aus Presseartikeln 84. Frankfurt am Main, November 11.

Schlesinger, Helmut. 1992. "Wege zu einer Europäischen Wirtschafts und Währungsunion und die Stellung Deutschlands darin" [Paths to a European Monetary and Economic Union and Germany's Role in This Development]. An der Freien Universität von Amsterdam, Deutsche Bundesbank. Auszüge aus Presseartikeln 83, Frankfurt am Main, November 5.

Schmemann, Serge. 1989. "Upheaval in the East: Germany; Cheers As Brandenburg Gate Reopens." *New York Times*, December 23.

Schmid, John. 1998. "They Soften Schröder's Position: Social Democrats Talk Up the Euro." *New York Times*, March 4.

Schmid, John. 2001a. "Economist Stresses Importance of Containing Inflation: ECB Defies Pressure on Rates." *New York Times*, October 18.

Schmid, John. 2001b. "Expectations Lowered for German Growth: Berlin Resists Resorting to Stimulus Package." *International Herald Tribune*, October 19.

Schneeweiss, Zoe. 2011. "Soros Says Exit Mechanism from Euro Is 'Probably Inevitable.'" Bloomberg, June 27.

Schneider, Friedrich. 2016. "Estimating the Size of the Shadow Economies of Highly-Developed Countries: Selected New Results." CESifo DICE Report 4/ 2016.

Schneider, Howard, and Anthony Faiola. 2010. "Hesitation by Leaders Drove Cost of Europe's Crisis Higher." *Washington Post*, June 16. http://www.washingtonpost.com/wp-dyn/content/article/2010/06/15/AR2010061505598.html.

Schrage, Michael. 2003. "Daniel Kahneman: The Thought Leader Interview." *Strategy+Business* 33, November. http://www.strategy-business.com/article/03409?gko=7a903.

Schubert, Christian. 2013. "3-Prozent-Defizitgrenze: Wie das Maastricht-Kriterium im Louvre entstand" [3 Percent Deficit Limit: How the Maastricht Criterion Arose in the Louvre]. *Frankfurter Allgemeine Zeitung*, September 26. http://www.faz.net/aktuell/wirtschaft/wirtschaftswissen/3-prozent-defizitgrenze-wie-das-maastricht-kriterium-im-louvre-entstand-12591473.html.

Schuman, Robert. 1950. "The Schuman Declaration." https://europa.eu/european-union/about-eu/symbols/europe-day/schuman-declaration_en.

Schwammenthal, Daniel, and William Echikson. 2003. "France Admits Worsening Deficit, Adding to Budget Crisis." Dow Jones Newswires, August 27.

Schwan, Heribert, and Tilman Jens. 2014. *Vermächtnis: Die Kohl Protokolle* [Legacy: The Kohl Transcripts]. Munich: Heyne. Kindle edition.

Schwartz, Nelson, and Katrin Bennhold. 2008. "European Leaders Vow to Fight Financial Crisis." *New York Times*, October 5.

Schwarz, Hans-Peter. 2012. *Helmut Kohl. Eine politische Biographie* [Helmut Kohl: A Political Biography]. Munich: Deutsche Verlags-Anstalt.

Sciolino, Elaine. 2003. "France and Germany Flex Muscles on Charter." *New York Times*, December 10. http://www.nytimes.com/2003/12/10/world/france-and-germany-flex-muscles-on-charter.html.

Sciolino, Elaine. 2005. "The Continental Dream: Will the French Shatter It?" *New York Times*, April 13.

Segreti, Giulia. 2014. "After Polarising Florence, Matteo Renzi Plans Renaissance in Rome." *Financial Times*, February 21.

Segreti, Giulia, and Guy Dinmore. 2012. "Eager Upstart Shakes Italy's 'Dinosaurs.'" *Financial Times*, November 21.

Séguin, Philippe, Daniel Vernet, and Pierre Servent. 1993. "Un entretien avec M. Philippe Séguin" [An Interview with M. Philippe Séguin]. *Le Monde*, February 6.

Seith, Anne. 2014. "Deep Divisions Emerge over ECB Quantitative Easing Plans." Spiegel Online, November 3.

Sengupta, Rajdeep, and Yu Man Tam. 2008. "The LIBOR-OIS Spread As a Summary Indicator." Federal Reserve Bank of St. Louis, *Economic Synopses* 25: 1. https://research.stlouisfed.org/publications/es/08/ES0825.pdf.

Sesit, Michael. 2000a. "Euro Slips to Another Low against Yen, Dollar on Lack of Firm Political Support." *Wall Street Journal Europe*, September 12.

Sesit, Michael. 2000b. "Many Old Factors Dragging Down New Currency." *Wall Street Journal Europe*, September 26.

Shah, Neil, and David Enrich. 2010. "Bank Aid Rankles Irish Voters; Ireland's Prime Minister Feels the Heat As Voters Stung by Years of Austerity Savage Dublin's Plan to Rescue Ailing Banks." *Wall Street Journal*, October 2.

Shah, Neil, Sara Schaefer Muñoz, Peter Stein, and Evan Ramstad. 2008. "Ireland, France Aid Banks, As Jitters Go Global." *Wall Street Journal*, October 1.

Shiller, Robert. 2015. *Irrational Exuberance*, 3rd ed. Princeton: Princeton University Press.

Shiller, Robert. 2017. "Understanding Today's Stagnation." Project Syndicate, May 23.

Shin, Hyun Song. 2012. "Global Banking Glut and Loan Risk Premium." *IMF Economic Review* 60, no. 2: 155–192.

Shleifer, Andrei, and Robert W. Vishny. 1998. *The Grabbing Hand Government Pathologies and Their Cures*. Cambridge: Harvard University Press.

Shrivastava, Anusha. 2012. "Funds Cut Euro-Zone Bank Debt." Wall Street Journal Online, July 25.

Silk, Leonard. 1972. "Klasen Hails the Strengthening Dollar." *New York Times*, September 20, 61.

Simensen, Ivar. 2007a. "D Bank Chief Told Regulator IKB Was in Trouble." *Financial Times*, August 3.

Simensen, Ivar. 2007b. "Subprime Woes Take Their Toll in Germany." *Financial Times*, July 31.

Sims, Christopher. 1999. "The Precarious Fiscal Foundations of the EMU." *Economist* 147, no. 4: 415–436.

Sims, Christopher. 2012. "Gaps in the Institutional Structure of the Euro Area." *Banque de France Financial Stability Review* 16: 216–223.

Sims, G. Thomas. 2001. "Euro-Zone Politicians Step Up Pressure on ECB to Cut Rates but Bank May Delay Action to Preserve Image of Independence: Calls from Italian and German Officials Grow Louder." *Wall Street Journal Europe*, June 27.

Sinn, Hans-Werner. 2003. "The Laggard of Europe." *CESifo Forum* 4: 1–32.

Sinn, Hans-Werner. 2013. "Why Draghi Was Wrong to Cut Interest Rates." *Financial Times*, November 13.

Skrekas, Nick. 2010. "IMF Pushes Blue Sky View of Greek Achievements." *Wall Street Journal*, August 9.

Sloan, Allan, and Roddy Boyd. 2008. "How Lehman Brothers Veered Off Course; Investment Bank Prided Itself on Real Estate Expertise." *Washington Post*, July 3.

Słomczyński, Wojciech, and Dariusz Stolicki. 2014. "National Interests in the European Parliament: Roll Call Vote Analysis." Center for Quantitative

Research in Political Science/Institute of Mathematics/Institute of Political Science and International Relations, Jagiellonian University, Krakow. http://paperroom.ipsa.org/app/webroot/papers/paper_64393.pdf.

Smith, David 1993. "The Unravelling of Europe—Focus: ERM." *Sunday Times*, August 1.

Smith, Fiona. 2014. "Germany's Merkel Hails 'Tremendous Success' of Irish Bailout." DPA International, March 7.

Smith, Helena. 2015. "Greece Stands Defiant As No Vote Rails against Wrenching Austerity." *Guardian*, July 6.

Smyth, Jamie. 2008. "Germany Takes a Swipe at British Economic Package." *Irish Times*, December 12.

Solletty, Marion. 2017. "Finland's Open Door Roils Its Politics." *Politico*, June 16.

Solomon, Robert. 1982. *The International Monetary System: 1945–1981*. New York: Harper & Row.

Spaak Committee. 1956. "Summary of the the Spaak Report." April. http://www.cvce.eu/content/publication/2007/2/27/4b911a0a-6bd0-4e88-bff9-4c87690aa4e8/publishable_en.pdf.

Spiegel, Peter. 2014. "Watch Your Words or Feed Populism, French Minister Warns Germany." *Financial Times*, December 8.

Spiegel, Peter. 2015. "Leaked Legal Opinion: EU Too Loose with Budget Rules?" *Financial Times*, May 4.

Spiegel, Peter, and David Oakley. 2010. "Irish Contagion Hits Wider Eurozone." *Financial Times*, November 11.

Spiegel, Peter, and Stefan Wagstyl. 2013. "ECB Split Stokes Fears of German Backlash; Frankfurt Rate Revolt Deepens Divisions." *Financial Times*, November 10.

Spiegel, Peter, Stefan Wagstyl, and Hugh Carnegy. 2014. "Renzi Leads Centre-Left Drive to Loosen Eurozone Fiscal Rules." *Financial Times*, June 19.

Spiegel Online. 2010a. "Dublin's Merkel Problem—Irish Debt Causing New Jitters across Europe," November 11.

Spiegel Online. 2010b. "Former Central Bank Head Karl Otto Pöhl: Bailout Plan Is All About 'Rescuing Banks and Rich Greeks,'" May 18.

Spiegel Online. 2010c. "German Finance Minister Wolfgang Schäuble: 'We Cannot Allow Greece to Turn into a Second Lehman Brothers,'" April 19.

Spiegel Online. 2010d. "Interview with German Finance Minister Schäuble: 'The US Has Lived on Borrowed Money for Too Long,'" November 8.

Spiegel Online. 2010e. "The World from Berlin—Merkel's Coalition Remains in Stand-By Mode," March 18.

Spiegel Online. 2011. "Outcome of Brussels Summit—Europe Takes Step Closer to Economic Government," July 25.

Spiegel Online. 2012a. "Behind the Scenes in Brussels—EU Summit Reveals a Paralyzed Continent," December 27.

Spiegel Online. 2012b. "The World from Berlin—The Real Problem Facing EU? It Is Not Trusted," August 20.

Standard and Poor's Global Ratings. 2011. "Research Update: Republic of Italy Outlook Revised to Negative on Risk of Persistent High Debt Ratio; 'A+/ A-1+' Ratings Affirmed." May 20. http://www.standardandpoors.com/en_EU/ web/guest/article/-/view/sourceId/6663704.

Stark, Jürgen. 2008. "Monetary Policy and the Euro." Speech at the conference on "Advantages and Benefits of the Euro—Time for Assessment," European Economic and Social Committee, Brussels, April 15.

Steelman, Aaron. 2011. "The Federal Reserve's 'Dual Mandate': The Evolution of an Idea." *Federal Reserve Bank of Richmond Economic Brief*, December.

Steen, Michael. 2012. "Weidmann Isolated As ECB Plan Approved." *Financial Times*, September 6.

Steinkamp, Sven, and Frank Westermann. 2014. "The Role of Creditor Seniority in Europe's Sovereign Debt Crisis." *Economic Policy* 29 (July): 495–552.

Stephens, Philip. 1997. "The Ragbag Treaty: EU Leaders Ignored the Real Issues at Amsterdam Summit." *Financial Times*, June 20.

Stevis, Matina. 2012. "EU Officials Set Cautious Vision of Integration." *Wall Street Journal*, December 6.

Stevis, Matina. 2013. "IMF and Europe Part Ways over Bailouts." *Wall Street Journal Europe*, October 11.

Stewart, Heather. 2015. "Euros 1tn 'Shock and Awe' Move to Save Eurozone: Central Bank to Pump Euros 60bn a Month into Economy Despite German Anger." *Guardian*, January 23.

Stothard, Michael. 2012. "Election Pledge Sees Finland Take Tough Line on Euro Crisis." *Financial Times*, July 13.

Strupczewski, Jan. 2008. "ECB Makes Record Rate Cut." Reuters News, December 4.

Sturdee, Simon. 2010. "German MPs Debate Unpopular Greek Aid," Agence France-Presse, May 7.

Summers, Peter. 2005. "What Caused the Great Moderation? Some Cross-Country Evidence." *Federal Reserve Bank of Kansas City Economic Review Third Quarter*: 5–32.

Sunday Business Post. 2009. "Our Banks Keep Going Back for More," December 6.

Sunday Business Post. 2015. "Greek Crisis: The Battle of the Bailout Boys," June 28.

Sunstein, Cass, and Reid Hastie. 2017. *Wiser: Getting beyond Groupthink to Make Groups Smarter*. Cambridge: Harvard Business Review Press. Kindle edition.

Suoninen, Sakari. 2009. "ECB Cuts Rates by Half-Point." Reuters News, January 15.

Sutherland, Peter. 1997. "The Case for EMU: More Than Money." *Foreign Affairs* 76, no. 1: 9–14.

Svensson, Lars. 1994. "Fixed Exchange Rates As a Means to Price Stability: What Have We Learned?" *European Economic Review* 38: 447–468.

Svensson, Lars. 1999. "Monetary Policy Issues for the Eurosystem." *Carnegie-Rochester Conference Series on Public Policy* 51, no. 1: 79–136.

Svensson, Palle. 1994. "The Danish Yes to Maastricht and Edinburgh: The EC Referendum of May 1993." *Scandinavian Political Studies* 17, no. 1: 69–82.

Swardson, Anne. 1997. "Events in France, Germany Threaten to Derail Europe's Single-Currency Plan." *Washington Post*, June 3.

Syal, Rajeev, et al. 2005. "Great and the Good Give Their Verdicts on European Project." *Times*, June 3.

Sylla, Richard, and John Joseph Wallis. 1998. "The Anatomy of Sovereign Debt Crises: Lessons from the American State Defaults of the 1840s." *Japan and the World Economy* 10: 267–293.

Syverson, Chad. 2017. "Challenges to Mismeasurement Explanations for the US Productivity Slowdown." *Journal of Economic Perspectives* 31, no. 2: 65–186.

Szász, André. 1999. *The Road to European Monetary Union*. New York: St. Martin's Press.

Tabellini, Guido, and Charles Wyplosz. 2004. "Réformes structurelles et coordination en Europe" [Supply-Side Policy Coordination in Europe]. Report for the French Council of Economic Analysis No. 51, La Documentation Française. http://www.cae-eco.fr/IMG/pdf/051.pdf.

Tanner, Henry 1968a. "De Gaulle Refuses to Devalue." *New York Times*, November 24, A1.

Tanner, Henry. 1968b. "For de Gaulle, Deep Trouble." *New York Times*, November 24, E1.

Tanner, Henry. 1968c. "Many Frenchmen Bitter at de Gaulle over Money Crisis." *New York Times*, November 23, A1.

Tanzi, Vito. 1998. "Corruption around the World: Causes, Consequences, Scope, and Cures." *IMF Staff Papers* 45, no. 4: 559–594.

Tarullo, Daniel K. 2008. *Banking on Basel: The Future of International Financial Regulation*. Washington, D.C.: Peterson Institute of International Economics. Kindle edition.

Taylor, John. 2001. "An Interview with Milton Friedman." *Macroeconomic Dynamics* 5: 101–131.

Taylor, Paul. 1997. "Politics Clashes with Fiscal Rectitude in Europe." Reuters News, May 29.

Taylor, Paul. 2000. "The Balance of Power in the European Union Is at Stake in a Tense Summit." Reuters News, December 4.

Taylor, Paul. 2008. "Europe Shows Limits in Credit Crisis Response." Reuters News, October 6.

Taylor, Paul. 2011. "Euro Debt Crisis Fells Governments, Legitimacy in Question." Reuters News, November 9.

Taylor, Paul. 2015. "Exclusive: Europeans Tried to Block IMF Debt Report on Greece: Sources." Reuters News, July 3.

Teasdale, Anthony. 2016. "The Fouchet Plan: De Gaulle's Intergovernmental Design for Europe." LSE Europe in Question Discussion Paper Series 117/2016.

Thacker, Strom. 1999. "The High Politics of IMF Lending." *World Politics* 52: 38–75.

Thal Larsen, Peter. 2017. "Stuck in a Rutte." Reuters, March 16.

Thatcher, Margaret. 2013. *Margaret Thatcher: The Autobiography*. London: HarperCollins. Kindle edition.

Thomas, Andrea. 2014. "Schäuble Calls on Italy to Pursue Structural Reform; German Finance Minister Says EU Rules Matter." Wall Street Journal Online, July 16.

Thomas, Andrea, and Costas Paris. 2010a. "Germany Struggles for Greek Consensus." Wall Street Journal Online, April 27.

Thomas, Andrea, and Costas Paris. 2010b. "World News: Merkel Puts Strings on Help for Greece—German Chancellor Says Athens Needs to Implement Deficit-Reduction Plan; ECB Chief Sees Swift Work on Aid Package." Wall Street Journal Online, April 27.

Thomas, Landon Jr. 2015 "Hopeful Start to Greek Debt Negotiations Quickly Soured." *New York Times*, July 2.

Thomas, Landon. 2016. "Italian Banks Continue to Lend to Stagnant Companies As Debt Pile Mounts." *New York Times*, August 18.

Thomas, Landon, and Jack Ewing. 2011. "Can Super Mario Save the Day for Europe?" *New York Times*, October 29.

Thomas, Landon Jr., and David Jolly. 2010. "Big Bond Sale Eases Pressure on Greece." *New York Times*, March 5.

Thomas, Pierre-Henri. 2012. *Dexia: Vie et mort d'un monstre bancaire* [Dexia: Life and Death of a Monster Bank]. Paris: Les Petits Matins.

Thomsen, Poul. 2013. "Transcript of a Conference Call on Greece Article IV Consultation." International Monetary Fund, Washington, D.C., June 5.

Thomson, Roddy. 2010. "Europe Turns Debt Screw As Greece Faces New Strikes." Agence France-Presse, February 16.

Thornhill, John. 2005b. "French Follies Undermine EU Constitution." *Financial Times*, April 5.

Thorpe, Jacqueline. 2005. "Europe in Crisis: French Heading for Polls to Vote on EU Constitution." *National Post*, May 27.

Thuburn, Dario. 2013. "Monti: Sober Academic Who Saved Italy from Default." Agence France-Presse, February 16.

Thurston, Michael, and Jitendra Joshi. 2003. "Euro Zone in Crisis As France, Germany Stitch Up Deficit Deal." Agence France-Presse, November 25.

Tietmeyer, Hans. 1994. "The Relationship between Economic, Monetary and Political Integration." In *Monetary Stability through International Cooperation: Essays in Honor of André Szász*, edited by Age Bakker, Henrik Boot, Olef Steijpen, and Win Vanthoor. Boston: Kluwer.

Tietmeyer, Hans. 2003. "From the Werner Report to the Euro." Pierre Werner Lecture, Luxembourg, October 21. http://www.bcl.lu/en/Research/conferences/Conferences/pierre_werner_lecture/discours_tietmeyer.pdf.

Tigges, Claus. 2007. "Zaubergriff statt ruhiger hand" [Magical Grasp Instead of a Steady Hand]. *Frankfurter Allgemeine Zeitung*, September 19.

Times. 1977. "Greek-EEC Talks Today." July 7, 8.

Times. 1980. "Rumours of Italian Devaluation Refuted." January 17.

Times. 1989. "The Strasbourg Summit." December 8.

Times. 1994. "Balladur Softens Kohl's Version of Hard-Core Europe." September 8.

Times. 2002. "Prodi's Conversion," October 22.

Timmermans, Frans. 2017. "Fog in Channel, Britain Cut Off." *Financial Times*, March 29.

Tirole, Jean. 2012. "The Euro Crisis: Some Reflexions on Institutional Reform, Banque de France." *Financial Stability Review* 16 (April): 225–242.

Tobin, James. 1978. "Harry Gordon Johnson, 1923–77." *Proceedings of the British Academy* 63: 443–458.

Tombs, Richard. 2014. *The English and Their History*. London: Allen and Lane.

Toomey, Christine. 1993. "German Plot to Derail Treaty." *Times*, May 23, 15.

Torry, Harriet. 2014. "German Finance Minister: Will Support Greece's Reform Efforts." Dow Jones Institutional News, December 29.

Traynor, Ian, and Larry Elliott. 2011. "Greek Crisis: EU Leaders Must Act Decisively or Face Disaster, Says IMF." *Guardian*, June 21.

Trean, Claire. 1992. "Genèse d'un traité" [Genesis of a Treaty]. *Le Monde*, April 30.

Trichet, Jean-Claude. 2005. "Monetary Policy and 'Credible Alertness'." Panel Discussion at Symposium Sponsored by Federal Reserve Bank of Kansas City, Jackson Hole, Wyoming, August 27. https://www.ecb.europa.eu/press/key/date/2005/html/sp050827.en.html.

Trichet, Jean-Claude. 2006. "Activism and Alertness in Monetary Policy." Lecture at Conference on Central Banks in the 21st Century, Banco de Espana, Madrid, June 8. https://www.ecb.europa.eu/press/key/date/2006/html/sp060608_1.en.html.

Trichet, Jean-Claude. 2007. "The Euro Area and Its Monetary Policy." Presented at Conference "The ECB and Its Watchers IX," Frankfurt am Main, September 7. https://www.ecb.europa.eu/press/key/date/2007/html/sp070907.en.html.

Trichet, Jean-Claude. 2008. "Address at the Ceremony to Mark the 10th Anniversary of the European Central Bank and the European System of Central Banks." Frankfurt am Main, June 2. https://www.ecb.europa.eu/press/key/date/2008/html/sp080602.en.html.

Trichet, Jean-Claude. 2011. "Remarks at the Farewell Event." Frankfurt am Main, October 19. https://www.ecb.europa.eu/press/key/date/2011/html/sp111019.en.html.

Trichet, Jean-Claude, and Vítor Constâncio. 2011a. "Introductory Statement to the Press Conference (with Q&A)." European Central Bank, April 7.

Trichet, Jean-Claude, and Vítor Constâncio. 2011b. "Introductory Statement to the Press Conference (with Q&A)." European Central Bank, June 9.

Trichet, Jean-Claude, and Vítor Constâncio. 2011c. "Introductory Statement to the Press Conference (with Q&A)." European Central Bank, July 7.

Trichet, Jean-Claude, and Vítor Constâncio. 2011d. "Introductory Statement to the Press Conference (with Q&A)." European Central Bank, October 6.

Trichet, Jean-Claude, and Mario Draghi. 2011. "Letter from the European Central Bank to Silvio Berlusconi," August 5. http://www.corriere.it/economia/ 11_settembre_29/trichet_draghi_inglese_304a5f1e-ea59-11e0-ae06-4da866778017.shtml?refresh_ce-cp.

Trichet, Jean-Claude, and Miguel Ángel Fernández Ordóñez. 2011. "Letter from Trichet and Fernández Ordóñez to Zapatero," August 5. http://www.ecb.europa. eu/pub/pdf/other/2011-08-05-letter-from-trichet-and-fernandez-ordonez-to-zapateroen.pdf.

Trichet, Jean-Claude, and Lucas Papademos. 2007. "Introductory Statement with Q&A." European Central Bank, November 8.

Trichet, Jean-Claude, and Lucas Papademos. 2008a. "Introductory Statement with Q&A." European Central Bank, January 10.

Trichet, Jean-Claude, and Lucas Papademos. 2008b. "Introductory Statement with Q&A." European Central Bank, February 7.

Trichet, Jean-Claude, and Lucas Papademos. 2008c. "Introductory Statement with Q&A." European Central Bank, April 10.

Trichet, Jean-Claude, and Lucas Papademos. 2008d. "Introductory Statement with Q&A." European Central Bank, June 5.

Trichet, Jean-Claude, and Lucas Papademos. 2008e. "Introductory Statement with Q&A." European Central Bank, November 6.

Trichet, Jean-Claude, and Lucas Papademos. 2008f. "Introductory Statement with Q&A." European Central Bank, December 4.

Trichet, Jean-Claude, and Lucas Papademos. 2009. "Introductory Statement with Q&A." European Central Bank, March 5.

Trotta, Daniel. 2008. "Europe Cuts Rates As Obama to Address Global Crisis." Reuters News, November 6.

Tversky, Amos, and Daniel Kahneman. 1973. "Availability: A Heuristic for Judging Frequency and Probability." *Cognitive Psychology* 5: 207–232.

Uhlig, Harald. 2008. "The Slow Decline of East Germany." National Bureau of Economic Research Working Paper 14553. http://www.nber.org/papers/ w14553.

Unmack, Neil. 2015. "Italy's Zero-Cost Bailout Is Too Good to Be True." Reuters News, November 23.

Unmack, Neil. 2017. "More Than Words." Reuters, June 29.

Usborne, David. 1991. "German Monetary Union a Disaster, Says Pohl." Independent, March 20.

Van Ark, Bart, Mary O'Mahony, and Marcel P. Timmer. 2008. "The Productivity Gap between Europe and the United States: Trends and Causes." *Journal of Economic Perspectives* 22, no. 1: 25–44.

Vanke, Jeffrey. 2001. "An Impossible Union: Dutch Objections to the Fouchet Plan, 1959–62." *Cold War History* 2, no. 1: 95–112.

Van Middelaar, Luuk. 2013. *The Passage to Europe: How a Continent Became a Union.* New Haven: Yale University Press.

Vannucci, Alberto. 2009. "The Controversial Legacy of '*Mani Pulite*': A Critical Analysis of Italian Corruption and Anti-Corruption Policies." *Bulletin of Italian Politics* 1, no. 2: 233–264.

Van Rompuy, Herman 2012. "Towards a Genuine Economic and Monetary Union." Brussels, December. http://www.consilium.europa.eu/uedocs/cms_Data/docs/pressdata/en/ec/134069.pdf.

Védrine, Hubert. 1996. *Les mondes de François Mitterrand: A l'Élysée 1981–1995* [The Worlds of François Mitterrand: At the Élysée 1981–1995]. Paris: Fayard.

Volcker, Paul. 1997. "An American Perspective on EMU." In *EMU and the International Monetary System*, edited by Paul Masson, Thomas Krueger, and Bart Turtleboom. Washington, D.C.: International Monetary Fund.

Volcker, Paul. 2008. "Keynote Speech at the Economic Club of New York," April 8. http://bazaarmodel.net/ftp/Project-C/Bazaarmodel/Materiaal/Xtradetail/pdf/2008-04--Transcript_Volcker_April_2008.pdf.

Von Hammerstein, Konstantin, and René Pfister. 2012. "A Cold Heart for Europe: Merkel's Dispassionate Approach to the Euro Crisis." Spiegel Online, December 12.

Wagstyl, Stephan. 2014. "Chemnitz Back from the Brink in Its Journey from East to West." *Financial Times*, November 6.

Walker, Marcus. 2005. "About-Face on Europe Inc.: Faced with Weak Economies, Politicians Blame Business." *Wall Street Journal Europe*, April 20.

Walker, Marcus. 2010. "Germany's Merkel Says Greece Doesn't Need Financial Support." Wall Street Journal Online, March 22.

Walker, Marcus. 2017. "Dutch Leader Takes Populist Turn to Fend Off Far-Right Party." Wall Street Journal Online, March 12.

Walker, Marcus, and Deborah Ball. 2014. "Q&A: Former Prime Minister Mario Monti on Italy's Prospects for Economic Growth; Architect of Austerity Policies during Financial Crisis Discusses Attempts to Lift Italian Economy." Wall Street Journal Online, April 29.

Walker, Marcus, and Charles Forelle. 2010. "In Shift, Germany Says It Is Open to IMF Aid for Greece." Wall Street Journal Online, March 19.

Walker, Marcus, and Charles Forelle. 2011. "Europe on the Brink: In Euro's Hour of Need, Aide Gets 'Madame Non' to Say Yes." *Wall Street Journal Asia*, April 15.

Walker, Marcus, Charles Forelle, and Stacy Meichtry. 2011. "WSJ: Deepening Crisis over Euro Pits Leader against Leader." Dow Jones News Service, December 29.

Walker, Marcus, and Matthew Karnitschnig. 2010. "Zeal and Angst: Germany Torn over Role in Europe." Wall Street Journal Online, May 8.

Walker, Marcus, and Neil Shah. 2010. "Contagion Fear Hits Spain; Cut to Credit Rating Opens New Phase in Crisis As Cost of Greece Bailout Debated." Wall Street Journal Online, April 28.

Wall, Denise. 2012. "Finnish Parliament Approves Spanish Bailout." Wall Street Journal Online, July 20.

Wallis, John J., and Wallace Oates. 1998. "The Impact of the New Deal on American Federalism." In *The Defining Moment: The Great Depression and the American Economy in the Twentieth Century*, edited by Michael D. Bordo, Claudia Goldin, and Eugene N. White. Chicago: University of Chicago Press.

Wallis, John Joseph, and Barry R. Weingast. 2008. "Dysfunctional or Optimal Institutions: State Debt Restrictions, the Structure of State and Local Governments, and the Finance of American Infrastructure." In *Fiscal Challenges: An Interdisciplinary Approach to Budget Policy*, edited by Elizabeth Garrett, Elizabeth A. Graddy, and Howell E. Jackson. New York: Cambridge University Press.

Wall Street Journal. 2010a. "Brussels vs. Bratislava; Slovakia Doesn't Want to Pay for Greece's Bailout," August 17.

Wall Street Journal. 2010b. "Europe's Bear Stearns; the Real Systemic Risk for the Euro-Zone Is Greek Bailout," April 24.

Wall Street Journal. 2010c. "The Price of Greece," April 30.

Wall Street Journal Europe. 2002. "Germany's Defense of VW May Hinder Takeover Law—Schröder Warns European Commission to Keep Its Hands Off Auto Maker—EU Officials Hope to Avoid Repetition of Last Year's Failure to Craft New Rules," February 27.

Walters, Alan. 1986. *Britain's Economic Renaissance: Margaret Thatcher's Reforms, 1979–1984*. Oxford: Oxford University Press.

Wardell, Jane. 2010. "UK Treasury Chief to Begin Major Spending Cuts." Associated Press, May 17.

Watanabe, Kota, and Tsutomu Watanabe. 2017. "Why Has Japan Failed to Escape from Deflation?" Understanding Persistent Deflation in Japan Working Paper Series 096, University of Tokyo, June.

Weiland, Severin. 2013. "Free Democrats Reel from Election Fiasco." Spiegel Online, September 22.

Weisman, Jonathan. 2010. "The New Political Landscape: Obama Faces Chillier Reception Abroad—Leaders at Asian Summits Back Austerity Moves Opposed by President; Ceding the Bully Pulpit to Republicans at Home." *Wall Street Journal*, November 5.

Werner, Pierre. 1970. "Report to the Council and the Commission on the Realization by Stages of Economic and Monetary Union in the Community." In *"Monetary Committee of the European Communities, 1986, Compendium of Community Monetary Texts."* Office of Official Publications of the European Communities, Luxembourg.

Wessel, David. 2009. *In FED We Trust: Ben Bernanke's War on the Great Panic.* New York: Crown. Kindle edition.

Wettach, Silke. 2015. "Juncker Speaks; The Greek Black Hole." *Handelsblatt Global*, February 27.

Wheatley, Alan. 1999. "Politicians Hail Euro Debut As Shares Soar." Reuters News, January 4.

White, Sarah. 2011. "Central Bank Steps Show Depth of Europe Bank Crisis— Update 1." Reuters News, November 30.

Whitney, Craig. 1994a. "Kohl Dismisses Vote Setback but Faces Harder Time." *New York Times*, October 18.

Whitney, Craig. 1994b. "The Victor (Again): Bonn's Long-Distance Runner— Helmut Kohl." *New York Times*, November 17, 10.

Whitney, Craig. 1996. "One European Currency: Is the 1999 Target Credible?" *New York Times*, January 29.

Wiegrefe, Klaus. 2010. "Germany's Unlikely Diplomatic Triumph: An Inside Look at the Reunification Negotiations." Spiegel Online, September 29.

Wiesmann, Gerrit. 2008. "Eurozone Inflation Soars to New High." *Financial Times*, June 30.

Williams-Grut, Oscar. 2017. "Deutsche Bank Is Paying $628 Million in Fines over Its $10 Billion Russian 'Mirror Trade' Scandal." Business Insider, January 31.

Willsher, Kim. 2017. "French Defence Minister Resigns over Inquiry into Misuse of Funds." *Guardian*, June 20.

Winestock, Geoff. 2000. "EU Commission Backs Greece's Euro-Zone Bid." *Wall Street Journal Europe*, May 4.

Winestock, Geoff, and Marc Champion. 2000. "Danish Vote on Euro Affirms EU Split—Britain, Sweden Unlikely to Join Any Time Soon." *Wall Street Journal Europe*, October 2.

Winning, Nicholas, and William Horobin. 2010. "Slovakia Resists EU in Aid Talks." Wall Street Journal Online, July 13.

Wittich, Günter, and Masaki Shiratori. 1973. "The Snake in the Tunnel." *Finance and Development*, June 1.

Yardley, Jim, Elisabetta Povoledo, and Gaia Pianigiani. 2014. "Political Star Rises on Vow to Upend Italy's Old Order." *New York Times*, February 15.

Ydstie, John. 2008. "Will the Fed's Latest Rate Cut Help the Economy?" NPR, October 29.

Yellen, Janet. 2011. "Pursuing Financial Stability at the Federal Reserve." Fourteenth Annual International Banking Conference, Federal Reserve Bank of Chicago, Chicago. https://www.federalreserve.gov/newsevents/speech/yellen20111111a.htm.

Za, Valentina. 2017. "Italy's 'Bitter' Bank Rescue Tsar Bemoans Strategy Vacuum." Reuters News, February 7.

Zampano, Giada. 2014. "Powerful Lobbies Stall Matteo Renzi's Reform Efforts in Italy; Resistance from Lawmakers, Unions Takes Teeth out of Moves to Overhaul Italy's Economy." Wall Street Journal Online, December 29.

Zampano, Giada. 2015. "Germany, Italy Leaders See More Work Still to Do." *Wall Street Journal*, January 24.

Zettelmeyer, Jeromin, Christoph Trebesch, and Mitu Gulati. 2013. "The Greek Debt Restructuring: An Autopsy." Peterson Institute of International Economics Working Paper 13-8, Washington, D.C.

Zingales, Luigi. 2016. "Are Newspapers Captured by Banks? Evidence from Italy." ProMarket Blog. May 12. https://promarket.org/are-newspapers-captured-by-banks.

Zysman, John. 1983. *Governments, Markets, and Growth: Financial Systems and the Politics of Industrial Change*. Ithaca: Cornell University Press.

INDEX

Figures and boxes are indicated by an italic *f* and *b* following the page number.

Europe Interbank Offered Rate
(EURIBOR), 196*f*
Eurostat, 135
eurozone. *See also* specific countries
banking struggles, 158, 159*f*,
227–229, 303–304
benefits of strong global
economy, 161
Britain's decision to stay out, 334
build-up to euro, 5–12
capital injection rules, 312–313
"core" inflation rate, 19, 354–355
crises, spreading of, 280–282
decisions on including countries,
396–397
declining industrial production
growth, 200*f*
Duisenberg on economy of, 139
economic disparities, 393–394
economic/financial
vulnerabilities, 158
economic growth problems,
127–130, 138–144
eurozone north's insulation from,
422–436
eurozone south, 396–408
falling interest, increasing
debt, 173*f*
financial bubble, 12–14
financial exuberance in, 172
financial system structure, 158
fiscal austerity in, 286–287, 392
France's shift to eurozone south,
400–408
Germany's move from commitments
to, 426
Germany's role in operations,
114–115
Greece's entrance into, 12,
129–135, 240
IMF economic assessments of, 127
incomes/employment
comparison, 340*f*

inflation rates, 291, 315–316,
316*f*, 338
initial eleven members, 121
low innovation (1997), 176*f*
Merkel and, 273, 335
mid-2017 short-term relief
rally, 19–22
monetary policy, 310
northern countries recovery, 393–394
north-south divergence,
394–396, 394*f*
political influence on ECB, 362–365
productivity-growth lag, 391–394
rolling crisis/response of
policymakers, 14–18
Schäuble's concern for future of,
244–246
southern eurozone countries,
396–400
stability ideology of, 158
unemployment, 156
unemployment rates, 11, 156, 392
U.S. financial crisis impact, 14–15
World Bank governance data, 398*f*
eurozone north. *See also* specific
countries
divergence from eurozone south,
394–396
Eastern Europeans as members
of, 433
France's shift to eurozone south,
400–408
Ireland's move from periphery to,
431–432
eurozone periphery. *See also* specific
countries
bank pressures in, 208, 209*f*
bond yields in, 173*f*
ECB and, 175
financial bubbles in, 14
financial/cognitive bubble in, 177–187
financial market/sovereign stress
in, 307

income benchmark, 339

income/employment
   comparison, 340f

increased debt burden ratio
   in, 95–96

inflation rates, 106, 174

irrational exuberance in, 172

Kohl's ten-point German unification
   plan, 79–84

Kreditbanken ("universal" banks), 162

loans to Greece, 16

loans to periphery countries, 13–14

London Debt Agreement with, 415

media insults in, 341

Merkel's distancing Europe from,
   322–326

mid-1960s economic
   dominance, 60, 61

Moody's "negative outlook" on debt
   of, 309

move from commitments to
   eurozone, 426

1971 consultations with
   France, 52–55

offer of aid to France, 402

OMT program and, 312–313

open violation of the SGP, 150

opinion of Greeks, 264

opposition to ECB's monetary
   policy, 320

opposition to monetary union, 6

political drift away from Europe,
   422–428

post-WWII gains, 34–35

public debt as percentage of GDP, 394f

rearming of, recommendation, 27–28

recessionary conditions in, 142, 149

recession in, 12, 142, 143, 144, 149

reduced exports to euro area, 171

resistance to opening borders, 30

reunification of, 73

Social Democratic Party, 42, 238,
   257, 425, 427

Solbes's/Prodi's blacklisting of,
   144, 151

stability ideology of, 51, 53, 91

subprime crisis and, 172, 195, 208,
   210, 215, 428, 475

trade shares, 171f

Treaty of Paris and, 27

trust in the European Union, 389f

2003-2008, capital inflows, 175f

unemployment in, 65, 81, 95, 96f

unification issues, 12

voting rights conflict, 137

World Bank governance data
   on, 398f

youth distress in, 394f, 395

Giavazzi, Francesco, 71b, 184

Giovanni, Alberto, 71b

Giscard d'Estaing, Valéry
   aid to Greece in joining EEC, 131
   bank expansion by, 163
   belief in monetary union, 8, 42,
      54–55, 93, 110–111
   biographical information, 54
   constitution project, 187–188
   defeat of Mitterrand, 101
   essay on political union, 76
   French presidency of, 58
   Mitterrand's defeat of, 67
   push to fix exchange rates, 57–59
   Schäuble-Lamers proposal and, 109
   Schmidt's support for, 58–59

Glick, Reuven, 171

global financial crisis (2007–2009).
   See also Greek crisis; Irish crisis;
   subprime mortgage crisis
   aftermath of, 283
   beginnings of, 192, 218
   different monetary policy response in
      the United States and eurozone,
      138–140, 198–202, 291–293
   eurozone economy and, 391
   ignoring of conditions leading to, 14
   IMF and, 262

unemployment, 232–233, 244

Wall Street Journal crisis coverage, 243, 247, 249, 250–252, 254

World Bank governance data on, 398*f*, 413

youth distress in, 394*f*, 395

Greek crisis

bailout, 241, 242, 245–258

ECB's response, 236, 243, 245, 248, 249, 252, 262, 299, 416–417

emergency liquidity arrangement and, 416, 418–419

endgame of, 249–250

falling forward thesis and, 263–267

fears of contagion from, 252, 253*f*, 255–258

Fischer's response, 247–248

FOMC's response, 241–242, 254

Geithner's response, 258

IMF's response, 16, 185, 232, 233, 247, 249–250, 253–255, 258–262, 414, 417–420

implosion in, 242–244

Lagarde's response, 244, 245, 252, 263

Legg's statement at the IMF Board meeting on May 9, 2010, 258–259

Lipsky at the IMF Board meeting on May 9, 2010, 258, 262

Lundsager's statement at the IMF Board meeting on May 9, 2010, 258

Merkel's response, 236–237, 239, 241–242, 245–248, 253, 255–258, 264

Obama's thoughts on, 415, 418

Papaconstantinou's response, 257

Papandreou/PASOK's response, 257

paying for, 250–255

repayment of creditors, 258–263

Schäuble's response, 240, 242, 244–246, 252, 285

Social Democrat's response, 257

sovereign/financial stress from, 263*f*

S&P rating downgrade, 237, 253

Strauss-Kahn's response, 254

Trichet's response, 252

U.S. Federal Reserve and, 241–242

Wall Street Journal coverage, 243, 247, 249, 250–252, 254

Greenspan, Alan

concerns about irrational exuberance phase, 159–160

economic deceleration concerns, 139–140, 139*f*

"light touch" banking regulation proposal, 167

subprime crisis response, 201–202

warning on prices of assets, 157

Greif, Avner, 50

Grexit (Greek exit from eurozone), 245, 259, 326–330, 340–341, 419

Grilli, Vittorio, 370

Grillo, Giuseppe "Beppe," 332, 341, 351, 363, 370. *See also* Five Star Movement

"Groundhog Day" discussions (Europe), 273

groupthink (of European leaders)

Akerlof's (Robert) analysis of, 51–52

cover for contradictions, 91

defined, 7, 51

ECB policy as a consequence of, 204

false beliefs of, 21

Greece's inclusion as a consequence of, 135

Kohl's legitimization of, 10, 11, 123

Krugman's comment on, 52

unwillingness to reconsider the Greek strategy, 422

Growth Plans, 170

Guigou, Elisabeth, 79, 94

Gulati, Mitu, 315

Gurría, José Ángel, 368

September 11, 2001 terrorist attacks, 142, 157
SGP. *See* Stability and Growth Pact
Shaalan, Shakour, 115
Sheets, Nathan, 252, 261, 270
Shiller, Robert, 157, 181, 219, 398
Shinzo, Abe, 382
Shleifer, Andrei, 118–119
Simitis, Konstantinos, 133
Sims, Christopher, 184, 312–313
single currency. *See* euro;
    monetary union
Single European Act (SEA, 1986), 67
Single Supervisory Mechanism
    (SSM), 371
Sinn, Hans-Werner, 147, 174, 320
Sløk, Torsten, 294
Slovakia, 266–267, 433, 445
"snake-in-the-tunnel" system, 8
Social Democratic Party (SPD), 42,
    238, 257, 425, 427
Social democracy, 434
    decline of in Europe, 238, 351,
    430, 434
Socialist Party (France), 351,
    358–359, 403
Social Security program (U.S.), 49
Société Générale, 161
Sócrates, José, 293
Solbes, Pedro, 144, 151, 183
Solow, Robert, 11, 89*b*, 90–91
South Korea, mid-2007 financial
    crisis, 128
sovereignty barrier, 22, 61, 443, 462
Soviet Union, 27, 77, 78, 124,
    153, 433
Spaak, Paul-Henri, 29
Spaak Committee Report (1956), 29
Spain
    bank branch density, 165
    Bankia (Spanish bank), 306–307
    Bank of Spain, 182–183
    bank pressures in, 209*f*

Barcelona summit, 145
bond yields, 173*f*, 311, 342
corruption in, 182
credit boom, 180*f*
debt burden/crisis, 308–310
deflation prevention, 356
ECB and, 299, 300, 307–308
economic contraction, 315
eurozone crisis in, 392
eurozone membership, 121
financial bubble, 181–183
financial/cognitive bubble in,
    181–183
Finland's approval of bailout for,
    307–308
French/German loans to, 172
government yields, 309–310
IMF and, 306
increased lending to, 172
inflation growth, 13
inflation rates, 291
investor's loss of confidence, 17,
    413*f*
low growth potential in, 408–412
LTROs and, 305
Operation White Whale, 182
property-credit boom, 14, 180*f*,
    181–183, 306
public debt as percentage of
    GDP, 394*f*
R&D/GDP ratio (1997), 176*f*
request for bailout, 307
rising sovereign-bond yields, 307
subprime crisis and, 224
2003-2008, capital inflows, 175*f*
World Bank governance data
    on, 398*f*
youth distress in, 394*f*, 395
Stability and Growth Pact (SGP, 1997),
    144–148
    aggravates recessions, 11
    agreement to abide by, 140
    conflict over wording of, 351–352